THE

PARISH REGISTER

OF

Christ Church, Middlesex County, Va.

FROM

1653 to 1812,

PUBLISHED BY

THE NATIONAL SOCIETY OF THE COLONIAL DAMES OF
AMERICA IN THE STATE OF VIRGINIA.

RICHMOND:

WM. ELLIS JONES, STEAM BOOK AND JOB PRINTER.

1897.

SOUTHERN HISTORICAL PRESS, INC.
c/o The Rev. Silas Emmett Lucas, Jr.
P.O. Box 738
Easley, South Carolina 29641-0738

ISBN 0-89308-631-2

PREFACE

The Blue Ridge Committee of the National Society of the Colonial Dames of America in the Commonwealth of Virginia, finding the *Christ Church Parish Register* wanting as a research tool, undertook to compare the 1897 edition with photocopies of the original manuscript which were in the Virginia State Library. It was discovered that Mrs. Sally Nelson Robins had done an excellent job of transcription, but that more than 1,200 names had been omitted from the index.

This new edition includes those names and in so doing will enable researchers to "discover" innumerable "lost" ancestors who were in the Register all the while.

In addition, the Blue Ridge Committee has prepared an index to the slaves whose births and deaths appear in the Parish Register. These approximately 4,000 slaves are grouped alphabetically under their owners' names for ease of research.

Acknowledgment is made to those members of the Blue Ridge Committee whose efforts made this re-indexing a reality: Mrs. James A. Bear, Jr., Miss Anne Page Brydon, Mrs. Charles Carnan, Mrs. Francis Duke, Mrs. Milton L. Grigg, and Mrs. Theodore Murphy. We are grateful to James A. Bear, Jr., Resident Director of Monticello, and to The Thomas Jefferson Memorial Foundation for access to their computer for this project; custom software was furnished by Information Dynamics, Inc.

Mary Caperton Bear
(Mrs. James Adam Bear, Jr.)

Mary Catharine Murphy
(Mrs. Theodore Murphy)

PUBLISHER'S PREFACE
CONCERNING CORRECTIONS,
OMISSIONS AND ADDITIONS

This edition of *The Parish Register of Christ Church, Middlesex County, Va., from 1653 to 1812* includes a new index and an Errata Section.

The Errata Section, beginning on page 314, points out some discrepancies found in this book, first published in 1897, and in its 1964 reprinting. In comparing it with a Xerox copy of the original Parish Register, furnished by the Virginia State Library, various errors and omissions were noticed, and it is with this in mind that the Errata Section is presented for the readers of this 1988 edition.

The letters "MSS" denote the original manuscript of the Parish Register of Christ Church, Middlesex County, Virginia.

INTRODUCTION.

The section in Virginia comprised within the present county of Middlesex, was at first included in Lancaster county and parish. Some time before 1666 that parish was divided into two portions, separated by the Rappahanhock river, and the new parishes were named Lancaster and Pyanketank. In 1666 they were reunited under the name of Lancaster, but a few years later again was separated and acquired the organization which they retained through the Colonial period, as Christ Church, Lancaster, and Christ Church, Middlesex. The register of the latter is printed in this book.

The vestry-book of Christ Church, Middlesex, beginning in 1663 and ending in 1767, which is now preserved at the Episcopal Theological Seminary, Alexander county, Va., shows that a Mr. Morris was minister from 1663 to 1666. He was succeeded in 1668 by Rev. John Shepherd, who at the time of his death in 1683, is described by his vestry as "our late worthy minister." In November of that year Major-General Robert Smith, one of the vestry, who had been commissioned to procure a minister, returned from England, bringing with him Rev. Duell Pead. This clergyman served the parish acceptably for seven years and then returned to England, where, it is believed, he became rector of Newland, St. Lawrence, Essex. Rev. Mathew Lidford, Mr. Pead's successor in 1692, only lived about a year, and was in turn followed by Rev. Samuel Gray, a most unworthy minister, who was tried for his life, for causing the death of one of his slaves by a severe whipping. This, it is presumed, caused his resignation or expulsion, as in 1699 the minister was Rev. Robert Yates, who continued until 1703 or 1704, when he returned to England in ill health. He appears to have been esteemed by his vestry, who continued his salary for some time in hope of his return. In 1704 he was succeeded by his son Bartholomew Yates, B. A., Brasenose College, Oxford, 1698, who continued to be the much loved and trusted incumbent, until his death on July 26, 1734. He was also a visitor and professor of William and Mary College. A tomb erected by his parishioners at Christ Church, bears testimony to the high regard in which he was held. Rev. John Klug succeeded to Mr. Yates in 1767, and, it is believed, continued until his death in 1795. He is represented to have been a pious and efficient minister.

The church now standing in the parish was built in 1712, and succeeded one, on the same spot, which was ordered to be built in 1666.

Bishop Meade says of the parish: "This being an early settlement, lying on one of the finest rivers in Virginia, and near the bay, we might expect to find here many of the ancestors of some of the most respectable families of Virginia. As the vestrymen were chosen from the leading citizens of each parish, we shall give, in the order in which they appear on the vestry-book for more than a hundred years, a full list of all who served the parish in that capacity. Those who have any acquaintance with the Virginia families, and with many who have dispersed themselves throughout the West and South, will readily trace great numbers to the parish of which we are treating. For the sake of brevity, we shall only mention the surnames. Corbin, Perrott, Chewning, Potter, Vause, Weeks, Willis, Cock, Curtis, Smith, Dudley, Thacker, Skipwith, Beverley, Wormeley, Jones, Miller, Scarborough, Woodley, Whitaker, Robinson, Warwick, Gordon, Chichester, Midge, Churchill, Burnham, Wormeley, 2d; Kemp, Smith, 2d; Cary, Dudley, 2d; Smith, 3d; Daniel, Price, Mann, Seager, Vause, 2d; Cock, 2d; Cant, Skipwith, 2d; Wormeley, 3d; Thacker, 2d; Grymes, Beverley, 2d; Kilbee, Kemp, 2d; Corbin, 2d; Robinson, 2d; Walker, Jones, 2d; Wormeley, 4th, Stanard, Churchill, 2d; Robinson, 3d; Walker, 2d; Robinson, 4th; Harden, Wormeley, 5th; Corbin, 3d; Smith, 4th; Grymes, 2d; Stanard, 2d; Reid, Carter, 2d; Elliott, Miles, Montague, Grymes, 3d; Nelson, Smith, 4th.''

The register here printed, was, together with the vestry-book, among those collected by Bishop Meade, and deposited in the Episcopal Theological Seminary, where it now is. The Virginia Society of Colonial Dames is indebted to the trustees of the Seminary for permission to bring the register to Richmond for the purpose of copying.

The copy here printed was made by one of the Virginia Dames, Mrs. Sally Nelson Robins, of Richmond, and compared with the original, and verified by Messrs. Edward W. James and William G. Stanard.

PARISH REGISTER,

MIDDLESEX COUNTY, VIRGINIA.

Novemb^r: the 19th. 1663.

At a Vestry held for the parish of Lancaster at the House of Mr Henry Corbin &c.

Whereas it doth appeare that there is an Act of Assembly Injoyning all Parishes to keep a perfect Register of all Christenings, Burialls and marriages, as by the said act will more at large appeare, In obedience whereunto we the Vestry of Lancaster parish being the Major part of us now mett together Doe hereby Authorize and appoint Mr Henry Corbin to keepe a true Register of Every thing Required by the Said Act for this Ensuing yeare and it is further agreed that Every Vestry man shall take the Charge of the said Register for a whole yeare, if a Clerk be not provided in the Interim.

CUTHBERT POTTER
ABRAHAM WEEKES
THOMAS WILLIS
ROBERT CHOWNING
JOHN VAUSE
HENRY CORBIN
RICHARD PERROTT.

Register of Christ Church Parish.

BURIALLS 1685.

Madam ffrances Wormeley the wife of Coll⁰ Christop Wormeley Esqr, Departed this Life on the 25th of May 1685 & was buried at home. In theire Garden the next Day following being 26th of May 1685.

Mrs Martha Boodle Departed this Life 10th and was buried 12th July 1685.

Thomas Allen (Smith of this County) Departed this Life 10th of Augᵗ 1685 being the same Day whereon he was Married to Lucy Blake & Dyed before night and was buried yᵉ next day following.

Mr John Batcheldor Departed this Life 4th Xemb & was Buried at home the 7th Xemb 1685.

Anthony Barlow Departed this Life 12th Xemb. and was buried at home ye 15th Xemb. 1685.

Matthew Bentley Departed this Life 8th of January & was buried 11th of January 1685.

Mrs Agatha Robinson wife of Mr Christopr Robinson Departed this Life 25th of January 168⅚ & was buried 27th January 168⅚.

John Dawd, Cooper & Servant to Major Robert Beverley Departed this Life 17th of Septemb 1686.

Thomas Beverley the Sone of Major Robert Beverley and Madam Katherine his Wife Departed this Life 20th of September 1686 and was buried at the Lower Chapˡˡ In the Ile 22th September 1686.

Rachell Dewd the Wife of Richard Dewd Departed this Life ye 29th of July 1681. and was buried in the Church Yard of our Lower Chapˡˡ ye 30th July 1681.

Elizabeth Poticarie Servᵗ Tho Dudley died ye po Sepᵗ & was buried 2th 1681.

William Allen Departed this Life 4th of Septemb 1681 & was buried in ye Lower Chapˡˡ Church yard ye next day following being 5th 9^{br} 1681.

William Watson Departed this Life 6th Xemb. & was buried in the Church yard of the great Church 8th of Xemb. — 1681.

Henry Stalker Departed this Life 12th Xemb. 1681 & was buried next day.

Robert Stephens Departed this Life 21th of Jan'y 1682 & buried 23th following.

Henry Chichley Kt. & his Majᵗˢ Deputy Governor of Virginia Departed this Life on Munday morning Early being 5th of ffebuary 168⅔ & was Buried in Christ Church Chancell Middlesex County neare the Comunion Table 9th of ffebuary 168⅔ following &c.

John Hunten Dyed at Major Beverley's & was buried there 23th of febr. 168⅔.

Mr John Sheppard, Minister of this parish Departed this Life 30th of June 1683 about 5 or 6 of ye Clock afternoone & was buried in ye Great Church at ye head of ye Ile on ye Second day of July following &c.

Elizabeth Stamper ye Wife of Jno. Stamper departd this Life 29th Aprill 1683.

Thomas Williams ye husband of Bridgt departd this Life 20th Xemb 1683 and was buried in ye Great Churchyard 23th Xemb. 1683.

John Smith Servant to Collo Chr Wormeley Esqr Departed this Life 10th March & was buried the 11th of March 168¾.

Capt Henry Creyke Departed this Life po June & buried at home 6th June 1684.

Christopher . . . . er Departed this Life 26th June & was buried yt very night.

Amie Orphan Departed this Life 26th June & was buried ye po July 1684.

John Slanter Departed this Life ye 18th & was buried 19th of August 1684.

William Young Departed this Life 26th & was buried 28th of Sept at Ed. Dockey.

Mrs Mary Bentley the wife of Mr Matthew Bentley Departed this Life ye 27th of Septemb. & was buried 29th of Septemb. 1684.

Mr Humphrey Jones Departed this Life 16th & was buried 20th of Octob. 1684.

Margaret Ashton Departed this Life 24th & was Buried 28th of March 1684.

The Honerable Lady Madam Katherine Wormeley Wife to the Honble Ralph Wormley Esqr Departed this Life 17th of May 1685 & was buried in the Chancell of the Great Church betweene ye Honble * * * * * Chickley & * * *

CHRISTENINGS &c.

Mary Daughter of John and Mary Batcheldor baptz Sept. 12th 1653.

Sarah Daughtr of Jno. and Mary Batcheldor born

Rebecca Daughter of Jno. & Mary Batcheldr was borne Octobr 2th 1658.

William Sone of Jno. & Mary Batcheldr was Born July 22th 1667 of a Munday betweene one and two of Clock.

Thomas Sone of Richard & Margt Williams Baptz Sept 22th 1670.

Sarah Daughter of Jno. & Jane Watts was Baptz Octobr 30th 1670.

Sarah Daughter of James & Mary Hopkins baptz October 30th 1670.

Ann Daughter of Richd and Anne Robinson baptz Novr 20th 1670.

William Sone of Wm and Eliza Wood was baptz July 17th 1670.

Sarah Williams was Baptized the 5th of March 1670.

Alice the Daughter of Tho. and Margt Weatherby baptz March 20th 1670.

Clemt the Sone of Mary Sanders was Christened the 16th of Aprll 1671.

Aliza Daughter of Daniell & Mary Banbry was Christd Aprll 16th 1671.

William the Sone ffrances Porter and Lucy the Daughter of John and
Jone Blake was Christened the 7th of May 1671.
Ann the Daughter of Tho. and Eliz^a Conaway Christn^d May 20th
1671.
Micoll the Daught^r of Jno. and Jone Blake was born Sept. 13th 1658.
Sarah Daughter of the above said was born Aprill 8th 1660.
George the sone of the ab. sd. the 8th of March, 1661.
Dianah Daughter of the ab. sd. borne 11th January 1663.
Eliz^a Daughter of ye ab. sd. was born 19th Sept. 1664.
Jone the Da^{tr} of the ab. sd. was born 10th of No^{br} 1664.
Lucy the D^r of the ab. sd. was Christn^d the 7th of May 16**.
   Being the age of seven Children of John and Jone Blake above
said &c.

1671 &c.   CHRISTININGS &c.

Jone the Daughter of Thomas and Grace Shoare and Amey the
Daughter of Ralph and Marg^t Smith were bap^{tz} Augt 20th 1671.
Andrew the Sone of William and Presilla Watson born ffeb^r 23th
1669.
Erasmus the son of John and Barbara Allin Christn^d Sept 10th 1671.
Sarah Daughter of Richard and Marg^t Williams Christn^d Octo^{br} 22th
1671.
Mary Daughter of David and Joane Allinson Christn^d Octo^{br} 29th
1671.
Bryan the son of Bryan and Hannah Harkins born ffeb^r 20th 1663.
Cornelius the sone of ye afores'd Bryan & Hannah Harkins was born
August the 25th 1666.
William the sone of Wm. and Presilla Watson was born Jan^r 17th
1671.
Cussandra ye Daughter of Jno. Sutton & Eliz^a Ellis Christn^d Decem^{br}
25th 1671.
ffrances Daughter of ffrances and Erasmus Withers Chr^d March 17th
1671.
Edward the sone of Edward Michaell Christened April 28th 1672.
Edward the son of Thomas Williams and Bridg^t Catt May 19th 1672.

BURIALLS Vizt.

Richard Rumiger Servant to Mr. Robert Chowning Drowned in his
Creek Decemb^r the 12th 1660.
Alice Daughter of Tho. and Mary Tugwell Dyed & was buried No-
vember the 22th 1660.
John Wilch dyed and was Buried 30th 1660.
Thomas Butterfield M^r. Boswel's Servant Dyed Decemb^r 5th 1660.
Arthur   M^r. Vaus man Dyed Jan^r 1st 166$^0_1$.
William Owen Servt to Henry Corbin Dyed July 13th 1661.
Matthew Booker Servant to Mr Jno. Vause was drowned May 26th
1661.
James Poynter Serv't to Mr Perrott Dyed Augst 28th 1661.
William Green Servant to Mr Perrott Dyed Augst 25th 1661.
Richard Travars Servant to Mr Perrott Dyed Augst 30th 1661.
Rich'd Woodcock Servant to Mr Boswell Dyed Octo^{br} 10th 1661.
Alice Ripinge Servant to M^r. Boswell Dyed July 20th 1661.

Mr Shereefes Servant to Mr Corbin Dyed Octo^{br} 11th 1661.
John Gibbor Servant to Mr Corbin Dyed Decemb^{br} 2th 1661.
John Ballard Servant to Mr Christo^r Withnell Dyed ffeb^r 20th 1661.
John Crispe Servant to Mr Batcheldor Dyed Septemb^r 30th 1661.
John Thomas Servant to Mr Thacker, Dyed March 5th, 1662.
Hugh Williams Servant to Mr Curtis Dyed July   th
Dorcas Stamper the wife of John Stamper Dyed July 16th 1667.
John Smyth Husband to Marg^t Smyth Dyed Decem^{br} 16th 1669.
Capt. Wormely's Wife's Son Aylmer Dyed the 16th and was Buried
    the 18th of January In the Chancell near the South end of y^e
    Communion Table 1669.
Mary wife to Tho. Reenes and her Sone were Buried in ye Alley
    Novemb^r 27th (neare her Pew) 1669.
William Hill was Buried in the Church Yard ffebruary 12th 1669.
Edward Thompson was Buried in the Entering into ye Chancell
    May 21th 167 .

CHRISTENINGS Viz^t.

Lettice Corbin the Daughter of Henry Corbin Esqr was born and
    Christened the 25th Day of   1657.
Alice Corbin Daughter of Henry Corbin Esqr was borne halfe an
    houre after five o'clock in the evening Feby 14th 1660.
Robert Chowning Sone of Robert and Jone Chowning was Chris-
    tened ffebruary 23th 1660.   Born 4th of May 1659.
Mary Willis Daughter of Tho. and Mary Willis Christened ffeb^r
    23th 1660.
Thomas Willis Sone of Tho. and Mary Willis was born Sept. 8th
    1660.
Ellianor Willis Daughter of Tho. & Mary Willis borne Aprill 18th
    1655.
Richard Willis Sone of Tho. & Mary Willis borne Augst 29th 1656.
John Willis Sone of Tho. and Mary Willis borne Novem^{br} 24th 1658.
Elizabeth Daughter of Tho. and Marg^t Williams Christ^{td} Ap^{rll} 4th
    1661.
Katherine Daughter of Abraham and Millicent Weekes christened
    the 15th of December 166 .
Winifrid Corbin daughter of Henry and Alice Corbin was borne the
    3^d Day of Novemb^r at 12 a Clock at night, and Christn^d the 12th
    of Aprill 1662.
George the Sone of Jno. and ffrances Hazlewood borne   25th 1661.
Diana Vause Daughter of Jno. and Ann Vause Christened April
    9th 1662.
Henry the Sone of Henry and Eltonhead Thacker was borne the
    9th Day of August 1663.
Ann Daughter of Henry and Alice Corbin was borne ffeb^r 9th and
    was Christened the 29th of the same Month 1664.
Henry Sone of Henry and Alice Corbin ffeb^r 12th At one a Clock
    in the Morning and was Christened on Easter Tuesday March
    22th, 1667.
Mary the Daughter of Andrew and Sarah Williamson was Borne the
    ffirst Day of Novemb^r about 3 a Clock in the After Noone 1669.
Ann Daughter of David and Jone Allinson was borne March 12th
    1665.

Catherine the Daughter of David and Jone Allinson borne March 18th 1667.

David Sone of David and Jone Allinson was borne the 18th Day of August about one of Clock in the after Noone 1669.

Margaret Daughter to William and Eliz^a Loyall was borne the 18th Day of August ab^t one of the Clock in ye afternoone 1669.

William Son of William and Eliz^a Downing was borne Novem^{br} 17th 1665.

Elizabeth Daughter of W^m & Eliz^a Downing was borne Sept. 23th 1670.

Thomas the Sone of Edward and Ann Bateman was Christned Sept. 1st 1672.

Ralph the Son of Jane Watts was Christned Septem^{br} the 22th 1672.

Edward Thacker the Sone of Henry and Eltonhead Thacker was Borne the 7th of January An. 1665.

Martha the Daughter of the above Named Thacker borne Decem^{br} 5th 1667.

Alice the Daughter of the above Named Thacker borne Decem^{br} 30th 1671.

Lettice the Daughter of the above Named Thacker borne ffebry 27th 1669.

Marke the Sone of Matthew Gibson and Eliz^a Lawright was borne the 29th of January 1667.

William and Ann Hares Childe, Named Ann was Christned March 30th 1673.

The Age of Severall Negroes of Mr Richd Perrott.

Thomas Mack Sone of Richard and Tugg borne 15th of July 1663.

ffrank Sone of Sampson and Kate borne the 12th of Aprill 1668.

Hannah Daughter of W^m and Kate borne Octo^{br} the 1st 1672.

Toney Sone of Toney and Sarah Borne 10th of Aprill 1672.

These negroes above were Entered April 30th 1673.

July 22th 1673 Doodis Minor's Negros Entred.

Mary Daughter of Deco and Phelis Borne July 1663.

Nann Daughter of the above Negro, was borne July 1666.

James Sone of the above Negro, was borne January 1669.

Betty Daughter of the above Negro, was borne March 1672.

Pallas Daughter of the abovs^d Negro, borne March 1672.

Mr Reeves three negros were Entered July 6th 1672.

James aged Nine yeares Octo^{br} next.

Tom aged Two yeares and a halfe.

Benn aged Two yeares and a halfe

MARRIAGES V$_{IZ}^t$.

William Baldwin and Magret Cook married Dec^{br} 19th 1660.

Robert Thompson and Marg^t Welch widow of Jno. Welch ffebruary 19th 1660.

Richard Howell and Ann Wilberton April 12th 1662.

Thomas Cordwell and Elizabeth Collyer

Robert Taylor and Elizabeth Welch April 11th 1662.

John Blewford and Elizabeth Parrat.

CHRISTENINGS.

Ann Daughter of Allexand^r and Mary Murra Christen^d Augst 24th.

Ann Daughter of Rich^d and Margaret Williams Christn^d Jan^r 18th 1673.

Ann Daughter of Tho. and Grace Shore Christened ffebry 8th 1673.

Mary Daughter of Tho. and Mary Tugwell born The Last Octo^{br} 1661.

Thomas Sone of ye above named Tugwell born June 16th 1664.

Ann Daughter of ye above named Tugwell born March 15th 1666.

Henry Sone of ye above named Tugwell borne Octo^{br} 7th 1670.

Marg^t Daughter of Ellianor and Jno° Carryer Christn^d Ap^{rll} 20th 1673.

William Son of W^m and Grace Copeland borne March 26th 1667.

John Sone of the above named Copeland borne March 21th 1669.

Mary Daughter of Allexand^r and Mary Murra Chrs^{td} Dec^{br} 20th 1674.

William Poole the Sone of W^m and Sarah Poole born March 7th 1668.

Maxamilian Petty the Sone of Maxamilian and Christian Petty was born 28th Novemb 1677.

Sarah Daughter of Jno. and Mary Wortham borne Novem^{br} 12th 1663 Between 11 and 12 a Clock at night, Sarah Departed this Life the 16th of January 1670.

Mary Daughter of the aboves^d Wortham borne the 11th ffeb^r 1665 about 8 a Clock at night, and Departed this Life the 21th of Decemb^{br} 1676.

John Sone of the aboves^d Wortham Borne September 27th 1669 about 4 a Clock after noone.

Margaret Daughter of the aboves^d Wortham borne ffeb^r 20th and Christened 26th of March 1671.

Margaret departed this Life the 9th of Aprill 1676.

Joseph Son of the aboves^d Wortham borne the 2th of July 1676 And Dyed the 9th of June the same yeare.

George Sone of the aboves^d Wortham was borne 20th of Aprill and Christened the 19th of May 1673.

Oswald Sone of Jno. and Eliz^a Wortham borne the first day of Ap^{rll} 1685.

Elizabeth Daughter of the above^{sd} Wortham borne ffebruary 20th 1686.

Chichley Corbin Thacker The Sone of Henry and Eltonhead Thacker was borne 4th January Ann° 1673.

Jn° Stamper the Sone of Jno. and Elizabeth Stamper was borne the 29th of August 1677 and was baptized at the house of the said Jn° Stamper p. Mr Sheppard, 8th of Octo^{br} 1677.

Thomas Ross the Sone of Andrew and Mary Ross borne the 22th of May and Baptized 22th of June ffollowing 1677.

Sarah Poole the Daughter of William and Sarah Poole was borne the 3th of Septemb. 1671.

The age of 3 children of David and Mary George Viz^t

Alice George was borne the 4th Xamb^r 1671.

David George was Borne the 12th of ffebruary 1673.

John George was Borne the 6th of July 1675.

The age of 4 children of Thomas & Jane Kidd Vizt.

Elizabeth Kidd was borne the ffirst of Septemb. 1672.

William Kidd was borne the 22 of March 1675.

Jane Kidd was borne the 12 of January 1677.

Mary Kidd was baptiz^d the   Day of August

   The age of 3 children of John and Sarah Davis vizt

Alice Davis was borne the 30th of June 1676.

Sarah Davis was borne the 31th of January 1678.

John Davis was borne the 7th of July 1681.

   Robert and Jane Price theire children Viz^t

Margaret Price was Borne the 14th of August 1670 about 12 a Clock
   and Baptized 12th of Septemb following.

John Price was Borne 29th of January about 5 afternoone and Baptized 2th of March 1672.

Robert Price was borne 19th of Novemb. and baptized 22th of the
   same 1674.

Jane Price was borne 10th of July 1676 about 4 afternoone and was
   bap^{tz} 14th of August.

Elizabeth Price was borne ye 7th of Novemb. 1681 and bap^{tz} at
   home 13th of Novemb. 1681.

Mary Price was Borne 3th of May 1679 and baptized at home the
   25th Ditto 1679.

Katherine Price was borne 6th of January and baptized at home
   13th January, 168$\frac{3}{4}$.

Elizabeth the Daughter of Mary Stradford was borne 3th of May and
   baptized the 24th of August 1679.

Hannah Daughter of Ann Nunnam was bap^{tz} 9th of ffebruary 167$\frac{8}{9}$.

Ann the Daughter of Mary Green was bap^{tz} at Lower Chap^{ll} May
   9th 1680.

William the Sone of Susanna Jaxon baptized at ye Gr^t Church Jan^y
   18th 167$\frac{9}{80}$.

Katherine Daughter of Ann Corell bap^{tz} at Maj^r Generall Smith's
   Octo^{br} 17th 1680.

Sarah the Daughter of William Hughs by Baptized Jan^r 16th 1680.

Elizabeth the Daughter of Wm Waller by Kath. Lestridge bap^{tz} feb^r
   20th 1680.

Elizabeth Daughter of Phillip Torksey by Mary ffrench bap^{tz} Aprill
   10th 1681.

Ann King Daughter of Julian & Rebeca King was borne 25th No-
   vemb^r 1676.

Elizabeth Daughter of Edm^d Sanders by ffrances was bap^{tz} 17th No-
   vemb^r 1681.

William the Illegitimate Sone of Hannah Majo^r Beverlys maid Jan^r
   8th 168$\frac{1}{2}$.

Ann the Illegitimate Daughter of Tho. Thompson by Jane Burk
   bap^{tz} June 4th 1682.

Rich'd Robinson Sone of Rich'd and Ann Robinson was borne
   12th of March 1674.

   The age of 3 children of John & Eliz^a Riseing:

William Riseing was borne the last Day of Aprill 1669.

Elizabeth Riseing was borne the 15^d of September 1672.

John Riseing was borne the 28th of March 1676.

The age of 3 children of William & Eltonhead Stanard:

Eltonhead Stanard was borne 2th of Septemb^r 1678.

Sarah Yates by marriage Sarah Stanard was borne 12th of July 1680.

William Stanard was borne 15th of ffebruary 1682.

Ann the Illegitimate Daughter of George Anderton by Sarah was baptized p. Mr Pead 7th of March 168$\frac{3}{4}$.

Walter the Illegitimate Son of Walter Lewis by Jane Burk baptized p. Mr Pead 6th of Aprill 1684.

The age of 4 children of Alexand^r & Mary Murrey:

Ann Murrey was borne the 12th of Aprill 1673.

Mary Murrey was borne the 22th of Novemb. 1674.

Rebecca Murrey was borne the 28th of Octo^{br} 1676.

John Murrey was borne the 20th of January 1678.

Francis the sone of ffrancis & Eliz^a Dodson borne 15th of July 1684.

Ann Smith Daughter of Anthony Smith & Ann his wife borne the 10 day of July, and baptized 11th of August 1678.

Elizabeth Lee Daughter of Tho. and Eliz^a Lee baptised 11th of Augst 1678.

John Atwood Sone of James and Mary Atwood was borne the 14th of July 1678, and was baptised 22th of Sep^t 1678.

Thomas Jones Sone of Tho. & Mary Jones bap^{tz} 3th of Novemb. 1678.

Richard Daniell sone of William & Jochebed Daniell was borne Sept. 30th 1678.

John Lee Sone of Majo^r Richard Lee and Mad^m Lettice Lee his wife was baptized 3th of Xember 1678.

George Davis the Sone of George & Susanna Davis bap^{tz} 22th Xemb 1678.

Sarah Clay Daughter of George and Sarah Clay borne 4th Xemb and was baptized 2th of ffebruary 1678.

Margret Askew Daughter of Rich^d and Eliz^a Askew bap^{tz} 2th Jan^{ry} 1678.

Christopher Sutton Son of Jno and Eliz^a Sutton borne ffeb^{ry} 27th 1678.

Mary Hill Daughter of Tho. & Ann Hill was borne the 14th of ffebruary and baptized the 6 of Aprill 1678.

Dianah Young the Daughter of William and Johan^r Young borne the 19th of ffebruary 1678 and was baptised 6th of Aprill 1678.

Richard Allen the Sone of Rich^d and Ann Allen borne 17th Jan^{ry} 1678 and Baptized 13th of Aprill 1679.

Gerrat Minor the Sone of Doodis and Eliz^a Minor was Baptized 13th of Aprill 1679.

Elizabeth Mins the Daughter of Thomas and Ann Mins borne the 29th of March, and baptized 11th May 1679.

Mary Colless the Daughter of Ambr's and Elizabeth Colless was borne the 25th of Aprill and baptized 18th of May 1679.

John Burk the Sone of Jno & Jane Burk borne 16th of Augst 1678 and baptized 18th of May 1679.

Elizabeth Tuydey Daughter of Eliz. Tudey borne March 24th 1678 bap^{tz} Ap^r 20th 1679.

Elizabeth Norman Daughter of Henry & Ann Norman borne 29th May 1679 and baptized 15th June Ditto yeare.

Jane Burnet Daughter of W^m & Loretta Burnet borne 14th May bap^tz 15th June 1679.

Susanna Gess Daughter of William and Eliz^a Guess borne 7th Ap^r bap^tz 13th July 1679.

Robena Hughs Daughter of Jno & Eliz^a Hughes borne 30th July bap^tz 31th August 1679.

Sarah the Daughter of Peter & Ellinor Brunwell was baptized 2th of November 1679.

Joseph Micham Sone of John & Micall Micham borne 17th Octo^br bap^tz 23th Novr 1679.

John & Elizabeth Patre the Sone and Daughter of Matthew & Eliz^a Patre bap^tz 7th Xmb. 1679.

Ann Thomas Daughter of Robert and Ancoretta Thomas baptized 21th Xemb. 1679.

Margaret the Daughter of Andrew and Sarah Williamson borne 16th of August 1679 and baptized 25th Xemb. 1679.

Robert Smith Sone of Tho. & Eliz. Smith bap^tz 18 Jan^ry 1679.

Thomas Stacey Sone of Tho. & Eliz^a Stacey bap^tz ffeb^r 18th 1679.

Mary Daughter of W^m & Eliz^a Wood bap^tz 22th ffeb^r 1679.

Katherine Wormeley Daughter of Capt. Ralph Wormeley Esqr was Bap^tz 4th March 1679.

Winifrid Seager Daughter of Randolph & Mary Seager bap^tz Ma^r 14th 1679.

Elizabeth Basket Dau^tr Jno. & Eliz^a Basket bap^tz 14th March 1679.

Jno. Charles Richman Son of Tho. and Eliz^a Richman borne 30th Jan^r 1679.

Winifrid Nichols Da^r of Henry & Alice Nichols bap^tz 14 feb.

An acco^t of Christenings and ages of Children for the yeare 1680 &c.

Elizabeth Weatherston the Daughter of Thomas & Elizabeth Weatherstone was baptised at the Lower Chappell p Mr Sheppard the 28th of March.

Mary Slanter the Daughter of John and Sarah Slanter was borne 4th of March 1679, and baptized 28th of March 1680.

Dorothy Long the Wife of Daniel Long aged   yeares was Baptized at the Upper Chappell p. Mr Shepard 4th of Aprill, the above yeare.

Ann Petty the Daughter of Maxamilian and Christian Petty was borne the 25th of March and was Baptized at home p. Mr Sheppard 11th of Aprill.

Elizabeth Jones the Daughter of Thomas and Mary Jones was bap^tz 2th of May.

Mary Slanter the Daughter of Anthony and Dorothy Slanter was bap^tz 25th Ap^rll.

Joseph Humphrys the Sone of John and Ann Humphrys bap^tz 9th of May.

Johannah Bristow the Daughter of Jno and Michall Bristow bap^tz 9th May.

Ann Mason the Daughter of Josiah and Eliz^a Mason Baptized 30th of May.

James Williams the Sone of John and Mary Williams baptized 6th of June.

Thomas Brookes the Sone of Richard and Mary Brooks bap^tz 27th of June.

Catherine Maynell the Daughter of Robert and Dorothy Maynell bap^tz 27th June.

Nicholas House the Sone of Nich° and Eliz^a House baptized 8th of August.

Joseph Orphin the Sone of Henry and Anne Orphin was borne 11th of July. and was baptized at the Lower Chap^ll p. Mr Sheppard 22th of August.

John Brent the Sone of Jn° and Jane Brent was bap^tz 22th of August.

Charles Brookes the Sone of Jonathan and Sarah Brookes was borne 12th Augt and baptized 29th Ditto.

Sarah Wilson the Daughter of Thomas and Mary Wilson bap^tz 12th of Septemb.

Ann Roberts the Daughter of Griffuth and Ann Roberts bap^tz 19th of Sept.

Benjamine Davis ye Sone of George & Susannah Davis baptiz^d 26th of 7temb.

John Gibbs the Sone of Grigory and Mary Gibbs was bap^tz p. Mr Shep^d 10th Octo^br.

William Burnett ye Sone of William & Loretta Burnett bap^tz 24th of Octob.

Peter Gates the Sone of Thomas and Roseamond Gates bap^tz 12th of Xemb.

William Parker Reymey Sone of Barnard and Ann Reymey bap^tz 2th of Jan^ry.

Elizabeth Summers Daughter of Jn° and Eliz^a Summers bap^tz 2th of of Jan^ry.

William Beverley Sone of Majo^r Robert Beverley & Katherine Beverley was Baptized 4th of January.

William & Ellianor Doss the Sone and Daughter of John and Ann Doss bap^tz 16th of Jan^ry.

Thomas Allen the Sone of Richard & Ann Allen borne 23th No^br bap^tz 23th Jan^ry.

Richard Atwood the Sone of James and Mary Atwood was bap^tz 30th of Jan^ry.

An Accompt of Christenings & Ages of Children For the Yeare 1681.

Ann Wooley Daughter of George & Sarah Wolley was baptized 10th of Aprill.

Mary Gardner the Daughter of Thomas and Diana Gardner was bap^tz 10th of Aprill.

Sarah Dudley the Daughter of James and Eliz^a Dudley Was bap^tz 27th ffebry.

William Baldwin the Sone of Tho. and Mary Baldwin borne 14th ffeb^r bap^tz 18th ditto.

Thomas Mins ye Sone of Tho. & Ann Mins baptized at ye Great Church 24th Aprill.

Elizabeth Tosely Daughter of Tho. & Eliz^a Tosely was bap^tz 29th of May.

Robert Murrey Sone of Alexd^r Murrey was borne 7th of Ap^rll & baptiz^d 4th of June.

William Gess the Sone of William & Eliz^a Guess was baptized 4th of June.

John Man ye Sone of Jno. Man & Dorothy his wife bap^{tz} at home 8th of June.

Elizabeth Webb Daughter of James & ffrancis Webb bap^{tz} 21st of Augst.

Jane Alldin the Daughter of Robert and Ellianor Alldin bap^{tz} Ditto Day.

John Vivion the Sone of Jno. and Marg^t Vivion baptized 28th of August.

Christian Worsdale Daughter of Richard & Martha Worsdale bap^{tz} 20th of August.

John Chayney the Sone of William and Penelope Chaney was borne 8th of August, and baptized p. Mr John Sheppard at the Upper Chap^{ll} 11th of Septemb.

Robert Guilliams Sone of Robert & Ann Guilliams borne 22th Augst bap^{tz} 18 7temb.

Thomas Davis Sone of Jno. & Sarah Davis bap^{tz} at ye Upper Chap^{ll} 16th of Octob.

Katherine Allen Daughter of W^m & Kath. Allen borne 2th Sep^t bap^{tz} 16th of October.

John Jones Sone of Rice & Jane Jones borne 31th Aug^t & bap^{tz} 3th of Octob. following.

Ann Goodlow the Daughter of George & Mary Goodlow bap^{tz} 23th of October.

Mary Carter ye Daughter of Wm. and Pen^o Carter was bap^{tz} 23th of October.

Richard Perrott Sone of Richd Perrott Junr by Sarah his wife borne 5th Octo^{br} bap^{tz} 17th Sep^t.

ffrances Weathers ye Daughter of John and Marg^t Weathers bap^{tz} 27th Novemb.

John Williams the Sone of Tho. & Mary Williams bap^{tz} 4th of September.

Mary Middleton Daughter of William & Mary Middleton bap^{tz} 4th Septmb.

Rice Curtis the Sone of Giles & Mary Curtis borne 4th No^{vr} bap^{tz} 15th January.

Christenings ffor the Year 1681—&c.

Katherine Seager the Daughter of Randolph & Mary Seager bap^{tz} 5th feb^r.

Thomas Smith Sone of Tho. & Eliz^a Smith was Baptized 5th of ffeb^{ry}.

Henry Ryder the Sone of John & Grace Rydr bap^{tz} 26th of ffebruary.

Robert & Ann The sone and Daughter of Eliz^a Wood was bap^{tz} 19th of March.

Alice Davis Daughter of Henry and Ann Davis bap^{tz} 19th of March.

MARRIAGES, &c.

Edward Ellis & Susannah Hill both of this pish was Married 7th July 1678.

William Loyall and Margaret Thompson was Married the 17th of Septemb. 1678

Joseph Mason and Elizabeth Burton was Married the 11th of July 1678.

Thomas Hedgcock & Margery Simmons was Married the 23th Xemb. 1678.

Richard Arrow and Ann Suckling was Married the 24th of Xemb. 1678.

Nicholas House and Elizabeth Hall Married the 20th of January 1678.

William Burnett & Loretta Pannell was Married 20th of January 1678.

Ambros Collis and Elizabeth Lawrence was Married 26th of January 1678.

William Cotterell and Rose Hollyday was Married p. License 2th ffebry 1678.

James Parker & Elizabeth Dudley Married p. Lycence the 21th of ffebruary 1678.

* * * gyn & Margaret Bridger was married p. Lycence the 27th of ffebruary 1678.

* * * Patris & Eliza Mayo was married the 4th of March 1678.

Major Robert Beverley & Mrs Katherine Hone was Married in Gloster 28th March 1679.

Thomas Wilson & Mary Seers both of this p'ish was Married 27th of Aprill 1679.

Robert Thomas & Ancoretta Wells was married ye 10th of June 1679.

John Vause and Elizabeth Calloway were Married p. Lycence 14th of June 1679.

Henry Davis and Ann West were Married the 29th of June 1679.

James Dudley & Mary Welch was Married in Gloster p. Lycence 18th of July 1679.

William King & Martha Richardson was Married 28th of July 1679.

Peter Brumwell & Ellianor Edwards was Married 10th of August 1679.

Thomas Smith and Elizabeth Clabor were Married 17th of August 1679.

Thomas Gates & Rose Stake was Married the 27th of August 1679.

Richard Hogans & Katherine Clarke was Married 9th of Septemb. 1679.

Major Phillip Lightfoot & Mrs Alice Corbin was Married p. Lycence 23 Septemb 1679.

Jonathan Stanly & Barbary Weybole was married the 28th of Septemb. 1679.

John Davis & Sarah Watts was Married the 26th of January 1679.

John Doss and Ann Taylor was Married the 26th of January 1679.

ffrancis Dodson & Eliza Harrelson was Married the 5th of ffebruary 1679.

Rice Jones & Jane Cock was Married p Lycence the 10th of ffebruary 1679.

Robert Deputy & Ann Wright was Married the 23th of ffebruary 1679.

Here Endeth the Acco't of Marriages for ye Yeare 1679.

CHRISTENINGS &c.

An Accompt of Christenings ffor the Yeare 1682.

ffrances the Daughter of Robert and Katherine Williamson was borne the 21th of Decemb 1682.

Thomas Basket sone of John and Eliz^a Basket was bap^{tz} 16th of Aprill.

Mary Brim Daughter of Jno. & Mary Brim was borne 7th of Jan^{ry} last and baptized the 16th of Aprill.

Elizabeth Douton the Daughter of Anthony & Eliz^a Douton was borne the 31th of Xemb^r 1681 and bap^{tz} ye 16th of Aprill ye Above Yeare.

Elizabeth Brim Daughter of Jno. & Mary Brim was borne 7th of Jan^{ry} and baptized 16th of Aprill.

Hance Erixson the sone of Hance and Judith Erixson was bap^{tz} 16th Aprill.

William Hughes sone of W^m and Eliz^a Hughes borne 17th March & bap^{tz} 14th of May.

John Mountague the sone of Peter and Mary Mountague was bap^{tz} 21th May.

Marvill Moseley the Sone of Marvill and Sarah Moseley bap^{tz} 21th May.

Thomas Blewford the Sone of Tho. & Mary Blewford bap^{tz} 21th of May.

John Ingram the Sone of James and Sarah Ingram bap^{tz} 21th of May.

Mary Jones the Daughter of Tho. & Mary Jones was bap^{tz} the 2nd of July.

Elizabeth Brumwell Daughter of Peter & Eliz^a Brumwell bap^{tz} 18th of July.

Ann Docker Daughter of Edward & ffrances Docker borne 3th of July and Baptized the 13th of August 82.

John West Sone of Nich^o and Hannah West was borne 5th of August and Baptized ye 3^d of September.

Thomas Brookes the sone of Richard and Eliz^a Brookes was borne the 22th of July and baptized the 3^d of September.

Rebecca Hill the Daughter of Tho. & Ann Hill borne 30th of August and Baptized 17th of September.

William Bristow Sone of Jno. & Michall Bristow was baptz^d 29th of October.

Robert Maynell the Sone of Robert & Dorothy Maynell borne 28th Septmb.

ffrances Hancock Daughter of Tho. & Eliz^a Hancock was borne 5th of Novemb.

Elizabeth Musgrane Daughter of Mich^{ll} Musgrane was baptiz^d 19th November.

Sarah Burnett the Daughter of W^m & Coretta Burnett was bap^{tz} 19th November.

MARRIAGES. 1681.

Edward Clark & Ann Allison was Married ye 13th of April 1681.

Benjamine Pickworth & Eliz^a Cooper was Married p Lycence 14th April 1681.

Hance Erickson & Judith Hayden was Married upon 17th of Aprill 1681.

Edward Docker & ffrances Dalley was Married 18th of Aprill 1681.

John Sheeres & Mary Osbondistall was Married 17th of May 1681.

Francis Frygore & Katherine Weaver was Married 8th of June 1681.

William Carter & Penelope Pew was Married upon 31th of August 1681.

John Weathers & Margaret Powell was Married at my Lady Skip-withs 3th Octo^{br} 81.

John Needles & Eliz^a Man was Married 24th of Octob. 1681.

John Lewis of New Kent County & Eliz^a O. Brissell of this prsh 24th Octob 1681.

William Hughs & Mary Drue was Married 28th of Novemb. 1681.

James Dyer & Ann Ashwin was Married the ffirst of Xemb. 1681.

William Thompson & Grace Elwood was Married 24th of ffebruary 1681–2.

Robert Williamson & Katherine Lewis were Married 27th of ffeb-ruary 168½.

Michaell Musgrane & Elizabeth Ball were Married 12th of Aprill 1680.

Robert Munday & Sarah Sackerman was Married the   of Aprill 1680.

Thomas Gardner & Diana Blake was Married the   of Aprill 1680.

Samuell Onely & Jane Parkes was Married the 25th of Aprill 1680.

John Payne & Ann Enos was Married the 9th of May 1680.

Joshua Lanson & Ann Smith was Married p. Lycence 17th of May 1680.

John Lanson & Mary Kilbey was Married p. Lycence 19th of Au-gust 1680.

Phillip Hunnings & Eliz^a Parris was Married 12th of Septemb 1680.

Richard Worsdall & Martha Woodgar was Married 26th Septemb. 1680.

David Nichols & Jone Barnett was Married 11th of November 1680.

John Johnson & Mary Broadbent Married 22th of November 1680.

William Allen & Katherine Smith were Marryed 2th Decemb. 1680.

Oswald Cary & Ann Jaxon Marryed p. Lycence 19th December 1680.

James Webb & ffrances Herbert was Married 19th December 1680.

John Brookes & Mary Hutchings were Marryed 23th of January 1680.

James Bendall & Eliz^a Blake was Marryed 30th January 1680.

John Ryder & Grace ffoster was Married the first Day of ffeb^{ry} 1680.

John Brewer & Mary English was Married upon 7th of ffebruary 1680.

Henry Bray & Ann Hodgekings was Married upon 12th ffeb^{ry} 1680.

Richard Dues & Rachell Norris was Married upon 14th ffebruary 1680.

Here Endeth ye Accompt of Marriages for the yeare.

MARRIAGES &c., 1682.

John Ross & Ann Humphreys was Married the 4th of June 1682.

George Guest & Mary Jones was Marryed the 2th of July 1682.

John Walcom of this parish & Eliz^a Coventry of Petso parish in Gloster Mar^d 10th July, 1682.

William Tignor Junr of ffairefield parish in the County of Northumberland and Dorothy Hill of this parish was Married the 18th of July 1682.

William ffitz Jeffreys & Ann Dudenfield were Married 3th of August 1682.

John Elee & Margaret Loyall of this parish was Married 2th of Aug^o 1682.

William Wakefield & Mary Barnes of this pish was Married 2th of Augt 1682.

David Barwick and Mary Michener of this psh Married 31st of Agust 1682.

Thomas Thompson & Eliza Hill of this parish was Married 17th of Septemb 1682.

Augustine Scarbrough & Dorothy Eddington was Married 6th of Octob^r 1682.

John Deverdall & Jone Blake of this pish. was Married ye 9th of Octob^r 1682.

Roger Prichard & Rebecca Yates of this parish Married 23th of Octob^r 1682.

Thomas Paine & Mary Mountague was Married 24th of October 1682.

Isaac Saserson & Mary Cooper both of this pish. Married 21th of November 1682.

Richard Gabriell & Johannah Buttersby were Married 31th of Xemb 1682.

Edmund Owen & Marg^t Thomas both of this pish. Married 5th of January 1682.

William Smith & Sissely Jones both of this pish. was Married 18th January 1682.

BURIALLS—1678.

Michaell Nickingson Departed this Life the 29th of July & was buried the 30th of July 1678.

Mary Daniel ye Daughter of William Daniel & Jochebed his Wife departed this Life upon 12th of September & was buried 13th Ditto 1678.

Ann Smith being the Second Daughter of that Name to Anthony & Ann Smith departed this Life 16th of Septemb. 1678.

Elizabeth Mins the Daughter of Thomas & Ann Mins Departed this Life 19th of October & was buried 20th Ditto 1678.

Elizabeth Boulton ye Wife of Daniell Boulton Departed this Life the 24th and was buried 25th of Octob. 1678.

Joseph Hill Servant to Joseph Harvey was found Dead in the Woods the 24th of January 1678.

Ellianor Jones the Wife of Humphry Jones departed this Life 9th Jan^ry 1678 and was buried in the Ile of the Upper Chap^ll 12th Ditto.

Daniell Boulton Departed this Life 11th Jan^r 1678 & was buried by his wife.

Edward Matthews departed this Life 25th & was burried 26th of ffebruary 1678.

21

Richard Collins Serv't to Jno Dudley departed this Life 4th August 1678 and was buried the same day in the Lower Chap[ll] Church Yard.

ffrancis Bridge the Sone of ffrancis & Marg[t] Bridge departed this Life 15th of Aug[t] 1679 and was buried in the Ile of Lower Chap[ll] the next day following &c.

Coll[o] Giles Brent of Potomac Departed this Life 2th of September 1679 and was buried in the Great Church Yard y[e] next day following &c.

John Pickworth Carpenter departed this Life 11th of Septemb 1679 & was buried in the great Church Yard ye day following.

John Comby departed this Life 26th of Septemb 1679 & was buried In the great Church Yard the next day following &c.

John Vause Departed this Life 26th of February 1679 & was buried In M[r] Christop[r] Robinsons orchard &c.

Elizabeth Vause the Wife of M[r] Jno. Vause Dec'd was buried 25th Xbr.

Coll[o] John Burnham Departed this Life y[e] 4th of January 1680 & was buried in the Chancell of ye Upper Chap[ll] 11th of Jan[ry] 1680.

ffrances Wormeley Daughter of Coll[o] Christop[r] & ffrances Wormely was Buried at home in theire Garden the 14th of January 1680.

William Sheffield depart[d] this Life 7th of ffebruary and was buried In the Lower Chap[ll] Yard 8th of Ditto.

1682 WEDDINGS OR MARRIAGES &c 1683.

John Tidbury & Eliz[a] Ball both of this parish was Married 25th Jan[ry] 1682.

Robert Roberts & Isabella Baker both of this parish was Married 13th ffebruary 1682.

Aron Williamson & Eliz[a] Waterton of this parish was Married 7th of June 1683.

Phillip Torksey & Mary ffrench y[e] 31th of July 1683.

Richard Reynolds and Margaret Smith was married y[e] 5th Aug[st] 1683.

John Pound and Elizabeth Joy was Married y[e] 28th of Octob 1683.

William Laurence and Johannah Sydnor both of Lancaster County was Married p. M[r] Duell Pead 16th Xemb 1683 p. Lycence.

Thomas Hickman & Martha Thacker was Married ye 18th Xemb. 1683 p Lycence.

John Dearclone & Katherine Clarke was Married 19th of Xemb. 1683.

Samuell Sharpe & Mary Simpson was Married 23th of Xemb. 1683.

John Cocking & Hannah Hollinsworth was Married 28th Xemb. 1683.

William Holley & Sarah Chaseman was Married 9th of January 1683.

Thomas Vahane & Mary Thompson was Married 10th of January 1683.

Robert Blackley & Jane Kidd was married 29th of January 168¾.

Hugh Watts & Johnna Marye was married p p'son Carr in New Kent 29th Jan[ry] 168¾.

John Collins & Marg[t] Weekes was married at M[r] Abra. Weekes ye po April 1684.

Richard ffarrell & Winifrid Watts was married ye 27th of Aprill 1684.

John Stamper and   was married p Mr Pead 8th of May 1684.

Richard Gabriell & Ann Taylor was married p Mr Pead po August 1684.

Henry Osbond and Mary Simpson was married p Mr Pead ye * *

William Woodard of Ware River & Bridg^{t} Williams of this p'ish was married 14th Ag^{t}–84.

Zachariah Mullins & Mary Mabraine of ye p'ish was married 7th of Septemb. 1684.

Nicholas Love & Eliz^{a} Thackston both of this p'ish was married 18th Septemb 1684.

Ezechias Rhodes & Eliz^{a} Nicholls both of this p'ish was married 22th Octob. 1684.

John Pitts & Mary Goodin both of this parish was married y^{e} 26th of Octob. 1684.

John Nicholls & Mary Lewis both of this p'ish was married 20th Novemb. 1684.

Tobias Mickleburrough & Eliz^{a} Minor both of this p'ish married 21th Xemb. 1684.

George Priestnall & Eliz^{a} Williams both of this p'ish was married po Jan^{ry} $168\frac{4}{5}$.

Thomas Stiff & Sarah Salter both of this p'ish was married 8th of ffebry 1684.

David Berwick Junr &   both of this p'ish was married 16th ffebruary 1684.

Ralph Cole & Eliz^{a} Hopkins both of this p'ish was marryed the

William Bennett & Mary Smith both of this p'ish marryed 18th ffebruary 1684.

WEDDINGS OR MARRIAGES 1685 &c.

George Haslewood & Ann Robinson both of this parish was marryed the 28th of ffebruary $168\frac{4}{5}$.

Peter Chilton and Susan Jaxon was marryed y^{e} 2th of March $168\frac{4}{5}$.

William Carter and Elizabeth Russell was marryed 18th of June 1685.

John Gordon and Mary Gordon was marryed y^{e} 17th of June 1685.

Edward Sanders and Elizabeth Teel was marryed y^{e} 6th of January 1685.

Humphry ffloyd & Marg^{t} King was marryed ye 19th of Octob^{r} 1685.

Robert Boodle and Elizabeth Best was married 19th of Octob^{r} 1685.

William Willis & Bridg^{t} Robinson was marryed 23th of June 1685.

William Loyal & Mary Masey was marryed August 6th 1685.

Thomas Allen & Lucey Blake was marryed 10th Augt 1685 & he dyed yt very Day.

Martin Masey & Elizabeth Kidd was married 17th of Septemb 1685.

John Bodgam of Gloster County & Mary Wallas of this parish was marry'd the 30th of Xemb $168\frac{5}{6}$.

Thomas Williams & Isabella Roberts both of this pish marryed 19th January $168\frac{5}{6}$.

Thomas Wadding & Mary Vuite both of this pish were marryed
19th January 168⅚.

Thomas Benson & Dorothy Sutton both of this pish was marryed
11th ffebry 168⅞.

CHRISTENINGS 1682 &c.

. . . . Clerk the . . . . of Richard & . . . . Clarke was baptized
12 Novemb. 1682.

Elizabeth Musgrane yᵉ Daughter of Michall & Elizᵃ Musgrane was
Baptized 19th of November 1682.

Sarah Burnett yᵉ Daughter of Wᵐ & Loretta Burnett bapᵗᶻ 19th
Novemb. 1682.

Lettice Shippey yᵉ Daughter of Richᵈ & Mary Shippey was bapᵗᶻ
19th Xemb. 1682.

William yᵉ Illegitimate Sone of Walter by Katherin Lestridge bapᵗᶻ
25th Xemb. 1682.

Mary Wilson yᵉ Daughter of Thomas & Mary Wilson was bapᵗᶻ yᵉ
31th Xemb. 1682.

Sarah Bendall Daughter of James & Elizᵃ Bendall was borne ye 26th
Xemb and baptized 11th of ffebruary 168⅔.

Margaret Orphin yᵉ Daughter of Henry & Amey Orphin borne 11th
Xemb. bapᵗᶻ 4. Maʳ 1682.

Elizabeth Sandford yᵉ Daughter of John & Sarah Sandford borne
17th January and baptized 4th of March following &c 168⅔.

Tobias Allen yᵉ Sone of Richard & Anne Allen borne yᵉ 30th of
January and Baptized 11th of March following &c 168⅔.

Humphry Jones yᵉ Sone of Humphry &   Jones borne in Lancaster County & bapᵗᶻ in Middlesex County at Mʳ Jones his
house p. Mʳ Shepard 11th march 168⅔

Ann Clay yᵉ Daughter of George & Sarah Clay was baptized 25th
of march 1683.

John Alldin yᵉ Sone of Robert & Ellianor Alldin borne po march
168⅔ (1683) and was Baptized yᵉ 8th of Aprill 1683 &c.

John Summers yᵉ Sone of John & Elizᵃ Summers was baptized yᵉ
8th Aprill 1683.

Margaret Weatherstone yᵉ Daughter of Tho. & Margᵗ Weatherstone bapᵗᶻ 6th May 1683.

Michall Micham yᵉ Daughter of John & Michall Micham was borne
7th apʳˡˡ and Baptized yᵉ 27th of May 1683.

Judith Wormeley yᵉ Daughter of Collᵒ Christopʳ Wormeley & ffrances Wormeley his wife was borne yᵉ 25th of May & baptized At
home 7th of June 1683.

Sarah Murrey yᵉ Daughter of Alexandʳ & Mary Murrey borne 10th
of May & Baptized 15th of July 1683.

William Dudley yᵉ Sone of William & Mary Dudley borne yᵉ po
Aprill and baptized yᵉ 29th of July 1683.

Katherine Wallis yᵉ Daughter of Vallentine & —— Wallis baptized
29th July 1683.

Thomas Patris ye Sone of Matthew & Elizᵃ Patris baptized 5th of
Augᵗ 1683.

Thomas Clincker ye sone of Tho. Clincker by Ginney Bess (a ffree
negro woman) was baptized 5th of Augᵒ 1683. mr. John Cocking Godfather &c.

Margaret ye Daughter of John Pound by Eliz. Joy bap^tz 5th of Augt 1683.

Thomas Weekes ye sone of ffrancis & Eliz^a Weekes baptized 5th August 1683.

Rose Gates Daughter of Tho & Rose Gates was baptized 5th of August 1683.

James Ross sone of Andrew & Mary Ross was baptized 5th of August 1683.

CHRISTENINGS—1683 & 1684.

John Stapleton ye sone of Tho. & ffrances Stapleton was borne 10th of August 1683.

Thomas Carter ye sone of William & Penelope Carter bap^tz 5th of Augt 1683.

Henry Guthridge ye sone of John & Rebe^a Guthridge bap^tz 5 of August 1683.

John Mynor ye sone of Doodis & Eliz^a Mynor was bap^tz 6th of Septemb. 1683.

Efforella Perrott ye Daughter of Rich^d & Sarah Perrott bap^tz 28th Septemb 1683.

Sarah Davis ye Daughter of John & Sarah Davis was bap^tz 4th of Novemb. 1683.

Phillip Phillips Jane Phillips sone and Daughter of Thomas & Eliz^a Phillips (both Capt Creeks Negroes) was baptized 2th of Xemb. 1683.

Elizabeth Butcher y^e Daughter of Richard & Mary Bucher bap^tz 16th Xemb. 1683.

Moses Norman ye sone of Tho. & Mary Norman was bap^tz 19th Xemb. 1683.

ffrances Gilliams ye Daughter of Robt. & Ann Gilliams bap^tz 26th Xemb. 1683.

Katherine Price y^e Daughter of Robert & Jane Price was bap^tz 13th Janry. 168$\frac{3}{4}$.

Agatha Daniell y^e Daughter of W^m & Jochabed Daniel bap^tz 6th of March 168$\frac{3}{4}$.

Henry Basket y^e sone of Jno. & Eliz^a Baskett bap^tz p. Mr Pead 23th of March, 168$\frac{3}{4}$.

Barnett ffreeman y^e sone of Barnett & Ann ffreeman was bap^tz 23th March, 168$\frac{3}{4}$.

Charles Lee y^e sone of Tho. & Eliz^a Lee was baptized p Mr Pead 23th of March, 168$\frac{3}{4}$.

Olliver Seager y^e sone of Randolph & Mary Seagur bap^tz 23th March 168$\frac{3}{4}$.

Margarett Dearelone y^e Daughter of Jno. & Katherine Dearelone bap^tz 30th Ma^r 1684.

Winifrid Williamson y^e Daught^r of Henry &   Williamson bap^tz po. April 1684.

John Burk y^e sone of Jno. & Mary Burk was bap^tz p. Mr Pead 2th of Aprill 1684.

Margarett Vivion y^e Daughter of Jno. & Marg^t Vivion bap^tz 2th of Aprill 1684.

Thomas Thompson ye sone of Tho. & Eliz^a Thompson bap^tz 6th of Aprill 1684.

John Sutton yᵉ sone of   & Elizᵃ Sutton was bapᵗᶻ p. Mʳ Pead 6th
of Aprill 1684.

Thomas Roberts yᵉ sone of Robert & Isabell Roberts bapᵗᶻ 6th of
Aprill 1684.

Joane Salter ye Daughter of Jno & Sarah Salter was bapᵗᶻ p. Mʳ
Pead 6th Aprˡˡ 1684.

Sarah Sadler ye Daughter of Samll & Elizᵃ Sadler bapᵗᶻ 6th of
Aprill 1684.

Elizabeth Guest yᵉ Daughter of George and Mary Guest bapᵗᶻ 13th
Aprill 1684.

John Smith yᵉ sone of Tho. & Elizᵃ Smith was babᵗᶻ 13th of Aprill
1684.

Abraham Trigg ye sone of Daniell and   Trigg baptizᵈ 4th of
May 1684.

Mary Ryder ye Daughter of Jnᵒ & Grace Ryder was bapᵗᶻ 4th of
May 1684.

Humphrey Dudding yᵉ sone of Humphrey & Sarah Dudding bapᵗᶻ
4th May 1684.

Phillip Torkes ye sone of Phill & Mary Torkes was bapᵗᶻ 8th of June
1684.

Mary Scarbrough yᵉ Daughter of Augustine & Dorothy Scarbrough
was Baptized the 8th of June 1684.

Mary Atwood yᵉ Daughter of James & Mary Atwood bapᵗᶻ 5th of
July 1684.

William Hill yᵉ Sone of Tho. & Ann Hill was baptized 20th of July
1684.

CHRISTENINGS.—1684 &c.

Thomas Chayney yᵉ Sone of William & Penelope Chayney borne
June 11th and Baptized 27th of July 1684.

Thomas Chowning yᵉ Sone of Robert & Ann Chowning was baptized
27th of July 1684.

Mary Breame ye Daughter of John & Mary Braeme was Bapᵗᶻ 27th
of July 1684.

Efferydytus Lawson ye Sone of John & Mary Lawson was bapᵗᶻ 10th
of August, 1684.

Charles Gibson Sone of Mary Gibson yᵉ widow of Gregory Gibson
bapᵗᶻ 7th Septemb 1684.

John Gabriell yᵉ Sone of Richard & Ann Gabriell was bapᵗᶻ ye 7th
of Septemb 1684.

Thomas Sharpe the Sone of Samˡˡ & Mary Sharpe was bapᵗᶻ 4th of
Septemb 1684.

James Webb the Sone of James & ffrances Webb baptized 28th of
Septemb 1684.

Robert Blackley yᵉ Sone of Robert & Jane Blackley was bapᵗᶻ 20th
of Octob. 1684.

Mary Watts yᵉ Daughter of Hugh & Johannae Watts was bapᵗᶻ 9th
of Novemb. 1684.

John Williams yᵉ Sone of Tho. & Elizᵃ Williams was baptized 18th
of Novemb. 1684.

John Guy the Sone of Tho. & Mary Guy was baptized 30th of
Novemb. 1684.

Mary Tignor ye Daughter of William & Dorothy Tignor bapᵗᶻ 4th
Xemb. 1684.

Jonathan Brookes y^e Sone of Jon. & Sarah Brookes was borne 4th Xemb. 1684.

Charles Stacy y^e Sone of Thomas & Eliz^a Stacy baptized 11th of January 168$\frac{4}{5}$.

Ann Breame the Daughter of John & Mary Breame bap^{tz} 11th January 168$\frac{4}{5}$

Thomas White the Sone of James & Eliz^a White of New Kent bap^{tz} 11th Jan^{ry} 168$\frac{4}{5}$.

Presilla Whealer y^e Daughter of Tho. & Ellianor Whealer bap^{tz} y^e po ffebruary 168$\frac{4}{5}$.

John Larking aged about   yeares was bap^{tz} at y^e Great Church p. Mr Duell Pead In the face of the Whole Congregation 8th of ffebruary 168$\frac{4}{5}$.

John Williams y^e Sone of Aron & Eliz^a Williams Bap^{tz} 18th of Novemb 168$\frac{4}{5}$.

William Vaughan y^e Sone of Tho. & Mary Vaughan bap^{tz} 15th of february 168$\frac{4}{5}$.

Michall Bristow y^e Daughter of Jno. & Michall Bristow bap^{tz} 15th ffebry 168$\frac{4}{5}$.

Mary Rhodes y^e Daughter Ezehias & Eliz^a Rhodes was bap^{tz} 15th ffeb^{ry} 168$\frac{4}{5}$.

Elizabeth Roe y^e Daughter of Thomas & Mary Roe was bap^{tz} 15th ffebruary. 168$\frac{4}{5}$.

Katherine Collins y^e Daughter of Jno. & Marg^t Collins bap^{tz} 22th ffebruary 168$\frac{4}{5}$.

Hannah ffletcher y^e Daughter of Edward & Mary ffletcher bap^{tz} po. March 168$\frac{4}{5}$.

William King y^e Sone of William & Martha King bap^{tz} y^e 15th of March 168$\frac{4}{5}$.

Henry Blewford y^e Sone of Tho. &   Blewford was bap^{tz} 15th of March 168$\frac{4}{5}$.

Ann Ingram y^e Daughter of James & Sarah Ingram bap^{tz} 15th March 168$\frac{4}{5}$.

Katherine ffarrell y^e Daughter of Rich^d & Winifrid ffarrell bap^{tz} 12th April 1685.

Arthur Bendall y^e Sone of James & Eliz^a Bendall borne 14th of Jan^{r}y 168$\frac{4}{5}$ & Baptized 12th of Aprill 1685.

Hannah Barbee y^e Daughter of W^m & Eliz^a Barbee bap^{tz} 12th of Aprill 1685.

CHRISTENINGS—1685 &c.

Margaret Brumwell ye Daughter of Peter & Ellinor Brumwell bap^{tz} 12th Aprill 1685.

Nicholas Jones y^e sone of Rice & Jane Jones was bap^{tz} at ye upper Chap^{ll} 3th May 1685.

Prissilla Middleton ye Daughter of William & Mary Middleton bap^{tz} 3th of May 1685.

Margarett Slawter ye Daughter of Jno & Eliz. Slawter was bap^{tz} 10th of May 1685.

James Micham ye sone of Jno & Michall Micham was bap^{tz} 17th of May 1685.

Thomas Hancock ye sone of Tho. & Eliz^a Hancock was bap^{tz} 24th of May 1685.

Phillip Brooks ye sone of Rich^d & Eliza Brooks was bap^{tz} ye 24th of May 1685.

Katherine Aldin ye Daughter of Robert & Ellianor Aldin bap^{tz} ye 24th of May 1685.

John Seager ye sone of Randolph & Mary Seager bap^{tz} 29th of May 1685.

James ye Illigitimate sone of Jno. Haddley by Mary Steeres bap^{tz} 17th of June 1685.

Edward James ye sone of Robert & Dorothy James bap^{tz} 16th of August 1685.

Elizabeth Prichett ye Daughter of Roger & Rebecca Prichett bap^{tz} 16th August 1685.

Richard Buttler ye sone of Rich'd & Mary Buttler bap^{tz} 30 of August 1685.

Katherine Williamson ye Daughter of Robert & Kath. Williamson bap^{tz} 6th Septemb. 1685.

Mary Dudding ye Daughter of Humphrey & Sarah Dudding bap^{tz} 6th Septemb. 1685.

John Walters ye sone of William & Katherine Walters was bap^{tz} 20th Septemb 1685.

Nathaniell Guess ye sone of William & Eliz^a Guess was bap^{tz} 4th of Octob. 1685.

Thomas Haslewood ye sone of Tho. & Mary Hazlewood bap^{tz} 18th of Octob. 1685.

Ann Dowlin ye Daughter of Antho. & Eliza Dowlin bap^{tz} 18th of Octob. 1685.

Oswald Wortham ye sone of John & Eliz^a Wortham bap^{tz} 4th of Aprill 1685.

John Sandersee ye sone of Edward & Eliza Sandersee bap^{tz} ye po. June 1685.

Robert Thackston ye sone of Rich^d & Eliza Thackston borne 2th Octob. bap^{tz} 22th Novemb 1685.

Robert Perrott y^e sone of Rich^d & Sarah Perrott Junr bap^{tz} 26th of Novemb. 1685.

Rose Curtis y^e Daughter of Charles & Rose Curtis bap^{tz} 26th of November 1685.

George Stapleton y^e sone of Tho. & ffrances Stapleton was borne 26th of Novemb. and Baptized at y^e great Church 10th of January 168$\frac{5}{6}$.

William Sandford y^e sone of Jno. & Sarah Sandford bap^{tz} 7th of ffebruary 168$\frac{5}{6}$.

Mary Scarbrough y^e Daughter of Augustine & Dorothy Scarbrough bap^{tz} 7th feb. 168$\frac{5}{6}$.

Richard Allen y^e sone of Richd & Ann Allen was bap^{tz} 14th of ffebruary 168$\frac{5}{6}$.

John Brim y^e sone of John & Mary Brim was bap^{tz} 14th of ffebruary 168$\frac{5}{6}$.

Elizabeth Mickleburrough y^e Daughter of Tobias & Eliz^a Mickleburrough bap^{tz} 14th feb. 168$\frac{5}{6}$.

Robert Benson ye Sone of Tho. & Dorothy Benson bap^{tz} 11th of ffebruary 168$\frac{5}{6}$.

WEDDINGS OR MARRIAGES 1686.

John Johnson & Lucina Blake both of this p'ish was married ye 6th of Aprill 1686.

Lewis Gasking & Ann Chambers both of this parish was marryed 6th of Aprill 1686.

Ralph Parr & Pheby Matthews both of this parish was married ye 1686.

William Sheppard & Sarah Edey both of this parish was married ye 20th May 1686.

Thomas Blackby & Margarett Jones both of this parish marryed 4th Octob. 1686.

William Humphreys & Sarah Davis both of this parish was maried 28th Nov. 1686.

William Nicholson & Grace Lewis both of this parish was married 2th Novemb 1686.

Richard Greenstead & Katherine Nicholls both of this parish was maried p. Mr. Pead ye 30th of Decemb. 1686.

Edward Canadey & Alice Nicholls both of this parish was married 30th Xemb. 1686.

Nicholas Rice & Ann Tugwell both of this parish was married 6th ffeb. 1686.

John Guthry & Eliz^a Basket both of this parish was marryed 6th ffeb. 1686.

William Jones of new Kent County & Alice Lee of this pish mary'ed 8th July 1686.

William Daniell Junr & Constance Vause both of this pish was married 24 July 1686.

William Williamson & Sarah Danger both of this pish marrid 23th August 1686.

John Perrin & Judith Spencer both of this parish was marryed 2th Sept. 1686.

John Williams & Mary Cordwell both of y^s parish married 10th of Octob. 1686.

George Johnston & Eliz^a White both of this pish marrid the   1686.

BURIALLS.—1686 &c.

Richard Dews Departed this Life 9th of Novemb. & was buried at Mr William Pooles 11th of Novemb. 1686.

Mr Richard Perrott Senr & president of Middlesex County Court departed this Life 11th and was buried 15th of November 1686.

Thomas Radley Departed this Life 13th & was buried 18th of January 1686.

Mrs Mabell Harvie wife of Joseph Harvie depart^d this Life 26th of Jan^ry & was buryed ye po. ffebruary 1686.

Theophylas Hone of this parish Departed this Life 3th & was buryd 5th of ffeb. 1686.

The Lady Ann Skipwith of this parish Departed this Life 5th of March and was Buryed 6th of March 1686.

Majo^r Robert Beverley of this parish Departed this Life 15th of March and was buryed 19th of March 1686.

Mrs Jane Price Departed this Life 27th of March and was Buryed at home the 29th of March 1687.

Peter Mynor the Sone of Doodis & Eliz⁴ Mynor was Baptized 7th of March 168⅚.

Jacob Stiff the Sone of Tho. & Sarah Stiff borne 11th of Jan' bap'ᵉ 21th March 168⅚.

Robert Dudley the Sone of William & Mary Dudley baptized 21th March 168⅚.

Henry yᵉ Illegitimate Sone of Tho. Ballard was baptized 21th of March 168⅚.

Issabella Willis yᵉ Daughter of William & Bridg' Willis bap'ᵉ 21th of March 168⅚.

Elizabeth Murrey Daughter Allˣ & Mary Murrey bap'ᵉ 4th of Aprill 1686.

Ann Brewer yᵉ Daughter of Jno. & Mary Brewer was bap'ᵉ 18th Aprill 1686.

Mary Standly yᵉ Daughter of Tho. & Rebecca Standly bap'ᵉ 18th Aprill 1686.

Thomasin Gates yᵉ Daughter of Tho. & Rose Gates was bap'ᵉ 9th of May 1686.

Thomas Musgrane yᵉ Sone of Michaell & Eliz⁴ Musgrane bap'ᵉ 23th May 1686.

Elizabeth Carter yᵉ Daughter of Wᵐ & Carter borne 6th of June 1686.

Theophilus Man ye Sone of John & Dorothy Man borne . . . bap'ᵉ 5th Xemb. 1686.

Henry yᵉ Sone of Henry & Ann Davis of Montagues Island bap'ᵉ 19th of Septemb. 1686.

Thomas ffitz Jeffryes yᵉ Sone of Wᵐ ffitz Jeffreys & Ann his wife borne 23th Augᵒ 1686.

William ffitz Jefferyes Sone of Wᵐ ffitz Jeffreys & Ann his wife borne 24th May 1682.

John Jefferyes yᵉ Sone of Wᵐ & ffrances Jefferyes borne 30th of Aug' 1686.

Sarah Cocking yᵉ Daughter of Jno. & Hannah Cocking borne 6th Augᵒ bap'ᵉ 7th Noᵇʳ 1686.

Ellianor yᵉ Illegitimate Daughter of Samˡˡ Banks by Mary Brown born 16th May and baptized 7th of Novemb. 1686.

John Summers the Sone of Jno. & Eliz⁴ Summers bap'ᵉ at yᵉ Uper Capˡˡ 14th Noᵇʳ 1686.

Charles Mullens yᵉ Sone of Zacheriah & Mary Mullens bap'ᵉ 14th Novemb. 1686.

George yᵉ Illegitimate Sone of Tho. Hucklescot by Eliz⁴ Ward borne 19th May and baptizᵈ 28th of Novembʳ 1686.

Rebecca Hill yᵉ Daughter of Tho. & Ann Hill bap'ᵉ at yᵉ lower Chapˡˡ 28th 9ᵇʳ 1686.

Sarah ffarrell yᵉ Daughter of Richᵈ & Winifrid ffarrell bap'ᵉ 19th Xemb. 1686.

Sarah Trigg yᵉ Dauᵗʳ of Daniell & Susannah Trigg bap'ᵉ 26th of Xemb. 1686.

Thomas Doss yᵉ Sone of Jno. & Ann Doss bap'ᵉ at yᵉ lower Chapˡˡ 9th January 1686.

ffrances Dudley yᵉ Daughter of Tho. & ffrances Dudley baptized 9th January 1686.

Eliz. Barwick ye Daught^r of Geo. & Mary Barwick bap^tz at ye Low^r
Chap^ll 20th ffeb. 1686.

Mary Elliott ye Daughter of Tho. & Sarah Elliott bap^tz at ye Upper
Chap^ll 27th ffeb^ry 1686.

Eliz^a Gellett ye Daught^r of Tho. & Ann Gellett baptized 27th of
ffebruary 1686.

Christop^r Beverly ye Sone of Robt. & Katherine Beverly bap^tz at
home 19th March 1686.

Habias Mugguire ye Dat^r of Jno. & Eliz^a Mugguire bap^tz at Mr Prices
29th March 1687.

Peter Guillams Sone of Ann & Robt Guillams bap^tz at home 29th of
March 1687.

James Curtis Sone of James & Eliz^a Curtis bap^tz at home 12th of
Aprill 1687.

Deuell Pead sone of Mr Deuel Pead & Mad^m Sarah Pead borne 14th
Xemb & bap^tz 21th Xemb 1687.

*An Acco^t of ye Register of Middlesex County Giving into the Secre-
taries office Beginning III. 78^r 1686.*

BURIED Viz^t.

11th Septemb. Mary the widow of James Hopkings.

17. Ditto. John Davis Servt to Majo^r Robt. Beverly.

22. Ditto. Tho. the Sone of Robert & Kath. Beverley.

10. Octob. William Rogers of Worchestershire Servt to Alexd^r
Murrey.

11. Novemb. Richd Dews of Yorkshire overseere to Majo^r Beverley.

15. Ditto Mr Richd Perrott Senr Presid^t of Midd^x County Court.

20. Xemb. Daniell Long &c.

— Ditto. John sone of William & Jochebed Daniell.

9 January Mrs Mary Mynor Widow of Mountagues Island.

— Ditto. Peter an negro of Mr John Worthams.

16 Ditto. Ann ye Wife of Richard Allen.

18 Ditto. Thomas Radley of London.

— Ditto. Mary ye Wife of John Bourk.

22 Ditto. John sone of Jno. & Mary Purvis.

— Ditto. Thomas sone of Thomas & Mary Williams.

— Ditto. Hannah Cock Servt to Mr Jno. Nicholls.

— Ditto. Thomas Williams of Hartford Shire.

BURIED.

po ffebry Mrs Mabell Harvey ye wife of Joseph Harvie.

5 Ditto Theophilus Hone native.

8 Ditto Richd Bishop Souldier buried at Mr Richd Robinsons.

10 Ditto Jonathan Brookes.

12 Ditto Samuell Simpson native.

15 Ditto Negro Harry Servt to Mr Richd Robinson.

17 Ditto Mary Payne.

— Ditto Jonathan Whitehead of Southworth London.

23 Ditto James Nicholson of Ixby in Cumberland In England.

27 Ditto William Thompson.

— Ditto Thomas Browne an Indian.

28 Ditto Mary Daughter to Tho. & Mary Haslewood.
4 March. Thomas Elliott of Chipping Orgur in Essex.
 6 Ditto The Lady Ann Skipwith &c.
 7 Ditto Thomas Chowning Native.
— Ditto Hannah Daughter to Christop^r & Katherine *Kilbee*.
— Ditto Hester Daughter to Timothy Davis native.
12 Ditto George ye Illigitimate sone of Nurse Dawny at Brandon.
19 Ditto Maj^r Robert Beverley of Yorkshire.
20 Ditto George Williams of Kent In England.
— Ditto Humphry Dudding &c.
23 Ditto Peter an Negro of Alice Thackers.
24 Ditto Richard Ellis.
25 Ditto 1687 Thomas Tugwell native.
26 Ditto John Davis of Bristow.
— Ditto Job. Gibson.
27 Ditto James Atwood a Yorkshire man.
28 March 1687 Susan wife to Daniell Trigg native.
— Ditto Israell Gray &c.
29 Ditto Jane wife to Robert Price.
— Ditto Vallentine Vallis Cooper.
— Ditto John sone to David George.
30 Ditto George Hanson.
          ffoure negros of Mr Chr. Robinson.
po. Aprill Alice Wife to William Jones native.
 4 Ditto Mary Widow of Jno. Davis, whose mayden name was
     Mary Greene.
 7 Ditto James Webb.
— Ditto William Olliver of ye Ile of Ely neare Cambridge.
— Ditto Thomas Standly.
11th Aprill Mary the Ellegitimate Daughter of Owen Fox and Mary
     Hudson native.
13 Ditto Henry Ballard ye Illegitimate son of Ballard.
— Ditto Eliz Wife to Tho. Stacy native.
16 Ditto Mary wife to Allexand^r Murrey She was of London.
18 Ditto Betty an negro of William Daniells.
— Ditto Betty an negro of Mr Robert Smiths at Brandon.
          65 in this acco^t Buried &c.

1686 CHRISTENED &c.

Septemb. Theophilus the sone of John & Dorothy Man.
 9 Ditto Henry ye sone of Henry & Ann Davis of Mountagus Islad.
Octob Thomas ye Sone of William & Ann ffitz Jeffereys of Rappa-
     hannock.
— Ditto John sone to William & ffrances Jefferys.
No^{br} 9 Nov^{br} Sarah Daughter to Jno & Hannah Cocking.

— Ditto Ellianor ye Illegetimate Daughter of Sam^{ll} Banks.   By
     Henry Browne &c.
14 Ditto John sone to Jno & Eliz. Summers.
— Ditto Charles sone to Zachariah & Mary Mullens.
20 Ditto. John ye Sone of W^m & Jochebed Daniell.
28 Ditto George ye Illegitimate sone of Tho. Hacklefoot by Eliz^a
     Ward.

— Ditto Rebecca Daughter of Tho. and Ann Hill.
19. Xemb. Sarah Daughter to Rich^d & Winifrid ffarrell.
— ditto. Sarah Daughter to Daniell & Susannah Trigg.
9 Jan^{ry} Thomas sone to John & Ann Doss.
— Ditto ffrances Daughter to Thomas and ffrances Dudley.
14 Ditto. John sone of George & Eliz^a Johnston.
10 ffeb^{ry} William sone to William & Grace Thompson.
14 Ditto William Sone to Nicholas & Rose Coleby.
20 Ditto Elizabeth Daughter to Geo. and Mary Barwick.
27 Ditto. Mary Daughter to Thomas & Sarah Elliott.
— Ditto Elizabeth daughter to Thomas & Ann Jellett of Rappahannock.
10 March Elizabeth daughter to John & Eliz^a Wortham.
19 Ditto Christopher sone to Robert & Katherine Beverley.
21 Ditto . Hobbs sone to ffrancis & Eliz^a Weekes.
29 Ditto Peter sone to Robert & Ann Guillams.
— Ditto Phebias Daughter to John & Eliz^a Mackguire.
12 Aprill James sone to James & Eliz^a Curtis.
27 In this Acco^t Christened &c.

1686 MARRIED.

2 Septemb. John Perin of Sussex in England & Judith Spencer
Widow of Kent in England.
21 Ditto. John Davis of Bristow and Mary Greene &c.
4 Octob. Thomas Blackey of Cumberland in England & Marg^t
Jones of Clamorganshire in Wales.
10 Ditto John Williams of Oxfordshire & Mary Cordwell of Shrop-
shire In England.
2 Novemb. William Nicholson & Grace Lewis &c.
20 Xemb. John Macguire and Elizabeth Dourey.
27 ditto John Purvis and Mary Shippey.
30 Novemb. Edward Canaday and Alice Nicholls.
— Ditto. Richard Greensted and Catherine Nicholls.
4 Jan^{ry}. Pythagorus Powell of Katesby in Northamptonshire & Ann
Reynor of Hartfordshire &c.
24 Ditto. William Daniell Junr & Constance Vause both Natives.
6 ffeb^r. John Guttery of Scotland & Eliz. Baskett &c.

65 Buried
27 Christened
12 Cupple Married
———
104 In all.

M^o

Whereas Mr Richard Perrott hath built a Pew in the Chancell on
the further side opposite to the Pulpitt in ye Upper Chappell of the
County of Middlesex, and a Stable also, which Pew and Stable Is
for the Use of Henry Corbin Esqr properly belonging to him and to
those that Shall have and Enjoy the house and Land Whereon he
now Liveth, on and for ever. It appeareth that ye Said Mr Richard
Perrott hath Received full Sattisfaction of Coll^o Henry Corbin Esqr
for building the abovesaid, by Virtue of a Receipt given Under his
hand which beareth Date from September the 29th 1669.

John Masey the Sone of Ralph & Margaret Masey bap^{tz} ye po. May 1687.

Mary ye Daughter of Sarah, widow of Jonathan Brookes bap^{tz} po. May 1687.

William Barbee Sone of W^m & Eliz^a Barbee bap^{tz} 15th of May 1687.

Avarilla Curtis ye Daughter of Charles & Rose Curtis bap^{tz} 15th May 1687.

Charles Grasson Sone of Tho. and Mary Grasson Baptized 15th May 1687.

William Watts ye Sone of Hugh & Johannah Watts bap^{tz} 22th of May 1687.

Thomas Bristow Sone of Jno. & Michall Bristow bap^{tz} 12th of June 1687.

Elizabeth ye Daughter of Patrick & Marg^t Goodridge bap^{tz} 12th June 1687.

John Blackley ye Sone of Robt. & Jane Blackley bap^{tz} 24th of Julye 1687.

Jane Curtis ye Daughter of Giles & Mary Curtis bap^{tz} 24th of Julye 1687.

Thomas the Sone of Ellianor Wheler Widow of Tho. Wheeler 31th of Julye 1687.

Alice Rhodes y^e Daugh^r of Ezekiah &   Rhodes bap^{tz} 7th of Aug^o 1687.

John y^e Illegitimate Sone of Eliz^a Servt to Mad^m Beverly bap^{tz} 28th Augt 1687.

Sarah King y^e Daughter of W^m & Martha King baptiz^d 25th of Septemb. 168$^6_7$.

Ann Guttrey y^e Daugh^r of Jno. & Eliz^a Guttrey was bap^{tz} 16th of Octob. 1687.

Thomas ffearne y^e Sone of Jno. & Mary ffee alias ffearne bap^{tz} po No^{br} 1687.

William Tignor Son of W^m & Dorothy Tignor bap^{tz} 30th of Octob. 1687.

William Carter y^e Sone of William & Penlopec Carter bap^{tz} 6th No^{br} 1687.

John ffearman sone of Jno. & Ursula ffearman bap^{tz} 6th of Novem^{br} 1687.

Peter ye sone of Peter & Susanna Shelton bap^{tz} y^t 15th Novem^{br} 1687.

James the sone of James & Eliz^a Bendall bap^{tz} 20th of November 1687.

William ye sone of John & Mary Bodgam bap^{tz} 7th Xemb 1687.

William the sone of William & Mary Loyall bap^{tz} 11th of January 1687.

Thomas the sone of George and Ann Clark baptized 4th of ffebruary 1687.

Eliz^a Daughter of James & Eliz^a Dudley bap^{tz} 12th of ffebruary 1687.

Sarah ye Daughter of Mr Deuell Pead & Madam Sarah Pead his wife was borne 7th of ffebruary 1687 and bap^{tz} 26th of ffeb^{ry} 1687.

John ye Sone of John & Sarah Hipkings baptized 20th of ffebruary 1687.

Ann ye Daughter of Samuell & Ann Ingram bap^tz 26th ffebruary 1687.

Judith ye Daughter of Robert and Sarah Clark bap^tz 11th of March 1687.

Here Ends the Acco^t of this Register The 10th of Aprill 1688.

WEDDINGS OR MARRIAGES 1687.

Edward Sanders & Mary Browne both of this parish was marryed 6th May 1687.

Thomas Chrisp & Dorothy Long both of this parish was marryed 18th of May 1687.

Martin Masey & Eliz^a Slanter both of this parish was marryed the—

Thomas Robey & Ann Wallis both of this pish was marryed 27th of June 1687.

James Pate & Eliz^a Eddington both of this pish marryed 27th of June 1687.

Abraham Depree & Rebecca Smith both of Rappahannock marryed 3^d July 1687.

Robert George & Sarah Elliott both of this parish was marryed 6th of July 1687.

Benjamin Marsh of New England & Katherine Allison of this pish was Marryed at Mr Robinsons house p Mr Pead 10th of July 1687.

James Shackleford   was marryed 14th of July 1687.

Nicholas ffowle & ffrances Webb both of this pish marryed 24th July 1687.

Joseph Carter & Mary Grant both of this parrish was marryed 4th Septemb 1687.

Joseph Smith & Eliza Rammage was marryed 22th of September 1687.

John ffearman & Ursula Roberts both of this pish mar^d 25th Septemb. 1687.

William Beamont & Eliz^a Hughs both of this pish marryed 10th October 1687.

Samuell Ingram & Ann Hartley both of this pish marryed 17th Octob. 1687.

Henry Emmerson & Eliz^a ffree both of this prish was marryed 17th Octob. 1687.

James Parker of New Kent of Southwell In Notinghamshire & Ellinor Abbott widow of Piscataway was married 18th of October 1687.

John ffearne of Gloster & Mary Lee of this pish Married ye po. November 1687.

William Brooks & Ann Cardwell both of this pish marryed 8th of Novemb. 1687.

John Littlefield & Susannah Sandeford was marryed 17th of Novemb. 1687.

Mr Christopher Robinson & Mad^m Katherine Beverly were mar^d 17th of 9^br 1687.

John Stone of Ridgely in Staffordshire & Mary O. Brissell native were Marryed ye 10th of November 1687.

Nicholas Payne of London & Mary Hackney Native Marryed 17th Xemb 1687.

Edward Sitterne of London & Jane Jones of this pish was marryed p° Janʳ 1687.

Mʳ John Vause & Eliz. Weekes both natives was married 19th of January 1687.

Robert Daniell & Margᵗ Price both natives of this pish mariᵈ 7th ffebʳʸ 1687.

The Honʳᵇˡᵉ Ralph Wormeley Esqʳ And Madam Eliz Armisted of Gloster was married at Collᵒ Armsteds in Gloster 16th of ffebruary 1687.

William Anderson & Ann Clever both of this pish was mᵈ 23th of ffebʳ 1687.

Thomˢ Stacy of Coulchester in Essex & Rebecca Standly was married 27th ffebʳ 1687.

Mʳ John Wortham & Mʳˢ Prudence Needham was married 26th of ffebruary 1687.

Jnᵒ Bloss of Coulchestʳ & Ann Ball Native was married 27th of ffebʳ 1687.

Here ended the Accoᵗ of this Register 10th Aprill 1688.

BURIALLS. Vɪᴢᵗ:

——— Curtis the Daughter of Charles & Rose Curtis Departed this Life the 18th of September 1687.

Samuell Smith yᵉ sone of Mʳ Alexdʳ Smith Departed this Life 5th of May 1687.

Jeremy Vynn of Norwidge departed this Life 17th of July 1687.

Nicholas Cock of this parish departed this Life 25th of Octob 1687.

Mʳ Robert Smith of this parish Departed this Life 27th of Octob 1687.

George Watson of the Barbadoes Servant to Mʳ Robert Smith Departed this Life 5th of December 1687.

Max Petty of this parish departed this Life 12th of Xember 1687.

Mary Bodgham of this parish (native) Departed this Life 12th Xemb. 1687.

Elizabeth Wortham of this parish Departed this Life 16th of Janʳ 1687.

John Loyall Sone of Jnᵒ Loyall Departed this Life 20th of January 1687.

Mʳˢ Margᵗ Perrott yᵉ Wife of Mʳ Richᵈ Perrott Senʳ departed 30th of Janʳ 1687.

Jane Sitterne of this parish departed this Life 4th of ffebruary 1687.

Nicholas Colbee of this pʳish Departed this Life 17th of ffebruary 1687.

Mary Athy of this parish departed this Life 23th of ffebruary 1687.

Sarah Martin of this pish hired Servᵗ to Tho. Norman departed 25th ffebʳ 1687.

Doctor William Poole of this parish departed this Life 29th ffebʳʸ Leap yeare 1687.

Thomas Purify Gardener to Ralph Wormely Esqʳ Departed 28th of ffebʳ 1687.

Here endeth The accoᵗ of this Register yᵉ 10th of Aprill 1688.

Samuell Smith Son of Allexand^r Smith Departed this Life 5th May 1687.

Mr Jeremy Vynn of Norwich Departed this Life 17th of July 1687.

Mr Nicholas Cock the 25th October 1687.

Mr Robert Smith 27th Octob^r 1687.

George Walton of ye Barbados 5th Xemb. 1687.

Max Petty the 12th Xembr 1687.

Mary Bodgham the 12th Xemb^r 1687.

Elizabeth Wortham the 16th January 1687.

John Loyall the 21th January 1687.

Jane Sitterne the 4th ffebruary 1687.

Nich^o Coleby the 17th ffebruary 1687.

Mary Athy the 23th ffebruary 1687.

Sarah Martin the 25th ffebruary 1687.

Do^r William Poole the 29th ffeb^r 1687.

Thomas Purify Gardener 28th ffeb^r 1687.

HERE WE BEGIN.   WEDDINGS &c.   AN NEW ACCO^t 1688.

Henry Osborne & Alice George both of this parish was Married p Mt Pead 15th of May 1688.

William Gough of New Kent & Alice Thacker of this parish were Marryed at Thackers 31th of May 1688.

William Southward & Marg^t Lewis both of this p^rish were mar^d 17th Ap^{rll} 1688.

Samuell Acton & Honour Berry both of this psh. were marryed at Mountagues 12th of July 1688.

Thomas Beamont & Mary Coster both of this pish marry^ed p. Lycence the 28th of June 1688.

Thomas Winger & Ann Doss of this parish were Marryed 15th of July 1688.

William Hobbs ye Shoemaker at Willis was marryed.

Edward Pierce & Katherine Humphryes of this pish was marryed 2th Sep^t 1688.

William Needler & Mrs Dorothy Man both of this pish was married 1688.

John Chedle & Millicent Hughs both of this pish was marryed 9th Octob. 1688.

Richard Bennett & Sarah Harrison both of this p. was maried 28th Octob. 1688.

William Johnson of Norwich & Mary Bennett of West Chester was Marryed 10th of ffebruary 168⅞.

Joyned together in ye State of Holy Matrimony by Mr. Deuel Pead;

David Davis & Martha King of this parish the . . . of . . . 168⅞.

Thomas Guy & Susannah Burford the 14th of Octob. 1689.

Paul Thilman & Mrs Margaret Price widow of Mr Robt Price Jan^r 27th 1689.

William Terrey & Elizabeth Cooper April 21th 1689.

John Nash (Native) and Mary Jenkinson of Cumberland in England were Marryed p. Lycence p. Mr Duel Pead the 12th of July 1690.

Ralph Wilkeson & the Widow Richans 25th of July 1690.

John Swift & Elizabeth Lone August 6th 1690.

Richard Davison and Katherine Downe the   of   1690.

Mr Randolph Seager and Madam Ann Cary were marryed 2th July 1691.

William Scarbrough and ffrances Macrory the —— —— 1691.

Here Endeth the acco^t of Marriages Given Into the Secretarys Office the 15th Day of October 1692.

Here we begin an New acco^t of

CHRISTENINGS—1688 &c.

Elizabeth ye Daughter of Nicholas & Mabell Paine borne 3th of March 1688 and baptized 3th of June 1688.

Alice ye Daughter of Jno & Mary Brim borne 10th ffeb^r bap^{tz} 16th June 1688.

George ye sone of Robert & Ann Chowning was borne 16th of ffeb^r 1688, and was baptized the 10th of June 1688.

Mary Daughter of Tho. & Mary Blewford borne 18th March bap^{tz} 10th of June 1688.

Thomas the sone of Anthony & Eliz^a Dowtin borne 9th May bap^{tz} 3th of June 1688.

Thomas the sone of W^m & Mary Dudley borne 31th of May bap^{tz} 24th of June 1688.

John the sone of Jno & Eliz^a Lane borne 10th of Aprill bap^{tz} ye po. May 1688.

Elizabeth Robinson ye Daughter of Mr Chr. Robinson and Mad^m Kath Robinson borne 18th of Augt Just at night & bap^{tz} at home 20th Augt 1688.

Robert the son of Mr Robert Boodle & Mary his wife borne 15th Novemb. 1688. ffebruary the 17th 168⅚. Baptized at ye Upper Chappell.

Richard sone to William and Ellinor Sadler.

Martha Daughter to Robert and Katherine Williamson.

Ralph ye Son of William and Mary Loyall.

Elizabeth Daughter to Robert and Dorothy James.

James sone to Jno. and Bloss.

Lettice Daughter to Nicholas & Eliz^a Lee.

Thomas Sone to John and Millicent Chedle.

March the 10th 168⅚ Baptized at ye Upper Chappell.

John ye Sone to Hugh and Johannah Watts.

Milliner Daughter to John & Ann Massey.

Aprill the 14th 1689 Baptised at Christ Church.

Elizabeth Daughter to Robert and Ann Gilliam.

Baptized at ye Upper Chappell the 7th of April 1689.

William ye sone of John ffearman and Ursula his Wife.

Thomas Sone of Thomas Gates and Rose his wife.

Sarah Daughter to John Alford and Lettice his Wife.

Baptized at the Upper Chappell 28th of Aprill 1689.

Ann Daughter to Henry Osborne and Alice his wife.

Mary Daughter to John Macguire and Eliz. his wife.

Katherine Daughter to Edward Berry and Sarah his wife.

Edward Sone to William Chayney and Pen his wife.

Agatha Daugh. to Mr Jno. Vause & Mrs Eliz^{a} Vause bap^{tz} 28th of ffeb^{r} $168\frac{8}{9}$.

Agatha Daughter of Deuel & Sarah Pead born 20th of Octob. ab^{t} 10 morning & bap^{tz} 27th ditto—1689.

BURIALLS—1688.

Mary the Daughter of Hugh & Johannah Watts Departed this Life 3th May 1688.

John Willis Departed this Life 4th and was Buried the 6th of May 1688.

Christopher ffisher of Ireland departed this Life y^{e} — June was bur^{d} 30th June 1688.

Walter Cane of Slaigh in Ireland Servt to Wm Tignor depart^{d} this Life p^{o} July. and was bury^{ed} 3th of July 1688.

Richard Askall Servt to James Dudley Departed this Life 6th of July 1688.

Eliz^{a} Dudley wife of James Dudley Departed this Life 8th of July 1688.

John Simpson of Barkin in Essex departed this Life 11th of July 1688.

Prudence Wortham ye Wife of Jno Wortham departed this Life 25th 7^{br} 1688.

Thomas Naylor serv^{t} to Mr Chr. Robinson Dyed the 23th of Nemb. 1688.

Mrs Ann Robinson Wife to Mr Richd Robinson Dyed 8^{br} 5th 1688.

John Cutter departed this Life the 11th of Octob 1688.

Elizabeth Atwood Departed this Life the 15th of Aprill 1689.

Mr Thomas Heyward Clerk of ye great Church Departed this Life 1689.

Mrs Eltonhead Stanard departed this Life October 28th 1689.

Two Servants belonging to Mr Robert Price (a man & a woman) Departed this Life in August—1689.

Thomas Pullen departed this Life 20th of December 1689.

Mr Robert Price Departed this Life the 11th of January $168\frac{9}{0}$.

Robert Porter Departed this Life the 27th of January $168\frac{9}{0}$.

Richard Thaxton departed this Life 2th of March $168\frac{9}{0}$.

Eusebias O.Bressell was buried the 7th of March $168\frac{9}{0}$.

Nicholas Lone Departed this Life the 7th of June 1690.

William Nicholson Dyed 19th & was buried the 21th of August 1690.

Edmund Mickleburrough Sen. departed this Life 27th of August 1690.

Honour Acton Dyed 3th and was buried 4th of Octob 1690.

Mary Wife of Mr Randolph Seager Departed this Life 8th of No^{br} 1690. and was buried in the Upper Chappell &c.

Richard the Son of Samuell Acton Dyed 9th of ffebruary $169\frac{0}{1}$.

Capt Oswald Cary Dyed the 17th of ffebruary $169\frac{0}{1}$.

Mr John Vause Dyed the 9th of September 1691.

John y^{e} Son of Do^{r} Robert Boodle was buried the 21th of Decemb 1691.

Mr John Wortham Departed this Life the 8th of June 1692.

Capt Walter Whittaker Dyed 27th of July 1692.

Here Endeth the Accot of Burialls Given into the Secretarys office the 15th of Octob. 1692.

CHRISTENINGS—1689 & 1690.

Elizabeth Daughter to Anthony & Ann Ridgaway borne 8th June 1689.

John ye Sone of John & Eliz^{a} Guthrey bapt^{z} 28th July 1689.

William sone of Mr Randolph Seagur and Mary his wife was borne 28th of August and baptized 8th of Septemb 1689.

John Sone to Richard & Eliz^{a} Brookes baptized 8th Septemb 1689.

William Sone to Mr William & Constance Daniell bap^{tz} at home the 8th of September 1689.

Christened at the Upper Chappell ye 1th day Xember 1689.

Mary Daughter to John Barlow and Pheby his wife.

Elizabeth Daughter to Zachariah Mullens & Mary his Wife.

Catherine Daughter to Robert George & Sarah his Wife.

Thomas Sone of Mr Thomas Stapleton & ffrancis his Wife.

Richans y^{e} Sone of John & Mary Brim bap^{tz} 23th ffeb^{r} 168$\frac{9}{0}$.

John y^{e} Sone of Jno & Jane Smith bap^{tz} at home 23th ffeb^{r} 168$\frac{9}{0}$.

Elizabeth Daughter to J^{no} & Eliz. Summers bap^{tz} 16th March 168$\frac{9}{0}$.

Baptized at y^{e} Upper Chappell the 6th of Aprill 1690.

Thomas the Sone of Humphrey and Jane Salt.

Samuell y^{e} Sone of Robert and Ann Chowning was Borne the 27th of ffebruary 1690, Baptized y^{e} 6th of Aprill.

Jane y^{e} Daughter of Patrick & Margaret Michaell y^{e} Same day.

Jeremiah ye Sone of Peter & Eliz^{a} Rawlings of New Kent County bap^{tz} p. Mr Pead 6th of Aprill 1690.

John the Sone of William & Marg^{t} Southward bap^{tz} at ye Great Church the 13th of August 1690.

John ye Sone of John & Pen. Evans was bap^{tz} at Upper Chap^{ll} 4th May 1690.

William ye Sone of W^{m} & Ann Brookes baptized 25th of May 1690.

Mayo & Sarah The sone and Daughter of John & Sarah Bourk borne 22th of May and baptized 15th of June 1690.

William ye Sone of Joseph and Mary Carter bap^{tz} 15th of June 1690.

Andrew the Sone of Jno & Sarah Hipkings was bore 11th of May and baptized 22th of June at ye Great Church 1690.

1690 1691 & 1692 &c.

Elizabeth ye Daughter of John & Michall Bristow bap^{tz} 6th of July 1690.

Rebecca ye Daughter of George & Eliz. Johnston bap^{tz} 6th of July 1690.

Thomas Sone of Robert & Sarah Clark bap^{tz} 6th of July 1690.

Sarah Daughter of Roger & Rebecca Prichard bap^{tz} 6th of July 1690.

Elizabeth Daughter of James & Sarah Ingram bap^{tz} 6th of July 1690.

Elizabeth Daughter of Anthony & Eliz. Dowlin bap^{tz} 21th of Augt 1690.

Katherine Vallott ye Daughter of Claud & Ann Vallott was borne the 2th of September 1690 and bap^{tz} 28th of the Same month 1690.

Ann y^{e} Daughter of George and Ann Haslewood borne the last day of November and baptized 28th of December 1690.

Theophilus y^{e} Sone of Mr Christop^{r} Robinson & Katherine his wife was baptized the ffirst day of January 169$\frac{0}{1}$.

Mary the Daughter of Mr Randolph & Mrs Mary Seager borne the
9th of Novemb. and baptized 11th of Ditto 1690.

William Sone of Tho. & Eliz^a Hancock bap^{tz} 20th of ffebruary 169$\frac{0}{1}$.

Clara the Daughter of Mr Christ^r & Mrs Kath. Robinson was borne
the 11th day of October 1689.

John the Son of Mr Robert & Mrs Mary Boodle was borne 24th of
January and bap^{tz} 19th of ffebruary 169$\frac{0}{1}$.

John Nash the Son of John & Mary Nash was borne 22th of Octob.
between Sun Sett and Darke and was bap^{tz} 13th of Novemb.
1691.

Henry the Sone of Ann Jones was baptized the 7th of Septemb 1689.

James the Sone of James & Jone Lewis baptized 30th of Novemb.
1690.

John the Sone of Robert & Kath Williamson bap^{tz} 30th of August
1691.

Henry the Sone of Peter & Abigall Chilton bap^{tz} 20th of Septemb.
1691.

Lucas the Sone of Robert & Ann Gilham bap^{tz} 27th of March 1692.

Rebecca the Daughter of James & Ann Cooper bap^{tz} 2th of Aug^t
1692.

Joseph the Sone of Robert & Eliz^a Humphreys bap^{tz} 11th Septemb.
1692.

William Hackney the Sone of Wm Hackney Junr borne 22th Jan^{ry}
1691.

George the Sone of William & Mary ffreeston borne ye 1st of Octo^{br}
1690.

William the Sone of Tho. & ffrances Dudley bap^{tz} 8th of October
1693.

John the Son of Jno. & Sarach Sandefford was Born the tenth of
October 1691.

Here Endeth the acco^t of Christenings Given Into the Secretarys
office the 15th of Octob. 1692.

The Age of Mr Richard Perrott & Sarah his wife.

Richard Perrott the Sone of Mr Richard Perrott Dec'd was Borne
the 24th of ffebruary 1650 Being the first Man Child that was
gott and borne In Rappahannock River of English parents &c.

Sarah Perrott was borne In Ware Parish in Gloster County on a
Sunday about 2 a clock afternoone the 16th of Augt 1657 being
the Daughter of Majo^r Tho. Curtis by Averilla his Wife, and
was marryed to the said Perrott 11th of ffeb^r 1672. Being then
the widow of one Mr Wm Halfhide &c.

The names of what children (& the Times When) have been born to
the abovesaid Mr Richard Perrott, and Sarah Perrott of Middlesex County.

Henry Perrott the Sone of the abovesaid Perrott was borne the 25th
of January—1657.

ffrank the Daughter of the above said was borne 28th of Augt 1677.

Sarah the Daughter of ye abovesaid was borne 21th of Sep^t 1679.

Richard the Sone of the abovesaid Perrott was borne 5th of Octob
1681.

Averilla the Daughter of the abovesaid was borne 3th of Augt 1683.
Robert the Sone of the abovesaid was borne 25th of Octo^{br} 1685.
Curtis the Sone of the abovesaid was borne 19th of Augt 1688.
Mary the Daughter of the abovesaid was borne 19th of Jan'y 1690.
Churchhill Blake the Sone of Thomas & Margaret Blake was borne
    30th of November 1690.
John Sandeford the Sone of Jno & Mary Sandeford was born the
    17th of Octob 1691.
Elizabeth Musgrane the Dauter of Michaell & Elizabeth Musgrane
    was borne 18th of August 1693.
ffrances Needles ye Daughter of W^m & Dorothy Needles was borne
    19th of March 1690.

CHRISTENINGS—1693 & 1694.

William ffurnelt ye Sone of Jno & Alice ffurnett bap^{tz} 16th of ffeb^{ry}
    1693.
John ye Sone of George & Eliz. Blake bap^{tz} 7th of Aprill 1693.
William & Roger begotten of Two Servant Wenches belonging to
    Coll^o Christopher Wormeley baptized the first of them on the
    30th of March the other on the 7th of Aprill 1693.
Edward Sone of Charles & Marg^t Whittaker bap^{tz} 18th of June 1693.
Sarah the Daughter of Tho. & Marg^t Chilton bap^{tz} 16th of July 1693.
Elizabeth Needles Daug^{tr} of W^m & Dorothy Needles borne 20th of
    March 169¾ and baptized 16th of July 1693.
Andrew ye Sone of Augustine & Eliz. Williamson bap^{tz} 30th of July
    1693.
Elizabeth the Daughter of Ezekias & Eliz^a Rhodes bap^{tz} 27th of
    Augt 1693.
Elizabeth ye Daughter of Ambros & Eliz^a Burfutt bap^{tz} 10th Sept.
    1693.
Thomas the Sone of Peter & Abig^{ll} Chilton bap^{tz} 20th of Septemb
    1693.
Katherine ye Daughter of W^m & Eliz^a Priest bap^{tz} 20th of Septemb.
    1693.
Elizabeth the Daughter of Hugh & Hannah Watts bap^{tz} 20th of
    Septemb. 1693.
Elizabeth ye Daughter of Anthony & Isabella Banks bap^{tz} 5th
    Novemb. 1693.
Thomas the Sone of James & Jone Lewis bap^{tz} 5th of Novemb.
    1693.
Mary the Daughter of James & Ann Dudley bap^{tz} 24th of ffebruary
    1693.
Mary the Daughter of Jno & Sarah Sandeford bap^{tz} 24th of March
    1693.
George the Sone of Edmund & Mary Sanders bap^{tz} 24th of March
    169¾.
Thomas the Sone of Peter & Ellianor Brumwell bap^{tz} 15th of Aprill
    1694.
Nicholas the Sone of Jno & Michall Bristow bap^{tz} 17th of June 1694.
Nicholas the Sone of Tho. & Eliz^a Stiff bap^{tz} 8th of July 1694.
John the Sone of Robert & Ann Gilham bap^{tz} 19th of July 1694.
ffrances the Daughter of Tho. & Cassandra Townsand bap^{tz} 9th Sept.
    1694.

Daniell the Sone of Jn° & Susannah Ress bap^tz 24th of Septemb.
1694.

Katherine a Mulatto Woman was baptized the 11th of Novemb. 1694.

Robert Wortham the Sone of George Wortham & Sarah his Wife
was borne 4th of October & baptized 16th of Ditto 1694.

Margaret the Daughter of Joshua & Mary Gore borne ye 1st Octob.
1694 and was baptized the 2th of Xemb. following.

HERE WE BEGIN—BURIALLS &c.

Mr Matthew Lidford (our late Minister) Departed this life the 22th of
March Anno Domo. 169$\frac{2}{3}$.

Mr Richard Robinson Senr was buried 19th of Xemb. 1693.

Mrs Ann Gray the Wife of Mr Samuell Gray (our minister) Departed
this life the 8th of August 1696.

Sarah y^e Wife of John Sandeford departed this Life May ye 8th &
Buried ye 9th 1706.

Mary ye Wife of Richard Alford departed this Life May ye 18th &
Buried ye 20th 1706.

Mary ye Wife of Robert Bigge departed this Life June ye 4th and
Buried ye 5th 1706.

Elizabeth ye Daughter of Mr Robert Dudley & Mrs Elizabeth his
Wife departed this Life June ye 20th and was Buried June ye
21st Anno Domi 1706.

Elizabeth ye Daughter of Ezekias Rhodes & Elizabeth his Wife
departed this Life July ye 20th and was Buried July ye 22nd
Anno Domi° 1706.

Elizabeth Sutton departed this Life Octob ye 27th & was Buried
Novemb^r ye 1st 1706.

Thomas Thompson Was Buried December ye 16th Anno Domi 1706.

Amy ye Wife of George Barack was Buried Decemb ye 25th Anno
Domi 1706.

George Dudly ye Son of Maj^or Robert Dudly departed this Life April
y^e 12th And was Interred April y^e 15th Anno Domini 1707.

John y^e Son of John & Mary Gibbs departed this Life March y^e 31st
and was Interred April y^e 1st Anno Domin 1708.

Edyth ye Wife of John Dudly departed this Life March y^e 4th and
was Interred March y^e 6th Anno Domi. 170$\frac{8}{9}$.

Margaret Goar y^e Daughter of Joseph Goar departed this Life May
y^e 1st and was Interred May y^e 2nd Anno Domi 1709.

Elizabeth Clifton departed this life febuary y^e 11th and was Interred
february y^e 12th: Anno Domi 170$\frac{8}{9}$.

Coll^nl John Grimes departed this Life August y^e 28th and was Interred
August ye 31st A. D. 1709.

CHRISTENINGS.—1694 & 1695.

Dorothy Wallis y^e Daughter of William & Ann Wallis was borne the
11th of November 1694.

Maccrora Scarbrough Sone of William & ffrances Scarbrough was
baptized the 3d of ffebruary 169$\frac{4}{5}$

Ann Hames the Daughter of Charles & Eliz^a Hames bap^tz 3th of
ffeb^r 169$\frac{4}{5}$.

Mary the Daug^r of Susannah & Edward Gough bap^tz 5th of ffeb^ry 169$\frac{4}{5}$.

43

Rebecca Hackney Daughter of W^{m} & Mary Hackney bap^{tz} 3th ffeb^{ry} $169\frac{4}{5}$.
Elizabeth the Daughter of Allexand^{r} & Eliz^{a} Mesan was borne the 11th of Xemb and bap^{tz} 10th of March $169\frac{4}{5}$.
John the Sone of John J. Johnson and Lucy his wife was borne the 6th of January and baptized 24th of March $169\frac{4}{5}$.
Rachell the Daughter of ffrancis and Mabell Dodson was born the 20th of ffebruary $169\frac{4}{5}$ and bap^{tz} 5th of May 1695.
George Gray the sone of Mr Samuell Gray and Mrs Ann Gray his wife was borne 23th of Aprill being St. George's Day and was baptized the 5th of May at his owne house, Mr William Churchhill and Capt William Daniell being God Fathers, and Mrs Ann Grimes God Mother 1695.
Joyce Bodgham the Daughter of John & Hannah Bodgham was baptized the 12th of May—1695.
Sarah Toxell the Daughter of Phillip and Mary Toxell was Baptized 12th of May 1695.
John Dudley the Sone of John & Eliz^{a} Dudley bap^{tz} 23th June 1695.
Elizabeth Gilley ye Da^{tr} of Tho. & Jane Gilley bap^{tz} 23th of June 1695.
ffrances Gressam ye Daughter of Tho. & Eliz^{a} Gresham was Borne 26th of March and baptized the 23th of June 1695.
Charles the Son of Tho. & Mary Williamson was Borne 15th of July and baptized the 4th of August 1695.
John the sone of Jno & Michall Miller bap^{tz} 4th of August 1695.
Elizabeth the Dau^{tr} of George & Eliz^{a} Blake bap^{tz} 18th of August 1695.

CHRISTENINGS—1695 &c.

Ann the Daughter of Jno & Mary Aston baptized 10th of Augt 1695.
Uriah the sone of Jno and Ann Boulton bap^{tz} 27th of Octob 1695.
Ann the Daughter of Samuell & Ann Ingram bap^{tz} 19th Novemb. 1695.
Susannah Jones Daughter of Roger & Mary Jones was borne the 19th of November and was Christened the same day at Mr Churchhills house p. Mr Samuell Gray 1695.
Christopher Kilbee the Sone of William & Johannah Kilbee was borne the   of Jan^{r} and bap^{tz} the 9th of ffeb^{ry} $169\frac{5}{6}$.
Robert Williamson the Sone of Robert & Katherine Williamson was Borne 19th of Jan^{r} and baptized 23th of ffeb^{r} $169\frac{5}{6}$.
William Newton the sone of William &   Newton was Borne 3th of January and Baptized the 2th of March $169\frac{5}{6}$.
Dorothy Dudley Daughter of Thomas & ffrances Dudley was Borne the   and baptized 10th of May 1696.
John Needles the sone of William and Dorothy Needles was Baptized the 10th of May 1696.
Sarah Sandeford the Daughter of John & Sarah Sandeford was bap^{tz} the 10th of May 1696.
Catherine Workley the Daughter of Benjamine & Elizabeth Workley was bap^{tz} 10th of May 1696.
Ezechias Rhodes the Sone of Ezechias & Elizabeth Rhodes was Baptized 10th of May 1696.

Katherine Baldwin Daughter of Edward & Keziah Baldwin was Baptized 5th of July 1696.

CHRISTENINGS.

William Dudley the Son of James & Ann Dudley bap^{tz} 2th of Augt 1696.

Benjamine Gray the Sone of Mr Samuell Gray Minister & Madam Ann Gray his wife was baptized at his house parson Vicaris and Mr John Grimes being God ffathers and Madam Elizabeth Wormeley God Mother. The 10th of August 1696.

The names and Ages of the Children of William and Grace Thompson.

Sarah the Daughter of the above said Thompson was borne the 13th of March 168$\frac{3}{4}$.

William the Sone of y^e abovesaid Thompson was borne the 10th of Octob 1685.

Mary the Daughter of the abovesaid was borne 2th of Sept. 1689.

Samuell the Sone of ye abovesaid was Borne 11th Novemb. 1691.

Elizabeth Smith ye Daughter of Robert & Elizabeth Smith was Bap^{tz} the 8th of November 1696.

Sarah Lawson the Daughter of Rowland & Ann Lawson was baptized 15th of November 1696.

Sarah Gore Daughter of Joshua Gore and Mary his wife was Borne 6th of Novemb. and baptized 6th Decemb 1696.

The Names and Ages of Two Children of Mr Henry Thacker & Elizabeth his wife &c.

Elizabeth Thacker was borne the 3th of December being Monday 1694.

ffrances Thacker was Borne the 19th Decemb^r being Satterday 1696.

CHRISTENINGS &c.

The Names and Ages of 3 Negros of Mr Henry Thacker's.

Dick the Sone of Nick and Jenney was borne 10th of March 1690.

Billey the Sone of Sampson & Nell was born 20th of ffeb^{ry} 1691.

Ned the Sone of Nick and Jeney was borne 20th of Aprill 1694.

Sarah Haines the Daughter of Charles & Eliz^a Haines bap^{tz} 7th No^{br} 1697.

Aimey Gresham ye Daughter of Tho. & Mary Gresham bap^{tz} 9th Nov. 1697.

Elizabeth Beverley the Daughter of Capt Henry Beverley & Mrs Elizabeth Beverley his wife was baptized p. Mr Gray at Esq. Wormeleys the 9th of Novemb 1697.

Richard Burnett the Sone of Jone Burnett was borne 16th Xemb. and baptized the —— —— 1697.

Churchhill Jones the Sone of Roger & Mary Jones was borne 15th of Jan^r and bap^{tz} 13th of March 169$\frac{6}{7}$.

William the Sone of William & Johannah Kilbee bap^{tz} 13th of March 169$\frac{6}{7}$.

James Duglas the Sone of James & Ann Duglas bap^{tz} 13th March 169$\frac{6}{7}$.

John ffurnett y^e Sone of Jno & Alice ffurnett bap^{tz} 13th of March 169$\frac{7}{8}$.

Ellianor Duglas the Daughter of James & Ann Dudlass was borne the 9th of June 1691.

Johannah Hackney the Daughter of William & Eliz^a Hackney was borne 8th of March & baptized 3th of Aprill 1698.

Isabella Hill the Daughter of William & Ann Hill was borne the ffirst of May 1698.

Arthur Nash The Sone of John & Mary Nash was Borne y^e 16th of November 1696 & was Bap^{tz} the 14th of ffebruary 169$\frac{6}{7}$.

The ages of two Children of Richard & Sarah Winn.

Mary Winn was borne 16th of Xember 169$\frac{6}{7}$.

Sarah Winn was borne 17th of January 169$\frac{8}{9}$.

CHRISTENINGS.—&c.

John Blake the Sone of George & Eliz^a Blake was bap^{tz} 1th May 1698.

Thomas Marston the Sone of Jno & Ann Marston was borne the 30th of August about 10 aClock & was bap^{tz} 15th Sept 1698.

William Roe y^e Sone of Jno & Katherine Roe bap^{tz} y^e 1st May 1698.

William Needles y^e Sone of W^m & Dorothy Needles bap^{tz} 22th June 1698.

Patrick Miller y^e Sone of Jno & Michall Miller bap^{tz} 22th of Jan^r 169$\frac{8}{9}$ and was borne the 29th of December 169$\frac{8}{9}$.

Mary Gore y^e Daughter of Joshua & Mary Gore was borne the 2th of Decemb. & baptized 22th of January 169$\frac{8}{9}$.

Elizabeth Gibbs y^e Daughter of Jno & Mary Gibbs bap^{tz} 22th Jan^r 169$\frac{8}{9}$.

James Cooper ye Sone of James & Ann Cooper was bap^{tz} 22th of Jan^r 169$\frac{8}{9}$.

Ambros Dudley the Sone of ffrancis & Dudley bap^{tz} 17th No^{br} 1698.

Elizabeth Ashton y^e Daughter of Tho. & Eliz. Ashton was baptized the 8th of ffebruary 169$\frac{8}{9}$.

Vallentine Wallis y^e Sone of William and Ann Wallis was Baptized 27th of March 1699.

Richard Phiney the Sone of Jno & Marg^t Phiney bap^{tz} 28th May 1699.

William Rhodes the Sone of Ezechias and Eliza Rhodes was baptized 28th of May 1699.

Sarah Daughter to John & Ann Boulton bap^{tz} 25th of June 1699.

Mary the Daughter of Capt Kemps Maide bap^{tz} 25th of June. 1699.

Richard the Sone of Jno Sandefords Maid bap^{tz} 25th of June 1699.

Rebecca Dennis the Daughter of Jno & Catherine Dennis was baptized the 22th of Septemb. 1699.

William Dunston the Sone of Thomas & Eliz^a Dunston was Baptized the 26th of July 1699.

Grace Sibley the Daughter of John Sibley was bap^{tz} 26th July 1699.

Zebulun the Sone of James & Jone Lewis bap^{tz} 22th of Octob 1699.

CHRISTENINGS &c.

Judith Cardis the Daughter of Uriah Cardis was borne 28th Sept. and baptized the 29th of Octob. 1699.

Ellianor the Daughter of Arthur & Mary Smith bap^{tz} 31th X^{br} 169$\frac{9}{100}$.

The names & Ages of Six Children of Ezechias and Elizabeth Rhodes &c.

Mary Rhodes was borne the 5th of January 1684.

Alice Rhodes was borne 18th of July 1687.

John Rhodes was borne the 12th of ffebruary 1689.

Elizabeth Rhodes was borne 7th of July 1693.

Ezechias Rhodes was borne the 6th of Aprill 1696.

William Rhodes was borne the 23th of Aprill 1698.

Thomas Berry son of Gerrat Berry was Born In January & Bap^tz 23th ffeb^r 1699.

Mary Beverley the Daughter of Mr Henry Beverley and Mrs Eliz^a Beverley was borne 11th of Novemb. 1699.

William Porter Sone of W^m & Jane Porter bap^tz 4th March 1690.

John Hackney Dodson the sone of ffrancis Dodson was Baptized the 4th of March 1690.

Margaret Martin the Daughter of Mrs Eliz^a Martin was Baptized 7th of March 1690.

CHRISTENINGS 1700.

William Scarbrough the Son of William & ffrances Scarbrough was Baptized 9th of May 1700.

Elizabeth Humphreys the Daughter of Robert & Rebecca Humphreys was baptized 19th of May 1700.

William Austine the Sone of John Austine bap^tz 19th of May 1700.

Sarah Blake the Daughter of John & Eliz^a Blake bap^tz 19th May 1700.

Margarett Cooper ye Daughter of James Cooper bap^tz 19th of May 1700.

Mary Chilton the Daughter of ——— Chilton baptized 9th of June 1700.

Mary Almond was bap^tz the 9th of June 1700.

Mussella a Negro Boy of Majo^r Dudleys bap^tz 9th of June 1700.

Lettice an Negro gile of Majo^r Dudleys bap^tz 9th of June 1700.

Clemence ye Daughter of Augustine & Jane Owen was borne the 4th of June and bap^tz 21th of July 1700.

Stephen Gibbs the Sone of Jno & Mary Gibbs bap^tz 21th of July 1700.

William Gardner the Sone of William & Mary Gardner was borne 2th of July and baptized 21th of July 1700.

John Marston the Sone of Jno & Ann Marston was borne the 13th of July and baptized 14th of August 1700.

Susannah Churchhill Jones the Daughter of Roger & Mary Jones was baptized the 14th of August 1700.

Mary Portwood the Daughter of Tho. & Barbary Portwood was borne 19th of ffebruary & baptized 24th of Xember 1699.

Charles Baker the Sone of William & Susannah Baker bap^tz 14th July 1700.

Zebulun Chilton the Sone of Peter & Abigall Chilton bap^tz 4th Aug^o 1700.

Ann Kemp the Daughter of Coll^o Matthew Kemp & Madam Ann Kemp his Wife was borne 12th of Sept. & bap^tz 22th Sept. 1700.

The ages of 5 Children of Tho. & Mary Gresham.

Charles Gresham was Borne the 10th of March 1687.
Thomas Gresham was borne the 9th of June 1689.
John Gresham was borne the 5th of January 1692.
Ffrancis Gresham was borne the 26th of March 1695.
Amey Gresham was borne the 12th of July 1700.
The Said Amey was by her first husband Gardner &c.

Hannah the Daughter of William &   Beamont was baptised the
    13th of October 1700.
Elizabeth Miller the Daughter of John and Michall Miller was borne
    26th of Sep^t and baptised 8th Novemb. 1700.
John Marchum the Sone of William & Eliz: Marchum was borne 6th
    of xember & bap^{tz} 9th of February 1700.
Elizabeth the Daughter of Tho. & Eliz: Still bap^{tz} 16th Feb^r 1700.
Joseph the Sone of Tho. & Barbary Portwood bap^{tz} 9th March 170$\frac{0}{1}$.
Mary the Daughter of Valentine & Ann Wallas was borne the 26th
    of February & baptized the 30th of March 1701.
Ann Newton the Daughter of William and Amey Newton, was bap-
    tized 30th of March 1701.
Ann Hill the daughter of W^m & Ann Hill bapt^{ed} 30th March 1701.
Elizabeth Gilley the Daughter of Tho. & Jane Gilley was baptised
    the 13th of June 1701.
Foure Negroes of the Widow Briscoe Baptized—Viz^t Frances, Sarah,
    Katherine, Phelis; all baptized the 6th of June 1701.

CHRISTENINGS.

Betty an Negro of Capt Smiths was borne 13th of July and was bap-
    tized the 13th of July 1701.
Thomas the Sone of Edward Williams was borne 7th of July and
    was baptized the 3^d of August 1701.
Robert an Illegitimate of a woman belonging to Do^r Stapleton was
    baptized the 3^d of August 1701.
John the Sone of Tho. & Eliz^a Baker borne 22th of Augt and bap-
    tized 14th of Septemb. 1701.
Susannah the Daught^r of Jno & Mary Michener was borne 19th of
    August and baptized 21th Septemb 1701.
Elizabeth Simms the Daughter of Tho. & Ann Simms was borne
    21th of September & baptized &c 1699.
Ann the Daughter of the aforesaid Simms was borne the 19th of
    August and baptized 16th of Septemb 1701.
Robert the Sone of Capt Henry Beverley and Madam Elizabeth
    Beverley his Wife was borne 6th of No^{vr} 1701.
Arthur the Sone of Edward & Keziah Ball born 14th March 1697.
Johannah the Daughter of the said Ball borne 14th Ap^{rll} 1699.
An the Daughter of Jno & Marg^t Phiney bap^{tz} 16th No^{vr} 1701.
Mary Godbee the Daughter of Edward & ffrances Godbee was borne
    the 13th of Octob. & bap^{tz} 23th of Ditto 1701.
Thompson the Sone of Patrick Quidley bap^{tz} 25th of Jan^{ry} 1701.
Marg^t the Daughter of Charles & Eliz^a Haines bap^{tz} 25th Jan^r 1701.
Edward the Sone of Ed. & Keziah Ball was bap^{tz} 1th of March 1701.
William the Sone of Augustine & Jone Dews was borne the 17th of
    December 1701.

Here ends the accot of Register Transcribed out of the Old Booke
In the Yeare 1702 &c.   p. John Nash.

The Birth of Negro Children.

Belonging to Mr Francis Weeks Junr.   Negro Peter was Born Anno
Dom. 1694.
Negro Jinny was Born Anno Dom 1696.   Negro Ben Was Born
An. Do. 1697.
Negro Dick was Born Anno Domi 1702.   Negro Numer was Born
An. Do. 1705.
Negro Milly Belonging to Mrs Milicent Weeks Was Born Anno.
Dom. 1695.
Negroes Belonging to John Bristow.   Negro Betty was Born in July
1696.
Negro Dy was Born in April, Anno Domini 1702.
Negroes Belonging to Mr Garrett Minor.   Palles was Born 8. Feb^{r}y
Year 1700.
Hannah a Negro was Born In April Anno Dom 1702.
Nan was Born In March Anno Domini 170$\frac{3}{4}$.
Negroes Belonging to Thomas Warrick were Born as followeth.
Frank was Born June Ye 14th 1699:   Peter was Born June Ye 14th
1701.
Negroe Cate Belonging to Mr Robert Daniel was Born May Ye 3d.
1704.
Negroes Belonging to Mr John Meacham.   Peter was Born Aug. Ye
8th 1702.
Moll was Born february Ye 13th Anno Domi. 170$\frac{4}{5}$.
Negroe Richard belonging to Mrs Pennellope Chainy was Born May
Ye 1st 1696.
Negroe Mat a Boy Belonging to Mr William Montague was Born In
Apr. 1695.
Negroes Belonging to Mr Thomas Montague were Born as followeth.
Negroe Moll was Born In feb^r 1692 & Ben was Born In May 1694.
Sam: A Negroe was Born in Jan: 1699.   Sara was Born May ye
2d 1704.
Lily a Negro Girl Belonging to John Hadly was Born february y^e
15th 170$\frac{5}{8}$.
Ye Birth of Negro Children Belonging Collo^{nl} William Churchhill
Esq Were Born as followeth; Betty a Negro Girl was Born June
y^e 21st 1705.
Sarah a Negro Girl was Born August y^e 27th Anno Domini 1705.
Sue a Negro Girl was Born Septemb y^e 29th Anno Domini 1705.
Nell a Negro Girl Belonging to Samuel Hoyl was Born in March
Anno Domi 170$\frac{2}{3}$.
Robbin a Negro Boy belonging to John Hipkings was Born In May:
1706.
Thamer a Negro Girl belonging to Mr Roger Jones was Born Sep-
tember the 7th Anno Domini 1707.
Will a Negroe Boy belonging to John Vivion born 8^{br} y^e 8th 1707.
Cate a Negroe Girl belonging to William Barbee Born Jan^r y^e 28th
Anno Domi 170$\frac{7}{8}$.
Jack a Negroe Boy belonging to John Adley was Born february y^e
27th 170$\frac{7}{8}$.

Robina Negroe Boy belonging to Matthew Hunt was Born April y^e 8th 1708.
Negroes belonging to Mr George Wortham Born as followeth
Gill Born In March 169⅞. Sue Born December 1703.
Cate Born Novemb^r Anno Domini 1706.

Here begins a Short Acco^t of Christenings Marriages & Burialls Transcribed out of a Book Kept at the Upper Chappell from ye 7th of Aprill Anno 1689 &c. Some of it being Recor^d before.

CHRISTENINGS—1690.

Richard the Sone of Samuell & Honour Acton was bap^tz at Mr Seagers p. Mr Sam^ll Gray the 10th of November 1690.

John the Sone of David and Martha Davis was bap^tz 10th of Novemb. 1690.

Sarah the Daughter of Jno & Ursula ffearman bap^tz 10th of Novemb. 1690.

Richard the Sone of Jno & Eliz^a Guttrey was bap^tz the 3d of Aprill 1691.

Benjamine the Sone of Jno & Mary Bowman bap^tz the 3th of April 1691.

Randolph the Sone of Joseph & Eliz^a Smith was borne 2th of Aprill and was bap^tz the 14th of June 1691.

Mary the Daughter of Martin Masey was baptized the 14th of June 1691.

Katherine the Illegitimate Daughter of Mary Nash, late servant to Mr Randolph Seager was baptized the 5th of July 1691.

Mary the Daughter of Richard & Katherine Davidson bap^tz 3th of Aprill 1691.

Mary the Daughter of Robert & Dorothy James baptized 5th of July 1691.

William the Sone of William & Sarah Batchelder bap^tz 26th of July 1691.

Thomas the Sone of Jno & Eliz^a Lewis was baptized the 26th of July 1691.

Henry the Sone of Henry & Eliz^a Emmerson bap^tz 18th of October 1691.

William the Sone of William & Ellianor Sadler borne 19th of October. 1691.

Robert the Sone of Robert & Margaret Daniell was borne 21th Septmb. 1691.

John the Sone of Anthony & Ann Ridgaway was bap^tz 16th of January 169½.

Elizabeth the Daughter of Mr William Chayney & Penellope his wife was baptized 31th of January 169½.

John the Sone of John & Millicent Chedle was bap^tz 31th of Jan^r 169½.

Alice Davis the Illegitimate Daughter of —— Davis by Mary Care was baptized the 31th of January 169½.

Paul the Sone of Jno & Eliz^a Swift was baptized 21th of ffebruary 169½.

John the Sone of William & Ann Brookes was bap^tz 21th of ffebruary 169½.

Martha the Daughter of David Davis was baptized 13th of March 169½.

Sarah the Daughter of Jnᵒ & Michall Bristow bapᵗ 13th of March 169½.

CHRISTENINGS.

John the Sone of Mʳ William Daniell & Constance his Wife was borne the ffirst Day of ffebruary & bapᵗ 10th of March 169½.

Elizabeth Daughter of Thomas & Hannah Haines bapᵗ 24th of Aprill 1692.

George the Sone of William & Mary Carter was borne 22th of Aprill and was baptized the 22th of May 1692.

Johannah the Daughter of John & Mary Brim baptized 12th of June 1692.

Ann the Daughter of Robert and Ann Chowning bapᵗ 12th of June 1692.

Rebecca the Daughter of Roger and Rebecca Prichard bapᵗ 12th June 1692.

Edward the Sone of William and Rebecca Hutson of Rappahannock County was baptized the 3d of July 1692.

William the Sone of William and Elizᵃ Marsh borne 5th July bapᵗ 24th Ditto 1692.

Agatha the Dauᵗ of Mʳ James Curtis & Elizᵃ his wife bapᵗ 25th of July 1692.

John the Sone of George and Rebecca Duffe borne 27th July bapᵗ 2th Augᵗ 1692.

Masey the Sone of Jnᵒ and Elizᵃ Guthery was bapᵗ 4th of Septemb 1692.

James the Sone of John & Penelope Evans of Rappᵃ bapᵗ 16th of Octob 1692.

Charles the Sone of Edward & Katherine Pierce was borne 1st of Augᵗ 1692.

George the Sone of George & Elizᵃ Johnston baptized 27th of Novemb 1692.

Elianor the Daughter of Jnᵒ & Elizᵃ Kersey bapᵗ 27th of November 1692.

Ann the Daughter of Nicholas & Mabell Paine bapᵗ 27th of November 1692.

Ann the Daughter of Nicholas & Ann Rice was bapᵗ 27th of November 1692.

Penelope the Daughter of Anthony & Elizᵃ Dowlin borne 12th of Octob. 1692 and Baptized the 26th of November 1692.

Pead the Sone of Jnᵒ & Michall Micham bapᵗ 8th of Janʳʸ 169¾.

John the Sone of Andrew & Isabella Wilson bapᵗ 12th of March 169¾.

Sarah Daughter of Robert and Sarah George bapᵗ 12th of March 169¾.

Ann the Daughter of Claud Vallott & Ann his Wife was borne the 31th of July, and was baptized the 14th of August 1693.

Elizabeth yᵉ Daughter of Martin & Elizᵃ Masey was borne 20th of Sepᵗ and was baptized 29th of Octob. 1693.

Lettice yᵉ Daughter of Jnᵒ and Mary Burk borne 24th Sepᵗ bapᵗ 29th Octob. 1693.

51

Mary Tugwell the Daughter of Henry & Mary Tugwell borne 20th of Sept. and baptized the 29th of October 1693.

Ann the Daughter of Barnard & Eliz^a Paine was borne 22th of Septemb and was baptized 29th of October 1693.

CHRISTENINGS.

Mary the Daughter of Charles Walker was baptized 29th of Octob 1693.

Ann the Daughter of Mr Thomas Stapleton by ffrances his Wife was borne the 14th of September 1693.

Jane the Daughter of ffrancis Taylor & Eliz^a his Wife was borne the 15th of November and baptized 31th of December 1693.

Phillip the Sone of William and Mary Carter borne 10th X^{br} bap^{tz} 4th Jan^r 169¾.

William the Sone of William & Bridget Willis baptized 4th of Jan^r 169¾.

Ann the Daughter of William and Ann Brookes bap^{tz} 21th of Jan^{ry} 169¾.

Hannah the Daughter of Jno & Millicent Chedle baptized 21th of Jan^{ry} 169¾.

Richard the Sone of Peter and Cary Tindall baptized 11th of ffebr. 169¾.

Eusebias the Sone of Jno & Eliz^a Lewis borne 22th Jan^r bap^{tz} 4th of March 169¾.

Sarah the Daughter of John and Eliz^a Pace was baptized 22th of Aprill 1694.

Jane the Daughter of Robert & Dorothy James bap^{tz} 22th of Aprill 1694.

Mary the Daughter of Michaell & Mercy Curtis bap^{tz} 3th of June 1694.

John ye Sone of Jno and Mary Bowmon bap^{tz} 15th of July 1694.

John the Sone of George & ⸺⸺ Cummings bap^{tz} 15th of July 1694.

Penelope Daughter of William & ⸺⸺ Carter bap^{tz} 15th of July 1694.

John the Sone of George & Mary Guest bap^{tz} 5th of August 1694.

Margaret ye Daughter of Robert & Katherine Williamson bap^{tz} 5th Augt 1694.

Hannah the Daughter of Jacob & Eliz^a Booseley bap^{tz} 5th of August 1694.

William Meacham the Sone of Jno & Michaell Meacham was Borne the 25th of ffebruary 1694.

John Lantor the Sone of Thomas Lantor was Borne the 30th Day of July and Baptized the 1st of Octo^{br} In the Yeare 1698.

Peter Lantor the Son of Thomas Lantor was born 25th Jan^{ry} and Baptized 18th of ffebruary In the yeare 16$\frac{99}{700}$.

Simon Son of William and Hannah Poobert was born y^e 22nd Septemb. 1699.

Mary Gardiner daughter of W^m & Ann Gardiner was born y^e 22nd day of September 1699.

WEDDINGS OR MARRIAGES.

Thomas Kidd and Alice Trigg were Marryed 18th of Septemb. 1690.

Jacob Booseley and Elizabeth Nash were Marryed 15th of June 1691.

Henry ffreeman and Ann Porter were Marryed the   1691.

William Carter and Mary Goodlow were Marryed 2th of July 1691.

George Duff and Rebecca Nash were Marryed 4th of July 1691.

Tobias Mickleburrough & Grace Nicholson were mar^d 17th Sept. 1691.

Mr Matthew Lidford & Mrs Lettice Weekes were Marryed 6th Jan^r 169½.

John Kersey and Elizabeth Priestnall were Marryed 2th of June 1692.

Henry Tugwell and Mary Baskett were Marryed 26th of Augt 1692.

Joseph Harrison and ffrances Haslewood Marryed 11th No^{vr} 1692.

John Waycomb and Eliz^a Micham were Marryed 31th Xm^{br} 169⅔.

Timothy Tracy and Rebecca Goodrich marry^d 19th ffeb. 169⅔.

Henry Meeres and Dorothy Hunt were married 22th of May 1693.

Thomas Spencer of King & Q^n County & Eliz^a Whelling of this parrish were Marryed 14th Xemb. 1693.

Angell Jacobus of ffarnum parish in Richmond County And Ann Vallott of this parish Widow were Marryed p Lycence the 12th of July Ann° 1694.

BURIALLS &c.

Frances the Daughter of M^r Jn° Sheppard Dec'd by ffrances his Wife Dyed the 24th of March 169⅟₁.

Theophylus the Sone of Mr Chr. Robinson and Mrs Katherine Robinson his wife was buried 14th of Aprill 1691.

Griffin the Sone of Jn° & Eliz^a Lewis was buried 28th of Sep^t 1691.

Amey a Servant Wench of Mr Chr. Robinson's buried 22th Octob. 1691.

Henry Nicholls Senr was buried the 9th of Aprill 1692.

Mary the Daughter of Mr Randolph Seager by Mary his Wife was buried in the Upper Chappell 17th of Aprill 1692.

Madam Katherine Robinson the wife of Mr Chr. Robinson Departed this Life 23th of Aprill 1692.

William Craine Dyed the 13th of August 1692.

Elizabeth Waycomb Dyed the 13th of August 1692.

Ann Jones Dyed the 14th of August 1692.

Elizabeth Willis Dyed the 17th of August 1692.

Elizabeth Swift Dyed 24th of August 1692.

Caleb Whelling Dyed the 3d of Septemb 1692.

George the Sone of Mr Geo. Haslewood Dyed 13th of Septemb. 1692.

John Guy the Sone of Tho. & Mary Guy Dyed 3th of Octo^{br} 1692.

Mr George Haslewood Departed this Life 10th of November 1692.

Mary Thompson Dyed the 5th of Decemb 1692.

Claud Vallott 29th and was buryed 31th of January 169⅔.

Ralph Wilkeson Dyed the 2d of ffebruary 169⅔.

Rebecca Duff Dyed the 15th of December 1693.

Mrs Sarah Perrott the Wife of Mr Richd Perrott Departed this Life the 26th of December 169¾.

Margaret Masey Dyed the 21th of December $169\frac{3}{4}$.

BURIALLS &c.

Mr William Chayney Dyed In January $169\frac{3}{4}$.
Richard Parry Dyed in January $169\frac{3}{4}$.
John Elee Dyed In January $169\frac{3}{4}$.
John Brewer Dyed the 5th of ffebruary $169\frac{3}{4}$.
Thomas Mins Dyed In ffebruary $169\frac{3}{4}$.
ffrances Docker was buried the 3d of March $169\frac{3}{4}$.
John Duff the Sone of George & Rebecca Duff Dyed 5th June 1694.
Thomas Marston Dyed the 24 Day of October In the year 1704.
Thomas Smith departed this life the 21st of May 1705.
Mary Y^{e} Wife of Theophilus Stanton departed this Life September Y^{e} 27th And was Interred September Y^{e} 29th Anno Domi. 1705.
Charls Williams was Interred July Y^{e} 27th Anno Domi 1706.
John Y^{e} Son of Nathan Underwood & Diana his wife departed this life October Y^{e} 24th And was Buried Y^{e} 25th of Y^{e} Same Anno Domini 1706.
Hannah Jones Y^{e} Wife of John Jones dyed 8^{br} Y^{e} 25th & Buried Y^{e} 27th of Y^{e} Same 1706.
John Nickols departed this Life Novem^{r} Y^{e} 27th & Buried Novemb^{r} Y^{e} 30th 1705.
Frances Y^{e} Wife of William Serdsborow Departed this Life Jan^{ry} Ye 17th & Buried Y^{e} 19th $170\frac{5}{6}$.
Mrs William Kilby departed this Life Feb^{r}y Ye 3d & was Buried feb^{ry} Y^{e} 5th Anno Domi $170\frac{5}{6}$.
William Porter departed this Life feb^{ry} Y^{e} 17th & was Buried feb^{ry} Y^{e} 20th Anno Dom. $170\frac{5}{6}$.
William Hartford departed this Life february Y^{e} 8th Anno Domini $170\frac{5}{6}$.
Sarah Y^{e} Wife of Richard Stevens departed this Life March Y^{e} 19th & Buried March Y^{e} 22nd $170\frac{5}{6}$.
John Sibley deceased April Y^{e} 7th & was Buried April Y^{e} 10th Anno Domi 1706.
Thomas Roberts departed this Life April Y^{e} 16th & was Buried April Y^{e} 18th 1706.
Henry Gale departed this Life May Y^{e} 2d & was Buried May Y^{e} 3d Anno Domini 1706.
Richard Stevens Departed this Life Decemb^{r} Y^{e} 18th & Buried Y^{e} 20th $170\frac{5}{6}$.

CHRISTENINGS.

Abraham Mountague the Sone of William & Lettice Mountague was baptized 28th of September 1701.
Richard Win the Sone of Rich^{d} & Sarah Win was baptiz^{d} Ditto day 1701.
Mary the Daughter of Jno & Mary Guthery bap^{tz} 23th of January $170\frac{1}{2}$.
Ann the Daughter of William & Mary Carter bap^{tz} 23th of January $170\frac{1}{2}$.
George the sone of Henry & Eliz^{a} Goodlow bap^{tz} 23th of Jan^{ry} $170\frac{1}{2}$.
Margaret the Daughter of Jno & Eliz^{a} Pace bap^{tz} 15th of March $170\frac{1}{2}$.

Jane the Daughter of Robert & Ann Blackley ⎫
Ann the Daughter of Rich⁴ & Eliz⁴ Allin
Elizabeth the Daughter of Michaell & Mercy Curtis ⎪ were
Sarah the Daughter of Ralph & Alice Masey ⎪ all 10
John the Sone of Edmund & Jane Mickleburrough ⎪ of them
Thomas the Sone of Nicholas & Dorothy Newton ⎬ Baptiz⁴
Richard the Illegitimate Sone of Ann Hughs ⎪ the 15th
Daniell the Sone of John & Michaell Micham ⎪ Day of
John the Sone of Joseph & Jane Micham ⎪ March 170½.
Henry the Sone of Robert & Marg⁴ Daniell ⎭

Margaret Murrow the Daughter of Ann Murrow, Bastard was born
yᵉ 1 Day of Aprill 1701.

Jane the Daughter of Robert & Sarah George bapᵗˣ 19th of Aprill
1702.

Katherine yᵉ Daughter of George & Katherine Twyman bapᵗˣ Ditto
day 1702.

Elizabeth the Daughter of William & Mary Danill was baptized 15th
of March 170½.

Peter Brim the Sone of Jnᵒ & Mary Brim was borne 6th of Aprill
and Baptized the 12th of May 1702.

William the Sone of William & Hannah Proverb was bapᵗˣ the 12th
of May 1702.

Margaret the Dauᵗʳ of Wᵐ and Marg⁴ Kidd was bapᵗˣ 12th of May
1702.

Charles the Sone of Charles & Mary Madcrions was borne the 10th
of ffebruary and bapᵗˣ on Whit Sunday 1702.

CHRISTENINGS.

William Mountague the Sone of Tho & Katherine Mountague was
Baptized 14th of June 1702.

ffrances the Sone of Jnᵒ & Eliz⁴ Summers bapᵗˣ 14th of June 1702.

Ann the Daughter of William & Ann Gardner bapᵗˣ Ditto Day 1702.

Jacob the Sone of Robert & Katherine Williamson was borne the
12th of June & was Baptized 22th of July 1702.

Thomas the Sone of Henry & Eliz⁴ Smith was borne 16th July And
Baptized 22th of the Same 1702.

Here endeth the Accoᵗ of the Whole Register Transcribed out of
Both yᵉ old Register Books of Christ Church parish In Midd˟
County.

Being Transcribed by order of Vestry held the 20th of Novemb.
An. 1701.

p. Jnᵒ Nash.

Robert yᵉ Son of Major Robert Dudley & Mʳˢ Elizabeth his Wife
was Born february yᵉ 14th Anno Domini 1691.

Elizabeth yᵉ Daughter of Mary Canidy was Born April yᵉ 4th. Anno
Domi 1704. An Illegitimate.

Att a generall Assembly begun at James Citty 8th of June 1680.

An Act for preventing Insurrections of Negros &c.

Whereas the ffrequent meeting of considerable Numbers of Negro
Slaves under pretence of Feasts and Burialls, is Judged & Deemed

of Dangerous Consequences, for prevention whereof for ye ffuture, Be it Enacted by the Kings most Excellent Majesty, by and with the Consent of this gen^erll Assembly, and it is hereby Enacted by the Authority aforesaid, that from and after the publication of this Law, it shall not be Lawfull for any Negro or other Slave, to carry or arme himselfe with any Club, Staff, Gun, Sword, or any other Weapon of Defence or offence, nor to goe nor Depart from his Masters Ground without a Citifficate from his Master, Mistris or Overseere, and Such permission not to be granted but upon particular and necessary occasions, and every Negro or Slave so offending not haveing a Certifficate as aforesaid, Shal be Sent to the next Constable who is hereby Impowered and Required to give the Said Negro Twenty Lashes on the bare back well laid on and So Sent home to his said Master, Mistriss or Overseer.

And it is further Enacted by the Authority aforesaid that if any Negro or other Slave Shall presume to lift up his hand in opposition against any Christian, Shall for every Such offence upon due proofe made thereof by the Oath of the party before a Majistrate have and receive Thirty Lashes on the bare back well laid on, And it is hereby further Enacted by the Authority aforesaid, that if any Negro or other Slave Shall absent himselfe from his Masters Service and ley hid and Lurking in obscure places, Committing Injuries to ye Inhabitents, and Shall Resist any pson or p^rsons that shall by any Lawfull Authority be Imployed to apprehend and take the Said Negro, that then in case of such Resistance, It shalbe Lawfull for such p^rson of p^rsons to Kill the Said Negro or Slave so lying out and Resisting, and this Law to be once every Six months published at the Respective County Courts and Parish Churches within this Collony.

CHRISTENINGS.

Anne daughter of Sr Wm Skipwith & Lady Sarah his Wife born July 31 1703.

Jonas Whitlock the Son of James & Margaret Whitlock his Wife was Baptized March ye 18th Anno Domini 170⅘

Ann Matthews the Daughter of William & Mary Matthews his Wife was born March ye 23d And Baptized April ye 6th Anno Domini 1705.

William Watliss the Son of Elizabeth Watliss was Baptized April ye 29th 1705.

Ann Dunkington ye Daughter of Elizabeth Dunkington was Bap. April ye 29th 1705.

James Townsend ye Son of John Townsend and Damaris his Wife was Born April ye 20th Anno Domini 1705.

John Smith Son of Thomas and Ruth Smith his Wife was Born January ye 24th Anno Domini 1704.

The Births of three children of James Smith and his Wife Ann Smith:

Elizabeth Smith was Born September ye 1st Anno Domini 1699.

James Smith was Born ye 25th of June Anno Domini 1702.

Ann Smith was Born ye 27th of October Anno Domini 1704.

Thomas Jones ye Son of Roger Jones & Mary his Wife was Born the 23rd of August Anno Domini 1704.

Benjamin Williamson y^e Son of Robert Williamson and Catherine his Wife was Born April y^e 21st & Baptized July y^e 1st 1704.

Ann Smith y^e Daughter of Thomas & Ann Smith his Wife was Born January y^e 10th Anno Domini $\frac{1699}{1700}$.

Ann Shepherd an Illegitimate the Daughter of Mary Shepherd was Baptized September y^e 2nd Anno Domini 1705.

John Finney y^e Son of John & Margaret Finney his Wife was Born March y^e 1st Ano. Domi 1697.

William Finney y^e Son of John & Margaret Finney his Second Wife was Baptized March y^e 10th Anno Domi 1706.

Francis ye Son of Samuel & Ann Loe his Wife was Born July ye 10th Anno Domini 1704.

Elizabeth Maxum ye Daughter of Thomas & Elizabeth Maxum his Wife was Baptized March ye 10th Anno Domi 1706.

William Gilley ye Son of Thomas Gilley and Jane his wife was Baptized March ye 22d Anno Domini 1706.

At a Gen^{rll} Assembly begun at James Citty November the 10th 1682. An additional Act for the better preventing Insurrections by Negros.

Whereas a certaine Act of Assembly held at James Citty ye Eight day of June In the Yeare of our Lord 1680 Intitaled an Act preventing Negros Irsurrections hath not had its Intended Effect for want of due Notice thereof being Taken, It is enacted by the Govern^r Councill and Burgisses of this p^{r}sent Grand Assembly and by the Authority thereof that for the better putting ye said Act in Due Execution the Church Wardens of Each parish in this Cuntry at the Charge of the parish by the first Day of January next, provide true Coppies of this and the aforesaid Act, and make or Cause Entry to be made thereof in the Register booke of the said parish and that ye minister or Reader of Each parish shall twice Every yeare vizt Some one Sunday or Lords day in Each of the Months of September and March in Each parish Church or Chappell of Ease in Each parish in the time of Divine Service after the Reading of the Second lesson, Reade and Publish both this p^{r}sent and the aforesaid Recited Act, under paine such Church Warden Minister or Reader Makeing Default to forfeit Each of them Six hundred pounds of Tobacco, one halfe to the Informer, and ye other halfe to the use of the poore of the said parrish and for the further better preventing Such Insurrections by Negros or Slaves Be it likewise Enacted and it is hereby Enacted by the Authority aforesaid, that noe Master or Overseer Shall at any time after the 20th Day of January next Knowingly permitt or suffer without the leave or Lycence of his or theire Master or overseere, any Negro or Slave not properly belonging to him or them, to Remaine or be upon his or theire Plantation above the space of ffoure hours at any one time. Contrary to the Intent of the before recited act, upon Paine to fforfeit being thereof Lawfully convicted before Some one Justice of the peace within the County where the ffact shall be comitted by the Oath of two Witnesses at the least, The Sume of Two hundred pounds of Tobacco in Caske for Each time so offending, to him or them that will sue for the same for which the Said Justice is hereby Impowered to award Judgment and Execution.

Transcribed out of the Register Booke at ye Upper Chappell &c.

John Nash and Ann Brewer both of Christ Church Parish in Middlesex County were Married ye 28th day of October, In the Yeare
of our Lord 1703.

The Births of Negro Children.

The Birth of Negro Children belong to Captn John Smith.

Negro Judith was Born ye 21st day of November Anno Domini
1702.

Negro Mulatto Charls was Born ye 8th day of April Anno Domini
1704.

Negro Cesar Belonging to Mr Roger Jones was Born 8^br ye 6th 1704.

The Birth of Three Negro Children belonging to James Curtis
Senr:

Negro Harry was Born In May 1698. Negro Frank was Born february 1699. Negro Tony was Born In february 1701.

Degal Negro belonging to Minor Minor was Born Octob^r ye 5th 1692.

Sue a Negro Girl belonging to James Smith was Born In May 1705.

The Ages of Negro Children Belonging to Mr Bartholomew Yates:
Alice Born Octo^br ye 15th 1694. Katey Born Novemb^r ye 1st 1695;
Gresham Born May the 28th 1700; Sue Born Octob^r ye 1st 1702.
Toney born Octob^r the 25th 1702; Harry born March ye 10th 170⅘.
Sarah Born June ye 14th 1705; Molly Born March 4th 1696.

Mary a Negro Belonging to Thomas Hipkins was Born July 1694.

Negro Will Belonging to Mr Roger Jones was Born June ye 16th
1706.

The Birth of Negro Children Belonging to Capt. John Smith:

Negro Anthony was Born July ye 21st Anno Domi 1705.

Negro Frank a Boy was Born february ye 9th 170⅝.

Negro Tom was Born June ye 21st Anno Domi 1706.

Rose a Negro Girl Belonging to Mrs Elizabeth Dudley was Born A.
D. 1702.

Robbin Mingoll A Negro Belonging to Robert Dudley was Born
An. Dom. 1706.

The Birth of Negroes belonging to Mr Frances Weeks Senr:

Negro Letty was Born March ye 17th Anno Domini 1701.

James Morris Son of Elizabeth A Mulatto Woman was Baptized by
Mr Andrew Jackson March ye 15th Anno Domi 170⅝.

Negroe Major a Boy Belonging to John Bristow was Born July y^e
31st 1706.

Negroe Frank a Girl belonging to Mrs Penelope Parrott was Born
Aug. ye 24th 1706.

Phillis Daughter of Nanney belonging to James Curtis Sen. born
June ye 1706.

CHRISTENINGS—1702.

James Smith the Sone of James and Ann Smith was borne the 5th
Day of June in the yeare of our Lord 1702.

John Man the Sone of John Man and Jane his wife was borne the
ffirst Day of May 1702.

58

Catherine Kilbie the Daughter of William and Johannah Kilbee was baptized the 9th of September 1702.

Robert Davis the Sone of Elisha and Elizabeth Davis was borne the 14th of October 1702.

John Gibbs the Sone of John and Mary Gibbs was Borne the 9th Day of October 1702.

Benjamine Gore the Sone of Joshua &   Gore was Baptized the 9th Day of December 1702.

James Rhodes the Sone of Ezechias and Elizabeth Rhodes was Baptized the 9th Day of December 1702.

Martha the Daughter of John and Ann Marston was borne the 7 Day of December 1702.

Judah the Daughter of Roger and Mary Jones was born the 26th Day of December 1702.

James Stiffe the Sone of Thomas and Elizabeth Stiffe was Baptized the 13th of January 170⅜.

George Blake the Sone of George and Elizabeth Blake was Baptized the 13th Day of January 170⅜

Francis Porter the Sone of William and Jane Porter was Borne the 9th of January 170⅜.

John the Sone of Uriah Cardis was Borne the 3ᵗh Day of January 170⅜.

This is Reserved for Registering the Birth of Negro Children in particular &c.

Nedd a Negro Boy Slave Belonging to Mʳ Edwin Thacker was Borne the 7th Day of January 1698.

Nanney a Negro Girle Slave belonging to Mʳ Edwin Thacker was borne the 15th Day of March in the Yeare 1698.

Moll a Negro Girle Slave belonging to Mʳ Richard Kemp was borne the 5th Day of August in the yeare 1700.

Cress a Negro Girle Slave belonging to Mʳ Richᵈ Kemp was born the 3th Day July in the yeare 1700.

Juda a Negro Slave of Mʳ Richard Kemp was borne the 7th Day of September In the Yeare 1697.

Nora a Negro Girle Slave belonging to Mʳ Richard Kemp was Borne the ffirst of October In the Yeare 1703.

Dinah a Negro Girle Slave belonging to Mʳ Richᵈ Kemp was Borne the 13th of November in the Yeare 1694.

Nedd a Negro Boy Slave belonging to Mʳ Richard Kemp was borne the 12th of August In the Yeare 1694.

Alice a Negro Girle Slave belong to Capᵗ Robert Daniell was borne the 2th Day of Septembʳ In the Yeare 1698.

Ben a Negro boy Slave belonging to the Said Capᵗ Robert Daniel borne the 4th Day of Aprill In the Yeare 1700.

Captain a Negro boy Slave of yᵉ Said Daniell was borne the ffirst Day of Aprill 1702.

Franck a Negro Girl Slave belonging to Mʳ Edwin Thacker Borne on the 15th Day of ffebruary In the Yeare 1702.

Billey a negro boy slave belonging to Mʳ Edwin Thacker Borne on the 27 day of March In yᵉ Yeare 1703.

Mingo a Negro boy Slave, son of Nan belonging to Mr Rice Curtis was born ye 15 Day of May 1704) Registered the 20th of July 1714.

CHRISTENINGS.

Joshua Lewis the Sone of James Lewis and Jone his wife was Borne the 27th Day of Decemb^r Anno Domini 1702.

Frances Berry the Daughter of Garrett Berry and Eliza his Wife was borne the 5th Day of ffebruary 170⅔.

Theophilus the Sone of Nicholas Branch and Mary his Wife was Baptized the 30th of March 1703.

Rebecca Godbee the Daughter of Edward Godbee & Frances his Wife was baptized ye 2th of June 1703.

William Bennett the Sone of William and Sarah Bennett was baptized the 2th of June 1703.

Abigall Smith the Daughter of Arthur and Mary Smith was Borne the 4th of August 1702.

Thomas the Sone of Henry Meacham and Mary his Wife was baptized the 26th of June 1703.

Christopher Robinson the Sone of Mr John Robinson and Maddam Catherine Robinson his Wife was borne 1th of July 1703.

Mabell Dodson the Daughter of Francis and Mabell Dodson was Baptized the ffirst Day of September 1703.

James Black the Sone of James and Ann Black was baptz^d the 26th Day of August In the Yeare 1702.

Frances the Daughter of Henry Tuggle and Mary his Wife was baptized the 26 Day of August 1702.

Sarah Preston the Daughter of Jacob and Mary Preston was Baptized the 23 Day of September 1702.

Jacob Brooks the Sone of William and Sarah Brooks Baptiz^d the 21 of Novemb^r In the Yeare 1702.

CHRISTENINGS.

Henry Johnston the Sone of George Johnston and Elizabeth his Wife was Baptized the 21 Day of Novemb^r In the Yeare 1702.

Margarett Lantor the Daughter of Thomas and Isabella Lantor was Baptized the 21th Day of Novemb^r In the Yeare 1702.

Winifrid Kidd the Daughter of Thomas and Alice Kidd was Baptized the 21th Day of Novemb^r In the Yeare 1702.

Ann Crank the Daughter of Matthew and Elizabeth Crank was Borne the 22th Day of August In the Yeare 1702.

Thomas Norman the Sone of Robert and Elizabeth Norman was borne the 9th Day of January and baptized 11th of March 170⅔.

Mary Hall the Daughter of Martin and Mary Hall was born the 2 Day of February And was baptized the 11th of March A^{nno} 170⅔.

Sarah Bird the Daughter of John and Elizabth Bird was Baptized the 24th Day of March In the Yeare 170⅔.

Sarah Siddon the Daughter of Edward & Ann Siddon was Baptized the 24 Day of March In the Yeare 170⅔.

Sarah the Daughter of Hermon and Elizabeth Church Yard was baptized the 24th Day of March In the Yeare 170⅔.

John George the Sone of David and Catherine George was Baptized the 18th Day of Aprill In the Yeare 1703.

Elizabeth Winn, the Daughter of Richard and Sarah Winn was
Baptized the 18th Day of Aprill In the Yeare 1703.
Edward Suthern the Sone of John and Catherin Suthern was Baptized the 23th Day of May In the Yeare 1703.
John Wood the Son of Thomas and Elizabeth Wood was Baptized
the 23 Day of June In the Yeare 1703.
Robert Kidd the Son of William and Marg^t Kidd was Baptized the
20th Day of July In the Yeare 1703.

CHRISTENINGS.

The Ages of thre Children of Mr Richard Kemp and Mrs Ellianor
Kemp his Wife.
Ann Kemp was Borne the 13th Day of August In ye Yeare 1694.
Rachell Kemp was Borne the 3th Day of April In ye Yeare 1696.
Richard Kemp was Born the 6th Day of Aprill In ye Yeare 1698.

The Ages of Three Children of Edmund Mickleburrough and
Jane his Wife.
Edmund Mickleburrough was Born the 22th Day of Decemb^r 1696.
Robert Mickleburrough was Born the 24th Day of October 1698.
John Mickleburrough was Born the 15th Day of Decemb^r 1701.

The Ages of Four Children of Michael & Mercy Curtis.
Mary Curtis was Born the 7th Day of March In ye Yeare 169¾.
Thomas Curtis was Born the 27th Day of Decemb^r In the Yeare
1695.
Michall Curtis was Born the 1st Day of Septemb^r In ye Yeare 1698.
Elizabeth Curtis was Borne the 25th of October In the Yeare 1701.

The Ages of Four Children of Richard and Ann Shurley.
Abraham Duff the Sone of George Duff Dec^d by Ann his Wife (the
now Wife of the Said Richd Shurley was borne the 15th of December 1696.
Ann Shurley was borne the 12th Day of Decemb^r In ye Year 1698.
Thomas Shurley was borne the 19th of Decemb^r In the Yeare 1700.
Richard Shurley was borne the 8th Day of August In ye Year 1703.

CHRISTENINGS.

Edwin Thacker the Son of Mr Edwin Thacker and Mrs Frances
Thacker his Wife borne on the Third Day of July at Twelve A
Clock in ye Day In the Yeare of our Lord 1695.
Ann Thacker the Daughter of Mr Edwin Thacker and Mrs Frances
Thacker his Wife Borne on the 27th Day of Septemb^r att Six a
Clock in the Morning In the Yeare 1696.
John Thacker the Son of Mr Edwin Thacker and Mrs Frances
Thacker his Wife Borne on ye 15th Day of January att Twelve
a Clock in ye Day In the Yeare 1697.
Sarah Meacham ye Daughter of Joseph Meacham and Jane his wife
was born ye 17 day of November 1703.
Elizabeth Hore y^e Daughter of John & Jane Hore Baptized y^e 22
Day of December 1703.
William Courlles y^e Son of Michaell and Mercy Curlls his Wife was
borne y^e 26 day of January 170¾.

Michaell Attwood y^e Daughter of Richard & Sarah Attwood was baptized y^e 26 Day of January 170$\frac{3}{4}$.

David Davis y^e Son of David & Mary Davis his Wife was Baptized y^e 26 day of January 170$\frac{3}{4}$.

Peter Chisman y^e Son of George & Catherine his Wife was borne y^e 29 day of August 1703.

Sarah y^e Daughter of William & Mary Daniell was Baptized ye 23 day of Febuary 170$\frac{3}{4}$.

Mary Mountague y^e Daughter of William & Leette his Wife was Baptized y^e 23 day of Febuary 170$\frac{3}{4}$.

John Medderus y^e Son of Charles & Mary Medderus his Wife was borne ye 21 day of ffebuary 170$\frac{3}{4}$.

Paul Thilman y^e Son of Paul & Sarah his Wife was Baptized y^e 23 day of ffebuary 170$\frac{3}{4}$.

CHRISTNINGS.

Richard Blackle y^e Son of Robert and Ann Blackle his wife was Baptized y^e 2 day of Aprill 1704.

Henry Goodlow y^e Son of Henry & Elizabeth Goodlow his wife was baptized y^e 2 day of Aprill 1704.

John Manuell y^e Son of Edmun & Ann Manuell his wife was bap^{tz} y^e 2 day of Aprill 1704.

Joseph Cartter ye Son of William & Mary Carter was Baptized ye 30 day of Aprill 1704.

John Maze ye Son of Ralph & Alice Maze was Baptiz^d ye 21 day of May 1704.

Thomas Emerson ye Son of Henry & mary his wife was baptized ye 21 day of May 1704.

Mary Pearce ye Daughter of John & Elizabeth Pearce was Baptized ye 23 day of July 1704.

Elizabeth Cranke ye Daughter of Mathew & Elizabeth Cranke was Baptized ye 23 day of July 1704.

Rite Curtis ye Son of Rite and Elizabeth Curtis was Baptized ye 3 day of September 1704.

Margrett Shurle ye Daughter of Rich^d & Ann Shurlle was Baptized ye 3 day of September 1704.

John George ye Son of Robert & Sarah George was Baptized ye 3d day of September 1704.

John George ye Son of Robert & Smith George was Baptized ye 24 day of September 1704.

Negro Children belonging to Mr William Churchhill Born as ffolloweth.

Major a Boy born July 1694.

Joan a Girl borne ye 2 day of September 1696.

Cott a Boy borne September 1697.

Tomboy a Boy borne August 1698.

Saturday a Boy borne June ye 1 day 1700.

May a Boy borne May ye 1 day 1701.

Mary a Girle borne ye 3 day of May 1701.

Sunday a Boy borne in Aprill 1703.

Thursday a boy Borne November 1703.

WEDDINGS OR MARRIAGES.

Hugh Finley & Mary Picket were Married Jan Ye 8th 1703.

Thomas Kingsley & Mary Ockoldham were Married ⎱ April y⁰ 14th
Robert Biggs & Mary Armistead were Married ⎰ 1703.

William Chelton & Margaret Wheatherstone were Married May y⁰ 18th 1703.

Mr John Lomax & Mrs Elizabeth Wormley were Married June Y⁰ 1st 1703.

Theophilus Staunton & Mary Percifull were Married June y⁰ 2nd

William Harfoot & Mary Caree were Married July y⁰ 14th 1703.

William Barber & Mary Gray were Married July y⁰ 22nd 1703.

Gabriel Roberts & Sarah Bendall were Married July y⁰ 26th

Mr William Churchhill & Mrs Elizabeth Wormley were Married Octob$_1$ y⁰ 5th.

William Hamock & Elizabeth Tight were Married Octob^r y⁰ 6th.

John Davis & Elizabeth Crank were Married Octob^r y⁰ 28th 1703.

Christopher Robinson & Judith Beverley were Married Octob^r ye 12th.

John Nash & Ann Brider were Married Octob^r y⁰ 28th 1703.

Christopher Sutton & Hope Branmount were Married Novembr^r ye 3d.

John Dangerfield & Mary Conway were Married Novemb^r y⁰ 11th.

Thomas Roberts & Mary Stevens were Married Novemb^r y⁰ 26th 1703.

Richard Straughan & Catherine Murrell were Married Decemb^r y⁰ 1st.

George Clay & Elizabeth Thompson were Married Decemb^r y⁰ 30th

Nicholas Harvey & Mary Norwood were Married Jan. ye 15th 1704.

James Daniel & Margaret Vivion were Married Jan y⁰ 27th 1704.

John Curles & Rebecca King were Married Feb. y⁰ 2d 1704.

Richard Rennall & Honnor Carvenoth were Married Feb. y⁰ 23d 1704.

James Jordan & Ann Burk Feb. y⁰ 23rd were Married 1704.

John Vivion & Christian Briscoe were Married Feb. y⁰ 23d 1704.

Walter Roberts & Jone Bocker were Married Apr. y⁰ 16th 1704.

Thomas Crank & Ann Goodlow were Married June y⁰ 22nd 1704.

Jeptha Edmunds & Ellener Doss were Married August y⁰ 18th 1704.

Thomas Pateman & Lettice Shippey were Married Aug. y⁰ 16th 1704.

Marvill Mosely & Aggatha Daniell were Married Aug y⁰ 31st 1704.

John Parson & Mary Osborn were Married Septem^{br} y⁰ 28th 1704.

John Gallifor & Mary Hues were Married Octob^r y⁰ 5th 1704.

Richard Moor & Alice Holly were Married Octob^r y⁰ 26th 1704.

Thomas Arle & Elizabeth Johnson were Married Octob^r y⁰ 26th 1704.

John Carbett & Catherine Alden were Married Novemb^r y⁰ 9th 1704.

William Bristow & Margaret Stark were Married Decemb^r y⁰ 7th 1704.

Bartholomew Yates & Sarah Mickleburrough Married Sept 14 1704.

CHRISTENINGS.

Armistead Churchhill ye Son of Mr William Churchhill and Elizabeth his Wife Was Borne att Rosegill in Christ Church parish In Middlesex County in Virginia ye 25 day of July 1704 being of a Tuesday about 5 or 6 a Clock in ye Afternoon and was Baptized ye 1 day of August following by Mr Bartholomew Yeats Minister

Margrett Haynes ye Daughter of Charles & Elizabeth Haynes was Borne ye 24 day of January 1705.

Mary Hunphrys ye Daughter of Joseph & Elizabeth Humphrys Was Borne ye 24 day of January 170¾.

George Wortham the Son of Mr George & Mrs Mary Wortham his Wife was Born Feb ye 5th Anno Domini 1699.

Sarah Wortham was Born Decemb^r ye 26th 1701.

John Wortham was Born Decemb^r ye 22d 1703.

Christopher Robinson ye Son of Mr John & Catherine Robinson his Wife was Born July ye 1st about six of the Clock In the Afternoon Anno Domini 1703.

John Robinson was Born feb: ye 3d About 10 of the Clock In the Afternoon his father and Mother Above Named Ann Dom 1704.

John Barnatt ye Son of John and Ann Barnatt his wife was Baptized Decemb^r ye 3d Anno Domini 1704.

Rachel Daniel ye Daughter of James and Margoret Daniel his Wife was Born Octob^r ye 14th and was Baptized Novemb^r ye 15th Anno Domini 1704.

Zacharias Gibbs the Son of John and Mary Gibbs his Wife was Baptized feb. ye 1st Anno Domini 1704.

Thomas Straughan the Son of Richard and Katherine Strauhan his Wife was Baptized feb. ye 1st Anno Domini 1705.

Edward Williams ye Son of Edward and Catherine Williams his Wife was Baptized feb. ye 4th Anno Domini 1705.

Howard Williams the Son of Charls and Ann Williams his Wife was Baptized Jan ye 3d Anno Domini 1705.

John a Negro of Mr Henry Thackers was Baptised feb ye 25th Anno Domini 1704.

CHRISTENINGS.

Richard Reynald Y^e son of Richard & Honor his Wife was Baptized Octob^r Y^e 15th Anno Domi 1704.

Ann Y^e Daughter of James Jordan & Ann his Wife Was Baptized Octob^r Y^e 15th Anno Domi 1704.

Jane Y^e Daughter of Thomas Stapleton and Mary his Wife was Baptized Octob^r Y^e 1st Anno Domi 1704.

John Y^e Son of Henry Tuggle & Mary his Wife was Baptized Novemb^r Y^e 5th Anno Domi 1704.

Thomas Y^e Son of Thomas Lanton and Ezebella his Wife was Baptized Novemb^r Y^e 5th Anno Domi 1704.

Abraham Y^e Son of James Baskett and Honor his Wife was Baptized January Y^e 7th Anno Domi 170⅘.

John Y^e Son of John Zachary And Eleanor his Wife was Baptized, Born January Y^e 7th Anno Domi. 170⅘.

Francis Thilman Y^e Son of Paul Thilman And Sarah his Wife was Born february Y^e 1st And Baptized Y^e 29th 1700.

Thomas Yᵉ Son of Thomas Williams and Elizabeth his Wife was Baptized february Yᵉ 18th Anno Domi 170$\frac{4}{5}$.

Henry Yᵉ Son of Edmund Mickleberry And Jane his Wife was Baptized February Yᵉ 18th Anno Domi 170$\frac{4}{5}$.

Peter Benet Yᵉ Son of William and Sarah Benet was Born November the Yᵉ 7th and was Baptized December Yᵉ 10th 1704.

Robert Yᵉ Son of Averila And Edward Couch was Born November Yᵉ 27th And was Baptized December Yᵉ 31st Anno Domi 1704.

John Yᵉ son of John and Jane Man his Wife was Born December Yᵉ 25th And was Baptized January yᵉ 21st Anno Domi 170$\frac{4}{5}$.

Elizabeth Yᵉ Daughter of Christopher And Hope Sutton his Wife was Born December Yᵉ 17th and Baptized January Yᵉ 21st 170$\frac{4}{5}$.

Elizabeth Yᵉ Daughter of Mʳ William and Killbee Namely Hannah Killbee his wife was Born January Yᵉ 13th And Baptized Yᵉ 11th of February Anno Domini 170$\frac{4}{5}$.

CHRISTENINGS.

Mary Yᵉ Daughter of Thomas and Mary Goddin his wife was Born December Yᵉ 19th And was Baptized february Yᵉ 11th Anno Domi 170$\frac{4}{5}$.

Robert Yᵉ Son of Robert and Judith Johnson his Wife was Born february Yᵉ 4th And Baptized, March Yᵉ 4th Anno Domi 170$\frac{4}{5}$.

John Yᵉ Son of Thomas And Mary Roberts was Born february Yᵉ 24th And Was Baptized March Yᵉ 25th Anno Domi 1705.

Elizabeth Yᵉ Daughter of Samuell and Margarett Philips was Born february Yᵉ 12th And was Baptized March Yᵉ 25th 1705.

John Yᵉ Son of John and Ann Morgan was Born March Yᵉ 17th And was Baptized April Yᵉ 15th Anno Domi 1705.

Hannah Yᵉ Daughter of John and Michal Miller his Wife was Born March Yᵉ 6th and was Baptized April Yᵉ 15th Anno Domi 1705.

John Yᵉ Son of John and Mary Millener was Born April Yᵉ 12th And Baptized May Yᵉ 6th Anno Domi 1705.

Sith Yᵉ Daughter of Hezekiah And Elizabeth Roads was Born June Yᵉ 2d And Baptized June Yᵉ 17th Anno Domi 1705.

William Yᵉ Son of Locklin and Ann Cannedy was Born february Yᵉ 1st And Baptized March Yᵉ 4th Anno Domi 1705.

Ann Yᵉ Daughter of Uriah and Sarah Carder was Born May Yᵉ 5th And Baptized June Yᵉ 17th Anno Domi 1705.

William Yᵉ Son of John and Rebecca Hughs was Born May Yᵉ 21st and Baptized July Yᵉ 1st Anno Domi 1705.

John Yᵉ Son of John and Rebecca Hughs was Born May Yᵉ 21st And Baptized July Yᵉ 1st Anno Domi 1705.

Thomas Yᵉ Son of William and Margaret Chelton was Born June Yᵉ 26th And Baptized July Yᵉ 29th 1705.

Ann Yᵉ Daughter of John and Ann Marston was Born * * Baptized August Yᵉ 19th.

Theodoret Yᵉ Son of Theophilus and Mary Stanton was * * And Baptized August Yᵉ 19th * *

Ann daughter of Wᵐ & Hannah Probent born 22d Decem * *

CHRISTENINGS.

Gray Skipwith Y^e Son of Sr William and Sarah Skipwith Lady his Wife was Born August Y^e 25th and Baptized Septem^{br} Y^e 20th 1705.

James Y^e Son of William and Mary Barley was Born August Y^e 16th and Baptized September Y^e 30th 1705.

John Y^e Son of Edward and Frances Godbee his Wife was Baptized April Y^e 1st 1705.

John Y^e Son of Patrick and Ann Manuel his Wife was Baptized April Y^e 1st 1705.

James Y^e Son of William and Mary Jones his Wife was Baptized April Y^e 1st 1705.

Aggatha Y^e Daughter of William & Margarett Kidd his Wife was Bap. April Y^e 1st 1705.

Elizabeth Y^e Daughter of John & Elizabeth Hickey his Wife was Bap. April Y^e 1st 1705.

Frances Y^e Daughter of Thomas & Alice Kidd his Wife was Baptized April Y^e 22nd 1705.

Averila Y^e Daughter of Joseph & Averila Hardee his Wife was Baptized April Y^e 22nd 1705.

Henry Y^e Son of John & Elizabeth Bird his Wife was Baptized May Y^e 13th 1705.

Robert Y^e Son of Robert & Mary Turrell his Wife was Baptized May Y^e 13th 1705.

Catherine Y^e Daughter of William & Ann Gardener his Wife was Bap. May Y^e 13th 1705.

Mary Y^e Daughter of David & Mary Davis his Wife was Baptized May Y^e 13th 1705.

Marvell Y^e Son of Marvell & Agatha Mosely his Wife was Bap. June Y^e 3d 1705.

John Y^e Son of John & Catherine Southern his Wife was Bap. August Y^e 12th 1705.

Joseph Y^e Son of Joseph & Jane Meacham his Wife was Baptized Y^e 7th of October and Born Y^e 15th Day of September Anno Domi 1705.

Mary Y^e Daughter of Jacob & Mary Preston his Wife was Bap. October Y^e 7th 1705.

Penelope Chany Y^e Daughter of Thomas & Mary Warwick his Wife was Bap. 9^{br} Y^e 7th 1705.

Edward Y^e Son of Edward & Ann Sidorn his Wife was Born October Y^e 1st And Baptized November Y^e 11th Anno Domi 1705.

Edward Wortham Y^e Son of Mr George & Mary Wortham his Wife was Born December Y^e 24th Anno Domini 1705.

John Nash Y^e Son of John and Ann Nash his Wife was Born November Y^e 19th & Baptized Y^e 20th of Y^e Same the Reverend Bartholomew Yates And Y^e Said John Nash Standing as Godfathers And Mercy Curtis as Godmother Anno Domini 1704.

John Jones Y^e Son of John & Hannah Jones his Wife was Baptized February Y^e 24th Anno Domi 170⅚

Richard Straughan Y^e Son of Richard & Catherine Straughan his Wife * * * May Y^e 12th Anno Domini 1706.

* * * Daughter of Edward & Kezia Ball his Wife Was Born March Y^e 31st * * * * * * Y^e 26th Anno Domini 1706.

* * * * * * * of Augustine & Jane Owen his Wife was Baptized * * * * Anno Domini 1706.

CHRISTENINGS.

Catherine Y^e Daughter of Edward & Keziah Ball was Born January Y^e 25th Anno Domini 1696.

Elizabeth Daughter of Y^e above Ball was Born May Y^e 1st 1704.

Thomas Y^e Son of Richard & Martha Basford his Wife was Baptized Septemb^r Y^e 8th Anno Domi 1706.

Illegitimate—Joanna Y^e Daughter of   a Servant to Mr Thomas Kemp In Gloucester County was Baptized Septemb^r Y^e 8th Anno Domi 1706.

Elizabeth Y^e Daughter of Nathan & Diana Underwood his Wife was Born Y^e 22nd Day of Novemb^r & Baptized Y^e 22d of Decemb^r it being Y^e Lords day In Stratton Major Parrish in King & Queen County, By Emmanuel Jones Minister of Petsoe Parish in Gloucester County her Sureties being James Overstreet & Elizabeth Potter, Derby Cauniff & Hannah his Wife Y^e day & time of her Nativity being Wednesday About Y^e dawning of Y^e day Anno Domini 1700.

John Y^e Son of Nathan & Diana Underwood his Wife was Born Y^e 24th Day of August About Y^e dawning of Y^e day it being Saturday & S^{nt} Bartholomew day, And was Baptized Septemb^r Y^e 29th being the lord's day, by ye Reverend Bartholomew Yates In Christ Church his Sureties being John Townsend Robert Johnson & Mrs Elizabeth Dudley Anno Domini 17 Peter Y^e Son of James & Margaret Daniel his Wife was Baptized Septemb Y^e 29th.

Hanna Y^e daughter of Thomas & Ann Symes his Wife was Baptized Sep. Y^e 29th Anno Domini.

William Y^e Son of John & Margaret Davis his Wife was Baptized Sep. Y^e 29th Anno Domini.

William Y^e Son of Matthew & Mary Hunt was Bap. 8^{br} Y^e 20th.

Mary Y^e Daughter of Thomas & Ezabella Lantor his Wife was Born about 12 of Y^e Clock Sept. Y^e 9th 1700.

Jeremiah Y^e Son of Thomas Early and Elizabeth his Wife was Bap. Dec Y^e 9th 1705.

Humphrey Y^e Son of Humphrey Jones & Jane his Wife was Born Nov. Y^e 25th and Bap. Y^e 20th of Jan. Anno Dom 1705.

John Y^e Son of Richard Win & Sarah his Wife was Bap Y^e Same day.

Anne ye Daughter William Probert & Hannah his wife was Bap. *

Elizabeth Y^e Daughter of John Aldin & Frances his Wife was Bap. Feb Y^e 10th 1704.

Anne Y^e Daughter of Robert Blackley & Ann his Wife was Bap Y^e same Day 17—

Matthew Y^e Son of Sara Brooks an Illegitimate was Bap: Y^e same day 170—

Catherine Daughter of Bartholomew & Sarah Yates Borne 24th of June 17—

CHRISTENINGS.

Aggatha ye Daughter of Thomas Buford & Elizabeth his wife was Born August ye 13th Anno Domini 1705.

Garrett ye Son of Mr Robert Daniel & Mrs Margaret his wife was Born July ye 7th Anno Domini 1705.

John ye Son of John Goodwin & Mary his Wife was Bap Aprill ye 7th 1706.

Joanna ye Daughter of David George & Catherine his wife was Bap ye same day 1706.

Joanna ye Daughter of Henry Emmerson & Mary his wife was Bap ye same day 1706.

Susanna ye Daughter of John Hore & Jane his wife was Bap ye same day 1706.

Margaret ye Daughter of William Simmons & Margaret his wife was Bap ye same day 1706.

Thomas ye Son of Philip Warrick & Catherine his wife was Bap. Ap^r ye 18th 1706.

Mary ye Daughter of James Brown & Elizabeth his Wife was Bap. ye Same day 1706.

John ye Son of William Balding & Sarah his Wife was Baptized May ye 9th 1706.

Mary ye Daughter of Abraham Trigg & Elizabeth his wife was Bap. ye Same day 1706.

Robert ye Son of William Carter & Mary his wife was Bap. June ye 30th 1706.

Henry ye Son of Richard Perrot & Sara his wife was Born ye 25th of feb^ry 1706.

Jane ye Daughter of John Pace & Elizabeth his wife Bap. Sep^tr ye 22nd 1706.

Elizabeth ye Daughter of Henry Goodlow & Elizabeth his wife was Bap. ye same day 1706.

Susanna ye Daughter of Mr. Harry Beverley & Mme Elizabeth his wife was Bapt. Novemb^r ye 17th Anno Domini 1706.

Ann ye Daughter of Thomas Sibley & Eleaner his wife was Born Novemb ye 3d and Baptized Decemb^r ye 23d Anno Domi 1705.

Jacob ye Son of Georg Blake & Elizabeth his wife was Born Decemb^r ye 8th and Baptized January ye 13th Anno Domi 170⅚.

Dorothy ye Daughter of Henry Mitcham & Mary his wife was Born Decemb^r ye 12th & Baptized ye Same Day Anno Domini 170⅚.

Averilla ye Daughter of Robert Dudley & Elizabeth his wife was Born March * * & Baptized March ye 31st Anno Domi 1706.

* * * ye Daughter of Robert Humphreys & Rebecca his wife was Born february 6th * * & Baptized february ye 18th Anno Domi 170⅚.

William ye Son of William Downing & Elizabeth his wife was Born June ye 3d and Baptized July ye 14th Anno Domini 1706.

Daniel ye son of Daniel Holland & Jane his wife was Born July ye 15th and Baptized August ye 4th Anno Domi 1706.

Robert ye Son of Richard Wait & Anne his wife was Born July ye 4th and Baptized August ye 4th Anno Domi 1706.

Catherine ye Daughter of John Phillips & Jane his wife was Born June ye 27th and Baptized ye Same day Anno Domini 1706.

Charles ye Son of Owen Selaman & Esther his wife was Born Septembr ye 14th & Baptized Octobr ye 6th Anno Domini 1706.

CHRISTENINGS.

Jane ye Daughter of Francis Dodson & Mable his wife was Baptized May ye 12th & Born April ye 13th Anno Domi 1706.

Edy ye Daughter of John Dudley & Edy his wife was Born April ye 12th & Baptized May ye 12th Anno Domi 1706.

Catherine ye Daughter of William Hamat & Elizabeth his wife was Born June ye 5th & Baptized July ye 14th Anno Domi 1706.

William ye son of Jonathan Herrin & Ann his wife was Born August ye 18th & Baptized Octobr ye 6th Anno Domi 1706.

Ann ye Daughter of Joseph Humphreys & Elizabeth his wife was Born Septembr ye 3d & Baptized Octobr ye 6th Anno Domi 1706.

Jane ye Daughter of William Wallis & Ann his wife was Baptized 8br ye 21st and Born Octobr ye 2d Anno Domini 1706.

John ye Son of Joseph Hutchinson & Mary his Wife was Baptized Novembr ye 17th 1706.

Hope ye Daughter of Christopher Sutton & Hope his wife was Bapt: ye Same Day 1706.

Mary Loe ye Daughter of Samuel Loe & Ann his Wife was Bap: Decembr ye 1st 1706.

Ann ye Daughter of Samuel Hoyl & Elizabeth his wife was Bap: December 22nd 1706.

Elizabeth ye Daughter of Edward & Aventa Couch his wife was Bap. Decembr 29th 1706.

Priscilla Churchhill ye Daughter of Collonl William Churchhill Esqr & Mme Elizabeth Churchhill his wife was Born of a friday Night about Nine or ten A Clock Being ye 21st of Decembr Anno Domi 1705, And was Baptized ye first day of January following Anno Domi $170\frac{5}{6}$ By ye Reverend Mr Bartholomew Yates our present Minister.

Sarah ye Daughter of James Smith & Ann his wife was Baptized Janry ye 12th $170\frac{6}{7}$.

Judith ye Daughter of Edward & Catherine Williams was Bap: Janry ye 12th $170\frac{6}{7}$

Agatha ye Daughter of Hugh Watts & Hannah his wife Bap. Janry ye 12th $170\frac{6}{7}$.

Diana ye Daughter of John Ashur & Susanna his wife was Bap. March ye 2d $170\frac{6}{7}$.

Elizabeth Ye Daughter of William hill & Ann his Wife Was Bap. Ye Same day $170\frac{6}{7}$.

Elizabeth Ye Daughter of William Bennett & Sarah his Wife was Bap Ye same day 17—.

Jacob Ye Son of Georg Blake & Elizabeth his Wife was Bap. March Ye 16th 1706.

Richard Ye Son of John Barnett & Ann his Wife was Bap. March Ye 16th 1706.

Catherine Ye Daughter of Mr Bartholomew Yates Minister And Mdm Sarah Yates his Wife was Born June Ye 24th & Baptized July Ye 4th Anno Domi 1706.

Mary Ye Daughter of Mr Roger Jones & Mdm Mary his Wife was Bap. March Ye 23d $170\frac{6}{7}$.

Mary Y^e Daughter of Mr John Robinson & M^{dm} Catherine Robinson his Wife was Born January Y^e 3d Anno Domini 170 6/7.

John Y^e Son of Edward Clark & Ann his Wife was Born March Y^e 31st And Baptized April Y^e 7th Anno Domini 1707.

Mary Y^e Daughter of Francis Coffly & Mary his Wife was Bap Apr^l Y^e 20th 1707.

Marrin Y^e Daughter of John Gibbs & Mary his Wife was Bap. Apr^l Y^e 20th 1707.

Sarah Daughter of Bartholomew & Sarah Yates Borne March 3d 1707.

CHRISTENINGS.

Elizabeth Y^e Daughter of Gabriel Roberts & Sarah his Wife was Baptized May Y^e 25th Anno Domini 1707.

Ruth Y^e Daughter of Thomas Maxum his Wife Baptized May Y^e 25th Anno Domini 1707.

Joice Y^e Daughter of Robert Johnson & Judith his Wife was Baptized June Y^e 22nd Anno Domini 1707.

Matthew an Illegitimate Born of an Irish Woman was Baptized Y^e Same Day Anno Domi 1707.

Mary Y^e Daughter of Robert Biggs & Elizabeth his Wife was Baptized August Y^e 3d Anno Domini 1707.

Christian Y^e Daughter of John Austin & Mary his Wife livers in Gloucester Was Baptized August Y^e 24th Anno Domi 1707.

Elizabeth Y^e Daughter of John Hughs And Rebecca his Wife was Baptized September Y^e 14th Anno Domi 1707.

Elizabeth Y^e Daughter of John Townsend & Damaris his Wife was Baptized September Y^e 28th Anno Domi 1707.

Benjamin Y^e Son of William Barbee & Mary his Wife Was Baptized October the 5th Anno Domini 1707.

Matthew Y^e Son of Matthew Evans & Elizabeth his Wife was Bap. Y^e Same day.

Catherine Y^e Daughter of William Southwort & Margaret his Wife Was Baptized Octob^r Y^e 19th Anno Domi 1707.

John & Jane being Twins Y^e Son & Daughter of Theophilus Staunton And Jane his Wife Were Baptized Octob^r Y^e 26th Anno Domi 1707.

Sara Carder Y^e Daughter of Uriah Carder & Sarah his Wife was Baptized Y^e same Day 1707.

William Y^e Son of Henry Brown & Elizabeth his Wife was Bap. Y^e Same day.

Ann Y^e Daughter of Benjamin Davis and Ann his Wife was Baptized November Y^e 6th Anno Domi 1707.

Susanna Y^e Daughter of William Matthews & Mary his Wife was Born July Y^e 4th Anno Domi 1706.

Samuel Y^e Son of William Matthews & Mary his Wife was Born Novemb^r Y^e 30th & Baptized Decemb^r Y^e 1st Anno Domi 1707.

Mary Y^e Daughter of Richard Straughan & Catherine his Wife was Baptized Decemb^r Y^e 7th Anno Domi 1707.

Michal Y^e Daughter of John Miller & Michal his Wife was Born Octob^r Y^e 31st & Baptized Decemb^r Y^e 7th 1707.

William Son of George & Mary Wortham borne 28th December 1707.

CHRISTENINGS.

Robert Y^e Son of James Dudley & Mary his Wife was Baptized January Y^e 18th Anno Domini 170$\frac{7}{8}$.

Susanna Y^e Daughter of John Davis & Margaret his Wife was Baptized Octob^r Y^e 1st Anno Domi 1707.

Nathan Underwood Y^e Son of Nathan Underwood & Diana his Wife was Born Y^e 9th being friday about nine of Y^e Clock in Y^e Morning & Was Baptized february Y^e 1st being Septuagesima Sunday. In christ Church by Y^e Reverend Mr Bartholomew Yates Minister of Y^e Same; his Sureties being Joseph Goear John Gibbs & Elizabeth Murry; Anno Domi 170$\frac{7}{8}$.

Simon Y^e Son of William & Anne Howard his Wife was Born January Y^e 11th & Baptized february Y^e 1st Anno Domi 170$\frac{7}{8}$.

William Y^e Son of Mr George Wortham & Mrs Mary his Wife was Born Decemb^r Y^e 28th & Baptized february Y^e 2d 170$\frac{7}{8}$.

Catherine Y^e Daughter of Thomas Robbason & Ann his Wife Was Baptized february Y^e 29th Anno Domi 170$\frac{7}{8}$.

Sarah Y^e Daughter of Thomas Davis & Mary his Wife Was Baptized Y^e Same Day Anno Domi 170$\frac{7}{8}$.

Abigail Y^e Daughter of John Marston & Ann his Wife Was Born January Y^e 25th & Baptized Y^e Same Day 170$\frac{7}{8}$.

John Y^e Son of John Burk & Michal his Wife Was Baptized Y^e Same Day 170$\frac{7}{8}$.

John Y^e Son of Willett Roberts & Mary . . . . his Wife B. Y^e Same Day Anno Domini Was Baptized 170$\frac{7}{8}$.

Judith & Elizabeth Daughters of Edward Williams & Catherine his Wife were Born March Y^e 4th & Baptized March Y^e 14th being Twins Anno Domini 170$\frac{7}{8}$.

Agnis Y^e Daughter of William Newberry & Agnis his Wife was Baptized April Y^e 2d Anno Domi 1708.

Mary Hoyt Y^e Daughter of Samuel Hoyt & Elizabeth his Wife was Baptized April Y^e 7th Anno Domi 1708.

Mary Y^e Daughter of Edward Ball & Kezia his Wife was Baptized April Y^e 26th Anno Domi 1708.

Rebecca Y^e Daughter of Francis Dodson & Mabel his Wife was Baptized May Y^e 2d Anno Domi 1708.

Edward Y^e Son of Edward Couch and Averilla his Wife was Baptized the Same Day Anno Domi 1708.

CHRISTENINGS.

Rebecca Y^e Daughter of John Jones & Parnell his Wife was Baptized May Y^e 16th Anno Domi 1708.

John Y^e Son of John & Mary Mitchener his Wife was Born April Y^e 4th Anno Domi 1705.

Alice Y^e Daughter of Charles Hayns & Ann his Wife was born Jan^r Y^e 21st 1704.

William & John Y^e Sons of Patrick Owen & Emary his Wife being Twins were Baptized May Y^e 23rd Anno Domi 1708.

Mary Y^e Daughter of John Mitchiner & Mary his Wife was Born June Y^e 16th Anno Domi 1699.

Averila Y^e Daughter of John Mundin & Frances his Wife Was Baptized June Y^e 13th 1708.

Anne Y^e Daughter of Thomas Chelton & Mary his Wife was Baptized Y^e Same Day 1708.

Samuel Y^e Son of William Marcum & Elizabeth his Wife was Baptized July Y^e 4th Anno Domini 1708.

James Y^e Son of Garrett Berry & Elizabeth his Wife Was Baptized August Y^e 8th Anno Domi 1708.

Richard Curtis Y^e Son of John Curtis Junr & Rebecca his Wife Born December Y^e 29th Anno Domi 1704.

John Y^e Son of Joseph Humphreys & Elizabeth his Wife Baptized Septemb^r Y^e 26th 1708.

Joanna Y^e Daughter of Robert Humphreys & Rebecca his Wife Was Baptized Octob^r Y^e 17th 1708.

Richard Wyett Y^e Son of Richard Wyett & Anne his Wife Was Baptized Novemb^r Y^e 7th Anno Domi 1708.

Christopher Y^e Son of Augustine Owen & Jone his Wife was Baptized Novemb^r Y^e 21st Anno Domi 1708.

Samuel Y^e Son of Samuel Loe & Ann his Wife Was Bap. this Day.

Thomas Y^e Son of Edmund Sanders & Mary his Wife was Bap. this Day.

Ann Y^e Daughter of Richard Daniel & Elizabeth his Wife was likewise Baptized this Day Anno Domi 1708.

CHRISTENINGS.

William Y^e Son of Joseph Hutchinson & Mary his Wife was Baptized Novemb^r Y^e 28th Anno Domi 1708.

John Ye Son of Thomas Symes & Ann his Wife was Baptized January Y^e 5th Anno Domi 170$\frac{8}{9}$.

Mary Y^e Daughter of Christopher Cutton & Hope his Wife was Baptized January Y^e 9th Anno Domi 170$\frac{8}{9}$.

Richard Y^e Son of John Dudley & Edith his Wife was Baptized the Same day Anno Domi 170$\frac{8}{9}$.

Nicholas Y^e Son of Jephtha Edmunds & Mary his Wife was Baptized Y^e Same Day Anno Domini 170$\frac{8}{9}$.

Mary an Illegitimate Y^e Daughter of Mary Rhodes was Baptized Y^e Same Day Anno Domi 170$\frac{8}{9}$.

Ruth Y^e Daughter of Edward Clark & Ann his Wife was Baptiz January Y^e 23d Anno Domi 170$\frac{8}{9}$

Marran Y^e Daughter of John Gibbs & Mary his Wife Baptized January Y^e 30th Anno Domi 170$\frac{8}{9}$

Sarah Y^e Daughter of John Barnatt & Ann his Wife was Baptized February Y^e 13th Anno Domi 170$\frac{8}{9}$.

Charles Y^e Son of James Daniel & Margaret his Wife Baptized 170$\frac{8}{9}$.

William an Illegitimate Son of Mary Canady was Born Octob^r Y^e 4th 1708 And Baptized March Y^e 13th A. D. 170$\frac{8}{9}$.

Elizabeth Y^e Daughter of Abraham Trigg & Elizabeth his Wife was Baptized March Y^e 27th Anno Domi 1709.

Christian Y^e Daughter of Benjamin Davis & Ann his Wife Was Baptized April Y^e 24th being Easter Day A. D. 1709.

Richard Y^e Son of William Bennet &   his Wife was Baptized May Y^e 1st A. D. 1709.

Mary Y^e Daughter of Thomas Lantor & Ezabella his Wife was Baptized May Y^e 22nd Anno Domi 1709.

Elizabeth Y^e Daughter of Lacklin Cannedy & Ann his Wife was Baptized the Same day Anno Domi 1709.

Edward Y^e Son of William Bristow & Margaret his Wife was Baptized July Y^e 6th Anno Domi 1709.

Elther Y^e Daughter of Thomas Maxum & Elizabeth his Wife was Baptized August Y^e 7th A. D. 1709.

CHRISTENINGS.

Sarah Y^e Daughter of Jonathan Herrin & Anne his Wife Was Baptized August Y^e 14th Anno Domi 1709.

William Y^e Son of Mr John Robinson & M^{dm} Catherine his Wife was Born March Y^e 25th Anno Domi 1709.

Gaffield Y^e Son of Henry Brown & Elizabeth his Wife was Born August Y^e 21st & Baptized Y^e 22d Anno Domi 17 .

William Y^e Son of John Ashur & Susanna his Wife was Baptized September Y^e 18th Anno Domi 1709.

Willet Y^e Son of Willett Roberts & Mary his Wife was Born August Y^e 11th & Baptized Septemb Y^e 25th 1709.

Roger Y^e Son of Mr Roger Jones & Mrs Mary his Wife was Baptized Decemb^r Y^e 18th Anno Domi 1709 Borne Y^e 18th October 1709.

Payton Y^e Son of Thomas Dudley Junr & Elizabeth his Wife Baptized January Y^e 22nd Anno Domi 170$\frac{9}{10}$.

Jane an Illegitimate Y^e Daughter of Ann an Irish Woman Servant to William Churchhill Esq. Baptized Y^e Same Day 170$\frac{9}{10}$.

Sarah Y^e Daughter of Francis Coffley & Mary his Wife was Baptized february Y^e 12th Anno Domi 170$\frac{9}{10}$.

Mary Y^e Daughter of Joseph Orphan & Constancy his Wife Was Baptized March Y^e 5th Anno Domi 170$\frac{9}{10}$.

Anne Y^e Daughter of John Owen & Michal his Wife Baptized Y^e Same Day Anno Domini 170$\frac{9}{10}$.

The Births of 5 Children of Henery & Eliz^a Thacker.

Henery Thacker borne Sunday Y^e 9th October 1698.

Martha Thacker borne Satturnday y^e 27th December 1701.

Chichely Thacker borne Sunday y^e 26th March 1704.

Lettice Thacker borne Satturnday y^e 26th ffebruary 1704.

Anne Thacker borne Wensday ye 5th October 1709.

Peter Harding Son of Nicholas and Elizabeth Harding borne 27th Aprill 1709.

The Births of six Negro Children belonging to Mr Henery Thacker.

Toney ye Son of Sambo & Jenny borne October ye 14th 1698.

Judith ye Daughter of Ditt^o borne September ye 6th 1701.

Sam the Son of Jack & Becka borne ffebruary ye 8th 1701.

Winey the Daughter of Cesar & Joane borne June ye 7th 1705.

Nanny the Daughter of Sambo & Jenny borne March 2d 1705.

Molley the Daughter of Jack & Beck borne June ye 28th 1706.

John a Negro belonging to Mr Jno Vivion borne December ye 19th 1709.

The Births of Seven Negroes belonging to Mr John Smith Senior (vizt).

Negro Hally borne 18th November 1704. Negro Moll borne 16th ffebruary 1705. Negro Judy borne 15th June 1707. Negro Sanco borne 12th May 1708. Negro Hannah borne 26th September 1708. Negro Dinah borne 6th March 1709. Negro ffranke borne 31th May 1710.

Negro Ben Jeney's Son belonging to Captn John Smyth borne July ye 31th 1710.

Negro Molly belonging to Mr Bartholomew Yates born May ye 27th 1709.

Negro Willm baptized was borne (belonging to Ditto) July ye 13th 1709.

The Births of Ten Negro Children belonging to Captn Henery Armistead Registred ye 26th day of June 1711.

Emmanuell borne 13th December 1700. Bess borne ye 12th ffebruary 1701. Rose borne 3d May 1702. Mingo borne 9th October 1703. George borne 10th Aprill 1707. Hannah borne ye 6th October 1707. Gabriell borne 29th ffebruary 1708. Sue borne ye 10th May 1708. Tom borne ye 29th Aprill 1709. Jacob borne 10th May 1709.

Ned a Negro belonging to Hen. Tuggell borne 7th ffeb^{ry} 1709.

Dick A Negro belonging to Mr Jno. Hipkins borne ye 27th March 1708.

The Births of three Negroes belonging to Mr Roger Jones Registred the 7th day of Aprill 1712.

Toney A Negro borne y^e 18th May 1711. Negro ffrank borne y^e 29th June 1711. Negroe Sarah borne y^e 11th Aprill 1711.

The Births of Three Negroes Belonging to Mr Rice Curtis Registered June ye 5th 17$\frac{1}{6}$.

ffrank borne y^e 20th of July 1708. Sarah borne y^e 25th of Aprill 1710. Judith borne y^e 2d of July 1711.

The Births of Sixteene Negroes Belonging to Mr Harry Beverley Registred Octob^r y^e 6th 171.

ffrank Daughter of Judith borne 15th July 1701. Maria Daughter of Judith borne 13th Octobo 1703. Sarah daughter of Judith borne 3d August 1705. Billy son of Phillis borne 15 November 1705. Bess daughter of Kate borne 26th August 1705. Moll daughter of Indian Fanny borne 2d May 1705. Moll daughter of Jenney borne 17th May 1706. Sarah daughter of Kate borne ye 25th September 1707. Ralph Son of Judith borne 10th August 1708. Harry Son of Jenney borne 15th of August 1708. Nanny daughter of Phillis borne 3d day of October 1709. Bob son of Kate borne 10th of October 1709. Anthony Son of Jenny borne 4th Aprill 1710. Beck daughter of Judith borne 5th March 1711. Peter son of Jenny borne 16th July 1712. Charles Son of Kate borne 2d day of October 1712.

The following Negroes Registred the 11th day of October 1712.

Charles A Negro belonging to Geo. Berwick borne ye 20th day of June 1707. Robin A Negro belonging to Do. borne August ye 4th day 1710.

Mingo A negro belonging to Oliver Seagar borne ye 26th day of May 1706.

Megg A negro belonging to Humphrey Jones borne ye 15th day of October 1706.

Peter a negro belonging to Garrett Minor borne ye 9th day of May 1707.

Winnie A negro belonging to Cap. Robt Daniell borne ye 5th day of Aprill 1707.

Jack A negro belonging to Phillip Warwick borne ye 9th day of May 1707.

Ned A negro belonging to John Aldin borne 10th day of October 1707.

Winifred Morris a Molatto belonging to Francis Weekes Junr baptized 25th day of Jan^ry 1707.

Tenny A negro belonging to Garrett Minor borne ye 20th day ffeb^ry 1709.

Cate A negro belonging to ffran. Weekes Junr borne ye 25th day of December 1709.

Mingo A negro belonging to Cap. Robert Daniell borne 10th day of Aprill 1710.

Jack A negro belonging to Thomas Hazlewood borne ye 23th day of ffeb^ry 1709.

Cate A negro belonging to Thomas Mountague borne ye 21th day of July 1710.

CHRISTENINGS.

Marvell Son of Samuell and Anne Loe was baptized 24th of September 1710.

Julian Son of John & Hannah King baptized 5th November borne 1st October 1710.

Mary Daughter of Garrett & Elizabeth Berry baptized 5th of November 1710.

Mary Daughter of Thomas and Elizabeth Golder baptized 5th of November 1710.

Samuell the Son of George & Mary Wortham was borne 28th January 1709.

Mary Daughter of J^no and Elizabeth Lewis baptized 3d January 1710.

John the Son of Augustine and Joane Owen baptized 22d Aprill 1711.

Mary Daughter of John & Mary Gibbs baptized 22d Aprill 1711.

Judith Daughter of Richard & Elizabeth Daniell baptized 22d Aprill 1711.

Thomas Son of Thomas & Eliza Maxum baptized 13th May 1711.

Stokeley Son of Henery & Hannah Toles baptized 3d June 1711.

Mary Daughter of Thomas & Mary Yarrow baptized 3d June 1711.

Mary Daughter of Edwd & Anne Clark baptized 3d June 1711.

John Son of John & Elizabeth ffoster baptized 3d June 1711.

Esther Daughter of Henery & Elizabeth Johnson baptized 3d June 1711.

Thomas Son of Sarah Palmer an Illegitimate baptized 7th September 1711.

Charles son of George & Mary Wortham borne 28th December 1711.

Ann Daughter of Edd^d &   Ball baptized 30th Aprill 1710.

Wm Son of J^no & Hannah Owen borne 15th of October 1711.

Mary Daughter of John & Elizabeth Saunders baptized 18th of November 1711.

Mary Daughter of William & Sarah Baldin baptized 9th December 1711.

Phebe Daughter of Edward & Keziah Ball baptized 2d March 1711.

Lower Chappel   { Margarett Daughter of James Smyth & Ann his wife borne 11th March 1708. Robert an Illegittimate Son of Marg^tt Child. David Son of Robert & Eliza Mackey & Dorothy Daughter of Robert & Avarilla Couch all baptized the 16th Aprill 1710.

John Son of Thomas & Mary Davis baptized 30th June 1710.

John son of Robert & Judith Johnson baptized 20th August 1710.

Thomas Son of John & Michall Burk. Susanna daughter of Peter Chelton Juni^or & Eliza his wife were all baptized 20th August 1710.

John Son of W^m & Ann Hill baptized October 1st 1710.

Eliz^a Daughter of W^m & Mary Barbee born 1st Septr baptized 1st October 1710.

Ruth daughter of Nathan & Diana Underwood born 13th Septr baptiz^d October 22d 1710.

Ann daughter of Joseph & Lucretia Gore baptized 4th ffebruary 1710.

John Son of Joseph & Mary Hutchinson baptized 25th ffebruary 1710.

Thomas Son of Thomas & Mary Chelton. Ezekiah Son of John & Ann Rhodes were all baptized ye 25th ffebruary 1710.

Sarah daughter of Geo. & Eliza Blake borne 14th January 1710.

Eliza daughter of Joseph & Eliza Humfreys baptized 8th Aprill 1711.

Joseph Son of John & Katherine Rowe baptizd 29th Aprill 1711.

William Son of John & Ann Barbee, Ann daughter of John & Rebecca Hughes were all baptized 29th Aprill 1711.

David Son of Geo. & Eliz^a Berick baptizd 20th May 1711.

William Son of Thomas & Ann Godwin baptizd July 1st 1711.

Eliz^a daughter of Robert & Eliz^a Biggs baptizd 1st July 1711.

Mary daughter of Ed^wd & Eliza Saunders baptizd 14th October 1711.

CHRISTENINGS.

John Son of Robert & Rebecca Humphreys. Mary Daughter of William & ffrances Sandiford. Eliz^a daughter of Hugh & Rebecca Roach. and Ezabell daughter of Willett & Mary Roberts baptized att home 25th November 1711.

Joseph Son of William & Elizabeth Marcum borne 18th November & baptized 16th December 1711.

Robert Son of John & Catherine Robinson born Octo: ye 20. baptizd Nov. 5: 1711.

The Births of Six Children of Mr Harry Beverley and Elizabeth his wife.

Robert Son of Harry & Elizabeth Beverley was borne 6th day of November 27th day of March 1701.

Margarett Daughter of Ditto borne 27th day of March 1704.

Sussanna Daughter of Ditto borne 15th day of November 1706.

Katherine Daughter of Ditto borne 7th day of December 1708.

Judith Daughter of Ditto borne 25th day of October 1710.

Peter Son of Ditto borne 2d day of July 1712.

Son of Henery & Eliz^a Browne borne 15th day of Aprill 1712.

Midle   ⎰ Benjamin Son of John & Margarett Davies baptized 3d
P'c'ncts ⎱   day of August 1712.

Mary Daughter of W^m & Agnis Newbery baptized 3d day of August 1712.

Mary Daughter of Jon^a & Ann Henning D^o 17th of ffeb^{ry} 1711.

Ann Daughter of Jno & Alice Church D^o 9th of March 1711.

John Son of Jos. & Constance Orphan Baptized 18th of May 1712.

James Son of Charles & Eliza Richardson Do 18th of May 1712.

John Son of Jos. & Mary Hutchinson Do 25th of ffeb^{ry} 1710.

Thos Son of Geo. & Eliz^a Hardin Borne 3d of May 1712.

ffrances daughter of Francis & Mary Coffley baptized 10th of August 1712.

John Son of Xtopher & Hope Sutton. Sarah daughter of John & Mary Dayly. John Son of W^m & Hannah Cane borne August 5th. All three baptized Aug. 31th 1712.

Robert Son of Sr Wm Skipwith & Lady Sarah his wife. Ezekiah & W^m being twin Sons of J^{no} & Mary Bradley were all baptized 21th day of September 1712.

George Son of Geo. & Eliz^a Berwick borne 26th day of 7^{br} 1712.

Katherine daughter of Patrick & Ann Mannell baptized ye 9th day of ffebruary 1706.

Upper   ⎧ Moses Son of W^m & Marg^{tt} Kidd baptized ye 30th day
          ⎨   of March 1707.
Chappell ⎩ Robert Son of John & Margarett Hardee baptized ye 30th
                  day of March 1707.

Elizabeth daughter of Thomas & Elizabeth Hardy Warrwick baptized ye 30th day of March 1707.

Robert son of Robert & Kattherine Perrott. Katherine daughter of Henery & Eliz^a Smith both baptized this 27th day of Aprill 1707.

Agatha daughter of Matthew & Elizabeth Cranck baptized the 18th day of May 1707.

Mary daughter of Charles & Mary Maderas baptized ye 24th Day of Aprill 1707.

Judith daughter of Richard & Ann Shurly baptized ye 29th day of June 1707.

Robt. Son of Thomas & Elizabeth Williams baptized ye 10th day of August 1707.

Joannah daughter of Joseph & Avarilla Hardy baptized ye 3d day of August 1707.

Elizabeth daughter of Rich^d & Honour Reynalds baptized ye 3d day of August 1707.

John Son of Thomas & Elizabeth Bewford. Jonathan Son of David & Mary Davids. Elizabeth daughter of James & Elizabeth Browne were all three baptized 21th day of 7^{br} 1707.

William son of W^m & Ann Gardiner baptized born ye 6th day of 7^{br} 1707.

William son of Sr Wm Skipwith & Lady Sarah his Wife was born September ye 15 1707.

CHRISTENINGS.

John Son of John & Johanna Degge born October ye 17. baptized 1707.

Thomas Son of Ralph & Mary Shelton baptized 9th day of November 1707.

John Son of Garrett & Diana Minor borne 29th day of June 1707.

Henery Son of Thomas & Alice Kid baptized 23th day of November 1707.

Thomas Son of Thomas & Lettice Bateman baptized 23th day of November 1707.

Philemon Son of James & Ann Black baptized 23th November 1707.

James Son of Robert & Marg^{rt} Daniell borne 5th November 1709.

George Son of Robert & Anne Blacklee baptized 14th day December 1707.

Alexander Son of Alexander & Mary Graves borne 8th day of Jan^{ry} 1707.

John Son of Richard & Martha Willis borne 1st day of Jan^{ry} 1707.

James Son of Joseph & Jane Meecham baptized 15th day of ffebruary 1707.

John Son of Henery & Mary Emmerson baptized Do. day &c 1707.

J^{no} Son of W^m & Mary Daniell baptized Do. day &c.

Jane daughter of Richard & Sarah Winn baptized Do. day &c.

ffrances daughter of ffrances & John Aldin baptized Do. day &c.

Richard Son of Richard & Sarah Perrott baptized 18th day of March 1708.

Mary daughter of Geo. & Hannah Guess baptized Do. day &c.

Elizabeth daughter of W^m & Mary Jones born ye 7th day of March 1708,

James Son of Jacob & Mary Pressnall baptized ye 9th day of March 1708.

Elizabeth daughter of Ralph & Alice Mazy baptized Do. day &c.

John Son of Thomas & Sarah Chowning borne 27th day of August 1707.

Charles son of Charles & Dorothy Lee baptized 30th day of May 1708.

Mary daughter of Willm & Mary Carter baptized 20th day of June 1708.

John Son of John & Jane Hoard baptized 1st day of August 1708.

Wm Son of Henery & Mary Bewford borne ye 17th day of June 1708.

Tobias Son of Edmond & Jane Mickleborough baptized ye 17th day of June 1708.

Elizabeth daughter of Thomas & Anne Crank baptized Do. day &c.

Ann daughter of Matthew & Elizabeth Cap baptized Do. day &c.

Hally son of David & Kattherine George baptized 3d day of October 1708.

Thomas son of William & Joannah Semour baptized Do. day &c.

Elizabeth daughter of Hobbs & Mary Weekes baptized Do. day &c.

Joseph Son of Robert & Anne Homes baptized ye 14th day of November 1708.

Macktyre Son of Thomas & Prudence Morris baptized Do. day &c.

Wm Son of J^{no} & Michaell Owen borne ye 4th day of November 1708.

Nickolas Son of Thomas & Mary Burk borne ye 29th day of November 1708.

Mary daughter of W^m & Hannah Probent borne 16th day of November 1708.
Newsome Son of John & Eliz^a Pace baptized 6th day of ffebry 1708.
William Son of W^m & Marg^tt Simonds baptized Do. day &c.
Sarah daughter of Robert & Katherine Perrott baptized Do. day &c.
Jane daughter of John & Marg^tt Hardee baptized Do. day &c.
John Son of W^m & Marg^tt Kidd baptized 27th day of ffeb^ry 1708.
Charles Son of John & Elizabeth Hickee baptized ye 10th day of Aprill 1708.
John Son of Richard & Sarah Attwood borne ye 3d day of March 1708.
John Son of James & Anne Jordan baptized the 8th day of May 1709.
Jane daughter of Henery & Eliz^a Goodloe baptized Do. day &c.
Mary daughter of W^m & Elizabeth Mullings baptized Do. day &c.
Richard Son of Robert & Sarah George baptized ye 29th day of May 1709.
Michall daughter of James & Mary Meecham baptized the 10th day of July 1709.
Edward Son of W^m & Marg^tt Bristoll borne ye 4th day of June 1709.
Barker daughter of Humphrey & Elizabeth Jones baptized ye 31th day of July 1709.
Henery Son of John & Mary Meecham borne ye 25th day of July 1709.
Wm Son of W^m & Sarah Rattenig baptized the 21th day of August 1709.
Eliz^a daughter of Richard & Martha Willes baptized Do. day &c.
Anne daughter of W^m & Elizabeth Brooks baptized 2d day of October 1709.
Joseph Son of Joseph & Avarilla Hardy baptized ye 23th day of October 1709.
Ralph Son of Ralph & Mary Shelton baptized Do day &c.
Martha daughter of Paile & Mary Cooper baptized Do. day &c.
Eliz^a daughter of Joseph & Mary Seares baptized ye 13th day of November 1709.

MARRIAGES D C^a 1–1704.1—Viz^t.

John Hughes and Rebecca Hill married ye 31th of December 1704.
Thos. Warwick & Eliz^a Goodrich ye 23d January 1704.
John Alding & ffrances Williamson ye 16th ffebruary 1704.
Humphrey Jones & Jane Hazlewood ye 18th ffebruary 1704.
Joseph Andrews & Eliz^a Terrill ye 20th of Aprill 1705.
John ffiney & Marg^tt Upton ye 12th of Aprill 1705.
John Goodwin & Mary Elliott ye 22nd of Aprill 1705.
John Price & Jane Smith ye 1st of May 1705.
Harman Churchyard and Eliza Perkins ye 26th of August 1705.
Phillipp Warwick & Catherine Twyman ye 5th of September 1705.
Robert Whitteker & Esther ffrancis ye 1st of October 1705.
Thos Maxam & Eliza Cooke ye 2nd of October 1705.
Sam^ll Hoyle & Eliza Elliott ye 23rd of October 1705.
John Maxkemett & Margarett Williams ye 28th of October 1705.
Dudley Jelley & Eliza Shelling ye 31th of October 1705.
Henery Ball & Alice Brookes ye 2nd of November 1705.

Patrick Owen & Mary Chills ye 23th of November 1705.
James Browne & Eliza Baldin ye 5th of December 1705.
Abraham Trigg & Eliza Guess ye 14th of December 1705.
Jeptha Edmunds & Mary Pain ye 24th of December 1705.
Joseph Hutchinson & Mary Needles ye 2nd of January 1705.
Richard Perrott & Sarah Pitts ye 15th of January 1775.
William Baldin & Sarah Lewis ye 17th of January 1705.
Richard Wait & Ann Dugless ye 3rd of ffebruary 1705.
Robert Perrott & Catherine Daniell ye 25th of March 1706.
Matthew Hunt & Mary Loyall ye 26th of March 1706.
Edward Parke & Anne fferne ye 26th of March 1706.
William Ryon & Elianour Jackson ye 18th of Aprill 1706.
Jonathan Horne & Anne Clay ye 14th of May 1706.
Henery Bailey & Catherine Denison ye 27th of May 1706.
ffrancis Coffley & Mary Wallis ye 24th of June 1706.
Thomas Davis & Mary Roberts ye 4th of August 1706.
Robert Biggs & Eliza Pate y^c 2nd of September 1706.
John Austain & Anne Bolton ye 2nd of September 1706.
William Johnson & Eliza Paine ye 8th of September 1706.
Garrett Minor & Diana Vivion ye 17th of October 1706.
Thomas Dudley & Eliza Meecham ye 22nd of October 1706.
Theophilus Stanton & Jane Porter ye 28th of November 1706.
Thomas Chowning & Sarah Davis ye 20th of December 1706.
Thomas Smyth & Jane Annis ye 26th of December 1706.
Benj^a Davis & Anne Williams ye 27th of December 1706.
John Custis & Avarilla Curtis ye 16th of January 1706.
John Degge & Johanna Killbee ye 21th of January 1706.
George Coleman & Martha Pressnall ye 27th of January 1706.
John Sandeford & Mary Walkell ye 13th of ffebruary 1706.
Edward Harrell & Margarett Brumwell ye 20th of Aprill 1707.
William ffiney & Honour Reardon ye 8th of May 1707.
James Walker & Clara Robinson ye 20th of May 1707.
Richard Attford & Mary Williams ye 29th of May 1707.
Henery Bewford & Mary Parsons ye 12th of September 1707.
Robert Deputy & Mary Huddle ye 9th of October 1707.
John Owen & Michaell Bristow ye 23th of October 1707.
James Areley & Jennett Ryell ye 18th of November 1707.
Samuell Samford & Isabella Langhee ye 21th of November 1707.
John Jones & Patrick Okendime ye 10th of ffebruary 1707.
Alexander Graves & Mary Stapleton ye 6th of Aprill 1708.
John Munday & ffrances Dudley ye 6th of Aprill 1708.
John Newton & Mary Michiner ye 6th of Aprill 1708.
Matthew Bowen & Eliz^a Wood ye 6th of May 1708.
John Whately & Mary Hurford ye 23th of May 1708.

MARRIAGES &c. 1708. Viz^t.

James Meecham & Mary fferne married ye 8th of July 1708.
Henery Bassett & Sarah Trigg ye 15th of July 1708.
Matthew Laundress & Eliz^a Jenkins ye 26th of July 1708.
John Meechan & Mary Atwood ye 27th of July 1708.
William Brookes & Eliz^a Cardwell ye 2d of September 1708.
John ffoster & Eliz^a Bailey ye 14th of September 1708.
Hobbs Weekes & Mary Perrott ye 16th of September 1708.

Stokeley Gales & Anne Velott ye 21th of October 1708.
John Owen & Sarah King ye 31th of October 1708.
William ffaulkener & Mary Weekes ye 3d of November 1708.
John Gibson & Eliz^a Willcocks ye 28th of November 1708.
Jonathan Brookes & Mary Tugell ye 27th of December 1708.
James Curtis & Agatha Vans ye 27th of December 1708.
Julian King & Sarah Snelling ye 30th of December 1708.
John Williams & Anne Shurley ye 17th of ffebruary 1708.
Thomas Olliver & Sarah Howes ye 21th of ffebruary 1708.
Michaell Smyth & Sarah Brookes ye 28th of Aprill 1708.
Joseph Alphin & Constantine Stiff ye 28th of Aprill 1708.
Matthew Perry & Sarah Murrey ye 28th of Aprill 1708.
Peter Chelton & Eliz^a Downing ye 1st of May 1708.
William Allford & Herodias Shibley ye 1st of May 1708.
William Stannard & Anne Hazlewood (Daughter of George Hazle-
    wood Son & Heire of Captn John Hazlewood late of Lond^o
    Marriner deced) and Anne daughter of Richard and Anne Ro-
    binson (the Widdow & Heire of Abraham Moore deced mar-
    ried ye 3d of May 1708.
Daniell Downing & Lettice Love ye 27th of May 1708.
John Saunders & Eliz^a Sibley ye 12th of June 1708.
William Hunt & Eliz^a Holland ye 13th of June 1708.
James Mackey & Eliz^a Brock ye 12th July 1708.
Isaack Hill & Marg^{tt} Jenings ye 28th of July 1708.
John Rhodes & Anne Paine ye 18th of August 1708.
Rinwing Gardiner & Anne Black ye 18th of August 1708.
Matthew Cock & Catherine Priest ye 12th of September 1708.
John Church & Alice Key ye 16th of October 1708.
ffrancis Parke & Anne Williams ye 18th of December 1708.
Wm Dess & Katherine Woodyard ye 18th of December 1708.
John King & Hannah Adams ye 23rd of December 1708.
John Barbee & Ann Miller ye 25th of December 1708.
John Gutterie & Sarah Stiff ye 5th of January 1708.
James M^{ac}tyre & Hannah Boseley ye 5th of January 1708.
Hugh M^{ac}tyre & Catherine George ye 5th of January 1708.
Thomas Golden & Eliz^a Goare ye 12th of January 1708.
Joseph Goare & Lucretia Tugwell ye 16th of ffebruary 1708.
Thomas Gilley & Mary Shephard ye 17th of ffebruary 1708.
John Owen & Hannah Probest ye 10th of Aprill 1708.
Powell Stampar & Mary Brookes ye 10th of Aprill 1708.
Edward Wallford & Rebecca Mason ye 10th of Aprill 1708.
Nicholas Jones & Anne Hoyle ye 11th of Aprill 1708.
William Tigwell & Priscella Snelling ye 20th of Aprill 1708.
William Elliott & Mary Neale ye 20th of Aprill 1708.
Edward Cambridge & Anne Nixson ye 1st of May 1708.
Thomas Clarke & Eliz^a Toseley ye 22th of May 1708.
George Barwick & Elizabeth Bristow ye 7th of June 1708.
Jacob Stiff & Eliz^a Clarke ye 5th of July 1708.
William Bushnell & Honour Reynalls ye 20th of July 1708.
Thomas Thornton & Agatha Curtis ye 25th of July 1708.
Thomas Cheedle & ffrances Godby ye 26th of July 1708.

Hugh Roach & Rebecca Bremont married y[e] 27th of July 1710.
John Gutterie & Jane Mitcham 4th of August 1710.
Minor Minor & Eliz[a] Norman 22th of August 1710.
Edward Saunders & Eliz[a] Austin 3d of August 1710.
William Hill & ffrances Needles 7th of September 1710.
Thomas Elliott & Eliz[a] Dudley 21th of September 1710.
William Daniell & ffrances Boseley 24th of October 1710.
Henery Tugell & Eliz[a] Browne 31th of October 1710.
Valentine Mayo & Anne Jordan 14th of November 1710.
Isaack Webb & Winifrid Hipkins 14th of November 1710.
Churchill Blakey & Sarah George 30th of November 1710.
William Sandeford & ffrances Townsend 25th of December 1710.
Arthur Donnelly & Lettice Downing 2d of January 1710.
Abraham Trigg & Judith Clarke 11th of January 1710.
John Mitcham & Mary Brame 1st of ffebruary 1710.
John Pinnell & Eliz[a] Ingram 4th of Aprill 1710.
James Monnoughon & Elianor Martin 5th of Aprill 1711.
Thomas Godin & Anne Webb 7th of Aprill 1711.
John Bell & Mary Key 20th of Aprill 1711.
William Wheeler & Eliz[a] Begerley 9th of May 1711.
Charles Richardson & Eliz[a] Carter 2d of June 1711.
Thomas Cheny & Jane Swepstone 16th of June 1711.
William Cain & Hannah King 4th of July 1711.
Thomas Salt & Anne Gabriell 3d of August 1711.
Thomas Warrick & Mary Jones 4th of August 1711.
Thomas Machen & Mary Chelton 8th of August 1711.
Hen: Ware & Marg[tt] Daniell 15th of August 1711.
Edward Radford & Mary Canady 23d of August 1711.
John Purvis & Winifred Nicholls 5th of September 1711.
John Johnson & Anne Stevens 21th of September 1711.
Arthur Thomas & Mary Saunders 26th of October 1711.
John Bradley & Mary Rhodes 2d of November 1711.
William Hackney & Alice Rhodes 2d of November 1711.
Rich[d] Gibbs & Penelope Dewton 16th of November 1711.
Joseph Timberlin & Eliz[a] Gray 11th of December 1711.
Daniell Hughes & ffrances Gresham 19th of December 1711.
Patrick Deacon & Rebecca Cooper 12th of January 1711.
Samuell Dagnell & Margarett Child 24th of January 1711.
Ralph Watts & Eliz[a] Mullins 5th of february 1711.
John Berry & Mary Dudley 17th of ffebruary 1711.
Edward Couch & Sarah Thomson 26th of ffebruary 1711.
Edward Prendergast & Elizabeth Hickey 26th of ffebruary 1711.
William Blazedon & Sarah Palmer 3d of March 1711.
Thomas Bristow & Catherine Wortley 1st of May 1711.
Robert Brine & Mary Matthew 25 May 1711.
John Hughes & Jayne Calaham 27 May 1711.
Richard Winn & Anne Cocke 28 May 1711.
John Vivion & Eliz[a] Thacker 19 June 1711.
Man Page & Judith Wormley 10 July 1711.
J[no] Marston & Mary Terrill 31 July 1711.
Henery ffollwell & Katharine Williamson 4 September 1711.

Augale Cummins & Ellianor Williamson 18 September 1711.
James Crosswell & Anne Brooke 22 October 1711.
John Nash & Mary Curlis 22 December 1711.
John South & Elizabeth Smith 7 Jan^ry 1711.
John Bristow & Mary Carter 8 Jan^ry 1711.

MARRIAGES.

Edward Moor & Margrett Symons married Feb^ry ye 13 1712.
James Bowman & Margrett Dearlow married Feb^ry ye 14 1712.
John Ingram & Mary Croony married Feb^ry ye 16 1712.
William Cheshire & Anne Davis married Aprill ye 12 1713.
Richard Wiat & Charity Beamont married Aprill ye 16 1713.
Peter Ballad & Mary Dabidie married June ye 2 1713.
John Cheedle & Lettice Southern married Sept. ye 14 1713.
James Riske & Anne Calvert married Sept. ye 24 1713.
Benjamine Woods & Elizabeth Wheeler married Novem^r ye 16 1713.
Gabriell Ray & Elizabeth Gibbs married Novem^r ye 22 1713.
Richard Allen & Mary Roebottom married Decem^r ye 27 1713.
Moses Norman & Alice Canady married Jan^ry ye 15 1713.
Samuell Batchelder & Catherine Vallott married Jan^ry ye 21 1713.
Robert Dudley & Elizabeth Curtis married Feb^ry ye 9 1713.
John Miller & Jane Hill married March ye 28 1714.
John Gresham & Anne Carnen married March ye 30 1714.
Thomas Hazlewood & Jane May married May ye 7 1714.
George Saunders & Anne Clark married May ye 9 1714.
Henry Ball & Sarah Bristow married May ye 12 1714.
John Watts & Elizabeth Worsell married June ye 17 1714.
Henry Barns & Johanna Lawrance married July ye 6 1714.
Ralph Lyall & Amy Mazey married August ye 19 1714.
Richard Steevens & Sarah Sandiford married Septemb^r ye 2 1714.
Curtis Perrott & Anne Daniell married Septemb^r ye 3 1714.
George Bonden & Sarah Bennett married Septemb^r ye 8 1714.
Thomas Keiling & Catherine Ball married Septemb^r ye 30 1714.
Aquilla Snelling & Mary Goar married Novem^r ye 24 1714.
John Smith & Anne Smith married Novem^r ye 24 1714.
Thomas Hackett & Mary Jarrett married Novem^r ye 28 1714.
Andrew Terry & Elizabeth Moxam married Decem^r ye 14 1714.
Jeffery Burk & Mary Ashton married Decem^r ye 19 1714.
William Markham & Elizabeth Wharton married Jan^ry ye 9 1714.
George Chowning & Elizabeth Daniell married Feb^ry ye 4 1714.
Edmond Hamerton & Sarah Thilman married Feb^ry ye 10 1714.
Henry Bridgforth & Mary Chelton married April ye 18 1715.
Thomas Paine & Catherine Lydford married May ye 26 1715.
John Hatton & Anne Godin married July ye 11 1715.
Thomas Blakey & Mary Meacham married Decemb^r ye 5 1715.
William Seagur & Anne Scinco married Decem^r ye 15 1715.
William Vanhan & Mary Wake married Decem^r ye 25 1715.
John Brame & Elizabeth Beamon married Jan^ry ye 24 1715.
James Hipkins & Mary Warner married Feb^ry ye 9 1715.
William Davis & Elizabeth Allen married Feb^ry ye 12 1715.
Eusebias Lewis & Mary Loyall married Ap. ye 5 1716.
John Watts & Elizabeth Foster married Ap. ye 12 1716.
John Pendergrass & Mary Alford married May ye 2 1716.

BURIALLS.

John Sadler buried the 31th day of October 1710.

John Meecham Dyed the 20th day of May 1712.

Phillipp Callvert dyed the 26th day of June 1712.

Elizabeth Sharlott dyed the 22th day of July 1712.

Ann daughter of Edward & Mary Radford buried 31th day of August 1712.

Jane daughter of Phillipp & Kath Warwick died ye 13th day of September 1712.

Mrs Ann Stannard wife Mr Wm Stannard departed this life on ffriday ye 5th day of X^ber 1712 about 12 of Clock att night aged twenty and two yeares and five days and having liv'd a married life three yeares Seven months and two days being great with child and near Eight months gone. Buried the 10th of December 1712.

William Son of Ralph and Alice Mazy buried ye 15th day of March 1712.

George Blake dyed ye 17th and was buried ye 19th day of July 1713.

Ralph Wormley Esqr dyed the 5th and was buried the 9th day of December 1713.

Mr William Mountague dyed the 7th and was buried the 10th day of X^ber 1713.

Mary Davies Widow dyed ye 7th and was buried the 9th day of March 1713.

Paul Thillman dyed the 14th and was buried the 17th day of March 1713.

Mrs Elizabeth Thacker Widow dyed the 22nd and was Interred the 25th May 1714.

Rebecca Johnson dyed ye 19th day of May & was buried ye 21th of May 1714.

Ben a negro belonging to Capt John Smith buried ye 7th of May 1714.

Elizabeth Marcum dyed ye 9th & was buried ye 11th of October 1713.

Thomas Tegnall dyed ye 10th & was buried ye 12th of October 1713.

John Okill dyed ye 25th of October & was buried 27th Ditto 1713.

Edmund Saunders dyed ye 1st and was buried ye 3d of November 1713.

John Curtis dyed November ye 8 & was buried 9^ber ye 10 1714.

Margrett Blakey dyed November ye 14 & was buried November ye 16 1714.

John Wacham dyed November ye 21 & was buried November ye 23 1714.

John Sandiford dyed Jan^ry ye 3 & was buried Jan^ry ye 6 1714.

Sarah Wormley dyed Jan^ry ye 12 & was buried Jan^ry ye 14 1714.

Alice Silvester dyed Jan^ry ye 6 & was buried Jan^ry ye 8 1714.

John Davies dyed Jan^ry ye 30 & was buried Jan^ry ye 31 1714.

John Watts dyed Decem. ye 17 & was buried December ye 18 1714.

Jack a negro belonging to John Smith Senr buried Feb. ye 9 1714.

Richard Hill dyed Jan^ry ye 23 & was buried Jan^ry ye 24 1714.

John Burk dyed March ye 13 & was buried March ye 14 1714.

Frank a negro belonging to John Smith buried March ye 27 1715.

Peter a negro belonging to George Wortham buried Feb^ry ye 22 1714.

Miles a negro belonging to James Walker buried March ye 15 1714.

Rinning Gardner dyed Ap: ye 7th was buried Ap: ye 9 1715.

Richard Allen dyed April ye 27th & was buried Aprill ye 30 1715.
Absolom Chowning dyed November ye 29 & was buried November ye 30 1714.
Kate a negro belonging to John Hoar buried May 22 1715.
William Bushnell dyed May ye 19 & was buried May ye 21 1715.
Edmund Saunders dyed July ye 31 & was buried Augs^t ye 1715.
Charles Lee dyed August ye 20 & was buried August ye 23 1715.
Anne Thacker dyed August ye 26 & was buried August ye 28 1715.
Alice Purvis dyed Septem^r ye 5 & was buried Septem^r ye 7 1715.
Griffin Nichols dyed Septem^r ye 14 & was buried Septem^r ye 15 1715.
Johanna Humpheries dyed Augst ye 29 & was buried August 31 1715.
Elizabeth Chelton dyed Septem^r ye 7 & was buried Septem^r ye 9 1715.
Macham Moor dyed Septem^r ye 9 & was buried Septem^r ye 10 1715.

Bar Yates Minister.

BURIALLS.

Thomas White dyed Septem^r ye 12 & was buried Septem^r ye 13 1715.
John Manuell dyed Octo: ye 3 & was burried October ye 4 1715.
Reuben Skelton dyed Octo. ye 8 & was buried October ye 10 1715.
Martin Gardner dyed Septem^r ye 12 & was buried Septem^r ye 14 1715.
Diana Gardner dyed Septem^r ye 21 & was buried Septem^r ye 23 1715.
Jane Lawson dyed Octo: ye 8 & was buried October ye 11 1715.
Clara Walker dyed Octo: ye 25 & was burid October ye 29 1715.
Mary Pendergrass dyed Septem^r ye 15 & was buried Septem^r ye 17 1715.
Johanna Barnes dyed October ye 16 & was buried October ye 18 1715.
Elizabeth Baldwin dyed October ye 16 & was buried October ye 18 1715.
William Southworth dyed Jan^ry ye 6 & was buried Jan^ry ye 7 1715.
Anne Marion dyed Jan^ry ye 6 & was buried Jan^ry ye 7 1715.
Bridgett Marion dyed Jan^ry ye 8 & was buried Jan^ry ye 9 1715.
William Lyall dyed Jan^ry ye 19 & was buried Jan^ry ye 21 1715.
George Pace dyed Jan^ry ye 19 & was buried Jan^ry ye 21 1715.
Dorothy Manuell dyed Jan^ry ye 1 & was buried Jan^ry ye 3 1715.
Richard Waitt dyed August ye 10 & was buried August ye 12 1715.
Francis Dodson dyed Jan^ry ye 8 & was buried Jan^ry ye 11 1715.
Elizabeth Curtis dyed Jan^ry ye 20 & was buried Jan^ry ye 24 1715.
George Bowden died Jan^ry ye 28 & was buried Jan^ry ye 31 1715.
Thomas Volve dyed Jan^ry ye 15 & was buried Jan^ry ye 17 1715.
Anne Cheshire dyed March ye 17 & was buried March ye 19 1715.
Mary Clay dyed Decem^r ye 2 & was buried Decem^r ye 4 1715.
Henry Goodloe dyed March ye 13 & was buried March ye 15 1715.
Thomas Smith dyed Jan^ry ye 15 & was buried Jan^ry ye 18 1715.
Nathan Underwood dyed ye 22 March & was buried March 24 1715.
William Kilpin dyed Ap. ye 14 & was buried Aprill ye 17 1716.
Mary an Indian Woman dyed May 16 & was buried May ye 18 1716.
Elizabeth Lee dyed July ye 26 & was buried July ye 27 1716.
Elizabeth Earley dyed July ye 6 & was buried July ye 8 1716.
Mary Nash dyed May ye 5 & was buried May ye 7 1716.
Ralph Mazey dyed July ye 20 & was buried July ye 22 1716.
Lydia Hamerton dyed August ye 9 & was buried August ye 10 1716.
Sarah Chowning dyed August ye 2 & was buried August ye 3 1716.

Violetta Seares dyed August y[e] 11 & was buried August y[e] 12 1716.
Hope Sutton dyed August y[e] 21 & was buried August y[e] 23 1716.
Sarah Haines dyed Sept. y[e] 4 & was buried y[e] Same day 1716.
John Warwick dyed Sept. y[e] 2 & was buried Septem[r] y[e] 4 1716.
Michal Owen dyed Sept. y[e] 10 & was buried Septem[r] y[e] 11 1716.
William Walker dyed Sept. y[e] 22 & was buried Septemr y[e] 23 1716.
Judith Lucas dyed August y[e] 15 & was buried August y[e] 16 1716.
Daniell Trigg dyed August y[e] 13 & was buried August y[e] 15 1716.
Benjamine Sparkes dyed Septem[r] 29 & was buried October y[e] 1 1716.
Valentine Mayo dyed Octo 5 & was buried October y[e] 7 1716.

Bar Yates Min[r]

CHRISTENINGS.

Thomas son of W[m] & Frances Hill born May y[e] 20 1711.
W[m] son of John & Hannah Owen was borne y[e] 15 October, baptized y[e] 2d December 1711.
Dianah daughter of John & Dianah Davies baptized 2d day of March 1711.
Martha daughter of John & ffrancis Alding baptized 16th day of March 1711.
Susannah daughter of Abraham & Judith Trigg baptized Do. day &c. 1711.
William Son of W[m] & Honour ffinny baptized 6th of Aprill 1712.
Thomas Son of Churchhill & Sarah Blacky baptized Do. day &c.
Sarah daughter of Thomas & Elizabeth Bewford baptized Do. day &c.
John son of Thomas & Mary Warwick borne 14th March 1711.
Mary daughter of Joseph & Avarilla Hardy borne 18th May 1712.
Henery Son of Jon[a] & Mary Brooks borne 1st day of May 1712.
Jane daughter of Edmond & Jane Mickleborough borne 8th of Aprill 1712.
Direll Son of W[m] & Marg[tt] Kidd borne 16th of March 1711.
William Son of Robert & Katherine Perrott borne y[e] 20th of May 1712.
Cary daughter of Powell & Mary Stampar borne 23d June 1712.
William Son of William & Elizabeth Brooks borne 10th May 1712.
Mary daughter of Thomas & Lettice Bateman borne Do. day &c.
Joshabee daughter of Marvell & Agatha Moseley borne 29th day of May 1712.
Agatha daughter of Robert & Ann Blackly borne 9th May 1712,
W[m] Son of Ralph & Alice Mazy borne 3d of August 1712.
Ann Daughter of James & Clara Walker borne 17th of January 1707.
John Son of James & Clara Walker borne 16th September 1709.
Katharine daughter of James & Clara Walker borne 3d November 1711.
Ann daughter of W[m] & Ann Stannard born Satturn day August 26th 1710 about two of the Clock in the afternoon and Baptized by y[e] Rev[rd] M[r] Bartho: Yates y[e] 17th of y[e] same month 1710.
Marvell Son of Sam[ll] & Ann Lee baptized y[e] 7th of December born y[e] 28th of October 1712.
Marg[tt] daughter of Thomas & Eliz[a] Elliott born y[e] 12th Jan[ry] baptized 8th ffeb[ry] 1712.

Ann daughter of Patrick & Rebecca Deagon born 30th Xber. baptize^d 8th ffeb^ry 1712.

Gregory Son of Thos & Ann Smyth born ye 31th Xber. baptized ye 8th ffebry 1712.

Bartho: Son of Bartho: & Sarah yates born ffeb^ry ye 9th baptiz^d ye 17th ffeb^ry 1712.

Robert Son of Thomas & Sarah Chowning born ye 20th day of March 1711.

John Son of Charles & Dorothy Lee born ye 28th August baptiz^d 5th day of October 1712.

Eliz^a daughter of Hugh & Catherine M^cctyre born 28th Septr baptiz^d 19th October 1712.

Eliz^a daughter of Richard & Penelope Gibbs born 5th Septem^r baptized 19th October 1712.

Penelope daughter of Thom^s & Susanna Carter born 26th September baptized 19th October 1712.

William Son of Thomas & Jane Cheyny baptiz^d 19th October 1712.

John & Winifred (twins) Son & daughter of John & Winifred Purvis born 24th March 1711.

William Son of Richard and Sarah Perrott born 27th December baptized 22nd day of ffebruary 1712.

Joseph Son of Humphrey and Elizabeth Jones born 14th December baptized 22nd ffebry 1712.

Mary daughter of James and Mary Meecham born 30th Jan^ry baptiz^d 25th of ffeb^ry 1712.

Mary Daughter of Elizabeth Worsdell born 7^ber 11th 1708, baptized March 1st 1712.

Thomas Son of Jacob Stiff and Eliz^a his wife was baptized Aprill 12th 1712.

Robert Son of John & Mary Wake baptized Aprill 12th 1713.

Mary daughter of William and Ann Hill baptized May 10th 1713.

Ann daughter of Sarah Bennett an Illegitimate baptized May 10th 1713.

Crisp Son of Ralph and Mary Shelton born Aprill 1st baptized May 17th 1713.

Mary daughter of Thomas and Katherine Bristow born May 1st baptized May 24th 1713.

William Son of William and Eliz^a Hammut baptized May 24th 1713.

John Son of Eliz^a Ballard Illegittimate baptized May 24th 1713.

Millicent daughter of Hobbs and Mary Weekes born 2d May baptized June 14th 1713.

Martha daughter of Henery and Sarah Baskett born May 15th baptized June 14th 1713.

Thomas Son of George and Eliz^a Blake baptized July 5th 1713.

Benjamine Son of John and Elianor Jones baptized August 2d 1713.

Thomas Son of Nathan and Diana Underwood born August 20th baptized Augt 24th 1713.

Jedidiah Son of John and Mary Bristow born August 10th baptized September 6th 1713.

George Son of George and Hannah Guest born August 3d baptized September 6th 1713.

Jane Daughter of Robert and Eliz^a Biggs baptized September 27th 1713.

Phillip Son of Phillipp and Katherine Warrick borne ye 20th of October 1713.

James Son of John & Elianor Medly was born ye 1st of August 1712.

Joseph Son of Mary and Joseph Seares baptized ye 15th of November 1713.

Judith daughter of David and Katherine George borne ye 2d of January. Alice daughter of John and Winifred Purvis borne ye 6th of December. Aaron Son of W^m and Marg^tt Kidd born ye 8th of December, Daniell Son of Abraham and Judith Trigg. All four baptized ye 24th of Jan^ry 1713.

William Son of Angeto & Elianor Comings born ye 6th October & baptized ye 6th November 1713.

Johanna Daughter of John & Johanna Degge born August ye 7. baptized 1711.

CHRISTENINGS.

William Son of William & Frances Hill born Novem^r ye 7 1712.

William Son of Mathew & Sarah Parry born March 27 baptized May ye 11 1712.

John Illegittimate Son of Martha Davies born y^c 27th of ffebruary. Mary Daughter of W^m & Mary Daniell. Margarett daughter of Thomas and Marg^tt Croucher. Jane daughter of John & Jane Guttery. Jane daughter of James and Hannah Macktyre. Anne daughter of Henery & Eliz^a Goodloe. Elizabeth daughter of John & Elizabeth Lewis. Were all Seven baptized the 7th day of March 1713.

James Son of John & Jane Hord. Ann daughter of John & Mary Riley both baptized March 21th 1713.

Mary daughter of James & Ann Smyth borne the 10th day of December 1713.

David Son of J^no & Elianor Zachary. Elizabeth daughter of W^m & Sarah Baldin. Unity daughter of Henery & Rebecca Smyth. All three baptized the 4th day of Aprill 1714.

Christopher Son of James & Agatha Curtis born the 11th baptized 19th of Aprill 1714.

Mary Daughter of Daniell & ffrances Hughes borne ye 21th August 1713.

Bartholomew Son of Edward and Ann Clark borne ye 5th October 1713.

Edward Son of Richard and Katherine Straughan borne ye 30th December 1713.

Daniell Son of Edward & Keziah Ball born ye 5th of Jan^ry 1713.

John Illegittimate Son of Sarah Allcock borne 26th December 1713.

Isaack son of John & Margarett Hardy. John Son of John & Elianor Medley. Hannah daughter of Alexander & Mary Graves. & Margarett daughter of Churchill & Sarah Blakey all 4 baptized the 18th day of Aprill 1714.

Thomas Son of Thomas & Mary Warrick baptized ye 2d day of May 1714.

Mary daughter of Abell & ffaith Ducksworth. & Sarah daughter of Robert & Ann Blackly were both baptized the 13th day of June 1714.

Moses Son of Moses & Alice Norman baptized ye 27th day of June
1714.

Thomas Son of John & Alice Duggin. & Katherine daughter of
W^m & Honour ffinney both baptized ye 8th day of August 1714.

Frances daughter of John & Ann Williams was borne ye 5th of
August, Millicent daughter of John & Lettice Cheedle were
both baptized ye 5th day of September 1714.

Ann daughter of George and Mary Wortham borne 28th May 1714.

Sarah daughter of Major Edmond Berkley and Lucia his wife was
borne ye 9th of ffebruary 1713.

Judith daughter of Thomas & Mary Mitcham was borne ye 4th of
November 1712.

Mary daughter of Augustine & Jone Owen baptized ye 25th of
October 1713.

John Son of Powell and Mary Stampar baptized ye 17th of October
1714.

Elizabeth daughter of W^m and Elizabeth Brookes baptized ye 17th
of October 1714.

William Son of John & Priscilla Brookes baptized ye 31th of October 1714.

Ann daughter of Richard and Mary Allen baptized ye 31th of October 1714.

Diana daughter Richard and Penelope Gibbs baptized ye 31th of
October 1714.

Frances daughter of Christopher & Judith Robinson born ye 8 of
Octo. baptized ye 17 of Octo. 1714.

Elizabeth & Martha daughters of W^m & Eliz^a Blackborn born Sept.
26th baptized Octo ye 24th 1714.

Sarah & Judith daughters of John & Eliz^a Wormley born June 20
baptized June ye 27 1714.

Henry Son of Sr Wm Skipwith & Lady Sarah his wife born Octo.
22 baptized Novem^r ye 21 1714.

Anthony Son of John & Johanna Degge born Novem^r ye 4 baptized
Novem^r ye 22 1714.

Anne daughter of George & Eliz^a Barwich born May ye 30 baptized
June ye 20 1714.

Absolom Son of Thomas & Sarah Chowning born Octo. ye 25 baptized Novem^r ye 28 1714.

William Son of William & Margrett Bristow born Feb. ye 2d baptized March ye 4 1713.

Betty daughter of Mathew & Sarah Parry born June 6 baptized
July ye 10 1714.

William Son of William & Priscilla Tignor born Octo. 23 baptized
Dec. ye 5 1714.

Mary daughter of John & Joice Tinny born Aug: 3 baptized Dec.
ye 12 1714.

Betty daughter of Robert & Catherine Perrott born Dec. 3 baptized
Dec. 25 1714.

Mary daughter of John & Rebecca Hues born   baptized Jan^ry
9 1714.

Richard Son of William & Frances Hill born Jan^ry 15 baptized Jan^ry
ye 22 1714.

Parnell daughter of John & Parnell Jones born Decem^r 19 baptized
Jan^{ry} ye 23 1714.
John son of Marvill & Agatha Mosely born Jan^{ry} 20 baptized Feb^{ry}
ye 4 1714.

Bartho: Yates. Minis:

CHRISTENINGS.

Thomas Son of William & Mary Elliott born Dec. 19. baptized Feb.
6 1714.
Mary daughter of William & Alice Hackney born Jan^{ry} 14. baptized
Feb. 6 1714.
John Stuart an illegitimate son of Frances Ingram born Feb. ye 1.
baptized ye 13. 1714.
John Son of John & Elizabeth Vivion born August ye 10. baptized
August ye 18. 1714.
Jane daughter of William & Jane Lawson born Feb^{ry} ye 12. baptized
Febry ye 15. 1713.
Christopher Son of Christopher & Hope Sutton born Jan^{ry} ye 13.
baptized Jan^{ry} ye 20. 1714.
Matthew Son of Thomas & Mary Yarrow born Feb'ry ye 4. bap-
tized March 6. 1714.
Jane daughter of John & Elizabeth Watts born Feb'ry ye 6. baptized
March 6. 1714.
John Son of Samuel & Catherine Batchelder born Feb'ry ye 5. bap-
tized March 13. 1714.
Mary daughter of Thomas & Catherine Batts born Decem^r ye 12.
baptized March 13. 1714.
Jacob Son of Jacob & Mary Presnall born Feb'ry ye 4. baptized
March 13. 1714.
Thomas son of Thomas & Jane Cheny born Feb^{ry} ye 18. baptized
March 13. 1714.
Thomas son of Thomas & Mary Machen born Feb. 22. baptized
March ye 20. 1714.
Thomas son of Robert & Elizabeth Wilson born Feb. 24. baptized
March ye 20. 1714.
Elizabeth daughter of Thomas & Elizabeth Elliott born March 5.
baptized Ap. ye 3. 1715.
William son of Joseph & Lucretia Goare born March 8. baptized
Ap. ye 3. 1715.
William son of Richard & Charity Waite born . . . . . . baptized
Ap. ye 3. 1715.
Lodswick son of Humphery & Elizabeth Jones born Feb'ry ye 20.
baptized Ap. ye 10. 1715.
Reuben son of Ralph & Mary Shelton born Febry ye 1. baptized
April ye 10. 1715.
Thomas an illegitimate Son of Mary Deputy born Jan^{ry} 15. baptized
April ye 10. 1715.
Anne daughter of Henry & Sarah Ball born March ye 3. baptized
Aprill 10. 1715.
Sarah daughter of Mathew & Elizabeth Crank born Feb'ry ye 20.
baptized Ap. 10. 1715.
Jane an illegitimate daughter of Anne Gerrard born Febry ye 14.
baptized Ap. 10. 1715.

Mary daughter of Thomas & Anne Crank born   baptized
    April 10. 1715.
Mary daughter of Joseph & Elizabeth Timberlin born March 28.
    baptized Ap. 24. 1715.
William son of William & Elizabeth Markham born March 29 bap-
    tized Ap. 24. 1715.
Henry son of Richard & Sarah Atwood born March 24. baptized
    May ye 1. 1715.
Elizabeth daughter of John & Hannah Owen born Ap. 2. baptized
    May ye 1. 1715.
Chichester son of Robert & Elizabeth Dudley born Ap: 8. baptized
    May ye 8. 1715.
John son of George & Sarah Bowden born Ap. 4. baptized May
    ye 15. 1715.
James son of Henry & Mary Bridgforth born May ye 12, baptized
    May 15. 1715.
George son of Charles & Dorothy Lee born Ap. 26. baptized May
    ye 22. 1715.
Sarah daughter of Hugh & Catherine Mactire born Ap. 10. baptized
    May 22. 1715.
Andrew son of John & Elizabeth South born Ap. ye 25. baptized
    May 29. 1715.
Ann daughter of John & Mary Murrey born Ap: 28 baptized May
    29. 1715.
John son of John & Elizabeth Peniell born Ap. 27. baptized June
    ye 5 1715.
Elizabeth daughter of John & Mary Bradley born May 18. baptized
    June 5. 1715.
Anne daughter of Jacob & Elizabeth Stiff born May 15. baptized
    June ye 5. 1715.
                Bar. Yates. Minis.

CHRISTENINGS.

James son of William & Frances Daniell born May ye 12. baptized
    June 12. 1715.
William son of Thomas & Elizabeth Baskitt born May 31. baptized
    June 26. 1715.
Sarah daughter of Samuel & Margret Dagnell born June 2. baptized
    July ye 3. 1715.
Edmund daughter of of George & Anne Saunders born July ye 2.
    baptized July 17. 1715.
Charles son of Charles & Mary Cooper born June 15. baptized July
    24. 1715.
Thomas Hobs son of Hobs & Mary Weeks born June 11. baptized
    July 30. 1715.
Martin son of Thomas & Mary Hackett born July 15. baptized Augst
    7. 1715.
Charles son of Joseph & Avarilla Hardee born July 19. baptized
    Augt 25. 1715.
John son of Richard & Sarah Steevens born May ye 31. baptized
    June 26. 1715.
William son of John & Anne Barnett born July 27. baptized Augst
    28. 1715.

Rachell daughter of Henry & Elizabeth Tuggell born Augst 8. baptized Augst 28. 1715.

Mary daughter of John & Mary Bristow born Augst 15. baptized Septem^r 4. 1715.

Griffin son of Henry & Alice Nicholls born Augst 23. baptized Septem^r 9. 1715.

Lydia daughter of Thomas & Catherine Keiling born Augst 12. baptized Septem 11. 1715.

Dianah daughter of William & Anne Hill born Augst 25. baptized Septem^r 25. 1715.

Jane daughter of John & Anne Smith born Septem^r ye 8. baptized Septem^r 25. 1715.

William son of Ralph & Amey Lyall born Augst 24. baptized Octob^r 2. 1715.

John son of Daniell & Frances Hues born Septem^r 24. baptized Octob^r 3. 1715.

Thomas son of Thomas & Anne Smith born Septem^r 15. baptized October ye 6. 1715.

Mary an illegitimate daughter of Elizabeth Guttery born Augst 24. bapt. 8^{br} 16. 1715.

Sarah daughter of Thomas & Sarah Chowning born Septem^r ye 3. baptized Octo: 16. 1715.

Diana daughter of William & Anne Gardner born Augst 26. baptized Septem^r 18. 1715.

Richard son of Thomas & Mary Davis born Sept. 15. baptized Octo. 23. 1715.

John son of John & Elizabeth Saunders born Sept. 28. baptized Octo. 23. 1715.

Anne an illegitimate mulatto daughter of Mary Whistler born Ap. 12. baptized Nov^{em} 4. 1715.

Mary daughter of John & Jane Miller born Sept. 26. baptized Novem. 6. 1715.

Mary daughter of William & Mary Barbee born Sept. 30. baptized Novem. 6. 1715.

George son of John & Winifred Purvis born Octo: 17. baptized Novem. 13. 1715.

Ralph son of John & Elizabeth Wormley born Octo: 5. baptized Novem. 9. 1715.

Anne daughter of Arthur & Mary Thomas born Nov. 5. baptized Decem. 4. 1715.

John son of Thomas & Catherine Bristow born Nov. 9. baptized Decem. 4. 1715.

Robert son of John & Prudence Reagen born Octo: 6. baptized Novem. 25. 1715.

Amey daughter of John & Jane Stuart born Octo 24 baptized Decem. 11. 1715.

Rachell daughter of John & Elizabeth Davies born Novem 20. baptized Decem. 11 1715.

Thomas son of John & Anne Gresham born Novem. 23. baptized Decem 18. 1715.

William an illegitimate son of Susanna Dainly born Novem. 27 baptized Decem. 19. 1715.

James son of James & Mary Meecham born Decem[r] 15. baptized
Jan[ry] 1. 1715.

Ellonar Daughter of William & Anne Cheshire born Novem. 24.
baptized Decem. 18. 1715.

Mary daughter of Edward & Sarah Couch born Decemb[r] 24. Baptized Jan. 2. 1715.

Judith daughter of John & Ethelred Lucas born Decem[r] 24 baptized
Jan[ry] 2. 1715.

Bridgett daughter of Patrick & Anne Marion born Jan[ry] y[e] 7. baptized Jan[ry] y[e] 8. 1715.

Frances daughter of George & Elizabeth Carter born Novem[r] 13.
baptized Jan[ry] y[e] 15. 1715.

George son of John & Elizabeth Pace born Jan[ry] y[e] 8. baptized Jan[ry]
16. 1715.

Robert son of Bartho: & Sarah Yates born Jan[ry] y[e] 8. baptized Jan[ry]
20. 1715.

Bar. Yates. Minis.

CHRISTENINGS.

Thomas son of Peter & Elizabeth Chelton born Decem[r] y[e] 24. baptized Jan[ry] 22. 1715.

Violetta daughter of Joseph & Mary Seares born Jan[ry] ye 1 baptized
Feb[r]y 12 1715.

Lydia daughter of Edmund & Sarah Hamerton born Janry 4. baptized Febry 12. 1715.

William son of John & Mary Berry born Feb[ry] ye 10. baptized
Febry 25 1715.

Mary daughter of Henry & Sarah Basket born Novem. 15. baptized
Decem. 18 1715.

Anne daughter of Ralph & Alice Mazey born Jan[ry] y[e] 25. baptized
Feb[ry] 26 1715.

Catherine daughter of John & Catherine Robinson born Feb[ry] 23.
baptized March 7 1715.

Sarah daughter of Valentine & Anne Mayo born Feb[ry] y[e] 10. baptized March 11. 1715.

William Son of Edward & Martha Brownley born Febry. y[e] 3. baptized March 4 1715.

Catherine daughter of Edward & Rebecca Peirce born Jan[ry] 10. baptized March 18. 1715.

Michal daughter of John & Michall Owen born Feb[ry] ye 19. baptized
March 18 1715.

John son of George & Elizabeth Barwick born Feb[ry] 22. baptized
March 18 1715.

Catherine daughter of John & Catherine Row born Feb[ry] 16 baptized
March 18. 1715.

Judith daughter of George & Elizabeth Chowning born March 21
baptized March 25. 1716.

Susanna daughter of Jonathan & Mary Brooks born March y[e] 6 baptized Ap: y[e] 8 1716.

Thomas son of Richard & Anne Winn born March y[e] 5 baptized
Ap: y[e] 8. 1716.

Constant Daughter of John & Margrett Davies born March ye 10.
baptized Ap: ye 15. 1716.

93

Sarah daughter of Michael & Sarah Smith born March ye 14. baptized Ap. ye 22. 1716.

William son of Thomas & Alice Kidd born Ap: ye 2d baptized Ap. ye 22. 1716.

James son of William & Margrett Kidd born March 27. baptized Ap. ye 22 1716.

Catherine daughter of Roger & Mary Jones born March ye 8. baptized Ap. ye 28 1716.

George son of George & Mary Roades born March 25. baptized Ap: ye 29. 1716.

Clara daughter of Curtis & Anne Perrott born Ap. 21 baptized Ap. ye 30. 1716.

John Son of John & Mary Gibbs born Ap. 5. baptized May 4 1716.

Elizabeth daughter of Gabriell & Elizabeth Ray born Ap. 3 baptized May 4. 1716.

George son of Churchhill & Sarah Blakey born Ap: 3. baptized May 6. 1716.

Thomas Son of Henry & Mary Beuford born Ap. 11. baptized May 6 1716.

John Son of Christopher & Sarah Chaffin born Ap. 1. baptized Ap. 29. 1716.

Martha daughter of John & Margrett Hardee born Feb^ry 12. baptized May 13. 1716.

Robert son of John & Elianor Medley born May 6. baptized June 3 1716.

William son of Edward & Anne Clarke born Ap. 26. baptized June 10 1716.

Anne daughter of Augastine & Joane Owen born May 6 baptized June 10. 1716.

Crispin son of Richard & Catherine Strauhan born May 10. baptized June 10. 1716.

Cary Son of James & Anne Smith born May 22 baptized June 10 1716.

William Son of Abraham & Judith Trigg born May 18 baptized June 17. 1716.

William son of Edward & Keziah Ball born May 25 baptized June 24 1716.

Avarilla daughter of Henry & Eliz^a Goodloe born June ye 20 baptized July 15 1716.

John Son of William & Bridget Gordon born July ye 12 baptized July 16 1716.

John Son of John & Frances Aldin born July ye 28, baptized August ye 26 1716.

John Son of John & Jane Guttery born August ye 16 baptized August ye 26 1716.

Sarah daughter of Jonathan & Mary Bell born July ye 3 baptized August ye 5. 1716.

George Son George & Anne Saunders born August ye 7 baptized August ye 31. 1716.

Bar. Yates Minis.

94

CHRISTENINGS.

John Son of Phillip & Catherine Warwick borne Augst 21, baptized Septem^r ye 1. 1716.

John son of Phillip & Catherine Warwick borne Augst 21. baptized Septem^r ye 1 1716.

James Son of George & Mary Wortham born Augst 17. baptized Septem^r ye 4 1716.

Lettice daughter of Thomas & Catherine Paine born Augst 8. baptized Septr 9 1716.

Alexander Son of Aquilla & Mary Snelling born July 23 baptized Septr ye 2 1716.

Anna daughter of Joseph & Elizabeth Humpheries born Augst 18 baptized Sept. 16 1716.

Mary daughter of Thomas & Elizabeth Bewford born Augst 20 baptized Septr 23 1716.

Avarilla an illegitimate daughter of Alice Davis born   baptized Sept. ye 16. 1716.

Elizabeth daughter of Richard & Elizabeth Daniell born Sept. ye 5. baptized Sept. 30. 1716.

West an illegitimate Son of Sarah Jarvise born Sept. ye 6. baptized Sept. 30 1716.

Thomas Son of Jeffery & Mary Burk born September ye 9 baptized October ye 5. 1716.

Agatha daughter of Harry & Elizabeth Beverley born Septr 22. baptized October ye 12 1716.

Randolph Son of W^m & Anne Seagar born October 10. baptized octo^r ye 23. 1716.

John an illegitimate Son of Rebecca Hackney born Septr 13 baptized october 14 1716.

Anne daughter of Wm Daniell Senr & mary his Wife born Octo. 12. baptized Novem^r ye 4. 1716.

John Son of Patrick & Rebecca Deagle born October 30 baptized Novem^r 25 1716.

William Son of Usebius & Mary Lewis born Novem^r ye 26 baptized Decem^r ye 2 1716.

Benjamine Son of William & Sarah Baldin born Novem^r 11. baptized Decem^r ye 7 1716.

William Son of Robert & Elizabeth Daniell born Decem^r ye 3 baptized Decem^r ye 16. 1716.

John Son of Jonathan & Anne Herring born Octo. 8 baptized Novem^r ye 10 1716.

Elizabeth daughter of Robert & Elizabeth Dudley born Dec. 27. baptized Jan^r ye 7 1716.

Phillip Son of Thomas & Mary Warwick born Novem^r 27 baptized Jan^r 13 1716.

Billington Son of Joseph & Elizabeth Williams born Dec^{mr} 10. baptized Jan^r 13. 1716.

John Son of John & Anne Williams born Decem^r 20. baptized Jan^r 13 1716.

Elizabeth daughter of Stokely & Anne Toles born Decem^r 17 baptized Decem^r 30. 1716.

Mildred daughter of John & mary Rily born Decem^r 2. baptized Jan^{r}y ye 27 1716.

Elizabeth daughter of Richard & mary Allen born Decem^r 24 baptized Jan^{r}y ye 27 1716.

Susannah daughter of Powell & mary Stamper born Decem^r 19. baptized Jan^{ry} ye 27 1716.

Richard Son of Richard & Sarah Steevens born Jan^{r}y 8. baptized Feb^{r}y 3. 1716.

Sarah daughter of Edward & Elizabeth Sanders born Decem^r 28 baptized Jan^r 20. 1716.

John Son of John & Lettice Cheedle born Jan^{r}y ye 5 baptized Feb^{r}y ye 10 1716.

Anne daughter of George & Elizabeth Hardin born Dec. 21 baptized Feb^{r}y ye 3. 1716.

Mary daughter of Ralph & Mary Shelton born Jan^{r}y 21 baptized Feb^{r}y ye 13 1716.

Anne daughter of Thomas & Jane Haslewood born Decem^r 30. baptized March ye 10. 1716.

James Son of Henry & Sarah Ball born Feb^{r}y ye 16 baptized March ye 10 1716.

James Son of John & Jane Price born Feb^{r}y ye 17 baptized March ye 10. 1716.

James Son of James & Margrett Daniell born Feb^{ry} ye 17 baptized March ye 17 1716.

William Son of Christopher & Judith Robinson born March ye 5 baptized March ye 17. 1716.

Roger Son of John & Anne Hatton born Decem^r ye 2d baptized Jan^{r}y ye 20 1716.

William Son of Samuell & Catherine Batchelder born March 11 1716. baptized Ap. ye 7. 1717.

Beamont Son of Christopher & Hope Sutton born March ye 5. 1716. baptized March 31. 1717.

William Son of John & Mary Sparkes born march 6. 1716 & baptized Ap. ye 7 1717.

Mary daughter of David & Katherine George born March 12. 1716. baptized Ap. 7. 1717.

Mary & Jane daughters of George & Hannah Guest born March 24 1716 baptized Ap. 7. 1717.

Daniell Son of Daniell & Frances Hues born March 14 1716. baptized Ap. 14 1717.

William Son of Thomas & Catherine Keiling born March the 7. 1716. baptized Ap. 14. 1717.

Russell Son of William & Frances Hill born Feb^{r}y ye 23. 1716 baptized Ap. 21. 1717.

Sarah daughter of Sr William Skipwith & Lady Sarah his wife born Ap. 11. baptized Ap. 25. 1717.

Bar. Yates. Minis.

CHRISTENINGS.

Elizabeth daughter of Humphery & Elizabeth Jones born March ye 19. 1716. baptized Ap. 28. 1717.

Elizabeth daughter of Thomas & Jane Cheney born March ye 19. 1716. baptized Ap. 28. 1717.

Elizabeth daughter of James & Hannah Mactire born March ye 23. 1716. baptized Ap. 28. 1717.

John son of Jacob & Elizabeth Stiff born April y⁰ 2. baptized May
y⁰ 5. 1717.
Mary daughter of John & Mary Murray born Ap. 25. baptized May
y⁰ 17. 1717.
Susanna daughter of John & Elizabeth Lewis born Ap. 23. baptized
May y⁰ 26. 1717.
Agatha daughter of William & Anne Gardner born Ap. 21. baptized
May y⁰ 26. 1717.
Judith daughter of Edward & Margrett Farrell born Ap. 25 baptized
June y⁰ 2. 1717.
Harry son of Joseph & Mary Seares born May y⁰ 19. baptized June
y⁰ 23. 1717.
Frances daughter of Robert & Anne Blackley born May y⁰ 29. bap-
tized June y⁰ 23. 1717.
William Son of William & Elizabeth Blackburne born June y⁰ 12
baptized July y⁰ 11. 1717.
Lucretia daughter of Hugh & Catherine Mactire born June y⁰ 17.
baptized July y⁰ 21. 1717.
John Son of John & Priscilla Brookes born June y⁰ 20 baptized July
y⁰ 21. 1717.
John Son of William & Elizabeth Brookes born June y⁰ 23 baptized
July y⁰ 21 1717.
Sarah daughter of Thomas & Sarah Chowning born June y⁰ 24.
baptized July y⁰ 21. 1717.
Judith daughter of Marvell & Agatha Moseley born July y⁰ 12 bap-
tized July y⁰ 21. 1717.
William Son of Thomas & Mary Cardwell born July y⁰ 7th baptized
August y⁰ 4 1717.
Elizabeth daughter of John & Micholl Owen born July y⁰ 28 bap-
tized August y⁰ 18. 1717.
Anne daughter of Christopher & Mary Kelshaw born July y⁰ 31.
baptized Sepᵗ y⁰ 8. 1717.
William Son of William & Alice Hackney born August y⁰ 13. bap-
tized Sept. y⁰ 8. 1717.
John Son of Samuell & Anne Low born August y⁰ 5 baptized Sept.
y⁰ 8 1717.
Elizabeth daughter of John & Elizabeth Vivion born August y⁰ 17.
baptized Sept y⁰ 9. 1717.
James Son of Robert & Elizabeth Biggs born August y⁰ 15 baptized
Sept y⁰ 15 1717.
Abel Son of Abel & Faith Ducksworth born Septemʳ y⁰ 13. bap-
tized Sept. y⁰ 29 1717.
Frances daughter of John & Prudence Reaguin born Sept. y⁰ 8.
baptized Sept y⁰ 29 1717.
Frances daughter of John & Anne Smith born Septemʳ y⁰ 16. bap-
tized Sept y⁰ 29 1717.
Joice daughter of Robert & Rebecca Humpheries born Sept. y⁰ 5
baptized Octo. 20 1717.
Elizabeth daughter of John & Eleonour Pemberton born Sept. y⁰ 10
baptized Octo 20. 1717.
Abraham Son of Hobs & Mary Weekes born Septemʳ 22. baptized
October 27. 1717.

James Son of John & Elizabeth Batchelder born Octo: 22. baptized
Novem^r 5. 1717.

Catherine daughter of Ralph & Elizabeth Watts born Octo: 8 baptized Novem^r 10. 1717.

Thomas Son of Thomas & Elizabeth Dudley born Sept. 18. baptized
October 20 1717.

Mary daughter of John & Rebecca Hues born Sept: 28 baptized
Novem^r 17 1717.

Martha daughter of Thomas & Anne Smith born Octo: 31. baptized
Novem^r 21 1717.

———— an illegitimate daughter of Susanna Ward born Octo. 24
1717.

John Son of Thomas & Mary Hackett born Octo: ye 19. baptized
Decem^r ye 5 1717.

Joseph Son of Joseph & Lucretia Goar born Novem^r ye 3. baptized
Decem^r ye 4 1717.

Josuah Son of John & Parnell Jones born Novem^r 3. baptized De-
cem^r ye 8 1717.

Sarah daughter of Hezekiah & Mary Ellis born Novem^r 7. baptized
Decem^r 15. 1717.

John Son of William & Elizabeth Marcum born Decem^r ye 1. baptized Decem^r ye 15. 1717.

John Son of Eusebius & Mary Lewis born Decem^r ye 8 baptized
Jan^r 19 1717.

Agatha daughter of John & Elizabeth Watts born Decem^r ye 25.
baptized Jan^r 19. 1717.

Henry Son of Henry & Elizabeth Brown born August ye 26. baptized Novem^r 17 1717.

Henry Son of Thomas & Mary Machen born Novem^r 29. Baptized
Jan^{ry} ye 5 1717.

William Son of Hugh & Rebecca Roach born Decem^r 27. baptized
Jan^{ry} ye 26 1717.

John Son of John & Sarah Fearn born Jan^{ry} ye 5 baptized Jan^{r}y
ye 26 1717.

Elizabeth an illegitimate daughter of Elizabeth Davis born Jan^{r}y y^e
16. baptized Jan^{ry} ye 26. 1717.

Bar. Yates: Min^t

CHRISTENINGS.

Smith Son of John & Elizabeth South born Jan^{r}y 24. baptized Jan^{r}y
30 1717.

John Son of John & Frances Smith born Decem^r 16. baptized Feb^{r}y
ye 5. 1717.

Gray Son of William & Mary Barbee born Jan^{r}y 7 baptized Feb^{r}y
ye 16 1717.

John Son of Lawrance & Anne Collings born Feb^{r}y ye 6 baptized
Feb^{r}y ye 16. 1717.

John Son of John & Elizabeth Nicholls born Jan^{r}y 24 baptized Feb^{ry}
2 1717.

Jemima daughter of Richard & Hannah Brine born Jan^{r}y 25 baptized Feb^{ry} 2 1717.

Thomas Son of Henry & Elizabeth Tugell born Jan^{ry} 26th baptized
Feb^{ry} 23 1717.

98

Thomas Son of Thomas & Jane Grindee born Feb^ry 4. baptized
Feb^ry 23 1717.

Anne daughter of David & Jane Murry born Jan^ry 20. baptized
Feb^ry 23 1717.

Bridgett & Margrett daughters of William & Bridgett Gordon born
& baptized March 5. 1717.

John Son of John & Anne Roades born Feb^ry ye 1 baptized March
ye 9 1717.

Mary daughter of John & Margrett Davies born Feb^ry ye 11 baptized March ye 9. 1717.

Henry & Robert Sons of John & Winifred Purvis born March 11.
baptized March 12. 1717.

Constant daughter of William & Frances Daniell born Feb^ry ye 6
baptized March 16. 1717.

Sarah daughter of William & Sarah Baldin born Feb^ry 22 baptized
March 16 1717.

Thomas Son of Thomas & Mary Yarrow born Feb^ry 28. 1717. baptized March 30 1718.

Joseph Son of William & Margrett Kidd born March 1: 1717 baptized Aprill 6. 1718.

Sarah daughter of John & Elizabeth Wormley born March 23. 1717
baptized April 6. 1718.

Henry Son of John & Katherine Robinson born Ap. 7 baptized
April 14 1718.

Henry Son of Mary Month a free Indian born Feb^ry 24 1717 baptized April 14. 1718.

William Son of William & Hanah Cain born March 15 1717 baptized April 20 1718.

Dorothy daughter of William & Priscilla Tignor born March 25.
baptized April 20 1718.

Peter Son of Thomas & Grace Mountague born March 28. baptized
April 27 1718.

Perrott Son of Joseph & Avarilla Hardee born April 4 baptized
April 27 1718.

Henry Son of George & Elizabeth Carter born May 13. baptized
May 18 1718.

George Son of John & Anne Johnson born April 13. baptized May
18 1718.

John Son of John & Mary Pendergrass born April 25. baptized June
1 1718.

Elizabeth daughter of John & Elizabeth Pinion born April 27 baptized June 1 1718.

Mary daughter of Edward & Sarah Couch born April 20. baptized
June 1 1718.

James Son of Edward & Anne Clarke born April 19. baptized May
25 1718.

Charles Son of William & Margrett Bristow born May 17. baptized
July 13. 1718.

John Son of John & Jane Stuart born June 3. baptized July ye 20
1718.

Avarilla Curtis daughter of John & Etheldred Lucas born July 23.
baptized Aug^st 3 1718.

Anne daughter of Thomas & Elizabeth Bewford born July 4. baptized August 10 1718.

Solomon Son of Matthew & Elizabeth Crank born July 17 baptized August 10 1718.

Thomas Son of Thomas Kidd jun^r & Margrett his wife born July 22. baptized August 10. 1718.

James Son of John & Johanna Degge born July 14. baptized August ye 23 1718.

Priscilla daughter of John & Sarah Miller born. July 24. baptized Augst ye 24 1718.

William Son of Henry & Sarah Ball born August ye 7. baptized August ye 31 1718.

Robert Son of Robert & Elizabeth Dudley born August ye 23. baptized Septem^r 14 1718.

Mary daughter of James & Anne Bristow born August ye 27 baptized Septem^r 21 1718.

Elizabeth daughter of James & Rebecca Jemson born Sept 14 baptized Octo. 5 1718.

Priscilla daughter of William & Anne Hill born Sept. 17. baptized Octo. 5 1718.

Mary daughter of Arthur & Mary Thomas born   baptized Octo 5. 1718.

Bar. Yates Min^r

CHRISTENINGS.

Anne daughter of Richard & Sarah Steevens born Novem^r 3. baptized Decem^r 7. 1718.

Mary daughter of William & Sarah Blazedon born Novem^r 4. baptized Decem^r 7 1718.

Christopher Son of Christopher & Sarah Chaffin born Novem^r 11. baptized Decem^r 7. 1718.

William Son of James & Mary Meacham born Septem^r 23. baptized Octo. 12 1718.

Sarah daughter of John & Mary Moseley born Octo. 2 baptized Octo. 12 1718.

Mary daughter of John & Anne Conner born Sept. 26. baptized Octo. 26 1718.

Elizabeth daughter of Thomas & Frances Vivion born Octo. 14. baptized Octo. 27 1718.

Sarah daughter of Thomas & Mary Burk born Octo ye 1. baptized Novem^r 2 1718.

Anne daughter of John & Margrett   born Septem^r ye 24. baptized Novem^r 16 1718.

Frances daughter of Bartho: & Sarah Yates born Novem^r ye 15. baptized Novem^r 17 1718.

John Son of John & Elizabeth Braine born Octo. 22. baptized Novem^r 23 1718.

Hannah daughter of Jacob & Elizabeth Rice born Novem^r 18. baptized Jan'ry 7 1718.

Anne daughter of John & Mary Berry born Novem^r ye 18 baptized ye 7 1718.

John Son of John & Mary Bradley born Octo. 28. baptized Decem^r ye 7 1718.

Anny daughter of Alexander & Mary Graves born Novem^r 16 baptized Decem^r ye 14. 1718.

Frances daughter of Edwin & Elizabeth Thacker born Dec ye 3. baptized Decem^r ye 19. 1718.

William Son of Ralph & Amey Lyall born Novem^r 24 baptized Decem^r ye 21 1718.

Edmund Son of John & Elizabeth Sanders born Decem^r ye 2. baptized Jan^{r}y ye 2 1718.

Robert Son of Edmund & Mary Pendergrass born Decem^r ye 10. baptized Jan^{ry} 4. 1718.

Elizabeth daughter of George & Elizabeth Guest born Decem^r ye 15. baptized Jan^{r}y 4. 1718.

John Son of John & Lucy Grymes born Jan^{r}y ye 1st baptized Jan^{r}y ye 15 1718.

Osborn Son of Thomas & Catherine Keiling born Decem^r 4 baptized Jan^{ry} ye 18 1718.

Samuel Son of John & Charity Ingram born Decem^r ye 9. baptized Jan^{ry} ye 18 1718.

Sarah daughter of Jacob & Elizabeth Stiff born Decem^r ye 15. baptized Jan^{ry} ye 18 1718.

John Son of Churchhill & Sarah Blakey born Decem^r ye 14. baptized Jan^{r}y 25. 1718.

Robert Son of Robert Daniell Junr & Elizabeth his Wife born Jan^{r}y 24. baptized Feb^{r}y 15. 1718.

Agatha daughter of William Daniell Senr & Mary his Wife born Jan^{r}y 29. baptized Feb^{r}y 15. 1718.

Grace daughter of William & Mary Tomson born Jan^{r}y 23. baptized Feb^{r}y ye 22 1718.

Benjamine Son of Jonathan & Ann Herring born Jan^{ry} 22. baptized March ye 1. 1718.

Curtis Son of Curtis & Anne Perrott born Jan^{ry} ye 30. baptized March ye 8 1718.

Nanny daughter of John & Jane Guttery born Jan^{r}y ye 31. baptized March ye 8. 1718.

John Son of Henry & Mary Bewford born Feb^{r}y ye 2. baptized March ye 8 1718.

Charles Son of Charles & Dorothy Lee born Feb^{r}y ye 8 baptized March ye 8 1718.

Peter Son of Christopher & Judith Robinson born March ye 1. baptized March ye 11. 1718.

Christopher Son of Christopher & Mary Kelshaw born Feb. ye 11. baptized March ye 22. 1718.

Frances daughter of Robert & Elizabeth Williamson born Feb. 21. 1718. baptized March 25 1719.

Anne daughter of John & Anne Barnett born Feb^{ry} 28. 1718. baptized March 27 1719.

Frances daughter of Daniel & Frances Hues born March 6. 1718 baptized April 3. 1719.

James Son of Augustine & Joan Owen born March 5. 1718. baptized Ap: 5. 1719.

Robert Son of Thomas & Susannah Clark born Jan^{ry} 20. 1718. baptized April ye 12. 1719.

Catherine daughter of William & Anne Seagur born Feb'y 25 1718. baptized Aprill ye 12. 1719.

Frances daughter of Thomas & Catherine Paine born March 15. 1718 baptized Ap. ye 12. 1719.

Tobias Son of Richard & Mary Allen born March ye 30: baptized April ye 12. 1719.

John Son of John & Jane Price born March ye 29 baptized April ye 12. 1719.

John Son of John & Elizabeth Dobbs born April ye 3 baptized April ye 12. 1719.

Betty daughter of William & Lettice Guttery born March ye 20. 1718. baptized April 19. 1719.

Anne daughter of Stokely & Anne Towles born April 23. baptized May ye 3 1719.

John Son of John & Elizabeth Lewis born April ye 11. baptized May ye 3. 1719.

Mary daughter of Jonathan & Mary Brooks born Ap: ye 3. baptized May ye 3. 1719.

Bar Yates minis.

CHRISTENINGS.

John Son of John & Anne Gresham born August ye 6. baptized Sep^t ye 13. 1719.

Joseph Son of Joseph & Elizabeth Humpheries born August ye 10. baptized Sep^t ye 20. 1719.

Hannah daughter of William & Elizabeth Blackburne born August 30. baptized Sep^t ye 29. 1719.

William Son of William & Catherine born Sep^t ye 6. baptized Octo. 4 1719.

Mary daughter of John & Elizabeth Wormley born Sep^t ye 21. baptized Octo. 6 1719.

Abraham Son of Abraham & Judith Trigg born Ap: 14. baptized May 10 1719.

Elizabeth daughter of John & Elizabeth Vivion born May 4. baptized May 19 1719.

Margrett daughter of Phillip & Margrett Brooks born Ap. 16. baptized May 24 1719.

Cassandra daughter of Thomas & Jane Cheney born Ap. 19. baptized May 24 1719.

Jonathan Son of Powell & Mary Stamper born April 21. baptized May 24 1719.

Anne daughter of Nicholas & Mary Bristow born April 26. baptized May 24 1719.

Henry Son of Joseph & Lucretia Goar born May ye 16. baptized June 7 1719.

William Son of William & Elizabeth Stanard born May ye 29 baptized June 8. 1719.

Rebecca daughter of Christopher & Rebecca Baines born Jan'y 20. 1718 baptized June 14. 1719.

Anne & Jane daughter of Thomas & Alice Kidd born May ye 7 baptized June 14. 1719.

John Son of James & Sarah Cole born May ye 16 baptized June ye 14 1719.

Thomas Son of Joseph & Mary Seares born May ye 18 baptized
June ye 14 1719.

William Son of George & Elizabeth Chowning born June ye 3d baptized June ye 14 1719.

Judith daughter of William & Frances Hill born June ye 2d baptized
June ye 28. 1719.

Judith daughter of Joseph & Elizabeth Williams born May ye 3. baptized May ye 30. 1719.

Frances daughter of Thomas & Mary Stapleton born June ye 17.
baptized July ye 5. 1719.

Kesiah daughter of Richins & Hannah Brame born July ye 2 baptized July ye 26. 1719.

Catherine daughter of John & Prudence Reagin born July y^e 7. baptized July y^e 26. 1719.

Jane daughter of John & Mary Murry born July y^e 4. baptized
Augst y^e 2 1719.

Jochebed daughter of Richard & Elizabeth Daniell born July y^e 14.
baptized Augt y^e 4. 1719.

Keziah daughter of John & Johannah Blake born July y^e 12. baptized $Augs^t$ y^e 9 1719.

Rachell daughter of John & Ann Smith born August y^e 17. baptized
Aug^{st} y^e 23 1719.

Mary daughter of Wm Chancellor by Mary Cole born July y^e 10.
baptized Aug^{st} y^e 30. 1719.

Anne daughter of Angello & Elionar Cummins born $Augs^t$ y^e 29.
baptized Octo. 4. 1719.

Francis Son of Francis & Anne Blunt born August y^e 29. baptized
Octo. 11 1719.

William Son of James & Anne Smith born Septem^r y^e 14. baptized
Octo. 11. 1719.

William Son of Charles & Mary Gresham born August y^e 15: baptized Octo y^e 11. 1719.

Mary daughter of George & Sarah Freestone born Sept. 22. baptized Octo. 18. 1719.

John Son of Edward & Elizabeth Sanders born Octo. ye 11. baptized Octo 25. 1719.

James Son of Benjamine & Mary Row born Octo. ye 2. baptized
Novem 1 1719.

William Son of Thomas & Mary Hackett born October ye 17. baptized Novem^r 8. 1719.

Harry Son of William & Sarah Anderson born Novem^r ye 5. baptized Novem^r 19. 1719.

Joseph Son of Joseph & Joanna Timberlake born Octo. ye 18. baptized Novem^r 22. 1719.

Joanna daughter of Christopher & Catherine Kilbee born Octo y^e
27. baptized Novem^r 22. 1719.

Benjamine Son of Edward & Keziah Ball born Novem^r ye 18. baptized Decem^r 13. 1719.

Elizabeth daughter of William & Sarah Davis born Nov. 15. baptized Dec. 22. 1719.

Anne daughter of Thomas & Mary Cardwell born Novem^r 20. baptized Dec. 20. 1719.

Thomas Son of John & Lettice Cheedle born Decem^r 10. baptized
Decem^r 20. 1719.

Henry Son of William & Anne Fleet born Octo: ye 10. baptized
Decem^r 30. 1719.

Sarah daughter of William & Alice Hackney born Novem^r ye 25.
baptized Jan^{ry} ye 3. 1719.

Anne daughter of Thomas & Anne Smith born Decem^r ye 24. baptized Jan^{r}y ye 17. 1719.

William Barbee Son of Christopher & Hope Sutton born Decem^r y^e
9. baptized Jan^{r}y ye 24. 1719.

William Son of William & Mary Webb born Jan^{ry} ye 5: baptized
Jan^{ry} ye 31. 1719.

Edwin Son of Edwin & Elizabeth Thacker born Jan^{ry} ye 17. baptized Feb^{ry} ye 4. 1719.

Bar Yates. Min^r

CHRISTENINGS.

Elizabeth daughter of Francis & Sarah Timberlake born Septem^r y^e
7. baptized Octo. 2. 1720.

Benjamine Son of John & Anne Roads born September ye 14. baptized Octo. ye 9. 1720.

Anne daughter of Thomas & Phrebe Tilley born September ye 16.
baptized Octo. ye 9. 1720.

Sarah daughter of Matthew & Mary Kemp born Feb^{r}y ye 2. baptized Feb^{r}y 14 1719.

Samuel Son of Samuel & Katherine Batchelder born Jan^{r}y ye 16.
baptized Feb^{r}y 21. 1719.

Willy Son of Robert & Anne Blackley born Jan^{r}y ye 16. baptized
Feb^{r}y 21 1719.

Ambrose Son of Robert & Elizabeth Dudley born Feb^{r}y ye 6 baptized Feb^{ry} ye 28 1719.

Thomas Son of Thomas & Grace Mountague born Feb^{r}y ye 20. baptized Feb^{r}y 28 1719.

George Son of John & Sarah Fearn born Feb^{r}y ye 4. baptized march
6 1719.

Mary Daughter of Hugh & Rebecca Roach born Jan^{r}y ye 23 baptized march ye 6. 1719.

Catherine daughter of Ralph & Mary Shelton born Jan^{r}y 26. baptized march ye 13. 1719.

William Son of Benjamine & Elizabeth Beamon born Feb^{r}y ye 9,
baptized march ye 13. 1719.

William Son of Charles & Alice Cooper born Feb^{r}y ye 16. baptized
march ye 13 1719.

Jemima daughter of John & Elizabeth Batcheldor born Feb^{r}y 24
baptized march 13. 1719.

Jane daughter of Thomas & Sarah Chowning born March ye 4. baptized March 13. 1719.

Mary daughter of John & Michal Williams born march ye 18. baptized march 21. 1719.

Edward Son of Edward & Margrett Farrell born Feb^{r}y 27 1719
baptized March ye 27. 1720.

Fuller Son of Sr Wm Skipwith & Lady Sarah his Wife born March
ye 2. 1719. baptized march 27. 1720.

Rachel a Mulatto daughter of Jane Tyre born Feb^ry 25. 1719. baptized April ye 3. 1720.

William Son of Mark & Sarah Wheeler born March ye 8. 1719.
baptized Ap. ye 3. 1720.

John Son of John & Elizabeth Watts born March ye 4. 1719. baptized Ap: ye 10. 1720.

Anne daughter of John & Sarah Miller born March 31. baptized Ap.
ye 24 1720.

Lucy daughter of John & Lucy Grymes born Ap. ye 18. baptized
Ap. ye 24 1720.

Jane daughter of William & Catherine Wood born Mar. 24 1719.
baptized Ap: ye 3. 1720.

Solomon Son of James & Margrett Ingram born April ye 5. baptized
May 1. 1720.

Martha daughter of William & Sarah Balden born April ye 5. baptized May 1. 1720.

George Son of Thomas & Sarah Oldner born March ye 9. 1719.
baptized Ap. ye 24. 1720.

Penelope a Slave belonging to James Walker baptized May ye 8 1720.

Anne daughter of Robert & Anne Spencer born Dec. 21. 1719. baptized May 15. 1720.

Joseph Son of Robert & Rebecca Humpheries born Ap: 8 baptized
May 15. 1720.

Humphery Son of William & Elizabeth Brookes born May 3. baptized May 22. 1720.

Anne daughter of Usebius & Mary Lewis born May ye 4. baptized
May 29 1720.

Catherine daughter of Henry & Elizabeth Goodloe born May 1 baptized June 12. 1720.

Samuell Son of William & Margrett Kidd born May ye 10 baptized
June 12. 1720.

John Son of James & Margrett Bowman born June 3. baptized June
19 1720.

Thomas Son of John & Priscilla Brookes born May ye 11. baptized
July ye 3 1720.

Anne daughter of Henry & Elizabeth Tugle born June ye 8. baptized July ye 3 1720.

John Son of Abell & Faith Ducksworth born June ye 10 baptized
July ye 3 1720.

Lucy daughter of Harry & Elizabeth Beverly born July ye 3 baptized July ye 10 1720.

Richard Son of Richard & Honor Taylor born June 20. baptized
July 24 1720.

Mary daughter of John & Frances Alldin born July ye 3. baptized
August 14 1720.

Betty daughter of Hugh & Chatherine Mactire born July ye 27.
baptized Sep^t 4 1720.

Anne daughter of George & Elizabeth Carter born August ye 8 baptized Sep^t 4 1720.

Agatha daughter of John & Elizabeth Wormeley born Septem^r y^e
10. baptized ye Same day 1720.

Ann daughter of Isaac & Elizabeth Allin born August ye 16. baptized Sep^t 11. 1720.

Samuell Son of Patrick & Rebecca Deagle born July ye 30. baptized Sept. 11 1720.

Joseph & Benjamine Sons of John & Parnell Jones born Septem^r 15. baptized Sep^t 18. 1720.

Ropert Son of Edmund & Elizabeth Mickleburrough born Sept. 11. baptized Sept. 25. 1720.

Elizabeth daughter of William & Elizabeth Stanard born Septem^r ye 18. baptized Sep^t 25. 1720.

CHRISTENINGS.

John Son of Ralph & Amy Lyall born Octo. 2. baptized Novem^r 13 1720.

Sarah daughter of William & Mary Tompson born Octo. ye 13 baptized Novem^r 13 1720.

Minor Son of Robert & Elizabeth Williamson born Octo ye 7. baptized Novemb^r 18 1720.

James Son of John & Margrett Davis born Octo. ye 17. baptized Novem^r 20 1720.

Lucy daughter of Thomas & Rose Wright born octo. ye 24. baptized Novem^r 20 1720.

Judith daughter of George & Anne Saunders born Octo: ye 27. baptized Novem^r 20 1720.

Sarah daughter of Joseph & Averella Hardee born Octo ye 19. baptized Novem^r 27 1720.

Jane Segar an illegitimate daughter of Elizabeth Nicholls born Octo. ye 19. baptized Novem^r 27. 1720.

John Son of Robert & Catherine Perrott born Novem^t ye 12. baptized Decem^r 7 1720.

Johannah daughter of William & Hannah Cain born Novem^r ye 15. baptized Dec. 11. 1720.

William Son of Bartholomew & Sarah Yates born Decem^r 10. baptized Dec. 14 1720.

Anne daughter of John & Lettice Cheadle born Decem^r ye 7 baptized Dec. 18. 1720.

Catherine daughter of Thomas & Catherine Keiling born Novem. 25. baptized Dec. 25. 1720.

Francis Son of Christopher & Mary Kelshaw born Decem^r ye 7. baptized Jan^{ry} 1. 1720.

Thomas Son of John & Elizabeth Lewis born Jan^{ry} ye 3. baptized Jan^{ry} ye 29 1720.

Anne daughter of Joseph & Jennett Jacobus born Jan^{ry} ye 15. baptized Jan^{ry} ye 29 1720.

Anne daughter of Daniell & Frances Hues born Jan^{ry} ye 15. baptized Feb^{r}y ye 5. 1720.

Aquilla Son of Aquilla & Mary Snelling born Feb^{r}y ye 4 baptized Feb^{r}y ye 10 1720.

Charles son of Charles & Dorothy Jones born Jan^{r}y ye 17. baptized Feb^{r}y ye 12 1720.

John Son of Paul & Susanna Philpots born March ye 4 baptized ye Same day 1720.

John Son of Henry & Judith Burk born Feb'y 27. baptized March ye 12 1720.

Kerenhappuch daughter of Richin & Hannah Brame born Feb'y 22. baptized March 12. 1720.

William Son of William & Mary Vaughan born Feb'y 3. 1720. baptized March 26 1721.

Sarah daughter of Thomas & Susannah Clarke born Feb'y 23. 1720. baptized Ap. ye 2 1721.

Robert Son of Churchhill & Sarah Blakey born March ye 7 1720. baptized Ap. ye 2. 1721.

John Son of George & Elizabeth Guess born March ye 24. 1720. baptized Ap. 2 1721.

William Son of John & Elizabeth Dobs born March ye 16. 1720 baptized Ap. 2 1721.

Jane a slave belonging to Capt John Smith baptized April ye 7 1721.

Catherine daughter of John & Jane Stuart born March ye 23. 1720. baptized Ap. 14. 1721.

Periot an illegitimate Son of Ann Pringle born March ye 1719 baptized Ap. 23. 1721.

Anne daughter of Thomas & Jane Haselwood born April 7. baptized May 4 1721.

Judith daughter of Samuel & Mary Spencer born March 22. 1720. baptized May 7 1721.

Susanna daughter of Henry & Elizabeth Blunt born March ye 31. baptized May 7. 1721.

Thomas Son of John & Elizabeth Peniell born April ye 8. baptized May ye 7 1721.

Elizabeth daughter of Henry & Sarah Emerson born April 10. baptized May 14 1721.

Sarah daughter of Ralph & Elizabeth Watts born April 11. baptized May 14 1721.

Ruben Son of Robert & Elizabeth Daniell born April 22. baptized May 14 1721.

Anna daughter of William & Anne Segar born May ye 15. baptized May 24 1721.

Thomas Son of Jacob & Elizabeth Stiff born Ap. ye 30. baptized May 28. 1721.

Morris Son of Richard & Sarah Steevens born May ye 6. baptized may 28. 1721.

Samuel Son of John & Jane Price born May ye 15. baptized May 30 1721.

Joseph Son of Joseph & Mary Seares born May ye 18. baptized June 4 1721.

William Son of John & Mary Sadler born June 5 baptized June 25 1721.

John Son of Henry & Sarah Ball born June ye 19 baptized July 11 1721.

Catherine daughter of Stokely & Anne Towles born July ye 5 baptized July 16 1721.

John Son of Nicholas & Mary Bristow born June ye 25 baptized July 16 1721.

James Son of James & Sarah Cole born June ye 24 baptized July 16 1721.

Avarilla daughter of Curtis & Anne Perrott born June ye 16. baptized July 16. 1721.

Bar. Yates Min^r

CHRISTENINGS.

Anthony Son of Thomas & Anne Smith born July ye 8. baptized July 23 1721.

Ransom Son of Joseph & Constantine Alphin born June ye 27 baptized July 30 1721.

Thomas Son of William & Elizabeth Blackburne born July ye 3. baptized July 30 1721.

Catherine daughter of Christopher & Catherine Kilbee born July y^o 5. baptized July 30 1721.

Alexander Son of John & Anne Smith born June 22. baptized July ye 4 1721.

John Son of John & Mary Murray born July ye 24 baptized August 2 1721.

Penelope daughter of Thomas & Jane Cheney born Aug. 6. baptized August 27 1721.

Agatha daughter of Marvell & Agatha Moseley born Aug. 12. baptized August 27 1721.

Mary daughter of Edwin & Elizabeth Thacker born Aug. 11. baptized Aug^st 27 1721.

Alexander Son of Andrew & Sarah Murray born August ye 19. baptized Sept. 5. 1721.

Mary daughter of Christopher & Sarah Chaffin born Septem^r 2. baptized Sept. 7 1721.

Jacob Son of Augustine & Joane Owen born August ye 12. baptized Sept ye 10 1721.

Agatha daughter of John & Elizabeth Wormley born Septem^r 14. baptized Sept. 24 1721.

Elizabeth daughter of Henry & Mary Elizabeth Thacker born Sept. 22 baptized Octo. 2 1721.

Catharine daughter of Richard & Mary Allen born Septem^r 16. baptized Octo 8. 1721.

Sarah daughter of Zebulon & Mary Chelton born Septem^r 18. baptized Octo. 15 1721.

William Son of Richard & Anne Moulson born Octo. ye 10 baptized Octo. 20 1721.

John Son of Hezekiah & Anne Roades born Septem^r 27. baptized Oct. 22 1721.

Margrett daughter of William & Sarah Blazeden born Septem^r 27. baptized Oct^o 22 1721.

Elizabeth daughter of Arthur & Mary Thomas born Septem^r 21. baptized Octo. 22 1721.

Anne daughter of James & Mary Micham born Septem^r 22. baptized Octo. 29 1721.

Jacob Son of Jacob & Elizabeth Rice born Septem^r 17. baptized Novem^r 4 1721.

Ruth daughter of Benjamine & Mary Row born Octo. 4. baptized Novem^r 12 1721.

Thomas Son of Thomas & Catherine Pain born Octo. 22. baptized Novem^r 19 1721.

Daniel & William Sons of Daniel & Frances Hues born Decem^r y^e
3. baptized Dec. 5. 1721.

Mary daughter of William & Jane Cardwell born Octo. ye 4 baptized Decem^r 10 1721.

Catharine daughter of William & Margrett Kidd born Novem^r ye 5.
baptized Decem^r 10 1721.

William Son of John & Mary Ryley born Novem^r ye 19: baptized Decem^r ye 10 1721.

John Son of James & Anne Jones born Novem^r ye 21. baptized
Decem^r ye 10 1721.

John Son of Thomas & Grace Mountague born Novem^r 23. baptized
Decem^r ye 14 1721.

Catherine daughter of James & Mary Bristow born Decem^r ye 15.
baptized Dec. 28. 1721.

Rachell daughter of George & Mary Barwick born Decem^r 17. baptized Jan^{ry} 14 1721.

Benjamine Son of William & Alice Hackney born Decem^r 25 baptized Jan^{ry} 14 1721.

Anne daughter of Jonathan & Anne Herring born July 29. baptized
August 20 1721.

Josiah Son of Oliver & Jane Segar born Dec. ye 16. baptized Jan^{ry}
ye 17 1721.

Jane daughter of John & Catherine Tompson born Dec. ye 27. baptize^d Dec. ye 28 1721.

Christopher Son of Richard & Honor Tayloe born Dec. ye 25. baptized Jan^{r}y ye 21 1721.

Hannah daughter of William & Elizabeth Batchelder born Jan^{r}y y^e
5. baptized Jan^{ry} ye 23. 1721.

Stephen Son of William & Mary Johnson born Decem^r ye 3. baptized Dec. ye 31 1721.

Thomas Son of Thomas & Mary Hackett born Jan^{r}y ye 9 baptized
Feb^{r}y ye 11 1721.

Jedidah daughter of John & Elizabeth Bream born Jan^{r}y 18. baptized Feb^{r}y ye 11 1721.

Christian daughter of Angello & Elianor Cummins born Decem^r y^e
27 baptized Jan^{r}y 28 1721.

John son of James & Margrett Daniel born Jan^{r}y ye 19. baptized
Feb^{r}y 18 1721.

Lucretia daughter of Joseph & Lucretia Goar born Feb^{r}y ye 12.
baptized Feb^{r}y 25 1721.

Robert Son of John & Mary Bradley born Jan^{ry} ye 21. baptized
Feb^{r}y 25 1721.

John Son of William & Catherine Rice born Jan^{r}y ye 26. baptized
March ye 4 1721.

Priscilla daughter of James & Margrett Ingram born Feb^{r}y ye 14.
baptized March ye 4. 1721.

Beverley Son of William & Elizabeth Stanard born Feb^{ry} ye 24. baptized March ye 4 1721.

Edward Son of Edward & Elizabeth Saunders born Feb^{r}y ye 4 baptized March ye 11 1721.

Mary daughter of John & Anne Fearn born Feb^{r}y ye 20. baptized
March ye 18. 1721.

Bar. Yates Min^r.

CHRISTENINGS.

Philip Son of John & Lucy Grymes born March ye 11. baptized March 18. 1721.

John Son of William & Sarah Davis born Feb'y 26. baptized March ye 25 1722.

Augustine an illegitimate Son of Mary Hargrow born March ye 8. 1721. baptized March ye 31. 1722.

John Son of John & Sarah Miller born March ye 16. 1721 baptized April ye 1 1722.

John Son of Joseph & Anne Pace born March ye 14 1721 baptized April ye 8 1722.

Richard Son of Richard & Elizabeth Daniel born March 17. 1721 baptized Ap: ye 15 1722.

Benoni Son of John & Ruth Vickars born April ye 9 baptized Ap. ye 18 1722.

Anne daughter of Henry & Anne Faulkner born March ye 20 1721, baptized Ap. ye 1. 1722.

John & Esther Son & daughter of Christopher & Mary Kelshaw born March ye 24. 1721, baptized Ap. ye 22. 1722.

John Son of Thomas & Elizabeth Dudley born Ap. ye 15. baptized April ye 22 1722.

Elizabeth daughter of Matthew & Mary Kemp born Ap. ye 28. baptized May ye 10 1722.

Benjamine Son of William & Sarah Anderson born Ap. ye 14 baptized May ye 13 1722.

Oswald Son of James & Anne Smith born May ye 1st baptized May ye 27 1722.

Jonathan Son of Jonathan & Mary Brooks born Ap. ye 6 baptized May ye 20 1722.

Margrett daughter of William & Anne Southworth born May ye 9. baptized June ye 10 1722.

William Son of Patrick & Rebecca Deagle born May ye 8. baptized June ye 10 1722.

Elizabeth daughter of Henry & Mary Tugle born June 22 baptized July ye 2 1722.

John Son of John & Anne Johnson born July ye 5 baptized July ye 9 1722.

Thomas Son of William & Frances Hill born June ye 17, baptized July ye 15 1722.

John Son of William & Elizabeth Gardner born August ye 1 baptized August ye 2 1722.

Elizabeth daughter of John & Johanna Blake born July ye 25. baptized August ye 5 1722.

John Son of Jonathan & Priscilla Johnson born July ye 31. baptized August ye 5. 1722.

Mary daughter of George & Elizabeth Guess born July ye 15. baptized August ye 12 1722.

John Son of Ralph & Mary Shelton born July ye 19 baptized August ye 12 1722.

Abraham Son of John & Margrett Hardee born July ye 5. baptized August ye 12 1722.

John Son of Thomas & Susanna Clark born July ye 5. baptized August ye 12 1722.

Michal daughter of William & Margrett Bristow born July ye 17. baptized August ye 19 1722.

Mary daughter of William & Mary Tomson born August ye 8. baptized Augst ye 21 1722.

William Son of Thomas & Susanna Oliver born July ye 27 baptized Augst ye 26 1722.

Robert Son of Robert & Elizabeth Williamson born July ye 31. baptized Septem^r 2 1722.

Elizabeth daughter of John & Anne Southworth born June ye 25. baptized July ye 29 1722.

Anne daughter of William & Lettice Guttery born Septem^r ye 12. baptized Sept. 22 1722.

Jacob Son of Jacob & Elizabeth Stiff born August ye 30 baptized Sept. ye 30 1722.

Anne daughter of William & Judith Dudley born Sept. ye 6. baptized October 7 1722.

Margrett daughter of William & Sarah Baldwin born Aug. ye 11. baptized Septr 23. 1722.

William Son of John & Margret Southern born August ye 16 baptized Septr 23 1722.

Benjamine Son of Henry & Elizabeth Tuggle born August ye 20. baptized Sept^{mr} 23 1722.

Jenny daughter of John & Mary Moseley born Octo. 1. baptized October ye 14 1722.

William Son of William & Margrett Johnson born Octo ye 8. baptized October ye 16. 1722.

James Son of Thomas & Elizabeth Greenwood born Octo. 12. baptized Octo. ye 16. 1722.

James Son of Samuel & Catherine Batchelder born Sept. ye 25. baptized Octo. ye 24. 1722.

Judith daughter of John & Rebecca Kidd born Octo. ye 8. baptized Novem^r 4. 1722.

Mary daughter of George & Elizabeth Harding born Novem^r 7. baptized Novem^r 9 1722.

Usebius Son of Usebius & Mary Lewis born Octo. ye 10 baptized Novem^r 11 1722.

Rowland Son of Christopher & Hope Sutton born Octo. ye 15. baptized Novem 18 1722.

Jane daughter of John & Micholl Williams born Octo. ye 27. baptized Novem^r 25 1722.

James Son of Robert & Chatherine Perrott born Novem^r ye 11. baptized Decem^r 18 1722.

Richins Son of Richins & Hannah Brame born Decem^r ye 3. baptized Decem^r 16 1722.

Betty daughter of Robert & Anne George born Decem^r ye 7 baptized Decem^r 16. 1722.

Anne daughter of Thomas & Mary Gibbs born Septem^r ye 30. baptized Novem^r 11. 1722.

Frances daughter of Edwin & Elizabeth Thacker born Octo. ye 2. baptized Octo. 28. 1722.

Anne daughter of George & Martha Chowning born Dec. 22. baptized Jan^{r}y ye 6. 1722.

Elizabeth daughter of Hezekiah & Anne Roades born Dec. 23. baptized Jan'y ye 20 1722.

Bar. Yates. Min^r

Mary daughter of Joseph & Mary Sears born Decem^r ye 27, baptized Jan'y ye 27 1722.

Elizabeth daughter of Thomas & Jane Norman born Jan'y ye 17, baptized Jan'y ye 27 1722.

Beverley Son of John & Catherine Robinson born Jan'y 11. baptized Feb'y 1 1722.

Samuel Son of William & Jennet Chowning born Feb'y ye 11 baptized Same day 1722.

Margrett daughter of John & Elizabeth Lewis born Jan'y ye 25 baptized Feb'y 17 1722.

Jacob Son of James & Sarah Cole born Feb'y ye 5, baptized Feb'y ye 17 1722.

Susanna daughter of John & Mary Berry born Feb'y ye 17. baptized March 3. 1722.

Mary daughter of Thomas & Rose Wright born Feb'y ye 7 baptized March ye 17. 1722.

William Son of John & Mary Guttery born Feb'y ye 14 baptized March ye 10. 1722.

Anne daughter of Hugh & Catherine Mactyre born Feb'y ye 15. baptized March 10 1722.

Mary daughter of John & Priscilla Brookes born March ye 3. 1722 baptized March 31. 1723.

Mildred daughter of Richard & Anne Greenwood born March ye 7 1722, baptized March 31. 1723.

Jane daughter of Oliver & Jane Segar born March ye 18. 1722 baptized March 31 1723.

George Son of George & Elizabeth Carter born Feb'y ye 27. 1722. baptized March 31 1723.

William Son of John & Jane Price born April ye 6 baptized April 28 1723.

Elizabeth daughter of Thomas & Anne Smith born Ap. ye 19. baptized May ye 5. 1723.

Daniel Son of William & Hannah Cain born March 10. 1722 baptized April ye 14 1723.

Isaack Son of John & Anne Rhodes born April ye 19. baptized May ye 12 1723.

Margret daughter of Robert & Elizabeth Daniell born Ap. ye 20. baptized May ye 19. 1723.

Judith daughter of Henry & Judith Burk born April 25. baptized May ye 19 1723.

Lucy daughter of William & Anne Daniel born April ye 21 baptized May ye 26 1723.

John Son of Henry & Sarah Putman born May ye 1. baptized June ye 2d 1723.

John Son of Patrick & Elizabeth Miller born June ye 4 baptized June ye 6 1723.

Charles Son of John & Lucy Grymes born May ye 31. baptized June ye 7 1723.

Mary daughter of Thomas & Jane Haslewood born May ye 16 baptized June ye 9 1723.

Anne daughter of Robert & Elizabeth Walker born May ye 17, baptized June ye 16. 1723.

Charles Son of Richard & Jane Moulson born June ye 9 baptized June ye 30. 1723.

James Son of John & Joyce Tiney born June ye 9 baptized June ye 30 1723.

Anne daughter of Henry & Elizabeth Ball born June ye 11. baptized June ye 30 1723.

Aquilla Son of Aquilla & Mary Snelling born June ye 28. baptized July ye 14 1723.

Thomas Son of John & Lettice Cheedle born July ye 6. baptized July ye 21 1723.

Elizabeth daughter of John & Anne Dudley born June ye 25. baptized July ye 28 1723.

Betty daughter of Henry & Sarah Emmerson born July ye 7. baptized August ye 11. 1723.

William Son of George & Anne Saunders born June ye 26 baptized August ye 4. 1723.

Sarah daughter of Francis & Sarah Timberlake born August ye 18. baptized August ye 21. 1723.

Clara daughter of John & Anne Smith born August ye 4 baptized Septem^r ye 8 1723.

Priscilla daughter of Rich^d & Sarah Steevens born August ye 11. baptized Septem^r ye 25 1723.

Charles Son of George & Amey Walker born Septem^r ye 3. baptized Septem^r ye 29 1723.

William Son of Jonathan & Mary Brooks born Septem^r ye 9. baptized Octo. ye 13 1723.

Thomas Son of Thomas & Susanna Clark born Septem^r ye 19. baptized Octo ye 13 1723.

Mary daughter of Richard & Mary Allen born Septem^r ye 23. baptized Novem^r ye 3. 1723.

Sarah daughter of Joseph & Elizabeth Smith born Septem^r ye 24. baptized Octo. ye 20. 1723.

Hezekiah Son of William & Hannah Roads born Octo. ye 8. baptized Octo ye 27. 1723.

Letitia daughter of Powel & Mary Stamper born Septem^r ye 22. baptized Novem^r ye 24. 1723.

Elizabeth daughter of John & Mary Saddler born Octo. ye 26. baptized Novem^r ye 24. 1723.

Mary daughter of Stockly & Anne Towles born Novem^r ye 1. baptized Novem^r ye 24. 1723.

Sarah daughter of William & Elizabeth Stanard born Novem^r ye 10. baptized Decem^r ye 2. 1723.

William Son of Arthur & Mary Thomas born Novem^r ye 15, baptized Decem^r ye 8. 1723.

William Still an illegitimate Son of   baptized Decem^r 15. 1723.

Betty daughter of Churchhill & Sarah Blakey born Novem^r ye 20. baptized Decem^r 15. 1723.

Elizabeth daughter of Jacob & Elizabeth Rice born Novemʳ yᵉ 16. baptized Decemʳ 20. 1723.

Constant daughter of Augustine & Jone Owen born Novemʳ yᵉ 16. baptized Decemʳ 22. 1723.

William Son of Christopher & Catherine Kilbee born Decemʳ yᵉ 19. baptized Janʳy 12. 1723.

Anna daughter of William & Elizabeth Blackbourn born Janʳy yᵉ 3. baptized Janʳy 19. 1723.

Bar Yates Minʳ.

John Son of Thomas & Catherine Pain born Decemʳ yᵉ 1. baptized Janʳy 22 1723.

Clement Son of Thomas & Grace Mountague born Decemʳ yᵉ 29 baptized Janʳy 22. 1723.

William Son of Edward & Mary Clark born Janʳy yᵉ 13. baptized Janʳy 22 1723.

Sarah daughter of Paul & Jane Thilman born Janʳy yᵉ 5. baptized Janʳy yᵉ 26 1723.

Thomas Son of John & Anne Southworth born Dec: yᵉ 22 baptized Febʳy yᵉ 2 1723.

John Son of William & Elizabeth Batchelder born Janʳy yᵉ 3. baptized Febʳy yᵉ 2. 1723.

Anne daughter of Wᵐ & Alice Hackney born Decemʳ yᵉ 18. baptized Janʳy 19. 1723.

Abby daughter of Zebulon & Mary Chelton born Janʳy yᵉ 5. baptized Febʳy 9. 1723.

Samuel Son of William & Jennett Chowning born Janʳy yᵉ 21 baptized Febʳy 16. 1723.

James Son of James & Margrett Ingram born Janʳy yᵉ 14. baptized Febʳy 16. 1723.

John Son of John & Elizabeth Wormley born Janʳy yᵉ 25. baptized Febʳy 13. 1723.

Charles Son of John & Jane Stuart born Janʳy yᵉ 27 baptized Febʳy yᵉ 23. 1723.

Mary daughter of Theophilus & Frances Branch born Janʳy 21. baptized March 15. 1723.

Robert Son of John & Mary Murray born Janʳy yᵉ 28. baptized March yᵉ 8 1723.

Jemima daughter of Nicholas & Mary Bristow born Janʳy yᵉ 30. baptized March yᵉ 8. 1723.

Anne daughter of William & Catherine Rice born Janʳy yᵉ 30. baptized March yᵉ 8 1723.

George Son of James & Mary Bristow born Febʳy yᵉ 7 baptized March yᵉ 8 1723.

Garritt Son of John & Mary Guttery born Febʳy yᵉ 19. baptized March yᵉ 8. 1723.

William Son of Henry & Elizabeth Blunt born Decemʳ 29 baptized March yᵉ 22 1723.

Anne daughter of Curtis & Anne Perrott born Febʳy yᵉ 20 baptized March yᵉ 24 1723.

John Son of John & Elizabeth Dobs born March yᵉ 8, 1723. baptized March yᵉ 29 1724.

Phebe daughter of James & Margrett Daniel born March yᵉ 12 1723 baptized April yᵉ 5. 1724.

Elizabeth daughter of Sr Wm Skipwith & Lady Sarah his Wife born March 22 1723. baptized Ap. 12. 1724.

William Son of William & Jane Cardwell born March ye 12. 1723, baptized April ye 29 1724.

Thomas Son of Daniel & Frances Hues born April ye 14 baptized May ye 3 1724.

William Son of William & Anne Segar born May ye 1. baptized May 9 1724.

Robert an illegitimate Son of Mary Mullens born   baptized May 10 1724.

Elizabeth daughter of Robert & Elizabeth Williamson born April ye 6 baptized May 31. 1724.

Nevill Son of Joseph & Elizabeth Bohannon born June ye 1. baptized June 28 1724.

Josee Son of Joseph & Lucretia Goar born June ye 2. baptized July ye 5 1724.

Benjamine Son of Ralph & Mary Shelton born June ye 18. baptized July ye 12. 1724.

Peter Son of William & Mary Bennett born June ye 21. baptized July ye 19. 1724.

Anne an illegitimate daughter of Dorothy Row born July ye 17. baptized July ye 26. 1724.

Aquilla Son of Jonathan & Priscilla Johnson born July ye 19. baptized August ye 16. 1724.

James Son of Thomas & Elizabeth Greenwood born July ye 17 baptized August 2. 1724.

Catherine daughter of John & Catherine Tomson born July ye 16. baptized August 2. 1724.

Alice daughter of John & Lucy Grymes born August ye 10. baptized August 16. 1724.

Edwin Son of Edwin & Elizabeth Thacker born July ye 16. baptized July ye 25. 1724.

Anne daughter of John & Elizabeth Harris born July ye 28. baptized Augt ye 18 1724.

Judith daughter of Peter Johnson & Anna both slaves to Morrice Smith baptized Aug^st ye 18. 1724.

Henry Son of John & Elizabeth Shorter born August ye 8. baptized August ye 22 1724.

Elizabeth daughter of Rice & Martha Curtis born August ye 19. baptized Aug^st 26. 1724.

William Son of Christopher & Sarah Chafin born July ye 27 baptized Aug^st ye 29. 1724.

John Son of Thomas & Rachel Amis born August ye 20. baptized Aug^st ye 30. 1724.

Mary daughter of Thomas & Ellis Faulkner born August ye 23 baptized Septem^r 27. 1724.

Lettice daughter of Peter Johnson & Anna both slaves to Morrice Smith baptized Aug^st ye 31. 1724.

Machen Son of John & Anne Fearn born August ye 16. baptized September ye 6 1724.

James Son of William & Anne Southworth born August 23. baptized Septem^r ye 13. 1724.

Samuel Son of William & Mary Tomson born Septem^r ye 3. baptized Septem^r ye 27 1724.

John Son of Jacob & Elizabeth Rice born October ye 16. baptized ye Same day 1724.

Anne daughter of John & Frances Heath born Septem^r ye 15. baptized Octo^r 25 1724.

Joannah daughter of John & Joannah Blake born Septem^r 20. baptized Novem^r ye 5. 1724.

John Son of Charles & Susanna Thomas born Octo. 13. baptized Novem^r ye 8. 1724.

Nathan Son of Christopher & Hope Sutton born Novem^r 22 baptized ye Same day 1724.

Thomas Son of John & Phobe Marston born Novem^r ye 9 baptized Novem^r ye 29 1724.

Diana daughter of James & Anne Smith born Novem^r ye 8. baptized Novem^r ye 29. 1724.

Bar. Yates Min^r.

Richard Son of John & Elizabeth Lewis born Novem^r ye 10. baptized Decem^r ye 6. 1724.

Anne illegitimate daughter of Elizabeth Guttery born   baptized Decem^r ye 6. 1724.

Mary daughter of John & Elizabeth Brame born Novem^r ye 5. baptized Decem^r ye 6 1724.

Stephen Son of John & Mary Riley born Novem^r ye 12. baptized Decem. 6. 1724.

Agnes daughter of Angello & Ellionar Commings born Novem^r ye 11. baptized Dec. 13. 1724.

George Son of Jonathan & Anne Herring born Novem^r ye 24. bap tized Decem^r ye 20. 1724.

Rachel daughter of William & Lettice Guttery born Novem^r 29 baptized Jan^{r}y 3 1724.

William Son of William & Hannah Roades born Dec. ye 3. baptized Jan^{r}y 3. 1724.

Joyce daughter illegitimate of Elizabeth Stapleton born Dec. ye 3. baptized Jan^{r}y 17. 1724.

Rachel daughter of John & Catherine Chowning born Decem: ye 26. baptized Jan^{r}y 17. 1724.

John Son of Thomas & Rosannah Wright born Decem^r ye 26. baptized Jan^{r}y 24. 1724.

Melchisedek Son of Richins & Hannah Brame born Decem^r ye 31, baptized Feb^{r}y 7 1724.

Ralph Son of Ralph & Elizabeth Watts born Jan^{r}y ye 1. baptized Feb^{r}y 7. 1724.

Frances daughter of Joseph & Mary Seares born Jan^{r}y ye 2. baptized Feb^{r}y 7 1724.

Lewis Son of William & Sarah Baldwin born Jan^{r}y ye 10. baptized Feb^{r}y 7 1724.

Benjamine Son of Edward & Mary Clark born Feb^{r}y ye 10. baptized March ye 7 1724.

John Son of Henry & Mary Tugle born Feb^{r}y 12. baptized March ye 21. 1724.

John Son of Robert & Anne George born Feb'y 13. baptized March ye 21. 1724.

Elizabeth daughter of Robert & Jane Mash born Feb'y ye 20 baptized March 21. 1724.

Thomas Son of Jacob & Elizabeth Stiff born March 3. 1724 baptized April ye 4 1725.

William Son of John & Elizabeth Saunders born March ye 5. 1724. baptized April 4. 1725.

Mary daughter of John & Sarah Miller born March ye 19, 1724 baptized April 4 1725.

Anne daughter of Matthew & Mary Kemp born March ye 31. baptized April 9. 1725.

Agatha daughter of John & Anne Ridgway born March ye 5. 1724. baptized April 11. 1725.

Mary daughter of Robert & Eliza Daniel born March ye 22. 1724. baptized April 11 1725.

William Son of John & Elizabeth Peniel born March ye 16. 1724. baptized April 25. 1725.

Mary daughter of John & Mary Sadler born April ye 1st baptized May ye 2 1725.

Mary daughter of Usebius & Mary Lewis born April ye 10. baptized May ye 2. 1725.

Chickley Son of Thomas & Mary Hackett born April ye 21. baptized May ye 2. 1725.

Susanna daughter of Adam & Dorothea Cockborn born May 8. 1724. baptized May 13. 1725.

Jane daughter of Thomas & Jane Cheney born Ap. ye 28. baptized May ye 23 1725.

Henry Son of Oliver & Jane Segar born May ye 2 baptized May ye 23 1725.

James Son of Patrick & Rebeckah Deagle born April 23. baptized May ye 30 1725.

Anne daughter of W^m & Margrett Bristow born May ye 4. baptized May ye 30 1725.

Sarah daughter of Thomas & Mary Gibbs born April ye 30. baptized May ye 30 1725.

William Son of Henry & Elizabeth Tuggle born May ye 28 baptized July ye 4 1725.

George Son of Joseph & Anne Pace born June 10. baptized July ye 4 1725.

Robert Son of Thomas & Jane Norman born June ye 20. baptized July ye 4 1725.

Natty daughter of George & Elizabeth Guest born June ye 18. baptized July ye 4. 1725.

James Son of William & Hannah Cain born June ye 11. baptized July ye 18. 1725.

Elizabeth daughter of George & Agatha Twyman born June 28. baptized July ye 25. 1725.

Henry Son of Richard & Mary Allen born June ye 27 baptized July ye 25. 1725.

Elizabeth daughter of John & Mary Moseley born July ye 14. baptized July ye 25. 1725.

Henry Son of Samuel & Catherine Batchelder born July ye 3. baptized Augst 1. 1725.

Mary daughter of George & Mary Barwick born July ye 29. baptized Augst 5. 1725.

Jane daughter of Richard & Anne Jones born July ye 15. baptized Augst ye 8. 1725.

Anne daughter of James & Anne Russel born   baptized Augst 8. 1725.

Sarah daughter of Joseph & Elizabeth Humphris born July ye 18. baptized Augst 8. 1725.

Anne daughter of John & Mary Bradley born July ye 5. baptized Augst 8. 1725.

Susanna daughter of John & Margrett Southern born July ye 22. baptized Augst 15. 1725.

George Son of George & Martha Chowning born July ye 24 baptized Augst 15 1725.

Josiah Son of W^m & Anne Daniel born July ye 13. baptized Augst ye 22 1725.

Jane daughter of Patrick & Elizabeth Miller born August ye 2 baptized Augst ye 29. 1725.

Elizabeth daughter of John & Michal Williams born July ye 28 baptized Septem ye 5 1725.

James Son of Henry & Sarah Emerson born Augst ye 6 baptized September ye 5. 1725.

—ert Son of Randolph & Sarah Rodes born August ye 13. baptized September ye 5. 1725.

Bar. Yates Min^r

Betty daughter of Joseph & Elizabeth Smith born Augst ye 5. baptized Septem^r ye 12 1725.

Needles Son of William & Frances Hill born August ye 12 baptized Septem^r ye 19. 1725.

Elizabeth daughter of James & Mary Micham born Augst 27. baptized Septem^r ye 26. 1725.

Mary daughter of Joseph & Mary Holland born Augst 31. baptized Septem^r ye 26. 1725.

John Son of John & Anne Southworth born Septem^r ye 14. baptized October ye 3. 1725.

Sarah daughter of William & Elizabeth Batchelder born Augst 31. baptized October ye 4. 1725.

Anne daughter of John & Anne Roads born Septem^r ye 5. baptized October 10 1725.

Isaack Son of Thomas & Susanna Oliver born Octo. ye 2 baptized October ye 10. 1725.

Catherine daughter of Henry & Catherine Weight born Sept: ye 26 baptized Novem^r ye 21. 1725.

Anne daughter of John & Anne Smith born Septem^r ye 30. baptized October ye 24 1725.

Armistead Son of Thomas & Margrett Alldin born Septem^r 23. baptized October ye 31. 1725.

Anne daughter of Patrick & Mary Knight born Octo. ye 7. baptized October ye 31. 1725.

Anne daughter of John & Sarah Fulsher born Octo. ye 26. baptized Novem^r ye 14 1725.

Ambrose Son of John & Anne Dudley born October yᵉ 20. baptized Novemʳ yᵉ 21. 1725.

Rebecca daughter of Abraham & Mary Wharton born Octo. yᵉ 29. baptized Novemʳ: 21. 1725.

William Son of William & Sarah Anderson born Novemʳ yᵉ 5. baptized Novemʳ: 21. 1725.

William Son of James & Agatha Jones born Octoʳ yᵉ 28. baptized Novemʳ yᵉ 28. 1725.

Elizabeth daughter of John & Anne Blake born Novemʳ yᵉ 5. baptized Novemʳ yᵉ 28. 1725.

Anne an illegitimate daughter of Mary Mullens born Octo. yᵉ 24. baptized Decemʳ: 19. 1725.

Thomas Son of John & Elizabeth Smith born Octo. yᵉ 30. baptized Decemʳ: yᵉ 7. 1725.

John Son of John & Keziah Scanland born Novemʳ: yᵉ 30. baptized Decemʳ 26 1725.

Elizabeth daughter of Edwin & Elizabeth Thacker born Novemʳ 26. baptized Janʳy 5. 1725.

Anne daughter of Richard & Anne Greenwood born Janʳy 22. baptized Janʳy 30 1725.

Benjamine Son of John & Lucy Grymes born Janʳy yᵉ 19. baptized Febʳy 6 1725.

Mary daughter of John & Elizabeth Wormley born Janʳy yᵉ 23. baptized Febʳy 7. 1725.

George Son of Richard & Jane Moulson born Janʳy yᵉ 17. baptized Febʳy 20 1725.

Jane daughter of Stokely & Anne Towles born Febʳy yᵉ 10. baptized Febʳy 20 1725.

Edmund Son of William & Eleanor Crutchfeild born Febʳy 13. baptized March 8. 1725.

Avarilla daughter of John & Margrett Hardee born Janʳy 21. baptized March 13. 1725.

Rachel daughter of John & Mary Goar born Febʳy 21. baptized March 13 1725.

Priscilla daughter of Aquilla & Mary Snelling born Febʳy 18 1725. baptized March 27 1726.

Frances daughter of John & Rebecca Kidd born April yᵉ 1 baptized April yᵉ 2 1726.

Jane daughter of Churchhill & Sarah Blakey born Febʳy 24. 1725. baptized April yᵉ 3. 1726.

Jennett daughter of William & Jennett Chowning born March yᵉ 6. 1725. baptized April 3. 1726.

Joshua an illegitimate son of Mary Jones (alias) Haywood born Ap. yᵉ 2. baptized April 5. 1726.

Conquest an illegitimate Son of Mary Jones alias Haywood born Ap. yᵉ 2: baptized April 5. 1726.

Frances daughter of Richard & Susanna Curtis born March yᵉ 25 baptized Ap: 10 1726.

Mary daughter of Rice & Martha Curtis born March 18. 1725 baptized Ap. 14. 1726.

Susanna daughter of Hezekiah & Anne Rodes born March yᵉ 19. 1725. baptized Ap: 17 1726.

Kerah daughter of Powell & Mary Stamper born March 21 1725. baptized Ap: 24 1726.

Jonathan Son of Jonathan & Priscilla Johnson born April y[e] 28. 1726.

John Son of Robert & Priscilla James born April y[e] 7. baptized April y[e] 24 1726.

Robert Son of Robert & Bridgett Wilkings born May y[e] 18. baptized 1726.

John Son of William & Alice Hackney born May y[e] 30. baptized 1726.

Averilla daughter of James & Margrett Ingram born May 19. baptized June 12. 1726.

Elizabeth daughter of William & Margrett Johnson born May 28. baptized June 12. 1726.

Catherine daughter of John & Elizabeth Dobbs born July y[e] 1. baptized Aug[st] 21 1726.

James Son of Arthur & Mary Thomas born August y[e] 22 baptized 1726.

Mary daughter of John & Catherine Tugle born August y[e] 13 baptized Septem[r] y[e] 4. 1726.

Hugh Son of Hugh & Catherine Mactire born July y[e] 19. baptized Septem[r] y[e] 4. 1726.

Thomas Son of William & Jane Cardwell born July y[e] 19. baptized Septem[r] y[e] 4. 1726.

James Son of Joshua & Martha Lewis born Septem[r] y[e] 5. baptized 1726.

Mary daughter of Charles & Susanna Thomas born Septem[r] y[e] 9. baptized 1726.

Benjamine Son of Christopher & Hope Sutton born August y[e] 27 baptized 1726.

Anne daughter of John & Elizabeth Weston born Octo: y[e] 10. baptized 1726.

John Son of John & Anne Johnson born October y[e] 24. baptized 1726.

Catherine daughter of John & Michall George born Octo y[e] 3. baptized October 16 1726.

Benjamine Son of Thomas & Elizabeth Greenwood born Octo y[e] 2. baptized October 16. 1726.

William Son of William & Sarah Cheseld born Octo y[e] 31. baptized Novem[r] 27 1726.

Robert Son of William & Judith Dudley born Novem[r] y[e] 10. baptized 1726.

Anna daughter of James & Mary Bristow born Octo y[e] 28 baptized Novem[r] 12. 1726.

William Son of Nicholas & Mary Bristow born Novem[r] y[e] 2. baptized Novem[r] 12. 1726.

William Son of Thomas & Susanna Oliver born Novem[r] y[e] 2 baptized 1726.

Mary daughter of William & Frances Mansfeild born Decem[r] y[e] 12. baptized Jan[ry] 8. 1726.

John Son of Christopher & Sarah Chaffin born Decem[r] y[e] 20. baptized 1726.

Vivion Son of James & Margrett Daniel born July y[e] 1st baptized July 29 1726.

Richard Son of Francis & Sarah Timberlake born August ye 19. baptized 1726.

Elizabeth daughter of John & Mary Murrah born August 14 baptized 1726.

George Son of Joseph & Elizabeth Bohannan born August ye 20 baptized 1726.

Mary daughter of George & Hannah Nevill born Novem^r ye 20 baptized 1726.

William Son of Thomas & Rose Wright born Decem^r ye 8. baptized 1726.

Betty daughter of Joseph & Mary Seers born Jan^ry ye 1 baptized Jan^ry ye 29 1726.

Catherine daughter of Thomas & Catherine Pain born Decem^r 19. baptized Jan^ry ye 29. 1726.

Mary daughter of Oliver & Jane Segar born Decem^r ye 11. baptized Jan^ry 29. 1726.

John Son of William & Anne Segar born Novem^r ye 9. baptized Novem^r 19. 1726.

Christopher Son of John & Sarah Miller born Jan^ry ye 27. baptized Feb^ry ye 2. 1726.

Mary daughter of John & Anne Southworth born Feb^ry 2. baptized Feb^ry ye 2 1726.

Clemence daughter of Edward & Sarah Ball born Jan^ry ye 15. baptized Feby 5. 1726.

Elizabeth daughter of Henry & Elizabeth Ball born Decem^r 28. baptized Jan^ry 29 1726.

Henry Son of John & Mary Guttery born Jan^ry 8. baptized Jan^ry ye 29 1726.

Ellis daughter of Thomas & Ellis Faulkner born Jan^ry ye 30. baptized Feb^ry 16. 1726.

James Son of John & Sarah Dazier born Feb^ry ye 17 baptized March 3 1726.

Eliz^a ye daughter of W^m & Mary Bennett born December ye 1 1726.

Elizabeth daughter of Daniel & Frances Hughes born Jan^ry ye 19. baptized March 5. 1726.

Dorothy daughter of John & Anne Fearn born Feb^ry ye 13. baptized March 5. 1726.

William Son of John & Elizabeth Thurston born Jan^ry 2d baptized Feb^ry 1 1726.

William Son of Armistead & Hannah Churchhill born Feb^ry ye 24th baptized March ye 16. 1726.

William Son of John & Frances Heath born Jan^ry ye 19 baptized Feb^ry 19 1726.

Josias Son of John & Catherine Chowning born March ye 6. baptized March 24 1726.

James Son of Ralph & Mary Shetton born Feb^ry 23. baptized March ye 23. 1726.

Francis a Slave belonging to ye Estate of James Walker dec'd baptized Ap. 23 1727.

Mary an illegitimate daughter of Jane Taylor born Feb^ry 1726 baptized Ap. 26 1727.

George Son of John & Hannah Blake born April ye 6. baptized April ye 30. 1727.

Charles Son of Edward & Elizabeth Whittacre born Ap. yᵉ 12. baptized April yᵉ 21. 1727.

Frances daughter of Jonathan & Mary Brooks born April yᵉ 19. baptized May yᵉ 18. 1727.

Ruth daughter of Richard & Mary Allen born May yᵉ 2. baptized May yᵉ 28. 1727.

William son of Thomas & Anne Lee born May yᵉ 6. baptized May yᵉ 28 1727.

Josiah Son of Joseph & Anne Pace born May 31. baptized June yᵉ 18. 1727.

Agatha daughter of Curtis & Anne Perrott born May 12. baptized June yᵉ 18. 1727.

William Son of George & Agatha Twiman born May yᵉ 20. baptized June yᵉ 18. 1727.

John Son of William & Elizebeth Crowder born May 1 baptized May yᵉ 28. 1727.

Elizabeth an illegitimate daughter of Mary Mullins born May yᵉ 5. baptized July yᵉ 9. 1727.

Elizabeth daughter of John & Elizabeth Braine born July yᵉ 10. baptized July yᵉ 30. 1727.

Frances daughter of John & Rebecca Kidd born   baptized August yᵉ 20 1727.

Edward Son of Edward & Mary Clark born August yᵉ 17. baptized August yᵉ 24 1727.

Ruth daughter of John & Elizabeth Smith born August yᵉ 25. baptized yᵉ Same day 1727.

Mary daughter of George & Amy Walker born July yᵉ 30. baptized August yᵉ 27 1727.

Millicent daughter of William & Elizabeth Blackburn born Sept. yᵉ 7. baptized Sept. 24. 1727.

George Son of Robert & Elizabeth Daniel born Septemʳ yᵉ 13. baptized October yᵉ 1. 1727.

Sarah daughter of Robert & Anne George born Septemʳ yᵉ 24. baptized October yᵉ 1. 1727.

Thomas Son of Thomas & Anne Berry born Septemʳ yᵉ 5. baptized October yᵉ 8. 1727.

Bar. Yates Minʳ

Ruth daughter of Jacob & Elizabeth Stiff born Septemʳ yᵉ 6 baptized October yᵉ 15 1727.

Anne daughter of John & Anne Ridgway born Septemʳ yᵉ 30 baptized October 22 1727.

Catherine daughter of Joseph & Elizabeth Smith born August yᵉ 24 baptized Sept. 24 1727.

Benjamine Son of William & Rachel Baker born Octo. yᵉ 28 baptized Novemʳ 5 1727.

Rose daughter of Richard & Susanna Curtis born October yᵉ 18, baptized Novemʳ 5 1727.

Elizabeth daughter of John & Rebecca Arther born Septemʳ yᵉ 25. baptized Novemʳ 19 1727.

Frances daughter of Theophilus & Frances Branch born Novʳ yᵉ 17. baptized Decemʳ 2 1727.

Robert Son of John & Mary George born Novem^r ye 17. baptized
Novem^r 18 1727.

Benjamine Son of Robert & Elizabeth Williamson born Novem^r 25.
baptized Dec. 3 1727.

George Son of George & Martha Chowning was born Novem^r 22.
baptized Decem^r 3 1727.

James Son of Robert & Bridgett Willkings was born Novem^r 27.
baptized Decem^r 11 1727.

John Son of William & Hannah Roads was born Novem^r ye 4 baptized Decem^r 17 1727.

Lucy daughter of William & mary Gayer was born Decem^r ye 17.
baptized Jan^ry 7 1727.

Anne daughter of Joshua & Martha Lewis was born Novem^r ye 8.
baptized Jan^ry 7 1727.

Joseph Son of John & Margrett Southern was born   baptized
Jan^ry 14 1727.

James Son of James & Rebecca Heptinstall was born Jan^ry ye 4th baptized Jan^ry ye 28. 1727.

Jane daughter of Francis & Elizabeth Porter was born Jan^ry ye 15.
baptized Feb^ry 2 1727.

Jane daughter of John & Mary Sadler born Jan^ry ye 15. baptized
Feb^ry ye 4 1727.

George son of George & Anne Wortham born Jan^ry 19. baptized
Feb^ry 11 1727.

Phoebe daughter of John & Phoebe Marston born Jan^ry 21. baptized Feb^ry 18 1727.

Joseph Son of Stockley & Ann Towles born Feb^ry ye 3. baptized
Feb^ry 25 1727.

Joseph Son of Samuel & Chatherine Batchelder born Feb^ry ye 9.
baptized Feb^ry 25 1727.

Maurice Son of John & Anne Smith born Jan^ry ye 12. baptized
March 4 1727.

Frances daughter of William & Frances Hill born Jan^ry ye 26. baptized March ye 10. 1727.

Meacham Son of John & Michal George born Feb^ry ye 23. baptized
March 17 1727.

William Son of William & Jennett Chowning born Feb^ry ye 21.
baptized March 17 1727.

Jacob Son of John & Anne Blake born Feb^ry 28. baptized March
ye 24 1727.

John Son of John & Michal Williams born March 19. 1727. baptized April ye 7 1728.

John Son of John & Mary Moseley born March 10. 1727 baptized
April ye 7 1728.

Jane daughter of Henry & Sarah Emerson born March 10. 1727.
baptized April ye 7 1728.

Henry Son of William & Margrett Johnson born March 2. 1727.
baptized April ye 7 1728.

John Son of John & Elizabeth Weston born Feb^ry ye 21. baptized
March ye 24 1727.

Mary daughter of Henry & Anne Barnett born Ap: ye 3. baptized
April 21 1728.

John Son of John & Frances Heath born April ye 14. baptized May ye 5 1728.

Michal daughter of George & Elizabeth Guess born April ye 5. baptized May ye 5 1728.

Thomas Son of Thomas & Sarah Older born   baptized May ye 19 1728.

Elizabeth daughter of John & Lettice Burk born May ye 24 baptized May ye 26 1728.

Elizabeth daughter of William & Margrett Bristow born May ye 14 baptized June 9 1728.

William Son of James & Jane Dudley born May ye 27. baptized June ye 9 1728.

Sarah daughter of Paul & Clement Phillpotts born July ye 5 baptized July 11 1728.

John Son of Michael & Anne Arrowy born July ye 4. baptized July ye 28 1728.

Jane daughter of John & Anne Good born July ye 14. baptized July ye 28 1728.

Margrett daughter of James & Jenney Daniel born July 5. baptized July ye 28 1728.

Ruth daughter of Edward & Mary Clark born July ye 29. baptized August ye 11 1728.

Sarah daughter of Joseph & Eliz^a Bohannan born August ye 5 baptized August ye 25 1728.

Anne daughter of Edwin & Elizabeth Thacker born August ye 3. baptized August ye 18 1728.

Mary daughter of John & Eliz^a Ellerson born August ye 13. baptized Septem^r 8. 1728.

Jane daughter of Henry & Frances Mickelburrough born August 19. baptized Septem^r 8. 1728.

William Son of Usebius & Mary Lewis born July ye 3. baptized August ye 18 1728.

Elizabeth daughter of Thomas & Penelope Mountague born Septem^r ye 10. baptized Septem^r 29. 1728.

Ruth daughter of John & Eliz^a Thurston born August ye 28. baptized Septem^r ye 29. 1728.

John Son of Samuel & Susanna Fleming born Septem^r ye 1 baptized Septem^r ye 22. 1728.

John Son of Joseph & Mary Hardee born September ye 27. baptized Octo ye 20. 1728.

Anne daughter of William & Judith Gardner born Octo. ye 10. baptized Novem^r 3. 1728.

Thomas Son of William & Anne Robinson born Octo. ye 7. baptized Novem^r 3 1728.

Bar. Yates Min^r.

Susanna daughter of John & Susanna Tomson born Octo. ye 21. baptized Novem^r ye 10 1728.

Thomas Son of Peter & Elizabeth Mountague born Octo. ye 28. baptized Novem^r ye 10 1728.

John Son of James & Margrett Ingram born Novem^r ye 13. baptized Novem^r 21 1728.

William an illegitimate Son of Susanna Williams born   baptized Novem^r 25 1728.

Mary daughter of John & Elizabeth Lewis born Novem^r ye 10 baptized Decem^r 1 1728.

Samuel Son of John & Elizabeth Dobbs born Novem^r ye 14. baptized Decem^r 1 1728.

Mary daughter of Matthew & Mary Kemp born Novem^r ye 25 baptized Decem^r 6 1728.

Betty daughter of George & Hannah Nevill born Decem^r ye 3. baptized Decem^r 14 1728.

Priscilla daughter of Jonathan & Priscilla Johnson born Novem^r ye 24 baptized Decem^r 15 1728.

Tabitha daughter of John & Catherine Tugell born Octo. ye 27. baptized Decem^r 22. 1728.

Elizabeth daughter of William & Catherine Southworth born Decem^r 5. baptized Decem^r 22. 1728.

Sarah daughter of Churchhill & Sarah Blakey born Novem^r 28. baptized Decem^r 22 1728.

John Son of Armistead & Hannah Churchhill born Decem^r ye 1 baptized Decem^r 23. 1728.

John Son of William & Elizabeth Long born Decem^r ye 1. baptized Decem^r ye 25. 1728.

Elizabeth daughter of Thomas & Rosamond Right born Decem^r ye 1 baptized Decem^r ye 29. 1728.

William Son of William & Mary Bennett born Decem^r ye 16. baptized Jan^ry ye 5 1728.

Mary daughter of William & Betty Wallis born Decem^r ye 15 baptized Jan^ry ye 12 1728.

Elizabeth daughter of Abraham & Mary Wharton born Decem^r ye 1. baptized Jan^ry ye 5 1728.

Elizabeth daughter of James & Edy Stiff born Jan^ry ye 14. baptized Jan^ry ye 26 1728.

Esther daughter of Richard & Jane Moulson born Jan^ry ye 2 baptized Jan^ry ye 30. 1728.

Mary daughter of Richard & Anne Greenwood born Jan^ry ye 5. baptized Feb^ry ye 2. 1728.

Michal daughter of Christopher & Hope Sutton born Jan^ry ye 11. baptized Feb^ry ye 16. 1728.

Edmund Son of Joshua & Martha Lewis born Jan^ry ye 20. baptized Feb^ry ye 16. 1728.

Mildred Orrill an illegitimate daughter of Averilla Hardee born Feb^ry 4. baptized Feb^ry 23. 1728.

Alexander Son of John & Mary Murray born Jan^ry ye 29. baptized March ye 2 1728.

Jacob Son of John & Anne Roads born Feb^ry ye 20. baptized March ye 5 1728.

Henry Son of Aquilla & Mary Snelling born Feb^ry 17 baptized March ye 9 1728.

John Son of John & Mary Rice born Feb^ry ye 23 baptized March ye 11 1728.

William Son of William & Frances Mansfeild born Feb^ry ye 11. baptized March ye 16. 1728.

Jane daughter of William & Jane Cardwell born Feb^ry ye 12. baptized March ye 16. 1728.

Henry Son of Henry & Mary Tugel born Feb'y ye 24. baptized March ye 16 1728.

William Son of William & Hannah Cain born Feb'y ye 10. baptized march ye 9. 1728.

Sarah daughter of Thomas & Ellis Faulkner born March ye 8. baptized March ye 24 1728.

Mildred daughter of Thomas & Mary Furgoson born March ye 8. 1728 baptized April ye 4. 1729.

John Son of Thomas & Hannah Lee born March ye 28. baptized ye Same day 1729.

William an illegitimate Son of Mary Pace born March ye 28 baptized April ye 6. 1729.

John Son of Thomas & Anne Berry born March ye 22d 1728 baptized April ye 20. 1729.

William & James Sons of John & Mary Guttery born April 19. baptized May ye 11. 1729.

Judith daughter of Oliver & Jane Segar born April ye 20th baptized May ye 11. 1729.

Dianah daughter of William & Elizabeth Wood born May ye 10. baptized May ye 18. 1729.

Anne daughter of Edward & Elizabeth Whittaker born May ye 18. baptized May 25. 1729.

Thomas Son of James & Agatha Jones born April ye 28. baptized June ye 1. 1729.

Catherine daughter of John & Sarah Carrell born May ye 9. baptized June ye 1. 1729.

Lucy daughter of Edmund & Mary Berkley born June ye 5. baptized June ye 10. 1729.

Frances daughter of John & Elizabeth Smith born May ye 20. baptized June ye 22. 1729.

Daniel Son of Ralph & Mary Shelton born May ye 17. baptized June ye 22. 1729.

Samuel Son of Thomas & Elizabeth Greenwood born May ye 25. baptized June ye 22. 1729.

Richard Son of John & Mary Green born June ye 7. baptized June ye 22. 1729.

James an illegitimate Son of Mary Hamilton born June ye 7. baptized June ye 22. 1729.

Catherine daughter of George & Agatha Twyman born June ye 13. baptized June ye 22. 1729.

Elizabeth daughter of John & Elizabeth Weston born June ye 19. baptized July 1. 1729.

Joseph Son of Joseph & Elizabeth Smith born June ye 4. baptized June ye 29. 1729.

Benjamine Son of James & Mary Meacham born June ye 17. baptized July ye 13. 1729.

John Son of Jeremiah & Elizabeth Earley born July ye 3. baptized July ye 17. 1729.

James Son of Hugh & Catherine Mactire born July ye 14. baptized July ye 20. 1729.

James & John Sons of John & Sarah Miller born July ye 10. baptized July ye 27. 1729.

Bar Yates Min^r

Rice Son of Rice & Martha Curtis born July ye 30. baptized August ye 3. 1729.

Benjamine Son of John & Catherine Williams born July ye 5 baptized August ye 3. 1729.

Oliver Son of William & Anne Segar born June ye 15. baptized August ye 3. 1729.

Agatha daughter of William & Anne Daniel born July ye 5. baptized August ye 10. 1729.

Mary daughter of Francis & Elizabeth Porter born July ye 24. baptized August ye 17 1729.

Joseph Son of William & Anne Anderson born July ye 26. baptized August ye 17 1729.

Joseph Son of William & Jennett Chowning born August ye 8. baptized August ye 24. 1729.

Thomas Son of Thomas & Anne Lee born August ye 23. baptized August ye 25. 1729.

Aggy daughter of Marvel & Mary Moseley born July ye 21. baptized August ye 24. 1729.

Thomas Son of John & Anne Fearn born August ye 29. baptized Septem^r ye 2. 1729.

John Son of Edward & Sarah Ball born July ye 29. baptized August ye 31. 1729.

William Son of William & Elizabeth Davies born August ye 9. baptized September ye 14. 1729.

Judith daughter of John & Jane Day born Septem^r ye 21. baptized Septem^r ye 23. 1729.

Benjamine & Mary Son & daughter of Thomas & Christian Sanders born Sept. ye 10. baptized Sept 28. 1729.

Daniel Son of James & Rebecca Heptenstall born Septem^r ye 14. baptized September ye 29 1729.

Moses Son of Richard & Mary Smither born August ye 2. baptized August ye 31 1729.

Bridgett daughter of Robert & Bridgett Wilkins born Septem^r ye 15 baptized Octo. 19. 1729.

Mary daughter of W^m & Elizabeth Crouders born September ye 26. baptized Octo. 26 1729.

John Son of William & Frances Thruston born Octo ye 6. baptized Octo. 26 1729.

Catherine daughter of Phillip & Elizabeth Brooks born Septem^r 3. baptized Octo. 26 1729.

William Son of William & Eleonar Harbinson born October ye 27. baptized Novem^r 1. 1729.

John Son of John & Johanna Blake born October ye 5. baptized October ye 19 1729.

Alexander Son of William & Susanna Saunders born Septem^r 19. baptized Octo. ye 19. 1729.

John Son of John & Anne Dudley born October ye 26. baptized Novem^r ye 9 1729.

Sarah daughter of John & Elizabeth Saunders born October ye 31. baptized Novem^r 9 1729.

Anne daughter of Henry & Sarah Putman born October ye 26. baptized Novem^r ye 9 1729.

William Son of Martin & Catherine Ferrell born Novem^r ye 6. baptized Novem^r 28. 1729.

Mary daughter of Joseph & Elizabeth Meacham born Novem^r ye 11. baptized Decem^r 7. 1729.

John Son of Zacharias & Mary Gibbs born Novem^r ye 17. baptized Decem^r 14. 1729.

Ellis daughter of Henry & Anne Jolly born Novem^r ye 28. baptized Decem^r 14. 1729.

William Son of Andrew & Elizabeth Davis born Octo ye 16. baptized Novem^r ye 9. 1729.

James Son of John & Rebecca Bradley born Decem^r ye 6. baptized Decem^r 21. 1729.

Edward Son of William & Elizabeth Blackburne born Novem^r 30. baptized Decem^r 21. 1729.

Thomas Son of Patrick & Ellionar Boswell born Decem^r ye 3. baptized Decem^r 21. 1729.

John Son of George & Anne Wortham born Decem^r ye 20. baptized Jan^{r}y 6. 1729.

Paul & Richard Sons of Paul & Jane Thilman born Jan^{r}y ye 17. baptized Jan^{r}y 21 1729.

Frances daughter of Henry & Frances Mickleburrough born Novem^r ye 30. baptized Decem^r 28. 1729.

Daniel Son of W^m & Margret Johnson born Jan^{r}y ye 11. baptized Jan^{r}y ye 21 1729.

Sarah daughter of John & Lucy Grymes born Jan^{r}y ye 29. baptized Feb^{r}y ye 6 1729.

Charles Son of Curtis & Anne Perrott born Jan^{r}y ye 22. baptized Feb^{r}y ye 8 1729.

William Son of William & Elizabeth Kidd born Decem^r ye 5. baptized Decem^r ye 28. 1729.

Robert Son of Robert & Anne George born Decem^r ye 15. baptized Decem^r ye 28. 1729.

Elizabeth daughter of James & Mary Bristow born Decem^r ye 18. baptized Feb^{r}y ye 8. 1729.

Harding Son of James & Margret Ingram born Decem^r ye 29. baptized Feb^{r}y ye 8. 1729.

Anne daughter of John & Catherine Chowning born Jan^{r}y ye 20. baptized Feb^{r}y ye 8. 1729.

Sarah daughter of Edwin & Elizabeth Thacker born Jan^{r}y ye 29. baptized Feb^{r}y ye 11 1729.

Jane daughter of Richard & Mary Allen born Jan^{r}y ye 7. baptized Feb^{r}y ye 8 1729.

William Son of Jacob & Elizabeth Stiff born Jan^{r}y ye 28. baptized Feb^{r}y ye 1. 1729.

Stapleton Son of William & Jane Crutchfeild born Feb^{r}y ye 14. baptized March 1. 1729.

Samuel Son of Robert & Elizabeth Daniel born Feb^{r}y ye 7. baptized March 1. 1729.

Margret daughter of Roger & Frances Linn born Feb^{r}y ye 9. baptized March 1. 1729.

Margret daughter of Henry & Mary Daniel born March ye 3. baptized March 22 1729.

Henry Son of John & Frances Heath born March ye 2. baptized
March 22 1729.

Jemima daughter of John & Rebecca Kidd born March ye 6. baptized March 22. 1729.

John Son of John & Isabell Jones born Feb^{r}y 26. 1729 baptized
March 29 1730.

Bar Yates. Min^r.

Daniel Son of Joseph & Anne Pace born Feb^{r}y ye 26. baptized
March ye 22 1729.

Caroline daughter of George & Amy Walker born March 13, 1729.
baptized April ye 3 1730.

Avarilla daughter of Joseph & Elizabeth Humphries born Jan^{r}y y^e
24. baptized Feb. 22 1729.

Mary daughter of William & Frances Guttery born March ye 26.
baptized April ye 3 1730.

Samuel Son of Nicholas & Mary Bristow born March ye 27 baptized
April ye 12 1730.

Elizabeth daughter of George & Martha Chowning born March y^e
20. 1729. baptized April ye 12. 1730.

John Son of Thomas & Elizabeth Marston born Ap: ye 3. baptized
April ye 26. 1730.

Thomas Son of Joseph & Mary Seares born Ap. ye 9. baptized May
ye 3 1730.

Williamson Son of John & Frances Bryant born April ye 21. baptized May ye 3. 1730.

Frances daughter of Stokeley & Anne Towles born May ye 8. baptized May ye 22 1730.

John Son of John & Mary Sadler born May ye 9. baptized May y^e
24 1730.

John Son of Richard & Sarah Wate born April ye 14 baptized May
ye 17 1730.

Dorothy daughter of Hugh & Anne Roach born May ye 14. baptized June ye 7 1730.

Catherine daughter of John & Anne Good born May ye 23 baptized
June ye 14 1730.

Elizabeth daughter of Robert & Anne Beverley born June 10. baptized June ye 13 1730.

William Son of Thomas & Penelope Mountague born June ye 14.
baptized June ye 23 1730.

Nathaniel Son of Armistead & Hannah Churchhill born June ye 16.
baptized July 8. 1730.

Mary daughter of John Elizabeth Weston born June ye 30. baptized
July 12 1730.

Elizabeth daughter of Charles & Johanna Curtis born June ye 30.
baptized July 24 1730.

Robert Son of George & Jane Goodwin born July ye 23. baptized
July ye 24. 1730.

Judith daughter of George & Elizabeth Guess born July 25. baptized
August ye 16 1730.

Margret daughter of Henry & Sarah Emerson born August 19.
baptized August 30. 1730.

Anna daughter of William & Frances Hill born July 25. baptized
August 30. 1730.

William Son of John & Elizabeth Humpheries born Septem^r y^n 1 baptized Septem 20. 1730.

Josias Son of John & Elizabeth Brim born Septem^r ye 7. baptized September 27. 1730.

Josiah Son of Hugh & Catherine Martin born Septem^r ye 9. baptized Octo. ye 18. 1730.

Judith daughter of Matthew & Mary Kemp born Octob^r ye 21. baptized Novem^r ye 4. 1730.

Elizabeth daughter of Aquilla & Margret Snelling born Octob^r ye 8. baptized Nov: 4. 1730.

John Son of Henry & Jochebed Nash born Octo: ye 19. baptized Novem^r ye 8. 1730.

Benjamine Son of John & Margret Southern born Octo: ye 29. baptized Novem^r ye 8. 1730.

John Son of John & Phebe Marston born October ye 13. baptized Novem^r 18 1730.

Sarah daughter of Jno & Mary Glen born October ye 30. baptized Novem^t 23. 1730.

Elizabeth daughter of William & Judith Baldwin born October 28. baptized Novem^r 29. 1730.

Elizabeth daughter of William & Elizabeth Wood born Novem^r ye 9. baptized Novem^r 29. 1730.

Jane daughter of John & Susanna Tomson born Novem^r ye 1. baptized Novem^r 29. 1730.

William Son of Joseph & Eliz^a Bohannan born Novem^r ye 19. baptized Novem^r ye 30. 1730.

William Son of Henry & Anne Barnet born Novem^r ye 6. baptized Decem^r ye 6 1730.

Christopher Son of William & Hannah Roads born Novem^r ye 25. baptized Decem^r ye 13. 1730.

Matthew Son of Usebius & Mary Lewis born Novem^r ye 23. baptized Decem^r ye 28. 1730.

Judith daughter of John & Anne Fearn born Decem^r ye 30. baptized Jan^{r}y ye 3. 1730.

William Son of James & Rebecca Heptinstall born Jan^{r}y ye 12 baptized Jan^{r}y ye 17 1730.

William Son of John & Agnes Bohannan born Jan^{r}y ye 3. baptized Jan^{r}y ye 17. 1730.

Edmund Son of Edmund & Mary Berkley born Decem^r ye 5. baptized Jan^{r}y 14. 1730.

James Son of Thomas & Mary Heath born Decem^r ye 1. baptized Jan^{r}y 10. 1730.

Mary daughter of Edward & Mary Clark born Decem^r ye 31. baptized Jan^{r}y 31. 1730.

John & William Sons of Oliver & Jane Segar born Jan^{r}y ye 17. baptized Jan^{r}y 19. 1730.

Chickeley Son of James & Jane Daniel born Jan^{r}y ye 16. baptized Jan^{r}y ye 31. 1730.

John Son of Eustace & Ruth Howard born Jan^{r}y ye 16. baptized Feb^{r}y ye 3. 1730.

Thomas Son of Thomas & Christian Saunders born Feb^{r}y ye 5. baptized March ye 7. 1730.

Susanna daughter of Richard & Susanna Curtis born Feb^{r}y ye 17. baptized March ye 7. 1730.

Elizabeth & Mary daughters of Thomas & Catherine Austin born March yᵉ 10. baptized yᵉ Same day 1730.

John Son of William & Betty Wallis born Janʳy yᵉ 8. baptized Febʳy yᵉ 21 1730.

Elizabeth daughter of Benjamine & Mary Pace born Janʳy yᵉ 17. baptized Febʳy yᵉ 21. 1730.

Anne daughter of Thomas & Mary French born Janʳy yᵉ 25. baptized Febʳy yᵉ 21. 1730.

Anne daughter of Michael & Anne Roan born Febʳy yᵉ 14. baptized Febʳy yᵉ 21. 1730.

Bar Yates Minʳ

Charles Son of John & Lucy Grymes born March yᵉ 11th baptized March yᵉ 18 1730.

Caroline daughter of John & Anne Smith born Febʳy yᵉ 17. baptized March yᵉ 21 1730.

Catherine Randal a Slave belonging to yᵉ estate of John Wormeley baptized March 21 1730.

John Son of John & Mary Goar born Febʳy yᵉ 2. baptized march yᵉ 14 1730.

Anna daughter of Marril & Mary Moseley born Febʳy yᵉ 19. baptized March yᵉ 14 1730.

Chicheley Corbin Son of Edwin & Elizᵃ Thacker born March yᵉ 17. 1730 baptized March 25 1731.

George Son of Henry & Mary Daniel born March yᵉ 17. 1730. baptized April yᵉ 4 1731.

George Son of George & Agatha Twyman born March yᵉ 29. baptized April yᵉ 4 1731.

Stanton Son of James & Jane Dudley born March yᵉ 17. 1730 baptized April yᵉ 25 1731.

John Son of George & Margret Best born April yᵉ 1. baptized April yᵉ 12 1731.

Mary daughter of Thomas & Anne Berry born April yᵉ 20. baptized May yᵉ 9 1731.

William Son of Abraham & Mary Wharton born April yᵉ 21. baptized May yᵉ 16 1731.

John Son of John & Sarah Carrel born Ap: yᵉ 10. baptized May yᵉ 2 1731.

John Son of William & Elizabeth Buford born Ap: yᵉ 2. baptized may yᵉ 2 1731.

Charles Son of Sampson & Elizabeth Darrill born May yᵉ 8. baptized May 30 1731.

Joseph Son of William & Mary Bennet born May yᵉ 2. baptized June yᵉ 6 1731.

Richard Son of Richard & Mabel Steevens born may yᵉ 3. baptized June yᵉ 6 1731.

Jonathan Son of Jonathan & Mary Brooks born May yᵉ 10. baptized June yᵉ 13 1731.

Hannah daughter of William & Hannah Cain born May yᵉ 8. baptized June yᵉ 6 1731.

Hannah daughter of William & Anne Robinson born May yᵉ 7. baptized June 20 1731.

Elizabeth daughter of Lunsford & Mary Lomax born June yᵉ 10. baptized July yᵉ 18 1731.

Reuben Son of John & Michal Williams born July ye 6. baptized July ye 15 1731.

Mary daughter of W^m & Rose Lewis born June ye 17. baptized August ye 1 1731.

William Son of Joseph & Elizabeth Smith born August ye 6. baptized August ye 8 1731.

James Son of Charles & Johanna Curtis born July ye 23. baptized August ye 14 1731.

Bartholomew Son of William & Jennet Chowning born July 2. baptized July 25 1731.

Garret Son of Edward & Agatha Southern born July ye 17. baptized July 25 1731.

Edmund Son of John & Rebecca Kidd born July ye 14. baptized August ye 15 1731.

Samuel Son of William & Margret Johnson born July ye 23. baptized August ye 15 1731.

Elizabeth daughter of Henry & Frances Mickleburrough born July ye 30. baptized August ye 15. 1731.

John Son of John & Elizabeth Smith born August ye 27. baptized Septr ye 5 1731.

Robert Son of Charles & Mary Carter born August ye 28. baptized Septem ye 6 1731.

Robert Son of William & Elizabeth Long born August ye 31. baptized Septem^r ye 12 1731.

William Son of Richard & Anne Jones born August ye 16. baptized September ye 19 1731.

Anna daughter of Francis & Elizabeth Porter born Septem^r ye 1. baptized Septem^r ye 19. 1731.

Jacob & Benjamine Sons of Samuel & Catharine Batchelder born Septr ye 29 bapti^d Sept 30. 1731.

Thomas Son of William & Jane Mountague born Sept. ye 9. baptized Octo^r ye 12 1731.

William Son of William & Frances Guttery born Sept. ye 7. baptized October ye 17 1731.

Mary daughter of Randolph & Sarah Rhodes born Augst 27. baptized Octob^r ye 17 1731.

Mary daughter of John & Elizabeth Pace born Septem^r 21. baptized October ye 17 1731.

Lettice daughter of Joseph & Anne Pace born Septem^r 26. baptized October ye 17 1731.

Thomas Son of Richard & Anne Greenwood born Octo. 27. baptized October ye 30 1731.

Robert Son of Robert & Elizabeth Wilkings born Septem^r ye 1. baptized October ye 10 1731.

Martha daughter of Hugh & Anne Roach born Septem^r ye 8. baptized October ye 10 1731.

Jane daughter of Hugh & Judith Stewart born Octo: ye 15. baptized October ye 31 1731.

John Son of Paul & Susanna Philpotts born Octo ye 21. baptized October ye 31 1731.

Elizabeth daughter of Henry & Anne Jolly born Octo: ye 13. baptized October ye 31 1731.

Henry Son of John & Catherine Tugel born Septem^r ye 27. baptized Novem^r ye 7. 1731.

William Son of John & Elizabeth Elerson born October ye 1. baptized November ye 7. 1731.

William Son of William & Frances Thurston born Octo: ye 24. baptized November ye 7. 1731.

James Son of John & Mary Rice born October ye 31. baptized Novem^r ye 28. 1731.

Henry Son of William & Hannah Churchhill born Novem^r ye 16. baptized Decem^r ye 2. 1731.

Elizabeth daughter of Edward & Elizabeth Whittacer born Novem^r ye 12. baptized Decem^r ye 5. 1731.

Jane daughter of Hezekiah & Anne Rhoades born Novem^r ye 11. baptized Decem^r 12 1731.

William Son of Henry & Sarah Nixon born Novem^r ye 28. baptized Decem^r 19. 1731.

Pleasant Son of Thomas & Betty Wakefield born Novem^r ye 23. baptized Decem^r 19. 1731.

Sarah daughter of Alexander & Lucy Lister born Jan^ry ye 9. baptized Jan^ry ye 11 1731.

Bar. Yates Min^r.

John Son of William & Anne Anderson born Decem^r ye 4. baptized Decem^r ye 12. 1731.

William Son of John & Anne Dudley born Decem^r ye 26. baptized Jan^ry ye 2 1731.

Judith daughter of Robert & Jane Dudley born Decem^r ye 26. baptized Jan^ry ye 24 1731.

Sarah daughter of William & Anne Daniel born Jan^ry ye 12. baptized Feb^ry ye 4. 1731.

William Son of William & Susanna Saunders born Jan^ry ye 12. baptized Feb^ry ye 13. 1731.

William Son of Churchhill & Sarah Blakey born Jan^ry ye 17. baptized Jan^ry ye 30. 1731.

William Son of Robert & Elizabeth Daniel born Jan^ry ye 22. baptized Jan^ry ye 30. 1731.

Agatha daughter of William & Jane Cardwell born Decem^r ye 12. baptized Jan^ry ye 30. 1731.

William Son of William & Mary Dawson born Jan^ry ye 29. baptized Feb^ry ye 3 1731.

Judith daughter of John & Johanna Blake born Feb^ry ye 6. baptized March ye 5 1731.

John Son of Thomas & Anne Lee born Feb^ry ye 26. baptized March ye 12 1731.

Richard Son of William & Anne Segar born Feb^ry ye 21. baptized March ye 12 1731.

William Son of William & Elizabeth Thurston born March 13. 1731. baptized April ye 2. 1732.

William Son of John & Anne Johnston born April ye 17. baptized May ye 7 1732.

Mary daughter of John & Michel George born April ye 21. baptized May ye 14. 1732.

Elizabeth daughter of William & Elizabeth Crowdas born April ye 22. baptized May ye 14. 1732.

Mary daughter of W^m & Jane Crutchfield born April ye 25. baptized June ye 4. 1732.

133

Martha daughter of Moses & Dorothy Kidd born May ye 7. baptized June ye 4. 1732.

Thomas Son of W^m & mary Southern born June ye 6. baptized June ye 25 1732.

Anne daughter of Samuel & Mary Sorry born May ye 29. baptized June 25. 1732.

Alexander Son of Jonathan & Priscilla Johnson born July ye 4. baptized July ye 9. 1732.

Avarilla daughter of Jacob & Eliz^a Stiff born June ye 11. baptized July ye 9 1732.

Charles Son of Ignatius & Mary Tureman born July ye 26. baptized July ye 27. 1732.

George Son of George & Amey Walker born July ye 13. baptized August ye 9 1732.

Catherine daughter of Thomas & Catherine Price born August ye 4. baptized August 27. 1732.

Esther daughter of Robert & Mary Daniel born August ye 5. baptized August 27 1732.

Josiah Son of John & Elizabeth Dobbs born August ye 17. baptized August ye 28 1732.

William Son of William & Mary Gayer born July ye 16. baptized August ye 20 1732.

James Son of Richard & Sarah Waight born August ye 23. baptized Septem^r ye 3. 1732.

Lucy daughter of Aquilla & Margret Snelling born August ye 21. baptized Septem^r ye 10. 1732.

Catherine daughter of Thomas & Penelope Mountague born August ye 4. baptized Septem^r ye 11. 1732.

James Son of Henry & Mary Tugle born August ye 20. baptized Septem^r ye 17. 1732.

William Son of William & Judith Baldwin born Aug^st ye 27. baptized Septem^r ye 17. 1732.

Catherine daughter of William & Elizabeth Wood born Septem^r ye 6. baptized Sept^t ye 17. 1732.

Daniel Son of Curtis & Anne Perrott born August ye 10. baptized September ye 17. 1732.

Elizabeth daughter of Sampson & Elizabeth Dorrell born Aug^st 23. baptized Septem. ye 24. 1732.

Mary daughter of John & Rebecca Bradley born Septem^r ye 11. baptized Octo. ye 1 1732.

Elizabeth daughter of John & Anne Chowning born August ye 25. baptized Septem^r ye 17. 1732.

Susanna daughter of John & Sarah Carrell born Septem^r ye 29. baptized Octo: ye 8. 1732.

Judith daughter of Robert & Elizabeth Johnson born Octo: ye 8. baptized Octo: ye 16. 1732.

Phillip Son of James & Rebecca Heptinstall born Octo: ye 15. baptized Octo: ye 22. 1732.

Edward Son of Edward & Sarah Ball born October ye 7. baptized Novem^r ye 5 1732.

William Son of Thomas Marston & Eliz^a his Wife born Octo: ye 1. baptized Octo^r ye 22. 1732.

John Son of James & Ann Gibson born Novem^r ye 3d baptized Novem^r ye 12 1732.

Charles Son of Charles & Mary Carter born Octo: ye 15. baptized
  Novem^r ye 15 1732.
Lettice daughter of William & Frances Guttery born Novem^r 17.
  baptized Nov. 26. 1732.
John Son of Thomas & Lucy Naish born Octo: ye 6. baptized De-
  cem^r ye 3. 1732.
Andrew Son of Andrew & Elizabeth Davis born Decem^r ye 30. bap-
  tized Jan^{r}y ye 14. 1732.
Nathaniel Son of Christopher & Hope Sutton born Decem^r ye 20.
  baptized Jan^{r}y ye 14. 1732.
Catherine daughter of Joseph & Mary Row born Decem^r ye 25.
  baptized Jan^{r}y ye 14. 1732.
George Son of Thomas & Christian Sanders born Jan^{r}y ye 11. baptized Jan^{r}y ye 14. 1732.
Susanna daughter of Thomas & Christian Sanders born Jan^{r}y ye 11.
  baptized Jan^{r}y ye 14. 1732.
Elizabeth daughter of Richard & Mary Hearn born Decem^r ye 29.
  baptized Jan^{r}y ye 14. 1732.

Bar Yates. Min^r.

Mary daughter of Eustace & Ruth Howard born Decem^r ye 25. bap-
  tized Feb^{r}y ye 7. 1732.
Thomas Son of Richard & Catherine Greenwood born Jan^{r}y ye 2.
  baptized Jan^{r}y ye 21 1732.
Samuel Son of John & Margrett Southern born Jan^{r}y ye 1. baptized
  Jan^{r}y ye 21 1732.
William an illegitimate Son of Mary Hardee born Decem^r ye 15.
  baptized Jan^{r}y ye 21. 1732.
John son of John & Susanna Tomson born Jan^{r}y ye 27. baptized
  Feb^{r}y ye 11 1732.
Anne an illegitimate daughter of Jane Tomson born   baptized
  Feb^{r}y ye 18 1732.
Lucy daughter of John & Anne Roades born Feb^{r}y ye 22 baptized
  Feb^{r}y ye 25 1732.
Ruth daughter of James & Jenny Daniel born Jan^{r}y ye 18. baptized
  Feb^{r}y ye 11 1732.
Hannah daughter of Nicholas & Mary Bristow born Jan^{r}y ye 9. bap-
  tized Feb^{r}y ye 11 1732.
Joseph Son of Benjamine & Mary Pace born Jan^{r}y ye 22. baptized
  Feb^{r}y ye 11 1732.
Sarah daughter of Charles & Mary Wood born Feb^{r}y ye 8. baptized
  March 4 1732.
James Son of Robert & Sarah Perrott born Jan^{r}y ye 25. baptized
  March ye 4 1732.
Mary daughter of George & Anne Wortham born Feb^{r}y ye 28. bap-
  tized March 6. 1732.
Thomas Son of John & Elizabeth Saunders born Jan^{r}y ye 25 bap-
  tized Feb^{r}y ye 4 1732.
Mary daughter of James & Jane Dudley born Feb^{r}y ye 16. baptized
  March ye 18. 1732.
Ruth daughter of John & Mary Murrah born Feb^{r}y ye 12. baptized
  March ye 11 1732.
Peter Son of Edward & Mary Clark born March ye 6. baptized March
  ye 23. 1732.

William Son of Marvel & Mary Moseley born March ye 29. baptized
April ye 8. 1733.
Avarilla daughter of James & Mary Bristow born March ye 13. 1732.
baptized April ye 8. 1733.
William Son of Thomas & Anne Berry born March ye 27. baptized
April ye 15 1733.
Ludwell Son of John & Lucy Grymes born April ye 26. baptized
May ye 6 1733.
Frances daughter of William & Betty Wallis born March ye 20. 1732
baptized April 29 1733.
Sarah daughter of James & Mary Meacham born March ye 29. bap-
tized April ye 29. 1733.
James Son of Michael & Anne Roan born April ye 1. baptized April
ye 29 1733.
Sarah daughter of Henry & Sarah Emerson born April ye 5. bap-
tized April ye 29. 1733.
Elizabeth daughter of John & Mary Sadler born April ye 15. bap-
tized April ye 29. 1733.
Jane daughter of William & Margrett Johnson born April ye 10.
baptized April ye 29 1733.
William Son of Michal & Anne Rudd born April ye 18. baptized
May ye 13 1733.
Jane daughter of James & Dianah Stuart born May ye 3. baptized
May ye 27. 1733.
Sarah daughter of John & Sarah Owen born May ye 1. baptized
May ye 27 1733.
Nelson Son of Edmund & Mary Berkeley born May ye 16. baptized
June ye 3 1733.
Benjamine Son of Richard & Mabell Steevens born May ye 17. bap-
tized June ye 3 1733.
Judith daughter of William & Jennet Chowning born April ye 22.
baptized May ye 20. 1733.
Thomas Son of William & Mary Gardner born May ye 15. baptized
May ye 20. 1733.
Reuben Son of Thomas & Mary Shelton born May ye 6. baptized
June ye 10. 1733.
Elizabeth daughter of Paul & Susanna Philpotts born May ye 24.
baptized May ye 27. 1733.
Mary daughter of John & Rebecca Arthur born May ye 6. baptized
June ye 17 1733.
William Son of John & Anne Lee born May ye 25. baptized June y^e
22 1733.
William & John Sons of Caleb & Margrett Brooks born June ye 27.
baptized June ye 27. 1733.
Sarah daughter of Usebius & Mary Lewis born May ye 28. baptized
July ye 1 1733.
Arthur Son of Henry & Jochebed Nash born June ye 29. baptized
July ye 22 1733.
Sarah daughter of John & Agniss Bohannan born July ye 17. bap-
tized July ye 29. 1733.
Anne daughter of John & Anne Fearn born July ye 9. baptized July
ye 25 1733.
Abraham Son of John & Elizabeth Pace born July ye 23. baptized
August ye 17 1733.

Margret daughter of Oliver & Jane Seagar born July ye 7th baptized August ye 12. 1733.

William Son of Thomas & Mary French born August 2. baptized August 23. 1733.

Antony a Slave belonging to Bar. Yates baptized Septem^r ye 2. 1733.

Jane daughter of Charles & Jane Daniel born August ye 18. baptized Septem^r ye 9. 1733.

Susanna daughter of Christopher & Elizabeth Owen born August ye 24. baptized Septem^r 12. 1733.

George Son of William & Anne Anderson born Septem^r ye 13. baptized Septem^r 16 1733.

Mary daughter of Henry & Rachel Perrott born August ye 18. baptized Septem^r ye 23. 1733.

Harry Wood a Slave belonging to Bar Yates baptized Septem^r ye 30. 1733.

Bar Yates. Min^r

John Son of John & Elizabeth Humphries born Septem^r ye 24. baptized Octo. ye 7. 1733.

Hannah Jackson a Slave belonging to Christopher Robinson baptized October ye 7. 1733.

Edmund Son of Henry & Frances Mickleburrough born Septem^r ye 21. baptized Octo: ye 14. 1733.

Frances daughter of James & Catherine Gardner born Augst ye 5. baptized August ye 12 1733.

Thomas Son of Thomas & Catherine Price born Octo: ye 13. baptized Novem^r ye 4. 1733.

Elizabeth daughter of Nicolas & Anne Mealer born Novem^r 7. baptiz'd Novem^r 18 1733.

Mary a Slave belonging to Christopher Robinson baptized Novem^r ye 18 1733.

Mayo Son of Jonathan & Mary Brooks born Septem^r ye 17. baptized Novem^r ye 25. 1733.

John Son of William & Elizabeth Kidd born Novem^r ye 3. baptized Novem^r ye 25. 1733.

Frances daughter of George & Martha Chowning born Novem^r ye 6. baptized Novem^r ye 25. 1733.

Armistead Son of Armistead & Hannah Churchhill born Novem^r ye 25. baptized Decem^r 14. 1733.

Penelope daughter of Jno & Elizabeth Bream born Novem^r ye 8. baptized Decem^r 16 1733.

Mary daughter of Patrick & Anne Knight born Decem^r ye 7. baptized Decem^r 30 1733.

Elizabeth & Mildred daughters of Jacob & Mary Faulkner born Dec: 14. baptized Dec. 30 1733.

Sarah daughter of Matthew & Mary Crank born Decem^r ye 8. baptized Decem: 23 1733.

Keziah daughter of Joseph & Elizabeth Smith born Decem^r ye 16. baptized Jan^{r}y ye 13 1733.

Benjamine Son of Aquilla & Margrett Snelling born Decem^r ye 22. baptized Decem^r 30 1733.

Nicholas Son of Anthony & Mary Anne Collins born Feb^{r}y ye 4. baptized Feb^{r}y ye 10 1733.

Robert Son of John & Jane Goodwin born Decem^r ye 30. baptized Jan^{r}y ye 27 1733.

Betty daughter of Richard & Catherine Greenwood born Jan^{r}y 15. baptized Jan^{r}y ye 27. 1733.

Mary daughter of Jno & Mary Henesey born Feb^{r}y ye 12. baptized Feb^{r}y ye 17 1733.

Mary daughter of George & Margrett Best born Jan^{r}y ye 20. baptized Feb^{r}y ye 17 1733.

John Son of Robert & Elizabeth Daniel born Feb^{r}y ye 17. baptized March ye 10 1733.

John Son of Edward & Agnes Southern born Feb^{r}y ye 13. baptized March ye 10 1733.

Mary daughter of Henry & Mary Daniel born Feb^{r}y ye 12. baptized March ye 10 1733.

John Son of William & Jane Mountague born Feb^{r}y ye 25. baptized March ye 10 1733.

Richard Son of William & Mary Bennet born Feb^{r}y ye 6. baptized March ye 3. 1733.

Anne daughter of William & Anne Robinson born Feb^{r}y ye 13. baptized March ye 3. 1733.

Benjamine Son of John Davis & Elizabeth his Wife born March ye 8. baptized March 24. 1733.

George Son of John & Judith Wortham born March ye 11. baptized March 24 1733.

John Son of John & Mary Crowdas born Feb^{r}y 15. 1733. baptized March ye 31 1734.

William a Slave belonging to Edwin Thacker baptized March ye 31 1734.

Richard Cooper a Slave belonging to Edwin Thacker baptized March ye 31 1734.

Jane a slave belonging to John Walker baptized March ye 31 1734.

Mary daughter of Anthony & Mary Betson born March 28. baptized Ap: ye 10. 1734.

Sarah daughter of William & Judith Baldwin born March ye 31. baptized Ap. 28. 1734.

Lucy daughter of Charles & Frances Grymes born April ye 26. baptized May ye 6 1734.

Priscilla daughter of John & Susannah Boss born April ye 14. baptized May 4 1734.

Elizabeth daughter of John & Sarah Carrill born April ye 26. baptized May ye 19. 1734.

Jemima daughter of Randolph & Sarah Rhodes born May ye 1. baptized May ye 19. 1734.

William Son of Thomas & Mary Shaw born May ye 3. baptized May ye 26 1734.

Thomas Son of John & Johanna Blake born May ye 4. baptized May ye 12. 1734.

Elizabeth daughter of John & Mary Rice born May ye 7. baptized June ye 9 1734.

Frances daughter of Phillip & Elizabeth Brooks born May ye 20. baptized June ye 9. 1734.

Benjamine Son of Jonathan & Priscilla Johnson born June ye 1. baptized June ye 23. 1734.

Robert Wormeley Son of Landon & Elizabeth Carter born June y^e
7. baptized June 27. 1734.
John Son of Charles & Mary Maderas born May ye 19. baptized
June ye 10 1734.
Sabrina a Slave belonging to Edwin Thacker baptized June ye 30 1734.

Bar Yates Min^r.

Sarah daughter of John & Catherine Walker born June ye 30. bap-
tized July ye 7th 1734.
Frances daughter of Edward & Martha Dillard born June ye 25. bap-
tized July ye 10. 1734.
William Son of John & Catherine Macheal born June ye 15. baptized
July ye 14. 1734.
William Son of Edward & Elizabeth Bristow born August 29 1734.
John Son of Jno & Mary Glen was born May 7th Baptiz'd June y^e
30th. 1734.
Benjamin Son of Jno & Michal Williams born June 24th Baptiz'd
June 30th 1734.
Elizabeth, Daughter of Charles & Elizth Fourget born June 23d.
Baptiz'd August 16th 1734.
John Son of Jno & Rebeckah Kid, born August 2d. Baptiz'd August
16 1734.
Thomas Son of Jno & Rachel Chowning born July 13th Baptiz'd
July 31st 1734.
Henry Son of William & Frances Thruston born July 22d. Baptiz'd
August 3d. 1734.
Sarah Daughter of Willm & Judith Owen, born August 3d Baptiz'd
Augst 3d. 1734.
Mary daughter of Henry & Sarah Brooks born Augst 10th Baptiz'd
Augst 16th. 1734.
William Son of James & Chatharine Brown, Born Septem^r 23d.
Baptiz'd Octr 13th 1734.
Susannah Daughter of Jno & Michal George Born Sep^t 30th Bap-
tiz'd Octr 13th 1734.
William Son of Willm & Elizth Wood, Born October 24th, Baptiz'd
November 12th 1734.
George Son of George & Jane Goodwin Born Oct. 12th Baptiz'd
Oct. 23d 1734.
Benjamin Son of   & Ann Jones Born Augst 25th 1734.
Paul Son of Paul & Susanna Phillpots born October 5th 1734.
John, Son of Abraham & Mary Wharton Born July 7th 1734.
Mical Daughter of Christopher & Ann Millar, Born Septr 19 1734.
Susannah, Daughter of Jno & Mary Berry, Born Octr 4th 1734.
Milecent, Daughter of Robt & Mary Daniel, Born Novr 18th Bap-
tizd Decr 15th 1734.
Sarah, Daughter of George & Jane Blackley, Born Nov: 28th Bap-
tiz'd Decr 15th 1734.
Ann, Daughter of Jno & Ann Dudley, Born Novr 4th Baptized Dec^r
1st 1734.
Rachel, Daughter of W^m and W^m and Ann Daniel born Nov. 9th
Baptiz'd Dec. 22nd 1734.
Frances Daughter of Curtis & Ann Parrott born Decr 6th Baptiz'd
Jan 5th 1734.

John Son of Robert & Mary Rogers born Decr 28th 1734.

Robert Son of John & Sarah Stamper born Decr 17th Baptiz'd Jan^ry 12th 1734.

Elizabeth, Daughter of W^m & Lucy Stapleton born Oct. 25th 1734.

Mary, Daughter of Jn° & Ann Johnston born Nov. 5th 1734.

Catherine Daughter of Jn° & Catherine Tuggle born Dec. 29. Baptiz'd Jan 26. 1734.

Lewis Son of Robt & Jane Dudley born Jan^ry 27th Baptiz'd Feb^ry 15th 1734.

Valentine Son of James & Ruth Mayo. born Feb^ry 2d Baptized Feb. 16th 1734.

William Son of W^m & Mary Southern born Decr 22d Baptiz'd Jan^ry 26th 1734.

Susanna Daughter of Churchhill and Sarah Blakey born Jan^ry 13th Baptiz'd Feb. 16 1734.

Mary Daughter of Andrew & Constant Hardee, born Jan^ry 19th Baptiz'd Jan: 26. 1734.

Abraham Son of James & Jane Daniel born Jan^ry 13th Baptiz'd Feb. 16th 1734.

Mary Daughter of Benjamine & Mary Pace born Jan^ry 20th Baptiz'd Feb. 16th 1734.

George a Slave belonging to Mrs Yates was Baptiz'd Feb^ry 16th 1734.

Elizabeth Daughter of James & Rebecka Hiptinstall born Ja^rn^y 26th Baptiz'd Feb. 23rd 1734.

Peter Son of Charles & Jane Daniel Born January 30th Baptiz'd Feb: 23d 1734.

William Son of John & Sarah Owen Born January 25th Baptiz'd Fcb. 23d 1734.

———— a Slave belonging to Mrs Wormley   Baptiz'd Feb. 23d 1734.

Jn° Reade Min^r

Rebecka Daughter of Hugh & Ann Rouch Born Novem^r 25th 1734.

Susanna Daughter of William &   Goare Born feb. 2d Bapt. March 2d 1734.

Jeremiah Son of Robt & Eliz: Wilkins born Dec. 11th 1734.

Elizabeth Elizabeth Kate Sarah William Slaves belonging to Maj^r Edm^d Berkley, Baptiz'd March 2d 1734.

Joyce a Slave Belonging to Lewis Berkley Baptiz'd March 2d 1734.

Lucy Daughter of Christopher & Mary Robinson born Feb: 27th Baptiz'd March 5th 1734.

Lodowick Son of Robert & Sarah Parrott born Jan^ry 26th Baptiz'd feb^ry 16 1734.

James Son of W^m & Hannah Rhodes born Feb. 1st Baptiz'd March 2d 1734.

William Son of Crispin & Lettitia Shelton, born March 4th Bap. March 30th 1735.

Avarilla Daughter of W^m & Margrett Johnston born Mar. 7th Bap. March 30th 1735.

Barbee Son of Andrew & Elizabeth Davis born Feb: 2d Baptiz'd March 2 1734.

Charles Son of Charles & Mary Wood born March 24th Baptiz'd Ap: 20th 1735.

Ann daughter of Rich^d & Eliz^th George born March 18th Baptiz'd
Ap: 20th 1735.
John Son of Edmund & Mary Day born March 10th Baptiz'd Ap:
13th 1735.
Judith Daughter of Stokely & Ann Towles born Ap 13. Baptized
May 11th 1735.
Ann Daughter of Willm & Mary Gardiner born Ap: 8th Baptizd
May 11th 1735.
Elizabeth Daughter of Willm & Hannah Pace born Ap. 18th Bap-
tiz'd May 11th 1735.
John Son of Ignatius & Mary Tureman, born May 16th Baptiz'd
June 1st 1735.
Samuel Son of Samuel & Mary Sorrow born May 5th Baptiz'd June
1th 1735.
Edmond Son of Thos & Sarah Laughlin born June 21st Baptiz'd
June 29th 1735.
Edward Son of Michael & Ann Reed born May 15th Baptiz'd June
8th 1735.
Benjamin Son of Jno & Elizabeth Thruston born June 4th Baptiz'd
July 13th 1735.
William Son of Jno & Mary Lawsoe born May 21 1735.
William Son of Thos & Lucretia Sanders born June 15th Baptiz'd
July 27th 1735.
Andrew Son of W^m & Ann Anderson of Petsworth parish born July
4th Baptiz'd July 27th 1735.
Henry Son of Henry & Jone Snow born May 5th Baptiz'd May 25th
1735.
Elizabeth Daughter of Edward & Mary Clark born Aug^st 22d Bap-
tiz'd Aug^st 31 1735.
Elizabeth Daughter of Caless & Marg^tt Brooks born Aug^st 10th Bap-
tized August 31 1735.
James Son of John & Judith Wortham born Aug^st 23d 1735.
John Son of W^m & Frances Guttery born July 25th Baptiz'd Aug^st
24th 1735.
Rachel Daughter of Phillip & Eliz^th Brooks born July 26th Baptiz'd
Aug^st 24th 1735.
Ann, Daughter of Duel & Judith Thurston born July 31. Baptiz'd
Aug^st 24th 1735.
Charles Son of Thos & Ann Lee Born Aug^st 10th Baptiz'd Aug^st
24 1735.
Henry Son of Rich^d & Catherine Greenwood born Aug^st 12th Bap-
tiz'd Aug^st 24th 1735.
Thomas, Son of John & Amy Burck born Aug^st 11th Baptiz'd Sep^t
14th 1735.
Margarett, Daughter of Jno & Margaret Southern Born Aug^st 18th
Baptized Sep^t 14th 1735.
Jean, Daughter of James & Jean Dudley, Born July 10th 1735.
Oliver, Son of Willm & Eliz. Willis born Septr 2d Baptiz'd Octr 5th
1735.
Henry, Son of Henry & Frances Mickleburrough born Septr 9th
Baptiz'd Oct. 5th 1735.
James Son of Thomas & Ann Berry born Septr 25th baptiz'd Oct^r
5th 1735.

John Son of W^m & Judith Owen born Octr 6th Baptiz'd Novr 13th 1735.

Ann, Daughter of Nicholas & Ann Meuler born Sept. 6th 1735.

Lewis, Son of Richard & Mabell Steevens born Sep^t 27th Baptiz'd Novr 9th 1735.

Leonard Son of Thos & Margrett Dawson born Octr 24th Baptiz'd Novr 2 1735.

Sarah, Daughter of Jno & Susanna Thomson born Novr 13th Baptiz'd Decr 7th 1735.

Mary Daughter of Willm & Jane Watts was born Sepr 14th Baptiz'd Novr 16th 1735.

J. Reade Min^r.

Peter Rebeccah Alice Clara Slaves belonging to Christopher Robinson Baptiz'd Decr 26th 1735.

Sarah daughter of Jno & Johanna Blake born Novr 30th Baptiz'd Decr 21st 1735.

Eustace Son of Eustace & Ruth Howard born Decr 26th Baptiz'd Jan^ry 25th 1735.

Joseph Son of W^m & Judith Baldwin born Decr 21st Baptiz'd Jan^ry 18th 1735.

Sarah daughter of Henry & Rachel Parrett born Dec. 6th 1735.

Martha daughter of George & Martha Chowning born Jan^ry 17th 1735.

Penelope daughter of Jno & Eliz^th Brame born Novr 30th Baptiz'd Decr 28th 1735.

Thomas, Son of Henry & Frances Bueford born Novr 22d 1735.

Sarah, daughter of Jno & Ann Fearn born Jan^ry 28th Baptiz'd Feb. 1st 1735.

John, Son of Willm & Ann Yarrington born Feb. 22d 1735.

Thomas, Son of Thomas & Mary French born Jany 10th Baptiz'd Feb: 8th 1735.

William, Son of George & Eliz^th Gest born Jan^ry 11. Baptiz'd Feb. 8th 1735.

Thomas, illegitimate Son of Mercy Hornsby a Servt to James Crosbee born Feb: 14. Baptiz'd Feb 22nd 1735.

Thomas Son of Jno & Lucretia Greenwood, born Feb. 13. baptiz'd Feby 29th 1735.

Leonard, Son of Thos & Catherine Price born March 20th baptiz'd March 28th 1735.

Elizabeth, Daughter of Benjamine & Judith Davis born January 4th, baptiz'd 1735.

Ann Daughter of Geo. & Ann Wortham born Decr 22. Baptiz'd 1735.

Sarah Daughter of Grigg & Eliz^th Yarbrough born Feb. 20th Baptiz'd March 21 1735.

Jane, Daughter of Jno & Jane Goodwin born Feb. 27. Baptiz'd March 21 1735.

John Son of Patrick & Eliz^th Calliham born Jan^ry 1st. Baptiz'd March 21 1735.

Jane, Daughter of Willm & Frances Thurston born Feb. 20th Baptiz'd March 21 1735.

Elizabeth, Daughter of Daniel & Mary Moor, born March 21. Baptiz'd April 11 1736.

<table>
<tr><td rowspan="4">Given into the S. O. Ap 1736</td><td>Nicholas, Son of John & Catherine Tuggle born March 9th Baptiz'd april 11 1736.</td></tr>
</table>

Given into the S. O. Ap 1736 {
Nicholas, Son of John & Catherine Tuggle born March 9th Baptiz'd april 11 1736.
Philip, Son of Thomas & Penelope Mountague born April 13th Baptiz'd Ap: 15 1736.
Willm Son of Henry a Slave belonging to Jn° Grimes Baptiz'd Ap: 25 1736.

Sarah, Daughter of Chloe a Slave belonging to Jn° Grymes, Baptiz'd Ap: 25 1736.

Elizabeth, Daughter of Jn° & Elizth Humphries born Feb. 3d. Baptiz'd Feb. 22 1736.

Benjamine, Son of Randal & Sarah Rhodes born Ap: 8th Baptiz'd May 9th 1736.

Hester, Daughter of George & Jane Blackey, born Ap^l 6th. Baptiz'd May 9th 1736.

Judith, Daughter of Christopher & Mary Robinson born June 2. Baptiz'd June 10th 1736.

Ann, Daughter of Joseph & Elizth Smith born May 19th, Baptiz'd May 27th 1736.

Benjamine, Son of W^m & Ann Robinson born May 21st 1736.

George, Son of Samuel & Elizth Major born June 13th Baptiz'd July 11th 1736.

Paul Son of Henry & Sarah Brookes born June 14th Baptiz'd July 11th 1736.

Thomas, Son of John & Mary Hennesey, born July 9th. Baptiz'd July 11th 1736.

Betty, Daughter of William & Elizth Kidd, born June 5th Baptiz'd July 11th 1736.

William, Son of Charles & Judith Gunter, born Augst 5th Baptiz'd Augst 22d 1736.

Joseph, Son of Jn° & Elizth White, born July 18th Baptiz'd Augst 22nd 1736.

Jane, Daughter of James & Mary Bristow, born July 22d Baptiz'd Augst 1st 1736.

Judith, Daughter of Jn° & Ann Robinson born Sept. 8th Baptiz'd Sept. 14th 1736.

Henry Son of John & Mary Goare, born Sept. 10th Baptiz'd Sept. 26 1736.

Given into ye Secret: off Octr 1736 {
Christopher, Son of Robt & Eliz. Daniel, born Sept. 27. Baptiz'd Octo^r 8th 1736.
Oliver, Son of Jn° & Margrett Towles, born Sept. 1st. Baptiz'd 1736.
Sarah, Daughter of Jn° & Elizth Blake born Sept. 7th 1736.

Mary, Daughter of Edwd & Martha Dillard born Sept: 28th. Baptiz'd Oct. 24, 1736.

Susanna, Daughter of Jn° & Elizth Davis born Oct. 17th Baptiz'd Oct. 30th 1736.

Ruth, Daughter of Robt & Betty Chowning, born Octr 9th Baptiz'd Oct: 21. 1736.

Willm Son of W^m & Mary Mullins born Octr 8th. Baptiz'd Novr 14th 1736.

Susanna, Daughter of Rich^d & Elizth George born Octr 28th. Baptiz'd Nov. 14th 1736.

Frances, Daughter of Christopher & Mary Ammon born Octr 28th Baptiz'd Nov^o 14th 1736.

Charles Thomas, a Slave belonging to Sarah Yates, Baptiz'd Novr 21 1736.

Lettice a Slave belonging to Sarah Yates Baptiz'd Novr 21 1736.

John Son of James & Martha Mayo born 9^{br} 14th & bapt. 9^{br} 14th 1736.

Hannah daughter of William & Elizabeth Backford born 9^{br} 9th & bapt. 10^{br} 10th 1736.

Henry Son of Joseph & Mary Tuggle born 9^{ber} 20th & bapt 10^{br} 10th.

Anny ye daughter of John Rachel Chowning born 10^{ber} 10th & bapt. 10^{ber} 26th 1736.

Mary ye daughter of Charles & Mary Wood born born Jan 2d & bapt Feb. 4th 1736.

Benjamin ye Son of Robert & Mary Daniel born January 4th 1736.

Edwin ye Son of Daniel & Mary Basket born 10^{ber} 27th & bapt. Feb. 4th 1736.

Mary ye daughter of William & Elizabeth Wood born Jan. 29th bapt. 4th Feb. 1736.

Ruth ye daughter of Richard & Catharin Bushrod Wood born Jan. 2d & bapt. Feb. 11th 1736.

William ye Son of William & Mary Fretwell born January 31th 1736.

Thomas ye Son of Phillip & Cassandra Warwick born January 27th 1736.

James ye Son of Duel & Mary Kidd born Feb 10th & bapt. March 4th 1736.

Molly ye daughter of Ann Whistler a mulatto born 10^{ber} 18th 1736.

Catherine ye daughter of Robert & Sarah Parrott born March 2?th & bapt. April 17th 1737.

Jane ye daughter of William & Jane Mountague born April 4th 1737.

Elizabeth daughter of Paul & Susanna Phillpots born May ye 27th 1737.

John ye Son of John & Sarah Stamper born April 14th & bapt. May 6th 1737.

Sarah ye daughter of William & Sarah Williams born May 5th & bapt. May 27th 1737.

George ye Son of Benjamine & Judith Kidd born May 3d & bapt. May 27th 1737.

William ye Son of Henry & Jochebed Nash born May 1st & bapt. May 27th 1736.

Edward ye Son of Robert & Elizabeth Bristow born August 13th 1736.

Martha ye daughter of Abraham & Elizabeth Wilson born Feb. 6th 1736.

Machen ye Son of John & Judith Wortham born February 25th 1736.

Charles ye Son of Charles & Jane Daniel was born Marth 2d 1736.

John ye Son of John & Mary Lawson was born March 4th 1736.

Mary ye daughter of William & Lucy Goar was born Feb: 1st 1736.

Judith daughter of Hugh & Ann Roach was born 9^{ber} 29th 1736.
Elizabeth daughter of John & Susannah Curtis was born March 18th
1736.
John ye Son of Christopher & Ann Miller was born Feb. 14th 1736.
Ann ye daughter of Aquilla & Margaret Snelling was born March
14th 1736.
Thomas & William twin Sons of Thomas & Hannah Lawson was
born January 17th 1736.
Ann ye daughter of Edmund & Mary Day was born 10^{ber} 26th 1736.
Lewis ye Son of William & Elizabeth Hackney was born Feb. 4th
1736.
George ye Son of David & Diana Barrick was born March 4th 1736.
James ye Son of John & Ann Johnson was born March 28th 1737.
John ye Son of Benjamin & Judith Davis was born April 2d 1737.
Alford ye Son of John & Sarah Boss was born Jan. 1st & bapt. June
3rd 1737.
Mary ye daughter of John & Ann Dudley was born July 4th & bapt.
July 31th 1737.
Ann ye daughter of John & Mary Matthews was born July 15th
1737.
Clara daughter of John & Catherine Walker was born 7^{ber} 7th &
bapt 7^{ber} 9th 1737.
Charles ye Son of Charles & Mary Madarius was born May 9th &
bapt. July 8th 1737.
Isaac ye Son of Peter & Elizabeth Hendson was born June 4th &
bapt. July 8th 1737.
James ye Son of James & Catharine Brown was born June 13th &
bapt. June 18th 1737.

Unto y^e
Secret:
Office
1737.

Joseph ye Son of Andrew & Constance Hardee was born
June 27th & bapt. July 8th 1737.
Agatha ye daughter of John & Agatha Hardee was born
June 30th & bapt. July 8th 1737.
Griffin ye Son of John & Catherine Tuggle was born Au-
gust 5th & bapt. August 28th 1737.
John ye Son of John & Michal George was born August
14th & bapt. August 25th 1737.
Ann ye daughter of Benjamin & Mary Pace was born Au-
gust 20th & bapt 25th 1737.
John ye Son of Caleb & Margaret Brooks was born 7^{ber}
2d & bapt: 7^{ber} 9th 1738.

Elizabeth Daughter of Ralph & Sarah Wormley born Sepr ye 3d
bapt ye 18th 1737.
Ann Daughter of Thomas & Christian Sanders born ye 25th of Sep^r
Baptized Novr ye 6th 1737.
Jane Daughter of William & Frances Thurston born ye 30th of Sep^r
Baptized Octo^r ye 23rd 1737.
Ratlif Son of Richard & Michal Jowel born ye 23d of Sepr 1737.
Ann Daughter of William & Ann Daniel born ye 18 of Octo^r Bap-
tized Novr ye 20th 1737.
Sarah Daughter of Richard   Wright born ye 9th of Sepr 1737.
Frances Daughter of William & Frances Guthery born ye 21st of
Sepr Baptized Octo^r ye 2d 1737.

James Son of Henry & Susanna Mickleburrough born yᵉ 18th of Octoʳ
Ruth Daughter of Richard & Catharine Street
born yᵉ 26th of Octoʳ
William Son of William & Judith Owen born
yᵉ 4th of Novʳ

⎫ Bap. Nov. 13th 1737.

Griffin Son of Grigg & Elizabeth Yarbrough born yᵉ 28th of Novʳ
Baptized Dec. 4th 1737.
Ann Daughter of Thoʳ & Mary Shaw born yᵉ 10th of March 1736.
James Son of Hugh & Elizabeth Martin born yᵉ 12th Janʳ 1736.
Frances Daughter of John & Ann Willcock born yᵉ 11. of March
1736.
John Son of Joseph & Mary Rowe born yᵉ 5th of Decemʳ 1735.
George Son of Andrew & Elizabeth Davis born yᵉ 7th of March
1737.
Francis Son of Richᵈ & Mabell Steevens born yᵉ 1st of Augˢᵗ 1737.
John Son of John & Ann Humphris born yᵉ 11th of Decemʳ 1737.
Richard Son of John & Mary Steevens born yᵉ 6th of Decemʳ 1737.
Humphry Son of Robert & Mary Rogers born yᵉ 28th Nov. 1737.
Richard Son of Arthur & Jane Dye born yᵉ 5th of Decemʳ baptized
yᵉ 5th of Febʸ 1737.
Elizabeth Daughter of Henry & Rachel George born Decemʳ yᵉ 8th
baptized Janʳy yᵉ 8th 1737.
Anny Daughter of William & Ann Yarrington born Janʳy yᵉ 11th
baptized Janʳy yᵉ 29th 173⅞.
Jane Daughter of William & Margaret Johnston born Janʳy yᵉ 21st
bapᵈ yᵉ 22 Died yᵉ 22. 173⅞.
Mary Daughter of Edmund & Mary Berkeley born Janʳy yᵉ 15th
baptized Janʳy yᵉ 30th 173⅞.
Ann Daughter of Robert & Mary Williams born Janʳy yᵒ 21st bap-
tized Febʳy yᵉ 19th 173⅞.
Lucy Daughter of Armistead & Hannah Churchhill born Janʳy yᵉ
17th baptized Febʳy yᵉ 8th 173⅞.
Robert Son of George & Jane Blackley born Janʳy yᵉ 29th baptized
Febʳy yᵉ 19th 173⅞.
John Son of Thomas & Catherine Price born Febʳy yᵉ 26th baptized
March yᵒ 22nd 173⅞.
John Son of John & Elizabeth Blake born Febʳy yᵉ 21st baptized
March yᵉ 19th 173⅞.
Charles Son of John & Ann Ginkins born Febʳy yᵉ 28th baptized
March yᵉ 26 1738.
Mary Daughter of Thomas & Mary Shelton bern Febʳy yᵉ 21st 173⅞.
William Son of Richard & Dorrity Gaines born March yᵉ 3d bap-
tized March yᵉ 19th 173⅞.
Christopher Son of Christopher & Mary Robinson born March yᵉ
9th bapᵉ March yᵉ 20th 173⅞.
Richard Son of Samˡ & Elizabeth Major born March yᵉ 24th bap-
tized April yᵉ 2d 1738.
Thomas Son of John & Ann Price born March yᵉ 13. baptized April
yᵉ 2d 1738.
Diana Daughter of John & Mary Crowdas born Febʳy yᵉ 25th bap-
tized April yᵉ 2 1738.

Tholomiah Son of Randal & Mary Rhodes born March y^e 15th baptized y^e 2d 1738.

Christopher Son of John & Anne Robinson born April y^e 2d baptized April y^e 10th 1738.

Judith Daughter of Edward & Mary Clark born March y^e 30th baptized April y^e 9th 1738.

William Son of Thos & Sarah Tignor born March y^e 9th baptized 173$\frac{7}{8}$.

Jane Daughter of Henry & Jone Snow born March y^e 10th 1738.

William Son of William & Patience Colley born March y^e 11th 1738.

James Son of John & Rebeckah Kidd born March y^e 30th baptized April y^e 23d 1738.

Josiah Son of William & Elizabeth Wallis born March y^e 31st baptized April y^e 23d 1738.

James Son of William & Mary Gardiner born April ye 27th baptized June ye 4th 1738.

Henry Son of Richard & Elizabeth Allin born May ye 28th baptized June ye 4th 1738.

Abraham Son of John & Agatha Warwick born May ye 19th baptized June ye 4th 1738.

Ruthe Daughter of Edmund & Martha Ditton born May ye 30th baptized June ye 18th. 1738.

Frances Daughter of George & Mary Guest born Jane ye 5th. baptized June 26th 1738.

Catherine Daughter of Churchhill & Sarah Blakey born July ye 2d. baptized July ye 16. 1738.

James Son of James & Martha Mayo born Augst 16th. baptized Augst ye 27th 1738.

Johannah Daughter of Thos & Keziah Maxwell born Augst ye 29th. bap^d Sepr ye 10th 1738.

Henry Son of John & Ann Hutson born Augst ye 13th baptized Sepr ye 17th 1738.

Richard Son of John & Susannah Tomson born Sepr ye 9th baptized Sepr ye 17th. 1738.

Nathan Son of David & Elizabeth Snodgrass born April 28th 1738.

Hezekiah Son of W^m & Hannah Rhods born June ye 8th. baptized July 9th 1738.

Daniel Son of Seth & Mary Hunter born Sepr ye 22. baptized 1738.

Sarah, Daughter of W^m & anne Robinson born ye Octo^r 27th. 1738.

Benjamin Son of Joseph & Elizabeth Smith born 25th Octr 1738.

Benjamin Son of John & Mary Rhodes born March 18th. 1738.

Thomas Son of W^m & Ann Segar born Augst ye 27. baptized Octo^r ye 8 1738.

Catherine Daughter of Thomas & Mary Trench born Sepr ye 15th. bap^d Octo^r 29. 1738.

Susana Daughter of Robt & mary Trueman born 8^{br} ye 15th. bap^d Octo^r 29 1738.

Ann Daughter of Patrick & Elizabeth Caleham born Octo^r ye 2d bap^d Octo^r 19. 1738.

Mary Daughter of Alexander & Anna Snelling born Octo^r 25th 1738.

Elizabeth Daughter of William & Mary Mullins born July 15th. bap^d Augst 6. 1738.

John Son of Hugh & Elizabeth Martin born July ye 10th. bap^d Augst 6. 1738.

Margaret Daughter Benjamin & Judith Davis born Octr 27th. 1738.

Robert Howrd born Novem^r 15th 1738.

Ann Daughter of Thos & Elizabeth Eliot born Octr 25th. Bap^d Novr 19th 1738.

Elizabeth Camel daughter of Elizabeth Ammon born Octr ye 2d. bap^d Novr 19th. 1738.

John Son of Augustine & Mary Owen born Novem^r ye 20th bap^d Decem^r 31th. 1738.

Edward Son of John & Judith Wortham born Novr ye 29th. 1738.

Cuffly Son of Henry & Sarah Brooks born Novr ye 22. bap^d Decr 11th 1738.

Agatha Daughter of Ave Daniel born Decem^r ye 22. bap^d Jan^{ry} ye 25th 173 8/9.

William Son of John & Mary Brooks born Novr ye 26th. 1738.

Mary Daughter of Edmund & Mary Day born Decr 8th. bap^d Decr ye 25th 1738.

Mary Daughter of William & Rachel Griffin born Decr 12th Bap^d Jan^{ry} 21th 1738.

Sarah Daughter of John & Agatha Hardee born Decr ye 6th bap^d Jan^{ry} 5th. 173 8/9.

Averilla Daughter of John & Margaret Southern born Decr 25th. bap^d Jan^{ry} 21th 173 8/9.

Catherine Daughter of Thos & Penelope Mountague born Decr 19th. bap^d Jan^{ry} 9th 173 8/9.

George Son of Philip & Casandra Warwick born Decr ye 13th. bap^d Jan^{ry} 9th 173 8/9.

Marlow Son of Robert & Jane Dudley born Novr ye 20th. bap^d Jan^{ry} 1st. 173 8/9.

Richard Son of Edward & Elizabeth Bristow born Jan^{ry} 7th bap^d Jan^{ry} 28. 173 8/9.

Lucy daughter of Armistead & Hannah Churchhill born Jan^{ry} 17th bap^d Feb. 8. 173 8/9.

Elizabeth daughter of Charles & Mary Wood born Feb^{ry} 15. bap^d March 4th. 173 8/9.

Garret Son of Robert & Elizabeth Daniel born Jan^{ry} 20th bap^d Feb^{ry} 19th. 173 8/9.

John Son of William & Mary Fretwel born Feb^{ry} 16th. bap^d March 4th 173 8/9.

Sarah Daughter of Thos & Ann Lee born Feb^{ry} 27th. bap^d March 4th. 173 8/9.

Powell Son of John & Sarah Stamper born March 20th bap^d April 25th 173 8/9.

Mary Daughter of Andrew & Elizabeth Davis born 11th of Feb^{ry} 173 8/9.

Elizabeth Daughter of Charles & Penelope Lee born Feb^{ry} ye 12th. bap^d March 4th 173 8/9.

Elizabeth daughter of Harry & Jane Sears born Jan^{ry} 8th bap^d April 15th 1739.

John Son of John & Elizabeth Davis born Feb^{ry} 26th bap^d 18th March 173 8/9.

Frances Daughter of Russel & Anne Hill born Feb^{ry} 25th bap
1738.

John Son of John & Mary Henesey born March 12th bap^d March
25th 1739.

William Son of George & Sarah Halcomb born March 27th 1739.

Charles Son of Robert & Betty Chowning born March 10th bap^d
March 25th 1739.

John Son of Edward & Martha Dillard born March 30th bap'd May
5th 1739.

Sarah Daughter of John & Ann Johnson born April ye 21st 1739.

John Son of John & Rachel Chowning born April ye 1st bap^d April
15th 1739.

Leonard Son of Honnor Renand born April 30th 1739.

Henry Son of William & Elizabeth Beuford born April 17th bap^d
May 6th 1739.

William Son of James & Elizabeth Dunlevy born April 29th 1739.

Elizabeth Daughter of Thos & Catherine Cheaney born May ye 1st
bap^d May 4th 1739.

John Son of James & Isabel Gibson born May ye 11th 1739.

Benjamin Son of William & Margaret Johnson born May 3d bap^d
May 27th 1739.

Catherine & Elizabeth Daughters of W^m & Jane Mountague born
May 24th 1739.

Margaret Daughter of Duel & Mary Kid born May 16th bap^d June
17th 1739.

Samuel Son of James & Catherine Brown born May 28th bap^d June
17th 1739.

James Son of Charles & Jane Daniell born June 15th 1739.

Lucy Daughter of Patrick & Ann Knight born May 28th bap^d July
22d 1739.

Rhoda Daughter of Andrew & Constant Hardee born July 9th bap^d
July 29th 1739.

Thomas Son of John & Ann Fearn born July ye 16th 1739.

Joseph Son of Joseph & Mary Tugle born July ye 2d bap^d July y^e
29th 1739.

Samuel Son of William & Elizabeth Wood born July ye 24th, bap^d
Augst ye 19th 1739.

James Son of James & Elizabeth Scrosby born Augst ye 13th bap^d
Sepr ye 5th 1739.

James Son of Mary Ratford born Augst ye 13th 1739.

John Son of John & Susana Serd born Sepr ye 4th bap^d Sepr ye 9th
1739.

Lucy Daughter of John & Johanne Blakes born March 25th bap^d
April 29th 1739.

John Son of John & Mary Matthews born Septr ye 19th 1739.

Benjamine Son of Paul & Margerret Phillpotts born Octo^r ye 13th
1739.

John Son of Rhodes & Elizabeth Geeenwood born Novr ye 19th
Bap^d ye 12th of Decem^r 1739.

Benjamin Son of Benjamin & Judith Kidd born Novr 18th Bap^d
23d of Decem^r 1739.

Ann Daughter of Daniel & Sarah Guthrie born Novr 12th 1739.

Jane Daughter of Henry & Betty Daniel born Novr ye 13th Bap^d
  Decr 5th 1739.
James Son of Christopher & Frances Curtis born Decem^r y^e 6th Bap^d
  Decr y^e 22d 1739.
Peter Son of Thomas & Judith Brumell born Decr y^e 25th 1739.
Mary Daughter of William & Mary Mullens born Jan^{ry} 30th Bap^d
  Feb^{ry} 24th 1739.
Elias Son of Robt & Mary Williams born Feby 9th Bap^d Feby y^e 24
  $173\frac{9}{40}$.
Peter Son of Robt & Eliz^a Daniel born Feb^{ry} y^e 6th $173\frac{9}{40}$.
Robert Son of John & Jane Aldin born Feb^{ry} y^e 17th $173\frac{9}{40}$.
Thos Son of George & Ann Wortham born Octo^r y^e 27th 1739.
Randal Rodes Son of Randal & Mary Rodes was born Fe^{bry} y^e 18th
  bap^d Feby y^e 24 $173\frac{9}{40}$.
Mary Shaw was born, Daughter of Thos & Mary Shaw January 13th
  $173\frac{9}{40}$.
Mary, Daughter of Charles & Mary Medarst was born Dec^{nb} 7th &
  Bap. Feb^{ry} y^e 3d $173\frac{9}{40}$.
Mary, Daughter of John & Sarah Doss was born Jan^{ry} 3d $173\frac{9}{40}$
Hugh Son Hugh & Ann Roach was born Feb^{ry} 6th $173\frac{9}{40}$.
Martha Daughter of John & Jane Blakey was born January 4th
  $173\frac{9}{40}$.
John Son of Henry & Jane Sears was born Dec^{mbr} 24th Bapt^d Jan^{ry}
  25th 1740.
James Son of John & Ann Croffield was born Jan^{ry} 25th Bapt^d Feb^{ry}
  15. 1740.
Martha, Daughter of Edward & Martha Dillard was born Jan^{ry} 8.
  Bapt^d Feb^{ry} 23rd 1740.
Leonard Son of John & Michal George was born Feb^{ry} 28. Bapt'd
  March 16 1740.
Thomas Son of Charles & Jane Daniel was born Decem^{ber} 11th &
  Bapt^d Feb^{ry} 3rd 1740.
William Son of Phillip & Cassandra Warwick was born March 6th
  Bapt^d March 8th 1740.
John Price Son of John & Ann Price was born March 11th Bapt^d
  April 6th 1740.
William Son of William & Frances Gutery was born March 16.
  Bapt^d April 6th 1740.
Ann Daughter of Richard & Elizabeth Allen was born March 28th
  Bapt^d May 18th 1740.
Martha Daughter of Edmund & Martha Dillon was born Aprill 14th
  1740.
Jane Daughter of Thomas & Catharine Price was born April 11th
  Bapt^d May 2d 1740.
John Son of James & Martha Mayo was born April 29th Bapt^d May
  18th 1740.
Sarah Daughter of John & Mary Breame was born April 9th 1740.
Elizabeth Daughter of William & Judith Owen was born April 6th
  1740.
Oliver Son of Hugh & Elizabeth Martin was born April 7th 1740.
William Son of David & Dianah Berrick was born May 24th 1740.
Thomas Son of Thomas & Mary Shelton was born May 2nd 1740.

Charles Son of William & Patience Colley was born Nov^{mb} 11th 1739 Bapt^d May 14th 1740.

Ann Daughter of Jacob & Ann Acre was born May 20th Bapt^d June 8th 1740.

James Son of George & Elizabeth Gest was born May ye 9th 1740.

Catharine Daughter of Charles & Penelope Lee was born May 12th & Bapt^d June 8th 1740.

Thomas Son of Edward & Elizabeth Whitaker was born June 24 1740.

John Son of John & Susanna Williams was born June 7th Bapt^d June 8th 1740.

John Son of Thomas & Kezia Maxwell was born June 8th Bapt^d July 6th 1740.

John Son of Henry & Ann Bohannan was born Sep^{mber} 17th 1740.

William Son of William & Mary Gardiner was born July 30th Bapt^d August 10. 1740.

John Son of Edward & Mary Clarke was born July 6th 1740.

Richard Son of Andrew & Elizabeth Davis was born August 17th 1740.

Mary Daughter of Cary & Ann Smith was born Augt 8th Bapt^d Augst 24 1740.

Elizabeth Daughter of Richard & Sarah Wait was born Augt 15th 1740.

Elizabeth Daughter of John & Agatha Warwick was born Augt 6 1740.

Richard Son of Richard & Catharine Street was born Sep^{mbr} 22d Bapt^d Oc^{ber} 12th 1740.

Robert Son of Robert & Dorothea Brownley was born Sep^{ber} 18th 1740.

Agnes daughter of John & Constance Uris was born Sep^{ber} 16th 1740.

George Son of Richard & Sarah English was born Sep^{mber} 26th 1740.

Judith Daughter of Joseph & Elizabeth Smith was born Sep^{ber} 18th 1740.

William Son of John & Lucretia Greenwood was born Sep^{ber} 28th Bap^t October 10. 1740.

Frances Daughter of William & Frances Thurston was born October 6th 1740.

Sarah Daughter of John & Rebekeh Kid was born Oct^{ber} 3d Bapt^d Nov^{mber} 2d 1740.

Martha Daughter of John & Mary Smith was born Nov^{ber} 12th 1740.

Samuel Son of John Judith Wortham born April ye 7th 1740.

Absolom Son of William & Elizabeth Hackney was born Oct^{ber} 7 1740.

Daniel Son of Daniel & Hannah Stringer was born Oct^{ber} 13th 1740.

Sarah Daughter William & Mary Southern was born Oct. 31st & Bapt. Nov^{ber} 23 1740.

John Son of William & Hannah Pace was born Oct^{ber} 31st & Bapt^d No^{ber} 23d 1740.

Augustine Son of Augustine & Mary Owen was born No^{ber} 1. & bapt. Nov^{ber} 23rd 1740.

Simon Son of Thomas & Sarah Laughlin was born Nov^{ber} 18th Bapt 24th 1740.

Frances Daughter of Will & Ann Daniel was born Nov^ber 9. Bapt
Dec^ber 5th 1740.
Elizabeth Daughter of William & Betty Wallis was born Nov^ber 3.
& Bapt Dec^ber 14th 1740.
Sarah Daughter of Samuel & Elizabeth Major was born Dec^mber 18th
1740.
George Son of George & Jane Blakley was born Dec^ber the 5th.
Bapt. 14th 1740.
Robert Son of Robert & Jane Dudley was born Dec^ber the 6th 1740.
Mary Daughter of William & Elizabeth Davis was born Dec^ber 9th.
Bapt Jan^ry 25 1740.
William Son of John & Martha Broocks was born Dec^ber 13th. &
Bapt^d 21st 1740.
Stephen Son of William & Margeret Johnson was born Feb^ry y^e 1st
Bapt^d March 14. 174$\frac{0}{1}$.
John Son of David & Ann Condon Ann Daughter of David & Ann
Condon were born Feb^ry y^e 20th 174$\frac{0}{1}$.
John Son of Jonathan & Mary Hearin born Feb^ry 15th 174$\frac{0}{1}$.
Henry Son of Henry & Beatey Daniel born March 7th Bapt. March
29 174$\frac{0}{1}$.
James Son of W^m & Jane Mountague born Feb^ry 18th Bapt^d March
8th 174$\frac{0}{1}$.
& Susanna Daughter of Charles & Mary Wood born March y^e 15th
Bap^t 29 174$\frac{0}{1}$.
Robert Chowning Son of Robert & Betty Chowning born March 2d
Bapt March 29th 174$\frac{0}{1}$.
Ann Daughter of Eustace & Ruth Howard born March 8th Bapt.
March 29 174$\frac{0}{1}$.
Hezekiah Son of John & Mary Rhodes born Jan^ry y^e 20th 174$\frac{0}{1}$.
Katherine Daughter of Robert & Mary Daniel born Feb^ry y^e 27th
174$\frac{0}{1}$.
Catherine Daughter of John & Catherine Tugle born Feb^ry 22nd
Bap^d March 29th 1741.
Nathaniel Son of Rich^d & Elizabeth Steevens born Feb^ry 28th Bap^d
April 12th 1741.
Anne Daughter of John & Mary Cloudus born March 12th 174$\frac{0}{1}$.
Frankey Daughter of Constant Daniel born March 31st Bap^d April
19th 1741.
James Son of Patrick & Eliz^a Callaham born April 5th Bap^d April
19th 1741.
William Son of John & Eliz^a Davis born March 30th Bap^d April 12th
1741.
Benjamine Son of Edwd & Eliz. Bristow born April 15th Bap^d April
26th 1741.
Robert Son of Robert & Eliz. Daniel born May 2d. Bap^d May 10th
1741.
John Son of James & Mary Overstreet born April ye 4th Bap^d May
10th 1741.
Elizabeth Daughter of James & Agatha Jones born April 16th Bap^d
May 10th 1741.
Mary Daughter of Thos & Dorothy Chilton born April 12th Bap^d
1741.
Anner Daughter of John & Susanna Thomson born April 14th 1741.

William Son of Henry & Eliz. Baden born April ye 27th Bap^d May 24th 1741.

John Son of John & Agatha Hardee born April ye 9th Bap^d May ye 10th 1741.

George Son of William & Mary Richeson born May ye 4th Bap^d May ye 31st 1741.

Rebecka Daughter of William & Mary Fretwell born May ye 23d. Bap^d May ye 31st 1741.

George Son of John & Ann Hudson born May ye 12th Bap^d June ye 21st 1741.

Henry Son of William & Eliz: Chowning born June 21st Bap^d July 12th 1741.

George Son of John & Ann Humphrys born May ye 19th 1741.

John Son of Jacob & Ann Acre born Augst ye 10th 1741.

William Son of John & Mary Matthews born Augst ye 21st 1741.

George Son of James & Ann Compton born Augst ye 21st 1741.

John Son of John & Sarah Stamper born Augst 17th Bap^d Sepr 13th 1741.

Lodowick Son of Thos & Sarah Tuggle born Sepr ye 14th. Bap^d Octo^r ye 4th 1741.

Sarah Daughter of John & Rachel Chowning born Augst ye 1st Bap^d Augst 23d 1741.

James Son of William & Eliz^a Wood born Augst ye 8th Bap^d Augst 23d 1741.

Henry Son of William & Mary Purcel born July ye 16th Bap^d Augst 23d 1741.

Mary Daughter of Obediah & Sarah Daniel born Sep^t 19th Bap^d Octo^r 4th 1741.

Jane Daughter of John & Mary Henesey born Sepr ye 23d Bap^d Octo^r ye 4 1741.

Luse Daughter of William & Eliz^a Hackney born Sepr ye 11th 1741.

Andrew Son of Andrew & Constance Hardee born Octo^r ye 10th Bap^d Octo^r 25th 1741.

Christopher Son of William & Ann Robinson born Novr ye 9th Bap^d 1741.

Sarah Daughter of John [&] Judith Wortham born Novr ye 14th 1741.

Elizabeth Daughter of William & Dorothy Parrott born Decr 13th Bap^d Decem^r 27th 1741.

Tomson Son of Jedediah & Catherine Bristow born Decr 14th 1741.

Thomas Son of Joseph & Mary Tugle born Decem^r 15th Bap^d Decr 17th 1741.

John Son of John & Mary Lawson born Jan^{ry} y^e 3d Bap^d Jan^{ry} y^e 31st 1741.

John & Sarah children of Thos & Lucretia Sanders born Jan^{ry} y^e 18th Bap^d Jan^{ry} 31st 1741.

Elizabeth Daughter of John & Susanna Serd born Jan^{ry} y^e 16th Bap^d Feb^{ry} 28th 174$\frac{1}{2}$.

Sarah Daughter of Edm^d & Mary Berkeley born Jan^{ry} y^e 27th Bap^d 174$\frac{1}{2}$.

Mary Daughter of James & Elizabeth Dunlevy born March y^e 11th 174$\frac{1}{2}$.

Sarah Daughter of Henry & Elizabeth Brooks born Feb[ry] y[e] 9th 174½.

George Son of Edward & Mary Clark born Aug[st] y[e] 11th 1742.

Catherine Daughter of John & Ann Prill born April y[e] 7th 1742.

Dorothy daughter of Richard & Phebe Jones born March 14th 174½.

Mary Daughter of John & Susanna Williams born May 6th Baptized May 23d 1742.

Catherine Daughter of Tho[s] & Catherine Cheney born May 5th Bap[d] May 23d 1742.

John Son of Edmund & Martha Ditton born May y[e] 21st 1742.

Elizabeth Daughter of John & Jane Alldin born May y[e] 23d 1742.

William Son of Tho[s] & Ann Lee born May 16th Bap[d] May y[e] 24th 1742.

Elizabeth & Sarah Daughters of Daniel & Hannah Stringer born July 5th Bap[d] 1742.

William Son of William & Hannah Pace born August y[e] 6th 1742.

Jane Daughter of Samuel & Ann Wood born August y[e] 21st Bap[d] Sep[r] 5th 1742.

Bernard or Barnit Son of James & Elizabeth Meacham born Aug[st] 27th Bap[d] Sep. 26th 1742.

Ann Daughter of William & Elizabeth Wood born Sep[r] y[e] 11th Bap[d] Sep[r] 26th 1742.

Reuben Son of George & Jane Blackly born Sep[r] y[e] 6th Bap[d] Sep[r] 26 1742.

Thomas Son of Tho[s] & Kezia Maxwell born Septem[r] y[e] 7th Bap[d] Octo[r] 1742.

William Son of Augustine & Mary Owen born Septem[r] 20th Bap[d] Nov[r] 7th 1742.

Letice Daughter of Tho[s] & Rachel Brooks born Octo[r] 11th Bap[d] Nov[r] 7th 1742.

William Son of John & Mary Henesey born Octo[r] 31st Bap[d] Nov[r] 7th 1742.

Henry Son of James & Isabell Gibson born Oct[r] 9th Bap[d] Oct[r] 10th 1742.

Sarah Daughter of Bartho[o] & Eliz[a] Yates born Octo[r] 29th bap[d] Nov[ber] 1742.

James Son of George & Mary Lee born Oct[r] 6th bap[d] Oct[r] 8th 1742.

Sarah Daughter of Robert & Dorothea Bromley born Oct[r] 11th 1742.

Elizabeth Daughter of Charles & Mary Medaris born Octo[br] 17th Bap[d] Dec 2nd 1742.

Sarah Daughter of Barth[o] & Elizabeth Yates born Octo[br] 29th Bap[d] Nov[r] 11th 1742.

Philiman Son of Joshua & Ann Jones born Nov[r] 9th Bap[d] 1742.

Benjamine Son of Daniel & Sarah Ball born Nov[r] 22d 1742.

David Son of David & Dianna Berrick born Decem[r] y[e] 1st 1742.

Elizabeth Daughter of William & Mary Jones born Decem[r] 10th Bap[d] 1742.

Jane Daughter of William & Mary Mullins born May y[e] 30th Bap[d] June 13th 1742.

Micajah Son of Tho[s] & Mary Shelton born June 20th Bap[d] July 4th 1742.

Reuben Son of Rich^d & Elizabeth Allin born July ye 18th Bap^d
Augst 15th 1742.
Francis Son of John & ——— White born Decem^r ye 5th 1742.
Jacob Son of William & Elizabeth Hackney born Decem^r 24th 1742.
Margaret Daughter of William & Frances Gutherie born Octo^r 9th.
Bap^d Novr 7th 1742.
John Son of John & Mary Deagle born Jan^{ry} 11th 1742.
Mary Daughter of Edward & Eliz^a Sanders born Jan^{ry} 11th 1742.
Michal Son Robert & Eliz^a Wake born Jan^{ry} 7th 1742.
Lucy Daughter of Thomas & Joyce Dudley born Jan^{ry} 4th 1742.
John Son of John & Mary Saunders born Jan^{ry} 20th. Bap^d Jan^{ry} 30th
1742.
Benjamin Son of W^m & Mary Greenwood born Jan^{ry} 16th. Bap^d Jan^{ry}
30th 1742.
Ann Daughter of W^m & Frances Thurston born Jan^{ry} 14th. Bap^d
Jan^{ry} 30th 1742.
Elizabeth Daughter of James & Catherine Brown born Jan^{ry} 4th.
Bap^d Jan^{ry} 30th 1742.
William Son of William & Lucretia Cooper born Feb^{ry} 13th 1742.
William Son of John & Christian Boss born Febuary 7th 1742.
Ann Daughter of Garritt & Clary Daniel born Feb^{ry} 21st 1742.
George Son of Richard & Sarah Wait born Feb^{ry} 8th 1742.
Samuel Son of William & Margeret Johnson born Feb^{ry} 19th 174$\frac{2}{3}$.
John Son of William & Clare Marks born Feb^{ry} 16. Bap^d March 13th
174$\frac{2}{3}$.
Josiah Son of John & Mary Bream born Feb^{ry} 8th bap^d Feb^{ry} 20th
174$\frac{2}{3}$.
Mary Daughter of James & Eliz^a Meacham born Feb^{ry} 12th 1743.
John Son of John & Jane Alldin born Jan^{ry} 10th 1743.
Milecent Daughter of Tabitha Shiprel born Jan^{ry} 9th. 1743.
Catherine & Elizabeth Daughters of John & Agatha Hardee born
Decemb 15th 1743 baptized Jan^{ry} 14th 1743.
George Son of George & Ann Wortham born March ye 20th 1743.
Milecent Daughter of Ann Croffield born Jan^{ry} 20th 1743.
John Son of William & Eliz^a Davis Jan^{ry} 22nd 1743.
Mary Daughter of Robert & Eliz^a Daniel born Jan^{ry} 28th. Bap^d Feb^{ry}
12th 1743.
John Son of John & Mary Brooks born April 11th 1743.
Easter Daughter of Robert & Betty Chowning born March 25. bap^t
Ap^{rl} 4 1743.
Solomon Son of William & Mary Gardner born May. 1st. bap^d May
3rd 1743.
Robert Son of John & Lucretia Greenwood born May 21th. 1743.
Elizabeth Daughter of Eustace & Ruth Howard born May 19th
bap^d June 28th 1743.
Elizabeth Daughter of John & Mary Barruck born June 30th 1743.
Mary Daughter of Robert & Elizabeth Elliot born June 15th 1743.
Ann Daughter of Randal & Mary Rodes born June 16th 1743.
Catherine Daughter of Henry & Betty Daniel born June 25th 1743.
Jane Daughter of Charles & Penelope Lee born June 20th Bap^d July
17th 1743.
Robert Son of William & Jane Mountague born July 14th. Bap^d
August 7th 1743.

Elizabeth Daughter of Edward & Elizabeth Whittakers born July
25 1743.

Mary Daughter of Charles & Ann Roane born August 20th Bap^d
Sep^ber 18. 1743.

Susanna Daughter John & Susanna Williams born August 25 1743.

Sarah Daughter of Edward & Elizabeth Bristow born August 28th
1743.

Ann Daughter of William & Eliz^a Chowning born August 12. Bap^d
Aug^st 18. 1743.

William Son of Patrick & Elizabeth Caleham born July 5th Bap^d
August 17th 1743.

Caty Daughter of Thomas & Sarah Tugle born August 26th Bap^d
Sep^ber 18 1743.

Susanna Daughter of Richard & Mary Paterson born August 24th
Bap^d Sep^ber 18. 1743.

Salley Daughter of Jacob & Ann Acrey born September 15. 1743.

Judith Daughter of John & Judith Wortham born September 15th
1743.

William Son of John & Constance Urie born September 8th 1743.

Mary Daughter of Aaron & Johanna Hudging born September 13th
1743.

Lucy daughter of William & Betty Wollace born October 25th
1743.

John Warwick Son of Phillip & Cossandra Warwick born Oc^ber 26.
bap^d Nov^ber 20. 1743.

Sarah Daughter of John & Sarah Stamper born Oc^ber 21th Bap^d
Novem^ber 20. 1743.

Sarah Daughter of John & Rachel Chowning born Oc^ber 14. Bap^d
Oc^ber 30. 1743.

Henry Son of Benjamine & Judith Kidd born Oc^ber 16th Bap^d Oc^ber
30. 1743.

Sarah Daughter of Peter & Elizabeth Hudson born October 3d
1743.

Elizabeth Daughter of Edward & Martha Dillard born October 20th
Bap^d No^ber 13. 1743.

Rachel Daughter of Charles & Mary Wood born October 6th 1743.

Frances Daughter of John & Catherine Smith born November 17th
1743.

Judith Daughter of Armstead & Hannah Churchill born Nov^ber 21th
Bap^d Dec^ber 4. 1743.

Elizabeth Daughter of Tobias & Margaret Allin born Dec^ber 1st Bap^d
Jan^ry 1. 1743.

Peggy Daughter of Humphrey & Catherine Jones born Dec^ber 25.
Bap^d Jan^ry 22 1743.

William Son of Harry & Mary Anderson born December 13th 1743.

Ann Daughter of John & Elizabeth Lyal born December 1st 1743.

Priscilla Daughter of William & Eliz^a Hackney born December 5th
1743.

Jane Jones Daughter of Sarah Clark born Feb^ry 16th Baptized March
4th 174¾.

William Son of Richard & Ann Daniel born March 9th Bap^d March
18th 174¾.

William an illegitimate Son of Eliz^a Davis born March 13th 174¾.

Mary Daughter of Samuel & Ann Wood born March 27th Bap^d
April ye 15th 1744.

Sarah Daughter of James & Ave Cole born March ye 25th Bap^d April
ye 20th 1744.

John Son of John & Frances Reade born June ye 19th Bap^d ye 20th
1744.

Mary Daughter of John & Mary Matthews born April ye 6th 1744.

Ann Daughter of Jonathan Herring and Mary born Novr the 3d
1743.

Mary Daughter of Richard & Catherine Street born March ye 25
bap^d April 15th 1744.

Jane Daughter of Harry & Jane Sears born April ye 13th Bap^d May
ye 6th 1744.

            Daughter of Henry & Susannah Mickleburrough born
Feb^{ry} ye 25th 1744.

Sarah Daughter of Arthur & Ann Dye born Sepr 16th bap^d Nov^r
11th 1744.

Robert Son of Henry & Betty Daniel born Octo^r ye 18th 1744.

Absalom Son of Richd Elizth Steevens born May ye 6th bap^d May y^e
20th 1744.

            Daughter of John & Loweresa Cooper born Sepr ye 30th
1744.

Nathanell Son of Thos & Christian Sanders born Sepr 14th 1744.

Lewis Son of John & Eliz^a Davis born Jan^{ry} ye 2d 1744.

Sarah Daughter of South & Rachel Smith born Sepr ye 1th 1744.

Jemima Daughter of John & Mary Bream born Sepr ye 13th bap^d
Sepr 30th 1744.

William Son of John & Ann Hudson born Sepr ye 18th bap^d Octo^r
ye 21st 1744.

Anna Daughter of William & Rachell Brooks born Sepr 13th bap^d
Octr ye 21. 1744.

Jane Daughter of George & Jane Blackly born Sepr 29th bap^d Nov^r
ye 11th 1744.

Thomas Son of John & ———— Bowles born ye 7th of Decem^r 1744.

Eliz^a Daughter of W^m & Eliz^a Chowning born Decem^r 16th bap^d
Jan^{ry} 13th 1744.

James Son of John & Mary Loson born Decem^r 27th 1744.

Bartholomew Son of Barth^o & Eliz^a Yates born Octo^r 22nd Bap^d
1744.

Mathew Kemp Son of Robert & Eliz^a Elliot born Jan^{ry} 10th 1744.

Mary Daughter of James & Mary Overstreet born Jan^{ry} 23d 1744.

Moseley Son of Obediah & Sarah Daniel born Jan^{ry} 13th bap^d Feb^{ry}
3d 1744.

Ann Daughter of William & Eliz^a Bueford born Novr 6th Bap^d Dec^r
2d 1744.

Elizabeth Daughter of John & Sarah Sanders Junr born July ye 2d
1744.

Elizabeth Daughter of John & Martha Brooks born Jan^{ry} 17th bap^d
Feb^{ry} 24th 1744.

Jonathan Son of Henry & Eliz^a Brooks born Jan^{ry} 19th bap^d Feb^{ry}
24th 1744.

Jane Daughter of John & Mary Guthrie born Feb^{ry} 3d bap^d Feb^{ry}
24th 1744.

Mary Daughter of James & Catherine Brown born April ye 6th bap^d ye 28th 1745.

Lucy Daughter of Daniel & Hannah Stringer born Feb^{ry} 8th 1744.

John Son of William & Mary Owen born April ye 18th 1744.

Margarett Daughter of Andrew & Constance Hardee born July 17th bap^d Augt 19th 1744.

Joanna Daughter of William & Eliz^a Healy born Feb^{ry} 22nd bap^d March 18th 1744.

Sally Porter Daughter of Janet Kelley born Decr 25th 1744.

Thomas Son of James & Catherine Parrott born Sepr ye 26th 1744.

Catherine Daughter of William & Eliz^a Cloudas born June 25th 1744.

Isaac Son of Charles [&] Penelope Lee born Octo^r 27th bap^d Decem^r 2d 1744.

John Hamment Son of John & Catherine Mack-Nell born Novr 13th 1744.

Prudence Daughter of Philip & Eliz^a Brooks born Feb^{ry} 28th Bap^d March 17th 174$\frac{4}{5}$.

Hannah Daughter of William & Hannah Pace born March y^e 9th 174$\frac{4}{5}$.

    Son of Charles & Ann Roan born Jan^{ry} 7th 174$\frac{4}{5}$.

Elizabeth Daughter of George & Mary Lee born y^e 6th of April 1745.

Ame Daughter of John & Eliz^a Loyal born June y^e 3d 1745.

John Son of John & Mary Rhodes born March y^e 29th 1745.

Mary Daughter of John & Redith Wortham born May 2d 1745.

Samuel Son of Edward & Mary Clark born April 11th 1745.

Thomas Son of William & Elizabeth Jones born June 5th 1745.

Thomas Son of Charles & Mary Hodges born June 12th 1745.

Ann Daughter of Thomas & Ann Lee born July ye 1st Bap^d July ye 14 1745.

Benjamine Son of John & Catherine Tugle born July ye 10th Bap^d Augst 11th 1745.

Blackly Son of John & Mary Gardner born July ye 13th Bap^d Augst 11th 1745.

Samuel Son of William & Jane Mountague born July ye 27th Bap^d Augst 11th 1745.

Ann Daughter of William & Frances Gutherie born Augst ye 4th Bap^d Sepr 1st 1745.

Jane Daughter of Edward & Mary Southern born Augst ye 23d 1745.

John Son of John & Martha Stuard born Octo^r ye 15th 1745.

John Son of David & Diannah Berrick born Novr ye 17th 1745.

Frances Daughter of Robert & Lucy Daniel born Novr ye 25th 1745.

Lodowick Son of John & Lucretia Greenwood born June 25th Bap^d Augst 11th 1745.

Thomas Son of Thomas & Catharine Cheyney born Sepr 20th Bap^d Octo^r 13th 1745.

Elizabeth Daughter of William & Frances Thruston born Sepr 2d Bap^d Octo^r 13th 1745.

Chowning Son of Benjamine & Judith Kidd born Octo^r 9th Bap^d Octo^r 13th 1745.

Sarah & Jane Daughters of Thos & Sarah Tugle born Novr 13th Bap^d Novr 16th 1745.

Hannah Daughter of John & Elizabeth Cornelius born Octo^r 20th Bap^d Decem^r 15th 1745.

Mary Daughter of John & Sarah Stamper born Novr 13th Bap^d Decem^r 15th 1745.

Frances Daughter of John & Jane Aldin born Decem^r 24th Bap^d Jan^{ry} 9th 1745.

Elizabeth Daughter of John & Jane Beamen born Novr 4th 1745.

William Son of James & Dorothy Davis born April 4th 1745.

Catherine Daughter of W^m & Mary Mullins born Sepr 29th Bap^d Novr 3d 1745.

Daniel Son of Daniel & Sarah Ball born Octo^r 30th 1745.

Benjamine Son of Charles & Mary Mederas born Sepr 4th Bap^d Octo^r 13th 1745.

Benson Son of Thos & Elizabeth Siblee born Augst 16th 1745.

Mary Daughter of William & Mary Jones born Decem^r y^e 10th 1745.

Jane Daughter of W^m & Elizabeth Wood born Sepr 8th Bap^d Sepr 22nd 1745.

John & Ann, Son & Daughter of George & Ann Wortham born Decem^r 29th Bap^d 1745.

Elizabeth Daughter of Thos & Christian Sanders born Feb^{ry} y^e 26th 174$\frac{5}{6}$.

Abraham Son of William & Mary Cloudas born March y^e 6th Bap^d March 30th 1746.

Mary Daughter of William & Anne Sadler born March 3d Bap^d March y^e 30th 1746.

Elizabeth Daughter of W^m & Mary Greenwood born Feb^{ry} 11th Bap^d March 30th 1746.

Sarah Daughter of Charles & Ann Roane born March 17th Bap^d April 20th 1746.

Ann Daughter of John & Constance Uric born March y^e 2d 174$\frac{5}{6}$.

Bernard Son of John & Susana Seward born March y^e 8th Bap^d March 30th 1746.

Martin Son of W^m & Mary Gardner born Feb^{ry} 14th Bap^d March 30th 1746.

Ann Daughter of W^m & Clare Marks born March 24th Bap^d April 20th 1746.

John Son of W^m & Sarah Robinson born Feb^{ry} y^e 15th 174$\frac{5}{6}$.

Elizabeth Daughter of Stephen & Anne Tenor born March y^e 30th Bap^d 1746.

Thomas Son of Humphrey & Amy Garret born Jan^{ry} 10th Bap^d Jan^{ry} 26th 174$\frac{5}{6}$.

Robert Son of John & Catharine Smith born Feb^{ry} 24th 174$\frac{5}{6}$.

Benjamine Son of W^m & Elizabeth Hackney born May 14th 1746.

Sarah Daughter of Harry & Mary Anderson born April y^e 19th 1746.

Elizabeth Daughter of Thos & Rose Blake born May y^e 19th 1746.

James Son of James & Cassandra Mackan born April 14th Bap^d Jany 1st 1746.

Lewis Son of John & Christian Boss born May 2d 1746.

Elizabeth Daughter of Edward & Elizabeth Bristow born May 7th 1746.

Daniel Son of David & Joshebed Jefferson born April 21st 1746.

Mary Daughter of Joathan & Mary Haren born July ye 6th 1746.

William Son of Jacob & Ann Acree born April 25th Bap^d June 22nd 1746.

Anne Daughter of Peter & Mary Hudson born June 17th Bap^d July 13th 1746.

William Son of John & Agatha Hardee born May 26th Bap^d June 22d 1746.

Lewis Son of W^m & Agatha Cardwell born June 8th Bap^d June 22d 1746.

John Son of Andrew & Rachel South born May 25th Bap^d June 22d 1746.

Sarah daughter of Edward & Mary Clark born May ye 2d 1746.

Ann Daughter of John & Ann Barrick born June ye 2d 1746.

Henry Son of Tobias & Margaret Allin born July 28th Bap^d Aug^st 24th 1746.

Elizabeth Daughter of John & Mary Matthews born July ye 20th 1746.

Elizabeth Daughter of James & Ave Cole born Sepr 26th Bap^d 1746.

Sarah Daughter of John & Mary Patison born Aug^st 5th 1746.

William Son of Samuel & Ann Wood born July 23d Bap^d Aug^st 3d 1746.

Nanny Daughter of Henry & Tabitha Shepherd born Aug^st 28th Bap^d Sepr 14th 1746.

Lucy Daughter of Philip & Mary Grymes born Aug^st 24th Bap^d Aug^st 26th 1743.

John Son of Philip & Mary Grymes born March ye 28th Bap^d April 5th 1745.

Philip Ludwell Son of Philip & Mary Grymes born April 5th Bap^d May 9th 1746.

John Son of Robert & Elizabeth Elliot born Sepr 20th. Bap^d 1746.

John Son of Richard & Ann Daniel born Sepr 23d 1746.

John Son of John & Mary Bream born Septr 22d. Bap^d Octo^r 26th. 1746.

Rachel Daughter of John & Rachel Chowning born Sepr 18th. Bap^d Oct° 5th. 1746.

Gregory Son of Robert & Eliz^a Durham born Novr 12th. Bap^d Decem^r 7th. 1746.

James Son of George & Mary Bristow born Novem^r 11th. Bap^d Decem^r 7th 1746.

Nanny Daughter of John & Mary Gutherie born Novr 8th. Bap^d Decem^r 7th 1746.

Roger Son of Churchhill & Millecent Jones born No^r ye 11th Bap^d 1746.

James Son of James & Judith Campbell born Decem^r 29th 1746.

James Son of John & Martha Brooks born Novr ye 1st 1746.

Oliver Son of William & Mary Moulson born Decem^r 5th. Bap^d 1746.

Lucy Daughter of Edward & Martha Dillard born Octo^r 20th. Bap^d Novr 16th 1746.

Salle Daughter of William & Eliz^a Hackney born Decem^r 3d 1746.

Dorrothy Daughter of John & Susanna Daniel born Decr 11th. Bap^d Jan^ry 22d. 1746.

Thomas & Elizabeth son & Daughter of W^m & Elizabeth Healy born Feb^ry 12th. 1746.

A Child of Robert & Eliz^a Chiles born Febry 16th 174$\frac{6}{7}$.

Agatha Daughter of Robert & Eliz^a Daniel born Jan^{ry} 6th 174$\frac{6}{7}$.

Elizabeth Daughter of George & Jane Blackley born Jan^{ry} 3d. Bap^d
Feb^{ry} 8th 1746.

Rachel Daughter of W^m & Elizabeth Chowning born Jan^{ry} 24. Bap^d
Feb^{ry} 8th 1746.

William Son of W^m & Elizabeth Buford born Feb^{ry} 10th 1746.

Mary Daughter of John & Ann Meacham born Feb^{r}y 1st. Bap^d April
12th 1747.

Hannah Daughter of Daniel & Hannah Stringer born Jan^{ry} 20th 174$\frac{6}{7}$.

Philemon Son of Harry & Jane Sears born March 10th 174$\frac{6}{7}$.

Sukey Daughter of W^m & Elizabeth Kidd born Feb^{ry} 17th. Bap^d
April 12th 1747.

Mary Daughter of Edward & Eliz^a Whittekar born Feb^{ry} 10th 174$\frac{6}{7}$.

George Son of Edward &   Blackbourn born Jan^{ry} 16th 174$\frac{6}{7}$.

Elizabeth Daughter of John & Judith Wortham born April 5th. Bap^d
April 17th 1747.

Sarah Daughter of John & Jane Beaman born April 8th. Bap^d May
3d 1747.

Elizabeth Daughter of Barth^o & Eliz^a Yates born June y^e 10th Bap^d
June 1747.

Colo James Kidd & Mrs Anna Fisher were married January 16th 1817
an he ran away from her on the 17th day of May following.

James Steptoe and Jane Syphax were married on the 29th day of
May 1819. and had a child on the 23d day of March 1821 (mu-
lattoe Child Something like his father.)

Robert Son of Spencer Clarke & Anne * * * 25th 1789.

Chichester Son of D^o born April 15th 1793.

Spencer Son of D^o born October 16th 1795.

Margaret Yarrington Daughter of D^o born December 15th 1797.

Ann & Wm Clark Son & Daughter of the above parents born March
23rd 1800 baptized 27th of October 1800.

Polly Meacham daughter of William & Penelope Segar was born
April 22nd 1803. Baptized March 29th 1804.

Mary Grymes Sayre was born May 19th 1805.

Births of Slaves for the Year of our Lord 1769.

John Saunders a Slave belonging to Anne Jones was born April 28th
1769 & was baptized July 9th.

Jenny a Slave belonging to William Jackson was born May the 18th
1769. & baptized July 9th.

Charles Nelson a Slave belonging to Anne Jones was born Octr 22d.
1769. & baptized March 18th 1770.

Ambrose a Slave belonging to William Jackson was born June 11th.
1773.

Tanna, a Slave belonging to John Seward Se^r was born May 30th
1774.

Winney a Slave belonging to William Pryor was born December
16th 1774.

Lucy a Slave belonging to John Seward was born Sepr 16th 1776.

MARRIAGES.

Dudley Jolly & Martha Gardner Married May ye 14th 1716.
Richins Brame & Hannah Cheedle Married May ye 15th 1716.
Thomas Cardwell & Mary Blackly Married June ye 22 1716.
Thomas Brumwell & Dianah Underwood Married July ye 8. 1716.
Christopher Kelshaw & Mary Easter Married August ye 10. 1716.
Robert Deshago & Elizabeth Nicholls Married August ye 13. 1716.
John Fearn & Sarah Wortham Married November ye 1. 1716.
William Wood & Susanna Dinely Married November ye 9. 1716.
Thomas Mountague & Grace Nicholson Married December ye 21. 1716.
Robert Williamson & Elizabeth Minor Married December ye 21. 1716.
John Batchelder & Elizabeth Davis Married Jan^{r}y ye 2. 1716.
John Nichols & Elizabeth Osborn Married Jan^{r}y ye 3. 1716.
William Guttery & Lettice Burk Married Jan^{r}y ye 24. 1716.
Richard Smother & Mary Davis Married June ye 6 1717.
Nicholas Bristow & Mary Gardner Married June ye 27 1717.
David Murray & Jane Clark Married July ye 18. 1717.
William Stanard & Elizabeth Beverley Married August ye 1st 1717.
John Williams & Michall Curles Married August ye 22 1717.
James Janison & Rebecca Hackney Married Septem^r ye 5. 1717.
Nicholas Lewis & Michall Burk Married Septem^r ye 19. 1717.
John Miller & Sarah Hadley Married Septem^r ye 26. 1717.
John Moseley & Mary Nichols Married October ye 10. 1717.
John Johnson & Anne Ingram Married October ye 13. 1717.
John Carter & Mary Rice Married October ye 24 1717.
John Pace & Elizabeth Mountague Married October ye 24 1717.
James Bristow & Anne Jones Married Novem^r ye 7. 1717.
John Conner & Anne Sittern Married Decem^r ye 19. 1717.
William Mountague & Elizabeth Minor Married Decem^r ye 24. 1717.
William Rice & Catherine Caniff Married Decem^r ye 26 1717.
Thomas Vivion & Frances Thacker Married Jan^{r}y ye 2. 1717.
William Ogilvie & Anne Riske Married Jan^{r}y ye 9. 1717.
Stephen Feild & Susanna Jones Married Jan^{r}y ye 16. 1717.
John Ingam & Charity Waite Married Feb^{r}y ye 20. 1717.
John Blake & Johannah Ball Married Feb^{r}y ye 24. 1717.
Arthur Nash & Anne Allen Married Feb^{r}y ye 25. 1717.
George Freestone & Sarah Atwood married Feb^{r}y ye 25. 1717.
George Guest & Elizabeth Basket married Feb^{r}y ye 25 1717.
Patrick Marion & Betty Baker Married April ye 13 1718.
Richard Eastree & Mary Gaffield Married April ye 15 1718.
William Tomson & Mary Sibley Married April ye 24 1718.
William Hunt & Sarah Brock Married May ye 1 1718.
John Mullinax & Bridgett Hearn Married May ye 1. 1718.

Bar Yates Min^r.

MARRIAGES.

William Davis & Sarah Pace Married June ye 16. 1718.
Charles Cooper & Alice Nichols Married June ye 26. 1718.
Robert George & Anne Nash Married July ye 28 1718.
Thomas Stapleton & Mary Williamson Married Augst ye 7. 1718.

Robert Gallbarth & Penelope Parrott Married Octo: ye 2. 1718.
Isaac Allin & Elizabeth Symes Married Octo. ye 7. 1718.
William Anderson & Sarah Goar Married Novr ye 19 1718.
William Pepper & Honor Finney Married Nov^m^r ye 27 1718.
Joseph Timberlake & Joanna Hackney Married Decem^r ye 9. 1718.
Christopher Kilbee & Catherine Lewis Married Jan^ry ye 1 1718.
Benjamine Row & Mary Jervis Married Feb^ry ye 5. 1718.
John Pace & Mary Murry Married Feb^ry ye 10 1718.
Joseph Hall & Catherine Ranson Married Ap: ye 23 1719.
James Ingram & Margrett Hardee Married July ye 24 1719.
Henry Burk & Judith Trigg Married August ye 13. 1719.
Thomas Gilly & Elizabeth Makerty Married August ye 13 1719.
Charles Gresham & Mary Arven Married August ye 15 1719.
Richard Taylor & Honor Pepper Married Octo. ye 9. 1719.
Edmund Mickleburrough & Eliz^a George Married November ye 19.
    1719.
Thomas Tilley & Phebe Syddern Married Novem^r ye 22 1719.
John Marston & Elizabeth Reades Married Decem^r ye 18 1719.
Robert Holderness & Abigal Chelton Married Feb^ry ye 11 1719.
Oliver Segar & Jane Daniell Married May ye 12. 1720.
Dennis O'Brian & Honor Bushnell Married May ye 19. 1720.
Henry Blunt & Elizabeth Biggs Married June ye 26. 1720.
John Dudley & Anne Hill Married June ye 26 1720.
Robert Mash & Sarah Mazey Married July ye 21 1720.
William Johnson & Mary Goodloe Married July y^a 21 1720.
Humphrey Jones & Sarah Hamerton Married July ye 21 1720.
William Gardner & Elizabeth Crank Married August ye 3. 1720.
Andrew Murrah & Sarah Perry Married Aug^st ye 16. 1720.
Massey Yarrington & Anne Chowning Married Septem^r ye 13. 1720.
Hezekiah Roads & Anne Hill Married Decem^r ye 8. 1720.
John Larke & Elizabeth Blake Married Decem^r ye 11. 1720.
George Barwick & Mary Edmonds married Decem^r ye 14. 1720.
Patrick Knight & Mary Pendergrass Married Jan^ry ye 12. 1720.
Richard Moulson & Anne Shurley Married Jan^ry ye 19. 1720.
Joseph Smith & Elizabeth Ball Married Feb^ry ye 7. 1720.
James Bristow & Mary Twyman Married Feb^ry ye 9. 1720.
John Southern & Margrett Kidd Married Feb^ry ye 17. 1720.
Zebulun Chelton & Mary Goar Married Feb^ry ye 20. 1720.
John Fearne & Anne Machen Married Feb^r ye 20. 1720.
John Kidd & Rebecca Godbee Married Feb^ry ye 21. 1720.
William Batchelder & Elizabeth Watts Married April ye 11 1720.
John Tomson & Catherine Twyman Married April ye 13. 1727.
                    Bar. Yates Mins^r.

MARRIAGES.

Joseph Pace & Ann Basford Married April ye 18 1721.
William Dudley & Judith Johnson Married April ye 27. 1721.
Tomson Betts & Anne Russell Married May ye 12 1721.
John Southworth & Anne Syms Married May ye 18 1721.
George Walker & Amey Lyall Married July ye 4. 1721.
Thomas Kidd & Elizabeth Laurance Married July ye 27 1721.
Robert Brown & Hannah owen Married August ye 3 1721.
William Southworth & Anne Jordan Married August ye 10 1721.

Richard Greenwood & Anne Baskitt Married August ye 10 1721.
William Johnson & Margrett Pace Married Septem^r ye 22 1721.
Alexander How & Mary Pace Married Septem^r ye 26. 1721.
Jonathan Johnson & Priscilla Tignor Married Septem^r ye 28 1721.
George Chowning & Martha Tugwell Married Octo. ye 19 1721.
Thomas Gilinwater & Elizabeth Marcum Married Novem^r ye 12 1721.
Thomas Norman & Jane Stapleton Married Novem^r ye 23 1721.
William Daniel & Anne Watts Married Decem^r ye 7 1721.
Lewis Neal & Sarah Micham Married Decem^r ye 26 1721.
William Chowning & Jannett Jacobus Married Decem^r ye 29 1721.
Henry Tugle & Mary Godbee Married March ye 30 1722.
Richard Callahan & Eliz^a Nutter Married March ye 31 1722.
Robert Walker & Elizabeth Alford Married March ye 31 1722.
Chichester Curtis & Mary Hargrove Married March ye 31 1722.
David Williams & Mary Ingram Married Augst ye 21 1722.
Henry Ball & Elizabeth Tugle Married Augst ye 23 1722.
William Roads & Hannah Miller Married Sept. ye 13 1722.
John Guttery & Mary Shay Married Sept ye 23. 1722.
Alexander Graves & Mary How Married Octo ye 9. 1722.
Patrick Miller & Elizabeth Hill Married Octo. ye 11. 1722.
Patrick Kelly & Catherine Nicholls Married Octo. ye 26 1722.
Edward Clarke & Mary Hunt Married Octo. ye 26 1722.
Thomas Amis & Rachel Daniel Married Novem^r ye 14 1722.
John Shorter & Elizabeth Underwood Married Decem^r ye 23 1722.
Paul Thilman & Jane George Married April ye 17 1723.
Robert Mash & Jane Roades Married April ye 23 1723.
Charles Thomas & Susanna Davis Married May ye 9 1723.
William Tomson & Mary Symes Married May ye 9 1723.
Thomas Faulkner & Ellis Ellis Married May ye 23 1723.
William Gray & Mary McCauley Married May ye 28 1723.
Richard Jones & Anne Davis Married August ye 1 1723.
John Ridgway & Anne Crank Married Septem^r ye 19 1723.
James Russell & Anne Hatton Married October ye 3 1723.
David Gutherie & Susanna Thruston Married October ye 11 1723.
John Chowning & Catherine Gardner Married October ye 24 1723.
John Burk & Lettice Dannolly Married Novem^r ye 6 1723.
John Robinson & Mary Storey Married Novem^r ye 8 1723.
Theophilus Branch & Frances Sandiford Married Decem^r ye 8 1723.
Rice Curtis & Martha Thacker Married Decem^r ye 26 1723.
    n Marston & Phebe Tilley Married Jan^{ry} ye 2 1723.

    Bar. Yates min^r

MARRIAGES.

Paulin Anderson & Judith Jones Married Jan^{r}y ye 9 1723.
William Bennit & Mary Humpherys Married April ye 9 1724.
George Twyman & Agatha Buford Married July ye 16 1724.
Richard Curtis & Susannah Curtis Married July ye 23 1724.
Thomas Wennan & Jane Porterfield Married August ye 14 1724.
Thomas Whitaker & Rebecca Hues Married August ye 20 1724.
John Smith & Elizabeth Alding Married Octo. ye 27 1724.
William Owen & Ruth Mayo Married Novem^r ye 12 1724.
Randolph Roads & Sarah Davies Married Novem^r ye 27 1724.

Joseph Carey & Anne Sargent Married Decem^r ye 3 1724.
Abraham Wharton & Mary Humpheries Married Jan^{ry} ye 7 1724.
James Jones & Agatha Crank Married Jan^{ry} ye 14 1724.
William Mansfeild & Frances Tuggle Married Jan^{ry} ye 21 1724.
John Scanland & Keziah Ball Married Jan^{ry} ye 27 1724.
Edward Ball & Sarah Owen Married Feb^{ry} ye 4 1724.
John Blake & Anne Johnson Married Feb^{ry} ye 9 1724.
John Evans & Catherine Nixon Married April ye 15 1725.
John Goar & Mary Madras Married May ye 13 1725.
Caleb Brooks & Elizabeth South Married June ye 17 1725.
George Neavill & Anna Symes Married June ye 22 1725.
John George & Michal Meacham Married July ye 29 1725.
Peter Mountague & Elizabeth Merry Married Augst ye 19 1725.
Thomas Allen & Margrett Haines Married Sept. ye 2 1725.
Joshua Lewis & Martha Marston Married Octo. ye 7 1725.
John Tugle & Catharine Kelly Married Octo. ye 8 1725.
James Daniel & Jenny Hicks Married Novem^r ye 11 1725.
John Soanes & Sarah Thilman Married Novem^r ye 25 1725.
John Gregory & Jane Kidd Married Decem^r ye 3 1725.
John Weston & Elizabeth Wright Married Decem^r ye 30 1725.
Thomas Lee & Anne Probart Married Jan^ry ye 6 1725.
Wm Chessells & Sarah Cole Married Feb^ry ye 10 1725.
Edward Whitaker & Elizabeth Hill Married Feb^ry ye 13 1725.
John How & Avarilla Hardee Married Feb^ry ye 22 1725.
Elias Burt & Anne Finney Married April ye 11 1726.
Wm Wallis & Betty Davies Married April ye 11 1726.
Robert Williamson & Elizabeth Mickleburrough Married Feb^ry y^e
    13 1726.
Anthony Ridway & Eliz^a Beaman Married April ye 3 1727.
Richard Steevens & Mabell Dodson Married April ye 14 1727.
John Good & Anne Gardner Married April ye 27 1727.
John Bently & Mary Ellis Married May ye 26 1727.
Joseph Hardee & Mary Mullins Married June ye 20 1727.
William Anderson & Anne Humpheries Married June ye 23 1727.
Henry Mickleburrough & Frances Alding Married July ye 20 1727.
Thomas Oneby & Mary Stamper Junr Married July ye 27 1727.
Henry Knight & Mary Tomson Married August ye 3 1727.
Paul Philpotts & Clement Owen Married August ye 10 1727.
James Dudley & Jane Stanton Married August ye 24 1727.
Thomas Mountague & Penelope Warwick Married August 31 1727.
William Southworth & Catherine Allen Married September ye 6
    1727.
                    Bar. Yates Min^r.

MARRIAGES.

William Baker & Rachel Dodson Married September ye 15 1727.
John Eberson & Elizabeth Brooks Married September ye 22 1727.
Frances Porter & Elizabeth Hughs Married September ye 28 1727.
James Heptinstall & Rebecca Bohame Married October ye 24 1727.
John Glen & Mary Brayerly Married Jan^{ry} ye 2 1727.
John Tomson & Susanna George Married Jan^ry ye 9 1727.
James Stiff & Edy Dudley Married Feb^ry ye 23 1727.
Thomas Brumell & Judith Ball Married April ye 25 1728.

John Mackneel & Catherine Hammett Married May ye 6 1728.
Robert Crawford & Joyce Fletcher Married June ye 3 1728.
William Saunders & Susanna Thomas Married June ye 5 1728.
Thomas Todd & Lettice Thacker Married June ye 7 1728.
John Williams & Catherine Perrott Married July ye 17 1728.
Joshua Allford & Anne Blackburne Married July y^r 21 1728.
John Allstone & Catherine Oneal married August ye 12 1728.
Henry Jolley & Anne Ellis Married August ye 15 1728.
John Bradley & Rebecca Jemson Married August ye 24 1728.
John Goodwin & Jane Gressett Married Septem^r ye 13 1728
William Davis & Elizabeth Shelton Married October ye 9 1728.
Jeremiah Earley & Elizabeth Buford Married October ye 16 1728.
John Barnett & Marran Gibbs Married Novem^r ye 13 1728.
William Kidd & Elizabeth Thurston Married Novem^r ye 13 1728.
William Thurston & Frances Kidd Married Novem^r ye 13 1728.
John Crockford & Lucretia Goar Married Novem^r ye 22 1728.
William Guttery & Frances Willbourn Married Novem^r ye 29 1728.
William Crutchfield & Jane Norman Married Decem^r ye 9 1728.
Joseph Meacham & Elizabeth Crutchfield Married Jan^ry ye 9 1728.
Andrew Davis & Elizabeth Barbee Married Jan^ry ye 10 1728.
George Godloe & Diana Minor Married Jan^ry ye 13 1728.
John Ridgway & Anne Batchelder Married Feb^ry ye 6 1728.
Henry Daniel & Mary Johnson Married Feb^ry ye 11 1728.
Patrick Boswell & Elioner Commings Married Feb^ry ye 18 1728.
William Balding & Judith Tugell Married April ye 8 1729.
John Bohannan & Agnes Newberry Married April ye 10 1729.
William Wood & Elizabeth Brown Married April ye 10 1729.
Robert Beverley & Anne Stanard Married April ye 10 1729.
Marvel Moseley & Mary Davis Married April ye 24 1729.
Henry Nash & Jochebed Moseley Married April ye 24 1729.
William Hill & Bridgett Mullinax Married April ye 24 1729.
William Thurston & Elizabeth Franks Married April ye 29 1729.
William Buford & Elizabeth Owen Married May ye 15 1729.
John Jones & Isabell Hill Married May ye 20 1729.
Hugh Roach & Anne Marston Married May ye 22 1729.
Thomas Saunders & Christian Davis Married June ye 4 1729.
Jacob Faulkner & Mary Crockford married June ye 19 1729.
George Nevill & Mary Gibbs Married June ye 20 1729.
Richard Waight & Sarah Blake Married July ye 16 1729.
Thomas Marston & Elizabeth Roach Married July ye 17 1729.

Bar. Yates Min^r.

MARRIAGES.

Roger Lin & Frances Hughes Married August ye 5th 1729.
George Goodwin & Jane Haselwood Married August Y^e 14th 1729.
John Humphries & Elizabeth Hackney Married August Y^e 28th 1729.
Charles Curtis Johannah Gordon Married September Y^e 11th 1729.
Thomas Walker & Elizabeth Shorter Married Novem^r Y^e 21 1729.
John Marshall & Mary Gilpin Married Novem^r Y^e 24. 1729.
William Mountague & Jane Price Married Decem^r Y^e 3 1729.
Peter Lee & Catherine Tuke Married Decem^r Y^e 15 1729.
Thomas French & Mary Callahan Married Jan^ry Y^e 20 1729.
William Bassett & Elizabeth Churchhill Married Jan^ry Y^e 29 1729.

James Edwards & Joice Crawford Married March Y^e 6 1729.
John Philips & Margret Cronan Married March Y^e 31 1730.
Christopher Owen & Elizabeth Davis Married April Y^e 9th 1730.
Eustace Howard & Ruth Davis Married April Y^e 28th. 1730.
Patrick Welch & Catherine Redman Married May ye 14th 1730.
Aquilla Snelling & Margret Allen Married May ye 14th 1730.
William Chaver & Rebecca Gillet Married July ye 8th 1730.
William Southern & Mary Saunders Married August ye 3rd 1730.
John Crowdas & Mary Parsons Married August ye 6th 1730.
Paul Philpots & Susanna Baxter Married October ye 27th 1730.
Sampson Darrell & Elizabeth Smith Married Novem^r ye 17th 1730.
Robert Wilkins & Elizabeth Miller Married Novem^r ye 19th 1730.
Henry Nixon & Sarah Daniel Married Decem^r ye 10th 1730.
John Brand & Martha Ambler Married Decem^r ye 10th 1730.
Paul Thilman & Elizabeth Vivion Married Decem^r ye 16th 1730.
Thomas Skelton & Mary Probert Married Jan'ry ye 14th 1730.
Hugh Stuart & Judith Machen Married Jan'ry ye 29th 1730.
Robert Dudley & Jane Moulson Married Feb'ry ye 5th 1730.
John Davis & Sarah Chaften Married Feb'ry ye 11th 1730.
George Best & Margret Cooper Married Feb'ry ye 11th 1730.
Matthias Allen & Anne Herrin Married April ye 19th 1731.
Robert Daniel & Elizabeth Carter Married April ye 29th 1731.
Ignatius Tureman & Mary Pace Married June ye 3th 1731.
Ralph Skelton & Mary Daniel Married June ye 10th 1731.
Richard Hearn & Mary Hackney Married August ye 13th 1731.
Bartholomew Scot & Elizabeth Northcoat Married Augs^t ye 18th
    1731.
David Davis & Barker Jones Married September ye 2nd 1731.
James Gibson & Anne Stiff Married Septem^r ye 10th 1731.
Robert Smether & Constant Davies Married Septem^r ye 24 1731.
Thomas Cheney & Dorothy Lee Married Septem^r ye 30 1731.
Thomas Wakefield & Betty Gardiner Married October ye 7 1731.
Robert Daniel & Mary Meacham Married October ye 8 1731.
Joseph Carter & Catherine Ammon Married December ye 1 1731.
Robert Johnson & Elizabeth Sutton Married December ye 31 1731.
John Wily & Elizabeth Clark Married Jan'ry ye 21 1731.
Joseph Row & Mary Sandiford Married Jan'ry ye 26 1731.
James Edmundson & Christian Gregory Married Feb'ry ye 2 1731.
Robert Perrott & Sarah Mactyre Married April ye 17 1732.

Bar Yates Min^r

MARRIAGES.

James Pressnall & Anne Daniel Married May ye 14th 1732.
Richard Greenwood & Catharine Seares Married May ye 18th 1732.
William Goar & Lucy Crockford Married May ye 19th 1732.
James George & Agatha Watts Married May ye 24th 1732.
John Lee & Anne Spyers Married June ye 8th 1732.
Henry Perrott & Rachell Bayn Married June ye 16th 1732.
Thomas Faulkner & Mary Owen Married June ye 18th 1732.
John Owen & Sarah Chaftin Married July ye 20th 1732.
John Bird & Alice Burnet Married August ye 31st 1732.
James Stuart & Dianah Davies Married August ye 31st 1732.

Charles Daniel & Jane Mickleburrough Married Septem^r ye 20th
1732.
Mathew Crank & Mary Basket Married October ye 26th 1732.
Charles Wood & Mary Baldwin Married October ye 29th 1732.
John Wortham & Judith Stewart Married Novem^r ye 2th 1732.
Patrick Knight & Anne Conner Married Novem^r ye 2th 1732.
Landon Carter & Elizabeth Wormeley Married Novem^r ye 16th 1732.
Michael Rudd & Anne Ball Married Movem^r ye 18th 1732.
Caleb Brookes & Margret Fox Married Novem^r ye 24th 1732.
John Berry & Mary Miller Married Novem^r ye 30th 1732.
Francis Samson & Margret Elliot Married Novem^r ye 30th 1732.
Nicholas Mealer & Anne Burnes Married Decem^r ye 26th 1732.
William Gardner & Mary Basket Married Jan^{r}y ye 12th 1732.
William Cheney & Elizabeth Cheney Married Jan^{r}y ye 22th 1732.
John Johnston & Anne Bennet Married Jan^{r}y ye 29th 1732.
Charles Maceras & Mary Eeles Married Feb^{r}y ye 4th 1732.
Anthony Collings & Mary ann Yates Married Feb^{r}y ye 24th 1732.
John Stamper & Sarah Perrot Married March ye 25th 1733.
John Davis & Elizabeth Rhoeds Married April ye 5th 1733.
Edward Dillard & Martha Alding Married April ye 6th 1733.
Edward Bristow & Elizabeth Daniel Married April ye 13th 1733.
John Walker & Catherine Yates Married (by Rev^d Em. Jones) May
ye 10th 1733.
George Blackley & Jane Pace Married May ye 16th 1733.
Peter Lee & Susanna Williams Married May ye 16th 1733.
William Owen & Judith Daniel Married June ye 1 1733.
Richard Carter & Mary Hill Married June ye 4 1733.
John Williams & Catherine Davis Married June ye 24 1733.
Patrick Purcell & Sarah Davis Married Septem^r ye 7 1733.
William Stapleton & Lucy Hardin Married September ye 21 1733.
John Chowning & Rachel Tuggle Married Octo. ye 3th 1733.
Richard Perrot & Elizabeth Greenwood Married Octo. ye 9th 1733.
James Broun & Catherine Wood Married Octo^r ye 17th 1733.
Henry Brooks & Sarah Cuffley Married Octo^r ye 19th 1733.
John O'neal & Jane Mactyre Married Decem^r ye 7th 1733.
John Curtis & Susanna Saunders Married Decem^r ye 7th 1733.

Bar Yates Min^r.

MARRIAGES.

William Pace & Hannah Booten Married Decem^r ye 26th 1733.
Arthur Ware & Jane Daniel Married Jan^{r}y ye 26th 1733.
Valentine Ball & Susannah Lewis Married Jan^{r}y ye 31th 1733.
Charles Dougherty & Sarah Parrot Married Feb^{r}y ye 26th 1733.
Edmund Day & Mary Yarrow Married April ye 14th 1734.
Charles Gunter & Judith Gutterie Married April ye 15th 1734.
Richard George & Elizabeth Mayo Married April ye 20th 1734.
John Connor & Mary Crosle Married May ye 2th 1734.
Benjamine Davis & Judith Packett Married May ye 28th 1734.
David Barwick & Dianah Hill Married May ye 30th 1734.
John Greenwood & Lucretia Mactyre Married (by C. Thacker) July
25th 1734.
Alexander Frazier & Ann Wood Married (by C. Thacker) 7ber 8th
1734.

John Hardee & Agathe Gardiner Married January 5th (Banns) 1734.
Andrew Hardee & Constant Sears Married January 5th (Banns) 1734.
Daniell Moor & Mary Hollan Married January 31st (Banns) 1734.
Thos: Dawson & Margrett Cain Married April 10th (Banns) 1735.
William Hackney & Elizth Wilkins Married April 10th (Banns) 1735.
Willm Phillips & Hannah Graves Married April 7th (Licence) 1735.
Dennis Obryant & Jane Floyd Married April 19th (Banns) 1735.
Jno Dobbs & Mary Stamper Married May 11th (Banns) 1735.
Jno Doss & Sarah Herring Married June 17th (Banns) 1735.
Sam^{ll} Major & Elizabeth Jones Married June 22d (Banns) 1735.
James Dunbery & Elizabeth Owen Married June 26th (Banns) 1735.
Grigg Yarborough & Elizabeth Lewis Married June 27th (Banns) 1735.
James Porter & Mary Mason Married July 31th. (Banns) 1735.
Phillip Warwick & Cassandra Cheaney Married August 3d. (Banns) 1735.
Roger Kain & Ann Johnson Married August 10th (Bann) 1735.
Jno Vivion & Jane Smith Married August 12th (Banns) 1735.
Wm Mullens & Mary Greenwood Married Augst 27 (Banns) 1735.
Jno White & Elizth Pace Married Sept. 15 (Banns) 1735.
Jno Towles & Margarett Daniel Married Octr 9th (Banns) 1735.
Jno Humpris & Ann Jones Married Octr 14th (Banns) 1735.
Curtis Hardee & Elizth Tillman Married Novr 13th (Licence) 1735.
Robert Chowning & Betty Guttery Married Decr 24th (Banns) 1735.
Christopher Ammon & Mary Bristow Married January 29th (Banns) 1735.
John Warwick & Agathee Twyman Married March 8th (Banns) 1735.
Richard Ham & Diana Gibbs Married May 9th (Banns) 1736.
Jno Williams & Susanna Brookes Married May 30th (Banns) 1736.
Duel Kidd & Mary Sorrow Married July 13th (Banns) 1736.
James Gibson & Elizth Crosby Married July 22nd (Banns) 1736.
James Brown & Mary Swepson Married July 26th (Banns) 1736.
John Blake & Elizth King Married Sept 29 (Banns) 1736.
Thos Duckworth & Ann Buford Married Octr 4th (Banns) 1736.
Richd Jowel & Michal Miller Married Oct^o 20th (Banns) 1736.

Jno Reade Min^r.

MARRIAGES.

Alexander Roane & Mary Hipkins Married 9^{ber} 8th 1736.
Benjamin Kidd & Judith Chowning Married 10^{ber} 10th. 1736.
William Jones & Mary Langdon Married 10^{ber} 13th. 1736.
Thomas Betts & Elizabeth Burnet Married February 4th 1736.
Henry Mickleburrough & Susannah Daniel Married February 17th. 1736.
John Stevens & Mary Hughes Married February 18th 1736.
Alexander Snelling & Anna Humphreys Married April 4th. 1737.
John Matthews & Mary Herring Married April 4th. 1737.
William Anderson & Constance Alphin Married April 23th. 1737.
Robert Williams & Mary Brookes Married May 6th. 1737.
Randal Rhodes & Mary Bristow Married May 15th 1737.
Benjamin Ball & Ann Owen Married May 20th 1737.

John Taliaferro & Frances Robinson Married Jun^e 30th 1737.
John Price & Ann Younger were Married June 17th 1737.
William Colley & Patience Bryant were Married July 4th. 1737.
James Amiss & Jane Seager Nichols were Married March 17th. 173$\frac{7}{8}$.
Nicholas Dillard & Mary Alldin Married Septem^r y^e 16th 1737.
Richard Allin & Elizabeth Thurston Married Octo^r y^e 23d 1737.
Thomas Tignor & Sarah Stiff Married Octo^r y^e 27th 1737.
Daniel Stringer & Hannah Batchelder Married Decem^r y^e 1st 1737.
George Lee & Mary Buford Married Decem^r y^e 4th. 1737.
John Dunston & Mary Tyley Married Decem^r y^e 20th 1737.
Robert Stureman & Mary Rice Married Decem^r y^e 23d 1737.
Carter Burwel & Lucy Grymes Married Jany y^e 5th 173$\frac{7}{8}$.
John Deagle & Mary Wharton Married Jany y^e 16th 173$\frac{7}{8}$.
Charles Lee & Penelope Cheany Married Jany y^e 24th 173$\frac{7}{8}$.
David Snodgrass & Elizabeth Banting Married Jany y^e 22d. 173$\frac{7}{8}$.
William Boughtoun & Judith Hill Married Jany y^e 22d. 173$\frac{7}{8}$.
John Reade & Frances Yates Married Feb^{ry} y^e 2d. 173$\frac{7}{8}$.
Augustine Owen & Mary Clark Married Feb^{ry} y^e 13th. 173$\frac{7}{8}$.
James Compton & Ann Steevens Married April y^e 3d. 1738.
Russell Hill & Anne Towles Married April y^e 11th 1738.
William Griffin & Rachel Smith Married April y^e 13th 1738.
Thomas Maxwell & Kezia Blake Married May y^e 2d 1738.

MARRIAGES.

George Goodwin & Elizabeth Warwick Married June y^e 15th 1738.
John Rhodes & Mary Davis Married June ye 16th 1738.
Robert Dudley & Jane Segar Married Augst ye 10th 1738.
William Collins & Elizabeth Macktyer Married   1738.
George Lee & Judith Wormeley Married Sep^{ber} ye 30th 1738.
William Bond & Constant Smithey Married Octo^r ye 24th 1738.
Thomas Chainey & Cathrine Bristow Married Octo^r ye 26th 1738.
Thomas Tyre & Catherine Jones Married Novr ye 28th 1738.
Henry Sears & Jane Watts Married Decr ye 7th 1738.
Paul Phillpotts & Margret Wilburn Married Decm^r ye 27th 1738.

MARRIAGES.

Stanton Dudley & Judith Jackson Saturday March 12. 1790.
James Stiffe & Susanna Wood March 17th 1796.
James Stamper & Catharine Jackson March 20th 1796.
John Boss & Anne Jackson May 4th 1796.
Daniel Ball Siblee & Nancy Davis Miller June 2d 1796.
Nicholas Sebre & Betsa Baines June 15. 1796.
Thos Fauntleroy & Isabella Loussier Sep^t 1. 1796.
Christopher Harwood & Elinor Craine Sepr 1st 1796.
John Jarvis & Mary Dame Novr 11th 1796.

Henry Heffernan Rector.

The above List was given to the Clerk of the County.

John Montague of Essex County Married Mary   of Spotsyl-
vania Novr 14th 1778.
James Burton & Sarah Currey of King & Queen County married
Decr 3rd 1778.

William Garton & Judith Jackson married Decr 15th 1778.
Thomas Dillard & Mary Dillard of King & Queen County married
 Decr 30th 1778.
James Cardwell & Ann Eubank of King & Queen County married
 January 28th 1779.
Griffin Tuggle & Frances Berry married January 10th 1779.
John Bristow & Frances Brooks married January 31st 1779.
Benjamin Minor & Betsy Ross married May 1st 1779.

Samuel Klug, Minis.

MARRIAGES.

William Peters & Henrietta Ridgway married Novr 12th 1780.
Jacob Stiff Sanders & Lucy Humphris married November 16th
 1780.
Alexander Anderson & Nancy Wilcox married Nov 26th 1780.
Johnston Wake & Nancy Jackson married January 6th 1781.
James Meggs & Mary Wilson married January 13th 1781.
Josiah Bristow & Elizabeth Wilkins married Feb'y 4th.
George Williams & Ann Chowning married February 24 1781.
Reuben Alderson & Mary Taff married February 19th 1781.
Thomas Roane & Sally Murray married March 4th 178 .
Samuel Thurston & Sarah Stamper Coats married March 9th 1   .
Benjamin Falkner & Anna Nichols married March 22nd 178 .
George Blake & Chrisse Saunders married March 22d 1781.

Samuel Klug. Minister.

Isaac Wilcox Son of —— —— Ann Wilcox was born 1776.
Richard Son of John & Clara Daniel was born February 6 1776.
John Son of Robert & Susanna Groom was born April 1st 1776.
Philip Son of Philip & Frances Mountague was born June 19th 1776.
William Jones Son of William & Ann Jones was born Sep.
Thomas Mitcham Son of Joseph & Judith Brooks was born Jan^ry 31st.
Elizabeth Daughter of of Lawrance & Frances Meacham was born—
Mary Daughter of John & Sukey Minter was born Oct^r
Jack Fearn Son of William & Sarah Stiff was born Novr 19th 1776.
Josias Son of John Parrish was born Octr 3d 1777.
Benjamin Son of Benjamin & Elizabeth Bristow was born March 19th
 1772.
Jack Phips Son of Benjamin & Sarah Bristow was born Septr 4th
 1775.
Randolph Son of Thomas & Mary Segar was born January 19th
 1778.
John Son of Thomas & Sarah Ann Harrow was born February 22d
 1778.
Thomas Son of James & Sarah Patterson was born February 17th
 1762.
John Son of James & Ann Patterson was born December 2d 1766.
Richard Son of James & Ann Patterson was born April 17th 1768.
James Son of James & Ann Patterson was born March 10th 1771.
James Son of Benjamin & Jane Kidd was born January 9th 1771.
Ruth Thurston Daughter of Edmund & Ruth Kid was born May
 8th 1771.

(Fragment)

Moll the Daughter of my negro woman Beas Dyed the thirtith of may laste.

Given under my hand this Seavententh of June 1739.

John Segar.

BURIALS.

John Mickleburrough dyed Octo^r ye 9 & was buried Octo^r ye 12. 1716.
Sarah Moseleey dyed Octo^r ye 9 & was buried October ye 11. 1716.
John Bristow dyed October ye 10 & was buried October ye 13. 1716.
Elizabeth Ray dyed October ye 22 & was buried October ye 25. 1716.
John Nash dyed October ye 10 & was buried October ye 12. 1716.
Thomas Winn dyed October ye 10. & was buried October ye 11. 1716.
Thomas Steel dyed October ye 21. & was buried October ye 22. 1716.
Agatha Curtis dyed October ye 22. & was buried October ye 24. 1716.
Elizabeth Ray dyed October ye 22 & was buried October ye 25. 1716.
John Clark dyed Novem^r ye 6 & was buried Novem^r ye 7. 1716.
William Gaffeild dyed October ye 25. & was buried October ye 28.1716.
John Davis dyed October ye 23 & was buried October ye 25. 1716.
William Sandiford dyed October ye 22 & was buried October ye 24. 1716.
Thomas Elliot dyed Novem^r ye 19. & was buried Novem^r ye 22. 1716.
William Elliot dyed Novem^r ye 22. & was buried Novem^r ye 27. 1716.
Elizabeth Churchhill dyed Novem^r ye 11 & was buried Novem^r ye 16. 1716.
Matthew Kemp dyed November ye 16 & was buried Novem^r ye 23. 1716.
Edmund Hamerton dyed Novem^r ye 27 & was buried Novem^r ye 30 1716.
Minor Minor dyed Novem^r ye 30 & was buried Decem^r ye 3. 1716.
Sarah Mayo dyed Novem^r ye 29 & was buried Novem^r ye 30. 1716.
Frances Ingram dyed Novem^r ye 30 & was buried Decem^r ye 2. 1716.
Sarah Adcock dyed Decem^r ye 1 & was buried Decem^r ye 2. 1716.
Mary Powell dyed Decem^r ye 2d & was buried Decem^r ye 4. 1716.
Thomas Bewford Senr dyed Decem^r ye 9. & was buried Decem^r ye 11. 1716.
John Ingram dyed December ye 17 & was buried December ye 19. 1716.
William Lewis dyed December ye 8 & was buried December ye 10. 1716.
Benjamine Baldin dyed December ye 8 & was buried December ye 10. 1716.
Elizabeth Southworth dyed December ye 21 & was buried December ye 22. 1716.
Morrice Griffin dyed December y^e & was buried December ye 1716.
Anne Ball dyed December ye 14 & was buried December ye 16 1716.
Tabitha Nichols dyed December ye 18 & was buried December ye 21 1716.
Richard Atwood dyed Jan^{r}y ye 1 & was buried Jan^{r}y ye 3. 1716.
Lucy Bartlett dyed December 16 & was buried December 24. 1716.
Hezekiah Roades dyed Jan^{r}y. ye 2 & was buried Jan^{r}y. ye 7. 1716.
Mary Sandiford dyed Jan^{r}y ye 3 & was buried Jan^{r}y. ye 5. 1716.

William Turnett dyed Jan'y. ye 10. & was buried Jan'y ye 12. 1716.
Elizabeth Chelton dyed Jan'y ye 10 & was buried Jan'y. ye 12. 1716.
James Roades dyed Jan'y. ye 11 & was buried Jan'y. ye 13. 1716.
Catherine Southern dyed December ye 31 & was buried Jan'y. ye 3.
1716.
John Mullins dyed Jan'y ye 20 & was buried January ye 21. 1716.
Hannah Cheedle dyed January ye 22 & was buried January ye 24 1716.
Elizabeth Dudley dyed January ye 11 & was buried January ye 13
1716.
Mary Sandiford dyed January ye 8. & was buried January ye 11. 1716.
Elizabeth Timberlake dyed January ye 8 & was buried January ye 11
1716.
Thomas Davis dyed January ye 10 & was buried January ye 13. 1716.
Mary Trigg dyed Jan'y ye 29 & was buried January ye 31. 1716.
John Williams dyed Feb'y ye 26 & was buried February ye 27. 1716.
Jacob Presenall dyed March ye 4 & was buried March ye 6. 1716.
Robert James dyed Feb'y ye 9 & was buried Febr'y ye 10 1716.

Bar. Yates. Minister.

BURIALS.

Sarah Perrott dyed March ye 13 & was buried March ye 15. 1716.
Sarah Bolton dyed Feb'y ye 3 & was buried Feb'y ye 6. 1716.
Jacob Blake dyed March ye 10. & was buried March ye 12. 1716.
Robert Couch dyed August ye 30. & was buried August ye 31. 1716.
Elizabeth Barwick dyed February ye 3. & was buried February ye 6.
1716.
Mathew Parry dyed April ye 2. & was buried April ye 4. 1717.
Anne Williams dyed April ye 4. & was buried April ye 6. 1717.
John Price dyed April ye 19. & was buried April ye 21. 1717.
James Mactire dyed April ye 26. & was buried April ye 27 1717.
Mary Allin dyed May ye 6. & was buried May ye 8. 1717.
James Riske dyed May ye 7 & was buried May ye 10. 1717.
Robert Murray dyed May ye 16 & was buried May ye 17. 1717.
Richard Reynolds dyed Ap: ye 30 & was buried May ye 1. 1717.
Hannah Guest dyed May ye 10 & was buried May ye 13. 1717.
Anne Austain dyed May ye 17 & was buried May ye 19 1717.
John Nash dyed June ye 30. & was buried July ye 1st 1717.
Elizabeth Pendergrass dyed July ye 27. & was buried July ye 29.
1717.
Thomas Cheedle dyed Sept ye 1. & was buried Septem^r ye 3. 1717.
Elizabeth Whiteacre dyed August ye 26. & was buried August ye 29.
1717.
Mary Hughs dyed September ye 9. & was buried Septem^r ye 11. 1717.
James Ball dyed September ye 24. & was buried Septem^r ye 25. 1717.
Paul Durham dyed September ye 28. & was buried Septem^r ye 29.
1717.
Sarah Ingram dyed September ye 29. & was buried October ye 1.
1717.
George Jennings dyed September ye 4. & was buried Septem^r ye 5.
1717.
John Sparkes dyed September ye 28. & was buried Septem^r ye 30.
1717.
Ruth Moxam dyed Octo. ye 11. & was buried Octo. ye 13. 1717.

Elizabeth Vivion dyed Octo. ye 23. & was buried Octo: ye 26. 1717.
Henry Anderson dyed Octo. ye 24 & was buried Octo. ye 26. 1717.
Thomas Underwood dyed Septem^r ye 9. & was buried Septem^r ye 11.
   1717.
Henry Barnes dyed October ye 23. & was buried October ye 25. 1717.
Mary Wilson dyed October ye 23. & was buried October ye 24. 1717.
John Smith Junr dyed Novem^r ye 15. & was buried Novem^r ye 18.
   1717.
Elizabeth Davies dyed Decem^r ye 1. & was buried Decem^r ye 2. 1717.
Joseph Goar sen^r dyed Decem^r ye 7. & was buried Decem^r ye 8 1717.
Uriah Bolton dyed Novem^r ye 19. & was buried Novem^r ye 21. 1717.
Peter Chelton dyed Decem^r ye 17. & was buried Decem^r ye 19. 1717.
William Marcum dyed Decem^r ye 17. & was buried Decem^r ye 19.
   1717.
Thomas Warwick dyed Decem^r ye 31. & was buried Jan'ry ye 3. 1717.
Elizabeth Pace dyed Decm^r ye 30. & was buried Jan'ry ye 1. 1717.
Henry Chelton dyed Decem^r ye 28. & was buried Jan'ry ye 2. 1717.
Mary Couch dyed Novem^r ye 4. & was buried Novem^r ye 6. 1717.
Edmund Saunders dyed Jan'ry ye 16. & was buried Jan'ry ye 19. 1717.
John Stiff dyed Jan'ry ye 23. & was buried Jan'ry ye 25. 1717.
Sarah Hadley dyed Decem^r ye 6. was buried Decem^r ye 9. 1717.
Mary Cooper dyed Jan'ry ye 18. & was buried Jan'ry ye 19. 1717.
Mabell Dodson dyed Feb'ry ye 8. & was buried Feb'ry ye 12. 1717.
William Hughes dyed March ye 10. & was buried March ye 12. 1717.

Bar. Yates. Minister.

BURIALS.

Bridgett Gordon dyed March ye 5. & was buried March ye 7. 1717.
Winnifred Nicholls dyed March ye 10. & was buried March ye 12.
   1717.
Anne Gardner dyed March ye 10 & was buried March ye 13. 1717.
Winnifred Purvis dyed March ye 15. & was buried March ye 16.
   1717.
Henry Nicholls dyed March ye 18. & was buried March ye 20. 1717.
John Burrow dyed October ye 28. & was buried October ye 30.
   1717.
John Hughes dyed April ye 5. & was buried April ye 7. 1718.
Abigall Marston dyed March ye 17. & was buried March ye 20 1717.
Mary Roberts dyed March ye 31. & was buried April ye 2. 1718.
Anna Hughes dyed April ye 28. & was buried April ye 30. 1718.
Mary Marston dyed April ye 4. & was buried April ye 7. 1718.
Jane Ballard dyed April ye 5. & was buried April ye 6. 1718.
John Conner dyed April ye 3. & was buried April ye 4. 1718.
William Jones dyed April ye 10. & was buried April ye 12. 1718.
Willet Roberts dyed April ye 11. & was buried April ye 13. 1718.
Thomas Stiff dyed April ye 11. & was buried April ye 13. 1718.
Mary Middleton dyed April ye 12. & was buried April ye 14. 1718.
Diana Minor dyed April ye 16. & was buried April ye 18. 1718.
Elizabeth Pemberton dyed April ye 20. & was buried April ye 22.
   1718.
Thomas Gates dyed May ye 9. & was buried May ye 11 1718.
Robert Purvis dyed May ye 24. & was buried May ye 25. 1718.
Rebecca Pearce dyed May 30. & was buried June ye 1. 1718.

Arthur Nash dyed May ye 16. & was buried May ye 17. 1718.
John Sandiford dyed May ye 25. & was buried May ye 27. 1718.
Sarah Betts dyed June ye 15. & was buried June ye 17. 1718.
Catherine George dyed Septem^r ye 26. & was buried Septem^r ye 28. 1718.
Peter Chilton dyed October ye 1. & was buried Octo. ye 4. 1718.
Anne Downey dyed October ye 14. & was buried Octo. ye 17. 1718.
Elizabeth Crank dyed October ye 26. & was buried Octo. ye 27. 1718.
Henry Month dyed Novem^r ye 14. & was buried Novem^r ye 14. 1718.
William Finney dyed Aprill ye 26. & was buried April ye 30. 1718.
Priscilla Miller dyed Novem^r ye 6. & was buried Novem^r ye 7. 1718.
William Baker dyed Novem^r ye 19. & was buried Novem^r ye 20. 1718.
Elizabeth Vivion dyed Decem^r ye 6. & was buried Decem^r ye 8. 1718.
Jeptha Edmunds dyed Novem^r ye 23. & was buried Novem^r ye 25. 1718.
Solomon Crank dyed Novem^r ye 24. & was buried Novem^r ye 25. 1718.
Mathew Crank dyed Decem^r ye 3. & was buried Decem^r ye 5. 1718.
Elizabeth Stiff dyed Decem^r ye 3. & was buried Decem^r ye 6. 1718.
Catherine Row dyed Decem^r ye 14. & was buried Decem^r ye 16. 1718.
Elizabeth Elliott dyed Decem^r ye 23. & was buried Decem^r ye 27. 1718.
Edmond Bartlett dyed Decem^r ye 15. & was buried Decem^r ye 22. 1718.
Joanna Humpheries dyed Decem^r ye 19. & was buried Decem^r ye 23 1718.
Joanna Diggs dyed Jan^{r}y ye 17. & was buried Jan^{r}y ye 22. 1718.
Andrew Foulk dyed Jan^{r}y ye 27. & was buried Jan^{r}y ye 29. 1718.
Alexander Murry dyed Feb^{r}y ye 19. & was buried Feb^{r}y ye 23. 1718.
John Pendergrass dyed Jan^{r}y ye 29. & was buried Jan^{r}y ye 31. 1718.
Mary Gilley dyed Feb^{r}y ye 6. & was buried Feb^{r}y ye 8. 1718.
Charles Bishop dyed March ye 9. & was buried March ye 12 1718.

Bar. Yates. Minister.

BURIALS.

Abraham Trigg dyed Feb^{r}y ye 25 & was buried Feb^{r}y. ye 27. 1718.
Patrick Owen dyed March ye 10 & was buried March ye 11. 1718.
Edward Syddern dyed March ye 12 & was buried March ye 14. 1718.
Charity Ingram dyed Feb^{r}y ye 28. & was buried March ye 2 1718.
Arthur Johnson dyed March ye 21. & was buried March ye 22 1718.
Ralph Broster dyed April ye 6 & was buried April ye 7 1719.
Anne George dyed April ye 7. & was buried April ye 9 1719.
Mary Daniel dyed March ye 26. & was buried march ye 27 1719.
Elizabeth Reynolds dyed March ye 14. & was buried march ye 16. 1718.
Philip Warwick dyed April ye 17. & was buried Aprill ye 20. 1719.
Robert Biggs dyed March ye 27. & was buried March ye 29 1719.
John Lucas dyed May ye 4 & was buried May ye 6. 1719.
Sarah Crank dyed July ye 12 & was buried July ye 14 1719.
Mary Shelton dyed July ye 18 & was buried July ye 19 1719.

Pearse Edward dyed August yᵉ 2. & was buried Augsᵗ yˢ 3 1719.
John Watts was killed September yᵉ 4. & was buried September yᵉ 9. 1719.
Joan Molloney dyed Septemʳ yᵉ 26. & was buried Septemʳ yᵉ 27. 1719.
Anne Bristow dyed Septemʳ yᵉ 23 & was buried Septemʳ yᵉ 24. 1719.
Elizabeth Jones dyed Octo. yᵉ 10. & was buried October yᵉ 13. 1719.
Daniel Hues dyed Octo. yᵉ 14. & was buried October yᵉ 15. 1719.
David Morgan alias Henry Smith dyed Octo. 28. was buried October yᵉ 31. 1719.
Alexander Graves dyed Novemʳ yᵉ 5. & was buried Novemʳ yᵉ 8. 1719.
Mildred Ryley dyed Novemʳ yᵉ 9. & was buried Novemʳ yᵉ 10. 1719.
John Dudley dyed Novemʳ yᵉ 25. & was buried Novemʳ yᵉ 27 1719.
William Stanard dyed Decemʳ yᵉ 27. & was buried Decemʳ yᵉ 29 1719.
Anne Brooks dyed Decemʳ yᵉ 21. & was buried Decemʳ yᵉ 23 1719.
Thomas Cheedle dyed Janʳy. yᶜ 10. & was buried Jannʳy. yᵉ 11. 1719.
Edwin Thacker dyed Febʳy. yᵉ 16. & was buried Febʳy. yᶜ 17. 1719.
Penelope Cheney dyed March yᵉ 22. & was buried March yᵉ 24. 1719.
William Hearn dyed Decemʳ yᵉ 12. & was buried Decemʳ yᵉ 14. 1719.
Samuel Shakpurr dyed Ap. yᵉ 1 & was buried Ap: yᵉ 2 1720.
Catherine Mountague dyed April yᵉ 19. & was buried Ap: yᵉ 21 1720.
Richard Finney dyed March yᵉ 20. & was buried March yᵉ 23. 1719.
Elizabeth Jennings dyed Ap: yᵉ 15. & was buried Ap. yᵉ 17. 1720.
Hezekiah Roades dyed Ap: yᵉ 14. & was buried Ap: yᵉ 16. 1720.
Thomas Tilley dyed Ap: yᵉ 17. & was buried Ap. yᵉ 19. 1720.
Edward Siddean dyed Ap: yᵉ 22. & was buried Ap: yᵉ 23 1720.
Sarah Fearn dyed Ap: yᵉ 15. & was buried April yᵉ 16 1720.
Jane Hardee dyed April yᵉ 10. & was buried April yᵉ 13 1720.
Elizabeth Berry dyed April yᵉ 17. & was buried April yᵉ 19. 1720.
Elizabeth Mactyre dyed March yᵉ 26. & was buried March yᵉ 28 1720.
John Johnson dyed April yᵉ 5. & was buried April yᶜ 7 1720.
Joseph Timberlake dyed March yᵉ 14 & was buried March yᶜ 17 1719.
Thomas Blunt dyed April yᵉ 1. & was buried April yᵉ 3 1720.
William Hill dyed May yᶜ 6 & was buried May yᵉ 8 1720.
James Lewis dyed May yᵉ 10. & was buried May yᵉ 12 1720.
Faith Ducksworth dyed June yᵉ 23. & was buried June yᵉ 24 1720.
Thomas Hill dyed August yᵉ 3. & was buried August yᵉ 4 1720.

Bar. Yates. Minister.

BURIALS.

Elizabeth Beverley dyed August yᵉ 6 & was buried August yᵉ 11. 1720.
John Curlett dyed August yᵉ 13 & was buried August yᵉ 14. 1720.
John Wignall dyed August yᵉ 9 & was buried August yᵉ 11. 1720.
Henry Ball dyed August yᵉ 27 & was buried August yᵉ 29. 1720.
Anne Wood dyed August yᵉ 18 & was buried August yᵉ 20. 1720.
Mary Lewis dyed August yᵉ 24 & was buried August yᵉ 25. 1720.
Agatha Wormeley dyed Sept. yᵉ 10 & was buried Septeʳ yᵉ 11. 1720.
Mary Ranstead dyed Sept. yᵉ 10 & was buried Septemʳ yᵉ 12. 1720.
Cary Stamper dyed Sept. yᵉ 2 & was buried Septemʳ yᵉ 4. 1720.
Robert Aldin dyed Sept. yᵉ 4 & was buried Septemʳ yᵉ 5. 1720.

William Beamon dyed August ye 24 & was buried Angust ye 26. 1720.

James Rowe dyed October ye 9 & was buried October ye 11. 1720.

James Curtis j^r dyed Novem^r ye 4 & was buried Novem^r ye 7. 1720.

William Gordon dyed Novem^r ye 14 & was buried Novem^r ye 17. 1720.

Roger Jones jun^r dyed October ye 26 & was buried October ye 29. 1720.

Judith Robinson dyed Novem^r ye 18 & was buried Novem^r ye 22. 1720.

James Curtis dyed Novem^r ye 18 & was buried Novem^r ye 23. 1720.

John Batchelder dyed Novem^r ye 26 & was buried Novem^r ye 29. 1720.

John Davis died Novem^r ye 27 & was buried Novem^r ye 29. 1720.

Avarilla Davis dyed Decem^r ye 2 & was buried Decem^r ye 4. 1720.

William Webb dyed Novem^r ye 28 & was buried Novem^r ye 30. 1720.

Sarah Batchelder dyed Decem^r ye 3 & was buried Decem^r ye 7. 1720.

Elizabeth Batchelder dyed Decem^r ye 6 & was buried Decem^r y^e — 1720.

Rals Lyall dyed Decem^r ye 5 & was buried Decem^r ye 7. 1720.

John Baskett dyed Novem^r ye 28 & was buried Novem^r ye 30. 1720.

Easter Moxham dyed Novem^r ye 28 & was buried Novem^r ye 30. 1720.

Henry Baskett dyed Decem^r ye 5 & was buried Decem^r ye 7. 1720.

Sarah Baskett dyed Decem^r ye 8 & was buried Decem^r ye 9. 1720.

Onnor Baskett dyed Decem^r ye 14 & was buried Decem^r ye 15. 1720.

Susanna Wood dyed Decem^r ye 12 & was buried Decem^r ye 14. 1720.

George Johnson died Decem^r ye 10 & was buried Decem^r ye 11. 1720.

Alice Kidd died Decem^r ye 14 & was buried Decem^r ye 15. 1720.

Elizabeth Chowing died Decem^r ye 10 & was buried Decem^r ye 11. 1720.

Judith Shurley died Decem^r ye 8 & was buried Decem^r ye 9. 1720.

Simon Probart died Decem^r ye 16 & was buried Decem^r ye 17. 1720.

Frances Thacker jun^r died Decem^r ye 23 & was buried Decem^r ye 24. 1720.

John Bird died December ye 19 & was buried Decem^r ye 20. 1720.

Thomas Cary died December ye 21 & was buried Decem^r ye 23. 1720.

Margret Southworth died Decem^r ye 16 & was buried Debem^r ye 18. 1720.

Mary Purvis died December ye 14 & was buried Decem^r ye 16. 1720.

Mary Whistler died December ye 19 & was buried Decem^r ye 19. 1720.

Robert Daniell died December ye 27 & was buried Decem^r ye 29. 1720.

William Gilley died December ye 15 & was buried Decem^r ye 17. 1720.

Thomas Moor died December ye 16 & was buried Decem^r ye 17. 1720.

John Camell died December ye 15 & was buried Decem^r ye 17. 1720.

John Micou died December ye 20 & was buried Decem^r ye 21. 1720.

Mary Pateman died December ye 15 & was buried Decem^r ye 16. 1720.

James Devolve died December ye 26 & was buried Decem^r ye 27. 1720.

Frances Williams died December ye 26 & was buried Decem^r ye 28. 1720.

Sarah Couch dyed October ye 19 & was buried October ye 22 1720.

Bar. Yates Minister.

BURIALS.

James Meacham dyed Decemr. ye 12 & was buried Decem^r ye 13. 1720.

Mary Buford dyed Decemr. ye 29 & was buried Decem^r y^c 30. 1720.

Samuel Kidd dyed Decem^r ye 26 & was buried Decem^r y^c 27. 1720.

Elizabeth Williams dyed Decem^r ye 26 & was buried Decem^r ye 27. 1720.

Frances Daniell dyed Decem^r ye 28 & was buried Decem^r ye 29. 1720.

William Curlis dyed Jan^{r}y ye 1 & was buried Jan^{r}y: ye 3. 1720.

William Brooks dyed Jan^{r}y. ye 4 & was buried Jan^{r}y ye 6. 1720.

Penelope Gilbreath dyed Jan^{r}y. ye 2 & was buried Jan^{r}y. ye 4. 1720.

Hugh Watts dyed Jan^{r}y. ye 2 & was buried Jan^{r}y: ye 4. 1720.

Timothy Callahan dyed Jan^{r}y: ye 3 & was buried Jan^{r}y ye 5. 1720.

William Ingram dyed Decem^r ye 10 & was buried Decem^r ye 12. 1720.

James Walker dyed Jan^{r}y. ye 12 & was buried Jan^{r}y ye 17. 1720.

Benjamine Goare dyed Jan^{r}y. ye 15 & was buried Jan^{r}y ye 17. 1720.

Betty Cooper dyed Decem^r ye 29 & was buried Decem^r ye 31. 1720.

Henry Nicholls dyed Jan^{r}y. ye 3. & was buried Jan^{r}y. ye 5. 1720.

Charles Cooper dyed Jan^{r}y. ye 15 & was buried Jan^{r}y. ye 17. 1720.

George Howard dyed Jan^{r}y. ye 23 & was buried Jan^{r}y. ye 25. 1720.

Catherine Perrott dyed Decem^r y^c 28 & was buried Decem^r ye 30. 1720.

Margret Kidd dyed Jan^{r}y ye 4 & was buried Jan^{r}y. ye 6. 1720.

George Stapleton dyed Jan^{r}y. ye 8 & was buried Jan^{r}y. ye 10. 1720.

Henry Buford dyed Jan^{r}y. ye 16 & was buried Jan^{r}y. ye 18. 1720.

Joseph Seares jun^r dyed Jan^{r}y. ye 17 & was buried Jan^{r}y. y^c 19. 1720.

Edward Cambridge dyed Jan^{r}y. ye 18 & was buried Jan^{r}y. y^c 20. 1720.

Henry Freeman dyed Jan^{r}y. ye 26 & was buried Jan^{r}y. ye 28. 1720.

John Pace dyed Jan^{r}y ye 20 & was buried Jan^{r}y. ye 23. 1720.

Alice Norman dyed Decem^r ye 20 & was buried Jan^{r}y ye 22. 1720.

John Owen dyed Jan^{r}y ye 23 & was buried Jan^{r}y ye 26. 1720.

Anne Deagle dyed Jan^{r}y ye 30 & was buried Jan^{r}y y^c 31. 1720.

Joseph Marcum dyed Jan^{r}y ye 11 & was buried Jan^{r}y. ye 12. 1720.

Garritt Minor dyed Feb^{r}y ye 2 & was buried Feb^{r}y ye 4. 1720.

Mary Graves dyed Feb^{r}y ye 2 & was buried Feb^{r}y. ye 4. 1720.

Mary Warwick dyed Jan^{r}y ye 8 & was buried Jan^{r}y. ye 11. 1720.

Charles Lee dyed Jan^{r}y ye 6 & was buried Jan^{r}y. y^c 9. 1720.

William Tignor dyed Feb^{r}y ye 5 & was buried Feb^{r}y ye 8. 1720.

Aquilla Snelling jun^r dyed Feb^{r}y. ye 10 & was buried Feb^{r}y ye 11. 1720.

Avarilla Hardee dyed Feb^{r}y. ye 7 & was buried Feb^{r}y. ye 9. 1720.

Sarah Freestone dyed Jan^{r}y y^c 7 & was buried Jan^{r}y. ye 9. 1720.

Thomas Russell dyed Jan^{r}y ye 21 & was buried Jan^{r}y. ye 23. 1720.

James Jameson dyed Jan^{r}y ye 17 & was buried Jan^{r}y. ye 19. 1720.

Benjamin Beamon dyed Jan^{r}y. ye 25 & was buried Jan^{r}y ye 27. 1720.

Mary Maderas dyed Feb^{r}y. ye 5 & was buried Feb^{r}y. ye 7. 1720.

Thomas Mountague Senr dyed Feb^{r}y. ye 9 & was buried Feb^{r}y. ye 14. 1720.

Charles Macarty dyed Feb^{r}y. ye 14 & was buried Feb^{r}y. ye 16. 1720.

Peter Bromwell dyed Feb^{r}y: ye 28 & was buried March ye 3. 1720.

Sarah Tomson dyed Feb^{r}y ye 28 & was buried March ye 1. 1720.

Thomas Walker dyed March ye 1 & was buried March ye 4. 1720.

Mary Robinson dyed March ye 5 & was buried March ye 9. 1720.
Mary George dyed Feb^ry: ye 22 & was buried Feb^ry. ye 24. 1720.
Phillip Carter dyed Feb^ry ye 27 & was buried Feb^ry ye 28. 1720.
Susanna Midleton dyed Feb^ry ye 28 & was buried March ye 1 1720.
William Probart dyed Feb^ry ye 13 & was buried Feb^ry ye 15 1720.

Bar Yates. Minister.

BURIALS.

Margrett Brooks dyed March ye 13 & was buried March ye 15 1720.
James Machen dyed March ye 22 & was buried   1720.
Sarah Mash dyed April ye 12 & was buried April ye 13 1721.
Edmund Mickelburrough jun^r dyed Ap: ye 15. & was buried April ye 17 1721.
Thomas Still dyed April ye 13 & was buried April ye 15 1721.
Anne Haselwood dyed April ye 28. & was buried April ye 30 1721.
Eloner Still dyed May ye 2d & was buried May ye 4 1721.
Joseph Jacobus dyed May ye 15. & was buried May ye 17 1721.
Dudley Jolly dyed May ye 9. & was buried May ye 11 1721.
John Guess dyed May ye 30. & was buried May ye 31 1721.
Sarah Ball dyed June ye 27 & was buried June ye 29 1721.
Lucy Beverley dyed July ye 6 & was buried July ye 8 1721.
John Dobs jun^r dyed July ye 13 & was buried July ye 14 1721.
Thomas Gresham dyed July ye 13 & was buried July ye 14 1721.
Eloner Williams dyed July ye 14. & was buried July ye 15. 1721.
Thomas Stiff dyed July ye 4. & was buried July ye 5 1721.
James Gilbert dyed August ye 14. & was buried August ye 15 1721.
James Gordon dyed August ye 19 & was buried August ye 20 1721.
Joseph Kidd dyed August ye 23. & was buried August ye 24 1721.
Grace Tomson dyed August ye 20. & was buried August ye 21 1721.
William Cottel dyed Sept. ye 4. & was buried Septem^r ye 5 1721.
William Ball dyed Septem^r ye 2. & was buried Septem^r ye 3. 1721.
Hannah Mactire dyed Septem^r ye 25 & was buried Septem^r ye 27 1721.
James Robbeck dyed Septem^r ye 28 & was buried Septem^r ye 30 1721.
Agatha Mosely dyed August ye 22. & was buried August ye 24 1721.
Mary Wormley dyed Octo: ye 14 & was buried Octo: ye 16. 1721.
Elizabeth Ingram dyed Octo. ye 7 & was buried Octo. ye 9. 1721.
Thomas Crank dyed Octo. ye 8. & was buried Octo. ye 10 1721.
Minor Williamson dyed Septem^r ye 27 & was buried Septem^r ye 29. 1721.
John Barnett dyed Octo: ye 31 & was buried Novem^r ye 2 1721.
Sarah Chowning dyed Novem^r ye 9. & was buried Novem^r ye 11 1721.
Thomas Chowning dyed Novem. ye 15. & was buried Novem^r ye 17 1721.
James Nutter dyed Novem^r ye 18. & was buried Novem^r ye 19 1721.
Thomas Diatt dyed Novem^r ye 5. & was buried Novem^r ye 7 1721.
Anne Nash dyed Decem^r ye 5. & was buried Decem^r ye 7 1721.
Catharine Canaday dyed Decem^r ye 1 & was buried Decem^r ye 3 1721.
Anne Moulson dyed Decem^r ye 8 & was buried Decem^r ye 10 1721.
John Purton dyed Novem^r ye 14. & was buried Novem^r ye 16 1721.
John Anderson dyed Novem^r ye 29. & was buried Decem^r ye 2 1721.
John Roads dyed Decem^r ye 25. & was buried Decem ye 27 1721.

Edward Canody dyed Jan'y ye 2 & was buried Jan'y ye 4 1721.
Alexander How dyed Jan'y. y^o 7 & was buried Jan'y y^o 9 1721.
Thomas Gibson dyed Jan'y. ye 18 & was buried Jan'y ye 19 1721.
John Vivion dyed Feb'y ye 12 & was buried Feb'y ye 16 1721.
Marvell Mosely sen^r dyed Feb'y ye 13 & was buried Feb'y ye 15 1721.
John Mickleburrough dyed Feb'y ye 13 & was buried Feb'y ye 15 1721.
William Lewis dyed Feb'y ye 28 & was buried March ye 2 1721.
John Smith Senr dyed Feb'y ye 19. & was buried Feb'y ye 23 1721.
Jacob Williamson dyed Feb'y ye 27 & was buried March ye 1 1721.

Bar Yates Minisster.

BURIALS.

William Sadler dyed Ap: ye 10 & was buried Ap. ye 12 1722.
John Blewford dyed Ap: ye 18 & was buried Ap: ye 20. 1722.
Owin Winn dyed Ap: ye 17 & was buried Ap. ye 19. 1722.
Thomas Williams dyed Ap: ye 20. & was buried Ap. ye 22. 1722.
Jane Guttery dyed Ap. ye 22 & was buried Ap. ye 24. 1722.
James Bowman died April ye 10. & was buried Ap. ye 12. 1722.
George Bonner was drowned July ye 15 & was buried July ye 17 1722.
Henry Diamond was drowned July ye 15 & was buried July ye 18. 1722.
Bridgett Gordon dyed July ye 17 & was buried July ye 19. 1722.
John Johnson dyed July ye 11 & was buried July ye 12. 1722.
William Roach dyed July ye 31 & was buried August ye 2 1722.
John Maderas dyed August ye 1 & was buried August ye 3 1722.
Brown Gordon dyed August ye 15 & was buried August ye 16. 1722.
Mary Tomson dyed August ye 19 & was buried August ye 21 1722.
William Hendring dyed August ye 17 & was buried August ye 18 1722.
Mary Foy dyed August ye 23 & was buried August ye 24 1722.
Mary Wisdale dyed August ye 22 & was buried August ye 23 1722.
Elizabeth Southworth dyed Septem^r ye 15 & was buried Septem^r ye 16. 1722.
Margrett Baldwin dyed Octo: ye 7 & was buried Octo: ye 9 1722.
Elizabeth Summers dyed May ye 29 & was buried May ye 30 1722.
Anne Goodloe dyed Septem^r y^r 7 & was buried Septem^r ye 8 1722.
James Greenwood dyed Octo: ye 16. & was buried Octo: ye 17 1722.
Elizabeth Emmerson dyed Octo. ye 1 & was buried Octo. ye 2 1722.
Robert Walker dyed Octo. ye 21 & was buried Octo. ye 22 1722.
Elizabeth Curtis dyed Novem^r ye 8. & was buried Novem. ye 9 1722.
James Mackmullen dyed Novem^r ye 14 & was buried Novem^r ye 15 1722.
James Brame dyed Septem^r ye 12. & was buried Septem^r ye 14 1722.
Dorothy Best dyed Jan'y ye 17 & was buried Jan'y ye 18 1722.
Jane Carnew dyed Decem^r ye 18 & was buried Decem^r ye 20 1722.
Thomas Langley dyed Feb'y ye 2. & was buried Feb'y ye 4 1722.
Anne Dudley dyed Feb'y ye 1 & was buried Feb'y ye 3 1722.
John Thilman dyed Feb'y ye 16. & was buried Feb'y ye 18 1722.
Elizabeth Pudduck dyed Feb'y ye 6 & was buried Feb'y ye 8 1722.
Edward Pearse dyed Feb'y ye 12 & was buried Feb'y ye 14 1722.
John Watts dyed Decem^r ye 17 & was buried Decem^r ye 19 1722.
Grace Southworth dyed Feb'y ye 24 & was buried Feb'y ye 25 1722.
Thomas Smith dyed March ye 11. & was buried March ye 14 1722.

William Anderson dyed April ye 7 & was buried April ye 9. 1722.
Arthur Donnolly dyed April ye 18 & was buried April ye 20 1723.
Alice Benson dyed April ye 17 & was buried April ye 19 1723.
William Guttery dyed April ye 27 & was buried April ye 29 1723.
Benjamin Taylor dyed June ye 5 & was buried June ye 7 1723.
William Daniel dyed May ye 29 & was buried May ye 31 1723.
Sarah Portwood dyed July ye 7 & was buried July ye 9 1723.
Catherine Lomax dyed August ye 12 & was buried August ye 15 1723.
Malcolme Towerd dyed July ye 31 & was buried August ye 2 1723.
Robert Perrott dyed August ye 9 & was buried August ye 11 1723.
Benjamine Robinson dyed August ye 23. & was buried August ye 26
    1723.
Grace Clay dyed Septem^r ye 20 & was buried September ye 22 1723.
James Cole dyed Septem^r ye 23 & was buried September ye 25 1723.
William Daniell dyed Octo ye 11. & was buried October ye 13 1723.

Bar Yates. Minister.

BURIALS.

Thomas Smith dyed Octo. ye 16. & was buried Octo. ye 18 1723.
William Huskett dyed Novem^r ye 11. & was buried Novem^r ye 13
    1723.
Elizabeth Newberry dyed Novem^r ye 5. & was buried Novem^r ye 8
    1723.
Richard Warren dyed Novem^r ye 12. & was buried Novem^r ye 14
    1723.
Elizabeth Banger dyed Novem^r ye 10. & was buried Novem^r ye 12
    1723.
Hezekiah Roades dyed Decem^r ye 10 & was buried Decem^r ye 12
    1723.
Samuel Worner dyed Decem^r ye 31 & was buried Jan^{r}y ye 1 1723.
William Newberry dyed Jan^{r}y ye 14 & was buried Jan^{r}y ye 19 1723.
John Davis died Jan^{r}y ye 27 & was buried Jan^{r}y ye 30 1723.
Chichester Curtis dyed Feb^{r}y ye 1 & was buried Feb^{r}y ye 5 1723.
John Miller dyed Jan^{r}y ye 28 & was buried Jan^{r}y ye 30 1723.
John Hickey dyed Feb^{r}y. ye 6 & was buried Feb^{r}y. ye 8 1723.
Frances Williams dyed Jan^{r}y. ye 21. & was buried Jan^{r}y ye 23 1723.
William Clark dyed Jan^{r}y ye 30. & was buried Feb^{r}y. ye 1 1723.
William Davis dyed Feb^{r}y. ye 18 & was buried Feb^{r}y. ye 20 1723.
John Mayo dyed March ye 5. & was buried March ye 10 1723.
Elizabeth Sadler dyed Feb^{r}y ye 16. & was buried Feb^{r}y ye 19 1723.
Sarah Watts dyed March ye 1. & was buried March ye 3 1723.
Jemima Batchelder dyed March ye 18. & was buried March ye 20.
    1723.
Thomas Cheedle dyed March ye 31. & was buried April ye 1 1724.
Patrick Kelly dyed May ye 6. & was buried May ye 8. 1724.
Christopher Kelshaw dyed May ye 2. & was buried May ye 4. 1724.
Anne Anderson dyed May ye 7. & was buried May ye 9. 1724.
John Roe dyed May ye 19. & was buried May ye 21. 1724.
John South dyed May ye 21. & was buried May ye 23 1724.
Aaron Williams dyed July ye 10. & was buried July ye 12. 1724.
Frances Vivion dyed August ye 16. & was buried August ye 21 1724.
Esther Kelshaw dyed August ye 20. & was buried August ye 22 1724.

Anne Mactire dyed Septem^r ye 15. & was buried Septem^r ye 17. 1724.
Pinchback Hamerton dyed Septem^r ye 23. & was buried Septem^r ye 26. 1724.
John Rice dyed October 17 & was buried October ye 20. 1724.
Daniell Cain dyed Novem^r ye 7. & was buried Novem^r ye 9. 1724.
Nathan Sutton dyed Novem^r ye 25. & was buried Novem^r ye 27. 1724.
Richard Waight dyed Dec. ye 10. & was buried Decem^r ye 12 1724.
John Thomas dyed Dec. ye 4. & was buried Decem^r ye 6 1724.
Anne Smith dyed Decem^r ye 20. & was buried Decem^r ye 23 1724.
Mary Goodrich dyed Jan^{r}y ye 17. & was buried Jan^{r}y. ye 19 1724.
Jane Price dyed March ye 5. & was buried March ye 8. 1724.
Elizabeth Tugle dyed March ye 7. & was buried March ye 9. 1724.
Elizabeth Skipwith dyed May ye 11. & was buried May ye 13. 1725.
Rebecca Roach dyed June ye 18. & was buried June ye 19. 1725.
Arthur Davis dyed July ye 10. & was buried July ye 12. 1725.
Margrett Wood dyed July ye 17. & was buried July ye 19. 1725.
Lewis Baldwin dyed August ye 8. & was buried August ye 10. 1725.
Garrett Berry dyed Octo. ye 1. & was buried October ye 2. 1725.
John Foster dyed Septem^r ye 6. & was buried Septem^r ye 7. 1725.
Agnes Cummins dyed Septem^r ye 26. & was buried Septem^r ye 28 1725.
Jane Miller dyed october ye 6. & was buried October ye 7. 1725.
Jemimah Bristow dyed Octo: ye 13. & was buried october ye 15. 1725.
George Pace dyed Septem^r ye 10. & was buried Septem^r ye 12. 1725.
John Miller jun^r dyed Octo. ye 19. — was buried Octo: y^o 23 1725.
Isaack Oliver dyed Octo. ye 16. & was buried Octo: ye 17 1725.
Robert Blackley dyed octo. ye 31. & was buried Novem^r ye 2 1725.

Bar. Yates. Minister.

BURIALS.

Angello Cummins dyed November ye 4 & was buried November ye 6 1725.
Henry Segar dyed November ye 28. & was buried November ye 30 1725.
Anne Hackney dyed Feb^{r}y ye 8. & was buried Feb^{r}y. ye 11. 1725.
Elizabeth Batchelder dyed Jan^{r}y ye 17. & was buried Jan^{r}y. ye 19. 1725.
John Gibbs dyed Jan^{r}y. ye 31. & was buried Feb^{r}y ye 3. 1725.
Phillip Warwick dyed March ye 7. & was buried March ye 9 1725.
Sarah Steevens dyed March y^o 11. & was buried March ye 13. 1725.
Robert Wharry dyed April ye 7. & was buried April ye 8. 1726.
Catherine Tomson dyed March ye 31. & was buried April ye 3. 1726.
Frances Kidd dyed April ye 2d, & was buried April ye 4. 1726.
John Merry dyed April ye 12. & was buried April ye 13. 1726.
Mary Gray dyed March ye 23 1725 & was buried March ye 25. 1726.
Robert Williamson dyed April ye 15. & was buried April ye 18. 1726.
Catherine Williamson dyed April ye 22. & was buried April ye 23. 1726.
Elizabeth Jones dyed March ye 29. & was buried March ye 31. 1726.
Elizabeth Mullens dyed April ye 2. & was buried April ye 4. 1726.
Benjamine Williamson dyed April ye 26. & was buried April ye 28. 1726.

Elizabeth Lee dyed June yᵉ 2d. & was buried June yᵉ 4. 1726.
Catherine Morgan dyed June yᵉ 18. & was buried June yᵉ 20. 1726.
Elizabeth Curtis dyed June yᵉ 29. & was buried July yᵉ 1 1726.
John Hackney Dodson dyed May yᵉ 8. & was buried May yᵉ 10 1726.
Anne Wingo dyed June yᵉ 15. & was buried June yᵉ 16 1726.
Mary Holland dyed July yᵉ 28 & was buried July yᵉ 29 1726.
Jane Tompson dyed Septemʳ yᵉ 2 & was buried Septemʳ yᵉ 4 1726.
James Baskett dyed August yᵉ 29 & was buried August yᵉ 31 1726.
Elizabeth Daniell dyed July yᵉ 27. & was buried July yᵉ 29. 1726.
Sarah Kemp dyed Septemʳ yᵉ 17. & was buried Septemʳ yᵉ 20. 1726.
Mary Gibson dyed Septemʳ yᵉ 27. & was buried Septemʳ yᵉ 29. 1726.
John Hackney dyed Septemʳ yᵉ 25. & was buried Septemʳ yᵉ 27. 1726.
John Degge dyed August yᵉ 28. & was buried August yᵉ 31. 1726.
John Penniell dyed Septemʳ yᵉ 3. & was buried Septemʳ yᵉ 5. 1726.
Anne Greenwood dyed Septemʳ yᵉ 26. & was buried Septemʳ yᵉ 28 1726.
Humphery Jones dyed Novemʳ yᵉ 11. & was buried Novemʳ yᵉ 14. 1726.
John Price dyed Novemʳ yᵉ 16. & was buried Novemʳ yᵉ 19. 1726.
Bathsheba Horn dyed Novemʳ yᵉ 23. & was buried Novemʳ yᵉ 25 1726.
David George dyed Decemʳ yᵉ 19. & was buried Decemʳ yᵉ 21. 1726.
Thomas Causer dyed Novemʳ yᵉ 10. & was buried Novemʳ yᵉ 12 1726.
Joseph Goar dyed Decemʳ yᵉ 8. & was buried Decemʳ yᵉ 10 1726.
Anne Goar dyed Decemʳ yᵉ 14, & was buried Decemʳ yᵉ 16. 1726.
Joseph Holland dyed Decemʳ yᵉ 11. & was buried Decemʳ yᵉ 13. 1726.
Wᵐ Cain junʳ dyed Decemʳ yᵉ 29. & was buried Janʳy. yᵉ 2 1726.
John Cain dyed Decemʳ yᵉ 30. & was buried Janʳy yᵉ 2 1726.
Hezekiah Ellis dyed Decemʳ yᵉ 23. & was buried Decemʳ yᵉ 26. 1726.
Anne Ball dyed Decemʳ yᵉ 22 & was buried Decemʳ yᵉ 23 1726.
Augustine Owen dyed Decemʳ yᵉ 31. & was buried Janʳy yᵉ 2 1726.
Anne Barwick dyed Janʳy yᵉ 12. & was buried Janʳy. yᵉ 14 1726.
Elizabeth Humpheries dyed Janʳy yᵉ 15. & was buried Janʳy. yᵉ 17 1726.
Anne Hill dyed Janʳy yᵉ 15. & was buried Janʳy yᵉ 17 1726.
Dorothy Blackburne dyed Janʳy yᵉ   & was buried Janʳy. yᵉ 7 1726.
Catherine Robinson dyed July 21 & was buried July yᵉ 22 1726.
George Read dyed May yᵉ 3. & was buried May yᵉ 5. 1726.
Martha Moor dyed July yᵉ 8. & was buried July yᵉ 10 1726.
George Bohannon dyed August yᵉ 23 & was buried August yᵉ 24 1726.
Susanna Knight dyed August yᵉ 21. & was buried Augsᵗ yᵉ 23 1726.
Edward Ball dyed Septemʳ yᵉ 4. & was buried Septemʳ yᵉ 6 1726.
Martha Micurday dyed July yᵉ 23. & was buried July yᵉ 25 1726.
Anne Farrell dyed Septemʳ yᵉ 29. & was buried Octo yᵉ 1. 1726.
Benjamine Clark dyed Octo. yᵉ 8. & was buried Octo yᵉ 10. 1726.
Alexander Smith dyed Octo: yᵉ 9. & was buried Octo yᵉ 11. 1726.
Joane Owen dyed Decemʳ yᵉ 12. & was buried Decemʳ yᵉ 14. 1726.
John Timberlake dyed Janʳy yᵉ 12 & was buried Janʳy yᵉ 14. 1726.
George Chowning dyed Janʳy yᵉ 8. & was buried Janʳy yᵉ 10. 1726.
John Merry dyed Janʳy yᵉ 15. & was buried Janʳy yᵉ 17 1726.
Agatha Smith dyed Janʳy yᵉ 19. & was buried Janʳy yᵉ 21. 1726.

William Chaffin dyed Jan'y y° 3. & was buried Jan'y y° 5. 1726.
Thomas Norman dyed Jan'y y° 12. & was buried Jan'y y° 15. 1726.
John Wormley dyed Feb'y y° 7. & was buried Feb'y y° 11 1726.
Anne Freeman dyed Feb'y y° 2 & was buried Feb'y y° 5 1726.
Mary Tompson dyed Jan'y y° 13 & was buried Jan'y y° 16 1726.
Christopher Robinson dyed Feb'y y° 20 & was buried Feb'y y° 23. 1726.
Francis Timberlake dyed Jan'y y° 20 & was buried Jan'y y° 23. 1726.
Mary Smith dyed Jan'y y° 28. & was buried Jan'y y° 31 1726.
John Micham dyed Feb'y y° 19. & was buried Feb'y y° 22 1726.
William Tompson dyed Feb'y y° 28. & was buried March y° 2 1726.
Elizabeth Maxsom dyed Jan'y y° 29. & was buried Jan'y y° 31. 1726.
Thomas Mahaffee dyed Feb'y y° 6. & was buried Feb'y. y° 8. 1726.
Robert Mahaffee dyed Feb'y y° 10. & was buried Feb'y. y° 12. 1726.
Peter Bennett dyed Feb'y y° 12. & was buried Feb'y y° 14. 1726.
Elizabeth Marston dyed Feb'y y° 25. & was buried Feb'y y° 27 1726.
John Sibley dyed Feb'y y° 28. & was buried March y° 2 1726.
Sarah Dozier dyed March y° 5. & was buried March y° 7. 1726.
Margrett Scanderett dyed March y° 1. & was buried March y° 2. 1726.
Avarilla Davis dyed Jan'y y° 14. & was buried Jan'y y° 16 1726.
Thomas Curtis dyed March y° 7. & was buried March y° 9. 1726.
W'" Heath dyed Feb'y y° 28. & was buried March y° 1. 1726.
Sarah Davis dyed March y° 9. & was buried March y° 11. 1726.
Richard Walker dyed March y° 11. & was buried March y° 13. 1726.
W'" Ball dyed Feb'y y° 20. & was buried Feb'y y° 23 1726.
Grace Mountague dyed March y° 20. & was buried March y° 23 1726.
James Edmunston dyed March y° 23. & was buried March y° 24 1726.
John Hardee dyed March y° 13. & was buried March y° 15. 1726.
Mary Fenwick dyed Decem' y° 29. & was buried Decem' 31 1726.
John Alding dyed April y° 1. & was buried April y° 3. 1727.
Ellis Faulkner dyed March y° 20. & was buried March y° 22. 1726.
Dorothy Tignor dyed April y° 5. & was buried April y° 7. 1727.
Sarah Chessells dyed March y° 17. & was buried March y° 19. 1726.
Moses Norman dyed March y° 21. & was buried March y° 23 1726.
Elizabeth Read dyed April y° 6. & was buried April y° 7. 1727.
James Smith jun' dyed April y° 13. & was buried April y° 15. 1727.
William White dyed April y° 16. & was buried April y° 17 1727.

Bar Yates Minister.

William Savage dyed April y° 17 & was buried April y° 19 1727.
Frances Berry dyed April y° 18 & was buried April y° 19 1727.
William Hunt dyed April y° 20. & was buried April y° 22. 1727.
Anne Crank dyed April y° 24. & was buried April y° 25. 1727.
William Hammelt jun' dyed Feb'y y° 14. & was buried Feb'y y° 16. 1726.
Isaac Burton dyed April y° 21 & was buried April y° 23 1727.
Charles Whitaker dyed April y° 26. & was buried April y° 28. 1727.
Margrett Kidd dyed March y° 24. & was buried March y° 25 1727.
William Kidd dyed April y° 29. & was buried April y° 30. 1727.
Ruth Thurston dyed April y° 4. & was buried April y° 6. 1727.
Isaac Hardee dyed April y° 16. & was buried April y° 18. 1729.
William Batchelder dyed April y° 30. & was buried May y° 1. 1727.

Tobias Mickleburrough dyed April ye 18. & was buried April ye 20 1727.

William Cummins dyed April ye 25. & was buried April ye 27. 1727.

Anne Cummins dyed May ye 10. & was buried May ye 12. 1727.

Thomas Kidd dyed May ye 11 & was buried May ye 13. 1727.

James Douglas dyed Feb^{r}y ye 4. & was buried Feb^{r}y ye 6. 1726.

George Sanders jun^r dyed May ye 13 & was buried May ye 15. 1727.

John Stuart jun^r dyed May ye 27 & was buried May ye 28. 1727.

Robert Waite dyed May ye 28 & was buried May ye 30 1727.

Margrett Daniel jun^r dyed May ye 5 & was buried May ye 8. 1727.

Mary Cufley dyed May ye 29 & was buried May ye 31. 1727.

Sarah Anderson dyed Decem^r 17. & was buried Decem^r ye 19. 1726.

Richard Estree dyed May ye 6. & was buried May ye 8. 1727.

Thomas Crank dyed May ye 6: & was buried May ye 7. 1727.

Powel Stamper dyed May ye 22. & was buried May ye 23. 1727.

Moseley Daniel dyed May ye 24. & was buried May ye 25. 1727.

Elizabeth Saunders dyed June ye 16. & was buried June ye 18. 1727.

Elizabeth Roads dyed July ye 18. & was buried July ye 20. 1727.

Robert Baker dyed July ye 30. & was buried July ye 31. 1727.

Lettice Cheney dyed August ye 5. & was buried August ye 6. 1727.

William Cheney dyed August ye 9. & was buried August ye 10. 1727.

Edward Clark jun^r dyed August ye 25. & was buried August ye 26. 1727.

Christopher Chaffin jun^r dyed August ye 22. & was buried August ye 23. 1727.

Patrick Miller jun^r dyed August ye 23 & was buried August ye 24. 1727.

Thomas Mason dyed September ye 6. & was buried September ye 7. 1727.

Elizabeth Twyman dyed August ye 29. & was buried August ye 30. 1727.

Anne Weston dyed August ye 16. & was buried August ye 17. 1727.

Thomas Blackburne dyed Septem^r ye 25. & was buried September ye 27. 1727.

Mary Wormeley dyed September ye 27. & was buried September ye 29. 1727.

Lettice Guttery dyed September ye 26. & was buried September ye 28. 1727.

Anne Ridgway dyed October ye 13. & was buried October ye 15. 1727.

Robert George jun^r dyed Novem^r ye 19. & was buried ye Same day 1727.

Elizabeth Green dyed Decem^r ye 21 & was buried Decem^r ye 23. 1727.

Thomas Shurley dyed Decem^r ye 22. & was buried Decem^r ye 23. 1727.

Lady Sarah Skipwith dyed Decem^r ye 26. & was buried Decem^r ye 30. 1727.

Charles Grymes dyed Decem^r ye 27 & was buried Decem^r ye 30. 1727.

Elizabeth Thacker dyed Decem^r ye 21. & was buried Decem^r ye 28. 1727.

John Smith dyed Novem^r ye 10. & was buried Novem^r ye 13. 1727.

John Johnson dyed Jan^{r}y ye 16. & was buried Jan^{r}y: ye 17. 1727.

William Humpheries dyed Jan[r]y y[e] 11. & was buried Jan[e]y. y[e] 13. 1727.
Anne Lewis dyed Jan[r]y y[e] 22. & was buried Jan[r]y y[e] 23. 1727.
Thomas Sears dyed Jan[r]y y[e] 9. & was buried Jan[r]y y[e] 11. 1727.
John Sears dyed Jan[r]y y[e]   & was buried Jan[r]y y[e] 20. 1727.

Bar Yates Min[st]

Catherine Evans dyed Jan[r]y y[e] 14 1727.
Elizabeth Murrah dyed Feb[r]y y[e] 14 1727.
Laurence orrill jun[r] dyed Feb[r]y y[e] 27 1727.
Mathew Hunt dyed March y[e] 4 1727.
Thomas Haslewood dyed March y[e] 5 1727.
John Horton dyed March y[e] 25 1728.
Mary Bradley dyed March y[e] 15. 1727.
Benjamin Barbee dyed April y[e] 21. 1728.
Patrick Miller dyed April y[e] 29. 1728.
Sarah Baldwin ju[r] dyed June y[e] 3. 1728.
Sarah Baldwin dyed June y[e] 17. 1728.
Maurice Dempsie dyed July y[e] 8 1728.
John Shorter dyed July y[e] 15. 1728.
James Smith dyed August y[e] 26. 1728.
Elizabeth daughter of Daniel Hues dyed August y[e] 15. 1728.
Elizabeth Thurston dyed September y[e] 3 1728.
George Wortham son of George Wortham jun[r] dyed September y[e] 6. 1728.
Mary Gibbs dyed September y[e] 13. 1728.
Susannah daughter of Hezekiah Rhoades dyed September 24. 1728.
George Blake dyed Septem[r] y[e] 21 1728.
Alice Canser dyed Septem[r] y[e] 26 1728.
Agnes Newberry Sen[r] dyed October y[e] 6. 1728.
John Mullines dyed October y[e] 19. 1728.
Mary Saunders dyed Novem[r] y[e] 13. 1728.
John Ingram dyed Novem[r] y[e] 21. 1728.
Adam Corkburne dyed Decem[r] y[e] 14 1728.
Mary Kemp dyed Decem[r] y[e] 9th. 1728.
Betty Nevill dyed Decem[r] y[e] 23 1728.
Daniel Hues dyed Octo: y[e] 17. 1728.
Hannah Nevill dyed Decem[r] y[e] 31. 1728.
Henry Gilpin dyed September y[e] 8. 1728.
Joseph Hardee Sen[r] dyed March y[e] 28 1729.
John Southern Sen[r] dyed October y[e] 1st. 1728.
John Son of Thomas Lee dyed March y[e] 28. 1729.
Robert Johnston dyed March y[e] 27. 1729.
Joanna Cain dyed July y[e] 1. 1729.
James M[c]tire dyed July y[e] 20. 1729.
James Roan dyed July y[c] 24. 1729.
John Marston dyed August y[e] 20. 1729.
Lilly Mahaffee dyed September y[e] 1. 1729.
Thomas Son of John & Ann Fearn dyed September y[e] 2nd 1729.
Anne daughter of John Weston dyed September y[e] 6. 1729.
Daniel Heptenstall dyed Octo y[e] 3. 1729.
Thomas Tuke dyed October y[e] 7. 1729.

Mary Branch dyed September ye 27. 1729.
Roger Hogg dyed Octo. ye 7. 1729.
Bridgett Wilkings dyed September ye 15 1729.
Thomas Marston dyed Octo. ye 7 1729.
William Gardner dyed September ye 1 1729.
Rebecca Dodson dyed October ye 10 1729.
Hugh Ridley dyed October ye 5 1729.
Mary Hatfeild dyed October ye 14 1729.
Abigall Holderness dyed October ye 17 1729.

Bar Yates Minister.

John Steward dyed November ye 15 1729.
William Ferrell dyed November ye 30. 1729.
Abraham Glenn dyed November ye 19. 1729.
Benjamine Sutton dyed October ye 27 1729.
Clemence Philpotts dyed Novem^r ye 17 1729.
Anne ye Wife of John Blake dyeed Decem^r ye 10 1729.
Margret ye Wife of John Davis dyed Novem^r ye 28. 1729.
Mary ye Wife of Aquilla Snelling dyed Decem^r ye 20 1729.
Robert Crawford dyed Jan^ry ye 7 1729.
Jane Thilman dyed Jan^ry ye 18 1729.
Daniel Johnson dyed Jan^ry ye 21 1729.
Edwin Thacker jun^r dyed Feb^ry ye 12 1729.
Mary Kelshaw dyed Feb^ry ye 1st 1729.
Mary Daniell dyed Feb^ry ye 12. 1729.
Thomas Greenwood dyed Feb^ry ye 10 1729.
Frances Thacker dyed March ye 21 1729.
Richard Moulson dyed April ye 7 1730.
Margret daughter of Henry Daniel dyed March ye 22 1729.
William Nancut drowned April ye 29 1730.
Thomas ye son of Peter Mountague dyed March ye 30 1730.
Mary daughter of William Guthrie dyed May ye 5. 1730.
John son of John Miller jun^r dyed April ye 8. 1730.
Jane daughter of Richard Allen dyed May ye 7. 1730.
Elizabeth daughter of William Bristow dyed May ye 26. 1730.
Ellis Faulkner dyed Seytember ye 6. 1730.
Daniel Son of Joseph Page dyed September ye 21. 1730.
Benjamine Son of Thomas Saunders dyed Octo ye 4. 1730.
Thomas Machen dyed October ye 12. 1730.
Robert Goodwin dyed September ye 26. 1730.
James Harvie dyed October ye 13. 1730.
Elizabeth daughter of Aquilla Snelling dyed Novem^r ye 11. 1730.
William Gray dyed Novem^r ye 14. was buried November ye 18. 1730.
Dorothy Roach dyed Octo. ye 20. 1730.
Hugh Huchison dyed Octo ye 3. 1730.
Nathaniel Churchhill dyed Decem^r ye 21 was buried Dec. ye 22. 1730.
Lucretia Crockford dyed Decem^r ye 16. 1730.
Thomas Chusick dyed Jan^ry ye 17. 1730.
Mary Moseley dyed Jan^ry ye 17. 1730.
Paul Thilman dyed Feb^ry ye 4 1730.
Elizabeth the Wife of Robert Daniel dyed March ye 3 1730.
Jane ye Wife of Thomas Cheney dyed March ye 10. 1730.
Elizabeth Austin dyed march ye 13. 1730.

Mary Austin dyed march ye 20. 1730.
Hugh Mactire dyed april ye 12. 1731.
Chicheley Corbin Thacker dyed August ye 14. 1731.
Ruth ye daughter of Jacob Stiff dyed October ye 2. 1731.
Sarah daughter of John Grymes dyed October ye 25 was buried October ye 29. 1731.
Anne ye Wlfe of Richard Greenwood dyed October ye 30. 1731.
Thomas Greenwood dyed Novem^r ye 1. 1731.
William son of William Guthery dyed Jan'y. ye 1. 1731.
Richard Hill dyed Jan'y ye 18. was buried Jan'y. ye 22 1731.
Elizabeth ye wife of Caleb Brooks dyed Jan'y: ye 19. 1731.
Catherine Lee dyed Jan'y: ye 11. 1731.

Bar Yates Min^r.

A child of Henry Emerson's dyed Decem^r ye 18 1731.
Frances Mansfield dyed Feb'y ye 21 1731.
Jane daughter of William Wood dyed March ye 9 1731.
Lucy Lister dyed Jan'y y^o 18 & was buried Jan^{ry} ye 26. 1731.
Charles ye Son of Sampson Darrell dyed Octo. ye 6 1731.
Anne ye Wife of John Johnston dyed Aprill ye 21 1732.
Thomas Blakey dyed May ye 17 1732.
Hugh Stewart dyed May ye 12 1732.
Hannah daughter of William Robinson dyed April ye 19 1732.
John Larke dyed July ye 9th. 1732.
Susanna Curtis dyed July ye 21. buried July ye 23 1732.
Lettice Wife of Jno Burk dyed August ye 27 1732.
Charles Grymes dyed Septem^r ye 19. was buried Septem^r 22 1732.
William Bohannan dyed Septem^r ye 20 1732.
Priscilla Johnson dyed Octo. ye 11. 1732.
Elizabeth ye Wife of Robert Johnson dyed October ye 17. 1732.
Elizabeth daughter of Henry Jolly dyed October ye 26 1732.
John Pollard dyed Novem^r ye 28 was buried Novem^r ye 30 1732.
William ye Son of John Johnson dyed Novem^r ye 28 1732.
William Stanard dyed Decem^r ye 3. was buried Decem^r ye 7. 1732.
John Davis dyed Decem^r ye 3 1732.
Elizabeth Larke dyed Novem^r ye 26. 1732.
William Gayer dyed Decem^r ye 14 1732.
John Gayer dyed Decem^r ye 16. 1732.
Elizabeth Vivion dyed Jan'y ye 12 was buried Jan'y ye 16 1732.
Matthew Son of Eusebius Lewis dyed Decem^r ye 16 1732.
Sarah Maccoy dyed Decem^r ye 25. 1732.
Thomas ye Son of Richard Greenwood dyed Jan'y. ye 30 1732.
Jacob Cole dyed Feb'y ye 24 1732.
Avarilla Curtis dyed March ye 2 was buried March ye 5 1732.
William Chessells dyed March ye 4 1732.
Richard Allen dyed March ye 8 1732.
Jane Stewart dyed March ye 12, was buried March ye 14. 1732.
Susanna Chelton dyed April ye 29 1733.
Sarah Ross dyed May ye 23 1733.
James Walker alias Weekes dyed June ye 21. 1733.
William Wood dyed July ye 25. was buried July ye 28 1733.
Elizabeth Philpotts dyed July ye 22 1733.
William Sanders dyed July ye 23 1733.

John Son of Caleb Brookes dyed August y[e] 1 1733.
John Son of Joseph Alphin dyed August y[e] 24 1733.
Susannah daughter of Christopher Owen dyed Septem[r] y[e] 9. 1733.
George Collett dyed Septem[r] y[e] 30. was buried October y[e] 1. 1733.
Susam Pace dyed October y[e] 6 1733.
Alice Cooper dyed Septem[r] y[e] 29 1733.
Thomas Smith dyed Septem[r] y[e] 1st 1733.
Frances Gardner dyed Septem[r] y[e] 16 1733.
Williamson Bryant dyed September y[e] 9. 1733.
John Guttery dyed October y[e] 24 1733.
Alexander Lister dyed Novem[r] y[e] 11. was buried Novem[r] y[e] 13.
  1733.
James Meacham dyed October y[e] 27. buried October y[e] 28. 1733.

Bar Yates Min[r].

Alice Nichols dyed Novem[r] y[e] 12 1733.
Mary daughter of John Tugle dyed Novem[r] y[e] 16 1733.
John Sadler dyed Novem[r] y[e] 11 1733.
Sarah daughter of Eusebius Lewis dyed Novem[r] y[e] 41733.
Mary Barwick dyed Decem[r] y[e] 8 1733.
Sarah Crank dyed Decem[r] y[e] 24 1733.
Robert George Sen[r] dyed January y[e] 21 & was buried January y[e] 23
  1733.
Betty Wakefield dyed January y[e] 5 1733.
Ann Chowning dyed January y[e] 2 1733.
Thomas Wakefield dyed Feb[r]y y[e] 4 1733.
Thomas Cheney dyed Feb[r]y y[e] 14 1733.
Mary y[e] Wife of Henry Daniel dyed Feb[r]y y[e] 21. 1733.
William Wood dyed March y[e] 7. 1733.
Thomas Wood dyed March y[e] 3 1733.
Elizabeth y[e] Wife of Ralph Watts dyed Feb[r]y y[e] 15 1733.
Thomas Godding dyed Feb[r]y y[e] 25 1733.
Susannah y[e] Wife of Thomas Clark dyed Feb[r]y y[e] 19. 1733.
Elizabeth Dobbs dyed March y[e] 9. buried March y[e] 11. 1733.
Margrett Segar dyed March y[e] 13. buried March y[e] 15. 1733.
Stephen Ryley dyed March y[e] 19. 1733.
John Bryant dyed March y[e] 24. 1733. buried March y[e] 26 1734.
Sarah Crowdoss dyed March y[e] 16 1733.
Oliver Segar dyed March y[e] 26 buried March y[e] 28. 1734.
George Walker dyed March y[e] 27. buried March y[e] 29. 1734.
Ralph Shelton dyed March y[e] 13. 1733.
Henry Tugle jun[r] dyed March y[e] 14 1733.
George Wortham Sen[r] dyed April y[e] 5. buried April y[e] 7. 1734.
John Williams dyed April y[e] 12 1734.
Margret Daniel dyed March y[e] 17 1734.
Margret Blackey dyed Ap: y[e] 15 1734.
Joseph Southern dyed February y[e] 7 1733.
Edward Bodenham dyed March y[e] 17 1733.
William Owen dyed May y[e] 2 1734.
Sarah Acree dyed May y[e] 24 1734.
Sarah George dyed April y[e] 14 1734.
Frances daughter of Philip Brooks dyed June y[e] 13.

The Rev⁴ Mʳ Bartholomew Yates dyed the 26th. day of July 1734. buried the 2d. day Augᵗ 1734.
Ann daughter of John & Ann Smith died the 6 day September 1734.
Jeremiah Clowder dyed August 12th 1734.
Margaret Daniel Dyed August 11th 1734.
Penelopy Breame Dyed October 19th 1734.
Lettice Guttery Dyed November 15th 1734.
Catharine Montague Dyed October 20th 1734.
Mary Beauford Dyed November 27th 1734.
John Pace Dyed November 25th 1734.
Abraham Pace Dyed November 27th 1734.
Thomas Dudley Dyed October 13th 1734.

Jnᵒ Reade Minʳ.

Robᵗ Wilkins Dyed October 1st. 1734.
Phebe Marston Dyed October 16th 1734.
John Thurston Dyed December 27th 1734.
Joseph Hardee Dyed December 2d. 1734.
Mary Goodwin Dyed November 24th 1734.
Willᵐ Gayre Dyed January 10th 1734.
Rich⁴ Parrott Dyed January 11th 1734.
Jnᵒ Burk Dyed February 11th 1734.
Ruth yᵉ Wife of James Mayo Dyed February 6th 1734.
Elizᵗʰ Robertson Dyed January 26th 1734.
Lucy Daughter of Christopher & Mary Robinson Dyed March 7th 1734.
Nickols Bristow Dyed January 27th 1734.
Willᵐ Watts Dyed March 15th 1734.
Ann Wife of Jnᵒ Gresham Dyed April 7th 1735.
Given unto yᵉ ⎰ William Thurston Senʳ Dyed March 30th 1735.
Secretary's office ⎰ Michal Williams Dyed March 25th 1735.
Ap. 1735. ⎱ Lucy Wife of Thoˢ Nash dyed June 2. 1735.
Amy Nickols Dy'd September 13th 1735.
Mary Brooks Dyed September 25th 1735.
Charged—Mary Wife of James Brown Dyed Novʳ 10th 1735.
Henry Ball Dyed Novʳ 21st (Elizᵗʰ Ball) 1735.
William Seagur Dyed Octoʳ 10th (Jane Seagur) 1735.
Eusebius Lewis Dyed Novʳ 21st (Mary Lewis) 1735.
Elizabeth Smith Dyed Novʳ 19th.
Jane Watts Decʳ 17th (Wᵐ Gardiner Senʳ) 1735.
Easter Moulson Dyed Decʳ 29th (Robᵗ Dudley) 1735.
Martha Daughter of George Chowning Dyed January 16th 1735.
William Son of Thoˢ & Ann Lee Dyed January 13th 1735.
Millicent Daughter of of Robert Daniel Dyed January 26th 1735.
Henry Parrott Dyed January 22nd (Rachel Parrott) 1735.
John Carrell Dyed January 3d (Jnᵒ Williams) 1735.
Thomas Son of Hen: & Frances Bueford Dyed January 5th 1735.
Ann Ryley Dyed Feb'y 6th (Jnᵒ Ryly) 1735.
Catherine Williams Dyed Feb'y 16th (Jnᵒ Williams) 1735.
Richard Patman Dyed Janʳʸ 25th 1735.
Jane Wife of Robᵗ Dudley Dyed March 2d 1735.
John Hughes Dyed March 12. 1735.

Given to the S: O: Ap: 1736.
{ Benjamin Greenwood Dyed Feb^ry 15th (Eliz^th Perrot) 1735.
George Gest Dyed March 22 (Geo. Gest. Senr) 1735.

Abraham Wharton Dyed March 25th 1736.
George Berwick Dyed April 13th 1736.
John Hipkins Dyed January 8th 1736.
James Hipkins Dyed March 27th 1736.
William Crooker Dyed May 23d 1736.
Joseph Alphin Dyed May 20th 1736.
Mary Hardee Dyed June 14th (Andrew Hardee) 1736.
Joseph Pace Dyed June 18th (Benjn Pace) 1736.
Wm Brown Dyed July 10th (James Brown) 1736.
Keziah Ball Dyed July 9th 1736.
Edmund Mickleburrough Dyed June 26th (Jane Mickleburrough) 1736.
Sarah Rhodes Dyed June 30th (Randal Rhodes) 1736.
William Baldwin Dyed July 26th (Judith Baldwin) 1736.

J^n° Reade Min^r.
Torn.   (Geo. Barbee) 1736.
Torn.   Best Dyed July 23d 1736.
Torn.   Registers omitted in ye year 1735.
Torn.   Octob^r 9th   (Tup. Tuggle) 1735.
Torn.   Octr 27th (Charles Wood) 1735.
Samuel Johnson Dyed Octr 19th (Wm Johnson) 1735.
Henry Allin Dyed Novr 1st (Mary Allin) 1735.
Thomas Mellican a Servt to Edwin Thacker Dyed Octr 4th 1736.
Sarah Perrott Daughter of Rachell Perrott Dyed Septr 12 1736.
Jane   a foundling Dyed Octr 3d 2736.

Given into ye Secret: Off. Otc° 1736.
{ Jane Mickleburrough Dyed Aug^st 10th (Charles Daniel) 1736.
Frances Smith Dyed Octr 2d 1736.
Susanna Daughter of J^n° & Susanna Curtis Dyed Sept 24th 1736.

Jane Thurston Dyed Octr 14th (Willm Thurston) 1736.
Nichols Tuggle Dyed Octr 12th (J^n° Tuggle) 1736.
Thomas Corbin Dyed Novr 4th 1736.
Ann Betts dyed October 27th 1736.
John Mayo dyed 9^ber 24th 1736.
Jane Johnson dyed 10^ber 14th 1736.
Catherine Greenwood dyed March 13th 1736.
Ann Duckworth died March 19th 1736.
Thomas Warwick died Feb. 19th 1736.
Ann Clark dyed March 15th 1736.
John Shanks dyed January 21th 1736.
Sarah Owen dyed February 20th 1736.
Elizabeth ye daughter of William & Elizabeth Blackburne dyed 10^ber 13th 1736.
Anna ye daughter of William & Elizabeth Blackburn dyed 10^ber 21th 1736.
Elizabeth Stevens dyed January 18th 1736.
Sarah Blasedon dyed January 20th 1736.
Mary ye Wife of James Brown dyed 9^ber 5th 1736.

Sarah ye Wife of Patrick Russel died January 19th 1736.
Martha daughter of Hugh & Ann Roach died May 22th 1737.
Mary ye daughter of John & Ann Johnson died January 4th 1736.
John ye Son of Elizabeth Humphries died June 21th 1737.
William ye Son of Thomas Sanders died June 9th 1737.
Sent to the Secret: Office October 1737. } Edward Hill died Feb. 20th 1736.
Sarah daughter of John & Martha Hardee died Sepr ye 28th 1737.
Ann Daughter of William Guthery died Sepr ye 8th 1737.
Christopher Sutton Senr died Octo^{r} ye 26th 1737.
Mary Gear died Novr y^{e} 3d 1737.
Joseph Son of Joseph & Elizabeth Humphris died Decem^{r} y^{e} 12th 1737.
Henry Son of Joseph & Mary Tugle died Decem^{r} y^{e} 12th 1737.
Robert Perrott died Decem^{r} y^{e} 13th 37.
Marget y^{e} Wife of Aquila Snelling Dyed Decem^{r} y^{e} 10th 37.
Ann Calahan dyed Feb^{r}y y^{e} 2d 173$\frac{7}{8}$.
Hannah Watts dyed Octr y^{e} 5th 1737.
Jane y^{e} Wife of George Goodwin dyed Jan^{r}y y^{e} 28th 173$\frac{7}{8}$.
James Son of William & Hannah Rhodes dyed April y^{e} 11th 1738.
Curtis Parrott dyed May y^{e} 14th 1738.
Churchhill Blakey dyed May y^{e} 8th 1738.
Elizabeth Terry dyed May y^{e} 26th 1738.
Bettey Daughter of John & Sarah Carrell dyed April y^{e} 8th 1738.
Hannah Jenkins daughter of John Jenkins dyed Sepr y^{e} 27. 1738.
John Losson dyed Octor y^{e} 14th 1738.
Benjamin Thurston dyed Novr y^{e} 30th 1738.
Catharine Walker dyed Octo^{r} y^{e} 5th 1738.
Cuffley Son of Henry & Sarah Brooks dyed Decem^{r} y^{e} 2d 1738.
Francis Kelshaw dyed Jan^{r}y: y^{e} 15th 173$\frac{8}{9}$.
John Son of John & Sarah Stamper dyed feb^{r}y: y^{e} 16th 173$\frac{8}{9}$
Garret Son of Robert & Elizabeth Daniel dyed Feb^{r}y: y^{e} 19th 173$\frac{8}{9}$.
Elizabeth Yarbrough dyed March y^{e} 4th 173$\frac{8}{9}$.
Frances Daughter of Russel & Anne Hill dyed March y^{e} 12th 173$\frac{8}{9}$.
Elizabeth Daughter of Charles & Penelope Lee dyed March y^{e} 23d 173$\frac{8}{9}$.
Mary Daughter of Andrew & Elizabeth Davis dyed March y^{e} 14th 173$\frac{8}{9}$.
Patrick Pussil died April y^{e} 23d 1739.
Edward Son of John & Judith Wortham died May y^{e} 25th 1739.
Ann Daughter of John & Mary Matthews died Augst y^{e} 2d 1739.
Edward Guthrie died Sepr 28th 1739.
Mary Daughter of Elizabeth Porter died Septr y^{e} 19th. 1739.
Thomas Trench died Septr ye 23d. 1739.
Avirilla Waldin died Septr ye 28th. 1739.
William Owen died Novr y^{e} 1st. 1739.
Hannah Brown died Novr y^{e} 6th 1739.
Joyce Edwards died Novr y^{e} 5 1739.
Isaac Rhodes Son of John & Ann Rhodes died Novr y^{e} 18th. 1739.
Ann Parrott died Novr y^{e} 16th 1739.
Charles Cooper died Decr y^{e} 14th 1739.
William Fares died Jan^{ry} y^{e} 4th. 173$\frac{9}{40}$.

Agnes Southern died Feb^{ry} y^e 11th. $173\frac{9}{40}$.

y^e 15th ⎫ Sons of Samuel Batchelder
elder Died Novr y^e 23rd ⎭   1739.

William Fluewelling Died March y^e 1st $173\frac{9}{40}$.
Elias Williams Died March y^e 2d. $173\frac{9}{40}$.
Peter Daniel Died March y^e 8th $173\frac{9}{40}$.
Roger Jones died April 13th 1739.
John Tylor Died November y^e 21th 1740.
George Harrod Died March y^e 19th $173\frac{3}{4}$.
Absolom Hackney Son of William & Elizabeth Hackney Died October y^e 13th 1740.
Henry Bohannan died July 28th 1740.
Jane Daniel Died March y^e 10th. 1739.
Elizabeth Dudley died March y^e 18. $173\frac{9}{40}$.
William Kid died April y^e 4th. 1740.
Jonathan Brooks died May y^e 17th 1740.
Elizabeth Pace died April y^e 6th 1740.
Thomas Hill Son William & Frances Hill died April 13th 1740.
Alexander Graves died June y^e 21th 1740.
Joseph Sears departed this Life June y^e 12th. 1740.
Ambrose Son of Paul Philpotts died August ye 9th 1740.
John Son of Paul Philpotts died August ye 9th 1740.
Edmund Fary died August ye 20th. 1740.
Judith Daughter of Richard & Sarah Wait died September 24th 1740.
Elizabeth Davis Died September 19th. 1740.
John Martin Son of Hugh & Elizabeth Martin died October y^e 10th 1739.
William Segar died October y^e 6 1740.
Sarah Laughlin Died November y^e 25 1740.
Edward Smith died January the 7th $173\frac{9}{40}$.
Elizabeth Lewis died January y^e 18th. $173\frac{9}{40}$.
Cufflee Brooks died January y^e 2d $173\frac{9}{40}$.
Sarah Williams died January y^e 13th $173\frac{9}{40}$.
John Greenwood Died January y^e 26th $173\frac{9}{40}$.
Diana Crowdas died January the 10th $173\frac{9}{40}$.
Robert Son of Robert & Jane Dudley Died January y^e 4th 1740.
George Wortham Son of John & Judith Wortham Died January y^e 28th 1740.
Catharine Wood died January y^e 30th 1740.
Elias Williams died March y^e 2th 1739.
Peter Daniel died March y^e 8th 1739.
John Segar died December 19th 1740.
Ann Smith died March 15th 1740.
Benjamine Reader died March 21st $174\frac{0}{1}$.
William Dobbs died February y^e 8th 1740.
Mary Wife of Robert Daniel died March y^e 9th $174\frac{0}{1}$.
Katherine Daughter of Robert & Mary Daniel died March 24th $174\frac{0}{1}$.
Robert Brown died March 31st 1741.
Elizabeth Daughter of Philip & Eliz. Brook died April y^e 13th 1741.
Dorothy wife of Thos Chilton died April y^e 25 1741.
Benjamine Meacham died April y^e 8th 1741.
Elizabeth Daughter of William & Jane Mountague Died May y^e 16. 1741.

Sarah Daughter of James & Ann Campton died June y° 4th 1741.
George Son of James & Ann Compton died Sep⁺ yᵉ 6th 1741.
James Wood died Sep⁺ yᵉ 28th 1741.
Susanna Wood died Sepʳ yᵉ 28th 1741.
Catherine Bristow died Decemʳ yᵉ 16th 1741.
John Carter died Janʳy. 24th 174½.
Anthony Collins died Janʳy yᵉ 27th 174½.
Lucy Stapleton died April y° 23d 1742.
Constant Anderson Wife of Wᵐ Anderson died May yᵉ 30th 1742.
Ann Daughter of George & Ann Wortham died April 6th 1742.
Sarah Daughter of John & Judith Wortham died April 6th 1742.
Ann Wife of James Compton died Octoʳ yᵉ 1st 1742.
John Pace died Septemʳ yᵉ 6th 1742.
Ann Wife of John Rhodes Senʳ died Septemʳ yᵉ 20th 1742.
William Bristow died Novʳ yᵉ 15th 1742.
Ruth Wife of William Owen died Novemʳ yᵉ 6th 1742.
William Paret died Octoʳ yᵉ 15th 1742.
Agatha Daughter of Ave Daniel died Sep⁺ 15th 1742.
Mary Wortham died May yᵉ 26th 1742.
Rebecca Kidd died June yᵉ 20th 1742.
Mary Daughter of Thoˢ & Mary Shelton died August yᵉ 5th 1742.
Sarah Chowning died August yᵉ 18th 1742.
Mary Daughter of John & Susanna Williams died Octoʳ yᵉ 1st 1742.
William Southern died Novʳ yᵉ 17th 1742.
Samuel Batcheler died Decemʳ yᵉ 12th 1742.
Samuel Sheepherd Son of Henry Sheepherd Died Janʳy 18 1742.
Elinor Morton Died October 30th 1742.
Robert Daniel Died July yᵉ 8th 1742.
Mary Turman Died March 12th 174⅔.
Elizabeth Humphris Died March yᵉ 7 174⅔.
Thomas Shelton died March yᵉ 24th 174⅔.
Milicent Daughter of John & Ann Croffield died Janʳʸ 23d 174⅔.
    Torn.   of Jacob Stiff died April 16th 1743.
    Torn.   iff Died May 1st 1743.
Benjamin Hackney died May 9th 1743.
John Fearn Died May yᵉ 1st 1743.
Jane Lee Died September 5th 1743.
Catherine Daughter of Henry & Betty Daniel Died August 21st
    1743.
Elizabeth Gest Died September 11th 1743.
Henry Daniel Died September 7th 1743.
Betty Wallace Died October 25th 1743.
Mary Guttrey Died Janʳʸ 2 1743.
Priscilla Stevens Died Janʳʸ 29th 1743.
Henry Tugle Died Janʳʸ 3d 1743.
Ann Croffield died Janʳʸ 24th 1743.
Sarah Wood Died Febʳʸ 27th 1743.
Jacob Rhodes Son of John Rhodes Senʳ Died Feb'y 26 1743.
Frances Sears Died Febʳʸ 16th 1743.
Robert Rodes Died Febʳʸ 23d 1743.
Richard Lewis Died Febʳʸ 29th 1743.
John Dose Died March 17th 1743.
John Henesey Died March 4th 1743.

Ann Chowning Died March 12th 1743.
John Chowning Died March 19th 1743.
John Walker died March 174¾.
Mary Daughter of James & Eliz^a Meachan died March ye 17th 1743.
Mary Rhodes died March ye 26th 1744.
Phillip Warwick died March ye 27th 1744.
Mary Wood died April ye 9th 1744.
William Ryley died April ye 6th 1744.
William Carrell died April ye 4th 1744.
Patrick Night died March ye 17th 174¾.
Eustace Howard died Feb^{ry} ye 28th 174¾.
George Chowning died April ye 1st 1744.
Eliz^a Johnson died April ye 23d 1744.
Martha Chowning died April ye 6th 1744.
Mary Daughter of James & Eliz^a Dunlevy died Octo^r 44.
Robert Alldin died June ye 21st 1744.
Mary Bristow died Sepr ye 5th 1744.
John Wortham died Jan^{ry} ye 21st 1744.
Mary Wife of Jacob Stiff died Decem^r 21st 1744.
Mary Wife of Wm Owen died April 24th 1744.
Elizabeth Wife of James Dunlevy died Sep^t ye 13th 1744.
Machen Son of John & Judith Wortham died Decem^r ye 30th 1744.
Elizabeth Wife of Curtis Hardee died Decem^r ye 26th 1744.
John Warwick died April ye 4th 1744.
Rachel wife of Harry George died Feb^{ry} ye 10th 1744.
Elizabeth Clowdas died Augst ye 7th 1744.
Mactyer Cornelius died Sep^t ye 28th 1744.
Elizabeth Gardner died July ye 13th 1744.
Sarah Wife of Henry Emberson died Feb^{ry} ye 4th 1744.
Nathaniel son of Thos & Christian Sanders died Sepr 24th 1744.
Thomas Cheney died Feb^{ry} ye 10th 1744.
Jemima Daughter of Randolph & Sarah Rhodes died March ye 2nd
    174⅘.
Ocany Santo died March ye 17th 174⅘.
Thomas Son of Joseph Tugle died Jan^{r}y ye 26th 174⅘.
Elizabeth Daughter of Thos Mountague died Feb^{ry} ye 5th 1744.
Garret Daniel died Jan^{r}y ye 28th 174⅘.
William Johnson Senr died March ye 10th 174⅘
Arthur Thomas died April ye 28th 1745.
Elizabeth Brooks died March ye 9th }
Philip Brooks died March ye 24   } 174⅘
William Cardwell died Decem^r ye 19th 1744.
Mary Sanders died Jan^{r}y ye 24th 1744.
James Jones died May ye 4th 1745.
Winnie Morris a Mulatto died Aprill ye 18th 1745.
Samuell Son of Edward & Mary Clark died June ye 19th 1745.
Mary Overstreet died May ye 25th 1745.
Mary Meacham died May ye 27th 1745.
Elizabeth Wife of Wm Jones died June ye 18th 1745.
Anne the Wife of Thomas Sovlt died Sep^t 19th 1745.
Elizabeth Daughter of Wm Jones died Sep^t 19th 1745.
William Pace Junr died Octo^r y^e 10th 1745.
William Son of Joseph Smith died Decem^r y^e 2d 1745.

Mary Blakey died Jan^{r}y y^{e} 16th 1745.
Jane Daughter of Henry Mickleburrough died Jan^{r}y y^{e} 26th 174$\frac{5}{6}$.
Frances Daughter of Henry Mickleburrough died Jan^{r}y y^{e} 30th 174$\frac{5}{6}$.
John Son of George Wortham died y^{e} 9th day of Jan^{r}y 174$\frac{5}{6}$.
William Son of Wm Hill died April y^{e} 25th 1746.
Elizabeth Brook died Novr y^{e} 14th 1746.
Robert Norman died Decem^{r} 23d 1746.
Thomas Clarke died Sep^{t} 18th 1746.
Catharine Dobbs died Octo^{r} y^{e} 31st 1746.
Rachel Daughter of Charles Wood died Septr y^{e} 10th 1746.
Frances Daughter of Wm Hill died May ye 30th 1746.
Ann Daughter of Wm Daniel died Novem^{r} ye 25th 1746.
William Daniel died Novr ye 28th 1746.
Josiah Daniel died Decem^{r} ye 21st 1746.
Agatha Daniel died Decem^{r} ye 29th. 1746.
John Son of John & Frances Ranes died May 15th. 1746.
Martha Dillion died April ye 26th. 1746.
Garett Son of Edmun Dillion died Sepr ye 11th. 1746.
Elizabeth Daughter of James Cole died Septr 29th. 1746.
Clare Marks died May y^{e} 16th. 1746.
Anthony Smith Died Decem^{r} y^{e} 1st 1745.
Blackley Son of John & Mary Gardner died Decem^{r} 12th 1746.
Elliner Devall Died Decem^{r} 7th 1746.
Rachel Chowning Junr Died Feb^{ry} 23d 174$\frac{6}{7}$.
Rachel Chowning Senr Died March y^{e} 27th. 1747.
Hannah Bristow died March y^{e} 10th. 174$\frac{6}{7}$.
Ruban Allin died April y^{e} 15th 1747.

Register of Births & Christen   for the Year of our Lord 1768.

Jane Daughter of Nathaniel & Mary Burwell was born Septem the 7th. 1768 & baptized January y^{e} 15th. 1769.
William Son of John & Dorothy Berry was born December the 21st. 1768. & baptized January 22d. 1769.
Charles Son of John & Anne Hodges was born * * the 12th 1768 & baptized the 28th. D^{o}.
Randolph, Son of William & Mary Segar was bo * * the 22d. 1768 & baptized December 26th. 176*.
the 23th 1769.
William, Son of Abraham & Anne Clowdas was born the 19th Day of March 1769. & baptized in April D^{o}.
Leonard Son of Robert & Mildred Stamper was born * * *
born December 14th 1769.
William Chadwick Son of John & Sarah * * was born October 8th. 1769.

Register of Births & Christenings for the Year of our Lord 1769.

William Son of Thomas & Mary Segar was born February the 20. 1769. & baptized the 7th. of March.
William Son of George & Mary Davis was born February * *
ances Daughter of Lewis & Frances Dudley was born September 19th 1769 & baptized October 21st.

* * Son of Joseph & Elizabeth Tuggle was born * the 6th 1769, & Baptized Decr 29th.

* * of James & Mary Kidd was born December 26th. 1769 * * January 15th. 1770.

* * orn Son of Benson & Susannah Siblie was born the 5th 1769.

Robert, Son of John Long & Sarah his Wife was born August 12th 1769.

Nelson, Son of John Humphries & was born September 24th 1769.

Naney & Betsey Daughters of William & Ann Gardener were born February 22d 1769.

Henry, Son of John & Sarah Hutson was born April 2d 1769.

Catherine Daughter of John & Elizabeth Seward was born May 23d 1769.

James Son of Edward & Margaret Crouch was born June 2d 1769.

Frances, Daughter of William & Rachel Taylor was born June 17th 1769.

Henry Son of Henry & Elizabeth Thurston * * *

Births & Christenings for the year of or 1771.

William Brookes son of John & Anne Hodges born January 11. 1771.

John Son of Thomas & Mary Segar was born the 13 of March 1771 & baptized March 24th 1771.

William Harrow, Son of Thomas & Sarah Anne Harrow was born January 20th 1771.

Burwell Laton, Son of Thomas & Elizabeth Laton March 30th 1771.

James Morris, Son of John & Elizabeth Morris was March 11th 1771.

Edward Jones Bristow, Son of Benj^m & Elizabeth B was born June 16th 1770.

Benjamin Batchelder, Son of Joseph & Michal Batchelder was born may the 4th 1771.

Hamstead & Ranson, Sons of John & Judith Wake were born august the 4th 1771 & Baptized the 6th of Octr following.

Jane Daughter of Lewis & Frances Dudley was born Septr the 25th 1771 & baptised Octr 12th.

Mary, Daughter of William & Susanna Jackson was born Sep^tr 10th 1771.

Elizabeth, Daughter of John & Elizabeth Daniel was born Decr 20th 1771, & baptized the 18th Jany following.

John, Son of John & Anne Crowdas born September 27th 1771.

John, Son of John & Mildred Layton born Novr 12. 1771.

Daniel Ball, Son of Benson & Susanna Sibley was born Decr 14th 1771.

Daughter of Humphrey & Elizabeth Wattkins s born September 16th 1771.

Catherine, Daughter of William & Rachel Taylor was born December 8th 1771.

John, Son of Abraham & Anne Crowdas was born the   September
1771.
    Stevens, Son of John & Sarah Mariah Craine born
March 23rd 1772.

Registry of Funerals Commencing May 19th 1795.

Henry Heffernan Rector.

Colonel Smith was interred on Friday June 26 1795.
John Jackson was interred on Thursday July 2nd.
Cap Tuning on Saturday July 11th 1795.
Sarah Berkeley on Sunday Augt 16th 1795.
——— Dennison on Sunday Sep^t 20th 1795.
——— Curtis on Tuesday Sep^t 22nd 1795.
——— Peachey on Monday October 5th 1795.
——— Muse on Saturday Decr 12th 1795.
——— Adkins on Sunday January 24th 1795.
Benjamin Churchill April 6th 1796.
Sarah Letitia Heffernan died July 12th 1796 at 5 oclock in the morn-
    ing, was buried on Thursday July 14th 1796. by the Rev^d M^r
    Smith.

Mrs. Hannah Kemp this 27th of april 1802 made oath before the
Court sitting in Urbanna Coart House that Mrs. Sarah Letitia Heffernan died on the day & hour above recorded, she being present
when Mrs. Heffernan died.

Ralph Wormeley.

Elizabeth Burwell Churchill died May 17th 1802.
Edmund Berkeley died July 8th 1802, 5^m past 7: p. m.
Mary Grymes died April 14th 1805.
Philip Ludwell Grymes died 18th of May 1805.
Jane Sayre died January 1st 1806.
Lucy Nelson Heffernan March 21st 1813.

Register of Marriages for the year of our Lord 1768.

John Dunlavy & Elizabeth Healey married nov^r 17th 1768.
Thomas Robinson & Mary Robinson Married December 10th 1768.
John Craine & Sarah Mariah Butterworth married Decr 10th 1768.
John Brown & Mary Acrey married Decr 10th 1768.
Steward Williams & Sarah Roan married Decr 11th 1768.
Robert Daniel jr. & Pene Lee married Decr 29th 1768.
William Acra & Elizabeth Blackley married Decr 30th 1768.

Marriages for the Year of Our Lord 1769.

Samuel Wood & Sarah Durham married Jany 19th 1769.
John Keys & Margaret Smith married Feby 4th 1769.
James Dunlavy & Elizabeth Falkner married Feby 17th 1769.
Henry Thurston & Elizabeth Brame married Feby 23rd 1769.
Alexander Rumage & Mary McDaniel married March 23rd 1769.
Howard Williams & Elizabeth Montague married March 23rd 1769.
John Layton & Mildred Sibley married March 25th 1769.
Bartholomew Yates & Anne Daniel married May 11th 1769.

Samuel Klug & Elizabeth Yates married. by the Rev^d Mr. Dunlap May 13th 1769.

Peter Kemp & Betty Daniel married May 18th 1769.

John Jackson & Elizabeth Boss married July 9th 1769.

William Degge & Mary Sutton married February 23rd 1770.

Edward Bristow Jr. & Mary Beaman married March 18th 177 .

Alexander Ramage & Hannah Chiles married april 10th 1770.

John Kidd & Elizabeth Jones married april 14th 1770.

Benjamin Williamson & Mildred Hutton Married april 26th 1770.

John Barrack s^r & Mary Sanders married April 30th 1770.

John Chapman & Elizabeth Elliott married May 12th 1770.

John Barrack Jr. & Mary Sanders married June 2nd 1770.

William Daniel & Lucy Guttery married July 26th 1770.

Lyne Rowe & Martha Clark married Septr 26th 1770.

Isaac Palmer & Elizabeth Taff married Sep^{tr} 28th 1770.

John Harwood & Mary Curtis married Novr 17th 1770.

William Smith & Nelly Livingston married Decr 1st 1770.

Humphrey Watkins & Elizabeth Thurston married Decr 2nd 1770.

James Bristow & Mary Brooks married Decr 9th 1770.

Roger Blackburn & Elizabeth Owen married Decr 15th 1770.

John Blake & Susannah Blake married Decr 24th 1770.

John Deagle & Hannah Sanders married Decr 25th 1770.

Thomas Brooks & Margaret Beaman January 29th 177–.

Edward Bristow jr. & Anne Brooks Married January 31st 177–.

Isaac Ware & Clara Stringer married March 16th 177–.

John Kemp & Sarah Batchelder married April 13th 1771.

Corbin Griffin (of York County) & Mary Berkeley married April 20th 1771.

Churchhill Gibson   M. Daniel married July 1771.
          son of ———— ———— August 17th 1773.

Lucy Blake, Daughter of Benjamin Seward was born January 1st 1773.

George, Son of Benjamin Kidd & Jane his Wife was born June 20th 1773.

Ann Chowning, Daughter of William & Rachel Taylor was born December 11th 1773.

John Thurston, Son of Benjamin & Frances Williams was born April 24th 1774.

William Son of Thomas & Mary Burton was born Novr 25th 17—.

William, Son of Henry & Elizabeth Thurston was born Sep^{tr} 11th 177–.

William, Son of John & Frances Dean was born January 16th 1775.

Thomas Mitcham, Son of Joseph & Judith Brooks was born January 31st 1775.

William, Son of William & Mildred Pryor was born December 10th 1774.

Nancy Vevel Parriott was born the 5th of January 1775.

William Chowning, Son of Churchhill & Ann Blakey was born January 30th 1775.

Nancy, Daughter of Benjamin & Ann Seward was born the 15th day of September 1775.

Samuel, Son of Robert & Mildred Stamper was born the 6th of october 1775.

Elizabeth, Daughter of John & Frances Dean was born February 14th 1776.

Fanny, Daughter of Philip & Elizabeth Brooke was born February 5th 1776.

James, Son of James & Betty Stiff was born April 3rd 1775.

John Blake, Son of James & Betty Stiff was born September 23rd 1776.

Elizabeth, Daughter of Lewis & Judith Steevens was born January 24th 1777.

Ann, Daughter of John & Ann Hodges was born March 12th 1777.

William, Son of William & Dorothy Hutson of the Parish of Stratton Major in King & Queen County was born October 26th 1776.

Elizabeth, Daughter of Daniel & Mary Jefferson was born February 5th 1775.

David, Son of Daniel & Mary Jefferson was born March 30th 1777.

Sally, Daughter of James & Mary Kidd was born March 12th 1776.

James Jones, Son of James & Elizabeth Dunlevy was born Jany 31st 1776.

George, Son of Robert & Mildred Stamper was born July 22nd 1777.

Edmond Abbott, Son of John & Mary Stevens was born Sep^tr 13th 1777.

Elizabeth Stannard, Daughter of John & Catherine Montague of the County of Essex was born October 30th 1777 & baptized Novr 11th at the House of Mr John Chinn of Lancaster County.

Simon Laughlin & Anne Scrosby married September ye 3rd 1772.

Robert Spratt & Anne Yates married Sepr 19th 1772.

James Crossfield & Anne Williams married October 27th 1772.

Churchhill Blakey & Anne Chowning married Octr 24th 1772.

Nathaniel Burwell & Susanna Grymes married Novr 28th 1772.

William Boldin & Mary Dunlevy married Decr 21st 1772.

John Seward & Rebekah Groom married Decr 27th 1772.

John Cornelius & Sarah Acra married Decr 27th 1772.

Abner Crowdas & Sally Haily married Decr 31st 1772.

William Keeling & Judith Hipkinstall married February 4th 1773.

Laurence Meacham & Frances Batchelder married February 4th 1773.

John Bryant & Mary Sears married March 6th 1773.

Michael Payne & Mary Elliott married March 26th 1773.

William Young & Jane Mickelburrough married April 8th 1773.

Philip Ludwell Grymes & Judith Wormeley married May 30th 1773.

Siah Cornelius & Jane Bray married May 30th 1773.

James Ware & Jane Machan married July 22nd 1773.

Robert Ware & Catherine Machan married July 22nd 1773.

John Askins & Anne Burton married Sep^t 4th 1773.

John Dean & Frances Smith married Sep^t 16th 1773.

Chowning Kidd & Catherine French married Sepr 23rd 1773.

John Chowning & Precilla Whitters married Sepr 24th 1773.

Thomas Wills & Sarah Dean married Sepr 25th 1773.

Benjamin Grymes & Sarah Robinson married October 9th 1773.

Joseph Brooks & Judith Hill married October 30th 1773.

William Pace & Cressy Sanders married November 4th 1773.

William Blake & Rachel Williams married Novr 4th 1773.

———— ———— Franky Garrett (King & Queen) married Novr 4th 1773.
Thomas Tenoe & Judith Belfare married May 21th 1774.
George Hauks & Mary Tuggle married July 2nd 1774.
John Chowning & Catharine Chowning married July 16th 1774.
Joseph Martin & Ann Deagle married August 15th 1774.
George Lorimer & Hannah Thacker Timberlake married October 8th 1774.
Melchizedeck Brame & Catharine Gibson married November 11th 1774.
William Jones & Betty Churchhill married Novr 24th 1774.
William Wood & Fanny Blake married Decr 4th 1774.
John Miller & Hester Christian married Decr 10th 1774.
John Boss & Judith Faulkner married Decr 12th 1774.
James Stiff & Betty Blake married Decr 17th 1774.
Thomas Blake & Ann Blake married Decr 24th 1774.
Benjamin Stevens & Joannah Barrick married Decr 25th 1774.
Benjamin Barrack & Frankey Clare married Decr 31st 1774.
Zebulum Hearing & Johannah Jackson married January 3d 1775.
William Deagle & Martha Boss married January 15th 1775.
George Warwick & Elizabeth Chowning married January 30th 1775.
Richard Layton & Elizabeth Stodix married February 4th 1775.
Daniel Dejarnatt & May Davis married February 12th 1775.
William Hutson & Jane Falkner married April 17th 1775.
Lodowick Jones & Lucy Tarpley married May 6th 1775.
William Taylor & Priscilla Segar married May 13th 1775.
John Wiat & Sarah Charles married June 3d 1775.
Charles Dudley & Nanny Sutton married Sep^{tr} 4th 1775.
James Turner & Martha Rowe married Septr 29th 1775.
John Montague & Catharine Yates married Decr 14th 1776.
Benj^a Rhodes & Patience Kelly married Decr 18th 1776.
Charles Whitticor & Mary Herrin married Decr 21st 1776.
William Shackelford & Catharine Daniel married Decr 21st 1776.
William Ware & Mary Bolden married Feby 15. 1777.
Thomas Crittendon & Catharine Shephard married Feby. 13th 1777.
Nicholas Tuggle & Susanna Abbot married Feby 16th 1777.
John Healey & Jane Warwick married March 30th 1777.
Thomas Willis & Mary Blake married May 3d 1777.
Richard Bird & Mary Pamplin married June 12th 1777.
Lunsford Daniel & Lydia Daniel married July 10th 1777.
John Owen & Mary Hill married Octr. 30th 1777.
Charles Howerton & Catharine Montague married Novr 3d 1777.
Charles Grymes & Mary Hubard married Decr 20th 1777.
Jonathan Eyre & Judith Kidd married Decr 28th. 1777.
Joseph Barwick & Ann Sanders married January 3d. 1778.
James Maury Fontaine & Betty Carter Churchhill married Jany 3d. 1778.
James Wortham & Franky Smith married Jany 4th 1778.
Michael Osborn & Ann Bowers married January 10th, 1778.
Jeremiah Powell & Agnes Dudley married Jany 17th 1778.
William Owen & Jane Batchelder married Jany 13th 1778.
George Lee & Peggy Hardy married Jany 22d 1778.
William Robinson & Ann Dunlevy married February 10th 1778.
Benjamin Williams & Esther Smith married Feby 25th 1778.

Thomas Gaines & Katy Wortham married April 19th 1778.
Abraham Currell Blade & Elizabeth Davis married August 18th 1778.
Thomas Harwood & Lucy Meacham married Sep^t 27. 1778.
Samuel Brooks & Priscilla Piper married October 31st 1778.
John Brooks & Anne Mickelburrough married May 13th.
John Carter & Hannah Baylor of King & Queen County married
    May 15th 1779.
Harry Beverley Yates & Lucy Murray married May 23d 1779.
John Groom & Catharine Ware married May 30th 1779.
Delphos Scott & Sarah Faulkner married May 30th 1779.
John Fenning & Mary Humphreys married May 31st 1779.
Daniel Jefferson & Priscilla Barrick married August 1st. 1779.
George West & Winney Shelton married August 28th 1779.
Joseph Sylvester & Fanny Hayton married Decr 1st. 1779.
William Murray & Ann Kemp married Decr 18th 1779.
Isaac Mitchell & Mary Johnson, of Essex County, married Dec^r
    19th. 1779.
George Brushwood & Sarah Garrett, of King & Queen County,
    married Decr 24th 1779.
William Bowden & Sarah Owen married Decr 26th 1779.
Edward Brook & Catharine Holleway married Decr 2 1779.
Roger Blackburn & Jane Hackney married Decr 30th 1779.
Oliver Daniel & Mary Stevens married January 1st 1780.
John Kidd & Lucy Collier married February 23d 1780.
William Moore & Elizabeth Swords married March 2d 1780.
Thomas Mountague & Ann Batchelder married March 23d. 1780.
William Elliot & Rebecca Deagle married May 18th 1780.
John Dance & Ann Ross married June 2d 1780.
Benjamin Kidd & Frances Dillard married June 3d 1780.
Matthew Elliot & Anne Hearing married Sep^{tr} 17th 1780.
Robert Heughen & Joanna Hearing married Sep^{tr} 17th 1780.
Isham Tatum & Rachel Garrett married Octr 19th. 1780.
Richard Cauthon & Anne Seward married Novr 9th 1780.
Samuel More & Martha Davis married March 28th 1781.
Sanders Bristow & Sarah Smith married March 29th. 1781.
William George & Ann Batchelder married April 8th 1781.
Reuben Lee & Sarah Williams married May 10th 1781.
Robinson Shackelford & Ann Bushrod Carpenter married May 12th
    1781.
John George & Susanna George married May 22d 1781.
Warner Dunstan & Susanna Brooking of Gloucester married May
    30th. 1781.
William Brown & Rhoda Callahan married August 18th. 1781.
George Rudolph & Elizabeth Hughes married in Kingston Parish
    Gloucester, September 13th. 1781.
John Flippen & Elizabeth Carney of Kingston Parish Gloucester
    married September 14th 1781.
Thomas Hayes & Mary Buckner Walker of Gloucester married
    Novr 3d. 1781.
Jonathan Denison & Jane Morgan married Decr 17th 1781.
Mordecai Cook & Elizabeth Scrosby married Decr 20th 1781.
Richard Crittendon & Frances Sykes, of King & Queen, married
    Decr 22d. 1781.

Robert Townley & Jane Anderson of King & Queen, married Dec[r] 29th. 1781.

John Coleman & Dorothy Wyatt, of Gloucester, married January 12th. 1782.

John Stephens & Elizabeth Collier, of King & Queen, married January 17th 1782.

Thomas Pierce & Milly Webb, of King & Queen, married January 19th 1782.

James Guthrie & Nancy Garrett, of King & Queen, married March 28th 1782.

John Dunn & Anne Cauthon, of Essex, married September 30th 1782.

William Bristow & Jane Chowning married October 5th 1782.

Thomas Patterson & Elizabeth Batchelder married Oct[r] 24th 1782.

Robert Coats & Mary Spann (of Gloucester) married Nov[r] 16th 1782.

Sydner Belfield (of Richmond) & Ann Young (of Essex) married November the 28th 1782.

John Pryor & Delphia Dilliard (of King & Queen) married Dec[r] 5th 1782.

William Hundley & Elizabeth Goode (of Essex) married Dec[r] 5th 1782.

William Moulson & Ann Guthrie (of King & Queen) married Dec[r] 6th 1782.

Benjamin Moore & Susanna Milbey (of King & Queen) married Dec[r] 19th 1782.

Christopher Brooke & Elizabeth Saunders married Dec[r] 24th 1782.

Thomas Bennet & Mary Hardy married Dec[r] 25. 1782.

James Hart & Milly Gest (of King & Queen) married Dec[r] 25th 1782.

Reubin Broadass & Elizabeth Garland (of Gloucester) married Dec[r] 26th 1782.

Francis Thornton & Elizabeth Hackney married Dec[r] 26th 1782.

James Cammiel & Heany Peters married January 2d 1783.

Michael Dixon & Catharine Didlake (King & Queen) married Jany 16th 1783.

Joseph Wyatt & Elizabeth Turner married January 23. 1783.

William Meredith & Ann Rootes married February 8th 1783.

Edward Trice & Ann Jeffries (King & Queen) married February 13th 1783.

John Groom & Elizabeth Curry (King & Queen) married February 14th 1783.

John Shackelford & Mary Drummond (King & Queen) married February 14th 1783.

John Mackendree & Ruthey Milby (King & Queen) married Sep[r] 28th 1783.

James Burton & Frances Yarrington (King & Queen) married October 23d 1783.

Miles Brown & Rachel Jordan (King & Queen) married Nov[r] 6th 1783.

James Clayton & Jane Dillard (King & Queen) married Nov[r] 13th 1783.

John Sadler & Mildred Corr (King & Queen) married Nov[r] 20th 1783.

John Dudley & Elizabeth Moulson married Novr 21st 1783.
Philip Gulley & Mary Sutton married November 27th 1783.
Gregory Perry & Mary Mills (Gloucester) married Novr 27. 1783.
Johnson Wake & Lucy Harvey married Decr 4th 1783.
Job. Stone & Elizabeth Oakes (King & Queen) married Decr 9th 1783.
Edmond Garret & Nancy Didlake (King & Queen) married Decr 18th 1783.
George Dejarnet & Anne Walker (Essex) married Decr 18th 1783.
John Downey & Rachel Sadler (Essex) married Jan'y 8th 1784.
Benjamin Kidd & Mary Guthrie (King & Queen) married Jan'y 8th 1784.
Reuben Layton & Martha Wilcox married February 19th 1784.
Benjamin Jacobs & Frances Blackley married March 27th 1784.
Richard Stalker & Elizabeth Emmerson married April 4th 1784.
John Robinson & Debby Dunlap married April 17th 1784.
John Good & Elizabeth Stevens married April 27th 1784.
Ralph Watts & Hanna Dunn married May 12th 1784.
Linzey Clark & Caroline Segar Brim married May 22d 1784.
Thomas Chowning & Elizabeth George married May 29th 1784.
Rlchard Gwathmey & Charlotte Spratt married June 3d 1784.
Thomas Cook & Kitty Meredith (King & Queen) married June 5th 1784.
George Fernald & Frances Madiex married June 26th 1784.
James Henderson & Elizabeth Milby married August
William Robinson & Ursule Robin
John Mickelburrough & Caty Allen married March 27th 1785.
Henry Batchelder & Elizabeth Dillard married March 31st 1785.
Benjamin Herring & Nancy Fleming married April 10th 1785.
George Sykes & Alice Mourning Livingston (King & Queen) married May 12th 1785.
Thomas Brooks & Anne Johnson married May 15th 1785.
Reubin Davenport & Jane Crump (King William) married May 28th 1785.
Benjamin Hackney & Jane George married June 2d 1785.
Lewis Boss & Sarah Boss married June 11th 1785.
Charles Whitaker & Elizabeth Stevens married June 30th 1785.
John Mitchell & Sally Gatewood (King & Queen) married June 30th 1785.
Thomas Wiatt & Catharine Robinson (Gloucester) married July 2d
George Blake & Betty Saunders married July 14th 1785.
Oliver Yarrington & Elizabeth Ware married July 15 1785.
Henry Chowning & Margaret Allen married Septr 11th 1785.
William Edwards & Nancy Robinson (Gloucester) married October 15th 1785.
Stubberfield Bowls & Sally Collier (King & Queen) married October 20th 1785.
John Cloudas & Elizabeth Cloudas (Essex) married Octr 27th 1785.
Thomas Healy & Sarah Mitchell married Octr 29th 1785.
John Buckner & Dorothy Scrosby married November 24th 1785.
Beverley Deane & Tilley Webb (King & Queen) married Decr 3d 1785.
John Hodges & Elizabeth Blackburn married December 3d 1785.

* * Woods & Elizabeth Brooks married December 17th 1785.
* * * & Catherine George married Feby 14th 1790.
* * * & Dolly Coleman (K. & Q.) married Feby 20th 1790.
George Haynes & Susanna Waller (K. & Q.) married March 20th 1790.
Thomas Hundley & Elizabeth McTyre (Essex) married April 1st 1790.
James Milby & Frances Ross married April 11th 1790.
Robert Didlick & Mary Baker (K. & Q.) married May 20th 1790.
William Curtis & Mary Robinson Whiting married June 5. 1790.
James Hall & Mary Walden (King & Q.) married June 24. 1790.

The above drawn off & sent to the Clks. of the several Counties wherein the marriages were solemnized.

Samuel Klug. Minister.

Lewis Hening & Jane Chapman married * *
Robert Mickleburrough & Elizabeth Dean married * *
Braxton Dunlevy & Mary Hibble married Decr 22d 1791.
Robert Lumpkin jr. & Lucy Roane (K. & Q.) married Decr 22d 1791.
William Healy & Elizabeth Bristow married Decr 24th 1791.
Charles Walden & Mary Ison (K. & Q.) married Decr 29th 1791.
Coleman Lumpkin & Sarah Calaun (Glos.) marie^d Jany 7th 1792.
William Bland j^r & Mary Ann Corr (K. & Q.) married Feby 20th 1791.
Staige Davis & Elizabeth Gardner (K. & Q.) married Feby 28th 17—.
James Batchelder & Mary Jackson married March
Thomas Sears & Anne Street (Essex) married February 11th 1786.
Thomas Brooke & Anne Taff. (Essex) married February 26th 1786.
Drury Bagwell & Catharine Ware (King & Queen) married Feby 28th 1786.
Batchelder Thurston & Peggy Daniel married March 16th 1786.
George Gardner & Elizabeth Dunn married March 16th 1786.
Richard Mountague & Charlotte Mountague married March 19th 1786.
Bartholomew Bristow & Ann Saunders married April 15th 1786.
Samuel Brooking & Mary Baker married July 8th 1786.
William Kidd & Rachel Chowning married August 3d 1786.
Robert Wilson & Betty Payne married October 8th 1786.
William Craine & Sarah Major Dillard married October 14th 1786.
Thomas Lambeth & Lucy Kidd (King & Queen) married October 18th 1786.
John Corr & Frances Campbell (King & Queen) married October 24th 1786.
Thomas Royston & Elizabeth Royston (Gloucester) married October 26th 1786.
Reuben Layton & Elizabeth Burton married October 29th 1786.
Henry Kidd & Catharine Swords were married by the Revd Mr Needler Robinson Novr 26. 1786.

The above drawn off for the Clerks of those County's wherein the above Marriages were solemnized.

Josiah Bristow & Fanny Bristow married December 24th 1786.

Richard Hopkins & Frances Blake married December 26th 1786.

William Didlake & Lucy Boyd (King & Queen) married January 7th 1787.

John McWilliams & Elizabeth Green (King & Queen) married January 20th 1787.

Charles Roane & Maretia Garrett (King & Queen) married Jany 26th 1787.

Thomas Spencer & Nancy Foster (King & Queen) married Feby 17th 1787.

Thomas Burk & Elizabeth Sutton married March 8th 1787.

James Taylor Horseley & Johannah Dudley (Glouster) married March 14th 1787.

Ralph Bland & Frances Corr (King & Queen) married April 15th 1787.

Christian Ryner & Rhoda Dudley (Gloucester) married March 14 1787.

Smith Horsley & Elizabeth Rilee Glou married 20th Decr 1787.

Edward Watts & Ann Garrett K. & Q. married Decr 21st 1787.

John Norris & Agatha Garrett, K & Q, married Decr 22d 1787.

Thomas Montague & Catharine Vass married Decr 22d 1787.

James Didlake and Mary Gardner, K. & Q. married Decr 22d 1787.

William James & Elzabeth Major married Decr 22d 1787.

Charles Curtis & Ann Murray married Decr 22d 1787.

David O'Dear & Nancy Shepherd K. & Q. Decr 23d 1787.

Niels Winning & Ann Miller married Decr 24th 1787.

John Whitely & Sally Saunders married Decr 25th 1787.

William Halyard & Frances Stedman (King & Queen married Decr 26th 1787.

Thacker Campbell & Hannah Montague (Essex) married Decr 27th 1787.

Drawn off for the Clks. of those Counties wherein the above Marriages were Solemnized.

James Davis & Elizabeth Humphris married Jany 28th 1788.

Robert Wake & Ann Elliott married February 1st 1788.

Thomas Robinson & Elizabeth Dillard (King & Queen) married February 9th 1788.

John Curry Montague & Charlotte Montague married March 23d 1788.

John Wood & Nancy Longest married April 2d 1788.

James Baker & Johanna Bray married May 3d 1788.

George West & Frances Barrick married July 20th 1788.

Saunders Bristow & Nancy Crossfield married August 17th. 1788.

Thomas Jones & Elizabeth Didlake (K. &. Q.) married Aug^st 23. 1788.

John Wilkines & Lucy Gibson married Aug^st 31st 1788.

James Boss & Susan Powell married Sep^tr 4th. 1788.

Lewis Walden & Judith Kidd married Septr 6th 1788.

Thomas Fargueson & Ann Didlak (K. & Q.) married Septr 7th 1788.

Robert Chowning & Fanny Abbott married January 1st. 1789.

William Kidd & Nancy Kidd married January 1st. 1789.

John Hebble & Elizabeth Haynes married January 17th 1789.

John Woodley & Mary Jefferson married January 19th 1789.
George Daniel & Lucy Clare married February 12th 1789.
Thomas Bray & Polly Bristow married February 21st. 1789.
Richard Bland & Mary Bowden K & Queen married March 14th
1789.
Beverley Carlton & Caty Drummond (K. & Q.) married March 19th
1789.
Robert Dudley & Ann Blake married April 19th 1789.
Zachariah Groom & Elizabeth Wyett married May 28. 1789.
Henry Chapman & Ann Bland (King & Queen) married June 11th
1789.
Philip Nelson & Sarah Nelson Burwell married June 27th 1789.
William Crittenden Webb & Fanny Wortham married July 11th
1789.
William Muire & Catharine Seward (K. & Q.) married Augst 20th.
1789.
John Hibble & Mary French married August 25th 1789.
Lewis Walden & Lucy Wallace (K. & Queen) married August 29th
1789.
John Crittenden & Polly Ware (King & Queen) married Decr 17th
1789.
Thomas Dudley & Betsey Shepard Crittenden (King & Queen) Dec^r
19 1789.
Henry Daniel Shepherd & Mary Daniel married December 19th
1789.
Philip Didlake & Lucy Falkner (King & Queen) married Decr 26th
1789.
Christopher Wake & Sarah Sommers married Decr 28. 1789.
Leonard George & Susanna George Daniel married Decr 31. 1789.
James Lee & Frances Thurston married January 5th 1790.
William Montague & Elizabeth Valentine married Jany 14th 1790.
Nathan Hall & Catharine Crossfield married January 28th 179 .
Nelson Daniel & Jean Blackburn married Februa— — ——.
Peter Wyatt & Josie Shepherd (King & Queen) married Octr 2d
1790.
Isaac Kidd & Polly Kidd married December 18th 1790.
George Davis Saunders & Charlotte Merchant married Decr 30th
1790.
Hudson Muse & Agnes Neilson married December 30th 1790.
William Jackson & Martha Vaughan married Jany 22nd 1791.
Simon Burton & Nancy Robinson married Jan^{r}y 23rd 1791.
Benjamin Walden & Mary Dudley (K. & Q.) married Jan'y 29th
1791.
Benjamin Kidd & Ann Spencer married Feb'y 5th 1791.
William Wood & Fanny Jones married Feb'y 10th 1791.
Thomas Bland Jr. & Sarah Waller (K. & Q.) married Feby 19th 1791.
Henry Goinge & Betsey Paggot (K. & Q.) married March 5th 1791.
Samuel Drummond & Isbell Gibson (King & Queen) married March
179 .
Benjamin Heningham & Rose Berryman Shackelford (K. & Q.)
married March 9th 1791.
Benjamin Collier & Rachel Ware (K. & Q.) married March 26th
1791.

Robert Jackman & Salley Hillen (Gloucester) married April 11th 1791.

William Shaw & Fanny Williams (K. & Q.) married April 26th 1791.

Richard Groom & Catharine Webb (K. & Q.) married April 21st 1791.

Thomas Siblee & Mary Layton married May 4th 1791.

John Gayle Sutton & Ann Wake married June 9th 1791.

William Holt & Polly Tisher married July 30th 1791.

James Groom & Frances Finley married Augst 6th 1791.

William Segar & Nancy Roane married Septr 24th 1791.

William Matthews & Elen Hunt married Octr 9th 1791.

Benjamin Dabney & Sarah Smith (K. & Q.) married Octr 8th —— Fragment.

William Reningham & Caty Kelligrew of Gloucester married March 29. 1782.

Bowden Newcomb & Rachel Currie, of King & Queen married April 3d 1782.

Abner Cloudas & Sarah Daniel married April 4th 1782.

Benjamin Hackney & Mary Stiff married April 6th 1782.

Charles Colly & Elizabeth Hudson, of King & Queen married April 14th 1782.

John Bennet & Elizabeth Richeson married April 21st 1782.

William Meredith & Judith Edmondson of King & Queen married April 30th 1782.

William Steptoe & Elizabeth Robinson married May 19th 1782.

Thomas Daniel & Judith Tool married May 24th 1782.

William Steward & Zena Medley (of Essex County) married May 24th 1782.

Pitman Wiatt & Martha Fuller (of King & Queen) married June 1st 1782.

Zachariah Crittenden & Eliz^a Ware (of King & Queen) married June 20th 1782.

John Tucker & Frances Pigg, King & Queen, married July 18th 1782.

Henry Lyn & Anne Parrott married July 30th 1782.

John Jesse & Catharine Beamon married August 4th 1782.

Jonathan Lewis & Sarah Gale Morgan married August 10th 1782.

William Booth & Mary Jones (Gloucester) married August 22d 1782.

John Sears & Lucy Medley married September 1st 1782.

John Clark & Frances Beamon married Septr 19th 1782.

Archibald Mullins & Susanna Beamon married Septr 19th 17

Samuel Klug, Minist.

John Cardwell & Elizabeth Stamper married February 27th 1783.

John Thurston & Sarah Sanders married February 27th 1783.

Harry Beverley Yates & Jane Montague married February 27th 1783.

Thomas Burk & Susanna Blake married March 2d 1783.

William Bristow & Jemima Blakemore married March 12th 1783.

John Jackson jr. & Mary Smith married March 22d 1783.

Major Odear & Rebecca Hooker (King & Queen) married March 27th 1783.

Adam Aldridge & Catharine Jackson married March 27th 1783.

William Wright & Mary Bowers (King & Queen) married March 30th 1783.

Gowen Jefferies & Ann Clark married April 14th 1783.

John Holderby & Ann Jordon married April 17th 1783.

George Sims & Susanna Dulany (Culpeper) married June 5th 1783.

Thomas Gord & Afia Lee married July 4th 1783.

James Healy & Ruth Bristoo married July 13th 1783.

William Kidd & Frances Tuggle married August 17th.

Thomas Griffin Peachy & Elizabeth Mills married September 22d 1783.

Peter Boles & Avery Hardy (of King & Queen) married September 25th, 1783.

Samuel Klug, Minister.

Lucy daughter of Anne a Mulatto in ye Service of Sr Wm Skipwith born Feb^{r}y ye 25 1722.

Nanny daughter of Kate a Slave belonging to John Gibbs born April ye 8 1722.

Rose daughter of Eve a Slave belonging to Hezekiah Ellis born April ye 30 1722.

Jon Son of Judy a Slave belonging to Robert Williamson jun^r May ye 12. 1722.

Phillis daughter of   a Slave belonging to Robert George Senr born May ye 31. 1722.

Ned Son of Jenney a Slave belonging to Rice Curtis born June ye 14. 1722.

Hylace daughter of Dinah a Slave belonging to Oliver Segar born June ye 27. 1722.

Bucker Son of Moll a Slave belonging to Thomas Smith born June ye 24. 1722.

Letty daughter of Jone a Slave belonging to John Bryan born June ye 1. 1722.

Jenny daughter of Betty a Slave belonging to John Smith Senr born July 25 1722.

Sam Son of Dinah a Slave belonging to Joseph Hardee born August ye 21. 1722.

Venus daughter of Kate a Slave belonging to John Shorter born August ye 20. 1722.

Monmouth Son of Sharlott a Slave belonging to Henry Thacker born Septem^r ye 11. 1722.

Will Son of Dido a Slave belonging to Capt John Smith born Septem^r ye 9 1722.

Charles Son of Beck a Slave belonging to Joseph Gour born August ye 18. 1722.

Nanny daughter of ——— a Slave belonging to Thomas Dudley born Sept. 16 1722.

Charles Son of Delah a Slave belonging to Humphrey Jones born Sept^{mr} 15. 1722.

Seberina daughter of Nell a Slave belonging to Humphrey Jones born Octo^{br} ye 5. 1722.

Pen daughter of Winney a Slave belonging to Edwin Thacker born Septm^r ye 20. 1722.

Gawin Son of Dinah a Slave belonging to William Segar born Octo. ye 10. 1722.

Tom Son of Nanny a Slave belonging to Richard Hill born Novem^r ye 28 1722.

Newman Son of Lucy a Slave belonging to Gawin Corbin born Decem^r ye 14. 1722.

Toby Son of Kate a Slave belonging to Margrett Daniel born Decem^r ye 22. 1722.

Peter Son of Letty a Slave belonging to Richard Taylor born novem^r ye 18. 1722.

Letty daughter of Hannah a Slave belonging to Maurice Smith born Jan^{r}y. ye 28 1722.

Thomas & William Sons of Penelope a Slave belonging to ye Estate of James Walker dec'd born March ye 4 baptized March 22 1722.

Frank daughter of Jenny a Slave belonging to Mathew Hunt March ye 21. 1722.

Nanny daughter of Jone a Slave belonging to Coll^o John Robinson born March 16. 1722.

Hannah daughter of Clary a Slave belonging to Coll^o John Robinson born March 22. 1722.

Sprigg Son of Hannah a Slave belonging to George Harding born March ye 20. 1722.

Charles Son of Dinah a Slave belonging to Henry Armistead born March ye 20. 1722.

Moll daughter of Sarah a Slave belonging to Robt Williamson born April 1. 1723.

Judy daughter of Sarah a Slave belonging to John Digge born March 27. 1723.

Letty daughter of Sarah a Slave belonging to Richard Taylor born Feb^{r}y. ye 15. 1722.

Toby Son of Frank a Slave belonging to Oliver Segar born Feb^{r}y ye 20. 1722.

Robin Son of Hannah a Slave belonging to Gawin Corbin born March ye 15. 1722.

Diana daughter of Frank a Slave belonging to Gawin Corbin born March ye 20. 1722.

George Son of Judy a Slave belonging to Thomas Mountague born April ye 18. 1722.

Jeffery Son of Margrett a Slave belonging to John Wormeley born April ye 19. 1722.

Jack Son of Doll a Slave belonging to William Blackburne born April ye 12. 1723.

Tom Son of Venus a Slave belonging to William Blackburne born April ye 15. 1723.

Jack Son of Nell a Slave belonging to ye estate of Edmund Berkley born April ye 28. 1723.

Harry Son of Monday a Slave belonging to Samuel Batchelder born May 17. 1723.

Percilla daughter of Sue a Slave belonging to Gawin Corbin born May ye 1. 1723.

Bristow Son of Beck a Slave belonging to Gawin Corbin born May ye 5. 1723.

Peter Son of Rachel a Slave belonging to ye Estate of Edm^d Berkeley dec'd born May 18. 1723.

Harry Son of Phillis a Slave belonging to Stockley Towles born May ye 22. 1723.

Walley Son of Dellow a Slave belonging to Thomas Haselwood born May ye 27. 1723.

Frank daughter of Judy a Slave belonging to Rice Curtis born June ye 5. 1723.

Beck daughter of Venus a Slave belonging to Frances Timberlake born May ye 29. 1723.

Frank daughter of Dye a Slave belonging to John Moseley born June ye 17. 1723.

Jack Son of Alice a Slave belonging to Margarett Daniel born June ye 12 1723.

Verina daughter of Lucy a Slave belonging to ye estate of John Vivian dec'd born June 22 1723.

Sawney Son of Phillis a Slave belonging to John Grymes born Ap. ye 1. 1723.

Del a Daughter of Margery a Slave belonging to John Grymes born April ye 9. 1723.

* Son of Kate a Slave belonging to John Grymes born June ye 11. 1723.

* daughter of Abigail a Slave belonging to John Grymes born June 25. 1723.

* daughter of Hannah a Slave belonging to ye estate of Wm Gordon dec'd. born April ye 15. 1723.

Antony Son of —— a Slave belonging to Armistead Churchhill born July ye 3. 1723.

Peg daughter of —— a Slave belonging to Armistead Churchhill born July ye 10. 1723.

Tony Son of Sarah a Slave belonging to John Cheadle born July ye 11. 1723.

Frank Son of Kate a Slave belonging to John Daniel born July ye 4. 1723.

Doll daughter of Jenny a Slave belonging to ye estate of Hobby Weeks born June 29. 1723.

Lena daughter of Sharlott a Slave belonging to Henry Thacker born July ye 16. 1723.

Rebecca daughter of Phillis a Slave belonging to Tho', Machen born July 20. 1723.

Isaac Son of Phillis a Slave belonging to Tho' Machen born July 31. 1723.

Nan daughter of Poll a Slave belonging to ye estate of Garritt Minor born July 27. 1723.

Eleanor daughter of Jenny a Slave belonging to ye estate of John Vivion born Augs^t 27. 1723.

Lyddee daughter of Kate a Slave belonging to John Smith jun^r born August 26. 1723.

Will Son of Frank a Slave belonging to Edmond Mickelborough born Septem^r ye 5. 1723.

Lucy daughter of Carter a Slave belonging to Thomas Norman born
Septem^r ye 1. 1723.
Tom Son of Jenny a Slave belonging to William Chowning born
Septem^r 15. 1723.
Jack Son of Mary a Slave belonging to John Wormeley born Septem^r ye 4. 1723.
Violett daughter of Kate a Slave belonging to John Gibbs born
Septem^r ye 21. 1723.
Hannah daughter of Sue a Slave belonging to John Price born August ye 23. 1723.
George Son of Moll a Slave belonging to Eliz^a Smith born Septem^r
ye 29. 1723.
Moll daughter of Judy a Slave belonging to John Price born October
ye 29. 1723.
Betty daughter of Moll a Slave belonging to Anne Thacker born
Sept. ye 15. 1723.
Jenny daughter of Kate a Slave belonging to John Wormeley born
Novem^r ye 5. 1723.
Kate daughter of Jenny a Slave belonging to ye estate of Wm Gordon
born Nov. ye 15. 1723.
Billy Son of Jenny a Slave belonging to John Murry born octo. 18.
1723.
Phillis daughter of Judy a Slave belonging to Wm Stanard born
Novem^r ye 24. 1723.
Antony Son of Hannah a Slave belonging to William Gray born
Octo. ye 16. 1723.
Peter Son of Judy a Slave belonging to William Blackbourne born
Nov. 15. 1723.
Dick Son of Lucy a Slave belonging to John Wormeley born Decem^r ye 5. 1723.
Judy daughter of Kate a Slave belonging to John Shorter born Decem^r ye 17. 1723.
George Son of Kate a Slave belonging to Margrett Daniel born Decem^r ye 21. 1723.
Dick Son of Nell a Slave belonging to Armistead Churchhill born
Jan^{ry} 2. 1723.
Margery daughter of Bess a Slave belonging to Henry Armistead
born Jan^{ry} ye 23. 1723.
Margery daughter of Betty a Slave belonging to Augustine Owen
born Jan^{r}y ye 23. 1723.
Letty daughter of Judy a Slave belonging to John Hipkings born
Feb^{r}y ye 11. 1723.
Sampson Son of Beck a Slave belonging to Joseph Goar born Feb^{r}y
ye 15. 1723.
Sampson Son of Bess a Slave belonging to Mathew Kemp born
March ye 4. 1723.
Frank Son of Judy a Slave belonging to John Smith Senr born
March ye 4. 1723.
Jemmy Son of Sarah a Slave belonging to Alexander Graves born
Feb^{r}y ye 12. 1723.
Titan Son of Sarah a Slave belonging to William Stanard born
Feb^{r}y ye 17. 1723.

Margret daughter of —— a Slave belonging to John Wormeley born March 12. 1723.

Rebecca daughter of Penelope a Slave belonging to James Walker decd. born. baptized Ap: 5. 1724.

Nell daughter of Judy a Slave belonging to John Degge born March ye 30. 1724.

Harry Son of Frank a Slave belonging to Mathew Kemp born April ye 7. 1724.

Charles Son of Pegg a Slave belonging to Henry Armistead born April ye 8. 1724.

Phillis daughter of Judy a Slave belonging to John Alding born March ye 24. 1723.

Tom Son of Megg a Slave belonging to Humphrey Jones born March 23. 1723.

Hanaball Son of Dinah a Slave belonging to Oliver Segar born April ye 1. 1724.

Sary daughter of Judy a Slave belonging to ye estate of Wm Daniel jun^r born Ap. ye 6. 1724.

Kate daughter of Nanny a Slave belonging to Bar. Yates born March ye 24. 1723.

Alice daughter of Phillis a Slave belonging to Thomas Churchhill born April ye 15. 1724.

Phillis daughter of Lucy a Slave belonging to ye estate of John Mayo born April 19. 1724.

Moll daughter of Flora a Slave belonging to John Wormeley born Ap. ye 10. 1724.

Nan daughter of Bridgett a Slave belonging to John Wormeley born May ye 1. 1724.

White Son of Nan a Slave belonging to John Wormeley born May ye 20. 1724.

Judy & Jenny daughters of a —— Slave belonging to ye estate of James Curtis jun^r decd. born May 25. 1724.

Charles daughter of Dinah a Slave belonging to Joseph Hardee born May ye 17. 1724.

Will Son of Peg a Slave belonging to ye estate of John Owen born May ye 25. 1724.

Winney daughter of Jenny a Slave belonging to John Alding born May ye 28. 1724.

Robin Son of a —— Slave belonging to Christopher Robinson born May 26. 1724.

Hannah daughter of a —— Slave belonging to Christopher Robinson born June 3. 1724.

Alice daughter of Sabrina a Slave belonging to Edwin Thacker born Ap. 22 1724.

Frank daughter of Moll a Slave belonging to Wm Mountague born June ye 3. 1724.

Frank Daughter of Sarah a Slave belonging to Jno Cheedle born June ye 3. 1724.

Silas Son of Dinah a Slave belonging to William Segar born June ye 8. 1724.

Kezia daughter of Winny a Slave belonging to ye estate of Henry Thacker born June 25. 1724.

Letty daughter of Frank a Slave belonging to Anne Thacker born June 20. 1724.

Nan daughter of Hannah a Slave belonging to y[e] estate of W[m] Gordon decd. born June 24. 1724.

Sam Son of Avey a Slave belonging to Humphrey Jones born May 26. 1724.

Nan daughter of Judy a Slave belonging to Robert Williamson jun[y] born June y[e] 9. 1724.

Harry Son of Alice a Slave belonging to John Wormeley born July y[e] 28. 1724.

Jane daughter of Beck a Slave belonging to Robert George jun[r] born May 24. 1724.

Kendall Son of —— a Slave belonging to Henry Gilpin born Septem[r] y[e] 5. 1724.

George Son of Bess a Slave belonging to Catherine Warwick born Septem[r] y[e] 3. 1724.

Sarah daughter of Alice a Slave belonging to y[e] estate of Edmund Berkeley born Septem[r] 8. 1724.

Will Son of Frank a Slave belonging to y[e] estate of Edmund Berkeley born Septem[r] 14. 1724.

Robin Son of —— a Slave belonging to Mathew Kemp born Septem[r] 19. 1724.

Will Son of Kate a Slave belonging to Robert George Sen[r] born Septem[r] 24. 1724.

Peter Son of Munday a Slave belonging to Samuel Batchelder born Septem[r] y[e] 17. 1724.

Harry Son of Betty a Slave belonging to John Smith Sen[r] born October y[e] 7. 1724.

Scipio Son of Arminto a Slave belonging to John Grymes born Sept. y[e] 19. 1724.

Simon Son of Ciss a Slave belonging to John Grymes born Sept. y[e] 30. 1724.

Jeptha Son of Phebe a Slave belonging to John Grymes born Octo. y[e] 8. 1724.

Enos Son of Phillis a Slave belonging to Rice Curtis born Octo. y[e] 21. 1724.

Dinah daughter of Hannah a Slave belonging to y[e] estate of Garritt Minor born Octo. y[e] 5. 1724.

Jenny daughter of Eve a Slave belonging to Hezekiah Ellis born Octo. y[e] 15. 1724.

Kate daughter of —— a Slave belonging to Robert Holderness born Octo. y[e] 7. 1724.

Minter Son of Jone a Slave belonging to Rice Curtis born Novem[r] y[e] 9. 1724.

Mingo Son of Frank a Slave belonging to David George born Octo: y[e] 27. 1724.

Amy daughter of Hannah a Slave belonging to Maurice Smith born Novem[r] 29. 1724.

Mary & Rachel daughters of Rebecca a Mollatto belonging to S[r] W[m] Skipwith born Nov. 30. 1724.

Nanny daughter of —— a Slave belonging to Francis Timberlake born Dec. 3. 1724.

Abigall daughter of Mary a Slave belonging to John Robinson born
Dec. 11. 1724.

Jack Son of Christain a Slave belonging to Thomas Causer born
Dec. 24. 1724.

Judy daughter of Jenny a Slave belonging to Matthew Hunt born
Novem^r 29. 1724.

Letty daughter of Judy a Slave belonging to John Price born De-
cem^r ye 17 1724.

Billy Son of Sue a Slave belonging to Richard Taylor born Jan^{r}y
ye 1. 1724.

Rose daughter of Dye a Slave belonging to John Marston Senr born
Jan^{r}y ye 13. 1724.

Moll daughter of Doll a Slave belonging to William Blackborne
Feb^{r}y 5. 1724.

Judith daughter of Sharlott a Slave belonging to Henry Thacker
born Feb^{r}y ye 13. 1724.

Jack Son of Frank a Slave belonging to Francis Porter born De-
cem^r 10. 1724.

Davy Son of Winny a Slave belonging to Edwin Thacker born
Jan^{r}y ye 10. 1724.

Joe Son of Kate a Slave belonging to Roger Jones born Feb^{r}y ye
28. 1724.

Matt Son of Nell a Slave belonging to Humphry Jones born Feb^{ry}
2 1724.

Jeffrey Son of Winny a Slave belonging to Thomas Hackett born
March 10. 1724.

Nanny daughter of Moll a Slave belonging to Anne Thacker born
Feb^{r}y 23 1724.

Austin Son of Hannah a Slave belonging to Robert Williamson born
March 17 1724.

Hampton Son of Judy a Slave belonging to Tho. Mountague born
April ye 1. 1725.

Nanny daughter of Sue a Slave belonging to Francis Porter born
April ye 16. 1725.

Nan daughter of Letty a Slave belonging to Richd Taylor born Ap.
25 1725.

George Son of Moll a Slave belonging to John Segar born Ap. 23
1725.

Jemmy Son of Betty a Slave belonging to John Robinson Esqr born
Ap. 6 1725.

Tamar daughter of Kate a Slave belonging to John Shorter born Ap.
26 1725.

Irene daughter of Judy a Slave belonging to William Stanard born
May ye 9 1725.

Jerrell Son of Moll a Slave belonging to William Stanard born May
ye 23 1725.

Driner daughter of Rosse a Slave belonging to Gawin Corbin born
May ye 16 1725.

Major Son of Winey a Slave belonging to Gawin Corbin born May
ye 25 1725.

Billy Son of Betty a Slave belonging to Armistead Churchhill born
May ye 16 1725.

Hannah daughter of Flounder a Slave belonging to Armistead Churchhill born May ye 12 1725.

Manuel son of Phillis a Slave belonging to Robert Holderness. born May ye 14 1725.

Joan daughter of Dellah a Slave belonging to Humphry Jones born May ye 23 1725.

Lettissha daughter of Judith a Slave belonging to Oliver Segar born May ye 31 1725.

Jamey Son of —— a Slave belonging to Mathew Kemp born June ye 21 1725.

Phillis Daughter of Dinah a Slave belonging to William Segar born June ye 6 1725.

Betty daughter of Dido a Slave belonging to John Smith senr born July ye 8.

Jack Son of Judy a Slave belonging to Rice Curtis born July ye 10 1725.

Jack Son of Dy a Slave belonging to John Mosely born July ye 9 1725.

Esther daughter of Abigal a Slave belonging to John Grymes born June ye 29 1725.

Peg daughter of Rachel a Slave belonging to John Grymes born July ye 11 1725.

Rose daughter of —— a Slave belonging to Mathew Kemp born Augs{t} ye 18 1725.

Judy daughter of Margrett a Slave belonging to John Wormley born Augs{t} 25. 1725.

Judy daughter of Kate a Slave belonging to John Wormley born August 29. 1725.

Peter Son of   a Slave belonging to John Murray born August 10. 1725.

Wonah daughter of Hannah a Slave belonging to George Hardine-born born July ye 23. 1725.

Dan Son of   a Slave belonging to Matthew Kemp born Septemr ye 19. 1725.

Betty daughter of Sarah a Slave belonging to Richd Taylor born Augst ye 18 1725.

Jemmy Son of Hannah a Slave belonging to Elizabeth Smith born Septemr ye 17. 1725.

Oriel Son of Lucy a Slave belonging to ye estate of John Vivion born Septemr 28 1725.

Betty daughter of Moll a Slave belonging to Eliza Smith born October ye 21. 1725.

Billy Son of Kate a Slave belonging to John Gibbs born October ye 27 1725.

Winne daughter of Jenny a Slave belonging to Rice Curtis born Novemr ye 12 1725.

Winne daughter of Kate a Slave belonging Margrett Daniell born Novemr 9 1725.

Silla daughter of Margery a Slave belonging to Oliver Segar born Novemr ye 28 1725.

Phillis daughter of Nell a Slave belonging to John Wormeley born Novemr ye 28 1725.

Jenny daughter of Megg a Slave belonging to Humphrey Jones born
Novem^r ye 26 1725.

Alce daughter of ——— a Slave belonging to John Wormley born
Decem^r ye 19 1725.

Silvia daughter of Judy a Slave belonging to Wm Blackbourn born
Octo. ye 14 1725.

Sara daughter of Nan a Slave belonging to Wm Blackbourn born
Octo ye 20. 1725.

Rose daughter of Betty a Slave belonging to Wm Blackbourn born
Decem. 12 1725.

Penelope daughter of ——— a Slave belonging to John Wormley
born Feb'y 9 1725.

Joan daughter of Kate a Slave belonging to Edwin Thacker born
Feb'y 19 1725.

Mingo Son of Judy a Slave belonging to John Price born April 3d
1726.

Jemima daughter of Judy a Slave belonging to ye estate of John Vivion born March 16. 1725.

Hannah daughter of Judy a Slave belonging to Christopher Sutton
born August 20 1725.

Sampson Son of Judy a Slave belonging to John Hipkins born April
ye 1st 1726.

Judy daughter of Frank a Slave belonging to Edmund Mickleburrough born Ap. 22 1726.

Jemny Son of Kate a Slave belonging to Armistead Churchhill born
March 16. 1725.

Rosegill Son of Wouna a Slave belonging to Armistead Churchhill
born March 16 1725.

Phillis daughter of Carter a Slave belonging to Tho: Norman born
April ye 26 1726.

Hampton Son of Hannah a Slave belonging to Martha Williamson
born May ye 19 1726.

Dick Son of Dellah a Slave belonging to Thomas Haslewood born
May ye 25 1726.

Agy daughter of Sabina a Slave belonging to Edwin Thacker born
June ye 21 1726.

Alice daughter of Rachel a Slave belonging to Edmund Berkley
born June ye 8 1726.

Davy Son of Phillis a Slave belonging to Thomas Machen born June
ye 28 1726.

Jemmy Son of Hannah a Slave belonging to John Minor born June
ye 25 1726.

Jenny daughter of Sarah a Slave belonging to Alexander Graves
born July ye 2 1726.

Ned son of Lucy a Slave belonging to John Tugle born July ye 13
1726.

Margery daughter of Dinah a Slave belonging to Jacob Stiff born
July ye 28 1726.

Abraham Son of Lucy a Slave belonging to Edwin Thacker born
July ye 30 1726.

Winny daughter of Poll a Slave belonging to William Mountague
born July 26 1726.

Moll daughter of Dinah a Slave belonging to Joseph Hardee born Septem^r ye 10. 1726.

Jack Son of Kate a Slave belonging to Robert George born Octo. 16. 1726.

Dinah daughter of Sarah a Slave belonging to Hezekiah Rhodes born Octo. ye 18. 1726.

Betty daughter of Letty a Slave belonging to Elizabeth Weekes born Novem^r ye 10. 1726.

Ned Son of Frank a Slave belonging to Anne Thacker born Decem^r ye 6. 1726.

Sam Son of Poll a Slave belonging to John Minor born Decem^r ye 22. 1726.

Abraham Son of —— a Slave belonging to Matthew Kemp born July ye 28. 1726.

Charlote daughter of —— a Slave belonging Matthew Kemp born Octo. ye 12. 1726.

Charles Son of Rachell a Slave belonging to John Grymes born Jan^{r}y ye 2. 1726.

Frances daughter of Frank a Slave belonging to John Wormeley born Ap. ye 11. 1726.

Jemima daughter of Rose a Slave belonging to Edwin Thacker born Octo: ye 6. 1726.

Beck daughter of Nan a Slave belonging to John Wormley born April 19. 1726.

Phillis daughter of Kate a Slave belonging to Edward Clark born July 7. 1726.

Judy daughter of Jenny a Slave belonging to Samuel Batchelder born Augst 1. 1726.

Charles Son of Jenny a slave belonging to Matthew Hunt born Augst 7 1726.

Moll daughter of Kate a slave belonging to John Smith born Decem^r ye 2 1726.

Nan daughter of Phillis a slave belonging to Stockly Towles born Decem^r 8 1726.

Will Son of Phillis a slave belonging to Rice Curtis born Jan^{r}y ye 17 1726.

Moll daughter of Moll a slave belonging to Elizabeth Smith born Feb^{r}y 25 1726.

Charles Son of Venus a slave belonging to Francis Timberlake born Decem^r 22 1726.

London Son of Sarah a slave belonging to William Stanard born May ye 10. 1726.

London Son of Frank a slave belonging to Gawen Corbin born Feb^{r}y ye 28. 1726.

Ned Son of Rose a slave belonging to Gawen Corbin born March ye 15. 1726.

Sarah daughter of —— a slave belonging to Armstead Churchhill born Feb^{r}y ye 27. 1726.

Winney daughter of Sarah a slave belonging to Robert Williamson born March ye 6 1726.

Charles Son of Winny a slave belonging to Edwin Thacker born March ye 8 1726.

Nimrod Son of Alice a slave belonging to Wm Stanard born April ye 8 1727.

George Son of Nathan a slave belonging to Marvil Moseley born March 1 1726.

Bristow Son of Jenny a slave belonging to Henry Tuggle born May ye 12. 1727.

Pat daughter of Juno a slave belonging to Matthew Kemp born May ye 17. 1727.

Phil Son of Rose a Slave belonging to George Harding born May ye 13 1727.

Jenny daughter of Dinah a slave belonging to ye estate of Tho. Smith born June ye 3 1727.

Sauney son of —— a slave belonging to ye estate of Jno. Wormley born May 13. 1727.

Abraham Son of Sue a slave belonging to Bar Yates born April ye 8 1727.

Judy & Winney daughters of Judy a Slave belonging to ye estate of Wm Daniell jun^r born May 24 1727.

Tom son of Winny a slave belonging to ye estate of Hen Thacker born May 24 1727.

Rose daughter of Hannah a Slave belonging to Eliz^a Smith born June ye 14 1727.

Jemmy Son of Jenny a slave belonging to John Murrah born June ye 11. 1727.

Sarah daughter of Dey a Slave belonging to John Roads born June ye 17. 1727.

Peter son of Bess a Slave belonging to Henry Armistead born July ye 2. 1727.

Jenny daughter of —— a Slave belonging to William Wood born July ye 10. 1727.

Harry son of   a Slave belonging to Richard Perrott born July ye 12 1727.

Nell daughter of Jenny a Slave belonging to Armistead Churchhill born July ye 19. 1727.

Harry son of Dy a slave belonging to John Moseley born August ye 15. 1727.

Will son of Mundy a Slave belonging to Samuel Batchelder born August ye 17. 1727.

Harry son of a Slave belonging to Clement Owen born July ye 23 1727.

Catherine daughter of Penelope a Slave belonging to ye estate of James Walker dec'd born Aug^st 19 baptized August 29 1727.

Lucy daughter of Lettice a Slave belonging to ye estate of Hobs Weeks dec'd born Aug^st ye 8 1727.

Will Son of Jane a Slave belonging to ye estate of Hobs Weeks decd born Aug^st ye 8 1727.

Peter son of Jone a Slave belonging to ye estate of John Wormley born August ye 27. 1727.

Frances daughter of Sue a Slave belonging to ye estate of John Wormley dec'd born Septem^r ye 5. 1727.

Jack Son of Kate a Slave belonging to John Shorter born August ye 27. 1727.

Frank daughter of Hannah a Slave belonging to Sr Wm Skipwith born Augst ye 27 1727.

Maria daughter of Kate a Slave belonging to Robert George born August ye 29. 1727.

Moll daughter of Pegg a Slave belonging to Thomas Cheney born Septem^r ye 7. 1727.

Ishmael Son of Frank a Slave belonging to Oliver Segar born Septem^r ye 8 1727.

Nanny daughter of Sharlot a Slave belonging to Henry Thacker born Septem^r ye 23 1727.

Phillis daughter of Beck a slave belonging to Robert George jun^r born August 27 1727.

Jenny daughter of Moll a slave belonging to Anne Thacker born June 16. 1727.

Dinah daughter of Abigail a slave belonging to John Grymes born September 25 1727.

Winny daughter of Judy a slave belonging to William Stanard born Octo. ye 6 1727.

Flora daughter of Cate a slave belonging to ye estate of John Wormeley born October 17 1727.

Bridgett daughter of a Slave belonging to Armistead Churchhill born Novem^r ye 6 1727.

Sawney Son of a Slave belonging to Roger Jones born Novem^r 14. 1727.

Harry Son of Kate a Slave belonging to William Channing born Octo^r 23 1727.

Ben Son of Cato a slave belonging to John Moseley born Novem^r ye 18 1727.

Juno daughter of Sarah a slave belonging to William Stanard born Decem^r ye 8 1727.

Ben Son of Judy a slave belonging to ye estate of Jno Alding dec'd born Novem^r 12 1727.

Bess ye daughter of Nell a slave belonging to Humphrey Jones born Novem^r 18 1727.

Dick Son of Jenny a slave belonging to Wm Chowning born Decem^r ye 4 1727.

Maud daughter of Judy a slave belonging to John Smith born Decem^r 26 1727.

Dinah daughter of Nan a slave belonging to ye estate of John Smith born Jan^{r}y 14 1727.

Phillis daughter of Jenny a slave belonging to Mathew Kemp born Feb^{r}y ye 2 1727.

Hannah daughter of Moll a slave belonging to William Mountague born Jan^{r}y 21 1727.

Nan daughter of Frank a slave belonging to Edmund Mickleburrough born Jan^{r}y 29 1727.

Bess daughter of Kate a slave belonging to Mary Gibbs born Feb^{r}y ye 1 1727.

Joan daughter of Joan a slave belonging to Jno Grymes born Feb^{r}y ye 8. 1727.

Mingo son of Moll a slave belonging to Jno Grymes born Feb^{r}y ye 9. 1727.

Nan daughter of Dillah a slave belonging to Henry Daniel born Febʳy yᵉ 8 1727.

Dick Son of Letty a slave belonging to Richard Tyler born Janʳy yᵉ 16. 1727.

Betty daughter of Jenny a slave belonging to Matthew Hunt born Febʳy 20 1727.

Sam & Crispin sons of Hannah a slave belonging to Laurence Orrell born yᵉ 20th of Febʳy 1727.

Phillis daughter of Jenny a slave belonging to yᵉ estate of Jn° Wormley born Febʳy 17. 1727.

Tom Son of Margrett a slave belonging to yᵉ estate of John Wormley born March 8. 1727.

Betty daughter of Alice a slave belonging to yᵉ estate of John Wormley born March 12. 1727.

Nell daughter of Bridgett a slave belonging to yᵉ estate of John Wormley born March 27. 1728.

Amy daughter of Alice a slave belonging to Margrett Daniell born March 28. 1728.

Beck daughter of Jenny a slave belonging to John Smith born April yᵉ 1 1728.

Sarah daughter of Venus a slave belonging to Wᵐ Southworth born March 31. 1728.

Crozier & Daphny son & daughter of Kate a slave belonging to Margrett Daniel born April 26. 1728.

Harry Son of Nanny a slave belonging to yᵉ estate of Jn° Wormley dec'd born April 24. 1728.

Lucy daughter of Sarah a free negro born at James Meacham's April yᵉ 8. 1728.

Charles Son of Doll a slave belonging to John Rhoads born April yᵉ 18. 1728.

Judith daughter of Phillis a slave belonging to Tho: Machen born April yᵉ 30 1728.

Amy daughter of a slave belonging to Armistead Churchhill born Febʳy yᵉ 20 1727.

Minter daughter of a slave belonging to John Grymes born April yᵉ 27 1728.

Toney Son of a slave belonging to Alice Causer born April yᵉ 24. 1728.

Betty daughter of Sue a slave belonging to Francis Porter born April yᵉ 21 1728.

Jenny daughter of Nanney a slave belonging to Lettice Thacker born June yᵉ 4. 1728.

Priscilla daughter of Alice a slave belonging to Edwin Thacker born June yᵉ 3 1728.

Nan daughter of Lucy a slave belonging to Edwin Thacker born May yᵉ 26. 1728.

Arabella daughter of a slave belonging to Gawin Corbin born Febʳy yᵉ 2. 1728.

Goy daughter of a slave belonging to Gawin Corbin born April yᵉ 13. 1728.

Sarah daughter of a slave belonging to Gawin Corbin born May yᵉ 21 1728.

Moll daughter of a slave belonging to Gawin Corbin born May ye 28 1728.

Frank daughter of a slave belonging to Gawin Corbin June ye 12 1728.

Grasheir son of a slave belonging to Gawin Corbin born June ye 14. 1728.

Lucy daughter of Phillis a slave belonging to Tho: Price born June ye 15. 1728.

Pompy son of Hannah a slave belonging to William Gray born April ye 22. 1728.

Caesar son of Judy a slave belonging to John Hipkins born June ye 26. 1728.

Cate daughter of a slave belonging to Gawin Corbin born June ye 24. 1728.

Cate daughter of Nell a slave belonging to ye estate of Jn° Wormley born July ye 3. 1728.

Mingo son of a slave belonging to John Grymes born July ye 13. 1728.

Edward son of Jenney a slave belonging to John Grymes born April 21. baptized July ye 14. 1728.

Bess daughter of Bess a slave belonging to Henry Armistead born July ye 25 1728.

Juno daughter of a Slave belonging to Henry Gilpen born July ye 10. 1728.

Betty daughter of Winne a Slave belonging to Elizabeth Weekes born July ye 22. 1728.

Charles Son of Daphney a Slave belonging to Frances Smith born August ye 15. 1728.

Joice daughter of a Slave belonging to Henry Armistead born August ye 11. 1728.

Oliver Son of Rachell a Slave belonging to Edmund Berkley born August ye 20 1728.

Robin Son of Dey a Slave belonging to John Roades born August ye 9 1728.

Jack Son of a Slave belonging to Armistead Churchhill born August ye 20. 1728.

Betty daughter of Jenny a Slave belonging to Armistead Churchhill born Septem^r 11. 1728.

Antony Son of Betty a Slave belonging to ye estate of Capt. Jn° Smith dec'd born Septem^r ye 8. 1728.

Ruth daughter of Sarah a Slave belonging to Anne daughter of James Smith born Septem^r ye 11. 1728.

Ben Son of Judy a Slave belonging to ye estate of John Vivion born Septem^r 21. 1728.

Peter Son of Pegg a Slave belonging to Robert Holderness born August ye 10. 1728.

Billey Son of Ben & Nan Slaves belonging to Wm Blackburne born Octo. 10. 1728.

Jeney daughter of Judy a Slave belonging to Eliz^a Smith born August ye 6. 1728.

Robin Son of Brinah a Slave belonging to Jonathan Brooks born Novem^r ye 4 1728.

Harry Son of Flora a Slave belonging to ye estate of Jn° Wormley dec'd born October ye 24. 1728.

Peter Son of a Slave belonging to Richard Hill born August ye 28. 1728.

Mary daughter of a Slave belonging to Richard Hill born August ye 29. 1728.

Betty daughter of Queen a Slave belonging to Gawin Corbin born Novem^r ye 17. 1728.

Tony Son of Sarah a Slave belonging to Hezekiah Roads born Novem^r ye 19. 1728.

Jenny daughter of Sharlott a Slave belonging to Henry Thacker born Novem^r 10. 1728.

Hannah daughter of   a Slave belonging to Ralph Shelton born Decem^r ye 6. 1728.

Gawin Son of Hannah a Slave belonging to Henry Mickleburrough born Decem^r ye 16. 1728.

Will Son of Kate a Slave belonging to Edwin Thacker born July ye 6. 1728.

Tony Son of Eve a Slave belonging to Edwin Thacker born Decem^r ye 3. 1728.

Robert Son of   a Slave belonging to Tho. Faulkner Senr born Novem^r ye 8 1728.

Neeton daughter of Hanah a Slave belonging to George Hardin born Decem^r ye 27. 1728.

Judy   a Slave belonging to John Crockford born Jan^ry ye 5. 1728.

Dianah daughter of Sarah a Slave belonging to William Stanard born Decem^r ye 19. 1728.

Phil Son of   a Slave belonging to Roger Jones born Janua^ry ye 9. 1728.

Judy daughter of Jenny a Slave belonging to Henry Tugel born Jan^ry ye 21. 1728.

Thom Son of a Slave belonging to ye Estate Thomas Smith decd born Jan^ry ye 26. 1728.

Judy daughter of Dillah a Slave belonging to Henry Daniell born Jan^ry ye 31. 1728.

Benjamine Son of Hagar a Mulatto belonging to Robt Johnson Senr born Feb^ry 2. 1728.

Molly daughter of a Slave belonging to John Crockford born Feb^ry ye 14. 1728.

Mary daughter of Jenny a Slave belonging to Armistead Churchhill born Feb^ry ye 21 1728.

Margery daughter of Jenny a Slave belonging to Francis Cheedle born Feb^ry ye 23. 1728.

Davy Son of   a Slave belonging to Sarah Jones born March ye 1 1728.

Amy daughter of Winney a Slave belonging to Edwin Thacker born March ye 15. 1728.

Rose daughter of Maria a Slave belonging to Edmund Berkley born April ye 16. 1729.

Doll daughter of Sabina a Slave belonging to Edwin Thacker born April ye 2. 1729.

Robin Son of Cate a Slave belonging to William Chowning born April yᵉ 29. 1729.

Will Son of Cate a Slave belonging to John Burk born May yᵉ 23. 1729.

Hannah daughter of Venus a Slave belonging to Sarah Timberlake born May yᵉ 24. 1729.

Billy Son of Moll a Slave belonging to Elizabeth Smith born May yᵉ 28. 1729.

Odo daughter of Peru a Slave belonging to John Bryant born May yᵉ 11. 1729.

Tom Son of   a Slave belonging to yᵉ estate of James Smith dec'd born June yᵉ 6. 1729.

Wonder Son of Rose a Slave belonging to George Hardin born May yᵉ 27 1729.

Kate daughter of Doll a Slave belonging to William Blackburne born 30th June 1729.

Judy daughter of Judy a Slave belonging to William Blackburn born June yᵉ 29 1729.

Frank daughter of Betty a Slave belonging to Gawin Corbin born June yᵉ 26 1729.

Jemmy Son of Frank a Slave belonging to Anne Thacker born July yᵉ 12 1729.

Ben Son of Sarah a Slave belonging to Alexander Graves born July yᵉ 15. 1729.

Sukey daughter of Dinah a Slave belonging to William Segar born July yᵉ 22 1729.

Edenburrough Son of Kate a Slave belonging to William Wood born Agust yᵉ 6. 1729.

Peter Son of Judy a Slave belonging to James Dudley born June yᵉ 14 1729.

Sampson Son of old Phillis a Slave belonging to Thos: Machen born July yᵉ 19. 1729.

Charles Son of young Phillis a Slave belonging Tho: Machen born August yᵉ 12. 1729.

Lucy daughter of Hannah a Slave belonging to Elizᵃ Smith born August yᵉ 12 1729.

Doll daughter of Sue a Slave belonging to Bar. Yates born September yᵉ 6. 1729.

Essex Son of Judy a Slave belonging to Thoˢ Mountague born September yᵉ 20. 1729.

Abigal daughter of Judy a Slave belonging to William Stanard born September yᵉ 12. 1729.

Mingo Son of Dye a Slave belonging to John Moseley born September yᵉ 20 1729.

Randolph Son of Dido a Slave belonging to yᵉ estate of Jnᵒ Smith decd. born Septemʳ yᵉ 14 1729.

Hamaton Son of Kate a Slave belonging to Robert George Senʳ born October yᵉ 15. 1729.

Della daughter of Peg a Slave belonging to Thomas Cheney born Novemʳ yᵉ 2. 1729.

George Son of Lucy a Slave belonging to Oliver Segar born Novemʳ yᵉ 7. 1729.

Gumbee Son of Phillis a Slave belonging to Jacob Stiff born Novem^r ye 25. 1729.

Guy Son of Anakey a Slave belonging to Edwin Thacker born Novem^r ye 30. 1729.

Gloster Son of Wilmuth a Slave belonging to Lawrance Orrill born Decem^r 27. 1729.

Mertilda daughter of Winney a Slave belonging to Chicheley Thacker born Dec. 13. 1729.

Bristow Son of Jenny a Slave belonging to ye estate of Hobs Weeks born Decem^r ye 19. 1729.

Tom Son of Letty a Slave belonging to ye estate of Hobs Weeks born Decem^r ye 22. 1729.

Murreah daughter of Nell a Slave belonging to Humphrey Jones born Decem^r ye 15. 1729.

Frank daughter of Kate a Slave belonging to Humphrey Jones born Decem^r ye 30. 1729.

Hampton Son of Jenny a Slave belonging to Henry Tugel Sen: born Jan'ry ye 25. 1729.

Billy Son of Jenny a Slave belonging to ye estate of Mathew Hunt born Jan'ry. ye 29. 1729.

Alice daughter of Sary a Slave belonging to Edmund Michelborough born Jan'ry 28, 1729.

Jenny daughter of Lucy a Slave belonging to Thomas Buford born Jan'ry ye 26. 1729.

Lucy daughter of Nattor a Slave belonging to Marvill Moseley born Jan'ry ye 9. 1729.

Numan Son of Frank a Slave belonging to Edmund Michelborough born Feb'ry. ye 9. 1729.

Cateena daughter of Lucy a Slave belonging to ye estate of John Vivion born Feb'ry 12. 1729.

Criss daughter of Lucy a Slave belonging to Edwin Thacker born Feb'ry 12. 1729.

Dick Son of Moll a Slave belonging to Bar. Yates born Decem^r 22. 1729.

Ned Son of Beck a Slave belonging to John Grymes born Novem^r ye 25. 1729.

Ben Son of Cris a Slave belonging to John Grymes born Feb'ry ye 5. 1729.

Joe Son of Alice a Slave belonging to Edwin Thacker born Feb'ry ye 22. 1729.

Moll daughter of Hanah a Slave belonging to Lawrance Orrill born March ye 8. 1729.

Joice daughter of   a Slave belonging to Hen: Armistead born March ye 9. 1729.

Daniel & Isaack Sons of Mary a Slave belonging to Armistead Churchhill born March 21. 1729.

Hannah daughter of Judy a Slave belonging to Thos Mountague born March ye 25. 1730.

Hannah daughter of Kate a Slave belonging to Richd Tyler born March ye 28. 1730.

Frank daughter of Sarah a Slave belonging to Ralph Shelton born March 4. 1729.

29

Margery daughter of Alice a Slave belonging to Margret Daniel born Ap. 1 1730.

Frank daughter of   a Slave belonging to Armistead Churchhill born March 27. 1730.

Peter Son of Lucy a Slave belonging to Christopher Sutton born March ye 31. 1730.

Cupid Son of Rose a Slave belonging to George Hardin born April ye 15. 1730.

Kate daughter of Dido a Slave belonging to Mathew Kemp born April ye 24. 1730.

Phillis daughter of Rose a Slave belonging to Edwin Thacker born May ye 2. 1730.

Isaac Son of Mary a Slave belonging to Armistead Churchhill born April ye 25. 1730.

Beck daughter of Daffine a Slave belonging to John Grymes born April ye 28. 1730.

Frank Son of Judy a Slave belonging to John Smith jun^r born May ye 17. 1730.

Kate daughter of Bett a Slave belonging to James Reid born April ye 24. 1730.

Frank Son of Sue a Slave belonging to ye estate of John Wormeley born May ye 13. 1730.

Boson Son of —— a Slave belonging to Paul Philpotts born March ye 13. 1729.

Amey daughter of Frank a Slave belonging to Robert Daniel born May ye 23. 1730.

Tom Son of Nanny a Slave belonging to ye estate of Jno Smith decd born June ye 20. 1730.

Jack Son of Jenny a Slave belonging to Frances Cheedle born June ye 13. 1730.

Gabriel Son of a Slave belonging to Zacarias Gibbs born July ye 2. 1730.

Frank daughter of Jenny a Slave belonging to Henry Tugel born June ye 28. 1730.

Jemmy Son of Daphne a Slave belonging to Frances Smith born June ye 25. 1730.

Patt Son of —— a Slave belonging to Roger Jones born July ye 16. 1730.

Harry Son of Venus a Slave belonging to Wm Southworth born June ye 20. 1730.

Betty daughter of Dinah a Slave belonging to ye estate of Tho. Smith decd. born Augst ye 4. 1730.

Charles Son of Dinah a Slave belonging to ye estate of Tho. Smith decd. born Augs^t 4. 1730.

Phillis daughter of Kate a Slave belonging to Wm Chowning born August ye 19. 1730.

Robin Son of Munday a Slave belonging to Samuel Batchelder born Septem^r ye 2. 1730.

Jack Son of Murrea a Slave belonging to Edmund Berkeley born Aug^{u}st ye 31. 1730.

Winney daughter of Moll a Slave belonging to Wm Mountague jun^r. born July ye 20. 1730.

Matt Son of Nancy a Slave belonging to ye estate of Jn° Wormeley decd. born Sept. 4. 1730.

Hampshire Son of Beck a Slave belonging to John Lewis born September ye 21. 1730.

Bob Son of Beck a Slave belonging to John Crockford born September ye 20. 1730.

Letty daughter of Jude a Slave belonging to Mary Bristow born September ye 28. 1730.

Laurance Son of Jone a Slave belonging to ye estate of Jn° Wormeley born Octo. ye 6. 1730.

Judy daughter of Hannah a Slave belonging to Sr Wm Skipwith born Octo. ye 20. 1730.

Peter Son of Sue a Slave belonging to Gawin Corbin born October ye 18. 1730.

Jenny Son of Bett a Slave belonging to John Moseley born Novem^r ye 7. 1730.

Sambo Son of Kate a Slave belonging to John Smith sen^r born Novem^r ye 18. 1730.

Tom Son of Jenny a Slave belonging to Coll° Gawin Corbin born Novem^r ye 29. 1730.

Kate daughter of Winney belonging to Gawin Corbin born Novem^r ye 30. 1730.

Hannah daughter of Verena a Slave belonging to Jonathan Brooks born Decem^r ye 3. 1730.

Jack Son of Hannah a Slave belonging to Eliz^a Smith Senr born Decm^r ye 23. 1730.

Criss daughter of Nell a Slave belonging to ye estate of Jn° Wormeley decd born Jan^ry 3. 1730.

Mingo Son of Beck a Slave belonging to John Grymes born Jan^ry ye 7. 1730.

Ben Son of Jenny a Slave belonging to Samuel Batchelder born Jan^ry ye 13. 1730.

Hannah daughter of Megg a Slave belonging to Humphrey Jones born Jan^ry ye 22. 1730.

Agie daughter of Judy a Slave belonging to William Stanard born Jan^ry ye 23. 1730.

Charles son of Nan a Slave belonging to Wm Blackbourne born July ye 31. 1730.

Moll daughter of Kate a Slave belonging to John Burk born Feb^ry ye 10. 1730.

Simon Son of Judy a Slave belonging to John Hipkins born Decem^r ye 18. 1730.

Lucy daughter of Hannah a Slave belonging to Laurence Orrill born March ye 3. 1730.

Judy daughter of Moll a Slave belonging to ye estate of Jn° Wormeley decd. born Feb^ry ye 20. 1730.

Polly daughter of Alice a Slave belonging to ye estate of Jn° Wormeley decd. born March 5. 1730.

Lettice daughter of Bridget a Slave belonging to ye estate of Jn° Wormeley decd. born March 6 1730.

Billy Son of Dinah a Slave belonging to Christopher Robinson born March ye 11. 1730.

Letty daughter of Betty a Slave belonging to Christopher Robinson born March ye 16. 1730.

James Son of Peg a Slave belonging to William Owen born March ye 5. 1730.

Robin Son of Jenny a Slave belonging to William Hill born April ye 2. 1731.

Jemmy Son of Sarah a Slave belonging to Hezekiah Rhoads born April ye 8. 1731.

Chance daughter of Bess a Slave belonging to the estate of Wm Gordon born March ye 14. 1730.

Kate daughter of Judy a Slave belonging to Frances Alding born April ye 13. 1731.

Nat Son of Moll a Slave belonging to Andrew Davis born April ye 20. 1731.

Ben Son of Sarah a Slave belonging to Edmund Michelborough born April ye 15. 1731.

Letty daughter of Winny a Slave belonging to Edwin Thacker born April ye 9. 1731.

Ned Son of Jenny a Slave belonging to Henry Tugell Junr born May ye 5. 1731.

Phil Son of —— a Slave belonging to Christopher Sutton born April ye 27. 1731.

Jack Son of Hannah a Slave belonging to Henry Mickelborough born April ye 6. 1731.

Dinah daughter of Ruth a Slave belonging to Edwin Thacker born May ye 8. 1731.

Sarah daughter of Willmut a Slave belonging to Lawrence orrill born May 7. 1731.

Hannah daughter of —— a Slave belonging to John Murrah born May ye 17. 1731.

Betty daughter of Sue a Slave belonging to Bar. Yates born April ye 24. 1731.

Phillis daughter of Phillis a Slave belonging to Mary Machen born May ye 18. 1731.

Judy daughter of —— a Slave belonging to Wm Anderson born May ye 4. 1731.

Beck daughter of Kate a Slave belonging to Edwin Thacker born May ye 22d 1731.

Bat Son of Betty a Slave belonging to Henry Armistead born May ye 20. 1731.

Nanny daughter of Sharlott a Slave belonging to Henry Thacker born May 28. 1731.

Davy & Jenny Son & daughter of Jenny a Slave belonging to ye estate of John Wormeley decd. born June 13. 1731.

Judy daughter of a Slave belonging to Alexander Graves born June ye 10. 1731.

Rose daughter of Carter a Slave belonging to Wm Crutchfeild born June ye 20. 1731.

Jemmy Son of —— a Slave belonging to Sampson Darrill born June ye 28. 1731.

Ruth daughter of —— a Slave belonging to Roger Jones born July ye 15. 1731.

Cate daughter of Dillah a Slave belonging to Henry Daniel born
June ye 15. 1731.

Daphney daughter of Beck a Slave belonging to John Grymes born
June ye 29. 1731.

Rosa daughter of Marjory a Slave belonging to Hugh Stewart born
July ye 14. 1731.

Miny Son of —— a Slave belonging to James Dudley born July y^e
24. 1731.

Frank Son of Moll a Slave belonging to Eliz^a Smith Senr born July
ye 19. 1731.

Winney daughter of Alice a Slave beloning to John Segar born July
ye 31. 1731.

Sary daughter of Flora a Slave belonging to ye estate of Jno Wormeley decd. born August ye 13. 1731.

Sue daughter of —— a Slave belonging to William Wood born August ye 10. 1731.

Ben Son of Margary a Slave belonging to Oliver Segar born June
ye 25. 1731.

Mil daughter of Lucy a Slave belonging to Oliver Segar born July
ye 10. 1731.

Sue daughter of Betty a Slave belonging to ye estate of Jno Smith
ded. born August ye 26. 1731.

Abram Son of Nanne a Slave belonging to ye estate of Jno Smith
decd. born Septem^r ye 1. 1731.

Frank Son of Phillis a Slave belonging to ye estate of James Smith
decd. born Septem^r ye 3. 1731.

Edy daughter of Alice a Slave belonging to Edwin Thacker born
August ye 18. 1731.

Alice daughter of Moll a Slave belonging to Armistead Churchhill
born August ye 23. 1731.

Margery & Lucy daughters of Judy belonging to ye estate of W^m
Daniel jun^r born August ye 24. 1731.

Peter Son of —— a Slave belonging to Rice Jones born August y^e
28. 1731.

Cromwell Son of Flora a Slave belonglng to John Grymes born August ye 31. 1731.

Ben Son of Dinah a Slave belonging to Margrett Daniel born Sep-
tem^r ye 15. 1731.

George Son of Kate a Slave belonging to Robert George Senr born
Septem^r ye 21. 1731.

Hannah daughter of Nan a Slave belonging to Wm Hackney born
Septem^r ye 24. 1731.

Numan Son of Sabina a Slave belonging to Edwin Thacker born
october ye 30. 1731.

Hannah daughter of Rose a Slave belonging to Wm Bristow born
october ye 24. 1731.

Jack Son of Moll a Slave belonging to Henry Thacker born Novem^r
ye 12. 1731.

Phil Son of Betty a Slave belonging to Sr Wm Skipwith born August
ye 26. 1731.

James Son of Kate a Slave belonging to Jno Marshall born Decem^r
ye 3. 1731.

Thamar daughter of Doll a Slave belonging to John Rhoads born Jan^ry. ye 15. 1731.

Ned Son of Chris a Slave belonging to John Grymes born Jan^ry ye 14. 1731.

Betty daughter of Eve a Slave belonging to Edwin Thacker born Jan^ry ye 18. 1731.

Deinah Son of Lucy a Slave belonging to Thomas Buford born Jan^ry ye 20. 1731.

Lucy daughter of Frank a Slave belonging to Edmund Mickelborough born Jan^ry. ye 16. 1731.

Nancey daughter of Judith a Slave belonging to Thomas Mountague born Decem^r ye 30. 1731.

Sango Son of Bellah a Slave belonging to ye estate of Thos Smith decd. born Jan^ry. ye 24. 1731.

Sam Son of Phillis a Slave belonging to Jno Segar born Jan^ry. ye 16. 1731.

Abram Son of Hannah a Slave belonging to Eliz^a Smith Senr born Feb^ry. ye 20. 1731.

Frank daughter of Beck a Slave belonging to James Ried born Feb^ry. ye 18. 1731.

Robin Son of Lucy a Slave belonging to Edwin Thacker born Feb^ry. ye 16. 1731.

Billy Son of Dido a Slave belonging to Christopher Robinson born Feb^ry. ye 22. 1731.

Phillis daughter of Jane a Slave belonging to Hugh Stewart born March ye 15. 1731.

Mingo Son of Kate a Slave belonging to John Smith Senr born April ye 9th 1732.

Billy Son of Alice a Slave belonging to Margrett Daniel born April ye 18. 1732.

Frank daughter of Kate a Slave belonging to Richard Tylor born April ye 28. 1732.

Phillis daughter of Moll a Slave belonging to Geo Wortham jun: born April ye 28. 1732.

Lucy daughter of Juno a Slave belonging to Mathew Kemp born May ye 21. 1732.

Bob Son of Winny a Slave belonging to Edwin Thacker born May ye 15. 1732.

Gilbert Son of Dinah a Slave belonging to ye estate of Thos Smith decd born May ye 15. 1732.

Tony Son of Peg a Slave belonging to Henry Armistead born May ye 20. 1732.

Sango Son of —— a Slave belonging to Anne Smith daughter of James Smith born June ye 2. 1732.

George Son of Sue a Slave belonging to ye estate of Jno Wormeley decd. born June ye 5. 1732.

Middlesex Son of Jenny a Slave belonging to Francis Cheadle born June ye 7. 1732.

Will Son of Cate a Slave belonging to John Moseley born June ye 18. 1732.

Cate daughter of Hannah a Slave belonging to Garrett Daniel born June ye 28. 1732.

Joe Son of Bess a Slave belonging to Paul Philpots born June ye 22 1732.

Phillis daughter of Letty a Slave belonging to John Davis born June ye 14. 1732.

Queen daughter of Bradford a Slave belonging to Gawin Corbin born July ye 25. 1732.

Cate daughter of Alice a Slave belonging to Gawin Corbin born July ye 28. 1732.

Hampton Son of Cate a Slave belonging to William Chowning born July ye 4. 1732.

Jenny daughter of Rose a Slave belonging to Edwin Thacker born July ye 30. 1732.

Abigal daughter of Clara a Slave belonging to Christopher Robinson born July ye 25. 1732.

Harry Son of Phillis a Slave belonging to ye estate of Jno Wormeley ded. born July ye 20. 1732.

Patt. daughter of Dye a Slave belonging to John Rhoads born July ye 24 1732.

Joe Son of Eve a Slave belonging to John Grymes born May ye 13. 1732.

Mar Son of Grace a Slave belonging to John Grymes born July ye 20. 1732.

Jenny daughter of Sara a Slave belonging to Ralph Shelton born Augus^t ye 10. 1732.

Pattey daughter of Annakey a Slave belonging to Edwin Thacker born Augs^t 14 1732.

Nan daughter of Peg. a Slave belonging to Thomas Cheney born Septem^r ye 10. 1732.

Betty daughter of —— a Slave belonging to Gawin Corbin born August 30. 1732.

Nell daughter of Hannah a Slave belonging to George Hardin born June ye 22 1732.

Ben Son of Kate a Slave belonging to John Burk born October ye 1 1732.

Sarah daughter of Nanny a Slave belonging to ye estate of Jno Wormley dec'd born Sept. 21 1732.

Caesar Son of Kate a Slave belonging to John Marshall born Septem^r ye 27. 1732.

Sawney Son of Beck a Slave belonging to William Goar born October ye 30. 1732.

Edy daughter of Cate a Slave belonging to Humphry Jones born Septem^r ye 12. 1732.

Ralph Son of Lucy a Slave belonging to Humphry Jones born Septem^r ye 27. 1732.

Winney daughter of Alice a Slave belonging to Robert George born Octo. ye 27. 1732.

Sampson Son of Moll a Slave belonging Wm Mountague born Novem^r ye 23. 1732.

Daniel Son of Betty a Slave belonging to Wm Blackburn born Novem^r ye 16. 1731.

Nan daughter of Nan a Slave belonging to Wm Blackburn born July ye 15. 1732.

Hannah daughter of Doll a Slave belonging to Wm Blackburn born
Septem^r 14. 1732.
Peter Son of Hannah a Slave belonging to John Marshall born No-
vem^r 12 1732.
Daphne daughter of Judy a Slave belonging to Thos Mountague
born Decem^r 28. 1732.
Scipio Son of Judy a Slave belonging to ye estate of Wm Stanard
decd. born Jan^ry ye 31. 1732.
Dick Son of Alice a Slave belonging to Edwin Thacker born Jan^ry
ye 31. 1732.
Sue daughter of Lucy a Slave belonging to Christopher Sutton born
Jan^ry ye 12. 1732.
Juno daughter of Nan a Slave belonging to William Hackney born
Jan^ry ye 26. 1732.
Billy Son of Moll a Slave belonging to William Wood born Feb^ry
ye 3d. 1732.
Yangar Son of Dido a Slave belonging to William Owen born Octo.
ye 14 1732.
Jenney daughter of Jenney a Slave belonging to Mary Hunt born
Decem^r 20. 1732.
Hannah daughter of Beck a Slave belonging to Jno Grymes born
Feb^ry ye 10. 1732.
Jenny daughter of Dinah a Slave belonging to Wm Saunders born
Feb^ry ye 7. 1732.
Winney daughter of Frank a Slave belonging to Robt Daniel born
Feb^ry ye 1. 1732.
Mingo Son of Bess a Slave belonging to ye estate of Wm Gordon
dec'd born March ye 4 1732.
Caesar & Dick Sons of Jenny a Slave belonging to Armistead
Churchhill born March ye 17. 1732.
Maud daughter of Judy a Slave belonging to Jno Smith jun^r born
Octo. ye 2. 1732.
Rose daughter of Dy a Slave belonging to John Moseley born
March ye 1. 1732.
Venus daughter of Phillis a Slave belonging to James Daniel born
March ye 19. 1732.
Peter Son of Eve a Slave belonging to Edwin Thacker born March
ye 31. 1733.
Flora daughter of   a Slave belonging to John Grymes born Ap.
ye 1. 1733.
Beck daughter of Betty a Slave belonging to Christopher Robinson
born March 22. 1733.
Sam Son of Dinah a Slave belonging to Christopher Robinson born
April 20. 1733.
Frank daughter of Wonnah a Slave belonging to Henry Armistead
born April 25. 1733.
Peter Son of Sarah a slave belonging to Hezekiah Rhoads born
April ye 30. 1733.
Pheebe daughter of Beck a Slave belonging to John Lewis born
April ye 29. 1733.
Cate daughter of Margrett a Slave belonging to ye estate of Jno
Wormeley dec'd born April 22 1733.

Blade Son of Rose a Slave belonging to George Hardin born May
ye 12. 1733.
Isaac Son of Dido a Slave belonging to Augustine Smith born June
ye 3. 1733.
Dum Son of Frank a Slave belonging to Roger Jones born May y^e
30 1733.
Dick Son of   a Slave belonging to Thomas Corbin born May y^e
1. 1733.
Alice daughter of Judy a Slave belonging to ye estate of Wm Daniel
dec'd born May ye 15 1733.
Nanny daughter of Kate a Slave belonging to William Wood born
June ye 11. 1733.
Robin Son of Sue a Slave belonging to Bar. Yates born June ye 9.
1733.
Neator daughter of Alice a Slave belonging to Christopher Robin-
son born May ye 29 1733.
Cela daughter of Molly a Slave belonging to Christopher Robinson
born May ye 20. 1733.
Hannah daughter of Kate a Slave belonging to Edwin Thacker born
June ye 30. 1733.
Jack Son of Sarah a Slave belonging to Edwin Thacker born July
ye 18. 1733.
Crumwell Son of Moll a Slave belonging to Elizabeth Smith born
July ye 10. 1733.
Cate daughter of Judy a Slave belonging to Mathew Kemp born
May ye 20. 1733.
Nanny daughter of Bess a Slave belonging to Mathew Kemp born
June ye 27. 1733.
Jenny daughter of Venus a Slave belonging to Aquilla Snelling born
July ye 29. 1733.
Phillis daughter of Jenny a Slave belonging to Henry Tugle jun^r born
Augu^st ye 5. 1733.
Abraham & Jacob Sons of Jenny a Slave belonging to ye estate of
Jno Wormeley decd. born July ye 18. 1733.
Esther daughter of Winny a Slave belonging to John Grymes born
August ye 1st 1733.
Sue daughter of Hannah a Slave belonging to Elizabeth Smith born
July ye 30. 1733.
Letty daughter of Bess a Slave belonging to John Segar born August
ye 9. 1733.
Roger Son of —— a Slave belonging to John Grymes born August
ye 20. 1733.
Isaac Son of Margery a Slave belonging to Oliver Segar born July
ye 13. 1733.
Marlebrough Son of Moll a Slave belonging to Wm Montague born
Aug^st 15. 1733.
Jeffery Son of Bradford a Slave belonging to Gawin Corbin born
Aug^st ye 22. 1733.
York Son of Willmott a Slave belonging to Laurance Orrill born
August ye 31. 1733.
Sangro Son of Jude a Slave belonging to John Hipkins born Sep-
tem^r ye 15. 1733.

233

Gabriel Son of Phillis a Slave belonging to Mary Machen born September y⁶ 24. 1733.

Lucy daughter of Nan a Slave belonging to William Hill born August y° 26. 1733.

Hagar daughter of Phillis a Slave belonging to Jacob Stiff born September y⁶ 22. 1733.

Jemmy Son of Margery a Slave belonging to Frances Alding born August y⁶ 31. 1733.

Johny Son of Hannah a Slave belonging to Laurance Qrrill born October y⁶ 2. 1733.

Priscilla daughter of Moll a Slave belonging to Christopher Robinson born May y⁶ 31. baptized Aug^st 19. 1733.

Toby Son of Kate a Slave belonging to Augustine Smith born October y⁶ 10. 1733.

Ned Son of Sharlote a Slave belonging to Henry Thacker born October y⁶ 25. 1733.

Sue daughter of Jenny a Slave belonging to John Murrah born October y⁶ 30. 1733.

Toby Son of Dillah a Slave belonging to Henry Daniel born October y⁶ 5. 1733.

Laurance Son of Flora a Slave belonging to y⁶ estate of Jn° Wormeley ded. born Octo^r y⁶ 12. 1733.

Margery daughter of Nell a Slave belonging to y⁶ estate of Jn° Wormeley decd. born Novem^r 15. 1733.

Jack Son of Jone a Slave belonging to Catherine Warwick born Novem^r y⁶ 30. 1733.

Sancho Son of Grace a Slave belonging to John Grymes born Novem^r y⁶ 9. 1733.

Jemmy Son of Billah a Slave belonging to y⁶ estate of Thos Smith born Decem^r y⁶ 23. 1733.

Dye daughter of Lucy a Slave belonging to Edwin Thacker born Novem^r y⁶ 25. 1733.

Sarah daughter of Sarah a Slave belonging to Edm^d Mickleburrough born Decem^r y⁶ 3. 1733.

Harry Son of Cress a Slave belonging to Jn° Grymes born Decem^r y⁶ 29. 1733.

Jenny daughter of Lett a Slave belonging to Anne Smith born Jan^ry y⁶ 14. 1733.

Nelly daughter of Molly a Slave belonging to Anne Wood born Feb^ry y⁶ 3. 1733.

Phillis daughter of —— a Slave belonging to Mary Bristow born Feb^ry y⁶ 9. 1733.

Susan daughter of —— a Slave belonging to Thomas Corbin born Jan^ry y⁶ 29. 1733.

Mack Son of —— a Slave belonging to Thomas Corbin born Feb^ry y⁶ 13. 1733.

Sarah daughter of —— a Slave belonging to Edmund Berkeley born March y⁶ 1. 1733.

Adam Son of Dinah a Slave belonging to y⁶ estate of Thos Smith decd. born March y⁶ 18. 1733.

Joe Son of Lucy a Slave belonging to Thomas Buford born March y⁶ 19. 1733.

Ben Son of Pegg a Slave belonging to William Owen born March ye 12. 1733.

Humphrey Son of Frank a Slave belonging to Christopher Robinson born Feb^{r}y ye 4. 1733.

Andrew Son of Jenny a Slave belonging to Christopher Robinson born March ye 12. 1733.

Bristow Son of Judy a Slave belonging to John Vivion born April ye 1. 1734.

Gawen Son of Sabrina a Slave belonging to Edwin Thacker born March ye 26. 1734.

Rose daughter of Rose a Slave belonging to Gawin Corbin born March ye 9. 1733.

Moll daughter of Kate a Slave belonging to Gawin Corbin born March ye 22. 1733.

Alice daughter of Sarah a Slave belonging to Charles Grymes born April ye 10. 1734.

Nan daughter of Munday, a Slave belonging to Samuel Batchelder born April ye 27. 1734.

Jack Son of Jenny, a Slave belonging to Armistead Churchhill born April ye 18. 1734.

Robin Son of Beck, a Slave belonglng to James Reid born May ye 3. 1734.

Windsor Son of Nanny, a Slave belonging to ye estate of Jno Worm· eley decd. born April ye 28. 1734.

Sary daughter of Nan, a Slave belonging to ye estate of Jno Smith Senr decd. born May ye 11. 1734.

Will Son of Rose, a Slave belonging to William Bristow born May ye 23. 1734.

Bristol Son of Sarah, a Slave belonging to Alexander Graves born June ye 1. 1734.

Gawin Son of Phillis, a Slave belonging to James Daniel Junr born May ye 22, 1734.

James Son of Nell, a Slave belonging to Humphrey Jones born April ye 15. 1734.

Mill daughter of Lucy, a Slave belonging to Humphrey Jones born March ye 2. 1733.

Antoney Son of Lucy, a Slave belonging to ye estate of oliver Segar born April ye 29. 1734.

Phil & Emanuel Sons of Hannah, a Slave belonging to Chris^{to} Robinson born June 16. 1734.

Dick Son of Betty, a Slave belonging to Xtopher Robinson born June ye 27. 1734.

Judee daughter of Betty, a Slave belonging to ye estate of Jno Smith ded. born June ye 7. 1734.

Moll daughter of Nany, a Slave belonging to James Crosbie born July 3. 1734.

Frank daughter of Judy, a Slave belonging to Eliza Annard born Oct. 20. 1734.

Phill Son of Mary, a Slave belonging to Co^{ll} Churchill born October 8th 1734.

Rose Daughter of Moll, a Slave belonging to George Worther born December 4th 1734.

Simon Son of Doll, a Slave belonging to Jn° Rhodes born June 29. 1734.

Peter Son of Dinah, a Slave belonging to Coll. Armistead born May 7. 1734.

Ben Son of Sue, a Slave belonging to Coll. Armistead born Augus 17. 1734.

Roger Son of Else, a Slave belonging to Jn° Blake born July 22d 1734.

Ben a Slave belonging to Coll. Churchill born October 24th 1734.

Dinah Daughter of Wonah, a Slave belonging to Coll. Armistead born Decr 2d 1734.

Dinah Daughter of Letty, a Slave belonging to Wm Daniel born June 24th 1734.

Sam Son of Kate, a Slave belonging to Churchhill Blacky born July 23rd 1734.

Europe Son of Jenny, a Slave belonging to Frances Cheedle born July 18th 1734.

Bristow Son of Kate, a Slave belonging to Jn° Moseley born October 12th 1734.

Sue Daughter of Hannah, a Slave belonging to Jn° Moseley born October 21st 1734.

Mintis Son of Alice, a Slave belonging to Jane Seager born Decr 7th 1734.

Jack Son of Hannah, a Slave belonging to Garrett Daniel born Novr 30th 1734.

Nanny Daughter of Sarah, a Slave belonging to Crispin Shelton born Novr 19th 1734.

Dick Son of Jone, a Slave belonging to Catherine Warwick born Decr 20th 1734.

Tom Son of ——, a Slave belonging to Thomas Corbin born Decr 19th 1734.

Ben Son of ——, a Slave belonging to Thos Corbin born Decr 20th 1734.

Jack Son of Flora, a Slave belonging to Jn° Grymes born Dec. 16th 1734.

Sam Son of Judee, a Slave belonging to Jn° Smith Junr born Dec. 19th 1734.

Judee Daughter of Kate, a Slave belonging to Jn° Burk born Jan^ry 2d 1734.

Johnny Son of ——, a Slave belonging to Matth: Kemp born March 17th 1733.

Jemmy Son of ——, a Slave belonging to Matth. Kemp born July 25th 1733.

Sam Son of —— a Slave belonging to Matth: Kemp born Jan^ry 8th 1734.

Dinah Daughter of Nan, a Slave belonging to Willm Hacknay born Decr 30th 1734.

Jenny Daughter of Virena, a Slave belonging to Jonathan Brooks born Feb^ry 24th 1734.

Doll Daughter of ——, a Slave belonging to Thomas Corbin born Feb. 14th 1734.

Siller Daughter of Frank, a Slave belonging to Roger Jones born March 24th 1734.

Dinah Daughter of Hannah, a Slave belonging to Eliz. Smith born March 30th 1735.

Harry Son of Jenny, a Slave belonging to Wm Hill born Ap. 3rd 1735.

Mille Daughter of Sue, a Slave belonging to Thos Price born March 3rd 1734.

Jn° Reade Min^r.

Judee, daughter of Winny, a Slave belonging to Edwin Thacker born Ap. 20th 1735.

Letty, Daughter of Rose, a Slave belonging to Edwin Thacker, born Ap. 6th 1735.

Wingo, Son of Dinah, a Slave belonging to Henry Daniel, born Ap: 24th 1735.

Dick, Son of Alice, a Slave belonging to Edwin Thacker, born May 31st 1735.

Jenny, Daughter of Rose, a Slave belonging to Geo. Hardin, born June 12th 1735.

Caesar, Son of Judy, a Slave belonging to Armistead Churchhill, born Ap: 10th 1735.

Phill, Son of Hannah, a Slave belonging to Armistead Churchhill, born Ap. 19th 1735.

Oliver, Son of Daffany, a Slave belonging to Jn° Grymes, born May 30th 1735.

Hannah, Daughter of Eve, a Slave belonging to Edwin Thacker, born Ap: 22nd 1735.

Phillis, Daughter of Bradford, a Slave belonging to Gawin Corbin, born May 13th 1735.

Jenny, Son of Cress, a Slave belonging to Jn° Grymes, born June 8th 1735.

Phill, Son of Phillis, a Slave belonging to Mary Machen, born June 12th 1735.

Jack, Son of Kate, a Slave belonging to Alexander Frazier, born June 22d 1735.

Hannah, Daughter of Sarah, a Slave belonging to Alexander Graves, born July 11th 1735.

Mille, Daughter of —— a Slave belonging to Gawin Corbin born June 29th 1735.

Lucy, Daughter of Jean, a Slave belonging to Mary Tugell born July 27th 1735.

Jemmy, Son of Kate, a Slave belonging to Alexander Frazeir, born June 23. 1735.

Sue, Daughter of Bess, a Slave belonging to Mathew Gale, born Aug^st 2. 1735.

Aaron, —— —— a Slave belonging to Gawin Corbin, born Aug^st 2. 1735.

Kate, Daughter of Jenny, a Slave belonging to Henry Tugle, born Sep^t 17th 1735.

Lucy, —— ——— a Slave belonging to Gawin Corbin, born Sept. 10. 1735.

Buchan, Son of Molly, a Slave belonging to Alexander Frazier, born Sep. 29. 1735.

Anthony, Son of Sharlot, a Slave belonging to Henry Thacker, born Sep^t 28th 1735.

Matt, —— —— a Slave belonging to Armistead Churchhill, born
Sep^t 10 1735.

Given into y^e ⎧ Annacle Daughter of Judee, a Slave belonging to
Secretary's office ⎪ Jn° Vivion, born Novr 4th 1735.
Decr 6th *1735* ⎨ Rose, Daughter of Sue, a Slave belonging to Coll.
Charged. ⎩ Armistead born Octr 29th 1735.

Letty, Daughter of Margery, a Slave belonging to Jean Seager born
Novr 2d 1735.

Phebe daughter of Sarah Oct^t 10th 1735. Sandy Son of Kate Dec^r
13th 1735. Slaves belonging to Gawin Corbin.

Will, Son of Sarah, a Slave belonging to Jn° Goodwin, Novr 27th
1735.

Nell, Daughter of Moll, a Slave belonging to Armistead Churchhill,
born Decr 3d 1735.

Bristow Son of Dillah, a Slave belonging to Henry Daniel born Dec:
17 1735.

Sary, Daughter of Hannah, a Slave belonging to Hen. Mickelburrough, born Jan. 2. 1735.

Nan, Daughter of Frank, a Slave belonging to Henry Armistead
born Decr 3d 1735.

Hannah, Daughter of Judy, a Slave belonging to James Daniel born
Jan^ry 27. 1735.

Pompey, Son of Venus, a Slave belonging to Eliz^th Thurston, born
Jan^ry 28th 1735.

Dick, Son of Sarah, a Slave belonging to Edm^d Mickelburrough,
born Jan^ry 20th 1735.

Adam, Son of Judy, a Slave belonging to Ch. Robinson, born Feb:
4th 1735.

Frank, Daughter of Jenny, a Slave belonging to Jn° Wortham,
born Feb. 3d 1735.

Nanny, Daughter of Beck, a Slave belonging to James Reid born
Feb: 12th 1735.

Duncan, Son of Sary, a Slave belonging to Eliz^th Stannard, born
Feb: 13. 1735.

Frank, Daughter of Lucy, a Slave belonging to Thos Buford, born
Feb: 19 1735.

Lucy, Daughter of Judy, a Slave belonging to Thos Mountague born
Jany 28 1735.

Phill. Son of —— a Slave belonging to Humphrey Jones, born Dec^r
29 1735.

Nan, Daughter of —— a Slave belonging to Humphrey Jones, born
Feb: 23 1735.

Three Negro Women named belonging to Christopher Robinson bap: Mar: 7 1735.

Tom, Son of Nanny, a Slave belonging to Ann Clarke, born Mar.
3d 1735.

Davy, —— —— a Slave belonging to Thomas Corbin, born Feb:
23 1735.

Frank, Daughter of —— a Slave belonging to Mathew Kemp born
Feb: 28. 1735.

Will Son of —— a Slave belonging to Thos Laughlin born Mar: 12th
1735.

Peter Son of Judy, a Slave belonging to Mathew Kemp born Sep[t]
  4th 1735.
Ursly Daughter of Lucy, a Slave belonging to Jane Seager Feb:
  21st 1735.
Given into y[e] ⎱ Dick Son of Jenny, a Slave belonging to Armis-
S. O. Ap. 1736. ⎰ tead Churchhill born March 31st 1736.
            Jn[o] Reade, Min[r]
Rose Daughter of Frank a slave belonging to Christ[r] Robinson born
  Ap 24. 1736.
Nicholas Son of Alice a slave belonging to Chris[r] Robinson born
  May 2d 1736.
Sam Son of Judith a slave belonging to Tho[s] Montague born Ap[l] 24
  1736.
Ave daughter of Sarah a slave belonging to Edwin Thacker born
  Nov[r] 10th 1735.
Simon Son of Phillis a slave belonging to Jacob Stiff born May 9th
  1736.
Dye Daughter of Judy a slave belonging to y[e] Estate of Jn[o] Hipkins
  dec'd born April 8th 1736.
Doctor Son of Bess a slave belonging to Alex Frazier born June 17th
  1736.
Harry Son of Letty a Slave belonging to y[e] Estate of W[m] Stannard
  deceas'd born July 6. 1736.
Sam Son of Bess a slave belonging to Math[w] Kemp. born May 19th
  1736.
Annaca Daughter of Grace a Slave belonging to Armistead Churehill
  born June 17th 1736.
—— —— —— a slave belonging to W[m] Gore born 17th June 1736.
Affrica Son of Winny a slave belonging to Edwin Thacker born
  July 19th 1736.
Chales Son of Jenny a slave belonging to Mary Murry, Seign[r] born
  July 28th 1736.
  The 3 following Registers omitted in 1735.
Mingo Son of Unity a slave belonging to Edward Dillard, born
  Sept[r] 26th 1735.
Cupid Son of Beck a Slave belonging to Jn[o] Lewis, born Oct[r] 17th
  1735.
Frank Daughter of Phillis a Slave belonging to Jn[o] Seager, born
  Oct[r] 20th 1735.
Gowin Son of Lucy a Slave belonging to Edwin Thacker born Oct[r]
  4th 1736.
Lemuel Son of Judith a Slave belonging to Eliz. Stannard born
  Aug[st] 31st 1736.
Hannah Daughter of Judy a Slave belonging to Jedediah Bristow,
  born March 18th 1735.
Harry Son of Hannah a slave belonging to y[e] Estate of Jn[o] Smith
  Dec[d] born Aug[st] 25th 1736.

Given unto ⎧ Tom Son of Lett a slave belonging to Ann Smith,
y[e] Secret off ⎪   born Oct[r] 14th 1736.
Oct[r] 1736. ⎨ Jane Daughter of Moll a slave belonging to Alex.
              ⎪   Frazier, born Sep[t] 30th 1736.
              ⎪ Eve Daughter of Winney a Slave belonging to Jn[o]
              ⎩   Grymes, born July 18th 1736.

Tom Son of Nan a Slave belonging to James Scrossby, born Octr 18th 1736.

Alce daughter of Pegg a slave belonging to William Owen was born 10^{ber} 15th 1736.

Doll daughter of Hannah a slave belonging to Matthias Gale was born Jan 25th 1736.

Jemmy Son of Hannah a slave belonging to Garret Daniel was born Jan 27th 1736.

Tamar daughter of Judy a slave belonging to Mr. John Smith (Aldin) born Jan. 25th 1736.

Pegg daughter of Cress a slave belonging to John Grymes Esq: born Jan. 30th 1736.

Isaac Son of Dinah a slave belonging to John Grymes Esq. born Feb 17th 1736.

Annica daughter of Cate a slave belonging to ye estate of John Burk deceased born Feb. 5th 1736.

Philip —— a slav^e belonging to ye estate of Collo Tho. Corbin deceased, born Feb. 15th 1736.

Sampson Son of Joan a Slav^e belonging to Philip Warwick born March 2d 1736.

Dick Son of Kate, a slav^e belonging to Thomas Salt, born March 15th 1736.

Ben Son of Kate, a slav^e belonging to Churchhill Blakey born March 16th 1736.

Letitia daughter of Alse a Slav^e belonging to Mrs. Jan^e Segar born April 4th 1737.

Catena daughter of Rose a Slave, belonging to Coll Edwin Thacker born May 4th 1737.

Caesar Son of Kate a Slave, belonging to Mr. Alexander Frazier born May 21th 1737.

Betty daughter of Molly a Slav^e belonging to Mrs Page born Jan. 21st 1736.

Jack Son of Betty a Slave belonging to William Lawson born March 6th 1736.

Beck daughter of Judy a Slave, belonging to Mr. Alexander Frazier born March 6th 1736.

Frank —— a Slav^e belonging to William Lawson born January 10th 1736.

Jenny daughter of Moll a Slave, belonging to George Wortham born March 17th 1736.

Moll daughter of Jenny a Slav^e belonging to Hannah Watts born July 10th 1735.

Hannah a negro-child belonging to Roger Jones born Jan. 16th 1737.

Peter a negro boy of Doll belong^{ng} to John Rhodes was born 10^{ber} 10th 1736.

Avith a negro girl of Nan belonging to William Hackney was Jan. 10th 1736.

—— a negro boy of Jenny belonging to Major Matt Kemp. born July 14th 1736.

Mingo a negro-boy of Coll Churchhill was born Feb. 25th 1736.

Sarah a negro girl of Major Berkeley was born June 7th 1737.

Sam a negro boy of Major Berkeley was born July 1737.

Molly a negro girl of Major Berkeley was born July 20th 1737.

Rose a negro girl of Major Berkeley was born July 24th 1737.

Charles a negro boy of Coll John Grymes was born July 12th 1737.

Frank a negro boy of Coll Churchhill was born April 1st 1737.

Billy a negro boy of Coll Churchhill was born April 18th 1737.

Luce daughter of Sharlot a Slav^e belonging to Mr Henry Thacker
    was born Aug 17th 1737.

Roger a slave belonging to ye Estate of Mr Thomas Corbin deceas'd
    born June 2d 1737.

Given to the
Secr^{e}t Offic^e
8ber. 1737.
  Primus ye son of Kate a slav^e belonging to Coll
    Gawen Corbin born May 30th 1737.
  Winny a slav^e belonging to Mr Humphrey Jones born
    July 9th 1737.
  Billy a slav^e belonging to Coll. Gawen Corbin born
    July 14th 1737.

A Negro child of Frank's belonging to Coll. Henry Armistead born
    Ausst ye 15th 1737.

Peter son of Jeney a Slave belonging to Henry Tugel born Octo^r y^e
    5th 1737.

Jemme Son of Dinner a slave belonging to Coll Henry Armstead
    born Sepr ye 18th 1737.

Margree a Negro child belonging to Edward Dillard born Octo^r y^e
    28th 1737.

Ealce Daughter of Letty a Slave belonging to Mrs Stanard born Nov^r
    ye 23 1737.

Robin Son of Jane a slave belonging to Mrs Hannah Watts born
    Sepr ye 17th 1737.

Ben Son of Janne a Slave belonging to Mary Hunt born July ye 3d
    1737.

Tony child of Dido a Slave belonging to Maj^r Kemp born April 17th
    1737.

Betty Daughter of Alice a Slave belonging to Christopher Robinson
    born Decem^r y^e 26. 1737.

Tamar daughter of Nan a Slave belonging to William Hill Senr born
    Decem^r y^e 27th 1737

Sprig Son of Juno a Slave belonging to George Hardin born Jan^y
    y^e 8th 173$\frac{7}{8}$.

Lucy daughter of Beck a slave belonging to James Reid born Jan^y
    y^e 14th 173$\frac{7}{8}$.

Billey Son of Phillis a Slave belonging to John Segar born Jany y^e
    27th 173$\frac{7}{8}$.

Davey Son of Cate a Slave belonging to John Segar born Feby y^e 2d
    173$\frac{7}{8}$.

Orson Son of Beck a Slave belonging to John Lewis born Feb^{ry} y^e
    14th 173$\frac{7}{8}$.

Jack Son of Letey a Slave belonging to Henry Tugel born March y^e
    21st 173$\frac{7}{8}$.

Mary Daughter of Penelope a Slave belong to John Walker born
    Novr 21st 1737.

Penalope Daughter of Jane a Slave belonging to John Walker born
    Novr 22d 1737.

—— Son of Kate a Slave belonging to Edward Thacker born Sep-
    tem^r y^e 10th 1737.

Ben belonging to William Bristow born Feb^ry 1737.

Simon Son of Venis a Slave belonging to Aquila Snelling born March ye 25th 1738.

Cloye Daughter of Cloye a Slave belonging to Co^ll Grymes born May ye 3d 1738.

Hannah Daughter of Hannah a Slave belonging to Co^ll Grymes born May ye 1st 1738.

Bowker Son of Kate a Slave belonging to Charles Daniel born May 24th 1738.

Nan daughter of Beck a Slave belonging James Mayo born March 25th 1738.

Charles Son of Judy a Slave belonging to George Hardin born April ye 1st 1738.

Harry Son of Bess a Slave belonging to James Crosby born May ye 15th 1738.

Frank daughter of Jude a Slave belonging to Jidediah Bristow born April ye 12th 1738.

Ann Daughter of Silvia a Slave belonging to Co^ll Grymes born May ye 7th 1738.

Jeny Daughter of Bess a Slave belonging to Alex^dr Frazier born May ye 13th 1738.

Jack Son of Judith a Slave belonging to Thos Mountague born June ye 11th 1738.

Nero Son of Jenny a Slave belonging to John Wortham born June ye 30th 1738.

Bess Daughter of Bess a slave belonging to Matthew Kemp born June ye 3rd 1738.

Oliver . . . . . belonging to John Smith born June ye 20th 1738.

Jene . . . . a Slave belonging to John Blake Senr born June ye 28th 1738.

Moll Daughter of Bess a Slave belonging to John Segar born June ye 29th 1738.

Peter Son of Hannah a Slave belonging to Co^ll Henry Armistead born June ye 19th 1738.

Simon Son of Hannah a Slave belonging to Geo. Hardin born June ye 20th 1738.

Lucy daughter of Beck a Slave born June ye 6th
Mary daughter of Beck a Slave born June ye 26th
} belonging to Chris^r Robinson 1738.

Jane daughter of Alice a Slave belonging to Co^ll Gawin Corbin born June ye 1st 1738.

Hampton Son of Phillis a Slave belonging to John Thompson born June ye 10th 1738.

Gloster Son of Judy a Slave belonging to Robt Daniel born July ye 8th 1738.

Will Son of Cres a Slave belonging to Co^ll John Grymes born July ye 10th 1738.

George Caine Son of Judy a Slave belonging to James Dunlevy born July ye 30th 1738.

James Son of Mortilly a Slave belonging to Co^ll Grymes born Aug^st 31st 1738.

Abygall daughter of Nell a Slave belonging to Humphrey Jones born Aug^st 29th 1738.
Sam Son of Hanna a Slave belonging to Henry Tugel born Aug^st ye 13th 1738.
Frank daughter of Rose a Slave belonging to Co^ll Thacker born Aug^st ye 19th 1738.
Mille daughter of Hannah a Slave belonging to John Smith Junr born Sepr ye 3rd 1738.
Ambrose & Sarah born of Murreah a Slave belonging to Edmund Berkeley   Sepr 16th 1738.
Mille daughter of Nan a Slave belonging to Mary Jackson born Octo^r 22nd 1738.
Harrow daughter of Dorender a Slave belonging to Richard Corbin born Oct 7 1738.
Jemima daughter of Verena a Slave belonging to Curtis Hardee born Novr ye 1. 1738.
Sarah daughter of Kate a Slave belonging to Eliz: Burk born Novr 18 1738.
Susannah Daughter of Alice a Slave born Aug^st 30th belonging to Co^ll Thacker 1737.
Harry Son of Kate a Slave born Septr 10th belonging to Coll Edwin Thacker 1737.
Hezekiah Son of Annaka a Slave belonging to Co^ll Edwin Thacker born Octr 6th 1737.
Kate Daughter of Kate a Slave belonging to Co^ll Edwin Thacker born Novr 7th 1738.
Newman Son of Sue a Slave belonging to Thos Price born Octr 27th 1737.
Lucy Daughter of Phillis a Slave belonging to Thos Price born April 4th 1738.
Winney Daughter of Daphne a Slave belonging to Thos Price born Novr 3rd 1738.
Simon Son of Venus a Slave belonging to Aquilla Snelling born April 9th 1738.
Sarah Daughter of Judy a Slave belonging to Hope Sutton born Aug^st ye 27th 1738.
Joe Son of Filles a Slave belonging to William Owen born Decm^r 25th 1738.
Rose Daughter of Judy a Slave belonging to Matthew Kemp born Novr 16th 1738.
Tom Son of Bradford a Slave belonging to Co^l Gawin Corbin born Novr 26th 1738.
Benjamin Son of Grace a Slave belonging to Co^ll John Grymes born Decem^r 2d 1738.
Jenny Daughter of Nan a Slave belonging to James Scrosby born Decr 14th 1738.
Motley Son of Kate a Slave belonging to Edmund Berkeley born Decr 31st 1738.
Phil ——— a Slave belonging to Thomas Laughlin born Jan^ry 8th 173$\frac{8}{9}$.
Pryscillia a Slave born June 1st. ⎫
Jeremy a Slave born June 16th. ⎬ these belonging to Ralph Worm-
Bridget a Slave born ⎭ ley—1738.

Simon Son of Jenny a Slave belonging to Matthew Kemp born Jan^{ry} 19th 173$\frac{8}{9}$.

Sary Daughter of Jenny a Slave born Jan^{ry} 20th. 〕 belonging to
Phebe Daughter of Tamar a Slave born Feb^{ry} 14. 〕 Richard Corbin 173$\frac{8}{9}$.

Rachel Daughter of Moll a Slave belonging to Co^{ll} Armistead Church-hill born Feb. 15th 173$\frac{8}{9}$.
Lewis Son of Sabina a Slave belonging to Co^{ll} Edwin Thacker born Feb^{ry} 20th 173$\frac{8}{9}$.
Hagar a Slave belonging to Roger Jones born Feb^{ry} y^e 18th 173$\frac{8}{9}$.
Lucy a Slave belonging to Co^{ll} Armistead Churchhill born Feb^{ry} y^e 14th 173$\frac{8}{9}$.
Frank a Slave belonging to Alexander Frazier born Feb^{ry} y^e 3d 173$\frac{8}{9}$.
Charles Son of Judy a Slave belonging to Chris^r Robinson born Feb^{ry} 24th 173$\frac{8}{9}$
Dick a Slave belonging to Alex^r Graves born Feb^{ry} y^e 28th 173$\frac{8}{9}$.
William Son of Winney a Slave belonging to Co^{ll} Edwin Thacker born March 1th 173$\frac{8}{9}$.
Parker a Slave belonging to John Smith born March y^e 5th 173$\frac{8}{9}$.
Harry Son of Judy a Slave belonging to Thos Mountague born Feb^{ry} 2d 173$\frac{8}{9}$.
Letty Daughter of Corinder a Slave belonging to Wm Mountague born March 5th 173$\frac{8}{9}$.
George Son of Doll a Slave belonging to John Rhodes born April 6th 1739.
Billey a Slave belonging to Richard Corbin born April y^e 14th 1739.
Harry Son of Hannah a Slave belonging to Mathias Gaille born April 19th 1739.
Lucy Daughter of Nan a Slave belonging to Wm Hackney born April 9th 1739.
Robin Son of Kate a Slave belonging to Alexander Frazier born April 27th 1739.
Betty Daughter of Jany a Slave belonging to Mary Murry born April 16th 1739.
Ned Son of Dido a Slave belonging to Matthew Kemp born April 15th 1739.
Frank Son of Lucy a Slave belonging to Thos Buford Senr born April 23d 1739.
Lucy Daughter of Judy a Slave belonging to Wm Gardiner Senr born May 20th 1739.
Judy Daughter of Judy a Slave belonging to John Smith born April 23d 1739.
Judy Daughter of Lucy a Slave belonging to Humphrey Jones born June 24th 1739.
Daphney Daughter of Pat a Slave belonging to Co^{ll} John Grymes born June 28th 1739.
Mingo ——— a Slave belonging to Alexander Graves born July ye 1st 1739.
Kate Daughter of Beck a Slave belonging to Co^{ll} Armistead born July 5th 1739.
Grace Daughter of Juner a Slave belonging to Matthew Kemp born Sepr 2d 1739.

Grabril Son of Bess a Slave born May 28th ⎫ belonging to Co^{ll}
Micall Son of Bettey a Slave born June 12th ⎬ Armistead 1739.
Sambo Son of Margery a Slave born July 7th ⎭

Judy Daughter of Rose a Slave belonging to Thos Chilton born
    Augst ye 8th 1739.

Amis Daughter of Betty a slave belonging to Edmund Berkeley born
    Novr 10th 1739.

Simon Son of Hannah a Slave belonging to Edmund Berkeley born
    Novr 15th 1739.

Morear —— —— a Slave belonging to William Jones born Augst y^e
    23. 1739.

Annaca —— —— a Slave belonging to Henry Mickelburrough born
    Octr ye 24th 1739.

Bess Daughter of Phillis a Slave belonging to John Fearn Senr born
    June 12th 1739.

Criss —— —— a Slave belonging to Richd Tyler born Novr ye 8th
    1739.

Margret Daughter of Phillis a Slave belonging to John Segar born
    Decr y^e 17th 1739.

Dick Son of Beck a Slave belonging to James Mayo born Decem^r
    y^e 7th 1739.

Hare Son of Cate a Slave belonging to John Carter born Jany y^e 2d
    1739.

Ampey Son of Margrey a Slave belonging to y^e Estate of Oliver
    Segar born Jan^{ry} 28th 173$\frac{9}{40}$.

Peter Son of Frank a Slave belonging to y^e estate Rog^r Jones born
    y^e 30th of Jany 173$\frac{9}{40}$.

Rachel daughter of Alice a Slave born Jan^y ⎫
    4th.   ⎬ these belonging to Co^{ll}
Betty daughter of Sarah a Slave born Jan^y ⎪ Thacker 173$\frac{9}{40}$.
    22d. ⎭

Harry Son Cate a Slave belonging to Constant Daniel born Feby y^e
    1st 173$\frac{9}{40}$.

Sarah daughter of Verena a Slave belonging to Jonathan Brooks
    born Feby 7th 173$\frac{9}{40}$.

Lemuel Son of Judith born 31st of Augst belonging to Eliz: Stanard
    1736.

Alice Daughter of Letty a Slave belonging to Eliz: Stanard born
    Novr y^e 27th 1737.

Billy Son of Judith a Slave belonging to Eliz: Stanard born May 7th
    1739.

Joe Son of Judith a Slave belonging to Eliz: Stanard born March
    23d 1740.

Judith Daughter of Sarah a Slave belonging to Eliz. Stanard born
    April 18th 1740.

Margret Daughter of Letty a Slave belonging to Eliz: Stanard born
    July 27th 1740.

George Son Winefred Morris a free Mullatto was born December
    19th 1740.

Letty Daughter of Sarah a Slave belonging to Richard Corbin was
    born May 2d 1740.

Bristow Son of Sarah belonging to Edwin Thacker was born March
    y^e 7th 1740.

Muria of Peg belonging to John Smith born October 15th 1740.

Newman a Slave belonging to Richard Corbin was born Jan^{ry} 8th 173$\frac{9}{40}$.

Charles Son of Hannah a Slave belonging to Wm Armistead born Febry 1st 173$\frac{9}{40}$.

Dinah daughter of Jenny born 25 of April belonging died the 6 Day of May 173$\frac{9}{40}$.

Peter Son of Jenny a Slave belonging to Daniel Stringer born November y^e 7th 1740.

Sam a Slave belonging to Nicholas Dillard was born April y^e 18th 1740.

Hannah Daughter of Sharlot a Slave belonging to Henry Thacker born April 15th 1740.

Dinah Daughter of Sue a Slave belonging to Wm Davis was born April 10th 1740.

Jubia Son of Rose a Slave belonging to Edwin Thacker born April 18th 1740.

Bess Daughter of Bess a Slave belonging to Alexander Frazier born May 1st 1740.

Diner Daughter of Diner a Slave belonging to William Armstead born May 21th 1740.

Emanuel & Daniel twin Sons of Sue belonging to William Armstead born May 12th 1740.

Wouna Daughter of Cate a Slave belonging to John Smith born May 20th 1740.

Guy Son of Phillis a Slave belonging to John Aldik born May 3d 1740.

Harry Son of Phillis a Slave belonging to John Thomson born July ye 21st 1740.

Dick A Slave belonging to John White born May ye 1st 1740.

Peter Son of Judy A Slave belonging to Robert Daniel born June 8th 1740.

Alice Daughter of Beck a Slave belonging to John Lewis born June 15th 1740.

Grace Daughter of Kate a Slave belonging to Edmund Berkley born May 20th 1740.

Febe a Slave belonging to John Blake born June the 17th 1740.

Buzbe Son of Judy a Slave belonging to Geo: Hardin born June 12th 1740.

Guy a Slave belonging to Armstead Churchill born June 11th 1740.

Nan Daughter of Hannah a Slave belonging to John Smith born June 11th 1740.

Cæsar Son of Judy a Slave belonging to Lawrence Orrill born July 25th 1740.

Eliza Daughter of Phillis belonging to John Smith born July 27th 1740.

Venus Daughter of Jude A Slave belonging to Thomas Mountague born Dec^{mb} 6. 1740.

Tom Son of Jude A Slave belonging to Jedidiah Bristow born Aug. 25th 1740.

Jack A Slave belonging to Charles Daniel born September 17th 1740.

Cate Daughter of Letty a Slave belonging to Henry Tugle born Sep^{ber} 13th 1740.

Jude Daughter of Dinah a Slave belonging to John Grymes born
Sep^ber 21. 1740.

Lewis a Slave belonging to Ann Smith born December 25th 1739.

Charles a Slave belonging to Ann Smith born February 17th 173$\frac{9}{4}$.

Will Son of Nan a Slave belonging to Mary Jackson born Decem^ber
1. 1740.

Harry a Slave belonging to the Estate of John Segar born No^ber &
died Decem^ber 19. 1740.

William Son of Beck a Slave belonging to James Reid was born
Jan^ry 22. 1740.

Joyce a Slave belonging to Mary Marshall born Jan^ry 11th 1740.

Phillip Son of Sarah a Slave belonging to Chris^r Robinson born June
y^e 23d 1740.

Beck Daughter of Frank a Slave belonging to Mary Lewis born
Jan^ry 28. 1740.

Betty Daughter of Lina a Slave belonging to Henry Thacker born
Feb^ry 17th 174$\frac{0}{1}$.

Glasco a Slave belonging to Henery Mickelburrough born Feb^ry 12.
1740.

Jack a Slave belonging to John Blakey born July 19th 1740.

Dina Daughter of Jenny a Slave belonging to Wm Fretwell born
May 6th 174.

Averilla a Slave belonging to Peter Hudson born July 31st 1740.

Jamey Son of Jane a Slave belonging to Thomas Mountague born
Dec^mb 6th 1740.

Frank Daughter of Jone a Slave belonging to Henry Daniel born
Feb^ry 25th 1740.

Randol Son of Nan a Slave belonging to Wm Hackney born March
9th 1740.

Joe Son of Clarinda a Slave belonging to Wm Mountague born March
29th 174$\frac{0}{1}$.

Phil Son of Judy a Slave to Ch^r Robinson born March y^e 1st. 1740.

Lucy Daughter of Moll a Slave belonging to Alex. Frazier born
April 1st 1741.

George Son of Kate a Slave belonging to Alex Frazier born April
8th 1741.

Sarah Daughter of Sarah a Slave belonging to Robert Mickleburr-
rough born March ye 2d. 1741.

Sampson Son of Nan a Slave belonging to Matthias Gale born May
ye 1st. 1741.

Jenny Daughter of Kate a Slave belonging to Co^ll Edwin Thacker
born April 29th 1741.

Robin Son of Daffiny a Slave belonging to the Honble John Grymes
Esqr born April 27th 1741.

Frank Son of Fortune a Slave belonging to Thos Laughlin born
May ye 9th. 1741.

Mole Daughter of Hannah a Slave belonging to Thos Laughlin born
May ye 23d 1741.

Ester Daughter of Bryner a Slave belonging to ye Estate of Oliver
Segar born March 29th 1741.

Peter Son of Margry a Slave belonging to ye Estate of Oliver Segar
born May ye 18th 1741.

Nat Son of Judeth a Slave belonging to Thos Mountague born May ye 24th 1741.

Hampton Son of Verena a Slave belonging to John Hardee born May ye 10th 1741.

Jeney Daughter of —— a Slave belonging to Robert Truman born June ye 15th 1741.

Diana Daughter of Letty a Slave belonging to ye Estate of Mr Stanard born July ye 12th 1741.

Glascow Son of a Slave belonging to ye Estate of John Shorter dec'd born July 15th 1741.

Richard Son of Alice a Slave belonging to Co^{ll} Thacker born July ye 3d 1741.

David Son of Doll a Slave belonging to John Rhodes born July ye 24th 1741.

Nan Daughter of Jane a Slave belonging to Henry Mickelburrough born Augst 19th 1741.

Dick Son of Sharlot a Slave belonging to Henry Thacker born Sepr ye 16th 1741.

Ben Son of —— a Slave belonging to Mary Murry born August ye 20th 1741.

Grace Daughter Cresce a Slave belonging to Co^{ll} John Grymes born Augst 10th 1741.

Frank a Slave belonging to Richard Corbin born Sepr ye 22d 1741.

Jack Son of a Slave belonging to Richd Corbin born Sepr 26th 1741.

Sukey daughter of Phillis a Slave belonging to ye Estate of Mr Stanard born Novr ye 18th 1741.

Pressilla daughter of Jenny a Slave belonging to Mrs Kemp born April ye 15th 1741.

Daniel Son of Judy a Slave belonging to Mrs Kemp born Octo^r ye 28th 1741.

Ann Daughter of Judy a Slave belonging to Lawrance Orril born Sepr ye 3d. 1741.

Sarah Daughter of Rose a Slave belonging to William Bristow born Decem^r ye 14th 1741.

Tom Son of a Slave belonging to William Gardiner Senr born Sepr ye 12th 1741.

Dick Son of hannah a Slave belonging to Mr Gaile born Octo^r ye 16th 1741.

Mary daughter of Frank a Slave belonging to Edm^d Berkeley born July ye 2d 1741.

Anthony & Nelly children of Sabina a Slave belonging to Co^{ll} Edwin Thacker born Sepr ye 6th 1741.

Harry Son of a Slave belonging to Co^{ll} Edwin Thacker born Novr ye 4th 1741.

Scipio Son of Rose a Slave belonging to Thos Chilton born March ye 6th 174½.

Daniel Son of Betty a Slave belonging to Edm^d Berkeley born Decem^r y^e 8th 1741.

Patty daughter of Kate a Slave belonging to Edm^d Berkeley born Jan^{ry} y^e 8th 174½.

Peter Son of —— —— a Slave belonging to Richd Allen born Jan^{ry} y^e 17th 174½.

Rose Daughter of Lettis a Slave belonging to Thos Saunders born Jan^{ry} y^e 2d 174$\frac{1}{2}$.

Alce Daughter of Alce a Slave belonging to Co^{ll} Gawin Corbin born Jan^{ry} y^e 1st 174$\frac{1}{2}$.

Dinah Daughter of —— a Slave belonging to William Jones born Feb^{ry} y^e 14th 174$\frac{1}{2}$.

Cate Daughter of Judah a Slave belonging to William Hackney born March 27th 1742.

Anthoney Son of Frank a Slave belonging to Samuel Batcheler born March 18th 174$\frac{1}{2}$.

Jane Daughter of Betty a Slave belonging to Cary Smith born March y^e 25th 1742.

Amy Son of   a Slave belonging to Ja^s Campbell born March y^e 28th 1744.

Sarah Daughter of Letty a Slave belonging to Jam^s Scrosby born March y^e 8th 174$\frac{1}{2}$.

Easter daughter of Bess a Slave belonging to Alexd^r Frazier born April y^e 19th 1742.

Jemmey Son of Kate a Slave belonging to y^e estate of John Burk dec'd born April 22d 1742.

Peter Son of —— a Slave belonging to John White born April y^e 25th 1742.

Anthony Son of Kate a Slave belonging to Charles Daniel born March 18th 174$\frac{1}{2}$.

Adam Son of Pegg a Slave belonging to John Robinson born May 10th 1742.

Sampson Son of Juda a Slave belonging to Robert Daniel born May 13th 1742.

Taylor Son of Phillis a Slave belonging to James Amis born May 28th 1742.

Anthony Son of Moll a Slave belonging to Geo. Wortham born Augst 2d 1742.

Jack Son of   a Slave belonging to Ralph Wormeley born April 26th 1742.

Pegg Daughter of   a slave belonging to Ralph Wormeley born June 22nd 1742.

Judy Daughter of Letty a Slave belonging to Henry Tugle born Sepr 14th 1742.

Nanny Daughter of Jenny a slave belonging to Henry Tugle born Sepr ye 6th 1742.

Jack Son of Judy a slave belonging to John Smith ald. born July ye 6th 1742.

Billey Williamson Son of —— a slave belonging to Edward Clark born Octo^r ye 6th 1742.

Mille Daughter of —— a slave belonging to Ralph Wormeley born Octr 2d 1742.

Phillis Daughter of —— a slave belonging to Ralph Wormeley born Octr 14th 1742.

Godfry Son of Lucy a Slave belonging to Wm Armistead born Sepr 15th 1742.

Doromb of Wounah a Slave belonging to Wm Armistead born Octr 10th 1742.

Tony Son of Hannah a Slave belonging to Co^{ll} Henry Armistead born Sepr 29th 1742.

Sam Son of —— a Slave belonging to Mary Roane born May ye 20th 1742.

Abram Son of —— a Slave belonging to Mary Roane born June 22th 1742.

Letty Daughter of Cate a Slave belonging to William Mountague born June 12th 1742.

Meriah Daughter of —— a Slave belonging to John Jones born born June 28th 1742.

Jeny Daughter of Cate a slave belonging to Matthias Gale born July 17th 1742.

Jack Son of Judy a Slave belonging to John Smith born July 6th 1742.

George Son of —— a Slave belonging to Churchhill Jones born July 7th 1742.

Neton Daughter of —— a slave belonging to Churchhill Jones born July 15th 1742.

Simon son of —— a slave belonging to Hugh Spotswood born July 18th 1732.

Peter Son of Jone a Slave belonging to Henry Daniel born Novr 24th 1742.

Dido Daughter of Fortin a Slave belonging to Thos Laughlin born Novr 28th 1742.

Jenny Daughter of —— a Slave belonging to John Smith born Novr 3d 1742.

Mirah Daughter of Sue a Slave belonging to Col^o John Grymes born Dec^{ber} 28. 1742.

Kezia Dughter of —— a Slave belonging to Curtis Hardee born Jan^{ry} 22.

Cate Daughter of —— a Slave belonging to Nicholas Dillard born Feb^{ry} 4th 1742.

Ben Son of Unity a Slave belonging to Edward Dillard born Feb. 26th 174$\frac{2}{3}$.

Jemme Son of Cloe a Slave belonging to John Willcox Feb^{ry} y^e 14th 174$\frac{2}{3}$.

Sue Daughter of —— a Slave belonging to Hope Sutton born Feb^{ry} 6th.

Agatha Daughter of —— a Slave belonging to Ralph Wormeley born March 15. 174$\frac{2}{3}$.

Newman Son of Beck a Slave belonging to John Lewis born March 20 174$\frac{2}{3}$.

Lewis Son of Wonna a Slave belonging to George Hardin born Jan^{ry} 2d 1743.

Judith Daughter of —— a Slave belonging to Thomas Laughlin born Jan^{ry} 10. 1743.

Will Son of Kate a Slave belonging to Charles Daniel born Feb^{ry} 27 1743.

Robin Son of Nan a Slave belonging to Charles Daniel born March 7. 1743.

Molly Daughter of Beck a Slave belonging to James Reid born April 9th 1743.

Booker Son of —— a Slave belonging to John Smith ju^{nr} born
April 14. 1743.

Judy Daughter of —— a Slave belonging to John Smith born Feb^{ry}
28th 174$\frac{2}{3}$.

Dick Son of Dy a Slave belonging to Wm Hill jun^r born May 29th
1743.

Phillis Daughter of Judy a Slave belonging to Law^r Orrill born May
29th 1743.

Jemmy Son of Frank a Slave belonging to Mary Lewis born May
1th 1743.

Billy Son of —— a Slave belonging to Robert Dudley born May
20th 1743.

George Son of Letty a Slave belonging to Ann Smith born May 29th
1743.

Kate Daughter of —— a Slave belonging to Churchill Jones born
June 4th 1743.

Massey Daughter of Dolly a Slave belonging to John Rhodes born
June 19th 1743.

Dinah Daughter of Nan a Slave belonging to —— Gail born July
8th 1743.

Jenny Daughter of Nan a Slave belonging to William Hackney Senr
born July 4th 1743.

Hannah Daughter of Judy a Slave belonging to Henry Thacker born
July 24th 1743.

Mary Daughter of Lena a Slave belonging to Henry Thacker born
August 3d 1743.

Tom Son of Judy a Slave belonging to Thomas Marston born August
29. 1743.

Harry Son of —— a Slave belonging to Ralph Wormeley born July
8th 1743.

Cupit Son of —— a Slave belonging to Ralph Wormeley born July
27. 1743.

George Son of —— a Slave belonging to Ralph Wormeley born August 5th 1743.

Eve Daughter of —— a Slave belonging to Col° Edwin Thacker
born August 21. 1743.

Sabina Daughter of Sabina a Slave belonging to Col° Edwin Thacker
born Sep^{ber} 9th 1743.

Annekin Daughter of a Slave belonging to Ralph Wormeley born
September 7. 1743.

Lucretia Daughter of Phillis a Slave belonging to Wm Mountague
born September 7. 1743.

Mary Daughter of Frank a Slave belonging to Charles Lee born
October 22. 1743.

Tom Son of Sharlot a Slave belonging to Henry Thacker born Oc^{ber}
5. 1743.

Edee Daughter of Judith a Slave belonging to Thomas Mountague
born Oc^{ber} 16. 1743.

James Son of —— a Slave belonging to Mary Jackson born November 30th 1743.

Cupid Son of Venus a Slave belonging to Richard Alleen born
Nov^{ber} 20th 1743.

Nassan Son of —— a slave belonging to Ralph Wormeley born Decem^ber 5th 1743.

Phalmoth Son of Lucy a Slave belonging to Chicheley Thacker born Dec^ber 28. 1743.

Simon Son of Letty a Slave belonging to Thomas Sanders born Dec^ber 16th 1743.

Kate Daughter of —— a Slave belonging to Col° Gawin Corbin born Jan^ry 14th 174¾.

Joe Son of —— a Slave belonging to Col° Gawin Corbin born Jan^ry 1. 174¾.

Jack Son of Jenny a Slave belonging to Henry Mickleburrough born Jan^ry 21. 174¾.

Ben Son of Jenny a Slave belonging to Thomas Buford Senr born Jan^ry 28 174¾.

Jenny Daughter of Daphney a Slave belonging to Ann Smith born July 17th 1743.

Hannah Daughter of Cate A Slave belonging to Moris Smith born Sep^ber 10. 1742.

Lucy Daughter of Letty a Slave belonging to Eliz^a Tugle born Feb^ry 12. 1743.

Tom Son of Hannah a Slave belonging to —— Gale born Feb^ry 22nd 1743.

Dinah Daughter of —— a Slave belonging to Hugh Spotswood born Feb^ry 24th 174¾.

Irenah Daughter of Phillis a Slave belonging to Beverley Stanard born Feb^ry 15th 174¾.

Frances Daughter of —— a Slave belonging to Ralph Wormely born March 10th 174¾.

Harry Son of Kate a Slave belonging to Eliz^a Burk born June ye 4th 1744.

Samuel Son of Ebo Frank a Slave born Octo^r ye 10th 1742, Alce Daughter of Betty a Slave born Novr ye 10th. 1742, Harry Son of Frank a Slave born Decem^r ye 15th 1742, Mareah Daughter of —— a Slave born Octo^r 14th 1742, Mingo Son of Cate a Slave born Octo^r ye 11th 1743, Cupit Son of Betty a Slave born Decem^r ye 16th 1744, James Son of Cates a Slave born Feb^ry ye 9th 174⅘, Isaac Son of Ebo Frank born March 20th 174⅘, these belong to Edmund Berkeley.

Susannah Daughter of —— a Slave belonging Mary Roane born March 19th 174¾.

Tom Son of Janey a Slave belonging to Thos Mountague born April 5th 1744.

James Son of —— a Slave belonging to Churchhill Jones born Marc^ ye 11th 1744.

Sam Son of —— a Slave belonging to John Jones born June 23d 1744.

Peter Son of Great Alice a Slave born Sepr 1744, Mary Daughter of Winny a Slave born Decem^r 15th 1744, Ralph Son of Little Alice a Slave born Feb^ry 23 1744, Ruben & Eliz^a Twins of Anaca a Slave born April 3d. 1745, Will Son of Jone a Slave born April 13th 1745, belonging to Edwin Thacker.

Cate Daughter of —— a Slave belonging to John Boss born May ye 20th 1744.

George Son of Rose a Slave belonging to John Rhoades born Feb^ry 26th 1744.

Mary Daughter of Rose a Slave belonging to Pat Cheops born Decr 14th 1744.

Dick Son of Sharlot a Slave born Novr 25, Billey Son of Jenney a Slave born Decr 20 1744, belonging to Henry Thacker.

Rachel Daughter of —— a Slave belonging to Obediah Daniel born Octo^r 26th 1744.

Patty Daughter of Phillis born Octo^r 1st. 1744.

Venus Daughter of Corender a Slave born Sepr 20th, Creasey Daughter of Cate a Slave born Octo^r 28th 1744, belonging to Wm Mountague.

Annaka Daughter of Judy a Slave belonging to Wm Daniel born Sepr 3d 1744.

Amee Daughter of —— a Slave belonging to Christian Miller born Sepr ye 1st 1744.

Aga Daughter of Cate a Slave belonging to Mary Carter born May 17th 1744.

Nanny Daughter of —— a Slave belonging to Mary Kemp born July 18th 1744.

Diner Daughter of betty a Slave belonging to Ann Smith born April 21st 1744.

Adam Son of Margerya a Slave born 1744, Peter Son of Moll a Slave born 1744, belonging to Coll Grymes.

Ned Son of Judy a Slave belonging to Mary Roane born June 13th 1744.

Mary Daughter of —— a Slave born Sepr 1st 1744, Edward Son of —— a slave born Novr 15th 1744, Sarah Daughter of —— a slave born Jan^ry 18th 174$\frac{4}{5}$, Thomas Son of —— a slave born Feb^ry 3d 174$\frac{4}{5}$, belonging to Ralph Wormley.

Francis Son of Betty a Slave born Sepr 27th belonging to Beverley Stanard.

Anne Daughter of —— a Slave belonging to y^e Estate of John Smith born April 28th 1744.

Anthoney son of Betty a Slave belonging to John Smith jun^r born April y^e 9th 1745.

Ben son of Beck a Slave belonging to Charles Roan born Jan^ry 14th 174$\frac{4}{5}$.

Tom Son of Jone a Slave belonging to James Machan born April 1st 1745.

Robin Son of —— a Slave belonging to y^e Estate of Gawin Corbin April 22d 1745.

Toney Son of —— a Slave belonging to Thomas Sanders born April 25th 1745.

George Son of —— a Slave belonging to John Mackneele born Feb^ry 21st 1744.

Will Son of —— a Slave belonging to Nicholas Dillard born May 2d 1745.

Sarah Daughter of Jeney a Slave belonging to John Wortham born June 22d 1744.

Susannah Daughter of Letty a Slave belonging to Bar: Yates born April 1745.

Jean Daughter of Diner a Slave belonging to Ann Wortham born
Feb^ry y^e 15th 174$\frac{4}{5}$.
Lucy Daughter of Beck a Slave belonging to George Wortham born
May 6th 1745.
Jane Daughter of —— a Slave belonging to Edward Dillard born
May 29th 1745.
Bristow son of Jeney a Slave belonging to John Kidd born July y^e
1st 1745.
Lewis Son of Beck a Slave belonging to Chris^r Robinson born July
19th 1744.
Tamer Daughter of Moll a Slave belonging to George Wortham
born July 13th 1745.
Judy Daughter of Mole a Slave belonging to Alexander Frazier born
July 17th 1745.
Sara Daughter of Nan a Slave belonging to William Hackney sen^r
born June 3d 1745.
Ben Son of Frank a Slave belonging to Eusebius Lewis born June
17th 1745.
Peter Son of Fillis a Slave belonging to William Hackney Junr born
July 12th 1745.
Newman Son of Ruth a Slave belonging to Margaret Johnson born
Aug^st 25th 1745.
Phebe Daughter of Helas a Slave belonging to Judith Segar born
Decem^r 28th 1745.
Ralph Son of —— a Slave belonging to Elizabeth Hardin born Octo^r
16th 1745.
Plymouth Son of Lena a Slave belonging to Henry Thacker born
Decem^r 17th 1745.
Kate Daughter of Dole a Slave belonging to John Rhodes born Sep^r
26th 1745.
Gowin Son of Frank a Slave belonging to Eliz^a Tugle born Decem^r
23d 1745.
Sarah Daughter of Nana a Slave belonging to Charles Daniel born
Octo^r 17th 1745.
Robin Son of Hannah a Slave belonging to Hugh Spotswood born
Novr 5th 1745.
Robing Son of —— a Slave belonging to Richard Corbin born Feb^ry
20th 1745.
Adam Son of Rose a Slave belonging to John Smith born Jan^ry
5th ——.
Rachel Daughter of Fortin a Slave belonging to Thos Laughlin born
April 23d 1745.
Chaney Daughter of —— a Slave belonging to John Berry born
March 2d 1745.
Anth^o Son of —— a Slave belonging to Churchhill Jones born Jan^ry
1st 1745.
Jane Daughter of Rose a Slave belonging to Thos Chilton born
Decem^r 12th 1745.
Peter son of —— a Slave belonging to Robert Elliot born Novr 16th
1745.
Milley Daughter of —— a Slave belonging to Robert Elliot born
Decem^r 26th 1745.

Isaac Son of —— a Slave belonging to Richard Corbin born Sep[r]
3d 1745.

Beck Daughter of —— a Slave belonging to Eliz[a] Hardin born
March 14th 1745.

Tom Son of Jone a Slave belonging to Tho[s] Buford Sen[r] born Octo[r]
19th 1745.

Jane Daughter of Margre a Slave belonging to Nicholas Dillard born
Sep[r] 28th

Sampson Son of Hannah a Slave belonging to George Lee born
March 4th 174⅚.

Simon Son of Judy a Slave belonging to Hope Sutton born Decem[r]
1745.

Susaner Daughter of Phillis a Slave belonging to Rand[h] Segar born
Feb[ry] 27th 1745.

Jemmy Son of Jude a Slave belonging to W[m] Gardner Sen[r] born
March 18th 1745.

Tom & Samson Son of Mareah a Slave belonging to Edmund Berkeley born in July or Aug[st] 1745.

Harry Son of Jenney a Slave belonging to Tho[s] Laughlin born Aug[st]
5th 1746.

Lewey Son of Moll a Slave belonging to Tho[s] Laughlin born Aug[st]
22d 1746.

Grace Daughter of Pate a Slave belonging to W[m] Armistead born
Feb[ry] 6th 174⅚.

Cella Daughter of Frank a Slave belonging to W[m] Armistead born
March 2d 174⅚.

Mingo Son of Rose a Slave belonging to Robert Trueman born July
15th 1746.

Jack Son of —— a Slave belonging to John Murry born Aug[st] 29th
1746.

Faney Daughter of —— a Slave belonging to Joseph Small born
Decem[r] 11th 1746.

Tho[s] Goselen Son of Ann a Slave belonging to Phillip Grymes born
Octo[r] 28th 1745.

Lucana Daughter of Nan a Slave belonging to Mary Jackson born
June 3d. 1746.

George Son of Hannah a Slave belonging to John Smith jun[r] born
July 20th 1746.

Tom Son of Bess a Slave belonging to Alex[or] Frazier born July 18th
1746.

Simon Son of —— a Slave belonging to John Berry born July 8th
1746.

Sary Daughter of —— a Slave belonging to John Jones born July
18th 1746.

Clara Daughter of Kate a Slave belonging to Alex[or] Frazier born
March 30th 1746.

Charles Son of —— a Slave belonging to Mary Kemp born July 2d.
1746.

Tamer Daughter of —— a Slave belonging to Churchhill Jones born
Nov[r] 22d. 1746.

Jeney Son of Kate a Slave belonging to Charles Daniel born April
1st 1746.

Lewis Son of Moll a Slave belonging to Mary Rone born April 15th 1746.

Phillis & Frank Daughters a Slave belonging to Mary Rone born May 7th 1746.

Lucy Daughter of Judy a Slave belonging to Charles Daniel born May 27th 1746.

Dolly White Daughter of Dina a Slave belonging to Ann Smith born May 16th 1746.

Milla Daughter of Daphine a Slave belonging to Ann.Smith born Novr 11th 1746.

Sue Daughter of Phillis a Slave belonging to Thos Price born April 26th 1746.

Daniel Son of Sabrina a Slave belonging to Jane Dudly born Octo^r 29th 1746.

Jacob Son of Frank a Slave belonging to Wm Mountague born Octo^r 25th 1746.

Isaac Son of Cate a Slave belonging to Wm Mountague born Novr 25th 1746.

Simon Son of —— a Slave belonging to Francis Bryant born Augst 14th 1746.

Esther Daughter of Margery a Slave belonging to John Smith Junr born Decem^r 26th 1746.

Mill Daughter of Jane a Slave belonging to Thos. Mountague born Novr 26th 1746.

Will Son of Letty a Slave belonging to Eliz^a Tugle born Novr 15th 1746.

Mille Daughter of —— a Slave belonging to George Blakey born Novr 1st 1746.

Lette Daughter of —— a Slave belonging to John Jones born Feb^{ry} 4th 1746.

Leaner Daughter of —— a Slave belonging to Massey Yarrington born Octo^r 10th 1746.

Abbie Daughter of —— a Slave belonging to Armistead Churchhill born December 12th 1746.

Anthony Son of —— a Slave belonging to Armistead Churchhill born Jan^{ry} 8th 1746.

Samson Son of Frank a Slave belonging to Catherine Batchelder born Sepr 17th 1746.

Lewis Son of Jeny a Slave belonging to Henry Mickleburrough born Jan^{ry} 28th 174$\frac{6}{7}$.

Rachel & Esther Daughter of a Slave belonging to Armistead Churchhill born in 1746.

—— Daughter of Dey a Slave belonging to Wm Hill Senr born April y^e 25th 1746.

Betty Daughter of Jeny a Slave belonging to Thos Beuford born March 6th 174$\frac{6}{7}$.

Abram Son of Hannah a Slave belonging to Wm Mountague born Jan^{ry} 6th 174$\frac{6}{7}$.

Bess Daughter of Chance a Slave belonging to Matthias Gale born March 28th 1747.

Daffery Daughter of —— a Slave belonging to y^e Estate of Wm Daniel born April 27th 1747.

Births of Negroes belonging to Samuel Klug.

Kate, Daughter of Nanny a Slave born April 1769.
George, Son of Nancy born 1773.
Randolph, Son of Nancy born 1775.
Matt, Son of Nancy born —— 1777.
Billy, Son of Nancy born September 1778.
Billy, Son of Peggy born ——— 1773.
Dolly, Daughter of Peggy born 1775.
Tom, Son of Peggy born October 1779.
James, Son of Nancy born Novr 9th 1780.
Ned, Son of Mary born August 1st 1781.
Jack son of Peggy born January 21st 1782.
Abram, Son of Mary born May —— 1784.
Jesse son of Peggy born —— 1785.

Births of Negroes belonging to Mary Yates.

Jack, son of Cilla born 1769.
Beck, Daughter of Peny born April 1st 1770.
Billy, son of Pene born August 1772.
Sukey, Daughter of Pene born June 1775.
Nancy Daughter of Pene born Novr 13th 1777.
Sarah, Daughter of Alice born February 1779.
Anthony son of Pene, born March 1781.
Robin, Son of Pene, born Novr 13th 1783.
Eveline Ann Graica Daughter of Kate born August 25th 1794.
Fanny Daughter of Nancy a Slave belon^g to S. Klug was born Nov^r
    7th 1785.
Frank, son of Peggy born July 1787.
Levie, son of Mary, born August 1787.
Peter son of Mary born March 1792.

Fragment 115 and 116.

John Walden & Frances Crittenden (K. & Q.) married March 24th
    1792.
James Hopkins & Mary Brooks married April 15th 1792.
Nelson Humphris & Lucy Jones married April 15. 1792.
Thomas Hugget & Frances Ware (K. & Q.) married April 22d.
    1792.
Francis Collier & Susannah Dillard (K. & Q.) married
William Jack   Martha Vass
The above * *
Richard Minie & Francis Leigh (K. & Q.) married June 29th 1793.
Burgess Kidd & Sarah Daniel married July 27th 1793.
Robert Watson & Mary Hibble married August 11th 1793.
    * * Keith & Mary Holden Taliaferao (K & Q.) married Au-
    gust 22nd 1793.
    * * * * Elizabeth Adams (K. & Q.) mar: Septr 12 1793.

Here begins ye Regester for ye death of Slaves from Septem^r in y^e
year 1715 w'ch before were Sett down together wth ye christian
burrialls.

Apollo a negro belonging to Wm Stanard dyed Septem^r ye 3 was buried Septem^r 4 1715.

Hester a negro belonging to Wm Stanard dyed Septem^r ye 24 was buried Septem^r 25 1715.

Toney a negro belonging to John Davies dyed Novem: ye 26 was buried Novem 27. 1715.

Bob a negro belonging to John Robinson dyed Octo: 20 was burid Octo: 21 1715.

Nanny a negro belonging to Frances Thacker dyed March 25 was buried March 26 1716.

Kitt a negro belonging to ye estate of Edwin Thacker dec'd dyed May ye 19 buried 20th 1716.

Hagar a negro belonging to Wm Sandiford dyed June ye 16. buried June ye 17 1716.

Sindab a negro belonging to Gawin Corbin dyed ye 2 of August buried August ye 3 1715.

Ned a negro belonging to ye estate of Hen: Thacker dec'd dyed Sept^mb 8 buried ye 9 1716.

Betty a negro belonging to Tho: Machen dyed March ye 17 buried ye 18 1715.

Grasheir a negro belonging to Tho: Machen dyed March ye 23 buried ye 24 1715.

Ben a negro belonging to Hen: Tugell dyed October ye 23 buried ye same day 1716.

Sarah a negro belonging to Thomas Warwick dyed Jan^ry ye 10 buried ye 11 1716.

Bess a negro belonging to Bar Yates dyed Feb^ry ye 4 buried ye same day 1716.

Dinah a negro belonging to Nicholas Bristow dyed Feb^ry 10 buried Feb^ry 11 1716.

Betty a negro belonging to Sarah Hadley dyed Feb^ry ye 4 buried ye same day 1716.

Jenny a negro belonging to John Robinson dyed Feb^ry ye 22 buried Feb^ry ye 23 1716.

Billy a negro belonging to ye estate of Henry Thacker dec'd dyed March ye 17. buried ye 18 1716.

Jack a negro belonging to Charles Lee dyed March ye 7. buried March ye 8 1716.

Rose a negro belonging to ye estate of Wm Churchhill dec'd dyed Feb^ry 10 buried ye 11 1716.

Jacob a negro belonging to ye estate of Wm Churchhill dec'd dyed Feb^ry ye 14 buried ye 15 1716.

Moll a negro belonging to ye estate of Wm Churchhill dec'd dyed March 5 buried ye 10 1716.

Rose a negro belonging to Wm Barbee dyed March ye 28 buried ye same day 1717.

Hannah a negro belonging to ye estate of Edwin Thacker dyed May ye 6 buried May ye 1717.

Will a negro belonging to Henry Armistead dyed June ye 4 buried June ye 5th 1717.

Emanuell a negro belonging to Henry Armistead dyed June ye 8. buried June 9 1717.

Burrows a negro belonging to Henry Armistead dyed June ye 10. buried June 11. 1717.

Tom a negro belonging to ye estate of Eliz^a Churchhill dyed May ye 10 buried May 11 1717.

Corey a negro belonging to John Murry dyed July ye 5 buried July ye 6 1717.

Jack a negro belonging to John Murry dyed July ye 13 buried July ye 14 1717.

Ben a Negro belonging to Matthew Hunt dyed Septem^r ye 7. buried ye same day 1717.

Alice a negro belonging to John Grymes dyed Feb^{r}y ye 1 buried Feb^{r}y ye 2 1716.

Judy a Negro belonging to John Smith Senr dyed Novem^r ye 15. buried Novem^r 16 1717.

George a Negro belonging to John Smith Senr dyed Novem^r ye 18. buried Novem^r 19 1717.

Harry a Negro belonging to Wm Barbee dyed Decem^r ye 2 buried Decem^r 3 1717.

Ned a negro belonging to Anne Thacker dyed Decem^r ye 6 buried Decem^r 8 1717.

Toney a Negro belonging to John Wormeley dyed Decem. ye 13 buried Dec. 15 1717.

Jack a Negro belonging to Jacob Stiff dyed Jan^{r}y ye 12 buried Jan^{r}y 13 1717.

Jack a Slave belonging to Wm Daniel jun^r dyed Feb^{r}y 26. buried Feb^{r}y 27 1717.

Poll a slave belonging to Phillip Warwick dyed March ye 11. buried March 12. 1717.

Dick a slave belonging to Christopher Sutton dyed Ap: 15: buried Ap: 16 1718.

Moll a Slave belonging to Gawin Corbin dyed March ye 10. buried March 11. 1717.

Kitt a slave belonging to John Robinson dyed June 30. buried July 1. 1718.

George a slave belonging to Jacob Stiff dyed August ye 28. buried August 29. 1718.

Billy a slave belonging to John Smith Junr dyed Septem^r 25. buried ye same day 1718.

Will a Slave belonging to John Vivion dyed August 30. buried August 31 1718.

Ibbo a slave belonging to John Smith dyed Octo: ye 16. buried Octo: 17 1718.

Captain a Slave belonging to Robert Daniel dyed Novem^r ye 20. buried Novem^r 21 1718.

Betty a slave belonging to William Ogilvie dyed Decem^r ye 20 buried Decem^r 21 1718.

Sue a slave belonging to Robert Dudley dyed Jan^{r}y ye 12. buried Jan^r ye 13. 1718.

Tony a slave belonging to ye estate of Wm Churchhill dec'd dyed Jan^{r}y 17. buried Jan^{r}y 18. 1718.

Bar Yates minister.

Sarah a slave belonging to Robt George jun^r dyed Decem^r 22 buried ye 23. 1718.

Betty a slave belonging to Edwin Thacker dyed Feb^{ry} 2. buried Feb^{r}y ye 3. 1718.

Toney a Slave belonging to John Aldin dyed March ye 23. buried ye same day 1718.

Ben a slave belonging to William Segar dyed Feb. 2. buried Feb. ye 3. 1718.

Dick a Slave belonging to John Vivion dyed May ye 7. buried May ye 8. 1719.

Megg a slave belonging to John Segar dyed May ye 26. buried May ye 26.

Jenny a slave belonging to James Smith dyed June ye 1. buried June ye 2. 1719.

Lucy a slave belonging to John Vivion dyed June ye 3. buried June ye 4 1719.

Jack a Slave belonging to Sam Loe dyed May ye 23. buried May ye 24 1719.

Tom a slave belonging to John Roades dyed July ye 20. buried July ye 21 1719.

Phill a slave belonging to Matthew Kemp dyed August ye 5. buried Augs^t ye 6 1719.

Harry a slave belonging to Thomas Cheney dyed Sept. ye 15 buried Sept. ye 16. 1719.

Margery a Slave belonging to Robert Dudley dyed Sept. ye 24. buried Sept. 24 1719.

Sam a slave belonging to William Segar dyed Octo ye 10. buried Octo. 11. 1719.

Thomas a slave belonging to Bartho: Yates dyed Jan^{r}y ye 10. buried ye 11. 1719.

Caesar a slave belonging to Mathew Kemp dyed Feb^{r}y ye 7. buried Feb^{r}y ye 8. 1719.

Toney a slave belonging to John Vivion dyed Jan^{r}y ye 20. buried Jan^{r}y ye 21. 1719.

Billey a slave belonging to Edwin Thacker dyed Feb^{r}y ye 29. buried ye same day 1719.

Catherine Lee a Slave belonging to Isaack Burton dyed Feb^{r}y 29. buried ye same day 1719.

Kate a slave belonging to Charles Cooper dyed Jan^{r}y 22. buried Jan^{r}y ye 23. 1719.

Dick an Indian Slave belonging to John Grymes dyed Ap: 2d buried Ap: 3. 1720.

Jack a slave belonging to John Grymes dyed Ap: ye 14. buried Ap. 15 1720.

Dinah a slave belonging to Henry Armistead dyed Ap: ye 8. buried Ap. 9 1720.

Sampson a slave belonging to Matthew Kemp dyed Ap: ye 26. buried Ap: 27 1720.

Jenny a slave belonging to John Smith Junr dyed May ye 1. buried May 2 1720.

Jenney a slave belonging to George Wortham dyed May ye 28. buried May 29. 1720.

Frank a slave belonging to Bar. Yates dyed June 25. buried June 26 1720.

Will a slave belonging to Henry Armistead dyed June ye 3. buried June 4. 1720.

Toby a slave belonging to John Smith jun^r dyed June 22. buried June 23 1720.

Frank a slave belonging to John Robinson dyed August 1. buried ye Same day 1720.

Frank a slave belonging to Armistead Churchhill dyed Augst. 3. buried ye same day 172

Doll a slave belonging to John Lewis dyed Septem^r ye 1. buried ye same day 172

Harry a Slave belonging to Mathew Kemp dyed Septem^r ye 7th 172

Nanny a slave belonging to James Curtis dyed Novem^r 15. buried Nov. 16 1720.

Aleck a slave belonging to James Curtis dyed Novem^r 16. buried Nov. 17 1720.

Will a Slave belonging to ye estate of ye abovesd James Curtis dyed Novem^r 21. buried 22. 1720.

Nan a Slave belonging to Anne Mayo dyed Novem^1 ye 20. buried Novem^r 21 1720.

Cæsar a Slave belonging to Henry Tugle dyed Novem^r ye 27. buried ye same day 1720.

Graysheir a Slave belonging to Bar Yates dyed Decem^r 16. buried Decem^r 17 1720.

Harry a Slave belonging to William Davies dyed Decem^r 16. buried Decem^r 17. 172 .

Peter a Slave belonging to James Meacham dyed Novem^r 27. buried Nov. 28 172 .

Jupiter a Slave belonging to Edwin Thacker dyed Novem^r 22. buried Novem^r 23 1720.

Dick a Slave belonging to Frances Thacker dyed Decem^r ye 2. buried Decem^r ye 5 1720.

Jemmy a Slave belonging to Edwin Thacker dyed Decem^r ye 4. buried Decem^r ye 5 1720.

Sarah a Slave belonging to Edwin Thacker dyed Decem^r ye 9. buried Decem^r 10 1720.

Charles a Slave belonging to Matthew Hunt dyed Decem^r ye 28. buried Decem^r 29 1720.

Ralph a Slave belonging to Roger Jones dyed Decem^r ye 11. buried Decem^r 12 172 .

Jemmy a Slave belonging to C: C: Thacker dyed Decem^r ye 30. buried Decem^r 31 1720.

Cornbonora a Slave belonging to Harry Beverley dyed Decem^r ye 31. buried ye Same day 1720.

Old Jack a Slave belonging to Bar. Yates dyed Jan^{r}y ye 3. buried Jan^{r}y ye 4 1720.

Jack a Slave belonging to Marvil Moseley dyed Decem^r ye 12 buried Dec. 13. 1720.

Kate a Slave belonging to Matthew Hunt dyed Jan^{r}y ye 11. buried Jan^{r}y 12. 1720.

Sawny a Slave belonging to John Grymes dyed Decem^r ye 22. buried Decem^r 23. 1720.

Absolom a Slave belonging to John Grymes dyed Jan^{r}y ye 4. buried Jan^{r}y ye 5 1720.

Harry a Slave belonging to John Grymes dyed Jan^{r}y ye 18. buried Jan^{r}y ye 19 1720.

Bar. Yates Minister.

Yoto a Slave belonging to Messrs Bell & Dee dyed Jan^{r}y ye 22 & buried ye 23 1720.

Jenny a Slave belonging to William Daniel Senr dyed Jan^{r}y ye 10. buried ye 11 1720.

Jack a Slave belonging to James Meacham dyed Jan^{r}y ye 17. & was buried 18 1720.

John a Slave belonging to Henry Thacker dyed Jan^{r}y ye 31. & was buried Feb. 1 1720.

Mingo a Slave belonging to James Curtis jun^r Estate dyed Feb^{r}y ye 2. buried Feb. 3 1720.

Della a Slave belonging to Humphery Jones dyed Jan^{r}y ye 23. buried ye 24 1720.

Roger a Slave belonging to Humphery Jones dyed Jan^{r}y ye 23. buried ye 24 1720.

Della a Slave belonging to Robt George Senr dyed Jan^{r}y ye 27. buried ye 28 1720.

Jemmy a Slave belonging to Robert George Senr dyed Jan^{r}y ye 29. buried ye 30 1720.

Hannaball a Slave belonging to Tho. Mountague Senr dyed Jan^{r}y ye 10. buried ye 11 1720.

Dina a Slave belonging to Frances Ransone dyed Feb^{r}y ye 18. buried Feb^{r}y ye 19. 1720.

Phillis a Slave belonging to William Segar dyed Feb^{r}y ye 13. buried Feb^{r}y ye 14 1720.

Guy a Slave belonging to Henry Goodloe dyed Feb^{r}y ye 18. buried Feb^{r}y ye 19 1720.

Adam a Slave belonging to Thomas Haselwood dyed Feb^{r}y ye 22. buried Feb^{r}y 23 1720.

Dublin a Slave belonging to Alexander Graves dyed March ye 7 1720.

Jenny a Slave belonging to Robt Williamson Senr dyed March 6 1720.

Sampson a Slave belonging to John Segar dyed March ye 20 1720.

Charles a Slave belonging to John Smith Junr dyed March ye 28 1721.

Cate a Slave belonging to Jacob Stiff dyed April 13 1721.

Peter a Slave belonging to Hen: Armistead dyed May ye 6 1721.

Peter a Slave belonging to Patrick Kelley dyed May ye 9 1721.

Judy a Slave belonging to Edwin Thacker dyed May ye 21 1721.

Joice a Slave belonging to Mathew Kemp dyed June ye 13 1721.

Billy a Slave belonging to John Robinson dyed July ye 7 1721.

Daniel a Slave belonging to ye estate of Edm^d Berkley dyed May ye 24 1721.

Bess a Slave belonging to George Harding dyed June ye 28 1721.

Degar a Slave belonging to ye estate of Garritt Minor dyed July ye 4 1721.

George a Slave belonging to ye estate of Garritt Minor dyed July ye 14 1721.

Cress a Slave belonging to ye estate of Coll^o Churchhill dyed 1721.

Frank a Slave belonging to ye estate of Coll^o Churchhill dyed 1721.

Winney a Slave belonging to Rice Curtis dyed July ye 24 1721.

Tom a slave belonging to Roger Jones dyed March ye 7. 1721.

Sarah a slave belonging to ye estate of Garritt Minor dyed Augs^t ye 6 1721.

Jemmy a Slave belonging to ye estate of Garritt Minor dyed Augs^t y^u 15: 1721.

Tom a slave belonging to James Daniel dyed August 30. 1720.

Jeffry a slave belonging to Christopher Robinson dyed Septem^r ye 10. 1721.

Sarah a Slave belonging to Robert George Senr dyed August ye 22. 1721.

Mary a slave belonging to Christopher Robinson dyed Septem^r ye 9 1721.

Harry a Slave belonging to John Berry dyed Septem^r ye 20. 1721.

Phillis a Slave belonging to Thomas Mountague dyed Novem^r ye 10. 1721.

Venus a slave belonging to Robt George Senr dyed Novem^r ye 11. 1721.

Letty a Slave belonging to Bar Yates dyed Novem^r 19. 1721.

Sarah a slave belonging to ye estate of Hen. Thacker dec'd dyed Decem^r ye 1. 1721.

Toby a slave belonging to Mathew Kemp dyed Decem^r ye 16 1721.

Sarah a slave belonging to Bar Yates dyed Decem^r ye 21. 1721.

Bristow a Slave belonging to Henry Tugle dyed Decem^r ye 16. 1721.

Roger a slave belonging to Mathew Kemp dyed Decem^r ye 29. 1721.

James a Slave belonging to Hen Armistead dyed Jan^{r}y ye 6. 1721.

Harry a slave belonging to Mathew Hunt dyed Jan^{r}y ye 5. 1721.

Cæsar a slave belonging to ye estate of Hen. Thacker dec'd dyed Feb^{r}y ye 1. 1721.

Penn a Slave belonging to Tho: Mountague dyed Jan^{r}y ye 24. 1721.

York a slave belonging to ye estate of Hen: Thacker dec'd dyed Feb^{r}y ye 1. 1721.

Jack a slave belonging to Stockly Towles dyed Jan^{r}y ye 31 1721.

Sarah a Slave belonging to Stockly Towles dyed Feb^{r}y ye 2 1721.

Robin a Slave belonging to Stockley Towles dyed Feb^{r}y ye 18 1721.

Jack an Indian Slave belonging to John Smith dyed Feb^{r}y ye 17. 1721.

Bar Yates—Minister.

Fragment—Dolly Daughter of John & Jane Bray was born January 2rd 1765.

By Henry Heffernan Rector.

Lura a Slave belonging to John Smith jun^r dyed Feb^{r}y ye 22 1721.

Antony a slave belonging to Bar Yates dyed March ye 5 1721.

Bess a slave belonging to Rice Jones dyed March ye 12 1721.

Jack a Slave belonging to John Segar dyed April ye 11 1722.

Abram a slave belonging to Hobs Weeks dyed April ye 18 1722.

Joe a slave belonging to John Smith dyed April yᵉ 26 1722.
Robert a Slave belonging to James Batchelder dyed May yᵉ 4 1722.
Alice a slave belonging to Elizᵃ Vivion dyed May yᵉ 3 1722.
Jenny a slave belonging to Bartho: Yates dyed May yᵉ 22 1722.
Bob a Slave belonging to John Robinson dyed May yᵉ 25 1722.
Sawney a slave belonging to Robert Williamson Senʳ dyed May yᵉ
    7. 1722.
Jack a slave belonging to Jonathan Johnson dyed August yᵉ 21 1722.
Monmouth a Slave belonging to Henry Thacker dyed Septemʳ yᵉ 20
    1722.
Charlott a slave belonging to yᵉ estate of John Vivion dec'd dyed
    August 15. 1722.
Sarah a slave belonging to Augustine Smith dyed Octo yᵉ 13 1722.
Letty a Slave belonging to John Moseley dyed Octo. yᵉ 16 1722.
Tom a slave belonging to Alexander Graves dyed Novemʳ yᵉ 16 1722.
Paul a slave belonging to Matthew Kemp dyed Decemʳ yᵉ 20 1722.
Tom a Slave belonging to Richard Hill dyed Decemʳ yᵉ 4 1722.
Toby a slave belonging to Margrett Daniel dyed Decemʳ yᵉ 29 1722.
Nanny a slave belonging to yᵉ estate of Garritt Minor dec'd dyed
    Octo yᵉ 20 1722.
George a slave belonging to Matthew Kemp dyed Janʳy yᵉ 24 1722.
Charles a slave belonging to Joseph Goar dyed Febʳy yᵉ 1 1722.
Betty a slave belonging to Paul Thilman dyed Janʳy yᵉ 29 1722.
Billy a slave belonging to John Segar dyed Janʳy yᵉ 29 1722.
Merenry a slave belonging to William Stanard dyed Febʳy yᵉ 28
    1722.
Nanny a slave belonging to John Robinson Esqʳ dyed March yᵉ 23
    1722.
Sarah a slave belonging to John Degge dyed April yᵉ 19. 1723.
Ned a slave belonging to John Cheadle dyed April yᵉ 15 1723.
Joe a slave belonging to Robert Williamson junʳ dyed April yᵉ 28
    1723.
Anne a slave belonging to John Gibbs dyed May yᵉ 26 1723.
Harry a slave belonging to Willlam Hackney dyed June yᵉ 15 1723.
Frank a slave belonging to Thomas Norman dyed June yᵉ 14 1723.
Nell a slave belonging to yᵉ estate of Edmund Berkley dec'd dyed
    June yᵉ 8 1723.
Harry a slave belonging to Samuel Batchelder dyed June yᵉ 30.
    1723.
Tom a slave belonging to John Price dyed July yᵉ 9 1723.
Kate a slave belonging to yᵉ estate of Wᵐ Gordon dec'd April yᵉ 28
    1723.
Collonell a Slave belonging to Armistead Churchhill dyed July yᵉ 10
    1723.
Old Alice a slave belonging to Bar Yates dyed August yᵉ 17 1723.
Jack a slave belonging to James Daniel dyed July yᵉ 28 1723.
Sam a slave belonging to Wᵐ Mountague junʳ dyed August yᵉ 13.
    1723.
Toney a slave belonging to John Cheadle dyed August yᵉ 19 1723.
Toby a slave belonging to Armistead Churchhill dyed Septemʳ yᵉ 8
    1723.
Frank a slave belonging to Gawin Corbin dyed Novemʳ yᵉ 16 1723.
Bristow a slave belonging to Gawin Corbin dyed Novemʳ yᵉ 18 1723.

Beck a slave belonging to Francis Timberlake dyed Novem^r ye 22.
1723.
Tom a slave belonging to Mathew Kemp dyed Novem^r ye 19 1723.
Frank a slave belonging to Mathew Kemp dyed Novem^r ye 25 1723.
Kate a slave belonging to Frances Thacker dyed Decem^r ye 2. 1723.
Hannah a slave belonging to Frances Thacker dyed Decem^r ye 20
1723.
Jo a slave belonging to John Wormeley dyed Decem^r ye 6. 1723.
Sarah a slave belonging to John Dodson dyed Decem^r ye 20 1723.
Tom a slave belonging to Stockly Towles dyed Decem^r ye 27 1723.
Nell a slave belonging to Armistead Churchhill dyed Jan^{r}y ye 2 1723.
Dick a slave belonging to Armistead Churchhill dyed Jan^{r}y ye 5.
1723.
Bar Yates Minister.

Brownstown a Slave belonging to William Blackbourn dyed Jan^{r}y y^e
14. 1723.
Pen a slave belonging to Edwin Thacker dyed Jan^{r}y ye 27 1723.
Will a slave belonging to Edmund Mickleburrough dyed Feb^{r}y ye 4
1723.
Peter a slave belonging to Thomas Cheney dyed Feb^{r}y ye 4 1723.
Betty a slave belonging to Anne Thacker dyed Feb^{r}y ye 22 1723.
Jack a slave belonging to Catharine Warwick dyed March ye 2 1723.
Will a slave belonging to ye estate of Thomas Smith, dec'd dyed
March ye 4 1723.
Peter a slave belonging to William Kidd dyed April ye 13 1724.
Kate a slave belonging to Charles Cooper dyed April ye 15 1724.
Joe a slave belonging to John Wormley dyed Septem^r ye 15 1723.
Tom a slave belonging to John Wormley dyed March ye 5 1723.
Nan a slave belonging to John Wormley dyed May ye 2 1724.
White a Slave belonging to John Wormley dyed May ye 21 1724.
Silas a slave belonging to William Segar dyed June ye 15 1724.
Bess a slave belonging to Roger Jones dyed June ye 16 1724.
Hannah a Slave belonging to John Wormley dyed July ye 15 1724.
Jack a slave belonging to John Alding dyed June ye 30 1724.
Jack a slave belonging to John Robinson dyed August ye 19 1724.
Simon a Slave belonging to John Grymes dyed Octo: ye 16 1724.
Jenny a slave belonging to ye estate of John Vivion dec'd was
drowned Sept. 15. 1724.
Jack a slave belonging to John Crockford hanged himself Octo: y^e
30 1724.
Lucy a Slave belonging to Thomas Norman dyed Novem^r ye 25 1724.
Mary daughter of Rebecca a Molatto belonging to Sr Wm Skipwith
dyed Decem^r ye 3 1724.
Rachel daughter of Rebecca a Molatto belonging to Sr Wm Skipwith
dyed Decem^r 17 1724.
Dick a Slave belonging to Sr Wm Skipwith dyed Decem^r ye 17. 1724.
Amey a slave belonging to Maurice Smith dyed Decem^r ye 26 1724.
Rachel a slave belonging to John Robinson dyed Jan^{r}y 15 1724.
George a slave belonging to Bar: Yates dyed Jan^{r}y ye 19 1724.
Will a Slave belonging to Edmund Bartletts estate dyed Jan^{ry} ye 4
1724.
Harry a slave belonging to Robert Daniel dyed Jan^{r}y ye 20 1724.

Jack a slave belonging to Bar. Yates dyed April ye 21 1725.
Beck a slave belonging to Colo John Robinson dyed May ye 2 1725.
Robin a Slave belonging to Mathew Kemp dyed May ye 19 1725.
Winney a slave belonging to John Alding dyed May ye 22 1725.
Jenny a slave belonging to John Wormley dyed June ye 8 1725.
Seymor a slave belonging to Christopher Robinson dyed July y^c 5 1725.
Charles a slave belonging to Joseph Hardee dyed October ye 18 1725.
Betty a Slave belonging to Elizabeth Smith dyed Novem^r y̓^{e} 9 1725.
Hannah a slave belonging to Armistead Churchhill dyed Novem^r ye 15 1725.
Dimond a slave belonging to John Wormley dyed Decem^r ye 20 1725.
Letitia a Slave belonging to Oliver Segar dyed Jan'ry ye 12 1725.
Sambo a slave belonging to Henry Tugle dyed Jan'ry ye 30 1725.
Rosegill a slave belonging to John Wormley dyed Jan'ry ye 20 1725.
Margrett a slave belonging to John Wormley dyed Feb'y ye 9 1725.
Anthony a Slave belonging to John Smith Senr dyed March ye 1 1725.
Moll a slave belonging to Thomas Cheney dyed March ye 5 1725.
Jenny a slave belonging to James Bristow dyed March ye 16 1725.
Cæsar a slave belonging to John Price dyed March ye 26 1726.
Bungy a Slave belonging to John Grymes dyed April ye 4 1726.
Sue a slave belonging to John Robinson dyed April ye 13 1726.
Hannah a slave belonging to John Robinson dyed April ye 14 1726.
Jemima a slave belonging to ye Estate of John Vivion dyed March ye 26 1726.
Irene a Slave belonging to Wm Stanard dyed August ye 24 1725.
Will a slave belonging to James Smith dyed April ye 8 1726.
Will a slave belonging to ye estate of John Owen dyed April ye 11 1726.
Sambo a slave belonging to Humphry Jones dyed April ye 30 1726.
Austin a Slave belonging to Martha Williamson dyed June ye 5 1726.

Bar Yates Min^r.

Robin a Slave belonging to John Segar dyed June ye 7 1726.
Ben a Slave belonging to John Price dyed July ye 1st 1726.
Dick a Slave belonging to Rice Curtis dyed July ye 29 1726.
Tony a Slave belonging to John Price dyed August ye 7 1726.
Cromwell a slave belonging to John Price dyed August ye 14 1726.
Jack a Slave belonging to Robt. George dyed October ye 18 1726.
Jack a Slave belonging to Nicholas Bristow dyed Novem^r ye 15 1726.
Dinah a Slave belonging to Mark Bannerman dyed Decem^r ye 3 1726.
Mintar a Slave belonging to Rice Curtis dyed Decem^r ye 10 1726.
Tom a Slave belonging to Rice Curtis dyed Decem^r ye 12 1726.
Jenny a Slave belonging to Joseph Goar dyed Decem^r ye 8 1726.
Charles a Slave belonging to Wm Blackburne dyed Decem^r ye 15 1726.
Venus a Slave belonging to Wm Blackburne dyed Decem^r ye 18 1726.
Corridon a Slave belonging to Wm Blackburn dyed Jan'ry ye 5 1726.
Silvia a Slave belonging to Wm Blackburn dyed Jan'ry ye 9 1726.
Sharp a Slave belonging to ye estate of Augustine Owen dyed Jan'ry 1. 1726.
Lucy a Slave belonging to Wm Owen dyed Jan'ry ye 19 1726.

Sarah a Slave belonging to Christopher Robinson dyed August ye 7 1726.

Mingo a Slave belonging to ye estate of John Price dyed Decem^r ye 17 1726.

Cate a Slave belonging to Edward Clark dyed Feb^{r}y ye 7 1726.

Tom a Slave belonging to Edward Clark dyed Febry ye 8 1726.

Matt a Slave belonging to Mark Bannerman dyed Febry ye 8 1726.

Commins a Slave belonging to ye estate of Francis Timberlake dyed Jan^{r}y ye 23 1726.

Lettice a Slave belonging to Thomas Machen dyed Jan^{r}y ye 28 1726.

Bridgett a Slave belonging to ye estate of Christopher Robinson dec'd dyed Febry 25 1726.

Sarah a Slave belonging to ye estate of William Daniel j^r dyed Febry ye 9 1726.

Toby a Slave belonging to Frances Smith dyed March ye 6 1726.

Dinah a Slave belonging to Jacob Stiff dyed Febry ye 2 1726.

Sampson a Slave belonging to ye estate of Wm Gordon dyed March ye 17 1726.

Robin a Slave belonging to ye estate of Wm Gordon dyed March ye 17 1726.

Dinah a Slave belonging to Rice Curtis dyed March ye 26 1726.

Isaak a Slave belonging to Gawen Corbin dyed Febry ye 26 1726.

George a Slave belonging to Gawen Corbin dyed Febry ye 28 1726.

Robin a slave belonging to Gawen Corbin dyed Febry ye 28 1726.

Ned a Slave belonging to Gawen Corbin dyed March ye 1 1726.

Joan a Slave belonging to Gawen Corbin dyed March ye 8 1726.

Hampshire a slave belonging to Gawen Corbin dyed March ye 10 1726.

Devonshire a slave belonging to Gawen Corbin dyed March ye 15 1726.

Aberry a Slave belonging to Gawen Corbin dyed March ye 23 1726.

Winny a slave belonging to William Mountague dyed March ye 5 1726.

Beck a slave belonging to John Grymes dyed Febry ye 16 1726.

Ruth a slave belonging to John Grymes dyed Feb^{r}y ye 18 1726.

Betty a slave belonging to John Grymes dyed Feb^{r}y ye 20 1726.

Hector a slave belonging to John Grymes dyed Feb^{r}y ye 26 1726.

Mars a slave belonging to John Grymes dyed March ye 10 1726.

Rose a slave belonging to John Grymes dyed March ye 10 1726.

Ralph a slave belonging to John Grymes dyed March ye 29 1726.

Sarah a slave belonging to John Smith dyed March ye 29 1726.

Hager a slave belonging to Armistead Churchhill dyed Feb^{r}y 25 1726.

Peter a slave belonging to Armistead Churchhill dyed Feb^{r}y 27 1726.

Sam a slave belonging to Armistead Churchhill dyed Feb^{r}y 16 1726.

Daniel a Slave belonging to Armistead Churchhill dyed Feb^{ry} 19. 1726.

Hagar a slave belonging to Armistead Churchhill dyed Feb^{ry} 23. 1726.

Arrow a slave belonging to ye estate of John Wormley dec'd dyed Feb^{r}y 10 1726.

Beck a slave belonging to ye estate of John Wormley dec'd dyed March ye 20 1726.

Sawney a Slave belonging to ye estate of John Wormley dec'd dyed
    March ye 12 1726.
Cæsar a slave belonging to William Gray dyed Jan^ry ye 28. 1726.
Greshear a slave belonging to ye estate of John Wormley dec'd dyed
    April 15 1727.
Tom a slave belonging to John George dyed April ye 22 1727.
Moll a Slave belonging to ye estate of Thomas Smith dyed May y^e
    5 1727.
Charles a slave belonging to Matthew Hunt dyed April ye 23 1727.
Nan a slave belonging to John Segar dyed May ye 12 1727.
Rachel a slave belonging to ye estate of John Wormley dyed May
    13. 1727.
Hannah a Slave belonging to ye estate of Garritt Minor dyed May
    ye 24 1727.
Judy a slave belonging to ye estate of John Price dyed April 30 1727.
Bess a slave belonging to ye estate of John Gibbs dyed June ye 17
    1727.
Petro a slave belonging to John Murrah dyed June ye 30 1727.
Peter a Slave belonging to Henry Armistead dyed July ye 9 1727.
Nell a slave belonging to Armistead Churchhill dyed July ye 24 1727.
Nanny a Slave belonging to Bar Yates dyed August ye 10 1727.
Sarah a slave belonging to John Rhodes dyed August ye 26 1727.
Nanny a slave belonging to Henry Thacker dyed october ye 1 1727.
Winny a Slave belonging to Thomas Cheney dyed Septem^r ye 14
    1727.
Tom Brideman a slave belonging to ye estate of John Wormley dec'd
    dyed October ye 5 1727.
Cromwell a slave belonging to Armistead Churchhill dyed August y^e
    4 1727.
Venus a Slave belonging to Daniel Listney dyed September ye 20
    1727.
Bridgett a slave belonging to Armistead Churchhill dyed Decem^r y^e
    15 1727.
Toney a slave belonging to Frances Alding dyed Decem^r ye 14 1727.
Jane a Slave belonging to William Stanard dyed Jan^ry ye 1 1727.
Harry a slave belonging to ye estate of John Wormley dec'd dyed
    Jan^ry ye 2 1727.
Pompey a slave belonging to Armistead Churchhill dyed Jan^ry ye 18
    1727.
Tom a slave belonging to Sarah Murrah dyed Feb^ry ye 5 1727.
Toby a Slave belonging to John Fearn dyed Jan^ry ye 20th 1727.
Natt a slave belonging to ye estate of Jno. Wormley dyed Feb^ry y^e
    17. 1727.
Hampton a slave belonging to Laurance Orrill dyed Feb^ry ye 8th 1727.
Nan a Slave belonging to Henry Daniel dyed Feb^ry ye 10 1727.
Oliver a slave belonging to Edmund Bartlett dyed Feb^ry ye 3 1727.
Robin a Slave belonging to Alexander Graves dyed Feb^ry ye 28 1727.
Jack a Slave belonging to Mary Hunt dyed March ye 15 1727.
Peter a slave belonging to Stockley Towles dyed March ye 17 1727.
James a slave belonging to Edmund Bartlett dyed March ye 4 1727.
Bacchus a slave belonging to Wm Stanard dyed Ap: ye 4 1728.
Nell a slave belonging to ye estate of Jno Wormley dec'd dyed April
    ye 19 1728.

Frank a Slave belonging to John Smith dyed April ye 20 1728.
Crosier a slave belonging to Oliver Segar dyed April ye 17. 1728.
Crispin a slave belonging to Laurance Orrill dyed April ye 13 1728.
Sam a slave belonging to Laurance Orrill dyed May ye 1 1728.
Dick a Slave belonging to Richd Taylor dyed May ye 18 1728.
Beck a slave belonging to ye estate of Jno. Wormley dyed June y^e
    19 1728.
Simon a slave belonging to ye estate of Jno Wormley dyed June y^e
    21 1728.
Peter a slave belonging to ye estate of Jno Wormeley dyed August
    ye 1 1728.
Scipio a slave belonging to Matthew Kemp dyed August ye 11.
    1728.
Dick a slave belonging to Henry Armistead dyed August ye 29.
    1728.
Sam a Slave belonging to William Thurston dyed August ye 25.
    1728.
William a slave belonging to Bar Yates dyed September ye 29 1728.
George a slave belonging to Marvell Moseley dyed September ye 14
    1728.

Bar Yates Min^r.

Dinah a slave belonging to Oliver Segar dyed ye 15. of September
    1728.
Winney a slave belonging to Christopher Robinson dyed Octo. ye 5
    1728.
Toney a slave belonging to Matthew Kemp dyed Octo: ye 20 1728.
Peter a slave belonging to William Segar dyed Octo: ye 12 1728.
Tom (son of Beck) a slave belonging to John Grymes Dyed Novem^r
    ye 3d 1728.
Cate (Daughter of Cate) a slave belonging to John Grymes dyed
    Novem^r ye 3d 1728.
Mingo a slave belonging to John Grymes dyed Novem^r ye 28 1728.
Lucy a slave belonging to John Tugell dyed Decem^r ye 10 1728.
Nan a slave belonging to Edwin Thacker dyed Decem^r ye 8 1728.
Robert a slave belonging to Tho: Faulkner Senr dyed Novem^r ye 13
    1728.
Ben a slave belonging to ye estate of John Vivion dyed Decem^r ye 16
    1728.
Judy a slave belonging to George Hardin dyed Decem^r ye 17 1728.
Judy a slave belonging to John Crockford dyed Jan^{r}y ye 10 1728.
Harry a slave belonging to ye estate of Tho: Smith dyed Jan^{ry} ye 1
    1728.
Gawen a slave belonging to Henry Mickleburrough dyed Jan^{r}y ye 3
    1728.
Judy a slave belonging to Henry Tugel jun^r dyed Feb^{r}y ye 16 1728.
Mary a slave belonging to Richd Hill dyed Feb^{r}y ye 23 1728.
Harry a Negro boy belonging to William Chowning dyed Feb^{r}y y^e
    21 1728.
Jack a Slave belonging to ye estate of Wm Daniel jun^r dyed March y^e
    13 1728.
Thom a slave belonging to Thomas Smith dec'd dyed March ye 12
    1728.

Maggy a slave belongin to Curtis Perrott dyed Feb'y ye 26 1728.
Betty daughter of Winny a molatto belonging to Elizabeth Weeks dyed April ye 10 1729.
Isaac Son of Jenny a slave belonging to ye estate of Jno Wormley decd dyed April ye 5. 1729.
Primas a slave belonging to Wm Owen dyed April ye 26 1729.
Wooser a Slave belonging to Humphrey Jones dyed May ye 1 1729.
Hannah a slave belonging to Ralph Shelton dyed May ye 27 1729.
Wonder a slave belonging to George Hardin dyed June ye 11. 1729.
Mingo a slave belonging to John Grymes dyed May ye 29 1729.
Will a slave belonging to Elizabeth Weeks dyed May ye 27 1729.
Dick a slave belonging to William Chowning dyed August ye 10. 1729.
Charles a slave belonging to Thomas Machen dyed August ye 26. 1729.
Jenny a slave belonging to Thomas Dudley dyed August ye 28 1729.
Abigall a slave belonging to John Grymes dyed August ye 30 1729.
Pancha a slave belonging to John Grymes dyed September ye 10 1729.
Jenny a slave belonging to William Wood dyed September ye 20 1729.
Della a slave belonging to Thomas Cheney dyed Novem^r ye 4 1729.
Jack a slave belonging to William Segar dyed Decem^r ye 5 1729.
Boson a slave belonging to Paul Philpott dyed Novem^r ye 10 1729.
Tom a slave belonging to ye estate of Hobs Weekes dyed Jan^ry ye 24 1729.
Toney a slave belonging to Edmund Mickleburrough dyed Feb'y ye 2 1729.
Frank a slave belonging to Francis Porter dyed Feb'y ye 14 1729.
Betty a slave belonging to Francis Porter dyed Feb'y ye 14 1729.
Oliver a Slave belonging to Edmund Berkley dyed Jan^ry ye 18 1729.
Rose a slave belonging to Edmund Berkley dyed Jan^ry ye 18 1729.
Cashus a slave belonging to Armistead Churchhill dyed Feb'y ye 14 1729.
Alice a Slave belonging to Edmund Mickleburrough dyed Feb'y ye 20 1729.
Ben a Slave belonging to Robert Daniell dyed Feb'y 25 1729.
Ned a Slave belonging to John Tugell dyed Feb'y ye 11 1729.
Lander a Slave belonging to ye estate of Wm Gordon dyed Feb'y ye 2 1729.
Maulkam a Slave belonging to Alexander Frazier dyed Feb'y ye 15 1729.
Syfax a Slave belonging to Armistead Churchhill dyed March ye 11 1729.
Robin a slave belonging to Armistead Churchhill dyed March ye 14 1729.
Moll a Slave belonging to Laurance Orrell dyed March ye 8 1729.
Alice a Slave belonging to William Stanard dyed Jan^ry ye 16 1729.
Samson a slave belonging to James Dudley dyed March ye 20 1729.
Harry a Slave belonging to Frances Alding dyed Jan^ry ye 16 1729.

Bar Yates. Min^r

York a Slave belonging to Matthew Kemp dyed April ye 10 1730.

Sarah a slave belonging to George Harding dyed April ye 25 1730.
Tom a slave belonging to Gawin Corbin dyed April ye 26 1730.
Diamond a slave belonging to Gawin Corbin dyed April ye 16 1730.
Ruth a Slave belonging to Anne Smith jun^r dyed April ye 21 1730.
Sampson a slave belonging to Thomas Machen dyed April ye 20 1730.
Bob a slave belonging to William Chowning dyed May ye 12 1730.
Jenny a Slave belonging to ye estate of Thomas Smith dec'd dyed
    May ye 25 1730.
Amey a slave belonging to Edwin Thacker dyed May ye 28 1730.
Judy a Slave belonging to ye estate of Wm Daniel jun^r dyed June y^e
    18 1730.
Winny a Slave belonging to ye estate of Wm Daniel jun^r dyed June
    ye 18 1730.
Charles a slave belonging to ye estate of Wm Daniel jun^r dyed June
    ye 20 1730.
Beck a Slave belonging to John Curtis dyed July ye 8 1730.
Mary a slave belonging to Thomas Cheney dyed July ye 4 1730.
Sawney a slave belonging to Oliver Segar dyed June ye 24 1730.
George a Slave belonging to Oliver Segar dyed June ye 27 1730.
Pat a slave belonging to Roger Jones dyed July ye 21 1730.
Frank a Slave belonging to John Smith Senr dyed March ye 30 1730.
Jenny a slave belonging to John Smith Senr dyed August ye 6 1730.
Tom Son of Nan a slave belonging to the estate of Jno Smith dec'd
    dyed Augs^t ye 24 1730.
Sarah a slave belonging to Edmund Berkley dyed August ye 27 1730.
Jemmy a slave belonging to Frances Smith dyed Septem^r ye 25 1730.
Daphney a slave belonging to Frances Smith dyed Septem^r ye 27
    1730.
Charles a slave belonging to ye estate of Tho. Smith dyed October
    ye 9 1730.
Bob a slave belonging to John Crockford dyed Novem^r ye 6 1730.
Jacob a slave belonging to George Harding dyed Novem^r ye 30 1730.
Harry a slave belonging to John Hipkings dyed Decem^r ye 14 1730.
Tom a Slave belonging to Gawin Corbin dyed Decem^r ye 24 1730.
Daniel a Slave belonging to Armistead Churchhill dyed Feb^ry ye 1
    1730.
Jeney a slave belonging to John Moseley dyed Feb^ry ye 1 1730.
Moll a slave belonging to John Burk dyed Feb^ry ye 16 1730.
Betty a slave belonging to ye estate of Thos Smith dec'd dyed Feb^ry
    ye 11 1730.
Liddey a slave belonging to Jno Smith Senr dyed Feb^ry ye 10 1730.
Criss a Slave belonging to Edwin Thacker dyed March ye 26 1731.
Jack a slave belonging to Henry Mickleburrough dyed April ye 25
    1731.
Jupiter a slave belonging to Hugh Stuart dyed April ye 21 1731.
Amy a slave belonging to Margret Daniel dyed May ye 15 1731.
Letty a slave belonging to Coll^o Edwin Thacker dyed June ye 25 1731.
Jack a slave belonging to Jacob Stiff dyed June ye 30 1731.
Cate a Slave belonging to ye estate of John Wormley dec'd dyed
    August ye 20 1731.
Antony a slave belonging to ye estate of Jno Smith dec'd dyed Au-
    gust ye 27 1731.

Tom a slave belonging to ye estate of James Smith dec'd dyed August ye 28 1731.

Lettey a Slave belonging to John Hipkings dyed Septem^r ye 6 1731.

Margery a slave belonging to ye estate of Wm Daniel jun^r dyed Septem^r ye 27 1731.

Phillis a slave belonging to Mary Machen dyed October ye 22 1731.

Jenny a slave belonging to Henry Thacker dyed October ye 18 1731.

Moll a Slave belonging to Henry Thacker dyed Novem^r ye 19 1731.

Jenny a slave belonging to Stokley Towles dyed Novem^r ye 21 1731.

Phil a slave belonging to Sr Wm Skipwith dyed Decem^r ye 26 1731.

Hannaball a Slave belonging to Mathew Kemp dyed Feb^ry ye 3 1731.

Cate a slave belonging to Margrett Daniel dyed Feb^ry ye 3 1731.

Rosa a slave belonging to Hugh Stewart dyed Jan^ry ye 27 1731.

Richmond a slave belonging to Armistead Churchhill dyed March ye 20 1731.

Ned a slave belonging to John Grymes dyed May ye 4 1732.

Bar Yates—Min^r.

Betty a Slave belonging to Edwin Thacker dyed May ye 28 1732.

Beck a slave belonging to Thos Corbin dyed May ye 15 1732.

Frank a slave belonging to ye estate of James Smith dyed June ye 10th 1732.

Sawney a slave belonging to Henry Armistead dyed April ye 20 1732.

Tom a slave belonging to ye estate of Jno Wormeley dyed June ye 18 1732.

Gunner a Slave belonging to ye estate of Jno Wormeley dyed July ye 6 1732.

Robin a slave belonging to Edwin Thacker dyed July ye 12 1732.

Harry a slave belonging to Edwin Thacker dyed August ye 3 1732.

Joe a slave belonging to John Grymes dyed August ye 5 1732.

Will a slave belonging to Margret Daniel dyed Septem^r ye 3 1732.

Old Frank a Slave belonging to ye estate of Jno Wormeley dec'd dyed Septem^r ye 1 1732.

Lucy a slave belonging to Matthew Kemp dyed Octo ye 8 1732.

Nan a slave belonging to John Crockford dyed Octo ye 20 1732.

Gilbert a slave belonging to ye estate of Tho: Smith dec'd dyed Novem^r 26 1732.

Kate a Slave belonging to John Marshall dyed Novem^r ye 15 1732.

Billey a slave belonging to William Wood dyed Feb^ry ye 11 1732.

Winney a slave belonging to Robt Daniel dyed Feb^ry ye 24 1732.

Frank a Slave belonging to Augustine Smith dyed March ye 11 1732.

Marlburrough a Slave belonging to Wm Mountague dyed March ye 12 1732.

Abraham a slave belonging to ye estate of John Smith dec'd dyed March ye 9. 1732.

Kate a slave belonging to Samuel Batchelder dyed April ye 27 1733.

Peter a Slave belonging to Hen: Armistead dyed April ye 10 1733.

Toney a slave belonging to Hen: Armistead dyed April ye 20. 1733.

Lucy a slave belonging to Thomas Price dyed May ye 20. 1733.

Phillis a slave belonging to Anne Smith dyed April ye 17. 1733.

Dinah a Slave belonging to ye estate of Hugh Steward dec'd dyed April ye 27 1733.

Toney a slave belonging to John Crockford dyed May ye 25. 1733.
Frank a slave belonging to Thos Corbin dyed May ye 26. 1733.
Flora a slave belonging to John Grymes dyed May ye 12. 1733.
Cæsar a slave belonging to Armistead Churchhill dyed March ye 18.
1732.
Dick a slave belonging to Armistead Churchhill dyed March ye 18.
1732.
Ralph a slave belonging to John Segar dyed June ye 16. 1733.
Ambrose a slave belonging to John Grymes dyed July ye 3 1733.
Yango a slave belonging to William Owen dyed July ye 13 1733.
Venus a slave belonging to James Daniel jun^r dyed August ye 14.
1733.
Mingo a slave belonging to ye estate of Wm Gordon dyed October y^e
2. 1733.
Jemmy a slave belonging to Frances Aldin dyed Septem^r ye 25 1733.
Jemmy a slave belonging to Stokly Towles dyed Decem^r ye 8. 1733.
Bess a Slave belonging to Stokly Towles dyed Decem^r ye 12. 1733.
Joe a slave belonging to Edwin Thacker dyed Novem^r ye 13. 1733.
Cyrus a Slave belonging to Edwin Thacker dyed Decem^r ye 8. 1733.
Dorinda a slave belonging to Edwin Thacker dyed Decem^r ye 15.
1733.
Robin a slave belonging to Jno Curtis dyed Novem^r ye 10. 1733.
Cyphax a slave belonging to Edwin Thacker dyed Novem^r ye 29 1733.
Scipio a slave belonging to ye estate of Wm Stanard dec'd dyed Jan'y
ye 1. 1733.
Jack a slave belonging to Catherine Warwick dyed January ye 13.
1733.
Jack a slave belonging to Matthias Gale dyed Jan^ry ye 26. 1733.
Sam a slave belonging to Frances Alding dyed Decem^r ye 15. 1733.
Judy a slave belonging to Frances Alding dyed Jan'y ye 6 1733.
Gabriel a slave belonging to Mary Machen dyed Feb'y ye 7. 1733.
Bess a Slave belonging to John Williams dyed Feb'y ye 21. 1733.
Judy a slave belonging to Thomas Saunders dyed March ye 2d 1733.
Sarah a slave belonging to Edmund Berkeley dyed March ye 24.
1733.

Bar Yates Min^r.

Ralph a Slave belonging to Christopher Robinson dyed Decem^r y^e
18 1733.
Simon a slave belonging to Christopher Robinson dyed Jan'y ye 3d
1733.
Phil a slave belonging to Christopher Robinson dyed Jan'y ye 20.
1733.
Harry a slave belonging to Christopher Robinson dyed Jan'y ye 10.
1733.
Diana a slave belonging to Christopher Robinson dyed Jan'y ye 10
1733.
Betty a slave belonging to Christopher Robinson dyed Jan'y ye 29
1733.
Phillip a slave belonging to Christopher Robinson dyed Feb'y ye 2
1733.
Joan a slave belonging to Christopher Robinson dyed Feb'y ye 16
1733.

George a slave belonging to Wm Buford dyed April ye 6 1734.
Bess a slave belonging to Wm Buford dyed March ye 23 1733.
Bluff a slave belonging to John Grymes dyed April ye 16 1734.
Gunner a slave belonging to ye estate of Thos Smith dec'd dyed May
   ye 2 1734.
Jenny a Slave belonging to ye estate of Jno Wormeley dec'd dyed
   April ye 15 1734.
Ben a Slave belonging to ye estate of Jno Wormeley dec'd dyed
   Aprill ye 22d 1734.
Toby a Slave belonging to ye estate of Jno Wormeley dec'd dyed
   May ye 7 1734.
Nocco a Slave belonging to John Grymes dyed May ye 20 1734.
Cromwell a Slave belonging to John Grymes dyed May ye 25 1734.
Bacchus a Slave belonging to John Grymes dyed June ye 2 1734.
Tom a Slave belonging to Mary Sadler dyed May ye 21 1734.
Peter a Slave belonging to Edwin Thacker dyed June ye 2d 1734.
George a Slave belonging to Frances Alding dyed May ye 30 1734.
Esther a Slave belonging to John Grymes dyed June ye 13 1734.
Sam a Slave belonging to Bar Yates dyed June ye 11 1734.
London a Slave belonging to ye Estate of Jeremiah Chouder dyed
   7^{ber} 1734.
Rose a Slave belonging to Honble Jno Grymes Dyed Decr 5th 1734.
Ben a Slave belonging to Coll: Armstead Dyed August 18th 1734.
Ben a Slave belonging to Coll. Churchhill Dyed October 30th 1734.
Jemmy a Slave belonging to Wm Mountague Dyed June 23d 1734.
Nal a Slave belonging to Frances Bryant Dyed Augst 12th 1734.
Exeter a Slave belonging to Henry Thacker Dyed July 31st 1734.
Bristow a Slave belonging to Alexander Graves Dyed July 24th 1734.
Harry a Slave belonging to ye Honble Jno Grymes Dyed Augst 27 1734.
Hanah a Slave belonging to Matthias Gale Dyed October 28th 1734.
Sam a Slave belonging to Henry Tugle Dyed November 4th 1734.
Jack a Slave belonging to ye estate of Jno Short Dec^d Dyed Novem-
   ber 6th 1734.
Jupiter a Slave belonging to Coll. Armstead Dyed Feb. 25 1734.
Peter a Slave belonging to Jno Curtis Dyed March 18 1734.
Dinah a Slave belonging to Jno Curtis Dyed March 25 1735.
Sam a Slave belonging to Robt Daniel Dyed March 26th 1735.
Judee a Slave belonging to Edwin Thacker Dyed June 21st 1735.
Will a Slave belonging to Mary Meacham Dyed July 8th 1735.
Buchan a Slave belonging to Alexander Frazier Dyed Octr 3d 1735.
Doll a Slave belonging to Thomas Corbin Dyed Sep^t 27th 1735.
Mille, Daughter of Lucy a Slave belonging to Jean Seager Dyed
   Octr 8th 1735.
Ben a Slave belonging to Coll. Armistead Churchhill Dyed Decr 11.
   1735.
Frank a Slave belonging to Robt Daniel Dyed January 17th 1735.
Fergus a Slave belonging to James Reed Dyed Feb. 3d 1735.
Aaron a Slave belonging to Gawen Corbin Dyed Jan^{ry} 26 1735.

     Jno Reade Min^r

Hannah a Slave belonging to Lawrence Orrell Dyed Feb 21st.
Ishmael a Slave belonging to ye estate of Thos Smith Dec'd Dyed
   March 2d 1735.

Nan a Slave belonging to Humphry Jones Dyed March 5. 1735.

Jenny a Slave belonging to John Ridgeway Dyed Feby 19. 1735.

Bookry a Slave belonging to Gawin Corbin Dyed March 19 1735.

Simon a Slave belonging to ye estate of Jno Hipkins dec'd Dyed May 4th 1736.

Kate a Slave belonging to Matthias Gale Dyed Decr 8th 1735.

Kate a Slave belonging to Henry Tuggle Dyed Septr 29th 1735.

Sampson a Slave belonging to Henry Thacker Dyed Octob^r 13th 1735.

Judee a slave belonging to ye Estate of Jno Shorter Deceas'd Dyed Octob^r 26th 1735.

York a slave belonging to Laurence Orrill Dyed Octob. 6th 1735.

Azor a Slave belonging to Gowen Corbin Dyed July 20th 1736.

———— a slave belonging to Wm Goare Dyed 1736.

Harry a slave belonging to ye Estate of Wm Stannard Deceas'd Dyed July 19th 1736.

Annaca a Slave belonging to Armstead Churchill Dyed Sep^t 29th 1736.

Jenny a slave belonging to Jno Curtis Dyed Octr 15th 1736.

Roger a slave belonging to Jno Ryly Dyed Octr 13th 1736.

Simon a slave belonging to Jno Rhodes Dyed Octr 28th 1736.

Guy a Slav^e belonging to William Blackburn dyed 1ober 10th 1736.

Ben a Slav^e belonging to William Blackburn dyed Jan. 2d 1736.

Peter a slav^e belonging to William Blackburn dyed Jan. 10th 1736.

Old-Will a slav^e belonging to William Blackburn dyed May 8th 1737.

Little-Nan a Slav^e belonging to William Blackburn dyed May 13th 1737.

Sarah a slave belonging to William Blackburn dyed May 17th 1737.

Phebe a slave belonging to Gowin Corbin dyed 10^{ber} 25th 1736.

Doll a Slav^e belonging to Matthias Gale dyed Feb. 1st 1736.

Joe a slav^e belonging to Thomas Burford dyed March 23th 1736.

Ben a slave belonging to Gowin Corbin dyed April 24th 1737.

Phillis a slave belonging to Mary Machen dyed 10^{ber} 20th 1735.

Judy a Slave belonging to Alexander Frazier dyed March 16th 1735.

Harris a slav^e belonging to Mr Ralph Wormley died January 173.

Lawrence a slave belonging to Mr Ralph Wormley died January 173.

Abram a Slav^e belonging to Mr Ralph Wormley died January 1736.

Alice a slav^e belonging to Mr Ralph Wormley died January 1736.

Sancho a slave belonging to Mr Ralph Wormley died January 173.

Sangro a slav^e belonging to Mr Ralph Wormley died Feb. 173.

Jack a Slave belonging to Coll Churchhill died Feb. 18th 1736.

Mingo a slave belonging to Coll Churchhill died Feb. 25th 1736.

Frank a slave belonging to Coll Churchhill died March 4th 1736.

Punch a slave belonging to Coll Churchhill died March 28th 1737.

Harry a Slave belonging to Coll Churchhill died April 7th 1737.

Brutus a slav^e belonging to Coll. Churchhill died April 9th 1737.

Dick a slave belonging to Coll Churchhill died April 9th 1737.

Rose-Gill a slave belonging to Coll Churchhill died April 10th 1737.

Hannah a Slav^e belonging to Coll Churchhill died April 18th 1737.

Will a slave belonging to Coll Churchhill died April 25th 1737.

Kate a slave belonging to Coll Churchhill died May 8th 1737.

Mingo a slave belonging to Coll Churchhill died May 10th 1737.

Em^l Jones, Minister.

Antony a Slav^e belonging to Coll. Churchhill died May 13th 1737.

Tony a slav^e belonging to Coll. Churchhill died May 1737.

York a slav^e belonging to Coll. Churchhill died Jun^e 1737.

Sango a Slav^e belonging to Coll. Churchhill died Jun^e 1737.

Robin a slav^e belonging to Coll. Churchhill died Jun^e 1737.

Bluff a slave belonging to Coll. Churchhill died June 1737.

Cæsar a Slav^e belonging to Coll Churchhill died June 1737.

Jenny a Slav^e belonging to Coll Churchill died June 23th 1737.

Scipio a Slav^e belonging to Coll Churchhill died July 10th 1737.

Betty a Slav^e belonging to Coll Churchhill died July 16th 1737.

Maria a Slav^e belonging to Major Berkeley died Jun^e 20th 1737.

Abraham a Slav^e belonging to Coll. John Grymes died April 29th 1737.

Easter a Slav^e belonging to Capt. William Blackburn died Jun^e 1737.

George a Slav^e belonging to Capt. William Blackburn died Jun^e 1737.

Billy a Slav^e belonging to Coll Churchhill died April 18th 1737.

Juno a Slav^e belonging to Coll Churchhill died June 5th 1737.

Beck a negro girl belonging to Coll Churchhill died June 23th 1737.

Jenny a Slave belonging to Coll Churchhill died June 23th 1737.

Betty a Slave belonging to Coll Churchhill died July 12th 1737.

Tony a Slav^e belonging to Coll Churchhill died May 6th 1737.

Nell a Slav^e belonging to Coll Churchhill died May 22th 1737.

Grace a Slave belonging to Coll Churchhill died May 25th 1737.

Venus a slave belonging to Coll Churchhill died June 2d 1737.

Daniel a Slave belonging to Mr Christopher Robinson died 10^{ber} 14th 1736.

Peter a slave belonging to Mr Christopher Robinson died Jan 3d 1736.

Kate a slav^e belonging to Mr Christopher Robinson died Jan 4th 1736.

Lucy a Slav^e belonging to Mr Christopher Robinson died Jan. 6th 1736.

Hannah a slav^e belonging to Mr Christopher Robinson died Feb. 4th 1736.

Betty a Slave belonging to Mr Christopher Robinson died Feb. 6th 1736.

Tony a slav^e belonging to Mr Christopher Robinson died Feb. 10th 1736.

Jenny a slav^e belonging to Mr Chick^ely Thacker died May 23th 1737.

Middlesex a slav^e belonging to Mr Alexander Frazier died August 14th 1737.

Jack a Negro belonging to William Owen dyed Novr ye 22nd 1737.

Frank a Negro child belonging to Armistead Churchhill dyed Novr ye 28th 1737.

Laurence a Slave belonging to Armistead Churchhill dyed Decem^r ye 16th 1737.

Mat a Negro Child belonging to Armistead Churchhill dyed Decem^r ye 20th 1737.

Middlesex a Slave belonging to Alexander Frazar dyed Augst y^e 14th 1737.

Yassum a Slave belonging to Mary Hunt dyed Octo^r 3th 1737.

Letty a slave belonging to William Mountague dyed Decem^r y^e 2d 1737.

a slave belonging to William Owen dyed Decem^r y^e 20th 1737.
Harry a Slave belonging to Edwin Thacker dyed Febry. y^e 6th 173$\frac{7}{8}$.
Minter a slave belonging to Co^{ll} Grymes dyed April y^e 29th 1738.
Judith a slave belonging to Roger Jones dyed May y^e 20th 1738.
Tony Son of Dido a slave belonging to Maj^r Kemp. dyed 1738.
Annica daughter of Kate a Slave belonging to Eliz^a Burk dyed June
    y^e 11th 1738.
Nanny a slave belonging to Alexander Frazier dyed July ye 7th 1738.
Toney a slave belonging to William Lawson dyed July ye 3d 1738.
Cenes a slave belonging to Co^{ll} Armistead Churchhill dyed June y^e
    28th 1738.
Titus a slave belonging to Co^{ll} Armistead Churchill dyed July ye 18th
    1738.
Rachel a Slave belonging to Co^{ll} Grymes dyed Augst ye 31th 1738.
Charles a Slave belonging to Co^{ll} Grymes dyed Sepr ye 6th 1738.
Jack a Slave belonging to Robt Daniel dyed Octr ye 19th 1738.
Jack a slave dyed June ye 12th, Will a slave dyed July ye 12th, Kate
    a slave dyed July ye 20th, Peter a slave dyed July ye 30th, Joe
    a slave dyed Augt ye 8th, these belonging to Matthew Kemp
    1737.
Dianah a slave died belonging to Ralph Wormley 1738.
Jane a slave belonging to Ralph Wormley Feb^{ry} 23d 1738.
Robin a slave belonging to Henry Tugle Died Novr ye 19th 1738.
Dick a slave belonging to Co^{ll} Armistead Churchhill died Decem^r y^e
    20th 1738.
Will a slave belonging to Thos Shelton died Decr y^e 14th 1738.
Jeney a slave belonging to John Blake Senr died Feb^{ry} y^e 29th 1738.
Charles a slave belonging to   died Feb^{ry} y^e 17th 1738.
Dick Son of Judey a slave belonging to y^e Estate of Oliver Segar
    died Feb^{ry} 10th 173$\frac{7}{8}$.
Gloster son of Judy a slave belonging to Robert Daniel died March
    y^e 11th 173$\frac{8}{9}$.
Sam a Slave belonging to y^e Estate of Oliver Segar died March y^e
    23th 1739.
Moll, Ails, & Rachel three Slaves belonging to Co^{ll} Armstead
    Churchhill died May y^e 5th 1739.
Moll Daughter of Bess a Slave belonging to John Segar died May y^e
    13th 1739.
Sarah Daughter of Mareah a Slave belonging to Edmund Berkeley
    died June 4th 1739.
Judy a slave belonging to Humphrey Jones died Augst ye 18th 1739.
Sue a slave belonging to Gawin Corbin died Jan^{ry} y^e 19th 173
Ambrus Son of Mareah died Octo^r y^e 10th belonging to Edmund
    Berkeley 1739.
Toney a slave belonging to y^e Estate of Olliver Segar died Novr y^e
    30th 1739.
Isaac Son of Margery a slave belonging to y^e Estate of Oliver Segar
    died Jan^{ry} 7th 173$\frac{9}{40}$.
Judith Daughter of Frank a slave belonging to y^e Estate of Oliver
    Segar died Jany y^e 19th 173$\frac{9}{40}$.
Margret Daughter of Letty a slave belonging to Eliz: Stanard died
    Augst 9th 1740.

Simon Son of Jenny belonging to the Estate of Matthew Kemp died March 20th 1740.

Betty daughter of Bess belonging to the Estate of Mathew Kemp died March 21st 1740.

Nanny belonging to the Estate of Richard Hill Died Feb^{ry} 8th 173$\frac{9}{40}$.

George belonging to Mathias Gaile died Feb^{ry} 2d 173$\frac{9}{40}$.

Letty belonging to Richard Corbin died January y^e 4th 1740.

Peter belonging to Churchill Jones died Feb^{ry} 28th 173$\frac{9}{40}$.

Ned Belonging to Matthew Kemp died Feb^{r}y 28th 173$\frac{9}{40}$.

Sambo belonging to Checkeley Thacker died Feb^{ry} 5th 173$\frac{9}{40}$.

Deal belonging to Henry Thacker died Feb^{ry} 6th 173$\frac{9}{40}$.

Malbrough belonging to Henry Thacker died Feb^{ry} 13th 173$\frac{9}{40}$.

Grace belonging to Matthew Kemp died June y^e 15 173$\frac{9}{40}$.

Letty belonging to William Mountague died May 27 1740.

Cate belonging to Henry Tugle died September y^e 20th 1740.

Jude belonging to Henry Daniel died October y^e 16th 1740.

Stafford belonging to Richard Corbin died December 26th 1740.

Busbee Son of Judy a Slave belonging to Geo: Hardin died January 28 174$\frac{0}{1}$.

Frank son of Fortune a slave belonging to Thos Laughlin died July y^e 19th 1741.

Betty a slave belonging to Cary Smith died July y^e 14th 1741.

Hannah Daughter of Sharlot a slave belonging to Henry Thacker died Sepr 22nd 1741.

Hannah a Slave belonging to Mary Murrah died April y^e 1st 1741.

Diego a free negro died Sep^t 3 1741.

Dick Son of Sharlot a slave belonging to Henry Thacker died Decem^r ye 17th 1741.

Will a Slave belonging to William Bristow died Augst ye 20th 1741.

Phillis Daughter of Juno born in King Wm County and died in Middlesex June y^e 8th (belonging to Edm^d Berkeley) 1741.

Simon Son of Juno born in y^e same County & died in Middlesex April 7th 1741.

Daniel Son of Betty a slave belonging to Edm^d Berkeley died Decem^r y^e 10th 1741.

Jenny a slave belonging to Robert Fureman died Jan^{ry} y^e 17th 174$\frac{1}{2}$.

Sarah a Slave belonging to Mary Graves died Jan^{ry} y^e 18th 174$\frac{1}{2}$.

Natt son of Judith a slave belonging to Thos Mountague died Novem^r y^e 15th 1741.

Phebe a slave belonging to John Blake died y^e 6th of April 1742.

Charles a slave belonging to Co^{ll} Armistead died June 1742.

Harry, Dick, Judy, Tamar & Chance, slaves belonging to George Hardin died in Feb^{ry} March 174$\frac{1}{2}$, & April 1742.

Sampson   belonging to Phillip Warwick died July y^e 15th 1742.

Phillis a slave belonging to Thos Chilton died Novr y^e 11th 1742.

Susanna a slave belonging to Mary Roane died March y^e 15th 174$\frac{1}{2}$.

Will a slave belonging to Mary Roane died May 19th 1742.

Catherine a slave belonging to Mary Roane died May 13th 1742.

Sampson a slave belonging to Matthias Gale died June 15th 1742.

Sampson a slave belonging to Robert Daniel died Feb^{ry} y^e 8th 1742.

Nassau a slave belonging to Jacob Stiff died April 26th 1743.

Ben a slave belonging to Mary Murrey died April 1743.
Simon a slave belonging to Hugh Spotswood Died May 1th 1743.
Tony Son of Willmott a slave belonging to Law^r Orrill Died June 12 1743.
Tony a slave belonging to John Rhodes died September 27th 1743.
Jack son of Rose a slave belonging to John Rhodes Senr died Sep^{ber} 27. 1743.
Scipio a slave belonging to Thomas Chelton died October 6th 1743.
John a slave belonging to Mary Graves died March 17th 1743.
Jenny Daughter of Daphny a slave belonging to Ann Smith died Sep^{ber} 28 1743.
Robin a Slave belonging to John Smith jun^r died December 16th 174–.
Sacco a slave belonging to Coll^o Gawin Corbin died Decem^{ber} 16th 174
Ann a slave belonging to Laurance Orrel died March 26th 1743.
Bob a slave belonging to Anthony Smith died March 17th 174¾.
George a slave belonging to Ann Smith died April 13th 1744.
Sampson a negroe child belonging to Bev. Stanard Died 174
Joe a slave belonging to Thos Laughlin died Feb^{ry} 19th 1743.
Moll Daughter of Hannah a slave belonging to Thos Laughlin died March 3d 1743.
Jeane a slave belonging to William Hill died Novr 29th 1743.
Hannah a slave belonging to ye Estate of Richard Hill died Jan^{ry} ye 3d 174¾.
Little Alice a slave belonging to Edwin Thacker died March 19th 1744.
Jeny a slave belonging to John Lewis died Octo^r ye 16th 1744.
Jeny a slave belonging to Eliz^a Tugle died Feb^{ry} 15 1744.
Phillis a Slave belonging to Jedediah Bristow died Decem^r ye 30th 1744.
Hannah a slave belonging to Jedediah Bristow died Jan^{ry} 7th 1744.
Willmuth a slave belonging to Law. Orrill died March 20th 1744.
Fillis a Slave belonging to John Alldin died July ye 2d 1744.
Judy a slave belonging to John Alldin died July ye 22d 1744.
Margret Daughter of Letty a slave belonging to B. Stanard Augst 14th 174.
Margere a Slave belonging to Jacob Stiff died 1744.
Gumbe a slave belonging to Jacob Stiff died 1744.
Cate a slave belonging to Robert Chowning died Novr 16th 1744.
Moll a Slave belonging to Mary Roane died April 30th 1744.
Bob a slave belonging to Charles Daniel died June ye 27th 1744.
Hannah a slave belonging to Thos Laughlin died Decem^r 23d 1744.
Jack Wilshire a Slave belong to Coll John Grymes died 1743.
Dick a slave belonging to Chicheley Thacker died April 17th 1745.
Kate a slave belonging to Eliz^a Burk died May ye 1st 1745.
Sam a slave belonging to ye Estate of John Smith died Feb^{ry} ye 9th 174⅘.
Glasgow a slave belonging to Matthew Gale Died July ye 9th 1745.
Alce a slave belonging to Clary Daniel Died Augst 2d 1745.
Tom a Slave belonging to Ann Smith Died Augst ye 16th 1745.
Daphina a slave belonging to Ann Smith Died Decem^r ye 22d 1745.
Mille a slave belonging to Ann Smith Died Jan^{ry} ye 11th 174⅚.

Isaac a Slave belonging to Richard Corbin died Feb^ry ye 28th 174⅚.
Robin a slave belonging to Richard Corbin died June ye 3d 1746.
Samson a slave belonging to Edmund Berkeley died Octo^r 1746.
Adam son of Rose a Slave belonging to John Smith Junr died Novr 3d. 1746.
George Son of Hannah a slave belonging to John Smith Junr died Novr 13th 1746.
Will a Slave belonging to Eliz^a Tugle died Decem^r ye 28th 1746.
Dinah a slave belonging to Edmund Dillion died March 31st 1746.
Daphne a slave belonging to John Grymes Esqr died April ye 30th 1746.
Sampson a slave belonging to George Lee died April 12th 1746.
Harington a Slave belonging to Alexander Frazier Died May 22d 1746.
Rachel a slave belonging to Armistead Churchhill died 174⅚
Tom a Slave belonging to George Wortham died Jan^ry 21st 174⅚.

———

A Fragment.

John Son of John & Sarah Sanders born Feby 18th, baptized March 13th 1757.

The above extracted from the Register of Christ Church Parish by

April 2d 1774.   Samuel Klug

MARRIAGES.

Drawn off & sent to the Clerks of Counties wherein the marriages * solemnized.

Samuel Klug, Minister.

    *   liam Corrie Beale & Anne Corbin (King & Queen) mar. May 26th 1792.
    *   er Minter & Mary Matthews married June 17th 1792.
Thomas Saunders & Mary Stiff married July 29 1792.
John Southern & Elizabeth Bowers (K & Q.) married Sept 1 17 * *
George Dillard & Molly Batchelder married Septr 6th 1792.
George Humphris & Nancy Foudry married Septr 9th 1792.
William Brooking & Betty Daniel married Septr 22d 1792.
John Miller & Avarilla Saunders married October 25th 1792.
Richard Walden & Hannah Dudley (K. & Q.) married October 25th 1792.
Gabriel Jones & Elizabeth Healy married Decr 13th 1792.
Joseph Boss & Elizabeth Barrick married Decr 27th 1792.
Robert Bowden & Mary Garret (K. & Q.) married Decr 27th 1792.
Thomas Spann & Patsey Hall (Gloucester) married Decr 29 1792.
Francis Anderson & Frances Spencer (K. & Q.) married Jan^ry 10th 1793.
William Palmer & Ursula Robinson married February 10th 1793.
Benjamin Walden & Mildred Didlake (K & Q.) married Feby 21st 1793.
Francis Shackelford & Mary Corr (K. & Q) married April 27th 1793.
John Darby & Lucy Harrison Churchhill married April 30th 1793.
William Kidd & Sally Stamper married May 18th 1793.

Tunstall Banks & Polly Murray Curtis married May 23d 1793.
Laurence Muse & Jane Southall married June 1st 1793.

A Fragment.

* iam C. Humphris & Elizabeth * * *
* liam Wake & Lucy Billups Powel Decr 21st 1799.
Augustine Blake & Sarah Robinson Decr 22nd 1799.
William Humphries & Elizabeth Davis March 2nd 1800.
Elliott Muse & Betty Tayloe Corbin May 3rd 1800.
Edwin Upshaw & Lucy Roane May 25th 1800.
Henry Hefferman & Lucy N. Berkeley Sep^t 28 1800.

by the Reverend Mr Smith.

Josiah Burns & Mary Garland Novr 29 1800.
John Mountain & Elizabeth Jones Decr 26 1800.

The above List given to the Clerk of the Court.

Henry Hefferman Rector.

* Do.

William George & Elizabeth Greenwood July 19.
Samuel William Sayre & Jane Grymes July 23.
James Healy Junr & Elizabeth M: Jones Octr 18.
Zachariah Crittenden & Catharine Jackson Octr 25th.
John Chowning & Catharine Blakey Decr 4th 1804.
Ralph Wormeley & Elizabeth Boswell May 7th 1805.
William Robinson & Martha Haines Stubbs August 22nd 1805.

The above List made out & Sent to the Clerk.

Thomas Cooke & Catharine B. Didlake Jan: 16th 1806.
Alexander Bristow & Nancy Brown August 9th 1806.
Benjamin Wiltshire & Nancy Kidd September 5th 1806.
Samuel William Sayre & Virginia Bassett Sepr 20 1806.

Henry Hefferman Rector.

Peter Son of John & Jane Bray was   June 10th 1767.
Betsy, Daughter of Jonn & Margaret Callaham born April ye 11.
     1768.
Benjamin Son of James & Mary Kidd was born October 23d 1761.
Nancy, Daughter of James & Mary Kidd was born September 1763.
Jane, Daughter of James & Mary Kidd was born February 11th
     1765.

From another book.

Robert Norman, Son of John & Alice Blake, Born May 29th 1775.
Samuel, Son of John & Alice Blake, Born February 17th 1777.
John, Son of William & Rachel Bristow, was born July 16th. 1777.
Thomas, Son of James & Mary Kidd was born June 15th 1778.
John Blake, Son of James & Betty Stiff was born September 23d
     1776.
Elizabeth Baker, Daughter of James & Betty Stiff was born Sep-
     tember 10th 1778.
Betty Daughter of John & Frances Thurston was born February
     21st 1776.

Levi, Son of James & Elizabeth Dunlevy was born September 16th
1778.
Charles, Son of Benjamin & Franka Blake was born Novr 21st 1778.
Alfred, Son of Joseph & Sarah Boss was born Decr 26th 1778.
John Son of William & Sarah Boss was born Novr 18th 1778.
Elizabeth, Daughter of Philip & Frances Montague was born Feb-
ruary 2d. 1779.
William Newcomb, Son of William & Anne Newcomb was born
February 4th 1779.
Elizabeth, Daughter of Charles & Ann Reade was born September
24th 1779. & baptized Octr 27th.
Rachel Murray Beverley, Daughter of Harry Beverley & Lucy
Yates was born February 24th & baptized March 3d. 1780.
Reuben Laten Son of John Parish & ———— his wife was born Dec^r
8th 1779.
William Lewis illegitimate Son of Elizabeth Lewis was born October
10th 1777.
Anthony Son of Thomas Harrow was born April 19th 1780.
Ann, Daughter of Francis & Mary Bland was born June 28th 1780.
Daniel, Son of Daniel & Priscilla Jefferson was born September 14th
1780.
John Archibald, Son of William & Ann Murray was born October
9th 1780.
James Son of George & Sarah Brushwood was born Octr 7th 1780.
Robert Beverley, Son of Beverley & Milly Daniel was born August
21st 1776.
Lucy Daughter of Beverley & Milly Daniel was born August 23d
1778.
Frances Ann Travers Daughter of Beverley & Milly Daniel was born
January 2d 1780.
Mary Daughter of John & Ann Hibble was born June 19th 1773.
Elizabeth Stanard, Daughter of Harry Beverley & Lucy Yates was
born August 7th 1781. and Baptized August 26th.
William Sourd Son of   Sourd in King & Queen was born Oct^r
8th 1781.
William Latané Son of Philip & Frances Mountague was born Nov^r
27th 1781.
John Son of Daniel & Priscilla Jefferson was born Jany 14th 1782.
Laban son of William Corr of King & Queen born Jany 3d 1782.
John son of W^m & Mary Bland born, Jany 21st 1782.
Robert Son of Josiah & Elizabeth Bristow was born 22d Day of Oc-
tober 1781.
Laban son of William Corr born 3d of January 1782.
John, son of Daniel & Priscilla Jefferson born January 14th 1782.
John son of William & Mary Bland born January 21st 1782.
Valentine Son of Robert & Susanna Groom born February 14 1782.
John Batchelder Son of William & Ann George born August 3d 1782.
Susanna Daughter of Lewis & Judith Stevens born Octr 27th 1782.
Mary Reeves, Daughter of Richard & Mary Bird was born Novem-
ber the 6th 1782.
Susanna Daughter of Lewis & Judith Stephens born Octr 27th 1782.
Richard Miller, Son of Thomas & Mary Segar was born December
16th 1782.

William Chowning son of Churchhill & Ann Blakey was born January 30th 1775.

* * * * ter of Churchhill & Ann Blakey was born * 2d 1778.

* * * * * * Churchhill, Ann Blakey was born * * * 1779.

* * * * lld Ann Blakey was born

William Son of John & Clara Daniel was born November 19th 1781.

William, Son of James & Betty Stiff was born March 19th 1783.

Thomas Meacham, Son of James & Betty Stiff was born June 7th 1785.

Kitty Taylor, Daughter of Mary Taylor was born December 14th 1776.

Patty Brooks, Daughter of John & Ann Brooks was born July 2d 1783.

Catherine George, Daughter of James & Mary Smith was born June 20th 1784.

John Richerson, Son of James & Mary Smith was born January 28th 1787.

Lewis Dudley, Son of William & Ann George was born the 16th of July 1785.

James Meacham, Son of William & Ann George was born the 27th September 1787.

Sarah, Daughter of Harry Beverly & James Yates was born January 13th 1788.

William Son of William George and Ann his Wife was born the 15th day of May. 1790.

John, Son of John & Lickey Minter, born January 30th 1783.

John son of Thomas & Judith Daniel born February 12th 1783.

Martin, son of Thomas & Sarah Ann O'Harrow was born April 16th 1783.

Lucy Daughter of Joseph Milbey was born May 23d 1783.

Thomas, son of Thomas Clark was born July 5th 1783.

Catharine, Daughter of Richard & Ann Cauthorn was born August 28th 1783.

Isaac Holloway, son of Edward & Catherine Brooks was born December 7th 1783.

Catharine Klug, Daughter of Harry Beverley & Jane Yates was born March the 1st 1784 & baptized March 14th.

John Draper, Son of John & Milly Parish was born March 12th 1784.

Martha, Daughter of Philip & Frances Montague was born April 30th 1784.

Frances Shackelford Daughter of William & Mildred Pryor was born June 22d 1783.

George, Son of George Dame & Mary his Wife was born March 8th 1784.

Thadeus, Son of George & Elizabeth Daniel was born the 18th July 1784.

Alice Berry, Daughter of John & Mildred Sadler was born July 25th 1784.

Lucy, Daughter of W^m & Mary Bland was born Sep^t 16th 1784.

Lucy, Daughter of Daniel & Priscilla Jefferson was born October 7th 1784.

James, Son of Thomas Harrow was born March 30th —aptised May 1st 1785.

John, Son of Richard & Anne Cauthorn was born February 15th 178.

Betsey, Daughter of Major & Phebe Guthree was born November 24th 1785.

Elizabeth, Daughter of James & Elizabeth Dunlevy was born April 1st 1782.

Nancy, Daughter of James & Elizabeth Dunlevy was born December 22d. 1785.

William Foster, Son of Cuthbert & Elizabeth Snow was born June the 2d. 1786.

Robert, Son of James & Elizabeth Wilkines was born August 30th 1786.

Thomas Hill, Son of Daniel & Priscilla Jefferson was born August 10th 1787.

Elizabeth Averilla, Daughter of John Parish was born May 22d 1787.

James Son of William & Mary Hall was born February 11th 1788.

Ambrose, Son of Robert & Ann Wake was born April 8th 1788.

James Son of Benjamin & —— Dudley was born June 8th 1788.

George Meacham Son of James & Mary Smith was born Feby 8th 1789 & Baptized June 7th 1789.

Caty Price, Daughter of Henry D. Shepherd & Mary his Wife was born 13th of November 1790.

Matthew French Son of John & Mary Hibble was born July 22d 1790.

John, Son of John & Lucy Wilkins was born January 26th 1791.

Lewis Dudly, Son of William George & Ann his Wife was born the 16th Day of July 1785.

James Meacham, Son of William George & Ann his Wife was born the 27th Septr 1787.

Susanna Brooking, Daughter of James Batchelder & Mary his Wife was born Septr 3d 1792.

* * * * * * & Sarah Tugle was born January 7th.

* * Son of William & Mary Bristow was born Sepr 1st.

* * ty Daughter of Kilman & Mary Calehan was born Sepr 12th.

Robert Son of —— —— Wilkins was born September 9th.

Clara Daught^r of William & Mary Williamson was born Novr 13th.

James Son of John & Joanna Dunlevy was born Septr 27th

Hannah Daughter of Samuel & Ann Wood was born Decem^r 10th.

Sarah Daughter of John & Eliz^a Batchelder was born June 7th.

Elizabeth Daughter of William & Elizabeth Owen was born.

John Son of Edward & Mary Kidd born Octr 15th & Bapt^d Octob^r 23d 17.

Ann Daughter of Jacob & Susanna Blake born Novr 13th 17.

Thomas Son of Stephen & Ann Tenoe was born Febry 23d 175.

Frances Daughter of John & Mary Yarrington was born May 29th 17.

Curtis Son of William & Eliz^a Daniel was born Augt 14th.

James Son of Charles & Mary Hodges was born April 28th 17 *

Fanny Bowles Daughter of John & Mary Bowles was born March
  27th 17   *
Josiah Son of Henry & Micah Blan was born July 5th 17   *
A Child was born (Daughter) of Daniel & Hannah Stringer Sep^r
  11th 17   *
Robert Son of John & Jane Chowning was born Decr 3d Bapt^d Janry
  13th: 1754: 17   *
Mary Daughter of John & Eliz^a Lewis was born Janry 6th & Bapt^d
  21st Do. 17   *
William Son of William & Jane Meacham was born June 12th 17 *
Philamon the Son of George & Mary Bristow was born Decr 31st 17 *
Ann Daughter of Robert & Ann Lenn was born Novr 20th 17   *
Elizabeth Daughter of William & Jane Mountague was born the
  26th Day Augt 17   *
William Son of James & Sarah Deagle was born April 26th 17   *
Elizabeth Daughter of Cornelius & Eliz^a Deforeest was born Dec^r
  10th Bap^d January 11 (1754) 175   *
David Son of Christopher & Ann Miller was born July 10th 175 *
John son of James and Jane Dunlevy was born Febry 15th 1754.
Joseph son of Joseph & Judith Eggleston was born Novr 25th &
  Bapt^d Decr 1st follg 1754.
James the son of William & Sarah Stiff was born March 4th 1754.
Mary Daughter of Philip & Mary Grymes was born Febry 12th 1754.
Gabriel son of Eusebius & Martha Lewis was born April 1st & Bapt^d
  28th 1754.
Thomas son of Samuel & Eliz^a Batchelder was born Jan^ry 19th Bapt^d
  Febry 1754.
Nelson Son of George & Mary Daniel was born Febry 8th 1754.
William Son to Henry & Elizabeth Johnson was born June 10th
  175   *
John Son of John & Mary Bowles was born Decr 24th 175   *
Benjamin Son of John & Martha born April 30th 175   *
Sarah Daughter of Benj^a & Dorothy Rhodes was born Augt 25th
  175   *
George Son of Thomas & Rose Blake was born Febry 17th 17   *
John the son of John & Eliz^a Bryant was born Janry 18th.
Charles Mechen Son of John & Judith Wortham born July 18th.
John Son of Meacham & Eliz^a George was born Sep^t 19th.
Ann Daughter of James & Mary Berry born Novr 25th.
        & Rebecah Dudley born Febru 26 & Bapt
    Daught^r of John & Jane Beaman born July 1st
  * * the Daughter of Edward & Rebecker Saunders born Febry
  5th 1754.
  * * Son of Edwd & Eliz^a Bristow born May 6th Bapt^d 26th 1754.
  * * ley Daughter of Henry & Tabbitha Shepherd born March
  7th 1754.
  * achel & Esther, Daughter of George & Mary Lee born May
  24th 1754.
  * * nnah, Daughter of John & Betty Cornelius Born May 21st
  1754.
  * rances Daughter of John & Lucresey Greenwood, Born June
  3d 1754.
Mary, Daughter of John & Eliz^a Howard, born July 17th 1754.

Anne Davis's Son John Born Janry 15th 1754.

Catherine Daughter of William & Eliz^a Chowning March 13th 1755.

Mary Daughter of James & Frances Smith born Febry 16th 1755.

William Son of James & —— Green born Janry 18th 1755.

Samuel Son of Joseph & Mikel Batchelder born Janry 1st 1755.

Elizabeth Daughter of William & Sarah Robinson born May 18th 1755.

Richard Son of George & Jane Blackley, born Janry 25th 1755.

Mary Daughter of John & Frances Taylor born Febry 5th 1755.

Leonard Son of Robert & Lucy Daniel born March 10th Bapt^d March 16th 1755.

Judith Daughter of Edward & Mary Southern born Jan'y 24th 1755.

Ann Daughter of George & Mary Blake born Febry 11th 1755.

John son of John & Eliz^a Lewis born Feby 17th Baptized March 30th 1755.

Ann Daughter of Lewis & Bettey Mountague born March 30th 1755.

Elizabeth Daughter of Richard and Ann Daniel born Dit^o 1st 1755.

Nelson son of Jacob and Winifred Rice born Dit^o 21st 1755.

Judith Heptinstall daughter of James & Judith Heptinstall born March 27th 1755.

Humphrey son of Needels & Jane Hill born April 7th 1755.

Stephen Son of Stephen & Ann Tenoe Born April 26th Bap^t May 4th 1755.

Mary Daughter of Henry & Jane Sears, Born March 24th 1755.

Francis Daughter of William & Sarah Roan Born April 3d 1755.

Josiah Son of Josiah & Eliz^a Brame born April 12th 1755.

Hannah Daughter of David & —— Snodgrass born Decr 3d Bapt^d Janry 17th 1747.

John son of John & Lucretia Greenwood born Augt 6th Bapt^d Sepr 6th 1747.

Mary Daughter of George & Mary Lee born April 22nd Bapt^d May 3d 1747.

* es son of Joseph & Eliza Collins born May 8th 1747.

ces son of W^m & Ruth Bristow born Sep^t 25th & Bapt^d Octr 2nd 1747.

* * * born August 18th

* * * Daughter was born March 4th

* * beth Lenn the Daughter of Robert Lenn & Ann his Wife was born Janry 28.

Margaret Beaman Daughter of John Beaman & Jane his Wife was born Novr 30th.

Frances Pain Daughter of Mary Guthery was born March 18th.

Elizabeth Thurston Daughter of John Thurston & Catherine his Wife was born March 3d.

Benjamin Pace Son of William Pace & Hannah his Wife was born January 28th.

William Bristow the son of John Bristow & Mary his Wife born Octob^r 6th.

Eliz^a Southren the Daughter of Edward Southren & Mary his Wife was born Sep^t 20th

John Mulins the Son of William Mulins & Mary his Wife was born August 23d.

Samuel Brooks the son of John Brooks & Martha his Wife born October 20th.

A Child of Tho⁸ Berry & Catharine his Wife born Oct ʳ 22nd.

Ann Deagle Daughter of William Deagle and Maryan his Wife was born July 6th.

Ann Daniel Daughter of Robert and Lucy Daniel was born 23d Augᵗ.

Elizabeth Baker the Daughter of Benjamin Baker and Frances his wife was born.

Jerusha Bowls ——— of John Bowls and Mary his Wife was born Sepʳ 20th.

Catey Horseley Daughter of Tho⁸ Horseley and Rhoda his wife born Octʳ 1st.

Anne Williams the Daughter of John & Susannah Williams was born Decʳ 10th.

John Son of Major & Ann Pryor his Wife born Augᵗ 24th.

Samuel Greenwood Son of Samuel Greenwood dec'd & Francis his Wife born Febry 26th.

Thomas son of Thomas Dudley & Joice his Wife was born April 21st.

Elizabeth Daughter of Lewis & Betty Mountague his Wife was born Augᵗ 28th.

William son of Amey Mylls born January 4th.

Mary the Daughter of Samuel Thompson & Mary his Wife was born Octʳ 26th.

William Son of William & Betty born April 14th.

Mary Daughter of John & Joanna Dunlevy born July 8th.

Josiah son of William & Eliza Daniel born Decʳ 30th.

William Son of Charles & Ruth Moulson born May 7th Baptᵈ 20th.

Alse Wilkin Daughter of James & Judith Heptinstall was born Sepʳ 7th.

Isham Son of Christopher & Ann Miller born Sepʳ 20th.

Jacob Urie Son of John & Constant Urie was born Decʳ 3d.

Rhoda Boss the Daughter of John Boss Senʳ & ——— ——— was born Sepᵗ 27th.

William Son of Churchhill & Millicent Jones was born Novʳ 17th.

Andrew Son of Andrew & Elizᵃ South was born Novʳ 1st.

Frances Daughter of John & Elizᵃ Batchelder born March 23d.

Agatha Daughter of James & Judith Campbell born Octʳ 8th.

Mary Daughter of Wᵐ Brooks & Catherine his Wife was born Augᵗ 5th Bapᵈ 25th.

John Son of Henry & Ann Washington born May 27th Bapᵈ the 29th & died 30th.

Jacob Son of John & Mary Rhodes was born May 6. Bapᵗ 17th Dᵒ.

Elizabeth Daughter of William & Mary Williamson was born May 12th.

Mary Daughter of Wᵐ & Jane Meacham was born July 18th: 1751.

John Son of Joseph & Mary Sinah born Octʳ 12.

Thomas Son of Thomas & Roase Blake was born Novʳ 8th.

Judith Daughter of Peter & Sarah Robinson was born Sepʳ 5th. Baptᵈ 21st. Do.

Churchhill Son of James & Isabel Gibson was born April 15th.

Sarah Daughter of John & Elizᵃ Cornelius was born April 22nd.

287

Molly Jones the Daugh^r of William & Sarah Jones was born April 20th 1751.
* * * of John & Martha Brooks was born Decr 29 * * *
* * * * * Betty Dean Born 1752.
* of W^m & Sarah Stiff was born Decr 3d 1752.
* Daughter of William & Marg^t Rountree born April 26th 1752.
* Son of William & Eliz^a Chowning was born Decr 11th 1752.
* Daughter of Ed^{wd} & Mary Southren was born October 23d 1752.
Daugh of William & Ruth Bristow born Jan'ry 12th Bap^t 28th 1752.
* iam Son of John & Catharine Thurston born Janry 3d 1752.
* Son of Rich^d & Ann Daniel born Novr 18th Bap^t 26th 1752.
* rles Son of John & Martha Shecard was born Octr 2nd 1752.
* Son of Jacob & Winney Rice was born Sep^t 28th 1752.
rh Son of David & Dinah Barrick was born Augt 18th 1752.
Daughter of Benjamin & Doritha Rhodes born July 13th 1752.
* s Son of Edward & Martha Dillard born Augt 25th 1752.
* * ma Daughter of John & Mary Patterson was born Decr 22nd 1752.
* * les Son of Charles & Ann Roane was born Octr 3d. 1752.
* * Son of William & Anne Sadler was born Decr 17th 1752.
Daught^r of Henry & Susanna Mickelburrough was born Jan^{ry} 15th 1752.
* * jamin Son of William & Mary Mullins was born Febry 8th 1752.
* * y Daughter of James & Jane Dunlevy was born March 26th 1752.
* * uel Son of George & Ruth Chowning was born June 15th 1752.
* uel Son of William & Frances Guthery was born July 8th 1752.
* * hel Daughter of John & Jane Beaman was born June 12th 1752.
* nnah Daughter of Philip & Mary Grymes was born March 4th 1752.
* nces Daughter of Needels & Jane Hill born Dit^o 22nd 1752.
* y Daughter of Meacham & Eliz^a George born Febry 20th 1752.
* iam Son of Samuel & Eliz^a Batchelder born Janry 7th Bapt^d 19th 1752.
* am Son of William & Eliz^a Owen born Dit^o 12th 1752.
* ery Goar Daughter of John & Mary Herring born May 22nd 1752.
* mas Son of Thomas & Sarah Tugle born March 29th 1752.
* m Daughter of John & Eliz^a Anderson born April 7th 1752.
* hn Son of Samuel & Mary Bristow born June 7th.
* hn Son of Alex. & Eliz^a Reade born Febry 5th Bap^t 15th Idem 1752.
* Son of Charles & Ruth Moulson born March 21st 1752.
* nry Son of Ric^d & Jane Overstreet born Febry 20th 1752.
* ncy Daughter of John & Judith Wortham born Janry 20th 1752.
* verley Son of Robert & Lucy Daniel born June 8th 1752.
* braham Son of Lewis & Betty Mountague born Janry 6th 1753.
* nhey Daughter of John & Ann Bird born March 27th 1753.

* argaret Goar Daughter of Harry & Mary Anderson born Febr^y 20th 1753.

* shsha Daughter of John and Mary Brooks born Dit° 5th 1753.

* lizabeth Daughter of Robert Clemons & Jane Warren born March 16th 1753.

* mas Son of Richard & Phebe Burk born Dit° 29th 1753.

* Daughter of James & Martha Green born March 27th 1753.

From another book.

Registry of Births & Christenings.

Henry Hefferman Rector.

Churchhill Anderson Son of John Hodges & Mary his Wife born August 12th 1795 baptized Jan. 31st 1796.

George Son of John & Lucy Croffield born Decr 30th 1795. and baptized on Sunday the 9th of May 1796.

Wm Son of Daniel & priscilla Jefferson born November 17th 1791.

Diana Daughter of Daniel & priscilla Jefferson born Jan: 29. 1795.

Registered this 4th of May 1796 at the request of Said Daniel Jefferson.

Eliza Churchill Daughter of John Darby and Lucy his Wife born on the 7th of November 1795. privately baptized & publickly received in Church on Sunday the 30th of October 1796.

Jacob & Elizabeth Blake Twins of Thomas Blake, and Inecy his Wife born the 11th of September 1791.

William Blake born 6th of January 1794. of the Same.

Anne Blake born the 15th of January 1796. D°

All baptized Sunday June 4th 1797.

Jefferson born Feb: 1798. baptized May 20th 1798 of Daniel & Priscilla Jefferson.

William Clark Son of Josiah Bristow & Fanny his wife born October 25th 1787.

Mariah Daniel Daughter of Said Parents born March 11th 1789.

Elizabeth Daniel born 24th of October 1793.

Frances Clark born July 10th 1796.

Robert Blakey Kidd Son of Thomas & Nancy Kidd born June 23d 1800. baptized Janu^y 1st 1805.

Mary Anne Kidd Daughter of the same parents born Decr 10th 1806 baptized January 1st 1808.

———

A Negro boy belonging to George Lee was born Octr 20th.

Negro boy belonging to Latané Mountague an Orphan was born Sepr 7th.

Negro Girl belonging to Christ^r Miller born Octr 19th.

Lucy the Daughter of Negro Maud belonging to ——— born Sepr 20th.

Patt a Negro Girl belonging to Edwd Blackburn born July 13th.

Will a Negro boy belonging to Gales Estate born Sep^t 12th.

Frank Daughter of Negro Jane belonging to George Fearn was born Novr 10.

Winney the Daughter of Daphne belonging to Thos Mountague was born Octr 14th.

Moll Rachel Serinah three Negro Girls belonging to Churchhill Jones born(at one birth) Augt 26th.

Winney a negro Girl belonging to John Jones was born Novr 15th.

Lucy the Daughter of Chloe belonging to Capt Wilcox was born Novr 16th.

Thomas a negro boy belonging to the Orphans of Hump^{ry} Jones dec'd was born Feb.

James the Son of Rose belonging to John Rhodes was born April 11th.

William Jackson the son of Phillis a slave belonging to Alex^r Reade born Augt 20th.

Mill a Negro Girl belonging to Wm Hackney jun^r was born March 20th.

Poll Daughter of Jenny belonging to Thos Buford was Born Janry 7th.

Judy the Daughter of Moll belonging to Mary Roane was born 9th Day of June.

Anna Daughter of Judy a slave belonging to Henry Thacker born Dec^r.

John Son of Lena a slave belonging to Henry Thacker, born Sep^t 7th.

Kate Daughter of Judy a slave belonging to Eliz^a Burk born Octr 21st.

Clara a Negro Girl belonging to Ann Daniel born August 1st.

Phill a slave belonging to Robert Daniel born August 10th.

Sarah a slave belonging to Henry Johnson born July 23d.

James a slave belonging to Gales Estate born July 12th.

Benjamin Son of Phillis a slave belonging to John Wortham born Decr 24th.

Abram son of Bess a slave belonging to Alexd^r Frazier born Novr 22nd.

Billey son of Phillis a slave belonging to Beverley Stanard born June 11th.

Margaret Daught^r of Betty a slave belonging to D^o born Febry 10th.

Jacob a slave belonging to the Estate of Hump^{ry} Jones dec'd born April 15th.

Nell a slave belonging to James Scrosby born May 2d.

Milly a slave belonging to George Wortham born Augt 18th.

Sarah a slave belonging to Judith Gunter was born June 28th.

Beck Daughter of Frank a slave belonging to James Reid born May 8th.

Juda Daughter of Dinah a slave belonging to John Blake Senr born May 5th.

Sampson a slave belonging to George Wortham born May 16th.

Agga Daughter of Jane a slave belonging to Thos Mountague born May 4th.

John Son of Ebo Frank a slave belonging to Edm^d Berkeley born Sep^t 10th.

Pompey Son of Rose a Slave belonging to John Smith born Decr 23d.

—— —— Slave belonging to Wm Mountague Born April 17th.

—— —— Slave belonging to Do. born July 19th.

—— —— Henry Mickelburrough.

—— Do. born Do. 25th.

——ghter of Lettice a slave belonging to Thomas Sanders.

  * * a Male child belonging to the Estate of George Wortham dec'd born 175 *

Slave belonging to George Wortham born Febry 23d 175*.
Son of Daphne a Slave belonging to Thomas Mountague born
Sep^t 23d 1752.
Daughter of Sue a Slave belonging to John Wilcox born Aug^t
6th 1752.
   the Son of Chloe a Slave belonging to Do. born Do. 12th 1752.
      Slave belonging to Joseph Sinath born 1752.
*   ard a Slave belonging to William Meacham born April 17th
1752.
Daughter of Oder a Slave belonging to Frances Bryant born
April 11th 1752.
a Slave belonging to Do. born June 4th 1752.
Daughter of Daphne a Slave belonging to Daniel Stringer born
May 23d: 1752.
*   aim a Slave belonging to Frances Bryant born Octr 9th 1752.
*   as a slave belonging to Charles Lee born September 22d 1752.
*   braham Son of Frank a slave belonging to Richard Tyler born
April 10th 1752.
*   ll a slave belonging to Henry Johnson born 16th July 1752.
*   Son of Doll a Slave belonging to John Rhodes born June 28th
1752.
a Son of —— belonging to John Berry born July 4th 1752.
*   ah Daughter of Juda a slave belonging to C. Henry Thacker
born Aug. 28. 1752.
*   arry son of Jenny a slave belong'g to Dit^o born Novr 27th 1752.
*   e Daughter of Ebo Frank a Slave belonging to Edmond Berkeley born Octr 1753.
*   chard a slave belonging to James Scrosby born Sepr 1st 1753.
*   arah Daughter of Jenny a slave belonging to Edm^d Berkeley
born April 24th 1753.
*   wis Son of Hannah, a Slave Dit^o born May 15th 1753.
*   umwell Son of Dudley Betty a slave Dit^o born June 24th 1753.
*   dia Daughter of Beck a slave Dit^o born June 13th 1753.
*   emmy a slave belonging to Mary Clark born April 3d 1753.
Ben a Slave belonging to Eliz^a Blake born Novr 30th 1753.
Sarah Daughter of Mary a Slave belonging to the Est^e of George
Wortham dec'd born Octr 10th 1753.
Harry a slave belonging to Christopher Robinson born Febry 24th
1753.
Sarah a slave Dit^o born June 2d 1753.
Beck the Daughter of Nanna a slave belonging to James Reid born
Novr 1st 1753.
   ccas Son of Sarah a Slave belonging to Lewis Mt'gue born
July 19th 1753.
*   Rey Daughter of Nancey a Slave belong^s to Thos Mt'gue born
June 8th 1753.
Bess a slave belonging to Christ^r Robinson born June 24th 1753.
   a Slave Dit^o born July 22nd 1753.
   a Slave belonging to George Lee, born April 25th 1753.
*   ert Son of Dinah a slave belonging to Ann Wortham jun^r born
Dec 11th 1753.
*   binah Daughter of Phillis a slave belonging to John * *
   *   *   of a Mulato Wench belonging to J.

Slave belonging Dit° born Oct' 7th.

a slave Dit° born Dec' 2nd.

* * ice a Slave belonging to John Smith jun' born June 15th.

Phillis a slave belonging to Ralph Wormeley born April 16th.

Abram a Male Slave belonging to D° born Sep' 10th.

Sam Do belonging to Dit° born Nov' 1st.

William Dit° born Janry 22rd.

Catherine a Female Dit° born May 24th.

Mille Dit° born July 24th.

Cate Dit° born Dit° 26th.

Beller Daughter of Jilson a Slave belong$ to Rich⁴ Corbin born April 1st.

Aaron Son of Nona slave Dit° born July 12th.

Felicia Daughter of Judy a slave belonging to Henry Thacker born Aug' 2nd.

Nan a Slave belonging to William Hackney born Oc'' 12th.

Adam a Slave belonging to George Wortham born June 28th.

Jane Daughter of Beck a slave belong$ to —— Daniel born March 18th.

Judy Daughter of Hannah a Slave belonging to George Lee born June 16th.

James Son of Chaney a Slave belong$ to Mary Jones born Dec' 1st.

Sarah Daughter of Beck a Slave belonging to John Lewis born Aug' 23d.

Davie Son of Moll a slave belong$ to Alex' Frazier born Sep' 16th.

Will son of Rose a Slave belonging to John Smith Jun' born Oct' 7th.

Simon son of Janna a slave belonging to W'' Buford, born Dec' 1st.

Dolly Daughter   a slave belonging to Edw⁴ Clark born June 26th.

Ann Daughter of Unity a slave belonging to Edw⁴ Dillard born March 16th.

Daphne Daughter of Nanna a Slave belonging to John Jones, born Febry 10th.

Peter Son of Frank a Slave belonging to Samuel Wood, born Janry 19th.

Jack Son of —— a slave belonging James Machan born Febry 16th.

Davy & Frank Son & Daught' of Frank a slave belong$ to Eusebius Lewis born Dec' 23 17 .

Sampson Son of Isbell a slave belonging to Rich⁴ Corbin born Janry 19th 17 .

Dick Son of Grace a slave Dit°   born D° 23d 17 .

Judy Daughter of Letty a Slave belong$ to Tho$ Sanders, born June 20th 17 .

Charles Son of —— a slave belonging to Churchhill Jones, born Dec' 24th 17 .

Ambrus Son of —— a slave Dit°   born Janry 2d 17 .

Jane Daught' of Daphne a Slave belong$ to the Estate of Rich⁴ Sheet decd born Janry 9th 17 .

Susanna Daughter of Mary a slave belonging to Tho$ Clark born Janry 23d 17 .

Dey the Daughter of Rose a Slave belonging to John Rhodes Sen' born Nov' 6th 17 .

Isaac Son of Dinah a slave belonging to Ann Smith born Febry 4 17 .

Frank son of —— a slave belong⁵ to George Wortham born March
5th 17 .

Winne Son of —— a Slave belonging to John Boss born April 10th.

Nanny Daughter of ——a slave belonging to Armistead Churchhill
born Jan^ry 24th 17 .

Joe Son of Cate a Slave belon⁵ to Matthias Gale born March 7th.

—— slave belon⁵ Dit° born Do 19th.

—— —— Ralph Wormeley born May 24th.
Do.

—— Son of —— a slave belong. to Armistead Churchhill born July.

—— Son of Moll a Slave belong. to George Wortham born Sep^t
14th.

—— Daughter of Maud a slave belong to John Smith dec'd born May
20th 1748.

—— Son of Rose a slave belong to Thomas Chilton born July 4th
1748.

—— Daughter of Phillis a slave belonging to Wm Hackney jun^r born
Apr^l 3d 1748.

—— Daughter of Hannah a Slave belong to George Lee born Oct^r
17th 1748.

—— D. of a slave belong to John Berry born April 19th 1748.

—llir Daughter of —— a Slave belong to Dit° born July 1st 1748.

—lle Daug^t of Nann a slave belong to Charles Daniel born April
21st 1748.

—llick Son of Kate a slave belong to Dit° born May 12th 1748.

—— Son of—— a Slave belonging to William Meacham born Janry
30th 1748.

—ll Son of Phillis a Slave belonging to John Wortham born Nov^r
3d 1748.

—ry Son of Moll a Slave belong to Alex^r Frazier born March 18th
174⁸⁄₉.

—ris Son of —— a Slave belonging to Armistead Churchhill born
Sep^t 25th.

—ry Daught^r of Ruth a Slave belonging to Margaret Johnson born
June 29th 1748.

—— Son of —— Margery a Slave belonging to Nicholas Dillard
born April 22nd 1748.

—— Daught^r of —— a slave belonging to Edwd Blackburn, born
April 24th 1748.

—ck Son of Dick & Judy a slave belonging to Mary Roane born
April 26th 1748.

—— Son of Jonay a slave belon⁵ to Thomas Buford Sen^r₁born Feb^ry
16th 1748.

—— son of Margery a slave belong to Nicholas Dillard born April
9th 1748.

—my Daugh^r of —— a slave belong to Mary Clark born March 7th
174⁸⁄₉.

—ewman Son of Frank a Slave belong to George Chowning born
March 25th 1748.

—ter Daught^r of Oder a Slave belong to Frances Bryant born April
10th 1748.

—— Daught^r of Moll a Slave belong to Mary Roane born Augt 20th
1748.

Peter Son of Ann a Slave belong to James Scrosby born Augt 28th 1748.

Billy By a Malato Wench Named Letty born Sep^t 16th belong to D° 1748.

—loa the Daughter of Prudence a Slave belonging to Frances Bryant born Janry 30th 174⅞.

Dick son of Sue a Slave belong to John Wilcox born March 12th 174⅞.

—ane Daughter of Ann a Slave belonging to Mary Jackson born Janry 31st 174⅞.

Harry son of Chloe a slave belonging to John Wilcox born March 28th 174⅞.

Moses Son of Penelope a slave belong^g to Beverley Stanard born Febry 10th 174⅞

Penelopy Daughter of Phillis a Slave belong to Dit° born March 26th 1749.

Kate Daughter of Lucy a slave belonging to D° born March 26th 1749.

Ben son of —— a slave belonging to Churchhill Jones born April 16th 1749.

—— Daughter of Lucy a slave belonging to Humphrey Jones born June 24th 1749.

Nell Daughter of Lucia a Slave belonging to Henry Mickelburrough born Sep^t 18th 1749.

Beck Daughter of a slave belon^g to Nicholas Dillard born Octr 15th 1749.

Peter son of Betty a slave belonging to John Smith jun^r born Octr 30th 1749.

Anna Daught^r of Judy a slave belonging to Henry Thacker born Decr 28th 1749.

—— Daught^r of Sue a Slave belonging to Alex^r Frazier born

—— Daughter of Nelley a Slave belonging to

—— Slave belonging to W^m

—— —gh^r of Phillis a slave bel:g to Judith Wortham born Apri

Harry Son of Moll a slave bel:g to Lewis Mountague born Jun

James Son of Jenny a slave belonging Henry Thacker born May 29th 17 .

Will Son of Nanne a slave belong^g to Sarah Jones born June 25th 17

George Son of Lucy a slave bel:g to John Seward born Octr 5th 17 .

Kate Daught^r of Jane a slave bel:g to George Fearn born Decr 25 17 .

Christopher Junkins, Son of Lena slave bel:g to Henry Thacker born January 28th 17 .

Brimer Daugh^r of —— a slave bel:g to Jam^s Brown born March 1st 1760.

Frank Daughter of Lucy a slave bel:g to James Reid born March 7th 1760.

Rachel Daught^r of Sarah a slave bel:g to Lewis Mountague born March 18 1760.

William Son of Nanny a slave bel:g to James Reid born April 23d 1760.

Cilla Daug^r of Jenny, a slave belong^g to Edm^d Berkeley born March 1760.

Peg, Daugh[r] of Kate a Slave blong to Dit° born April 1760.

Unity, Daughter of Moll Carter bel:g to W[m] Meacham born Aug[t] 28th 1760.

Will, Son of Jane, a slave bel:g to Penelope Mountague born July 7th 1760.

George, Son of Hannah a slave bel:g to Philip Mountague born Nov[r] 11 1760.

Jack a slave belonging to the Est[e] of George Wortham dec'd born Sep[t] 15. 1760.

Kitt son of —— a slave bel:g to Nicholas Dillard born April 15th 176 .

Toney Son of —— a slave bel:[g] to Anne Jones born Janry 3d 17

Lede Daught[r] of Render a slave belong:[g] to Tho[s] Sanders born Janry 24th 17

Lucy Daug[r] of Nanny a slave —— born April 17th 17

Lewis, son of Jane, a slave bel:[g] to George Fearn born July 7th 17.

Tom son of —— a slave belonging to John Seward born Nov[r] 5th 1760.

James Son of —— a slave belong:[g] to John Humphris born Dec[r] 20th 1760.

Births of Negro Children.

Lewis Son of —— a slave belonging to Ralph Wormeley born April 24th.

David son of —— a slave belonging to Dit° born Sept[r] 17th.

Izbel Daught[r] of —— Dit° belonging to Dit° born Oct[r] 22nd.

Laurence son of —— Dit° belonging to Dit° born Janry 18th.

Betty Daughter of —— Dito belonging to Dit° born Febry 23d.

Jenny Daughter of —— Dit° belonging to Dit° born March 7th.

Mason son of —— Dit° belonging to Dit° born Febry 14.

Nicholas son of —— Dit° belonging to Dit° born Dit° 19. 17 .

Minne Son of —— Dito belonging to Dit° born March 7.

Dick Son of Rose belonging to Edmund Berkley born July 17.

Abram son of —— Dit° belonging to Dit° born May.

Penny Daught[r] of —— Dit° belonging to Dit° born July 5.

Joshua son of —— a slave belonging to George Wortham born Nov[r] 12th.

Stephen Son of —— a slave belonging to Massey Yarrington born Sept[r] 30th 1751.

Nell Daughter of Beck a slave belonging to Edmond Berkeley born June 1751.

Johnny son of Ebo Frank Dit° belonging to Dit° born Oct[r], Thomas son of Mariah Dit° belonging to Dit° born Nov[r] 30 1751.

Sarah Daught[r] of —— a Dit° belonging to Nicholas Dillard, born Aug[t] 1751.

A Negro child a slave belonging to Thomas Boothe born Aug[t] 13th 1751.

Judy Daughter of Hannah a slave belon[g] to Frances Meacham Daniel born Nov. 20. 1751.

George son of —— a slave belonging to Churchhill Jones born Aug[t] 2nd 1751.

Judy Daughter of —— a slave belonging to Dit° born Dec[r] 19th 1751.

Dinah Daught^r of —— Dit° belonging to Dit° born Octr 3rd 17

Hary Son of Hannah Dit° belonging to Thomas Mountague born March 14th

Daniel son of —— Dit° belonging to Mary Jackson born Febry 8th

Moll Daughter of —— Dit° belonging to John Gardner born March 8th.

Jemmy son of —— a slave belonging to Churchhill Jones born March

James son of Great Nan a slave belonging to Lewis Mountague born Januy 11th 175 .

Lucy Daught^r of Jenny a slave belonging to Thomas Buford born March 22 1755.

Jack son of Jane a slave belonging to Thomas Mountague born April 27th 7

William Smith son of Lena a slave belon:^g to Henry Thacker born Mar 14th.

Sarah Daugh^r of Frank, a slave belonging to Henry Daniel born Feb^y.

George son of —— a slave belong:^g to Gales Est^e born March 17th 1756.

Phill son of —— a slave bel:^g to Wm Meacham born April 12th 1756.

Moll Daugh^r of —— a slave bel:^g to Wm Roane born May 26th 1756.

Easter Daugh^t of a slave bel:^g to Dit° born June 26th 1756.

—— Daught^r of —— a slave bel:^g to the Est^e of Geo. Wortham dec'd born Ap^l 1756.

—— a slave bel^g to Gales Est^e Born.

—— Daugh^r of a Slave belong^g to Wm Jone.

—bin Son of —— a slave belong^g to Nicho^s Dillard born May 5 1756.

—bin Son of —— a slave belong^g to the Estate of John Alldin dec'd born July 15 1756.

Fill Son of —— a Slave belonging to Edwd Ware born Sep^t 6th 1756.

Sally Daug^r of Letty a slave belong^g to Thos Saunders born Novr 20th 1756.

—nny Daug^r of Phebe a slave belong^g to John Bryant born Decr 26th 1756.

Cloe Daughter of —— a slave belong^g to Mary Clark Ma^{ch} 25th 1757.

Easter Daugh^r of Hannah a slave bel^g to Philip Mountague born Ap^l 11th 1757.

—h Daugh^r of Moll a Slave bel^g to Lewis Mountague born May 7th. 1757.

—ler Daughter of Jane a Slave bel^g to Geo. Fearn born June 5th 1757.

Sally Daugh^r of Hannah a Slave bel^g to James Daniel, born Aug 20th 1757.

Cate Daugh^r of Juday a slave bel^g to Dit° born Augt 26th 1757.

Ben Son of Lucy a slave belong^g to Martha Orril born Sep^t 2rd 1757.

Jane Daugh^r of Jane a Slave bel^g to Penelope Mountague born Octr 15th 1757.

Bristow Son of Nanny a slave bel^g to Philip Mountague born Octr 19th 1757.

Sue Daug^r of Jane a slave bel^g to John Meacham born Octr 20th 1757.

Harry Son of Nanny a slave bel^g to James Reid born Octr 26th 1757.

Antony Son of Jenny a slave bel^g to Henry Thacker born Novr 6th 1757.

—— Son of Sue, a slave belong^g to Alex^r Frazier born Novr 23rd 1757.

—y Daug^r of a Slave belong^g to Dit^o born Novr 24th 1757.

—— Son of Lucy a slave bel^g to James Reid born January 10th 1758.

—z Son of Lena a Slave bel^g to Henry Thacker, born Janry 18th 1758.

Newman, Son of Odour, a slave bel^g to John Yarrington born Jany 6. 1758.

Moses, Son of Hannah a Slave bel^g to Nicholas Dillard born Feby 1st 1758.

Hope, Daug^r of Kate a slave bel^g to Gale's Est^e born Febry 27th 1758.

—ses son of —— a slave bel^g to the Est^e of George Wortham dec'd born May 19. 1758.

—te Daug^r of —— a slave belonging to Dit^o born May 27th 1758.

Milly, Daug^r of —— a slave bel^g to James Brown born July 6th 1758.

Nelson, Son of a slave bel^g to Willm Roane born July 12th, 1758.

Mansor, and James Son of Alice a Slave bel^g to Wm Chowning born Augt 27. 1758.

Betty, Daug^r of —— a slave bel^g to the Est^e of Gale born Sep^t 23d 1758.

Joanna Daughter of Nanny a Slave bel^g to Henry Thacker born Novr 20th 1758.

—— a slave belong^g to Henry Thacker born.

—— slave belonging to Betty

———

—— born Sep^t 7th Bapt^d 27th Do.

—— Daughter of —— & —— South born Janry 16th.

—— Son of John & Ann Meacham, was born Febry 5th.

Lucy Daughter of Robert & Lucy Daniel born Decr 4th Bapt^d 26th Do.

Lucy Daughter of John & Mary Bowles born April 4.

William Son of John & Agathy Hardee born Novr 19th & Bapt^d Janry 10.

James Son of James & Jane Dunlevy born June 6th Bapt^d 7th Do.

James Son of John & Tabitha Fox born Octr 21st.

Ann Daughter of William & Hannah Pace born Novr 18th Bapt^d Decr 20th.

George son of Smith & Rachel South born Jan 11th & Bap^d Jan. 31st.

Judith Daughter of John & Christian Boss Febry 7.

Mary Daughter of Jacob & Ann Acree born June 9th.

Richard Son of Eusaleus & Martha Lewis born Novr 1st.

George Son of John & Martha Hudson born Janry 10th.

Frances Williams Daughter of John & Susanna Williams born Janry 31st.

Elizabeth Daughter of W^m & Rachel Brooks born June 17th.

Jane Daughter of James & Frances Smith born Sep^t 12th & Bapt^d Octr 18th.

Vivion Son of Henry & Susanna Mickelburrough born Novr 6th.

Thomas Son of James & Cassandra Machan born Febry 14th & Bapt^d March 3d.

Richard Son of Charles & Ruth Moulson born Octr 9th & Bapt^d Novr 8th.

Thomas the Son of Thomas & Ann Waid born Octr 26th.

Peter Son of W^m & Jane Mountague born May 13th.

Mary Daughter of William & Mary Blackburn born July 23d & Bapt^d Augt 9th.

Hannah Daughter of Jacob & Barshebe Rice born Febry 9th.

George Son of Charles & Penelopa Lee born May 17th.

Henry Son of Henry & Betty Daniel born June 6th.

Jane Daughter of George & Mary Fearn born July 5th & Bapt^d 17th.

William Son of Edward & Mary Southern born Augt 5th.

James Son of Richard & Phebe Jones was born Sepr 14th.

William Son of Edward & Ann Blackburne born Octr 18 & Bapt^d 23d Do.

Josiah Son of James & Averiler Cole born May 5th.

John Son of Jacob & Sarah Vallentine born July 11th.

Churchhill Son of W^m & Sarah Jones born Decr 30th.

Mary Daughter of John & Judith Faulkner born Novr 23d.

Christopher Son of W^m & Sarah Morgain born May 18th.

Ann Daughter of John & Eliz^a Lewis born Augt 3d Bapt^d 28 Do. 17 .

Lucy Daughter of John & Jane Chowning born Sep^t 1st 17 .

Elizabeth Daughter of John & Mary Rhodes born March 14 17 .

—— Son of Robert & Mary Bonds born April 4th & Bapt^d 11th Do. 17 .

—hn Son of John & Martha Brooks born Augt 28th 17 .

—hn & James Sons of Humphrey & Amy Garret born Augt 23d 17.

—ge Sons of Charles & Penelopy Lee born Augt 19th Bap^t 17 .

—— —— —— Tugle born Augt 25th.

—les Wood & Margaret Elegitimate son & Daughter of C.

—hanne Daughter of Charles & Mary Medeiras born May 26th & Bap^t June.

—lliam son of John & Anne Wormeley born June 26th.

—ah Daughter of Armistead & Hannah Churchhill born Sepr 4th Bapt^d 11. Do. 1748.

—mes son of John & Mary Bream born Octr 18th & Bapt^d Novr 20th 1748.

—lliam son of William & Elizabeth Healy born July 29th 1748.

Agatha Daughter of Rich^d & Ann Daniel born March 29th 1748.

—ess son of John & Constant Urie born July 8th 1748.

—— Daughter of W^m & Mary Williamson born Sep^t 7th Bapt^d 18th Do. 1748.

Mary Daughter of John & Catharine Smith born Sep^t 2nd 1748.

Elizabeth Daughter of John & Frances Taylor born Sep^t 17th 1748.

Churchhill son of Churchhill & Millicent Jones born Sep^t 27th 1748.

Mary Daughter of John & Mary Bowles born Sep^t 21st Bapt^d Octr 9th 1748.

—— son of Charles & Ann Roan born Novr 14th Bapt^d Decr 11th 1748.

John son of George & Mary Bristow born Novr 7th 1748.
—uel son of Samuel & Ann Wood born Novr 2nd & Bapt^d 20th Do. 1748.
—abeth Daughter of W^m & Ann Summers born Decr 6th 1748.
—— Daughter of Edwd & Eliz^a Bristow born Decr 8th 1748.
—— Daughter of William & Mary Greenwood born April —th Bapt^d 24 Do. 1748.
—— Daughter of W^m & Mary Mullins born April 4th Bapt^d 24 Do. 1748.
John son of George & Mary Blake born March 30th 1748.
Benjamin son of John & Susanna Seward born May 29th Bapt^d June 26th 1748.
—— Daughter of Robert & Mary Gibson born June 14th 1748.
Thomas son of John & Mary Norman born March 4th 1748.
—— Daughter of John & Jane Beaman born Decr 17th 1748. Bapt^d Janry 22. 174 8/9.
—— son of George & Jane Blakey born Janry 18th Bapt^d Feb^ry 12th 174 8/9.
George son of Robert & Ann Trueman born Febry 17 174 8/9.
—atha Daughter of Henry & Tabatha Shepherd born — th 174 8/9.
Mildred Daughter of John & Jane Hutton born Janry 13th 174 8/9.
Mary Daughter of Lewis & Betty Mountague born Febry 24th 1748 Bapt^d Mar^h 26th 1749.
—— son of John & Frances Robinson born April 11 1749.
—— Daughter of John & Agatha Hardee born April 9th 1749.
Martha Daughter of John & Martha Steward born March 24th 1749.
Elizabeth Daughter of James & Dorrithy Davis born April 2nd 1749.
Doroth Daughter of George & Mary Lee born March 31st 1749.
John son of John & Betty Cornelius born Janry 10th Bapt^d Febry 12th 174 8/9.
Ransom son of Robert & Eliz^a Durram born Janry 18th 1750.
—anna Daughter of John & Susanna Sords born May 20th 1750.
—jamin son of Thomas & Sarah Tugle born June 11th
—rah Daughter of Henry & Susanna Mickelburrough born May 22nd
—atherine Daughter of Samuel & Eliz^a Batchelder born April 29th
Mary Daughter of Joseph & Elen Beard born Sep^t 23d
William son of William & Eliz^a Dean born April 15th
—bert son of John & Frances Robinson born Augt 29th
—alph son of Harry & Mary Anderson born April 15th
—— —— —— Henry Gardner born Augt 11th 17 .
—— ——ghter of John & Mary Gardner born Augt 17th 17 .
——ions Son of Cornelius & Sarah Deforces born Sepr 27th 17 .
Judith Daughter of William & Eliz^a Haley born May 18th 17 .
William Son of John & Elizabeth Lewis born July 31st & Bapt^d Septr 2nd 1750.
Richard Son of Rich: & Ann Daniel, born April 16th. 1750.
Ignatious & Ann Son & Daugh^r of Robert & Ann Turman born Decr 4th. 1750.
William Son of William & Elizabeth Owen, born Febry 10th 175 .
Robert Son of Robert & Elizabeth Elliot, born July 14th 175 .
Thomas Son of Jacob & Ann Acree, born June 5th 175 .
Anne Daughter of George & Jane Blackley, born June 2d 175 .
Ann Daughter of Parrott & Eliz^a Prindle born June 25th 175 .

Ann Daughter of Tobias & Margaret Allen, born April 2nd 175 .
George Son of George & Mary Bristow, born March 27th.
Thomas Son of William & Mary Bristow born March 27.
Charles Son of Edward & Eliz^a Bristow born April 27.
Persilah Daughter of Edward & Eliz^a Whittecar born Augt 16th 1 .
Josiah Son of John & Agatha Hardee born, June 19th 1751.
Mary Daughter of Samuel & Ann Wood born, Dit° 19 175 .
William Son of Daniel & Hannah Stringer born Sep^t 20th 175 .
Mary Daughter of James & Dorothy Davis, born Octr 18 175 .
John Son of John & Jane Chowning born Oct^or 4th 17 . ·
William Son of Henry & Tabitha Shepherd born Novr 24th 175 .
Elizabeth Daughter of Ambrus & Kezia Dudley, born Decr 27th 175.

Births of Negroes.

Dinah Daughter of Peg a Slave belonging to the Est^e of Charles
Gunter decd, born Febry 7th 1754.
Esther Daught^r of Cate a slave belonging to Edmon Berkeley, born
Febry. 1754.
Johnny Son of Jenney a slave belonging to Dit° born January 175 .
Edward Skinner Son of Nanny a Slave belonging to Henry Thacker,
born June 26th 175 .
Phil Son of —— a slave belong.g to Churchhill Jone, born June 27th
175 .
Phillis Daughter of —— a slave belong.g to Dit° born July 2nd 175.
Cate Daughter of —— a slave belon—g to Wm Meacham born Febry
21st 17 .
Rose Daughter of —— a slave belon.g to William Jones decd, born
May 4th –7 .
Charlot Daughter of Jenny a Slave belonging to Henry Thacker,
born Febry 7th 175 .
—— Johnson son of Hagar a slave belonging to Jacob Stiff born
March 18th 175 .
—— Daught^r of —— a slave belonging to Martha Orriell born April
8th 1754.
—— Daught^r of —— a slave belonging to Christ^r Robinson born
April 15th 175 .
—m Son of Hannah a Slave belonging to Nicholas Dillard born
May 5th –75 .
—n Son of —— a slave belonging to William Bristow born June
4th –7 .
Mary Clark born Decr 26th.
—upe Son of —— a Slave belonging to Gale's Estate born Sep.
—ster Daught^r of Jeany a slave belonging to Alex^r Frazier born Dec^r.
Joyce Daughter of Ebo Frank a slave belonging to Edmon Berkeley
born Dec.
Hannah Daught^r of Tamer a slave belon:g to John Rhodes born
Sep^t 5th 1754.
Betty Daught^r of Nanny a Slave belonging to James Reid born Dec^r
27th 1754.
Betty Daughter of Sue a Slave belonging to John Meacham born
Sep^t 9th 1754.
Sam Son of Moll a Slave belonging to Lewis Mountague born Oct^r
1. 1754.

Ailce Daught^r of —— a slave belonging to the Est^e of George Wortham Decd born Novr 21st 1754.

Nann Daught^r of —— a slave belonging to Christ^r Robinson born June 14th 17 .

Grace Daught^r of —— a slave belonging to Dit° born Novr 28. 175 .

Penny Daughter of —— belonging to Henry Mickelborough born Apr^l 10th 175 .

James Son of Prudence a Slave belonging to Frances Bryant born March 14th 1755.

Wall Son of Daphne a Slave belonging to Thomas Mountague, born Febry 6th 1755.

Peg Daught^r of —— a slave belonging to Christ^r Robinson, born Janry 11th 1755.

Will Son of —— a slave belonging to Dit° born February 21st 1755.

Ned & Tom Sons of —— belonging to Dit° born Dit° 27th 1755.

Booker Son of Frank a slave belonging to John Wortham born Janry 4th 1755.

Meney Son of —— a slave belonging to Thomas Sanders born Janry 15th 1755.

Nathaniel Wilson, Son of Phillis, a slave belonging to John Wortham born July 27th 1755.

Tom Son —— belonging to John Berry born Feby 4th 1755.

John Son of a Slave belonging to Frances Orril, born May 12th 1755.

Peter, Son of Jane a slave belonging to Thos Mountague born May 17th 1755.

Margery, Daugh^r of a Slave belonging to Nicholas Dillard born May 25th 1755.

Henry, Son of Lena a Slave belonging to Henry Thacker born June 10th 1755.

Peter Son of a slave belonging to Joseph Batchelder born July 9th 1755.

Sam, Son of Bess belonging to Wm Jones's orphans born July 25th 1755.

Criss Daughter of Nann a slave belonging to Sarah Jones born June 20th 1755.

Lettey Daughter of Phebe a slave belonging to John Bryan born Sepr 7th 1755.

Daphney, Daug^r of Frank a slave belonging to Richd Taylor born Octr 3. 1755.

William & Harry sons of Moll a slave belonging to Jane Whan, born Octr 20th 175 .

Robert, Son of Kate a slave belonging to Charles Lee born Octr 18th 17 .

Dilce Daug^r of Betty a slave belonging to Beverley Stanard born Novr 23d 175 .

Thomas Son of Jenny a slave belonging to Henry Thacker born Decr 8th.

Frances, Daughter of Nanny a slave a slave belonging to Dit° born Dec.

Isan Daughter of Lucy a a slave belong^g to Dit° born Aug^t

Elizabeth, Daughter of a slave belonging to James Green born Decr 14th.

* ank Daughter of a slave belonging to the Estate of George Wortham dec'd born Decr 17th.

Beck Daugh^r of Rose a slave belong^g to John Rhodes born

* amuel, son of a slave belg to Chr^r Robinson born Janry 16th

* A Female Negro * *

From another book.

Registry of Marriages Commencing May 19th 1795.

Henry Hefferman Rector.

Leonard George & Margaret Vance married by Licence August 6th 1795.

James Kidd & Caty Meckelborough married by License August 15 1795.

Richard Cooke & Eliza Blueford married by Licence September 6th 1795.

Vincint Yarrington & Elizabeth B. Stiffe married by Licence November 5th 1795.

Meacham Wortham & Joana Wake married by Licence November 14th 1795.

George Shepherd & Unice Tuning married by Licence November 21st 1795.

Francis Corbin & Ann Munford Beverley of Essex C° married by Licence at Blandfield December 3rd 1795.

The above List made off & sent to the Clerk of the County.

Marriages commencing January 1st 1796.

William Nelson Stiffe & Sarah Healy married by Licence Thursday January 28th 1796.

Peter Robinson & Nancy Stiffe Thursday Feb: 18th 1796.

Tom Stiffe & Elizabeth Davis Saturday Feb. 20th 1796.

John Layton Junr & Lucy Wilkins Novr 17th 1796.

Paulin Anderson Blackburn & Sally Hodges Jan: 10th 1797.

John Seward & Mary Shepherd February 2nd 1797.

Richard Henry Corbin & Betty Tayloe Corbin Feb: 10th 1797.

John Trigg & Susanna Collier of Gloucester March 30th 1797.

William Layton & Mary Atkins April 1st 1797.

Thomas Healy & Frances Montague May 6th 1797.

Charles Brown & Catharine Hackney July 8th 1797.

Archibald Richie & Patsey Hepkins Roane July 25th 1797.

John Quarles & Elizabeth S. Yates October 12th 1797.

Stapleton Davis & Alice Blake Novr 23rd 1797.

Zachariah Collins & Ann Burton Decr 1st 1797.

Henry Heffernan Rector.

The above List was given to the Clerk of the County.

Matthew Glen & Elizabeth Garland Decr 26th 1797.

James Owen & Winny Bennett January 27th 1798.

Augustine Blake & Peggy Marshall June 23rd 1798.

Robert Long & Johanna Blake July 5th 1798.

Samuel Blake & Sarah Wood Sep^t 20th 1798.

James Wiatt & Fanny Curtis October 10th 1798.

Robert U. Blake & Letetia Baldry November 20th 1798.
John Murray & Lucy Sutton December 25th 1798.
John Blake Long & Sarah Blake Decr 30th 1798.

Henry Heffernan Rector.

The above List was given to the Clerk of the County.
Thomas Cooke & Rachel Murray Beverley Yeates married Jan: 15th
    1799.
John Tayloe Corbin & Juliet Muse married January 31st 1799.
John Spencer & Molly Cooke of King & Queen February 7th
William Robinson & Frances Healy February 28th.
John Waller & Nancy Sears of Gloucester March 7th 1799.
Eli Taylor & Elizabeth Dudley May 4th 1799.
Samuel Montague & Elizabeth Stannard Montague July 11th 1799.
Thomas Sears & Catey Collier August 1st 1799.
—— —— Harriet Murray September 16th 1799.
—— —— Wiatt Novr 14th 1799.
John B. Stiffe & Lucy Siblee January 3rd 1801.
Thomas Kidd & Anne Blakey February 5th 1801.
Samuel Stamper & Sally Kidd April 4th 1801.
Robert Barrick & Lucinda L. Jackson April 23rd 1801.
Matthew Kemp & Lucy Daniel May 21st 1801.
Thomas L. Churchill & Elizabeth B. Berkeley May 28th
Berrin Abbot & Nancy Dejarnett June 18th 1801.
Thomas R. Corr & Mary Anne Bland August 27th 1801.
William C. Humphrees & Sarah McGeehee Sep^t 15th 1801.
Edward McGehee & Caroline C. Jones Decr 7th 1801.
Benjamin Marable Junr & Mary Lyell Decr 10th 1801.
Staige Humphries & Diana Barrick December 12th 1801.
Thomas T. Montague & Elizabeth Montague Decr 19th 1801.
Meacham Wortham & Lucy Bristow January 6th 1802.
William C. Blakey & Jane Healy January 28th 1802.
John Major & Mary Murray February 6th 1802.
William Curtis & Ariana Maria Grymes February 6th 1802.
Charles Robinson & Elizabeth Wood February 18th 1802.
Henry Blakey & Frances O. George August 29th 1802.
Isaac Reveer & Sarah Barrick Dec^l 30th 1802.
John Siblee & Ann Barrick Novr 4th 1802.

The above List made out & given to the Clerk.

Nelson Stamper & Elizabeth Meacham Jan: 13th 1803.
Ransone Wake & Mary Elliot February 10th 1803.
Henry Gaines & Mira Muse March 10th 1803.
Edmund Read & Lucy Cloudas June 30th 1803.
William St. John & Nancy Harwood Sepr 1st 1803.
James Hopkins & Susanna Davis Novr 10th 1803.
John Robinson & Susanna Blake Jan. 1 1804.
Charles Gibson & Nancy Mickleborough   13th 1804.
Tayloe Braxton & Anna Frances Maria Corbin Mar: 6th 1804.
John George & Jane Meacham March 29th 1804.
William George & Patty Jacobs married April 12th.
Philip Grymes & Sarah R. Steptoe May 20th.
George Layton & Catharine Adkinson May 20th 1807.
Beverley A. Blake & Nancy Reed July 15th 1807.

John Battaile & Mary Willis Dangerfield Novr 18. 1807.
John Darby & Lucy B. Churchill Decr 15. 1807.
James Baytop & Catharine K. Yates Decr 31. 1807.
Matthew Major & Elizabeth Blakey Jany 30. 1808.
John Bristow & Mary Watson Jan. 31. 1808.
    The above List sent to the Clerk Middlesex.
Robert Blakey & Frances D. Roane Octr 12. 1808.
Thomas Street & Nancy Owen Decr 14. 1809.
George Henly & Harriet Roane Decr 21st 1809.
Thomas Evans & Sarah S. Montague Jan 22. 1810.
James Chowning & Maria Sutton June 7th 1810.
Isaac Kidd & Lucy Lee Sepr 3rd 1811.
George D. Nicolson & S. T. Wormeley Decr 4. 1811.
Richd M. Segar & P. Roane January 16. 1812.
John Bristow & Nancy Walden Feb. 1st 1812.
Isaac Jones & Betsey Owen June 5th 1811.
Southey Derby & Agnes Powell married July 7.
Jeremiah Spencer & Mary Blackburn married July 15th 1769.
Thomas Roberts & Mildred Goslin married August 20th 1769.
Daniel Jefferson & Mary Dunlavy married October 19th 1769.
Thomas Layton & Elizabeth Rhodes married October 27th 1769.
John South & Sarah Sears married November 2d 1769.
Churchhill Jones & Judith Churchhill married November 11th 1769.
George Blake & Judith Healy married December 23d 1769.
William Matthews & Lucy Hudgings married Decr 24th 1769.
John Hibble & Anne Robinson married December 24th 1769.
    Marriages for the Year of our Lord 1770.
John Clare & Susanna Davis married January 14th 1770.
Hugh Walker & Catherine Morgan married January 20th 1770.
Philip Sears & Frances Bryan married January 23d 1770.
William Jeffries & Esther Lee married February 10th 1770.
Daniel Turner & Catharine Montague married February 17th 1770.
        Samuel Klug, Minister.

David Ker of King & Queen County & Frances Tucker married
    August 8th 1771.
Lewis Boss & Anne Deagle married August 14th 1771.
John Mactyer & Susanna Clark married Octr 16th 1771.
Anderson Miller & Dorothy Berry married Octr 17. 1771.
Asher Bray & Sally Tuggle married Novr 3d 1771.
James Dunlevy & Anne Belfore married Novr 30th 1771.
Benjamin Seward & Anne Blake married Decr 12th 1771.
John Sanders & Anne Clare married Decr 14th 1771.
Isaac Stephens & Elizabeth Wroe married Decr 17 1771.
Robert McTyer & Fanny Lee married Decr 24 1771.
William Patterson & Elizabeth Southern married Decr 28 1771.
John Bagot & Mary Wortham married January 8th. 1772.
Moses Matthews & Alice Hiptinstall married Jany 9th 1772.
John Richeson & Mary George married March 29th 1772.
Robert Longest & Betty Dudley married July 5th 1772.
John Daniel & Clara Williamson married August 2d 1772.
        Samuel Klug, Minister.

Births & Christenings for the Year of our Lord. 1770.

Felicia Daughter of Gawin Corbin & Johanna his Wife was born February 1st 1770 & baptized Feby 11th.

Len Son of Richard & Mary Bristow was born January 18th 1770. & baptized Feby 13th.

William Nelson Son of William & Sarah Stiff was born Jan 30th 1770. & baptized Feby 28th.

Sally Willcocks Daughter of Mary Willcocks was * January 1st 1770 & baptized March 18th.

Bartholomew Son of Bartholomew & Anne Yates * January 17th 1770 & baptized March 25th.

William Blake, the Son of Jacob & Susanna Blake was born September 2d. 1770.

William Robinson Son of Charles & Anne Robinson was born June 10th 1770.

Edward Jones Bristow Son of Benj^m & Elizabeth Bristow was born June 16th 1770.

William Son of John & Margaret Callaham was born January 1st 1770.

Polly, Daughter of Daniel & Mary Jefferson was born Novr 7th 1770.

Dorothy Daughter of Joseph & Ann Parrott was born February 25th 1770.

Johnny Son of Jenney a Slave belonging to Harry Beverley born Feb'y 1.

Hannah daughter of Kate a slave belonging to Henry Tugell born March 2.

Lucy daughter of Frank a slave belonging to Matthew Kemp born March ye 30.

Hannah daughter of Dye a Slave belonging to John Mosely born Ap: ye 6.

Dinah daughter of Alice a slave belonging to Robt Daniel sen^r born May 17.

James Son of Sarah a Slave belonging to ye estate of Tho: Warwick born Sept. 21.

Frank daughter of Jenney a slave belonging to Hobbs Weeks born Feb^ry ye 17.

Jefferey Son of Jenney a slave belonging to Humphery Jones born May 12 17 .

Betty daughter of Poll a Slave belonging to Garritt Minor born June 20 17 .

Ben Son of Phillis a slave belonging to William Segar born June 28 17 .

Peter Son of Moll a slave belonging to Roger Jones born July ye 7th 17 .

Billy Son of Sarah a Slave belonging to John Smith jun^r born July 25 17 .

Phillip Son of Mary a slave belonging to Edm^d Bartlett baptized July 13. & about 1 year old.

Frank daughter of Jane a slave belonging to Frances Ransom born July 12.

Letty daughter of Judy a Slave belonging to John Aldin born July 20.

Frank daughter of Judy a slave belonging to Robt Williamson jun^r born Augs^t 1.

Robin Son of Phillis a Slave belonging to Anne Mayo born July 25.

Robin Son of Moll a slave belonging to John Smith Senr born August 26.

Dinah daughter of Sarah a slave belonging to George Harding born Novem^r 19.

Rose daughter of Phillis a Slave belonging to Tho: Meacham born Decem^r 20.

Roger Son of Nell a Slave belonging to Humphery Jones born July 25.

Peter Son of Bess a slave belonging to Philip Warwick born Feb^ry 14.

Osman Son of Kate a Slave belonging to Frances Thacker born 25 June.

Billy Son of Lettey a slave belonging to Edwin Thacker born Novem^r 22.

Eve daughter of Venus a slave belonging to Hezekiah Ellis born Jan^ry ye 30.

Kate daughter of Dina a slave belonging to Jacob Stiff born March ye 15 171 .

Simon Son of Rebecca a Slave belonging to Sr Wm Skipwith born Jan^ry 11. 171 .

Frank daughter of Sarah a slave belonging to Alexander Graves born Decem 15. 171 .

Sarah daughter of Sarah a slave belonging to Gawin Corbin born March 25 17 .

Charles & Easter Son & daughter of Frank a Slave belonging to Gawin Corbin born April 1 171 .

Anthony Son of Lettice a slave belonging to Bar Yates born Ap: 2. baptized May 17. 171 .

Jack Son of Wan a slave belonging to James Daniell born May ye 17. 171 .

Nanny daughter of Jeney a Slave belonging to Rice Curtis born May ye 5. 171 .

Betty daughter of Sarah a slave belonging to Richard Hill born Ap: ye 30. 171 .

Toby Son of Sue a Slave belonging to William Barbee born June ye 18. 171 .

Essex Son of Rose a slave belonging to Gawin Corbin born June ye 16. 1719.

Randall Son of Phillis a slave belonging to Gawin Corbin born June ye 22. 171 .

Sarah daughter of Poll a Slave belonging to Garritt Minor born June ye 30. 1719.

Lucy daughter of Jenny a slave belonging to John Vivion born May ye 24 1719.

Jack Son of Flownder a slave belonging to ye estate of Mr Churchhill born May 6. 1719.

Harry Son of Wonna a slave belonging to Mathew Kemp born July ye 2d. 1719.

Cyrus Son of Judy a slave belonging to William Stanard born June ye 24 1719.

Jemmy Son of ——- a slave belonging to William Hackney born June ye 5 1719.

Tom son of —— a slave belonging to John Roads born July ye 15 1719.

Phill son of Juno a slave belonging to Matthew Kemp born July ye 18 1719.

Primus son of a slave belonging to Lewis Tomkies born August ye 12. 1719.

Harry son of Guinea a slave belonging to Thomas Dudley born Augst ye 6 1719.

Wonna daughter of Jeny a slave belonging to John Degge born July ye 1 1719.

Winney daughter of Pegg a slave belonging to Thomas Cheney born Sept. ye 9. 17

George Hooper son of Han a slave belonging to Garritt Minor born Sept ye 14. 17

Kate daughter   a slave belonging to Edmund Mickleburrough born Sept 26.

Ben negro Son of Soll belonging to R. Grymes.

Katy negro daughter of Kate belonging to Frances Thacker born May 25 17

—artin a negro son of Letty belonging to Wm Young born Feb. 10 1714.

Judith a Negro daughter of Sarah belonging to Thos. Warwick born May 6 1716.

Dick a negro Son of Sarah belonging to George Harding born May 14 1718.

Alice a negro Daughter of Alice belonging to Jno Grymes born baptized July 22 17

Betty a negro Daughter of Phillis belonging to Gawin Corbin born Feb^{ry} 20th 1715.

Pompey a negro son of Sue belonging to Gawin Corbin born Ap: 2 1715.

Syndab a negro son of Moll belonging to Gawin Corbin born June 25 1715.

Hannah a negro daughter of Sarah belonging to Gawin Corbin born March 27 1716.

Jack a negro Son of Frank belonging to Gawin Corbin born Ap: 19 17

Suke a negro Daughter of Rose belonging to Gawin Corbin born May 21 17

Natt a negro Son of Jeney belonging to Rice Curtis born Augt 24 1714.

Jack a negro son of Moll belonging to Peter Mountague born Augst 3 1716.

Poll a negro Daughter of Bess belonging to Phillip Warwick born Augst 13 1716.

Ben a negro son of Cate belonging to John Hord born Septem^r ye 5 1716.

Margery daughter of Judy a negro belonging to Robt Dudley born Septem 27 1716.

Dina negro daughter of Bess belonging to Nicholas Bristow born Dec. 16 1716.

Toney a negro Son of Jeney belonging to John Degge born Augst
ye 5 1716.
Letty a negro daughter of Alice belonging to Wm Stanard born Octo:
ye 22 1716.
Thomas a negro Son of Letty belonging to Bar Yates born Decem.
28. baptized Feb^{ry} 9.
Cummah Son of Betty a negro belonging to Thomas Smith born
Jan'y 3 1716.
Letty daughter of Alice a negro belonging to Wm Stanard born Octo:
24 1716.
Molly daughter of Hannah a negro belonging to Wm Stanard born
Ap: 30 1717.
Charles son of   a negro belonging to Thomas Dudley born
May 24
Will son of Phebe a negro belonging to Thomas Mountague born
June 17
Ben son of Jenney a negro belonging to Capt James Bristow born
June 26
Frank daughter of Dido a negro belonging to Capt John Smith born
June 14
Nimine daughter of Jenney belonging to Capt. John Smith born
June 26
Sampson son of Phillis a negro belonging to Roger Jones born May
25
Harry son of Sue a negro belonging to Wm Barbee sen^r May 30
Sam Son of Moll a negro belonging to Gawin Corbin born Novem^r 13
Alice daughter of Kate a negro belonging to Gawin Corbin born
Jan^r 12
Sanco son of Sue a negro belonging to Gawin Corbin born June 11
Harry Son of Della a negro belonging to Thomas Haselwood born
May ye 14 1717.
Billy son of Moll a negro belonging to John Segar born June ye 14
1717.
Phillis son of Judy a negro belonging to Robert Daniell born June y^e
23 1717.
Jenny daughter of Letty a slave belonging to William Young born
June ye 18
Sam Son of Janey a slave belonging to Rice Curtis born July ye 30
James son of Jane a slave belonging to John Grymes born June 23
Baptized.
George Son of Peg a Slave belonging to Thomas Cheney born Au-
gust ye 9.
Ned Son of Betty a Slave belonging to Capt John Smith born Au-
gust ye 24.
Frank Son of Bess a Slave belonging to Henry Armistead born Sept.
Peter Son of Mentas a slave belonging to John Grymes born Jan'y.
Sarah Daughter of Judy a Slave belonging to John Grymes born
March 25.
Sue Daughter of Rose a slave belonging to John Grymes born No-
vem^r 6.
Robin Son of Flora a Slave belonging to John Grymes born Octo. 21.
John Son of Lucy a slave belonging to John Grymes born July 29
17 .

Hannah daughter of Judy a slave belonging to John Degge born Septem^r 25. 17 .

Bob Son of Beck a slave belonging to William Davis born Novem^r ye 1717.

Clarinda daughter of Kate a slave belonging to William Stanard born Novem 3. 1717.

Toney Son of Mary a slave belonging to ye estate beth Churchill born D. 14.

Phillis daughter of Phebe a slave belonging to Tho. Mountague born Jan^{r}y y^e

Nan daughter of Judy a slave belonging to Wm Daniel jun^r born Novem^r ye 6.

Bridgitt daughter of Sarah a slave belonging to Gawin Corbin born Jan^{r}y ye 4.

Cate daughter of Letty a slave belonging to Fran: Weekes born Jan^{r}y ye 6 1719.

Jenny Son of Letty a slave belonging to Catherine Young born Jan^{r}y ye 10 1719.

Dick Son of Frank a slave belonging to Matthew Kemp born Feb^{r}y ye 6 1719.

Moll daughter of Mary a slave belonging to ye estate of Armistead Churchhill born Dec. 28. 1719.

Wonna daughter of a slave belonging to ye estate of Armistead Churchhill born Jan^r 4. 1719.

Charles Son of Sarah a slave belonging to John Smith jun^r born Feb^{r}y ye 11 1719.

Scipio Son of a slave belonging to John Grymes born March ye 13 1719.

Mary daughter of a slave belonging to John Grymes born March ye 13 1719.

Rose daughter of Rose a slave belonging to John Grymes born March ye 17 1719.

Sue daughter of a slave belonging to John Grymes born March ye 27 172 .

Peg daughter of Dinah a slave belonging to Henry Armistead born March 20 17 .

Abram Son of Lucy a Slave belonging to Henry Armistead born March 23 1719.

Sampson Son of Dido a slave belonging to Matthew Kemp born April 21 1720.

Tom Son of Phillis a slave belonging to Stokely Towles born May ye 4 1720.

Beck daughter of Kate a slave belonging to Augustine Smith born June ye 18 1720.

Kate daughter of Munday a slave belonging to John Batchelder born July 4 1720.

Ben Son of Frank a slave belonging to David George born July 4 1720.

Frank daughter of Diana a slave belonging to Armistead Churchhill born June 5. 1720.

Letty daughter of Moll a slave belonging to Tho: Mountague born Octo. ye 17. 1713.

Jack Son of Frank a slave belonging to Tho: Mountague born Jan^{r}y
27. 1713.

Cæsar Son of Frank a slave belonging to Tho: Mountague born Ap:
ye 30 1716.

Sampson Son of Frank a slave belonging to Tho: Mountague born
Feb^{r}y ye 28 1717.

Eugene Son of Moll a Slave belonging to Tho: Mountague born
Octo: ye 25. 1719.

Dinah daughter of Kate a slave belonging to Charles Jones born
July ye 25.

Nan daughter Felicia a salve belonging to Anne Mayo born Augst 30.

Clarinda daughter of a slave belonging to James Curtis jun^r born
June 20 17 .

Gabrill Son of Nell a slave belonging to ye estate of Edm^d Berkley
born Sept 4 17 .

Judy daughter of Alice a Slave belonging to Robert Daniell July y^e
17 17 .

Ben son of Kate a slave belonging to William Daniel Senr born Sep^t
ye 8 1720.

Hampton son of Judy a slave belonging to John Aldin born Sep^t y^e
27 1720.

Juno daughter of Hannah a slave belonging to George Harden born
Sept. 23. 1720.

Ned Son of   a slave belonging to John Smith jun^r born Sept. y^e
10. 1720.

Penn daughter of Sarah a slave belonging to Robert Williamson
born Sept. 29. 1720.

Will son of Dellow a slave belonging to Tho: Hazelwood born Octo:
ye 10. 1720.

Lucy daughter of Judy a slave belonging to Robert Williamson jun^r
Novem 1. 1720.

Sabrinah daughter of Frank a slave belonging to Oliver Segar born
Sept. 18 1720.

Gawin son of Dinah a slave belonging to Oliver Segar born Sept. 22
1720.

Charlott daughter of Jeney a slave belonging to John Vivion born
Novem^r 15. 1720.

Frank daughter of Alice a slave belonging to Edmond Bartlett's estate born 9^{ber} 28. 1720.

Betty daughter of Mary Whistler a mulatto in ye Service of John
Price born May 2

Will son of Mary Whistler a mulatto in ye Service of John Price born
April 26

Toney son of Judy a slave belonging to John Price born April ye 6

Alice daughter of Sue a slave belonging to John Price born Sept.
ye 14

Mercury son of Judy a slave belonging to Wm Stanard born Novem^r
ye 17

Beck daughter of Jenney a slave belonging to Matt: Hunt born De-
cem^r ye 10

Gawin son of Nell a slave belonging to Humphery Jones born De-
cem^r ye 9

Ben Son of Jeney a slave belonging to John Smith born Decem^r ye 18

Phillis daughter of Eve a slave belonging to Hezekiah Ellis born Novem^r ye 21

Jack son of Phillis a slave belonging to Roger Jones born Decem^r y^e

Kate daughter of Moll a slave belonging to John Segar born Decem^r ye 10

Flora daughter of Judy a slave belonging to John Degge born Jan^{ry} ye 3

Stephen Monday son of   a slave belonging to   born Decem^r ye 21

Jude daughter of hannah a slave belonging to   born Jan^{r}y

Jemmy Son of Hannah a slave belonging to Garritt Minor born Feb 20 1720.

Nero son of Phillis a slave belonging to Thomas Machen born March 27 1721.

Joice daughter of Dido a slave belonging to Matthew Kemp born April ye 13 1721.

Hannah daughter of Beck a slave belonging to Robt George jun^r born April 4 1721.

Peter son of Bess a slave belonging to Henry Armistead born April 21 1721.

Winney daughter of Jenny a slave belonging to Rice Curtis born April 27 1721.

Dego son of Poll a slave belonging to ye estate of Garritt Minor born April ye 28. 1721.

Ross son of Hannah a slave belonging to William Gray born April ye 18 1721.

Judy daughter of Winney a slave belonging to Edwin Thacker born Ap: ye 10. 1721.

Harry son of Sarah a slave belonging to Armistead Churchhill born Ap: ye 29 1721.

Sprigg son of   a slave belonging to Henry Gilpin born May ye 5. 1721.

Tamar daughter of Sarah a slave belonging to George Harding born May ye 30. 1721.

Johny son of Coss a slave belonging to Harry Beverly born May 25. 1721.

Billy son of Betty a slave belonging to John Robinson born July ye 2. 1721.

Cross son of Wonna a slave belonging to ye estate of Armistead Churchhill born June 6 1721.

Letty daughter of   a slave belonging to John Moseley born June 15. 1721.

Frank daughter of   a slave belonging to Thomas Norman born July 11 1721.

Jack son of Letty a slave belonging to Hobs Weeks born July ye 1 1721.

Tom Son of Wonne a slave belonging to Mathew Kemp born July ye 27 1721.

Moll Daughter of Frank a slave belonging to Edmund Mickleburrough born July 20. 1721.

Sue daughter of Jenny a slave belonging to Armistead Churchhill born May ye 1, 1721.

Judey daughter of Pugg a Slave belonging to Armistead Churchhill born July 15. 1721.

Dinah daughter of Kate a slave belonging to Roger Jones born August ye 6. 1721.

Pen daughter of Judy a slave belonging to Tho: Mountague born August 7. 1721.

Frank daughter of Jenny a Slave belonging to Samuell Batchelder born August 12. 1721.

Ned Son of Sarah a slave belonging to John Cheadle born Septem^r ye 1. 1721.

Robin Son of Sarah a slave belonging to Alexander Graves Septem^r ye 10. 1721.

Jack Son of Sarah a slave belonging to Henry Armistead born Septem^r ye 16. 1721.

Corridan Son of Judy a Slave belonging to William Blackburne born Sept. 10. 1721.

Roger Son of Juno a slave belonging to Mathew Kemp born Sept. 15. 1721.

Sarah daughter of Winny a slave belonging to ye estate of Henry Thacker dec'd born Sept 24. 1721.

Frank daughter of Sarah a slave belonging to William Stanard born Sept. 17. 1721.

Kate daughter of Judy a Slave belonging to William Daniell jun^r born Novem^r 1. 1721.

Judy daughter of Kate a slave belonging to William Hackney born Nov. 6. 1721.

Bristow Son of Sue a slave belonging to John Price born Novem^r 28. 1721.

Letty daughter of Sue a Slave belonging to Bar Yates born Jan^ry ye 5. 1721.

Lura daughter of Sarah a slave belonging to John Smith jun^r born Feb^ry ye 5. 1721.

Ishmael Son of Moll a Slave belonging to John Smith Senr born Jan^ry ye 18. 1721.

Kate daughter of Frank a slave belonging to Anne Thacker born Octo. ye 4 1721.

Toney Son of Dinah a slave belonging to John Marston born Jan^ry ye 25. 1721.

Cæsar Son of Judy a Slave belonging to John Price born Feb^ry ye 15. 1721.

Moll daughter of Moll a slave belonging to James Hipkings born Novem^r ye 4. 1721.

Sawney Son of Mary a slave belonging to Armistead Churchhill born March 10. 1721.

Frank Daughter of Dido a slave belonging to Matthew Kemp born April ye 1. 1722.

Betty daughter of Jenny a Slave belonging to John Grymes born May 28. baptized August ye 13. 1721.

Sarah daughter of Margery a slave belonging to John Grymes born Feb^ry ye 16. 1721.

Margery daughter of Rose a Slave belonging to John Grymes born
    Feb⁷ yᵉ 27. 1721.
Daniel Son of Flora a slave belonging to John Grymes born March
    yᵉ 29. 1722.
Ben Son of Phillis a slave belonging to Anne Mayo born Feb⁷ yᵉ 14
    1721.
Poll daughter of Frank a Slave belonging to David George born
    April yᵉ 4 1722.
Simon Son of Frank a slave belonging to Matthew Kemp born April
    3d. 1722.
Judy Daughter of Dina a slave belonging to Jacob Stiff born Aprill
    yᵉ 9 1722.
Abram Son of Jeny a Slave belonging to Hobs Weeks born April yᵉ
    11 1722.
Kate daughter of   a slave belonging to Wᵐ Mountague born
    March yᵉ 30 1722.
Alice daughter of Jenny a slave belonging to Elizᵃ Vivion born May
    yᵉ 2 1722.
Lucy daughter of   a slave belonging to Garritt Minor born May
    yᵉ 11 1722.
Jenny daughter of   belonging to Thomas Mountague born
    May 19. 1722.

                                        Bar Yates Minʳ.

ERRATA

Dewd, Rachell; mss Dews 7
Richard; mss Dews 7
Harkins, Cornelius; mss
Cornelias 9
Sutton, Cussandra; mss
Cassandra p
Smyth, Margt.; mss Smith 10
Thacker, Eltonhead; mss
Elconhead 10
Edward; mss Edwin 11
Wilberton, Ann; mss
Welberton 11
Stamper, Jno.; mss John 12
Price, Margaret; mss
Margret 13
King, Rebeca; mss Rebecka
13
Young, Johanr.; mss Johana.
14
Hughs, Robena; mss Rebecca
15
Hughes, Jno.; mss Hughs 15
Eliza.; mss Hughs 15
Brunwell, Sarah; mss
Brumwell 15
Peter; mss Brumwell 15
Ellinor; mss Brumwell 15
Patre, John; mss Patris 15
Elizabeth; mss Patris 15
Matthew; mss Patris 15
Eliza.; mss Patris 15
Wormeley, Ralph, Esqr; mss
Wormley 15
Long, Daniel; mss Daniell
15
Brookes, Charles; mss Brooks
16
Reymey, William Parker;
mss Parks 16
Wooley, Ann; mss Woolley
16
Worsdale, Richard; mss
Richd. 17
Lawrence, Elizabeth; mss
Laurence 18
Bridger, Margaret; mss
Bridge 18
Mayo, Eliza; mss Eliza. 18
Clarke, Katherine; mss
Clerke 18
Harrelson, Eliza.; mss
Harelton 18
Hughes, William; mss
Hughs 19
Wm.; mss Hughs 19
Eliza.; mss Hughs 19
Allison, Ann; mss Allinson
19
Sheeres, John; mss Skeeres
20
Lanson, Joshua; mss Lawson
20
John; mss Lawson 20
Parris, Eliza.; mss Elliza.
20
Hill, Eliza; mss Eliza. 21
Saserson, Isaac; mss
Sasorson 21
Hill, Joseph; mss-servant
to Joseph Harvey 21
Thacker, Martha; mss
Thaker 22
Dearclone, John; mss
Dearelone 22
Mullins, Zachariah; mss
Mullens 23

Berwick, David, Junr.; mss
Barwick 23
Loyal, William; mss Loyall
23
Roberts, Isabella; mss
Issabella 23
Clerk, ----; mss Clark 24
Sandford, Elizabeth; mss
Sandeford 24
John; mss Sandeford 24
Sarah; mss Sandeford 24
Daniel, Wm.; mss Daniell
25
Jochabed; mss Daniell 25
Basket, Henry; mss Baskett
25
Seagur, Randolph; mss
Seager 25
Mary; mss Seager 25
Dudding, Humphrey; mss
Humphry 26
Humphrey; mss Humphry 26
Braeme, John; mss Breame
26
Mary; mss Breame 26
Rhodes, Ezehias; mss
Ezekias 27
Brooks, Phillip; mss
Brookes 28
Hazlewood, Tho.; mss
Haslewood 28
Mary; mss Haslewood 28
Dowlin, Eliza; mss Eliza.
28
Sandersee, Eliza; mss
Eliza. 28
Thackston, Eliza; mss
Eliza. 28
Sandford, William; mss
Sandeford 28
Jno.; mss Sandeford 28
Sarah; mss Sandeford 28
ffitz Jeffreys, Wm.; mss
Jeffereys 30
Ann; mss Jeffereys 30
Brown, Mary; mss Browne 30
Elliott, Mary; mss Elliot
31
Tho.; mss Elliot 31
Sarah; mss Elliot 31
Gellett, Eliza.; mss
Gellet 31
Guillams, Peter; mss
Guilams 31
Browne, Henry; mss Mary 32
Dourey, Elizabeth; mss
Dowrey 33
Baskett, Eliz.; mss Baskitt
33
Wheeler, Thomas; mss
Wheler 34
Tho.; mss Wheler 34
Allison, Katherine; mss
Allinson 35
Rammage, Eliza; mss Eliza.
35
Abbott, Ellinor; mss
Abbot 35
Brissell, Mary O.; mss
O'Brissell, Mary 35
Stacy, Thoms.; mss
(illegible Standly) 36
Osborne, Henry; mss Osbone
37
Needler, William; mss
Needles 37

Bennett, Mary; mss Bennet
37
Thaxton, Richard; mss
Thackston 39
Bressell, Eusebias O.;
mss O'Brissell 39
Seagur, William; mss Seager
40
Randolph; mss Seager 40
Mary; mss Seager 40
Stapleton, ffrancis; mss
ffrances 40
Humphryes, Joseph; mss
Humphryes 41
Robert; mss Humphryes 41
Eliza.; mss Humphryes 41
ffurnelt, William; mss
ffurnett 42
Hames, Ann; mss Haines 43
Charles; mss Haines 43
Eliza.; mss Haines 43
Johnson, John J.; mss no
"J" 44
Dudlass, James; mss Dudlas
46
Ann; mss Dudlas 46
Humphreys, Elizabeth; mss
Humphryes 47
Robert; mss Humphryes 47
Rebecca; mss Humphryes 47
Chilton, Zebulun; mss
Zebulon 47
Marchum, Eliz.; mss Eliza.
48
Wallas, Valentine; mss
Vallentine 48
Cummings, John; mss
Cummins 52
George; mss Cummins 52
----; mss Cummins 52
Madcrions, Charles; mss
Maderious 55(2)
Mary; mss Maderious 55
Weeks, Frances; mss Francis
58
Kilbie, Catherine; mss
Kilbee 59
Yard, Sarah; mss Church-
Yard 60
Herman; mss Church-Yard
60
Elizabeth Church; mss
Church-Yard 60
Curtis, Michael; mss
Michaell 61
Courlles, Michaell; mss
Curlis 61
Mercy; mss Curlis 61
George, Robert; not in mss
62
Smith; not in mss 62
Branmount, Hope; mss
Branmont 63
Vivion, Margaret; mss
Margoret 63
Curles, John; mss Curtis
63
Parson, John; mss Parsons
63
Lanton, Ezebella; mss
Ezabella 64
Philips, Samuell; mss
Samuel 65
Cauniff, Derby; mss Canniff
67
Hannah; mss Canniff 67

Win, Richard; mss Winn 67
Sarah; mss Winn 67
Perrot, Henry; mss Parrot
68
Richard; mss Parrot 68
Sara; mss Parrot 68
Phillips, Catherine; mss
Philips 68
John; mss Philips 68
Jane; mss Philips 68
Couch, Aventa; mss Averilla
69
Goear, Joseph; mss Gear 71
Roberts, Willett; mss
Willet 71
Cutton, Mary; mss Sutton
72
Christopher; mss Sutton
72
Hope; mss Sutton 72
Bennet, Richard; mss Bennit
72
William; mss Bennit 72
Roberts, Willett; mss
Willet 73
Ball, Eddd.; mss Edwd. 76
Mackey, Eliza; mss Eliza.
76
Chelton, Eliza; mss Eliza.
76
Blake, Eliza; mss Eliza.
76
Humfreys, Eliza; mss
Eliza. 76(2)
Rowe, Joseph; mss Row 76
John; mss Row 76
Katherine; mss Row 76
Barbee, Ann; mss Anne 76
Saunders, Eliza; mss
Eliza. 76
Davies, Benjamin; mss
Benjamine 77
Richardson, Eliza; mss
Eliza. 77
George, Hally; mss Harry
78
Goodwin, John; mss Goodin
79
Churchyard, Harman; mss
Church Yard 79
Cooke, Eliza; mss Eliza. 79
Jelley, Dudley; mss
Jolley 79
Shelling, Eliza; mss Eliza.
79
Guess, Eliza; mss Eliza.
80
Pate, Eliza; mss Eliza. 80
Meecham, Eliza; mss
Eliza. 80
Custis, John; mss Curtis
80
Attford, Richard; mss
Allford 80
Meechan, John; mss Meecham
80
Atwood, Mary; mss Attwood
80
Olliver, Thomas; mss
Oliver 81
Howes, Sarah; mss Hewes 81
Moore, Abraham; mss Moon
81
Gardiner, Rinwing; mss
Rinning 81
Miller, Ann; mss Ann
Hiller 81
Tugwell, Lucretia; mss
Tigwell 81
Toseley, Eliza.; mss
Boseley 81
Probest, Hannah; mss
Probert 81

Bremont, Rebecca; mss
Beomont 82
Cheny, Thomas; mss Cheney
82
Wortley, Catherine; mss
Worthey 82
Croony, Mary; mss Cromy 83
Canady, Alice; mss Canaday
83
Hazlewood, Thomas; mss
Hazelwood 83
Worsell, Elizabeth; mss
Worsdell 83
Bondon, George; mss Bouden
83
Jarrett, Mary; mss Jarrott
83
Seagur, William; mss
Seagar 83
Saunders, Edmund; mss
Edmond 84
Marion, Anne; mss Manion
85
Bridgett; mss Manion 85
Mazey, Ralph; mss Masey 85
Lucas, Judith; mss Lucass
86
Blacky, Churchhill; mss
Churchill 86
Brooks, Henery; mss Brookes
86
Jona.; mss Brookes 86
Mary; mss Brookes 86
William; mss Brookes
86(2)
Elizabeth; mss Brookes
87
Gibbs, Richard; mss Richd.
87
Comings, Angeto; mss
Angelo 88
Straughan, Edward; mss
Stroughan 88
Richard; mss Stroughan 88
Katherine; mss Stroughan
88
ffiney, Katherine; mss
ffiney 89
Wm.; mss ffiney 89
Honour; mss ffiney 89
Barwich, Anne; mss Barwick
89
George; mss Barwick 89
Eliza.; mss Barwick 89
Parry, Mathew; mss Matthew
89
Perrott, Betty; mss Perrot
89
Robert; mss Perrot 89
Catherine; mss Perrot 89
Elliott, Thomas; mss
Elliot 90
William; mss Elliot 90
Mary; mss Elliot 90
Cheny, Thomas; mss Cheney
90(2)
Jane; mss Cheney 90
Elliott, Elizabeth; mss
Elliot 90
Thomas; mss Elliot 90
Elizabeth; mss Elliot 90
Jones, Lodswick; mss
Lodowick 90
Nicholls, Griffin; mss
Nichols 92
Henry; mss Nichols 92
Alice; mss Nichols 92
Hues, Daniell; mss Daniel
92
Lucas, Ethelred; mss
Etheldred 93
Basket, Mary; mss Baskett
93
Henry; mss Baskett 93
Sarah; mss Baskett 93

Owen, Augastine; nee
Augustine 94
Ball, Keziah; mss Kesiah
94
Haslewood, Anne; mss
Haselwood 96
Thomas; nee Haselwood 96
Jane; mss Haselwood 96
Blackley, Frances; mss
Blackly 97
Robert; mss Blackly 97
Anne; mss Blackly 97
Brine, Jemima; mss Brane
98
Brine, Richard; mss Rickins
Brame 98
Hannah; mss Brame 98
Cain, Hannah; mss Hanah 99
Clarke, James; mss Clark
99
Edward; mss Clark 99
Anne; mss Clark 99
Lucas, Ethelred; mss
Etheldred 99
----, Anne; mss Anne Har-
dee 100
----, John; mss John
Hardee 100
----, Margrett; mss
Margrett Hardee 100
Barnett, Anne; mss Barrett
101
John; mss Barrett 101
Anne; mss Barrett 101
Seagur, Catherine; mss
Seagar 102
William; mss Seagar 102
Anne; mss Seagar 102
Yates, Bar. Minis.; mss
Mint. 102
----, William; mss William
Rice 102(2)
----, Catherine; mss
Catherine Rice
Smith, Ann; mss Anne 103
Chancellor, Mary; mss dau.
William Chancellor by
Mary Cole 103
Ball, Keziah; mss Kesiah
103
Yates, Bar. Minr.; mss
Mint. 104
Tilley, Phrebe; mss Phoebe
104
Mickleburrough, Ropert;
mss Robert 106
Tompson, Sarah; mss Tomson
106
William; mss Tomson 106
Mary; mss Tomson 106
Hardee, Averetta; mss
Averilla 106
Towles, Stokely; mss
Stokley 107
Barwick, Rachell; mss
Rachel 109
Tayloe, Christopher; mss
Taylor 109
Richard; mss Taylor 109
Honor; mss Taylor 109
Yates, Bar. Minr.; mss
Mint. 109
Hargrow, Mary; mss Har-
grove 110
Saddler, Elizabeth; mss
Sadler 113
John; mss Sadler 113
Mary; mss Sadler 113
Bohannon, Nevill; mss
Bohannan 115
Joseph; mss Bohannan 115
Elizabeth; mss Bohannan
115

Backford continued
Hannah 144; William 144
Baden, Eliz. 153; Henry
153; William 153
Bagot, John 304
Bagwell, Drury 205
Bailey, Eliza. 80; Henery
80
Baines, Betsa 170;
Christopher 102; Rebecca
102(2)
Baker, Benjamin 287;
Benjamine 122; Betty 162;
Charles 47; Eliza. 48;
Elizabeth 287; Frances
287; Isabella 22; James
206; John 48; Rachel 122;
Robert 185; Susannah 47;
Tho. 48; William 47,122,
165,175
Balden, Martha 105; Sarah
105; William 105
Baldin, Benjamine 95,172;
Eliza 80; Elizabeth 88;
Mary 76; Sarah 76,88,95,
99(2); William 76,80,95,
99; Wm. 88
Balding, John 68; Sarah
68; William 68,166
Baldry, Letetia 303
Baldwin, Edward 45;
Elizabeth 85,130; Joseph
142; Judith 130,134,138,
142,191; Katherine 45;
Keziah 45; Lewis 116,
182; Margrett 111,180;
Mary 16,168; Sarah 111,
116,138,186; Sarah, jur.
186; Tho. 16; William 11,
16,111,116,130,134(2),
138,191; Wm. 142
Ball, ---- 67,76; Ann 36,
76; Anne 90,113,168,172,
183; Arthur 48; Benjamin
169; Benjamine 103,154;
Catherine 67,83; Clemence
121; Daniel 154,159(2);
Daniell 88; Ed. 48; Eddd.
76; Edward 48(2),67(2),
71,76,88,94,103,121,127,
134(2),165,183; Eliza.
22; Elizabeth 20,67,113,
121(2),163; Elizth. 190;
Henery 79; Henry 83,90,
96,100,107,113,121,164,
176,190; James 96,173;
Johannah 48,162; John
107,127; Judith 165;
Kezia 67,71; Keziah 48
(2),67,76,88,94,103,165,
191; Mary 71; Phebe 76;
Sarah 90,96,100,107,121,
127,134,154,159,179;
Valentine 168; William
94,100,179; Wm. 184
Ballad, Peter 83
Ballard, ---- 32; Eliza.
87; Henry 30,32; Jane
174; John 10,87; Tho. 30
Banbry, Aliza. 8; Daniell
8; Mary 8
Banger, Elizabeth 181
Banks, Anthony 42;
Elizabeth 42; Ellianor
30; Isabella 42; Samll.
30,32; Tunstall 281
Banks (?), Ellianor 32
Bannerman, Mark 266,267
Banting, Elizabeth 170
Barack, Amy 43; George 43
Barbee, Ann 76; Benjamin
70,186; Eliza. 27,34,76;
Elizabeth 166; Geo. 191;
Gray 98; Hannah 27;

Barbee continued
John 76,81; Mary 70,76,
92(2),98; William 34,49,
70,76,92,98,306; Wm. 27,
34,76,258,259; Wm., Senr.
308
Barber, William 63
Barley, James 66; Mary 66;
William 66
Barlow, Anthony 7; John
40; Mary 40; Pheby 40
Barnatt, Ann 64,72; John
64(2),72; Sarah 72
Barnes, Henry 174; Johanna
85; Mary 21
Barnet, Anne 130; Henry
130; William 130
Barnett, Ann 69; Anne 91,
101(2),123; Henry 123;
John 69,91,101,166,179;
Jone 20; Mary 123;
Richard 69; William 91
Barns, Henry 83
Barrack, Benjamin 201;
John, Sr. 199; John, Jr.
199
Barrick, ----rh 288; Ann
160(2),303; David 145,
288; Diana 145,303;
Dinah 288; Elizabeth 280;
Frances 206; George 145;
Joannah 201; John 160;
Priscilla 202; Robert
303; Sarah 303
Barruck, Elizabeth 155;
John 155; Mary 155
Bartlett, Edmd. 305;
Edmond 175,310; Edmund
265,268(2); Lucy 172
Barwich, Anne 89; Eliza.
89; George 89
Barwick, Anne 183; David
21,168; Eliz. 31;
Elizabeth 33,93,173;
Geo. 31,33; George 81,
93,109,118,163; John 93;
Joseph 201; Mary 31,33,
109,118(2),189; Rachell
109
Basford, Ann 163; Martha
67; Richard 67; Thomas
67
Basket, Daniel 144; Edwin
144; Eliza. 15,19,29;
Elizabeth 15,162; Henry
25,93; Jno. 15; John 19;
Mary 93,144,168(2);
Sarah 93; Thomas 19
Baskett, Abraham 64; Eliz.
33; Eliza. 25; Henery
87; Henry 177; Honor 64;
James 64,183; Jno. 25;
John 177; Martha 87;
Mary 53; Onnor 177;
Sarah 87,177
Baskitt, Anne 164; Eliza-
beth 91; Thomas 91;
William 91
Bassett, Henery 80;
Virginia 281; William
166
Batchelder, ----iam 288;
----therine 299; Ann
202(2); Anne 166;
Benjamin 197; Benjamine
132; Catharine 132;
Catherine 90,96,111,118;
Chatherine 123; Eliza.
284,285,287,288,299;
Elizabeth 98,109,114,
118,177,182,203; Frances
200,287; Hannah 109,170;
Henry 118,204; Jacob
132; James 98,111,205,264;

Batchelder continued
Jane 201; John 90,98,114,
162,177,284,287,309;
Joseph 123,197,286,301;
Katherine 104; Michal
197; Mikel 286; Molly
280; Samuel 90,104(2),
111,118,123,132,193,210,
214,218,219,226,227,235,
264,272,285,286,288,299;
Samuell 83,96,312; Sarah
50,118,177,199,284;
Susanna Brooking 284;
Thomas 285; William 50(2),
96,109,114,118,184
Batcheldor, ---- Mr. 10;
Elizabeth 104; Jemima
104; Jno. 8; John 8,104;
Mr. 7; Mary 8(3); Sarah
8
Batcheldr, Jno. 8(2); Mary
8(2); Rebecca 8; William
8
Batcheler, Samuel 194,249
Bateman, Ann 11; Edward 11;
Lettice 78,86; Mary 86;
Thomas 11,78(2),86
Battaile, John 304
Batts, Catherine 90; Mary
90; Thomas 90
Baxter, Susanna 167
Baylor, Hannah 202
Bayn, Rachell 167
Baytop, James 304
Beale, ---liam Corrie 280
Beaman, ---- 285; ----hel
288; Eliza. 165; Jane
161,285,286,288,299;
John 161,285,286,288,299;
Margaret 199,286; Mary
199; Sarah 161
Beamen, Elizabeth 159; Jane
159; John 159
Beamon, Benjamin 178;
Benjamine 104; Catharine
208; Elizabeth 83,104;
Frances 208; Susanna 208;
William 104,177
Beamont, ---- 48; Charity
83; Hannah 48; Thomas 37;
William 35,48
Beard, Elen 299; Joseph
299; Mary 299
Beauford, Mary 190
Begerley, Eliza. 82
Belfare, Judith 201
Belfield, Sydner 203
Belfore, Anne 304
Bell, ---- Mr. 262; John
82; Jonathan 94; Mary 94;
Sarah 94
Bendall, Arthur 27; Eliza.
24,27,34; James 20,24,
27,34(2); Sarah 24,63
Benet, Peter 65; Sarah 65;
William 65
Bennet, Anne 168; John 208;
Joseph 131; Mary 131,138;
Richard 72,138; Thomas
203; William 72,131,138
Bennett, Ann 87; Eliza.
121; Elizabeth 69; Mary
37,115,121,125; Peter
115,184; Richard 37;
Sarah 60,69,83,87;
William 23,60(2),69,115,
125(2); Winny 302; Wm.
121
Bennit, William 164
Benson, Alice 181; Dorothy
28; Robert 28; Tho. 28;
Thomas 24
Bentley, Mary Mrs. 8;
Matthew 7; Mr. 8

Bently, John 165
Berick, David 76; Eliza.
    76; Geo. 76
Berkeley, ---- Major 240,
    241; Maj. 276; Edm. 291;
    Edmd. 153,211,248(2),
    278,290,294,295; Edmon
    300(2); Edmond 291,295;
    Major 89; Edmund 136,
    146,198,214,226,234,243
    (2),245,252,255,273,
    277(2),280; Elizabeth B.
    303; Lucia 89; Lucy N.
    281; Mary 136,146(2),
    153,199; Nelson 136;
    Sarah 89,153,198
Berkley, Edmd. 262,310;
    Majr. 140; Edmund 126,
    130(2),210,217,222,223,
    246,264,270,271,295;
    Lewis 140; Lucy 126;
    Mary 126,130
Berrick, David 150,154(2),
    158; Dianah 150; Dianna
    154; Diannah 158; John
    158; William 150
Berry, Ann 141,285; Anne
    100,122,126,131,136;
    Catharine 287; Dorothy
    196,304; Edward 38;
    Eliza 60; Elizabeth 72,
    75,176; Frances 60,171,
    184; Garrett 60,72,75,
    182; George 293; Gerrat
    47; Honour 37; James 72,
    141,285; Jno. 139; John
    82,93,100,112,126,168,
    196,254,255,263,291,293,
    301; Katherine 38; Mary
    75,93,100,112,131,139,
    285; Sarah 38; Susanna
    112; Susannah 139; Thomas
    47,122(2),126,131,136,
    141; Thos. 287; William
    93,136,196
Berwick, David, Junr. 23;
    Eliza. 77; Geo. 74,77;
    George 77,191
Bess, Ginney 24
Best, ---- 191; Dorothy
    180; Elizabeth 23;
    George 131,138,167; John
    131; Margret 131; Mar-
    grett 138; Mary 138
Betson, Anthony 138; Mary
    138(2)
Betts, Ann 191; Sarah 175;
    Thomas 169; Tomson 163
Beuford, Elizabeth 149;
    Henry 94,149; Mary 94;
    Thomas 94; Thos. 256;
    William 149
Beverley, Major 8; ---- 31;
    Agatha 95; Ann Munford
    302; Anne 129; Catharine
    Klug 283; Christopher
    33; Eliza. Mrs. 47;
    Elizabeth 45,76,95,129,
    162,176; Elizabeth
    Stanard 282; Elizabeth
    Madam 48; Mme. 68; Mrs.
    45; Harry 95,261,282(2),
    283,305; Mr. 68,74,76;
    Henry Capt. 45,48; Mr.
    47; Jane Yates 283;
    Judith 63,77; Kath. 31;
    Katherine 16,33,76;
    Madam 7; Lucy 179;
    Lucy Yates 282(2);
    Margaret 76; Mary 47;
    Peter 77; Rachel Murray
    282; Robert 31,33,48,
    76,129,166; Major 7,16,
    18,29; Majr. 32;

Beverley continued
    Susanna 68; Sussanna
    76; Tho. 31; Thomas 7;
    William 16
Beverly, ---- Madm. 34;
    Major 13; Christopr. 31;
    Elizabeth 105; Harry
    105,283,311; Katherine
    31; Madm. 35; Lucy 105;
    Robert 31; Major 31;
    Sarah 283
Bewford, Anne 100; Eliza-
    beth 77,86,95,100;
    Henery 78,80; Henry 101;
    John 77,101; Mary 78,95,
    101; Sarah 86; Thomas
    77,86,95,100,172; Wm. 78
Bigge, Mary 43; Robert 43
Biggs, Eliza. 76(2),87;
    Elizabeth 70,97,163;
    James 97; Jane 87; Mary
    70; Robert 63,70,76,80,
    87,97,175
Bird, ----nhey 288; Ann
    288; Elizabeth 66;
    Elizabth. 60; Henry 66;
    John 60,66,167,177,288;
    Mary 282; Mary Reeves
    282; Richard 201,282
Bishop, Charles 175;
    Richd. 31
Black, Ann 60,78; Anne 81;
    James 60(2),78; Philemon
    78
Blackborn, Eliza. 89;
    Elizabeth 89; Martha 89;
    Wm. 89
Blackborne, William 215
Blackbourn, ---- 161; Anna
    114; Edward 161; Eliza-
    beth 114; George 161;
    William 114,265; Wm. 217
Blackbourne, William 212;
    Wm. 227
Blackburn, Anna 191; Edwd.
    289,293; Elizabeth 122,
    191,204; Jean 207; Mary
    298(2),304; Millicent
    122; Paulin Anderson
    302; Roger 199,202;
    William 122,191,224,275,
    298; Capt. 276; Wm. 231,
    232
Blackburne, Ann 298; Anne
    166; Dorothy 183; Edward
    128,298; Elizabeth 97,
    102,108,128,191(2);
    Hannah 102; Thomas 108,
    185; William 97(2),102,
    108,128,191,210,224,298,
    312; Wm. 222,266
Blackby, Thomas 29
Blackey, George 143;
    Hester 143; Jane 143;
    Margret 189; Thomas 33
Blackle, Ann 62; Richard
    62; Robert 62
Blacklee, Anne 78; George
    78; Robert 78
Blackley, Ann 55,67; Anne
    67,97,104,299; Elizabeth
    161,198; Frances 97,204;
    George 139,146,161,168,
    286,299; Jane 26,34,55,
    139,146,161,286,299;
    John 34; Richard 286;
    Robert 22,26(2),55,67,
    97,104,146,182; Robt.
    34; Sarah 139; Willy 104
Blackly, Agatha 86; Ann
    86,88; George 154,157;
    Jane 154,157(2); Mary
    162; Reuben 154; Robert
    86,88; Sarah 88

Blacky, Churchhill 86,236;
    Sarah 86; Thomas 86
Blade, Abraham Currell 202
Blake, Alice 281(2),302;
    Ann 201,207,284,286;
    Anne 119,123,187,289,304;
    Augustine 281,302;
    Benjamin 282; Betty 201;
    Beverley A. 303; Charles
    282; Churchhill 42;
    Diana 20; Dianah 9; Eliz.
    42; Eliza 76; Eliza. 9,
    20,44,46,47,87,291;
    Elizabeth 44,59,68,69,
    110,119,146,159,163,289;
    Elizth. 143; Fanny 201;
    Frances 206; Franka 282;
    Geo. 76; Georg 68,69;
    George 9,42,44,46,59(2),
    84,87,121,171,186,204,
    285,286,299,304; Hannah
    121; Inecy 289; Jacob 68,
    69,123,173,284,289,305;
    Jno. 9,142,143,236;
    Joanna 116; Joannah 116;
    Johanna 110,127,133,138,
    142,302; Johannah 103;
    John 9(2),42,46,47,103,
    110,116,119,121,123,127
    (2),133,138,146(2),162,
    165,169,187,199,246,278,
    281(2),299; John, Senr.
    277,290; John, senr. 242;
    Jone 9(4),21; Judith 133;
    Kezia 170; Keziah 103;
    Lucey 23; Lucina 29; Lucy
    9(2); Lucy (Lucey) 7;
    Margaret 42; Mary 201,
    286,299; Micoll 9; Roase
    287; Robert Norman 281;
    Robert U. 303; Rose 159,
    285; Samuel 281,302;
    Sarah 9,47,76,142,143,
    166,303; Susanna 208,284,
    303,305; Susannah 199;
    Thomas 42,87,138,201,285,
    287(2),289; Thos. 159;
    William 200,289,305
Blakemore, Jemima 208
Blakes, Johanne 149; John
    149; Lucy 149
Blakey, ---- 283(2); Ann
    199,283; Anne 303; Betty
    113; Catharine 281;
    Catherine 147; Churchhill
    94,101,107,113,119,125,
    133,140,147,192,199,200,
    240,283; Churchill 82,88;
    Elizabeth 304; George 94,
    256,299; Henry 303; Jane
    119,150,299; John 101,
    150,247; Margarett 88;
    Margrett 84; Martha 150;
    Mary 196; Robert 107,304;
    Sarah 88,94,101,107,113,
    119,125(2),133,140,147;
    Susanna 140; Thomas 83,
    188; William 133; William
    C. 303; William Chowning
    199,283
Blakley, George 152(2);
    Jane 152
Blan, Henry 285; Josiah
    285; Micah 285
Bland, Ann 207,282; Francis
    282; John 282; Lucy 283;
    Mary 282(2),283; Mary
    Anne 303; Ralph 206;
    Richard 207; Thomas, Jr.
    207; William, Jr. 205;
    Wm. 282,283
Blandon, Sarah 191
Blazeden, Margrett 108;
    Sarah 108; William 108

Blazedon, Mary 100; Sarah 100; William 82,100
Blewford, ---- 27; Henry 27; John 11,180; Mary 19,38(2); Tho. 19,27,38; Thomas 19
Bloss, Ann 38; James 38; Jno. 36,38
Blueford, Eliza 302
Blunt, Anne 103; Elizabeth 107,114; Francis 103(2); Henry 107,114,163; Susanna 107; Thomas 176; William 114
Bocker, Jone 63
Bodenham, Edward 189
Bodgam, John 23,34; Mary 34; William 34
Bodgham, Hannah 44; John 44; Joyce 44; Mary 36,37
Bohame, Rebecca 165
Bohannan, Agnes 130; Agniss 136; Ann 151; Eliza. 124, 130; Elizabeth 121; George 121; Henry 151, 193; John 130,136,151, 166; Joseph 121,124,130; Sarah 124,136; William 130(2),188
Bohannon, Elizabeth 115; George 183; Joseph 115; Nevill 115
Bolden, Mary 201
Boldin, William 200
Boles, Peter 209
Bolton, Anne 80; Sarah 173; Uriah 174
Bond, William 170
Bondon, George 83
Bonds, Mary 298; Robert 298
Bonner, George 180
Boodle, John 39,41; Martha Mrs. 7; Mary 38; Mrs. 41; Robert 23,38; Dor. 39; Mr. 38,41
Booker, Matthew 9
Booseley, Eliza. 52; Hannah 52; Jacob 52,53
Booten, Hannah 168
Booth, William 208
Boothe, Thomas 295
Boseley, ffrances 82; Hannah 81
Boss, Alford 145; Alfred 282; Christian 155,159, 297; Elizabeth 199; James 206; John 138,145, 155,159,170,201,252,282, 287,293,297; Joseph 280, 282; Judith 297; Lewis 159,204,304; Martha 201; Priscilla 138; Rhoda 287; Sarah 145,204,282 (2); Susannah 138; William 155,282
Boswel, ---- Mr. 9
Boswell, ---- Mr. 9(2); Elizabeth 281; Ellionar 128; Patrick 128,166; Thomas 128
Boughtoun, William 170
Boulton, Ann 44,46; Daniell 21(2); Elizabeth 21; Jno. 44; John 46; Sarah 46; Uriah 44
Bourk, John 31,40; Mary 31; Mayo 40; Sarah 40(2)
Bowden, George 85,91; John 91; Mary 207; Robert 280; Sarah 91; William 202
Bowen, Matthew 80

Bowers, Ann 201; Elizabeth 280; Mary 209
Bowles, ---- 157; Fanny 285; John 157,285(3), 297,298; Lucy 297; Mary 285(2),297,298(2); Thomas 157
Bowls, Jerusha 287; John 287; Mary 287; Stubberfield 204
Bowman, Benjamine 50; James 83,105,180; Jno. 50; John 105; Margrett 105; Mary 50
Bowmon, Jno. 52; John 52; Mary 52
Boyd, Lucy 206
Bradley, Anne 118; Elizabeth 91; Ezekiah 77; James 128; Jno. 77; John 82,91,100(2),109, 118,128,134,166; Mary 77,91,100,109,118,134, 186; Rebecca 128,134; Robert 109; Wm. 77
Braeme, John 26; Mary 26
Braine, Elizabeth 100, 122(2); John 100(2),122
Brame, Eliza. 286; Elizabeth 116,198; Elizth. 142; Hannah 103,107,111, 116; James 180; Jno. 142; John 83,116; Josiah 286(2); Kerenhappuch 107; Kesiah 103; Mary 82,116; Melchisedek 116; Melchizedeck 201; Penelope 142; Richin 107; Richins 103,111(2),116, 162
Branch, Frances 114,122(2); Mary 60,114,187; Nicholas 60; Theophilus 60,114, 122,164
Brand, John 167
Branmount, Hope 63
Braxton, Tayloe 303
Bray, Asher 304; Dolly 263; Henry 20; Jane 200, 263,281; Johanna 206; John 263,281; Peter 281; Thomas 207; William 201
Brayerly, Mary 165
Bream, Elizabeth 109,137; Jedidah 109; Jemima 157; Jno. 137; Johm 160; John 109,155,157,160, 298; Josiah 155; Mary 155,157,160,298; Penelope 137
Breame, Ann 27; John 27, 150; Mary 26,27,150; Penelopy 190; Sarah 150
Bremont, Rebecca 82
Brent, Giles Collo. 22; Jane 16; Jno. 16; John 16
Bressell, Eusebias O. 39
Brewer, Ann 30,58; Jno. 30; John 20,54; Mary 30
Brider, Ann 63
Bridge, ffra..cis 22(2); Margt. 22
Bridger, Margaret 18
Bridgforth, Henry 83,91; James 91; Mary 91
Brim, Alice 38; Caroline Segar 204; Elizabeth 19, 130; Jno. 19(2),38; Jno. 55; Johannah 51; John 28(2),40,51,130; Josias 130; Mary 19(3),28,38, 40,51,55; Peter 55; Richans 40

Brine, Hannah 98; Jemima 98; Richard 98; Robert 82
Briscoe, ---- the Widow 48; Christian 63
Brissell, Eliza. O. 20; Mary O. 35
Bristoll, Edward 79; Margtt. 79; Wm. 79
Bristoo, Ruth 209
Bristow, ---- 285; ----hn 288; Alexander 281; Anna 120; Anne 100,102,117, 176; Avarilla 136; Banjamin 171; Bartholomew 205; Benjamin 171(2); Benjamine 152; Benjm. 197,305; Catherine 92, 109,153,194; Cathrine 170; Charles 99,300; Edward 73,139,144,148, 156,159,168,300; Edward Jones 197,305; Edward, jr. 199; Edward, Jr. 199; Edwd. 152,285,299; Eliz. 152; Eliza. 285,299,300; Elizabeth 40,81,124,128, 139,144,148,156,159(2), 171,187,197,205,282,305; Fanny 206,289; George 114,160,285,299,300(2); Hannah 135,196; Jack Phips 171; James 100,109, 114,120,128,136,143,160, 162,163,199,266; Capt. 308; Jane 143; Jedediah 153,239,279; Jedidiah 87, 246; Jemima 114; Jemimah 182; Jidediah 242; Jn. 51; Jno. 15,19,27,34,42; Johannah 15; John 40,49, 58,83,87,92(2),107,171, 172,281,286,299,304(2); Josiah 171,206,282,289; Katherine 87; Len 305; Lucy 303; Margaret 73; Margrett 89,99,111,117, 124; Mariah Daniel 289; Mary 87(2),92(2),100,102, 107,109,114(2),120(2), 128,129,135,136,143,160, 169(2),195,227,234,284, 285,286,288,299,300(2), 305; Michaell 80; Michal 111; Michall 15,19,27(2), 34,40,42,51; Nicholas 42,102,107,114,120,129, 135,162,258,266,307; Nickols 190; Philamon 285; Polly 207; Rachel 281; Richard 148,305; Robert 144,282; Ruth 286, 288; Samuel 129,288; Sanders 202; Sarah 51, 83,156,171; Saunders 206; Thomas 34,82,87,92,300; Tomson 153; William 19, 63,73,89(2),99,111,120, 124,139,187,194,203,208, 235,242,248,278,281,284, 286,288,300(2); William Clark 289; Wm. 117,229, 286
Broadass, Reubin 203
Broadbent, Mary 20
Brock, Eliza. 81; Sarah 162
Bromley, Dorothea 154; Robert 154; Sarah 154
Bromwell, Peter 178
Broocks, John 152; Martha 152; William 152
Brook, Edward 202; Eliz. 193; Elizabeth 193,196; Philip 193

Brooke, Anne 83; Christopher 203; Elizabeth 200; Fanny 200; Philip 200; Thomas 205
Brookes, Alice 79; Ann 40, 50,52(2); Caleb 168,189; Charles 16; Eliza. 19, 40; Elizabeth 89(2),97, 105; Henry 143; Humphery 105; John 20,40,50,89, 97(3),105,112,189; Jon. 27; Jonathan 16,27,31, 34,81; Mary 34,81,112, 169; Paul 143; Priscilla 89,97,105,112; Richard 19,40; Sarah 16,27,34, 81,143; Susanna 169; Thomas 16,19,105; William 40,50,52,80,89, 97,105; Wm. 40,89
Brooking, Samuel 205; Susanna 202; William 280
Brooks, ----shsha 289; Ann 283; Anna 157; Anne 79, 176,199; Caleb 136,145, 165,188; Caless 141; Catherine 127,283,287; Cufflee 193; Cuffley 192; Cuffly 148; Edward 283; Eliza. 28,157,158; Elizabeth 79,86,127,138, 141,154,157,165,188,195, 205,297; Elizth. 141; Frances 122,138,171,189; Henery 86; Henry 139,148, 154,157,168,192; Isaac Holloway 283; Jacob 60; James 160; John 136,145, 148,155(2),157,160,202, 283,287,288,289,298; Jona. 86; Jonathan 93, 102,113,122,131(2),137, 157,193,222,227,245; Jonathon 110(2),236; Joseph 171,199,200; Judith 171,199; Letice 154; Margaret 145; Margrett 102(2),136,179; Margtt 141; Martha 157, 160,287,288,298; Mary 16,86,93,102(2),110,113, 122,131,137,139,148,155, 190,199,257,287,289; Matthew 67; Mayo 137; Patty 283; Philip 158, 189,195; Phillip 28,102, 127,138,141; Prudence 158; Rachel 141,154,297; Rachell 157; Richard 16; Richd. 28; Samuel 202, 287; Sara 67; Sarah 60, 139,148,154,192; Susanna 93; Thomas 199,204; Thomas Mitcham 171,199; Thos. 154; William 35, 60,86(2),113,136,148,157, 178; Wm. 79,287,297
Broster, Ralph 175
Broun, James 168
Brown, Catharine 145; Catherine 149,155,158; Charles 302; Chatharine 139; Elizabeth 68,70,73, 98,155,166; Gaffield 73; Hannah 192; Henry 70,73, 98(2); James 68,139,145 (2),149,155,158,169,190, 191(2),297; Jams. 294; John 198; Mary 30,68, 158,190,191; Miles 203; Nancy 281; Robert 163, 193; Samuel 149; William 70,139,202; Wm. 191

Browne, ---- 77; Eliza. 77,82; Elizabeth 77(2); Henery 77; Henry 32; James 77,80; Mary 35; Thomas 31
Brownley, Dorothea 151; Edward 93; Martha 93; Robert 151(2); William 93
Brumell, Judith 150; Peter 150; Thomas 150,165
Brumwell, Eliza. 19; Elizabeth 19; Ellianor 42; Ellinor 27; Margaret 27; Margarett 80; Peter 18,19,27,42; Thomas 42, 162
Brunwell, Ellinor 15; Peter 15; Sarah 15
Brushwood, George 202,282; James 282; Sarah 282
Bryan, Frances 304; John 209,301
Bryant, Eliza. 285; Frances 129,274,291(2), 293,294,301; Francis 256; John 129,189,200, 224,285(2),296; Patience 170; Williamson 129,189
Bucher, Mary 25; Richard 25
Buckner, John 204
Bueford, Ann 157; Eliza. 157; Frances 142,190; Hen. 190; Henry 142; Thomas 142,190; William 157
Buford, Agatha 164; Aggatha 68; Ann 169; Elizabeth 68,131,161, 166; Henry 178; John 131; Mary 178; Thomas 68,225, 230,234,252,296; Thomas, Senr. 293; Thos. 238, 290; Thos., Senr. 255; Thos., senr. 244; William 131,161,166; Wm. 161,274,292
Burck, Amy 141; John 141; Thomas 141
Burford, Mary 170; Susannah 37; Thomas 275
Burfutt, Ambros 42; Eliza. 42; Elizabeth 42
Burk, ----mas 289; Ann 63; Eliz. 243,279; Eliza. 252,277,290; Elizabeth 124; Henry 107,112,163; Jane 13,14(2); Jeffery 83,95; Jno. 14,25,51, 188,190,236; John 14,25, 71(2),76,84,107,124,164, 224,227,231,240,249,271; Judith 107,112(2); Lettice 51,124,162,188; Mary 25,51,78,95,100; Michal 71; Michall 76, 162; Nickolas 78; Phebe 289; Richard 289; Sarah 100; Thomas 76,78,95, 100,206,208
Burnes, Anne 168
Burnet, Alice 167; Elizabeth 169; Jane 15; Loretta 15; Wm. 15
Burnett, Coretta 19; Jone 45; Loretta 16,24; Richard 45; Sarah 19,24; William 16(2),18; Wm. 19,24
Burnham, John Collo. 22
Burns, Josiah 281
Burrow, John 174

Burt, Elias 165
Burton, Ann 302; Anne 200; Elizabeth 18,205; Isaac 184; Isaack 260; James 170,203; Mary 199; Simon 207; Thomas 199; William 199
Burwel, Carter 170
Burwell, Jane 196; Mary 196; Nathaniel 196,200; Sarah Nelson 207
Bushnell, Honor 163; William 81,85
Butcher, Elizabeth 25
Butterfield, Thomas 9
Buttersby, Johannah 21
Butterworth, Sarah Mariah 198
Buttler, Mary 28; Rich'd. 28; Richard 28
Cain, Daniel 112; Daniell 182; Hannah 99,106,112, 117,126,131(2); James 117; Joanna 186; Johannah 106; John 183; Margrett 169; William 82,99(2), 106,112,117,126(2),131; Wm., junr. 183
Calaham, Jayne 82
Calahan, Ann 192
Calaun, Sarah 205
Caleham, Ann 147; Elizabeth 147,156; Patrick 147,156; William 156
Calehan, Kilman 284; Mary 284
Callaham, Betsy 281; Eliza. 152; James 152; John 281, 305; Margaret 281,305; Patrick 152; William 305
Callahan, Mary 166; Rhoda 202; Richard 164; Timothy 178
Calliham, Elizth. 142; John 142; Patrick 142
Calloway, Elizabeth 18
Callvert, Phillipp 84
Calvert, Anne 83
Cambridge, Edward 81,178
Camell, John 177
Cammiel, James 203
Campbell, Agatha 287; Frances 205; James 160 (2),287; Jas. 249; Judith 160,287; Thacker 206
Campton, Ann 194; James 194; Sarah 194
Canaday, Catharine 179; Edward 33
Canadey, Edward 29
Canady, Alice 83; Mary 72, 82; William 72
Cane, Hannah 77; John 77; Walter 39; Wm. 77
Canidy, Elizabeth 55; Mary 55
Caniff, Catherine 162
Cannedy, Ann 65,73; Elizabeth 73; Lacklin 73; Locklin 65; William 65
Canody, Edward 180
Canser, Alice 186
Cap, Ann 78; Elizabeth 78; Matthew 78
Carbett, John 63
Carder, Ann 65; Sara 70; Sarah 65,70; Uriah 65,70
Cardis, John 59; Judith 46; Uriah 46,59
Cardwell, Agatha 133,160; Ann 35; Anne 103; Eliza. 80; James 171; Jane 109, 115,120,125(2),133;

Cardwell continued
  John 208; Lewis 160; Mary
  97,103,109; Thomas 97,
  103,120,162; William 97,
  109,115(2),120,125,133,
  195; Wm. 160
Care, Mary 50
Caree, Mary 63
Carey, Joseph 165
Carlton, Beverley 207
Carnen, Anne 83
Carnew, Jane 180
Carney, Elizabeth 202
Carpenter, Ann Bushrod 202;
  John Pickworth 22
Carr, p'pson 22
Carrel, John 131(2); Sarah
  131
Carrell, Bettey 192;
  Catherine 126; John 126,
  134,190,192; Sarah 126,
  134,192; Susanna 134;
  William 195
Carrill, Elizabeth 138;
  John 138; Sarah 138
Carryer, Ellianor 12; Jnoo.
  12; Margt. 12
Carter, ---- 30,52; Ann
  54; Anne 105; Charles
  132,135(2); Eliza. 82;
  Elizabeth 30,93,99,105,
  112,139,167; Frances 93;
  George 51,93,99,105,112
  (2); Henry 99; John 162,
  194,202,245; Joseph 35,
  40,62,167; Landon 139,
  168; Mary 17,40,51,52,
  54,62,68,78(2),83,132,
  135,253; Penelope 25,52,
  87; Penlopec 34; Peno.
  17; Phillip 52,179;
  Richard 168; Robert 68,
  132; Robert Wormeley 139;
  Susanna 87; Thomas 25;
  Thoms. 87; William 20,
  23,25,34(2),40,51,52(2),
  53,54,62,68; Willm. 78;
  Wm. 17,30
Carvenoth, Honnor 63
Cary, Ann Madam 38; Oswald
  20; Capt. 39; Thomas 177
Catt, Bridgt. 9
Cauniff, Derby 67; Hannah
  67
Causer, Alice 221; Thomas
  183,215
Cauthon, Anne 203; Richard
  202
Cauthorn, Ann 283; Anne
  284; Catharine 283; John
  284; Richard 283,284
Chadwick, William 196
Chaffin, Christopher 94,
  100(2),108,120;
  Christopher, junr. 185;
  John 94,120; Mary 108;
  Sarah 94,100,108,120;
  William 184
Chafin, Christopher 115;
  Sarah 115; William 115
Chaften, Sarah 167
Chaftin, Sarah 167
Chainey, Thomas 170
Chainy, Pennellope Mrs. 49
Chambers, Ann 29
Chancellor, Mary 103; Wm.
  103
Chaney, Penelope 17;
  William 17
Channing, William 220
Chapman, Henry 207; Jane
  205; John 199
Charles, Sarah 201

Chaseman, Sarah 22
Chaver, William 167
Chayney, Edward 38;
  Elizabeth 50; John 17;
  Pen. 38; Penellope 50;
  Penelope 26; Thomas 26;
  William 26,38; Mr. 50,54
Cheadle, Anne 106; Francis
  230; John 106,211,264
  (2),312; Lettice 106
Cheaney, Cassandra 169;
  Catherine 149; Elizabeth
  149; Thos. 149
Cheany, Penelope 170
Chedle, Hannah 52; Jno.
  52; John 37,38,50(2);
  Millicent 38,50,52;
  Thomas 38
Cheedle, Frances 223,226,
  236; Hannah 162,173;
  Jno. 213; John 83,89,
  96(2),104,113; Lettice
  89,96,104,113; Millicent
  89; Thomas 81,104,113,
  173,176,181
Chelton, Abby 114; Abigal
  163; Anne 72; Eliza 76;
  Elizabeth 85,93,173;
  Henry 174; Margaret 65;
  Mary 72,76,82,83,108,
  114; Peter 81,93,174;
  Peter, Junor. 76; Sarah
  108; Susanna 76,188;
  Thomas 65,72,76(2),93,
  279; William 63,65;
  Zebulon 108,114; Zebulun
  163
Cheney, Cassandra 102;
  Catherine 154(2); Eliza-
  beth 96,168; Jane 96,
  102,108,117(2),187;
  Lettice 185; Penelope
  108,176; Thomas 96,102,
  108,117,167,187,189,195,
  220,224,231,260,265,266,
  268,270,271,307,308;
  Thos. 154; William 168,
  185
Cheny, Jane 90; Thomas 82,
  90(2)
Cheops, Pat 253
Cheseld, Sarah 120;
  William 120
Cheshire, Anne 85,93;
  Ellonar 93; William 83,
  93
Chessells, Sarah 184;
  William 188; Wm. 165
Cheyney, Catharine 158
  Thomas 158; Thomnas 158
Cheyny, Jane 87; Thomas
  87; William 87
Chichley, Henry 7
Chickley, ---- Honble 8
Child, Margarett 82;
  Margtt. 76; Robert 76
Chiles, ---- 161; Eliza.
  161; Hannah 199; Robert
  161
Chills, Mary 80
Chilron, Thos. 193
Chilton, ---- 47; Abigall
  41,47; Abigll. 42;
  Dorothy 152,193; Henry
  41; Margt. 42; Mary 47,
  152; Peter 23,41,42,47,
  175; Sarah 42; Tho. 42;
  Thomas 42,293; Thos.
  152,245,248,254,278;
  Zebulun 47
Chinn, John Mr. 200
Chisman, Catherine 62;
  George 62; Peter 62

Chouder, Jeremiah 274
Chowing, Elizabeth 177
Chowning, ----uel 288;
  Absolom 85,89; Ann 26,
  38,40,51(2),156,171,189,
  195; Anne 111,128,134,
  163,200; Anny 144;
  Bartholomew 132; Betty
  143,149,152,155; Catharine
  201; Catherine 116,121,
  128,286; Charles 149;
  Easter 155; Eliz. 153;
  Eliza. 156,157(2),286,
  288; Elizabeth 93,103,
  129,134,161,201; Frances
  137; George 38,83,93,103,
  111,118(2),123(2),129,
  137,142,164,183,190,195,
  288,293; Henry 153,204;
  James 304; Jane 104,203,
  285,298,300; Jennet 112,
  132,136; Jennett 114,
  119(2),123,127; Jno. 139;
  John 78,116,121,128,134,
  144,149(2),153,156,160,
  164,168,195,200,201,281,
  285,298,300(2); Jone 10;
  Joseph 127; Josias 121;
  Judith 93,136,169; Lucy
  298; Martha 111,118,123,
  129,137,142(2),190,195;
  Rachel 116,139,144,149,
  153,156,160(2),161,205;
  Rachel, Junr. 196; Rachel,
  Senr. 196; Robert 10(2).,
  26,38,40,51,87,149,152
  (2),155,169,206,279,285;
  Mr. 9; Robt. 143; Ruth
  143,288; Samuel 112,114;
  Samuell 40; Sarah 78,85,
  87,89,92(2),97(2),104,
  153,156,179,194; Thomas
  26,32,78,80,87,89,92,97,
  104,139,179,204; William
  103,112,114,119,123(2),
  127,132,136,153,156,164,
  212,224,231,269,270,271,
  286,288; Wm. 157,161,
  220,226,297
Crisp, Thomas 35
Christian, Hester 201
Church, Alice 77; Ann 77;
  Jno. 77; John 81
Churchhill, ---- Coll. 236;
  ---- 240,241; Collo. 263;
  Coll. 274,275,276(2); Mr.
  44,306; Armistead 64,121,
  125,129,137(2),146,148,
  211,212,215,216,217,219,
  220,221,222,223,225,226
  (2),229,232,235,237,238
  (2),239,256,261,264(2),
  265,266,267,268(4),270
  (2),271,272,273,276,280,
  293(3),298,309(2),311(2),
  312(2); Coll. 244(2),
  274,277(2); Armstead 218;
  Coll. 277; Betty 201;
  Betty Carter 201; Eliza.
  259; Elizabeth 64,166,
  172; Mme. 69; Hannah 121,
  125,129,133,137,146,148,
  298; Henry 133; John
  125; Judith 304; Lucy
  146,148; Lucy Harrison
  280; Nathaniel 129,187;
  Priscilla 69; Thomas 213;
  William 73,121,133;
  Colloul. 49; Mr. 44,62,
  63,64; William, Esqr.
  Collo. 69; Wm. 258,259
Churchill, ----- Coll. 235;
  ----beth 309; Armistead
  239,256; Armstead 156,

Crittendon, Richard 202;
Thomas 201
Crockford, John 166,223(2),
227,265,269,271,272,273;
Lucretia 187; Lucy 167;
Mary 166
Croffield, Ann 150,155,
194(2); George 289;
James 150; John 150,194,
289; Lucy 289; Milecent
155; Milicent 194
Cronan, Margret 167
Crooker, William 191
Croony, Mary 83
Crosbee, James 142
Crosbie, James 235
Crosby, Elizth. 169; James
242
Crosle, Mary 168
Crossfield, Catharine 207;
James 200; Nancy 206
Crosswell, James 83
Crouch, Edward 197; James
197; Margaret 197
Croucher, Margarett 88;
Margtt. 88; Thomas 88
Crouders, Elizabeth 127;
Mary 127; Wm. 127
Crowdas, Abner 200;
Abraham 198; Anne 197,
198; Diana 146,193;
Elizabeth 133(2); John
138(2),146,167,197(2),
198; Mary 138,146;
William 133
Crowder, Elizebeth 122;
John 122; William 122
Crowdoss, Sarah 189
Crump, Jane 204
Crutchfeild, Edmund 119;
Eleanor 119; Jane 128;
Stapleton 128; William
119,128; Wm. 228
Crutchfield, Elizabeth 166;
Jane 133; Mary 133;
William 166; Wm. 133
Cuffley, Sarah 168
Cufley, Mary 185
Cukmmins, Anne 103
Cummings, ---- 52; George
52; John 52
Cummins, Agnes 182; Angello
103,109,182; Anne 185;
Augale 83; Christian
109; Elianor 109;
Elionar 103; William 185
Curles, John 63; Michall
162
Curlett, John 176
Curlis, Mary 83; William
178
Currey, Sarah 170
Currie, Rachel 208
Curry, Elizabeth 203
Curtis, ---- 36,198; Mr.
10; Agatha 51,81,88,172;
Avarilla 34,80,188;
Averilla 41; Charles 28,
34,36,129,132,166,206;
Chichester 164,181;
Christopher 88,150;
Eliza. 31,33,51; Eliza-
beth 55,61,62,83,85,115,
129,145,180,183; Fanny
302; Frances 119,150;
Giles 17,34; James 31
(2),33,81,88,132,150,
177,261; Mr. 51; James,
jr. 177; James, junr.
213,262,310; James, Senr.
58; James, Sen. 58;
Jane 34; Jno. 191,273,
274,275; Johanna 129,
132; John 84,145,168,271;

Curtis continued
John, Junr. 72; Martha
115,119,127; Mary 17,
34,52,61,119,199; Mercy
52,55,61,66; Michael 61;
Michaell 52,55; Michall
61; Polly Murray 281;
Rebecca 72; Rice 17,115,
119,127(2),164,209,211,
214(2),216(2),218,263,
266(2),267,306,307,308,
311; Mr. 60,74; Richard
72,119,122,130,164; Rite
62(2); Rose 28(2),34,36,
122; Sarah 41; Susanna
119,122,130(2),188,191
(2); Susannah 145,164;
Tho. Major 41; Thomas
61,184; William 205,303
Custis, John 80
Cutter, John 39
Cutton, Christopher 72;
Hope 72; Mary 72

Dabidie, Mary 83
Dabney, Benjamin 208
Dagnell, Margret 91;
Samuel 91; Samuell 82;
Sarah 91
Dainly, Susanna 92; William
92
Dalley, ffrances 20
Dame, George 283(2); Mary
170,283
Dance, John 202
Danger, Sarah 29
Dangerfield, John 63; Mary
Willis 304
Daniel, ---- 292; ----ver-
ley 288; Abraham 140;
Agatha 127,148,161,194,
196,298; Ann 72,139,145
(2),152,155,156,160,196,
286,287,288,290,299;
Ann. 298; Anne 112,118,
127,133,167,198; Ave
148,194; Beatey 152;
Benjamin 144; Betty 150,
155,157,194,199,280,298;
Beverley 282; Catharine
201; Catherine 155,194;
Charles 72,137,140,144
(2),150,168,191,242,246,
249,250,254,255,256,279,
293; Chickeley 130;
Christopher 143; Clara
171,283; Clary 155,279;
Constant 152,245; Curtis
284; Dorrothy 160; Eliz.
143,152; Eliza 117,287;
Eliza. 150,155,161,284;
Elizabeth 72,110,122,
128,133,138,148,168,187,
192,197(2),283,286,289;
Esther 134; Frances 152,
158; Frances Ann Travers
282; Frances Meacham
295; Frankey 152; Garret
148,192,195,240; Garrett
68,230; Garrit 155;
George 122,131,207,283,
285; Henry 128,131,138,
150,152(2),155,157,166,
187,189,194(2),221,229,
234,237,238,247,250,268,
278,296,298(2); James
63,64,67,72,109,114,
120,124,130,135,140,165,
232,238,263,264,273,296;
James, junr. 235; Jane
130,137(2),140(2),144,
150(2),168,193; Jenney
124; Jenny 135; Jochabed
25; Jochebed 21;

Daniel continued
John 109,138,160(2),171,
197,211,283(2),304;
Josiah 118,196,287;
Judith 168,283; Katherine
152,193; Leonard 286;
Lucy 112,158,282,286,287,
288,297(2),303; Lunsford
201; Lydia 201; M. 199;
Margaret 67,72,190; Mrs.
68; Margarett 169,211;
Margoret 64; Margret 128,
187,189,226,271,272;
Margrett 109,114,120,124,
210,212,221,229,230,264,
272; Margrett, junr. 185;
Mary 21,117,128,131,134,
138(2),139,144,152,153,
155,167,175,187,189,193
(2),207,285; Milecent
139; Millicent 190; Milly
282; Moseley 157,185;
Nelson 207,285; Obediah
153,157,253; Oliver 202;
Peggy 205; Peter 67,140,
150,193(2); Phebe 114;
Rachel 64,139,164; Rich.
299; Richard 72,110(2),
156,160,171,286,299;
Richd. 288,298; Robert
112,117,122,128,133,134,
138,144,148,152(2),155,
157,158,161,167(2),187,
190,192,193,194,226,246,
249,259,265,277,278,286,
287,288,290,297; Mr. 49,
68; Robert Beverley 282;
Robert, jr. 198; Robt.
139,143,150,232,242,272,
274,277; Robt., Senr.
305; Ruth 135; Samuel
128; Sarah 133,153,157,
167,208,257; Susanna 160;
Susanna George 207;
Susannah 169; Thadeus
283; Thomas 150,208,283;
Vivion 120; Will 152;
William 12,112,127,133
(2),145,156,164,181,196,
199,267,283,284,287;
William, Junr. 213;
William, Senr. 262,310;
Wm. 25,118,139,196,233,
236,253,256,259; Wm.,
junr. 271,272,309; Wm.,
junr. 229
Daniell, Agatha 25,101;
Aggatha 63; Anne 83,95;
Catherine 80; Charles
149; Constance 40,51;
Constant 99; Elizabeth
75,83,95(3),101,103,107,
112,183; Frances 91,99,
178; Garrett 236; Henry
55,223; James 78,91,96
(2),149,306; Jane 149,
163; Jno. 78; Jochebed
14,31,32,103; John 31,32,
51; Judith 75; Margaret
50; Margret 112; Margrett
96,216,221; Margt. 55;
Margtt. 78,82; Mary 62,
78,88(2),95,101; Richard
14,75,95,103; Robert 36,
50(2),55,78,95,101,107,
177,270,308,310; Capt.
59; Cap. 75; Robert,
Junr. 101; Robt. Capt.
75; Ruben 107; Sarah 62;
William 14,31,32,40,62,
82,91,95,99,181; Capt.
44; Mr. 40,51; William,
junr. 312; William, Junr.
29,33; William, Senr. 101;

Daniell continued
wm. 32,78,95; Wm., jun.
219; WM. 88
Danill, Elizabeth 55;
Mary 55; William 55
Dannolly, Lettice 164
Darby, Eliza Churchill 289;
John 280,289,304; Lucy
289
Darrell, Charles 188;
Sampson 167,188
Darrill, Charles 131;
Elizabeth 131; Sampson
131,228
Davenport, Reuben 204
Davids, David 77; Jonathan
77; Mary 77
Davidson, Katherine 50;
Mary 50; Richard 50
Davies, Benjamin 77; Betty
165; Constant 93,167;
Dianah 86(2),167; Eliza-
beth 92,127,174; John 77,
84,86,88,92,93,99,258;
Margarett 77; Margrett
93,99; Martha 88; Mary
84,99; Rachell 92;
William 127(2),261
Davis, ---- 50; Alice 13,
17,50,95; Andrew 128,
135(2),140,146,148,151,
166,192,228; Ann 17,30,
32,70(2),72; Anne 83,
164,286; Arthur 182;
Avarilla 95,177,184;
Barbee 140; Benja. 80;
Benjamin 70,72,145,148;
Benjamine 16,138,142,168;
Catherine 168; Christian
72,166; David 37,50,51,
62(2),66,167; Dorothy
159,300; Dorrithy 299;
Elisha 59; Eliza. 152,
155,156,157; Elizabeth
59,98(2),103,128,135,
138,140,142,146,148(2),
151,152,162,167,192,193,
202,281,299,302; Elizth.
143; George 14(2),16,
146,196; Henry 17,18,30
(2),32(2); Hester 32;
James 106,159,206,299,
300; Jno. 17,32,143;
John 13(2),18,25,31,32,
33,50,63,67,71,76,106,
110,138,145,148(2),152,
155,157,167,168,172,177,
181,187,188,231,286;
Judith 142,145,148;
Lewis 157; Margaret 67,
71,148; Margret 187;
Margrett 106; Martha 50,
51,202; Mary 32,62,66(2),
71,76,92,148,152,162,166,
170,192,196,300; May 201;
Richard 92,151; Robert
59; Ruth 167; Sarah 13
(2),17,25(2),29,71,80,
103,110,164,168,184;
Staige 205; Stapleton
302; Susanna 14,71,143,
164,303,304; Susannah 16;
Thomas 17,71,76,80,92,
173; Timothy 32; William
67,83,103,110,128,152(2),
155,156,159,162,166,181,
196,309; Wm. 246
Davison, Richard 38
Dawd, John 7
Dawson, Leonard 142;
Margrett 142; Mary 133;
Thos. 142,169; William
133(2)

Day, Ann 145; Edmund 141,
145,148,168; Jane 127;
John 127,141; Judith
127; Mary 141,145,148(2)
Dayly, John 77; Mary 77;
Sarah 77
Dazier, James 121; John
121; Sarah 121
Deacon, Patrick 82
Deagle, Ann 201,287; Anne
178,304; James 117,285;
John 95,155(2),170,199;
Mary 155; Maryan 287;
Patrick 95,106,110,117;
Rebecca 95,106,110,202;
Rebeckah 117; Samuell
106; Sarah 285; William
110,201,285,287
Deagon, Ann 87; Patrick
87; Rebecca 87
Dean, Betty 288; Eliza.
299; Elizabeth 200,205;
Frances 199,200; John
199,200(2); Sarah 200;
William 199,299(2)
Deane, Beverley 204
Dearclone, John 22
Dearelone, Jno. 25;
Katherine 25; Margarett
25
Dearlow, Margrett 83
Dee, ---- Mr. 262
Deforces, Cornelius 299;
Sarah 299
Deforeest, Cornelius 285;
Eliza. 285; Elizabeth
285
Degge, Anthony 89; Hannah
309; James 100; Johanna
78,88(2),89,100; John
78(2),80,88,89,100,183,
213,264,307,308,311;
William 199
Dejarnatt, Daniel 201
Dejarnet, George 204
Dejarnett, Nancy 303
Dempsie, Maurice 186
Denison, Catherine 80;
Jonathan 202
Dennis, Catherine 46; Jno.
46; Rebecca 46
Dennison, ---- 198
Depree, Abraham 35
Deputy, Mary 90; Robert
18,80; Thomas 90
Derby, Southey 304
Deshago, Robert 162
Dess, Wm. 81
Devall, Elliner 196
Deverdall, John 21
Devolve, James 177
Dewd, Rachell 7; Richard 7
Dews, Augustine 48; Jone
48; Richard 29; Richd.
31; William 48
Dewton, Penelope 82
Diamond, Henry 180
Diatt, Thomas 179
Didlak, Ann 206
Didlake, Catharine 203;
Catharine B. 281; Eliza-
beth 206; James 206;
Mildred 280; Nancy 204;
Philip 207; William 206
Didlick, Robert 205
Digge, John 210
Diggs, Joanna 175
Dillard, Edward 139,149,
150,156,160,168,239,241,
250,254,288; Edwd. 143,
292; Elizabeth 156,204,
206; Frances 139,202;
George 280; Jane 203;

Dillard continued
John 149; Lucy 160;
Martha 139,143,149,150
(2),156,160,288; Mary
143,171; Nicholas 170,
246,250,253,255,293,294,
295(2),297,300,301;
Nichos. 296; Sarah Major
205; Susannah 257; Thomas
171
Dilliard, Delphia 203
Dillion, Edmun 196; Edmund
280; Garett 196; Martha
196
Dillon, Edmund 150; Martha
150(2)
Dinely, Susanna 162
Ditton, Edmund 147,154;
John 154; Martha 147,154;
Ruthe 147
Dixon, Michael 203
Dobbs, Catharine 196;
Catherine 120; Elizabeth
102,120,125,134,189; Jno.
169; John 102(2),120,
125,134; Josiah 134;
Samuel 125; William 193
Dobs, Elizabeth 107,114;
John 107,114(2); John,
junr. 179; William 107
Docker, ffrances 19,54;
Ann 19; Edward 19,20
Dockey, Ed. 8
Dodson, ffrancis 14,18,44,
47; Eliza. 14; Francis
14,60,69,71,85; Jane 69;
John 265; John Hackney
47,183; Mabel 71; Mabell
44,60(2),165,174; Mable
69; Rachel 165; Rachell
44; Rebecca 71,187
Donnelly, Arthur 82
Donnolly, Arthur 181
Dorrell, Elizabeth 134(2);
Sampson 134
Dose, John 194
Doss, Ann 16,30,33,37;
Ellener 63; Ellianor 16;
Jno. 30,169; John 16,18,
33,150; Mary 150; Sarah
150; Thomas 30,33;
William 16
Dougherty, Charles 168
Douglas, James 185
Dourey, Elizabeth 33
Douton, Anthony 19; Eliza.
19; Elizabeth 19
Dowlin, Ann 28; Antho. 28;
Anthony 40,51; Eliz, 40;
Eliza 28; Eliza. 51;
Elizabeth 40; Penelope 51
Downe, Katherine 38
Downey, Anne 175; John 204
Downing, Daniell 81; Eliza.
11(2),81; Elizabeth 11,
68; Lettice 82; William
11(2),68(2); Wm. 11
Dowtin, Anthony 38; Eliza.
38; Thomas 38
Dozier, Sarah 184
Drue, Mary 20
Drummond, Caty 207; Mary
203; Samuel 207
Ducksworth, ffaith 88;
Abel 97(2); Abell 88,105;
Faith 97,105,176; John
105; Mary 88
Duckworth, Ann 191; Thos.
169
Dudding, Humphrey 26(2),
28; Humphry 32; Mary 28;
Sarah 26,28
Dudenfield, Ann 21

Dudlass, Ann 46; James 46
Dudley, ---- 284; Major
47; --ances 196; ffrances
30(2),33(2),41,44,80;
ffrancis 46; Agnes 201;
Ambros 46; Ambrose 104,
119; Ambrus 300; Ann 42,
45,139(2),145; Anne 111,
113,119,127,133,180;
Averilla 68; Benjamin
284; Betty 304; Charles
201; Chichester 91;
Dorothy 44; Edith 72;
Edy 69(2),165; Eliza. 16,
34(2),39,44,82; Elizabeth
18,43,68,73,91,95(2),98,
100,104,110,113,173,193,
300,303; Mrs. 43,55,58,
67; Frances 196,197;
Hannah 280; James 16,18,
34,39(2),42,71,124,131,
135,141,165,224,229,270,
284; Jamess 45; Jane
124,131,133,135,140,148,
152,190,193,197; Jean
141(2); Jno. 22,139;
Johannah 206; John 44(2),
69,72,110,113,119,127(2),
133,145,163,176,204;
Joice 287; Joyce 155;
Judith 111,120,133; Kezia
300; Lewis 140,196,197;
Lucy 155; Marlow 148;
Mary 24,30,38,42,71,82,
135,145,207; Payton 73;
Rebecah 285; Rhoda 206;
Richard 72; Robert 30,
55,58,68,71,83,91,95,
100(2),104,120,133,148,
152(2),167,170,193(2),
207,251,259,260; Major
55; Mr. 43; Robt. 140,
190(2),307; Sarah 16;
Stanton 131,170; Tho 7;
Tho. 30,41; Thomas 33,
38,44,80,98(2),110,155,
190,207,209,270,287(2),
307,308; Thomas, Junr.
73; William 24(2),30,
41,45,111,120,124,133,
163; Wm. 38
Dudly, Edyth 43; George
43; Jane 256; John 43;
Robert Major 43
Dues, Richard 20
Duff, Abraham 61; Ann 61;
George 53,54,61; John
54; Rebecca 53,54
Duffe, George 51; John 51;
Rebecca 51
Duggin, Alice 89; John 89;
Thomas 89
Duglas, Ann 45; Ellianor
46; James 45(2)
Dugless, Ann 80
Dulany, Susanna 209
Dunbery, James 169
Dunkington, Ann 56;
Elizabeth 56
Dunlap, ---- Revd. Mr. 199;
Debby 204
Dunlavy, James 198; John
198; Mary 304
Dunlevy, Ann 201; Braxton
205; Eliza. 195; Eliza-
beth 149,153,195,200,
282,284(2); James 149,
153,195(2),200,242,282,
284(2),285,288,297(2),
304; James Jones 200;
Jane 285,288,297; Joanna
284,287; John 284,285,
287; Levi 282; Mary 153,
195,200,287; Nancy 284;

Dunlevy continued
William 149
Dunn, Elizabeth 205; Hanna
204; John 203
Dunstan, Warner 202
Dunston, Eliza. 46; John
170; Thomas 46; William
46
Durham, Eliza. 160;
Gregory 160; Paul 173;
Robert 160; Sarah 198
Durram, Eliza. 299; Ransom
299; Robert 299
Dye, Ann 157; Arthur 146,
157; Jane 146; Richard
146; Sarah 157
Dyer, James 20

Earley, Elizabeth 85,126;
Jeremiah 126,166; John
126
Early, Elizabeth 67;
Jeremiah 67; Thomas 67
Easter, Mary 162
Eastree, Richard 162
Eberson, John 165
Eddington, Dorothy 21;
Eliza. 35;
Edey, Sarah 29
Edmonds, Mary 163
Edmondson, Judith 208
Edmunds, Jephtha 72;
Jeptha 63,80,175; Mary
72; Nicholas 72
Edmundson, James 167
Edmunston, James 184
Edward, Pearse 176
Edwards, Ellianor 18;
James 167; Joyce 192;
William 204
Eeles, Mary 168
Eggleston, Joseph 285(2);
Judith 285
Elee, John 21,54
Elerson, Elizabeth 133;
John 133; William 133
Eliot, Ann 148; Elizabeth
148; Thos. 148
Ellerson, Eliza. 124; John
124; Mary 124
Elliot, Eliza. 157; Eliza-
beth 155,160,299; John
160; Margret 168; Mary
155,303; Mathew Kemp
157; Matthew 202; Robert
155,157,160,254,299(2);
Thomas 172; William 172,
202
Elliott, Ann 206; Eliza
79; Eliza. 86; Elizabeth
90(2),175,199; Margtt.
86; Mary 31,33,79,90,
200; Sarah 31,33,35;
Tho. 31; Thomas 32,33,
82,86,90(2); William 81,
90
Ellis, Anne 166; Edward
17; Eliza. 9; Ellis 164;
Hezekiah 98,183,209,214,
306,311; Mary 98,165;
Richard 32; Sarah 98
Elwood, Grace 20
Emberson, Henry 195;
Sarah 195
Emerson, ---- 188; Eliza-
beth 107; Henry 62,107,
118,123,129,136,188;
James 118; Jane 123;
Margret 129; Mary 62;
Sarah 107,118,123,129,
136(2); Thomas 62
Emmerson, Betty 113; Eliza.
50; Elizabeth 180,204;
Henery 78; Henry 35,50(2),

Emmerson continued
Henry cont.: 68,113;
Joanna 68; John 78; Mary
68,78; Sarah 113
English, George 151; Mary
20; Richard 151; Sarah
151
Enos, Ann 20
Erickson, Hance 20
Erixson, Hance 19(2);
Judith 19
Estree, Richard 185
Eubank, Ann 171
Evans, Catherine 186;
Elizabeth 70; James 51;
John 40(2),51,165;
Matthew 70(2); Pen. 40;
Penelope 51; Thomas 304
Eyre, Jonathan 201

Falkner, Benjamin 171;
Elizabeth 198; Jane 201;
Lucy 207
Fares, William 192
Fargueson, Thomas 206
Farrell, Anne 183; Edward
97,104(2); Judith 97;
Margrett 97,104
Fary, Edmund 193
Faulkner, Anne 110(2);
Elizabeth 137; Ellis 115,
121(2),126,184,187; Henry
110; Jacob 137,166; John
298; Judith 201,298; Mary
115,137,298; Mildred 137;
Sarah 126,202; Tho. 223,
269; Thomas 115,121,126,
164,167
Fauntleroy, Thos. 170
Fearn, Ann 109,115,121,127,
130,136(2); Dorothy 121;
Geo. 296; George 104,
289,294,295,298; Jane
298; Jno. 142; John 98
(2),104,109,115,121,127,
130,136,149,162,186,194,
268; John, senr. 245;
Judith 130; Machen 115;
Mary 109,298; Sarah 98,
104,142,176; Thomas 127,
149,186
Fearne, John 163
Feild, Stephen 162
Fenning, John 202
Fenwick, Mary 184
Fernald, George 204
Ferrell, Catherine 128;
Martin 128; William 128,
187
Finley, Frances 208; Hugh
63
Finney, Anne 165; Honor
163; John 57(3); Margaret
57(2); Richard 176;
William 57,175
Fisher, Anna Mrs. 161
Fleet, Anne 104; Henry 104;
William 104
Fleming, John 124; Nancy
204; Samuel 124; Susanna
124
Fletcher, Joyce 166
Flippen, John 202
Floyd, Jane 169
Fluewelling, William 193
Fontaine, James Maury 201
Foster, Elizabeth 83; John
182; Nancy 206
Foudry, Nancy 280
Foulk, Andrew 175
Fourget, Charles 139;
Elizabeth 139; Elizth.
139

Fox, James 297; John 297; Margret 168; Owen 32; Tabitha 297
Fox (?), Mary 32
Foy, Mary 180
Franks, Elizabeth 166
Frazar, Alexander 276
Frazeir, Alexander 237
Frazier, Alex. 239(2),247, 293; Alexander 168,237 (2),244(2),246,254,270, 274,275,277,280; Mr. 240(2),276; Alexdr. 242, 249,290; Alexer. 255(2); Alexr. 292,294,297,300
Freeman, Anne 184; Henry 178
Freestone, George 103,162; Mary 103; Sarah 103,178
French, Anne 131; Catherine 200; Mary 131,137,142, 207; Thomas 131,137,142 (2),166; William 137
Fretwel, John 148; Mary 148; William 148
Fretwell, Mary 144,153; Rebecka 153; William 144(2),153; Wm. 247
Frygore, Francis 20
Fuller, Martha 208
Fulsher, Anne 118; John 118; Sarah 118
Fureman, Robert 278
Furgoson, Mary 126; Mildred 126; Thomas 126
Gabriell, Ann 26; Anne 82; John 26; Richard 21,23, 26
Gaffeild, William 172
Gaffield, Mary 162
Gail, ---- 251
Gaile, ---- Mr. 248; Mathias 278
Gaille, Mathias 244
Gaines, Dorrity 146; Henry 303; Richard 146; Thomas 202; William 146
Gale, ---- 252,289,290, 296(2),297(2),300; Henry 54; Mathew 237; Matthew 279; Matthias 240,247, 250,256,273,274,275(2), 278,293
Gales, Stokeley 81
Gallbarth, Robert 163
Gallifor, John 63
Gardener, Ann 66,197; Betsey 197; Catherine 66; Naney 197; William 66,197
Gardiner, Agathe 169; Ann 52,77,141; Betty 167; James 147; Mary 52,141, 147,151; Rinwing 81; William 77,147,151(2), 248; Willm. 141; Wm. 52, 77; Wm., Senr. 190; Wm., senr. 244
Gardner, Agatha 97; Amey 48; Ann 55(2); Anne 92, 97,124,165,174; Blackly 158,196; Catherine 137, 164; Diana 16,85,92; Elizabeth 110,149,205; Frances 137,189; George 205; Henry 299; James 137; John 110,158,196, 296,299; Judith 124; Martha 162; Martin 85, 159; Mary 16,47,48,136, 155,158,159,162,196,206, 299; Rinning 84; Solomon 155; Thomas 16, 20,136; William 47,55,

Gardner continued
William cont.: 92,97, 110,124,136,155,163,168, 187; Wm. 159,255
Garland, Elizabeth 203, 302; Mary 281
Garret, Amy 159,298; Edmond 204; Humphrey 159,298; James 298; Mary 280; Thomas 159
Garrett, Agatha 206; Ann 206; Franky 201; Maretia 206; Nancy 203; Rachel 202; Sarah 202
Garton, William 171
Gasking, Lewis 29
Gates, Peter 16; Rose 25 (2),30,38; Roseamond 16; Tho. 25,30; Thomas 16, 18,38(2),174; Thomasin 30
Gatewood, Sally 204
Gayer, John 188; Lucy 123; Mary 123,134; William 123,134(2),188
Gayre, Willm. 190
Gear, Mary 192
Gellett, Ann 31; Eliza. 31; Tho. 31
George, Alice 12,37; Ann 141,282,283(2),284; Anne 111,117,122,128,175; Betty 111; Catherine 40, 60,68,81,120,175,205; David 12(2),32,60,68,78, 88,96,183,214,309,313; Eliz. 163; Eliza. 285, 288; Elizabeth 146,204; Elizth. 141,144; Frances O. 303; Hally 78; Harry 195; Henry 146; James 167; James Meacham 283, 284; Jane 55,164,204; Jno. 139; Joanna 68; John 12,32,60,62(2),117, 120,123(2),133,145(2), 150,165,202,268,285,303; John Batchelder 282; Judith 88; Katherine 88, 96; Katherine 78; Leonard 150,207,302; Lewis Dudley 283; Lewis Dudly 284; Mary 12,96, 123,133,179,304; Meacham 123,285,288; Michal 123, 139,145,150; Michall 120; Michel 133; Rachel 146,195; Richard 79,168; Richd. 141,144; Robert 35,40,51,55,62(2),79, 111,117,122,123,128(2), 162,218,220,231,266; Robert, junr. 185,214, 220; Robert, senr. 229; Robert, Senr. 189,209, 214,224,263; Robt. 260, 311; Robt., Senr. 262, 263; Sarah 40,51(2),55, 62,79,82,122,189; Smith 62; Susanna 144,165,202; Susannah 139; William 202,281,282,283(3),284, 303
Gerrard, Anne 90; Jane 90
Gess, Eliza. 15; Susanna 15; William 15,17
Gest, Elizabeth 151,194; Elizth. 142; Geo., Senr. 191; George 142,151,191; James 151; Milly 203; William 142
Gibbor, John 10
Gibbs, Anne 111; Diana 89, 169; Eliza. 87;

Gibbs continued
Elizabeth 46,83; Grigory 16; Jno. 46,47; John 16, 43(2),59(2),64,70,71,72, 75,94(2),128,182,209,212, 216,264,268; Marran 72, 166; Marrin 70; Mary 16, 43,46,47,59,64,70,72,75 (2),94,111,117,128,166, 186,220; Penelope 87,89; Richard 87,89; Richd. 82; Sarah 117; Stephen 47; Thomas 111,117; Zacarias 226; Zacharias 64,128
Gibson, Ann 134; Catharine 201; Charles 26,303; Churchhill 199,287; Gregory 26; Henry 154; Isabel 287; Isabell 149, 154; Isbell 207; James 134,149,154,167,169,287; Job. 32; John 81,134,149; Lucy 206; Marke 11; Mary 26,183,299; Matthew 11; Robert 299; Thomas 180
Gilbert, James 179
Gilbreath, ---- 178
Gilham, Ann 41,42; John 42; Lucas 41; Robert 41,42
Gilinwater, Thomas 164
Gillet, Rebecca 167
Gilley, Elizabeth 44,48; Jane 44,48,57; Mary 175; Tho. 44,48; Thomas 57, 81; William 57,177
Gilliam, Ann 38; Elizabeth 38; Robert 38
Gilliams, ffrances 25; Ann 25; Robt. 25
Gilly, Thomas 163
Gilpen, Henry 222
Gilpin, Henry 186,214,311; Mary 166
Ginkins, Ann 146; Charles 146; John 146
Glen, Jno. 130,139; John 139,165; Mary 130,139; Matthew 302; Sarah 130
Gless, Abraham 187
Glou, Elizabeth Rilee 206
Goar, Anne 183; Henry 102; John 119,131(2),165; Josee 115; Joseph 43,98 (2),102,109,115,183,212, 264,266; Joseph, senr. 174; Lucretia 98,102,109, 115,166; Lucy 144; Margaret 43; Mary 83,119, 131,144,163; Rachel 119; Sarah 163; William 167, 231; Willliam 144
Goare, ---- 140; Benjamine 178; Eliza. 81; Henry 143; John 143; Joseph 81, 90; Lucretia 90; Mary 143; Susanna 140; William 90,140; Wm. 275
Godbee, ffrances 48; Edward 48,60,66; Frances 60,66; John 66; Mary 48,164; Rebecca 60,163
Godby, ffrances 81
Goddin, Mary 65(2); Thomas 65
Godding, Thomas 189
Godin, Anne 83; Thomas 82
Godloe, George 166
Godwin, Ann 76; Thomas 76; William 76
Goear, Joseph 71
Goinge, Henry 207
Golden, Thomas 81
Golder, Elizabeth 75; Mary 75; Thomas 75

Good, Anne 124,129;
Catherine 129; Jane 124;
John 124,129,165,204
Goode, Elizabeth 203
Goodin, Mary 23
Goodloe, Anne 88,180;
Avarilla 94; Catherine
105; Eliza. 79,88,94;
Elizabeth 105; Henery
79,88; Henry 85,94,105,
262; Jane 79; Mary 163
Goodlow, Ann 17,63; Eliza.
54; Elizabeth 62,68(2);
George 17,54; Henry 54,
62(2),68; Mary 17,53
Goodrich, Eliza. 79; Mary
182; Rebecca 53
Goodridge, Elizabeth 34;
Margt. 34; Patrick 34
Goodwin, George 127,139(2);
166,170,192; Jane 129,
138,139,142(2),192; Jno.
142,238; John 68(2),79,
138,166; Mary 68,190;
Robert 129,138,187
Gord, Thomas 209
Gordon, Bridget 94;
Bridgett 99(2),174,180;
Brown 180; James 179;
Johannah 166; John 23,
94; Margrett 99; Mary
23; William 94,99,177;
Wm. 211,212,214,228,232,
264,267,270,273
Gore, ---- 59; Ann 76;
Benjamine 59; Joseph 76;
Joshua 43,45,46,59;
Lucretia 76; Margaret 43;
Mary 43,45,46(2); Sarah
45
Goslin, Mildred 304
Gough, Edward 43; Mary 43;
Susannah 43; William 37
Gour, Joseph 209
Graky, Samll. Mr. 50; Mary
35
Grasson, Charles 34; Mary
34; Tho. 34
Graves, Alexander 78(2),
80,88,101,164,176,193,
212,217,224,228,235,237,
244,262,264,268,274,306,
312; Alexr. 244; Anny
101; Hannah 88,169; Mary
78,88,101,178,278,279
Gray, ---- Mr. 45; Ann
Madam 45; Mrs. 43,44;
Benjamine 45; Eliza. 82;
George 44; Israell 32;
Mary 63,182; Samuell Mr.
43,44(2),45; William
164,187,212,222,268,311
Green, ---- 286; Ann 13;
Elizabeth 185,206;
James 286,289,301; John
126; Martha 289; Mary
13,126; Richard 126;
William 9,286
Greene, Mary 32,33
Greenstead, Richard 29
Greensted, Richard 33
Greenwood, -rances 285;
Anne 112,119(2),125,132,
183,188; Benjamin 155,
191; Benjamine 120;
Betty 138; Catherine
135,138,141,191; Eliza-
beth 111,115,120,126,
149,159,168,281; Francis
287; Henry 141; James
111,115,180; Jno. 142;
John 149,151,155,158,
168,193,285,286(2);
Lodowick 158; Lucresey 285;

Greenwood continued
Lucretia 142,151,155,
158,286; Mary 125,155,
159,169,299; Mildred
112; Rhodes 149; Richard
112,119,125,132,135,138,
164,167,188(2); Richd.
141; Robert 155; Samuel
126,287(2); Thomas 111,
115,120,126,132,135,142,
187,188(2); William 151,
299; Wm. 155,159
Gregory, Christian 167;
John 165
Gresham, ffrances 82; Aimey
45; Amey 48; Ann 190;
Anne 92,102; Charles 48,
103,163; Eliza. 44;
Ffrancis 48; Jno. 190;
John 48,83,92,102(2);
Mary 45,48,103; Tho. 44,
45,48; Thomas 48,92,179;
William 103
Gressam, ffrances 44
Gressett, Jane 166
Griffin, Corbin 199; Mary
148; Morrice 172; Rachel
148; William 148,170
Grimes, Ann Mrs. 44; Jn.
143; John Collnl. 43;
Mr. 45
Grindee, Jane 99; Thomas
99(2)
Groom, James 208; John
171,202,203; Rebekah
200; Richard 208; Robert
171,282; Susanna 171,
282; Valentine 282;
Zachariah 207
Grymes, ---- Coll. 242(3),
253,277(2); ----nnah 288;
Alice 115; Ariana Maria
303; Benjamin 200;
Benjamine 119; Charles
112,131,138,185,188,201,
235; Frances 138; Jane
281; Jno. 232,234,236,
237(2),239,307; Honble.
274(2); John 101(2),105,
110,112,115,119,128,131,
136,160,188,211,214,216,
218,220(2),221,222,225,
226,227,229(2),230,231,
232,233(2),234,240,247,
259,260,262,265,266,267,
269,270(2),272(2),273
(2),274(3),308(2),309,
312,313; Coll. 241,242,
243,244,248; Colo. 250;
Coll. 276,279; John,
Esqr. Honble. 247; John,
Esqr. 280; Lucy 101,105
(2),112,115,119,128,131,
136,138,160,170; Ludwell
136; Mary 160(3),198,
285(2),288; Philip 110,
160(3),285,288,303;
Philip Ludwell 160,198,
200; Phillip 255; R.
307; Sarah 128,188;
Susanna 200
Guess, Eliza 80; Eliza.
17,28; Elizabeth 107,
110,124,129; Geo. 78;
George 107,110,124,129;
Hannah 78; John 107,179;
Judith 129; Michal 124;
Michal 124; Nathaniell
28; William 17,28
Guest, Elizabeth 26,101
(2),117; Frances 147;
George 20,26,52,87,96,
101,117,147,162; Goerge
87; Hannah 87,96,173;

Guest continued
Jane 96; John 52; Mary
26,52,96,147; Natty 117
Guillams, Ann 31,33; Peter
31,33; Robert 33; Robt.
31
Guilliams, Ann 17; Robert
17(2)
Gulley, Philip 204
Gunter, Charles 143,168,
300; Judith 143,290;
William 143
Gutery, Frances 150;
William 150(2)
Gutherey, William 188(2)
Gutherie, David 164; Frances
155,158; John 160;
Margaret 155; Mary 160;
Nanny 160; William 155
Guthery, ----uel 288; Ann
192; Eliza. 51; Frances
145(2),288; Frances Pain
286; Jno. 51,54; Mary
54(2),286; Masey 51;
William 145,192,288
Guthree, ---- Major 284;
Betsey 284; Phebe 284
Guthrey, Eliza. 40; John
40(2)
Guthridge, Henry 25; John
25; Rebea. 25
Guthrie, Ann 149,158,203;
Daniel 149; Edward 192;
James 203; Jane 157;
John 157; Mary 157,187,
204; Sarah 149; William
158,187
Guthry, John 29
Gutterie, John 81,82;
Judith 168
Guttery, Anne 111,116;
Betty 102,169; Elizabeth
92,116; Frances 129,132,
135,141; Garritt 114;
Henry 121; James 126;
Jane 88(2),94,101,180;
John 33,88,94(2),101,112,
114,121,126,141,164,189;
Lettice 102,111,116,135,
185,190; Lucy 199; Mary
92,112,114,121,126,129;
Nanny 101; Rachel 116;
William 102,111,112,116,
126,129,132(2),135,162,
166,181; Wm. 141
Guttrey, Ann 34; Eliza.
34,50; Jno. 34,50; Mary
194; Richard 50
Guy, John 26,53; Mary 26,
53; Tho. 26,53; Thomas
37
Gwathmey, Richard 204

Hackett, Chickley 117;
John 98; Martin 91; Mary
91,98,103,109,117; Thomas
83,91,98,103,109(2),117,
215; William 103
Hacklefoot, George 32; Tho.
32
Hacknay, Willm. 236
Hackney, Absolom 151,193;
Alice 90,97,104,109,114,
120; Anne 114,182;
Benjamin 194,204,208;
Benjamine 109,159;
Catharine 302; Eliza.
46,153,156,160; Elizabeth
145,151,155,159,166,193,
203; Jacob 155; Jane 202;
Joanna 163; Johannah 46;
John 95,120,183; Lewis
145; Luse 153; Mary 35,
44,90,167; Priscilla 156;

Hackney continued
  Rebecca 44,95,162; Salle
  160; Sarah 104; William
  41,46,82,90,97(2),104,
  109,120,145,151,153,155,
  156,160,169,193,232,240,
  249,264,292,307,312;
  William, Junr. 254;
  William, Senr. 251,254;
  Wm. 44,114,159,229,244,
  247; Wm., junr. 290,293;
  Wm., Junr. 41
Haddley, James 28; Jno. 28
Hadley, Sarah 162,174,258
Hadly, John 49
Haily, Sally 200
Haines, Charles 45,48;
  Eliza. 45,48; Elizabeth
  51; Hannah 51; Margrett
  165; Margt. 48; Sarah
  45,86; Thomas 51
Halcomb, George 149; Sarah
  149; William 149
Haley, Eliza. 299; Judith
  299; William 299
Halfhide, Sarah 41; Wm.
  Mr. 41
Hall, Elizabeth 18; James
  205,284; Joseph 163;
  Martin 60; Mary 60(2),
  284; Nathan 207; Patsey
  280; William 284
Halyard, William 206
Ham, Richard 169
Hamat, Catherine 69;
  Elizabeth 69; William 69
Hamerton, Edmond 83;
  Edmund 93,172; Lydia 85,
  93; Pinchback 182; Sarah
  93,163
Hames, Ann 43; Charles 43;
  Eliza. 43
Hamilton, James 126; Mary
  126
Hammelt, William 184
Hammett, Catherine 166
Hammut, Eliza. 87; William
  87(2)
Hamock, William 63
Hancock, ffrances 19;
  Eliza. 19,27,41; Tho.
  19,27,41; Thomas 27;
  William 41
Hanson, George 32
Harbinson, Eleonar 127;
  William 127(2)
Hardee, Abraham 110;
  Agatha 145(2),148,153,
  155,160,299,300; Agathy
  297; Andrew 140,145,149,
  153(2),158,169,191;
  Avarilla 91,99,119,165,
  178; Averella 106;
  Averila 66(2); Averilla
  125; Catherine 155;
  Charles 91; Constance
  145,153,158; Constant
  140,149; Curtis 169,195,
  243,250; Elizabeth 155,
  195; Isaac 184; Jane 79,
  176; John 77,79,94,110,
  119,124,145,148,153(2),
  155,160,169,184,192,248,
  297,299,300; Joseph 66,
  91,99,106,124,145,165,
  190,209,213,218,266;
  Joseph, Senr. 186;
  Josiah 300; Margarett
  77,158; Margrett 94,110,
  119,163; Margtt. 79;
  Martha 94,192; Mary 124,
  135,140,191; Mildred
  Orrill 125; Perrott 99;
  Rhoda 149; Robert 77;

Hardee continued
  Sarah 106,148,192;
  William 135,160,297
Harden, George 310
Hardin, Anne 96; Eliza.
  77,255; Elizabeth 96,254;
  Geo. 77,237,246,278;
  George 96,223,224,226,
  231,233,241,242(2),250,
  269,270,278; Lucy 168;
  Thos. 77
Hardine, George 216
Harding, Elizabeth 73,111;
  George 111,210,219,262,
  271(2),306,307,311; Mary
  111; Nicholas 73; Peter
  73
Hardy, Avarilla 77,79,86;
  Avery 209; Isaack 88;
  Joannah 77; John 88(2);
  Joseph 77,79(2),86;
  Margarett 88; Mary 86,
  203; Peggy 201
Haren, Joathan 159; Mary
  159(2)
Hares, Ann 11(2); William
  11
Harfoot, William 63
Hargrove, Mary 164
Hargraves, Augustine 110;
  Mary 110
Harkins, Bryan 9(3);
  Cornelius 9; Hannah 9(2)
Harrell, Edward 80
Harrelson, Eliza. 18
Harris, Anne 115; Elizabeth
  115; John 115
Harrison, Joseph 53; Sarah
  37
Harrod, George 193
Harrow, Anthony 282; James
  284; John 171; Sarah Ann
  171; Sarah Anne 197;
  Thomas 171,197,282,284;
  William 197
Hart, James 203
Hartford, William 54
Hartley, Ann 35
Harvey, Joseph 21; Lucy
  204; Mabell Mrs. 3I;
  Nicholas 63
Harvie, James 187; Joseph
  29,31; Mabell Mrs. 29
Harwood, Christopher 170;
  John 199; Nancy 303;
  Thomas 202
Haselwood, Anne 107,179;
  Jane 107,166; Thomas
  107,211,262,308
Haslewood, ffrances 53;
  Ann 40(2); Anne 96;
  Geo. Mr. 53; George 23,
  40,53; Mr. 53; Jane 96,
  113; Mary 32(2),113;
  Tho. 32; Thomas 28,96,
  113,186,217
Hatfeild, Mary 187
Hatton, Anne 96,164; John
  83,96; Roger 96
Hauks, George 201
Hayden, Judith 20
Hayes, Thomas 202
Haynes, Charles 64; Eliza-
  beth 64,206; George 205;
  Margrett 64
Hayns, Alice 71; Ann 71;
  Charles 71
Hayton, Fanny 202
Haywood, Conquest 119;
  Joshua 119; Mary Jones
  (alias) 119(2)
Hazelwood, Tho. 310
Hazlewood, ffrances 10;
  Anne 81; George 10,81;

Hazlewood continued
  Jane 79; Jno. 10; John
  Capn. 81; Mary 28; Tho.
  28; Thomas 75,83
Healey, Elizabeth 198;
  John 201
Healy, Eliza. 158; Eliza-
  beth 160(2),280,298;
  Frances 303; James 209;
  James, Junr. 281; Jane
  303; Joanna 158; Judith
  304; Sarah 302; Thomas
  160,204,302; William 158,
  205,298; Wm. 160
Hearin, John 152; Jonathon
  152; Mary 152
Hearing, Anne 202; Joanna
  202; Zebulum 201
Hearn, Bridgett 162;
  Elizabeth 135; Mary 135;
  Richard 135,167; William
  176
Health, Anne 116; Frances
  116,121,124,129; Henry
  129; James 130; John 116,
  121,124(2),129; Mary 130;
  Thomas 130; William 121;
  Wm. 184
Hebble, John 206
Hedgcock, Thomas 18
Hefferman, Henry 281;
  Rector 281(2),289,302
Heffernan, Henry 198,263;
  Rector 170,302,303; Lucy
  Nelson 198; Sarah Letitia
  198; Mrs. 198
Henderson, James 204
Hendring, William 180
Hendson, Elizabeth 145;
  Isaac 145; Peter 145
Henesey, Jane 153; Jno.
  138; John 149(2),153,154,
  194; Mary 138(2),149,153,
  154; William 154
Hening, Lewis 205
Henly, George 304
Hennesey, John 143; Mary
  143; Thomas 143
Henning, Ann 77; Jona. 77;
  Mary 77
Henningham, Benjamin 207
Hepstinstall, Judith 287
Heptenstall, Daniel 127,
  186; James 127; Rebecca
  127
Heptinstall, Alse Wilkin
  287; James 123(2),130,
  134,165,286,287; Judith
  286(2); Phillip 134;
  Rebecca 123,130,134;
  William 130
Herbert, ffrances 20
Herrin, Ann 69; Anne 73,
  167; Jonathan 69,73;
  Mary 201; Sarah 73;
  William 69
Herring, ----ery Goar 288;
  Ann 101,157; Anne 95,109
  (2),116; Benjamin 204;
  Benjamine 101; George
  116; John 95,288; Jonat-
  han 95,101,109,116,157;
  Mary 157,169,288; Sarah
  169
Heughen, Robert 202
Heyward, Charity (mother)
  34; Elizabeth (daughter)
  34; Tho. (father) 34;
  Thomas Mr. 39
Hibble, Ann 282; John 207,
  282,284,304; Mary 205,
  257,282,284; Mathew
  French 284

Hickee, Charles 79;
Elizabeth 79; John 79
Hickey, Elizabeth 66(2),
82; John 66,181
Hickman, Thomas 22
Hicks, Jenny 165
Hill, ---nces 288; Ann 14,
19,26,30,33,46,48(2),69,
76,87; Anna 129; Anne
92,100,149,163(2),183,
192; Dianah 92,168;
Dorothy 21; Edward 192;
Eliza 21; Elizabeth 69,
164,165; Frances 86,88,
89,96,103,110,118,123(2),
129,149,192,193,196;
Humphrey 286; Isaack 81;
Isabell 166; Isabella
46; Jane 83,286,288;
John 76; Joseph 21;
Judith 103,170,200; Mary
14,87,168,201; Needels
286,288; Needles 118;
Priscilla 100; Rebecca
19,30,33,79; Richard 84,
89,188,210,223,264,278,
279,306; Richd. 269;
Russel 149,192; Russell
96,149,170; Susannah 17;
Tho. 14,19,26,30,33;
Thomas 86,110,176,193;
William 10,26,46,69,82,
87,88(2),89,92,96,100,
103,110,118,123,129,166,
176,193,196,228,234,279;
William, senr. 241; Wm.
48,76,86,196(2),237,256;
Wm. junr. 251
Hillen, Salley 208
Hipkings, Andrew 40; James
312; Jno. 40; John 34(2),
49,212,271,272; Sarah
34,40
Hipkins, James 83,191; Jno.
239,275; Mr. 74; John
191,217,222,227,233;
Mary 169; Thomas 58;
Winifrid 82
Hipkinstall, Judith 200
Hiptinstall, Alice 304;
Elizabeth 140; James 140;
Rebecka 140
Hoar, John 85
Hoard, Jane 78; John 78(2)
Hobbs, William 37
Hodgekings, Ann 20
Hodges, Ann 200(2); Anne
196,197; Charles 158,
196,284; Churchhill
Anderson 289; James 284;
John 196,197,200,204,
289; Mary 158,284,289;
Sally 302; Thomas 158;
William Brookes 197
Hogans, Richard 18
Hogg, Roger 187
Holderby, John 209
Holderness, Abigall 187;
Robert 163,214,216,222
Hollan, Mary 169
Holland, Daniel 68(2);
Eliza. 81; Jane 68;
Joseph 118,183; Mary
118(2),183
Holleway, Catharine 202
Holley, William 22
Hollinsworth, Hannah 22
Holly, Alice 63
Hollyday, Rose 18
Holt, William 208
Homes, Anne 78; Joseph 78;
Robert 78
Hone, Katherine Mrs. 18;
Theophilus 31;

Hone continued
Theophylas 29
Hooker, Rebecca 208
Hopkings, James 31; Mary
31
Hopkins, Eliza. 23; James
8,257,303; Mary 8;
Richard 206; Sarah 8
Hord, James 88; Jane 88;
John 88,307
Hore, Elizabeth 61; Jane
61,68; John 61,68;
Susanna 68
Horn, Bathsheba 183
Horne, Jonathan 80
Hornsby, Mercy 142; Thomas
142
Horseley, Catey 287; James
Taylor 206; Rhoda 287;
Thos. 287
Horsley, Smith 206
Horton, John 186
House, Eliza. 16; Nicho.
16; Nicholas 16,18
How, Alexander 164,180;
John 165; Mary 164
Howard, Ann 152; Anne 71;
Eliza. 285; Elizabeth
155; Eustace 130,135,
142(2),152,155,167,195;
George 178; John 130,
285; Mary 135,285; Ruth
130,135,142,152,155;
Simon 71; William 71
Howell, Richard 11
Howerton, Charles 201
Howes, Sarah 81
Howrd, Robert 148
Hoyl, Ann 69; Elizabeth
69; Samuel 49,69
Hoyle, Anne 81; Saml. 79
Hoyt, Elizabeth 71; Mary
71; Samuel 71
Hubard, Mary 201
Huchison, Hugh 187
Hucklescot, George 30;
Tho. 30
Huddle, Mary 80
Hudging, Aaron 156;
Johanna 156; Mary 156
Hudgings, Lucy 304
Hudson, Ann 153,157; Anne
160; Elizabeth 156,208;
George 153,297; John
153,157,297; Martha 297;
Mary 32,160; Peter 156,
160,247; Sarah 156;
William 157
Hues, Anne 106; Daniel
101,109(2),115,176,186
(2); Daniell 92,96(2),
106; Elizabeth 186;
Frances 92,96,101(2),
106,109,115; John 89,
92,98; Mary 63,89,98;
Rebecca 89,98,164;
Thomas 115; William 109
Hugget, Thomas 257
Hughes, ffrances 88; Ann
76; Anna 174; Daniel
121; Daniell 82,88;
Eliza. 15,19; Elizabeth
121,202; Frances 121,
166; Jno. 15; John 76,
79,82,174,190; Mary 88,
169; Rebecca 76; William
19,174; Wm. 19
Hughs, Ann 55; Eliza. 35;
Elizabeth 70,165; John
65(3),70; Mary 173;
Milicent 37; Rebecca
65(2),70; Richard 55;
Robena 15; Sarah 13;
William 13,20,65

Humfreys, Eliza 76(2);
Joseph 76
Humpheries, Anna 95; Anne
165; Elizabeth 95,102,
130,183; Joanna 175;
Johanna 85; John 130;
Joice 97; Joseph 95,102
(2),105; Mary 165; Rebecca
97,105; Robert 97,105;
William 130,186
Humphreys, Mary 164
Humphrees, William C. 303
Humphreys, ---- 68; Ann
20,69; Anna 169; Eliza.
41; Elizabeth 47,69,72;
Joanna 72; John 72,76;
Joseph 41,69,72; Mary
202; Rebecca 47,68,72,76;
Robert 41,47,68,72,76;
William 29
Humphries, ---- 197;
Avarilla 129; Elizabeth
129,137,143,192; Elizth.
143; Jno. 143; John 137
(2),166,192,197; Joseph
129; Nelson 197; Staige
303; William 281
Humphris, ----iam C. 281;
Ann 146; Elizabeth 118,
192,194,206; George 280;
Jno. 169; John 146(2),
295; Joseph 118,192(2);
Lucy 171; Nelson 257;
Sarah 118
Humphryes, Katherine 37
Humphrys, Ann 15,153;
Elizabeth 64; George 153;
John 15,153; Joseph 15,64
Hundley, Thomas 205;
William 203
Hunnings, Phillip 20
Hunt, Dorothy 53; Elen 208;
Mary 67,164,232,241,268,
276; Mathew 186,210,225,
263; Matt. 310; Matthew
50,67,80,215,218,221,259,
261(2),268; William 67,
81,162,184
Hunten, John 8
Hunter, Daniel 147; Mary
147; Seth 147
Hurford, Mary 80
Huskett, William 181
Hutchings, Mary 20
Hutchinson, John 69,76,77;
Jos. 77; Joseph 69,72,
76,80; Mary 69,72,76,77;
William 72
Hutson, Ann 147; Dorothy
200; Edward 51; Henry
147,197; John 147,197;
Rebecca 51; Sarah 197;
William 51,200(2),201
Hutton, Jane 299; John 299;
Mildred 199,299
Hymphrys, Mary 64

Ingam, John 162
Ingram, Ann 27,35(2),44(2);
Anne 162; Averilla 120;
Charity 101,175; Eliza.
82; Elizabeth 40,179;
Frances 90,172; Harding
128; James 19,27,40,105,
109,114(2),120,124,128,
163; John 19,83,101,124,
172,186; Margret 128;
Margrett 105,109,114,120,
124; Mary 164; Priscilla
109; Samuel 101; Samuell
35(2),44; Sarah 19,27,
40,173; Solomon 105;
William 178
Ison, Mary 205

Jack, William 257
Jackman, Robert 208
Jackson, Andrew Mr. 58;
 Anne 170; Catharine 170,
 209,281; Elianour 80;
 Johannah 201; John 198,
 199; John, Jr. 208;
 Judith 170,171; Lucinda
 L. 303; Mary 197,205,
 243,247,251,255,294,296;
 Nancy 171; Susanna 197;
 William 161,197,207
Jacobs, Benjamin 204;
 Patty 303
Jacobus, Angell 53; Anne
 106; Jannett 164; Jennett
 106; Joseph 106,179
James, Dorothy 28,38,50,
 52; Edward 28; Elizabeth
 38; Jane 52; John 120;
 Mary 50; Priscilla 120;
 Robert 28,38,50,52,120,
 173; William 206
Jameson, James 178
Janison, James 162
Jarrett, Mary 83
Jarvis, John 170
Jarvise, Sarah 95; West 95
Jaxon, Ann 20; Susan 23;
 Susanna 13; William 13
Jeffereys, Ann 32
Jefferies, Gowen 209
Jefferson, ---- 289;
 Daniel 159,200(2),202,
 282(3),284(2),289(2),
 304,305; David 159,200;
 Diana 289; Elizabeth 200;
 John 282; Joshebed 159;
 Lucy 284; Mary 200(2),
 207,305; Polly 305;
 Priscilla 282(2),284(2),
 289(2); Thomas Hill 284;
 Wm. 289
Jefferyes, ffrances 30;
 John 30; Wm. 30
Jefferys, ffrances 32;
 John 32; William 32
Jeffreys, William ffitz 21
Jeffries, Ann 203; William
 304
Jellett, Ann 33; Elizabeth
 33; Thomas 33
Jelley, Dudley 79
Jemson, Elizabeth 100;
 James 100; Rebecca 100,
 166
Jenings, Margtt. 81
Jenkins, Eliza. 80; Hannah
 192; John 192
Jenkinson, Mary 37
Jennings, Elizabeth 176;
 George 173
Jervis, Mary 163
Jesse, John 208
Johnson, Alexander 134;
 Ann 145,149,169,192;
 Anne 99,110,120,165,204;
 Aquilla 115; Arthur 175;
 Benjamin 149; Benjamine
 138; Daniel 128,187;
 Eliza. 195; Elizabeth
 63,75,120,134,188,285;
 Esther 75; George 99;
 Henery 75; Henry 123,
 285,290,291; James 145;
 Jane 136,191; John 20,29,
 44,76,82,99,110(3),120
 (2),145,149,162,176,185,
 188,192; John J. 44;
 Joice 70; Jonathan 110,
 115,120(2),125,134,138,
 164,264; Judith 65,70,
 76,134,163; JOhn 180;
 Lucy 44; Margaret 149,

Johnson continued
 Margaret cont.: 254,293;
 Margeret 152,155; Margret
 128,132; Margrett 111,
 120,123,136; Mary 109,
 166,192,202; Priscilla
 110,115,120,125(2),134,
 138,188; Rebecca 84;
 Robert 65(2),67,70,76,
 134,167,188; Robt., Senr.
 223; Samuel 132,155,191;
 Sarah 149; Stephen 109,
 152; William 37,80,109,
 111,120,123,132,136,149,
 152,155,163,164,188,285;
 William, Senr, 195;
 Willliam 111; Wm. 128,191
Johnston, Ann 140; Anne
 133,188; Avarilla 140;
 Eliz. 40; Eliza. 33,51;
 Elizabeth 60; George 29,
 33,40,51(2),60; Henry
 60; Jane 146; Jno. 140;
 John 33,133,168,188;
 Margaret 146; Margrett
 140; Mary 140; Rebecca
 40; Robert 186; William
 133,146; Wm. 140
Jolley, Henry 166
Jolly, Anne 128,132;
 Dudley 162,179; Eliza-
 beth 132,188; Ellis 128;
 Henry 128,132,188
Jone, Wm. 296
Jones, ---- 24,139; Mr.
 24; Agatha 119,126,152;
 Alice 32; Ann 41,53,139,
 154,169,171; Anne 109,
 118,132,161,162,295;
 Barker, 79,167; Benjamine
 87,106,139; Caroline C.
 303; Catherine 94,156,
 170; Charles 106(2),310;
 Churchhill 45,160,250,
 252,254,255,287,289,292,
 294,295,296(2),298(3),
 300,304; Churchill 251,
 278; Dorothy 106,154;
 Elianor 87; Elizabeth
 15,78,79,87,90,96(2),
 152,154,158,169,176,182,
 195(2),199,281; Elizabeth
 M. 281; Ellianor 21; Em
 Minister 275; Revd. 168;
 Emmanuel 67; Fanny 207;
 Gabriel 280; Hannah 54,
 66; Henry 41; Humphery
 163,262,305,310; Humphrey
 67(2),75,79(2),87,90,96,
 156,183,209,213,214,217,
 220,225,227,235,238,243,
 244,270,277,294,306; Mr.
 8,241; Humphry 21,24(2),
 215,216,231,266,275;
 Humphry. 290; Humpry.
 290; Isaac 304; Isabell
 129; James 66,109,119,
 126,152,165,195,298;
 Jane 17,27,36,67,118,
 156; John 17,54,66(2),
 71,80,87,90,98,106,109,
 129(2),166,250,252,255,
 256,290,292; Joseph 87,
 106; Joshua 154; Josuah
 98; Judah 59; Judith
 164; Lodowick 201; Lods-
 wick 90; Lucy 257;
 Margarett 29; Margt. 33;
 Mary 14,15,19(2),20,44,
 45,47,56,59,66,69,78,
 82,94,154,159(2),208,
 292; Mdm. 69; Mrs. 73;
 Millecent 160; Millicent
 287,298; Molly 288;

Jones continued
 Nicholas 27,81; Parnell
 71,90(2),98,106; Peggy
 156; Phebe 154,298;
 Philiman 154; Rebecca 71;
 Rice 17,18,27,229,263;
 Richard 118,132,154,164,
 298; Roger 44,45,47,56,
 59,73,94,160,193,215,220,
 223,226,228,233,236,240,
 244,261,263,265,271,277,
 305,308,311,312; Mr. 49,
 58(2),69,73,74; Roger,
 junr. 177; Rogr. 245;
 Sarah 223,288,294,298,
 301; Sissely 21; Susanna
 162; Susannah 44; Susan-
 nah Churchhill 47; Tho.
 14,19; Thomas 14,15,56,
 126,158,206; William 29,
 32,66,119,132,154,158,
 159,169,171(2),174,201,
 245,249,287,288,300; Wm.
 78,195(2),298,301
Jordan, Ann 64(2); Anne 79,
 82,163; James 63,64,79;
 John 79; Rachel 203
Jordon, Ann 209
Jowel, Ann 209; Michal 145;
 Ratlif 145; Richard 145;
 Richd. 169
Joy, Eliz. 25; Elizabeth 22

Kain, Roger 169
Keeling, William 200
Keiling, Catherine 92,96,
 101,106(2); Lydia 92;
 Osborn 101; Thomas 83,92,
 96,101,106; William 96
Keith, ---- 257
Kelley, Janet 158; Patrick
 262
Kelligrew, Caty 208
Kelly, Catharine 165;
 Patience 201; Patrick
 164,181
Kelshaw, Anne 97; Christopher 97,101(2),106,110,
 162,181; Esther 110,181;
 Francis 106,192; John
 110; Mary 97,101,106,110,
 187
Kemp, ---- Capt. 46; Majr.
 241; Maj. 277; Mrs. 248;
 Ann 47,61,202; Madam 47;
 Anne 117; Elizabeth 110;
 Ellianor Mrs. 61; Hannah
 198; John 199; Judith
 130; Mary 104,110,117,
 125(2),130,186,253,255;
 Mathew 212,213,214,216(2),
 220,226,230,233,238,239,
 260,261,262,263(2),265,
 266,272,306,311,312;
 Mathw. 239; Matt. Major
 240; Matth. 236; Matthew
 104,110,117,125,130,172,
 216,218,219,242,243,244
 (3),260(2),264(2),269(2),
 270,272,277,278(3),303,
 305,307,309(2),311,312,
 313; Collo. 47; Peter
 199; Rachell 61; Richard
 61(2); Mr. 59(2); Sarah
 104,183; Thomas Mr. 67
Ker, David 304
Kersey, Elianor 51; Eliza.
 51; Jno. 51; John 53
Key, Alice 81; Mary 82
Keys, John 198
Kid, Alice 78; Duel 149;
 Edmund 171; Henery 78;
 Jno. 139; John 139,151;
 Margaret 149; Mary 149;

Mederas, Benjamine 159;
Charles 159; Mary 159
Medley, Elianor 88,94; John
88(2),94; Lucy 208;
Robert 94; Zena 208
Medly, Elianor 88; James
88; John 88
Meecham, Eliza 80; Henery
79; James 78,79,80,87,
93(2); Jane 78; John 79,
84; Joseph 78; Mary 79
(2),87(2),93; Michall 79
Meechan, John 80
Meeres, Henry 53
Meggs, James 171
Mellican, Thomas 191
Merchant, Charlotte 207
Meredith, Kitty 204;
William 203,208
Merry, Elizabeth 165;
John 182,183
Mesan, Allexandr. 44;
Eliza. 44; Elizabeth 44
Meuler, Ann 142(2);
Nicholas 142
Michael, Margaret 40
Michaell, Edward 9(2);
Jane 40; Patrick 40
Micham, Anne 108; Daniell
55; Eliza. 53; Elizabeth
118; James 27,108,118;
Jane 55; Jno. 27,51;
John 15,24,55(3),184;
Joseph 15,55; Mary 108,
118; Micall 15; Michaell
55; Michall 24(2),27,51;
Pead 51; Sarah 164
Michelborough, Edmund 225,
228
Michelborrough, Edmund 225
Michener, Jno. 48; Mary
21,48; Susannah 48
Michiner, Mary 80
Mickelborough, Edmond 211;
Edmund 230; Henry 228,
301
Mickelborrough, ----rah
299
Mickelburroug, Edmd. 238
Mickelburrough, Anne 202;
Edmund 179,307,311;
Frances 124; Hen. 238;
Henry 124,245,247,248,
288,294,298,299; Jane
124,200; John 204;
Robert 247; Susanna 288,
298,299; Vivion 298
Mickleberry, Edmund 65;
Henry 65; Jane 65
Mickleborough, Edmond 78,
86; Jane 78,86(2);
Nancy 303; Tobias 78
Mickleburrough, ---- 157;
Edmd. 234; Edmund 55,61
(2),106,137,163,191,217,
220,265,270(2); Edmund,
Senr. 39; Eliza. 28;
Elizabeth 28,106,132,
165; Frances 128(2),132,
137,141,196; Henry 128,
132,137,141(2),146,157,
165,169,196(2),223,252,
256,269,271,290; James
146; Jane 55,61,168,191
(2),196; John 55,61,172,
180; Robert 61,205;
Ropert 106; Sarah 63;
Susanna 146; Susannah
157; Tobias 23,28,53,185
Micou, John 177
Micurday, Martha 183
Middleton, Mary 17(2),27,
174; Prissilla 27;
William 17,27

Midleton, Susanna 179
Milbey, Joseph 283; Lucy
283; Susanna 203
Milby, Elizabeth 204;
James 205; Ruthey 203
Millar, Ann 139; Christo-
pher 139; Mical 139
Millener, John 65(2); Mary
65
Miller, Anderson 304; Ann
81,145,206,285,287;
Anne 105; Christian 253;
Christopher 121,145,285,
187; Christr. 289; David
285; Elizabeth 48,112,
118,167; Hannah 65,164;
Isham 287; James 126;
Jane 92,118,182; Jno.
44,46; John 44,48,65,70,
83,92,100,105,110(2),
112,117,121,126(2),145,
162,181,187,201,280;
John, junr. 182,187;
Mary 92,117,168; Michal
65,70(2),169; Michall
44,46,48; Nancy Davis
170; Patrick 46,112,118,
164,186; Patrick, junr.
185; Priscilla 100,175;
Sarah 100,105,110,117,
121,126
Mills, Elizabeth 209; Mary
204
Minie, Richard 257
Minor, Benjamin 171; Diana
78,166,174; Doodis 11,
14; Eliza. 14,23; Eliza-
beth 162(2); Garrett 75
(2),78,80; Mr. 49; Garrit
311(2),313; Garritt 178,
211,214,263(2),264,268,
305,306,307; Gerrat 14;
John 78,217,218; Minor
58,82,172
Mins, Ann 14,16,21; Elizabeth 14,21; Tho. 16;
Thomas 14,16,21,54
Minter, ----er 280; John
171,283(2); Lickey 283;
Mary 171; Sukey 171
Mitcham, Dorothy 68; Henry
68; Jane 82; John 82;
Judith 89; Mary 68,89;
Thomas 89
Mitchell, Isaac 202; John
204; Sarah 204
Mitchener, John 71(2);
Mary 71
Mitchiner, John 71; Mary
71(2)
Molloney, Joan 176
Monnoughon, James 82
Montague, Catharine 190,
201,304; Catherine 200;
Charlotte 206; Elizabeth
198; Elizabeth Stannard
200; Elizabeth 282;
Elizabeth Stannard 303;
Elizabeth 303; Frances
282,283,302; Hannah 206;
Jane 208; John 170,200,
201; John Curry 206;
Martha 283; Philip 282,
283; Samuel 303; Sarah
S. 304; Thomas 206; Mr.
49; Thomas T. 303; Thos.
239; William 207; Mr.
49; Wm. 233
Month, Henry 99,175; Mary
99
Moor, Daniel 143; Daniell
169; Edward 83; Eliza-
beth 143; Macham 85;
Martha 183; Mary 143;

Moor continued
Richard 63; Thomas 177
Moore, Abraham 81; Benjamin
203; William 202
More, Samuel 202
Morgain, Christopher 298;
Sarah 298; Wm. 298
Morgan, Ann 65; Catherine
183,304; David 176; Jane
202; John 65(2); Sarah
Gale 208
Morris, Elizabeth 197;
George 245; James 197;
John 197; Macktyre 78;
Prudence 78; Thomas 78;
Winefred 245; Winnie 195
Morton, Elinor 194
Moseleey, Sarah 172
Moseley, Agatha 86,97,108
(2); Aggy 127; Anna 131;
Elizabeth 117; Jenny 111;
Jno. 236; Jochebed 166;
John 100,111,117,123(2),
162,211,219,220,224,227,
230,232,264,271,311;
Joshabee 86; Judith 97;
Marril 131; Marvel 127,
136,166; Marvell 86,97,
108,269; Marvil 219,261;
Marvill 19(2),225; Mary
100,111,117,123,127,131,
136,187; Sarah 19,100;
William 136
Mosely, Agatha 66,90,179;
John 90,216,305; Marvell
66(2),180; Marvill 63,90
Moulson, Anne 108,179;
Charles 113,287,288,298;
Easter 190; Elizabeth
204; Esther 125; George
113,119,125,167; Mary
160; Oliver 160; Richard
108,113,119,125,163,187,
298; Ruth 287,288,298;
William 108,160,203,287
Mountague, ---- 37; -braham
288; Abraham 54; Ann 286;
Bettey 286; Betty 287,
288,299; Catherine 134,
148,149,176; Charlotte
205; Clement 114; Eliza-
beth 124(2),149,162,193,
195,285,287; Frances 171,
282; Grace 99,104,109,
114,184; James 152; Jane
132,138,144(2),149,152,
155,158,193,285,298;
John 19,109,138; Katherine
55; Latane 289; Leette
62; Lettice 54; Lewis
286,287,288,294(2),296
(2),299,300; Mary 19,21,
62,299; Penelope 124,129,
134,143,148,295,296;
Peter 19,99,124,165,187,
298,307; Philip 143,171
(2),282,295,296(2);
Richard 205; Robert 155;
Samuel 158; Tho. 55,215,
262,263,309(2),310,312;
Thomas 75,99,104(2),109,
114,124(2),129,132,134,
143,162,165,187,202,210,
230,246,247,251,263,291,
296(2),301,308,313; Tho-
mas, Senr. 178; Thos. 148,
195,224,225,232,238,242,
244,248,252,256,278,289,
290,301; William 54,55,
62,129,132,138,144,155,
158,162,166,193,217,220,
250,267,276,278,285; Mr.
84; William Latane 282;
Wm. 149,152,213,226,231,

Owen continued
Michaell 78; Michal 73,
86,93; Michall 93;
Micholl 97; Nancy 304;
Patrick 71,80,175; Ruth
194; Sarah 136(2),139,
140,165,191,202; Susanna
137; Susannah 189;
William 9,71,140,146(2),
150,154,158,164,168,189,
192,194,201,228,232,235,
240,243,273,276,277,284,
288,299(2); Willm. 139;
Wm. 76,78,86,142,195,
266,270

Pace, Abraham 136,190; Ann
145,297; Anne 110,117,
122,129,132; Benjamin
145,286; Benjamine 131,
135,140; Benjn. 191;
Daniel 129; Eliza. 52,
54,79; Elizabeth 68,93,
131,132,136,141,174,193;
Elizth. 169; George 85,
93,117,182; Hannah 141,
151,154,158(2),286,297;
Jane 68,168; Jno. 54;
John 52,68,79,93,110,
132,136,151,162,163,178,
190,194; Joseph 110,117,
122,129,132,135,163,191;
Josiah 122; Lettice 132;
Margaret 54; Margrett
164; Mary 126,131,132,
135,140(2),145,164,167;
Newsome 79; Sarah 52,162;
Susan 189; William 126,
151,154(2),158,168,200,
286,297; William, Junr.
195; Willm. 141
Packett, Judith 168
Page, ---- Mrs. 240; Daniel
187; Joseph 187; Man 82
Paggot, Betsey 207
Pain, Catherine 108,114,
121(2); John 114; Mary
80; Thomas 108(2),114,
121
Paine, Ann 51,52; Anne 81;
Barnard 52; Catherine
95,102; Eliza 80; Eliza.
52; Elizabeth 38; Frances
102; Lettice 95; Mabell
38,51; Nicholas 38,51;
Thomas 21,83,95,102
Palmer, Isaac 199; Sarah
75,82; Thomas 75; William
280
Pamplin, Mary 201
Pannell, Loretta 18
Paret, William 194
Parish, Elizabeth Averilla
284; John 282,283,284;
John Draper 283; Milly
283; Reuben Laten 282
Parke, ffrancis 81; Edward
80
Parker, James 18,35
Parkes, Jane 20
Parr, Ralph 29
Parrat, Elizabeth 11
Parrett, Henry 142; Rachel
142; Sarah 142
Parriott, Nancy Vevel 199
Parris, Eliza. 20
Parrish, John 171; Josias
171
Parrot, Sarah 168
Parrott, Ann 139,192,305;
Anne 208; Catherine 144,
158; Curtis 139,192;
Dorothy 153,305; Eliza-
beth 153; Frances 139;

Parrott continued
Henry 190; James 158;
Joseph 305; Ludowick 140;
Penelope 163; Mrs. 58;
Rachel 190; Richd. 190;
Robert 140,144; Sarah
140,144; Thomas 158;
William 153
Parry, Betty 89; Mathew
88,89,173; Richard 54;
Sarah 88,89; William 88
Parson, John 63
Parsons, Mary 80,167
Pate, Eliza 80; James 35
Pateman, Mary 177; Thomas
63
Paterson, Mary 156; Richard
156; Susanna 156
Patison, John 160; Mary
160; Sarah 160
Patman, Richard 190
Patre, Eliza. 15; Eliza-
beth 15; John 15; Matthew
15
Patris, ---- 18; Eliza.
24; Matthew 24; Thomas
24
Patterson, ----ma 288;
Ann 171(3); James 171
(5); John 171,288; Mary
288; Richard 171; Sarah
171; Thomas 171,203;
William 304
Payne, Betty 205; John 20;
Mary 31; Michael 200;
Nicholas 35
Peachey, ---- 198
Peachy, Thomas Griffin 209
Pead, ---- Mr. 14(2),23
(3),25(3),26(2),29,35,
37,40; Agatha 39; Deuel
39; Mr. 31,37; Deuell
31; Mr. 34; Duel 37;
Duell 22,27; Sarah 34,
39; Madm. 31; Madam 34
Pearce, Elizabeth 62; John
62; Mary 62; Rebecca 174
Pearse, Edward 180
Peirce, Catherine 93;
Edward 93; Rebecca 93
Pemberton, Eleonour 97;
Elizabeth 97,174; John
97
Pendergrass, Edmund 101;
Elizabeth 173; John 83,
99(2),175; Mary 85,99,
101,163; Robert 101
Peniel, Elizabeth 117;
John 117; William 117
Peniell, Elizabeth 91,107;
John 91(2),107; Thomas
107
Penniell, John 183
Pepper, Honor 163; William
163
Percifull, Mary 63
Perin, John 33
Perkins, Eliza 79
Perrin, John 29
Perrot, Elizth. 191; Henry
68; Richard 68,168; Sara
68; Sarah 168
Perrott, ---- Mr. 9(3);
ffrank 41; Agatha 122;
Anne 94,101,108,114(2),
122,128,134; Avarilla
108; Averilla 42; Betty
89; Catherine 90,106,
166,178; Charles 128;
Catherine 111; Clara 94;
Curtis 42,83,94,101(2),
108,114,122,128,134,270;
Daniel 134; Efforella
25; Henry 41,137,167;

Perrott continued
James 111,135; John 106;
Katherine 77,79,86;
Margt. Mrs. 36; Mary 42,
80,137; Rachel 137;
Rachell 191; Richard 17,
41(2),78(2),80,87,219;
Mr. 33,41(3); Richard,
Senr. 29; Richd. 25,28;
Mr. 11,53; Richd. Junr.
17; Richd., Senr. Mr. 31,
36; Robert 28,42,77(2),
79,80,86,89,106,111,135,
167,181,192; Sarah 17,25,
28,41(4),78,79,87,135,
173,191; Mrs. 53; William
86,87
Perry, Gregory 204; Matthew
81; Sarah 163
Peters, Heany 203; William
171
Petty, Ann 15; Christian
12,15; Max 36,37; Maxa-
milian 12(2),15
Pew, Penelope 20
Philips, Elizabeth 65; John
167; Margarett 65;
Samuell 65
Phillips, Catherine 68;
Eliza. 25; Jane 25,68;
John 68; Phillip 25;
Thomas 25; Willm. 169
Phillpots, Elizabeth 144;
Paul 139(2),144; Susanna
139
Phillpotts, Benjamine 149;
Clement 124; Margerret
149; Paul 124,149,170;
Sarah 124
Philpots, John 106; Paul
106,167,231; Susanna 106,
144
Philpott, Paul 270
Philpotts, Ambrose 193;
Clemence 187; Elizabeth
136,188; John 132,193;
Paul 132,136,165,193(2),
226; Susanna 132,136
Phiney, An 48; Jno. 48;
Margt. 46,48; Richard 46
Phiney, Jno. 46
Picket, Mary 63
Pickworth, Benjamine 19
Pierce, Charles 51; Edward
37,51; Katherine 51;
Thomas 203
Pigg, Frances 208
Pinion, Elizabeth 99(2);
John 99
Pinnell, John 82
Piper, Priscilla 202
Pitts, John 23; Sarah 80
Pollard, John 188
Poobert, Hannah 52; Simon
52; Williams 52
Poole, Sarah 12(3); William
12(2); Doctor 36; Dor.
37; Mr. 29; Wm. 12
Porter, ffrances 9; Ann
53; Anna 132; Elizabeth
123,127,132,192; Frances
165; Francis 59,123,127,
132,215(2),221,270;
James 169; Jane 47,59,
80,123; Mary 127,192;
Robert 39; Sally 158;
William 9,47,54,59; Wm.
47
Porterfield, Jane 164
Portwood, Barbary 47,48;
Joseph 48; Mary 47;
Sarah 181; Tho. 47,48
Poticarie, Elizabeth 7
Potter, Elizabeth 67

Pound, John 22,25;
Margaret 25
Powel, Lucy Billups 281
Powell, Agnes 304; Jere-
miah 201; Margaret 20;
Mary 172; Pythagorus 33;
Susan 206
Poynter, James 9
Prendergast, Edward 82
Presnall, Jacob 90(2),173;
Mary 90
Pressnall, Jacob 78; James
78,167; Martha 80; Mary
78
Preston, Jacob 60,66; Mary
60,66(2); Sarah 60
Price, ---- Mr. 31; Ann
146,150; Catharine 150;
Catherine 134(2),137,
142,146; Elizabeth 13;
James 96; Jane 13(2),25,
32,96,102,107,112,150,
166,182; Mrs. 29; John
13,79,96,102(2),107,112,
146(2),150(2),170,173,
183,212(2),215,217,264,
266(3),267,268,310,312
(2); Katherine 13,25;
Leonard 142; Margaret
13; Mrs. 37; Margt. 36;
Mary 13; Robert 13(2),
25,32; Mr. 39(2); Robt.
37; Samuel 107; Tho.
222; Thomas 134,137(2),
146(2),150,272; Thos.
142,237,243,256; William
112
Prichard, Rebecca 40,51(2);
Roger 21,40,51; Sarah 40
Prichett, Rebecca 28
Priest, Catherine 81;
Eliza. 42; Katherine 42;
Wm. 42
Priestnall, Elizabeth 53;
George 23
Prill, Ann 154; Catherine
154
Prindle, Ann 299; Eliza.
299; Parrott 299
Pringle, Ann 107; Periot
107
Pritchett, Elizabeth 28;
Roger 28
Probart, Anne 165; Simon
177; William 179
Probent, Ann 65; Hannah
65,79; Mary 79; Wm. 65,
79
Probert, Anne 67; Hannah
67; Mary 167; William 67
Probest, Hannah 81
Proverb, Hannah 55; William
55(2)
Pryor, ---- Major 287; Ann
287; Frances Shackelford
283; John 203,287;
Mildred 199,283; William
161,199(2),283
Pudduck, Elizabeth 180
Pullen, Thomas 39
Purcel, Henry 153; Mary
153; William 153
Purcell, Patrick 168
Purify, Thomas 36,37
Purton, John 179
Purvis, Alice 85,88; George
92; Henry 99; Jno. 31;
John 31,33,82,87(2),88,
92,99; Mary 31,177;
Robert 99,174; Winifred
87(2),88,92,99; Winnifred
174
Pussil, Patrick 192

Putman, Anne 127; Henry
112,127; John 112; Sarah
112,127

Quarles, John 302
Quidley, Patrick 48;
Thompson 48

Radford, Ann 84; Edward
82,84; Mary 84
Radley, Thomas 29,31
Ramage, Alexander 199
Rammage, Eliza 35
Ranes, Frances 196; John
196(2)
Ransom, Frances 305
Ranson, Catherine 163
Ransone, Frances 262
Ranstead, Mary 176
Ratford, James 149; Mary
149
Rattenig, Sarah 79; Wm.
79(2)
Rawlings, Eliza. 40;
Jeremiah 40; Peter 40
Ray, Elizabeth 94(2),172
(2); Gabriell 83,94
Read, Edmund 303; Eliza-
beth 184; George 183
Reade, ----hn 288; Alex.
288; Alexr. 290; Ann
282; Charles 282; Eliza.
288; Elizabeth 282;
Frances 157; J. Minr.
142; Jno. 191; Minr. 140,
169,190,237,239; Min.
274; John 157(2),170
Reader, Benjamine 193
Reades, Elizabeth 163
Reagen, John 92; Prudence
92; Robert 92
Reagin, Catherine 103;
John 103; Prudence 103
Reaguin, Frances 97; John
97; Prudence 97
Reardon, Honour 80
Redman, Catherine 167
Reed, Ann 141; Edward 141;
James 274; Michael 141;
Nancy 303
Reenes, Mary 10; Tho. 10
Reeves, ---- Mr. 11; James
226,235,238,241,247,250,
290,291,294(2),297(2),
300; Honnor 149; Leonard
149
Reningham, William 208
Rennall, Richard 63
Ress, Daniell 43; Jno. 43;
Susannah 43
Reveer, Isaac 303
Reymey, Ann 16; Barnard
16; William Parker 16
Reynald, Honor 64; Richard
64(2)
Reynalds, Elizabeth 77;
Honour 77; Richd. 77
Reynalls, Honour 81
Reynolds, Elizabeth 175;
Richard 22,173
Reynor, Ann 33
Rhoades, Anne 133; Hezekiah
133,186; Jane 133; John
222; Susannah 186
Rhoads, Hezekiah 228,232;
John 221,230,231,253
Rhodes, ---- 34; Alice 34,
47,82; Ann 76,192,194;
Anne 112; Benja. 201,
285; Benjamin 147,288;
Benjamine 143; Doritha
288; Dorothy 285; Eliza
46; Eliza. 27,42;

Rhodes continued
Elizabeth 42,43(2),44,
47(2),59,298,304;
Ezechias 23,44(2),46,47
(2),59; Ezehias 27;
Ezekiah 34,76; Ezekias
42,43; Hannah 140,192;
Hezekiah 152,218; Isaac
192; Isaack 112; Jacob
194,287; James 59,140,
192; Jemima 138,195; Jn.
236; Jno. 275; John 47,
76,81,112,147,152,158,
170,192,240,244,248,251,
254,268,287,290,291,298,
300,302; John, Senr. 194
(2),279,292; JOhn 158;
Mary 27,47,72(2),82,132,
147(2),152,158,195,287,
298; Randal 143,147,169,
191; Randolph 132,138,
195; Sarah 132,138,143,
191,195,285; Tholomiah
147; William 46,47,192;
Wm. 140
Rhods, Hannah 147; Hezekiah
147; Wm. 147
Rhoeds, Elizabeth 168
Rice, Ann 51(2); Anne 114;
Barshebe 298; Catherine
109,114; Elizabeth 100,
108,114(2),116,138;
Hannah 100,298; Jacob
100,108(2),114,116,286,
288,298; James 133; John
109,116,125(2),133,138,
182; Mary 125,133,138,
162,170; Nelson 286;
Nicholas 29,51; William
109,114,162; Winifred
286; Winney 288
Richans, ---- The Widow 37
Richardson, Charles 77,82;
Eliza 77; James 77;
Martha 18
Richeson, Elizabeth 208;
George 153; John 304;
Mary 153; William 153
Richie, Archibald 302
Richman, Eliza. 15; Jno.
Charles 15; Tho. 15
Ridgaway, Ann 40,50; Anthony
40,50; Elizabeth 40;
John 50
Ridgway, Agatha 117; Anne
117,122(2),185; Henrietta
171; John 117,122,164,166
Ridley, Hugh 187
Ridway, Anthony 165
Ried, James 230
Right, Elizabeth 125;
Rosamond 125; Thomas 125
Riley, Ann 88; John 88,116;
Mary 88,116; Stephen 116
Rily, John 95; Mary 95;
Mildred 95
Ripinge, Alice 9
Riseing, Eliza. 13; Eliza-
beth 13; John 13(2);
William 13
Riske, Anne 162; James 83,
173
Roach, Ann 145,150,192;
Anne 129,132; Dorothy
129,187; Eliza. 76;
Elizabeth 166; Hugh 76,
82,98,104,129,132,145,
150(2),166,192; Judith
145; Martha 132,192;
Mary 104; Rebecca 76,98,
104,182; William 98,180
Roades, Anne 99,108,112,
135; Elizabeth 112;

Roades continued
George 94(2); Hannah 116;
Hezekiah 108,112,172,176,
181; James 173; Jane 164;
John 99(2),108,135,260;
Lucy 135; Mary 94;
William 116(2)
Roads, Anne 104,118(2),
125; Benjamine 104;
Christopher 130; Eliza-
beth 65,185; Hannah 113,
123,130; Hezekiah 65,
113,163,223; Jacob 125;
John 104,118,123,125,
179,219,307; Randolph
164; Sith 65; William
113,123,130,164
Roan, ---- 158; Ann 158,
298; Anne 131(2),136;
Charles 158,253,298;
Francis 286; James 136,
186; Michael 131,136;
Sarah 198,286; William
286
Roane, ----les 288;
Alexander 169; Ann 156,
159,288; Charles 156,
159,206,288; Frances D.
304; Harriet 304; Lucy
205,281; Mary 156,250,
252,253,278,279,290,293
(2); Nancy 208; P. 304;
Patsey Hepkins 302;
Sarah 159; Thomas 171;
Willm. 297; Wm. 296
Robbason, Ann 71; Catherine
71; Thomas 71
Robbeck, James 179
Roberts, Ann 16(2); Elizabeth 70; Ezabell 76;
Gabriel 63,70; Griffuth
16; Isabell 26; Isabella
23; John 65,71; Mary 65,
71,73,76,80,174; Robert
22,26; Sarah 70; Thomas
26,54,63,65,304; Ursula
35; Walter 63; Willet
73,174; Willett 71,73,
76
Robertson, Elizth. 190
Robey, Thomas 35
Robin, Ursule 204
Robinson, ---- Mr. 35;
--bert 299; Agatha Mrs.
7; Ann 8,13,23,143(2),
153; Mrs. 39; Anne 8,
81(2),124,131,138,147
(2),304,305; Benjamine
143,181; Beverley 112;
Bridgt. 23; Catharine
204; Catherine 76,93(2),
112,183; Maddam 60; Mdm.
70,73; Mrs. 64; Ch. 238;
Charles 303,305; Chr.
247; Mr. 32,38,39,53(3);
Chrisr. 242,244,247,
254; Christo. 235;
Christopher 60,63,64,89,
96,101,137(2),140,142,
143,146(2),147,153,184,
190,213,227,228,230,231,
232,233,234,235,238,
241,263(2),266,267(2),
269,273,291; Mr. 35,276;
Christopr 7; Christopr.
22,40; Christr. 239,
291,300,301(2); Mr. 41;
Chrr. 302; Clara 41,80;
Elizabeth 38,208,286;
Frances 89,170,299(2);
Hannah 131,188; Henry
99; Jno. 143; John 64
(2),76,93,99,112,147,
159,164,204,215,249,

Robinson continued
John cont.: 258(2),259,
261,262,264,265(2),266,
299(2),303,311; Collo.
210; Colo. 266; Mr. 60,
70,73; John, Esqr. 215;
John, Esqr 264; Judith
89,96,101,143(2),177,
287; Kath Madm. 38;
Kath. Mrs. 41; Katherine
40,99; Madam 53; Mrs.
53; Lucy 140,190; Mary
70,140,143,146,179,190,
198; Nancy 204,207;
Needler Revd. Mr. 205;
Peter 101,287,302;
Rich'd. 13(2); Richard
81; Richard, Senr. Mr.
43; Richd 8; Richd. Mr.
31(2),39; Robert 76;
Sarah 147,159,200,281,
286,287; Theophilus 40;
Theophylus 53; Thomas
124,198,206; Ursula 280;
William 73,96,124,131,
138,153,188,201,204,281,
286,303,305; Wm. 143,
147,159; Xtopher 235
Rodes, ---ert 118; Ann
155; Anne 119; Hezekiah
119; Mary 150,155; Randal
150(2),155; Randolph 118;
Robert 194; Sarah 118;
Susanna 119
Roe, Elizabeth 27; Jno.
46; John 181; Katherine
46; Mary 27; Thomas 27;
William 46
Roebottom, Mary 83
Rogers, Humphry 146; John
140; Mary 140,146; Ro-
bert 140,146; William 31
Rone, Mary 256
Rootes, Ann 203
Ross, Andrew 12,25; Ann
202; Betsy 171; Frances
205; James 25; John 20;
Mary 12,25; Sarah 188;
Thomas 12
Rouch, Ann 140; Hugh 140;
Rebecka 140
Rountree, Margt. 288;
William 288
Row, Anne 115; Benjamine
103,108,163; Catherine
93(2),135,175; Dorothy
115; James 103; John 93;
Joseph 135,167; Mary
103,108,135; Ruth 108
Rowe, James 177; John 76,
146; Joseph 76,146;
Katherine 76; Lyne 199;
Martha 201; Mary 146
Royston, Elizabeth 205;
Thomas 205
Rudd, Anne 136; Michael
168; Michal 136; William
136
Rudolph, George 202
Rumage, Alexander 198
Rumiger, Richard 9
Russel, Anne 118(2); James
118; Patrick 192; Sarah
192
Russell, Anne 163; Eliza-
beth 23; James 164;
Thomas 178
Ryder, Grace 26; Henry
17; Jno. 26; John 20;
Mary 26
Rydr, Grace 17; John 17
Ryell, Jennett 80
Ryley, Ann 190; John 109;
Mary 109; Mildred 176;

Ryley continued
Stephen 189; William 109,
195
Ryly, Jno. 190,275
Ryner, Christian 206
Ryon, William 80

Sackerman, Sarah 20
Saddler, Elizabeth 113;
John 113; Mary 113
Sadler, Alice Berry 283;
Anne 159,288; Eliza. 26;
Elizabeth 136,181;
Ellianor 50; Ellinor 38;
Jane 123; John 84,107,
117,123,129(2),136,189,
203,283; Mary 107,117(2),
123,129,136,159,274;
Mildred 283; Rachel 204;
Richard 38; Saml1. 26;
Sarah 26; William 38,50
(2),107,159,180,288
Salt, Humphrey 40; Jane 40;
Thomas 40,82,240
Salter, Jno. 26; Joane 26;
Sarah 23,26
Samford, Samuel1 80
Samson, Francis 168
Sandefford, Jno. 41; John
41; Sarach 41
Sandeford, Jno. 42(2),46;
John 42,43,44,80; Mary
42(2); Sarah 42,43,44(2);
Susannah 35; William 82
Sanders, ffrances 13; Ann
145,201; Benjamine 127;
Christian 127,135(2),145,
157,159,195; Clemt. 8;
Cressy 200; Edmd. 13;
Edmund 42,72,101; Edward
23,35,96,103,155; Eliza.
155; Elizabeth 13,96,101,
103,157,159; George 42,
135; George. junr. 185;
Hannah 199; Jacob Stiff
171; John 101,103,153,
157,280(2),304; Lucretia
141,153; Mary 8,42,72,
127,155,195,199(2);
Nathanel1 157; Nathaniel
195; Sarah 96,153,157,
208,280; Susanna 135;
Tho. 292,295; Thomas 72,
127,135(2),145,192,252,
253,290,301; Thos. 141,
153,157,159,195; William
141,188,192
Sandersee, Edward 28; Eliza
28; John 28
Sandford, Elizabeth 24;
Jno. 28; John 28; Sarah
24,28; William 28
Sandiford, ffrances 76;
Frances 164; John 84,
175; Mary 76,167,172,
173; Sarah 83; Wm. 258
Santo, Ocany 195
Sargent, Anne 165
Saserson, Isaac 21
Saunders, ---- 285;
Alexander 127; Ann 205;
Anne 91,94,106,113;
Avarilla 280; Benjamine
187; Betty 204; Chrisse
171; Christian 130;
Edmund 84,85,91,174;
Edward 82,109(2),285;
Edwd. 76; Eliza 76;
Elizabeth 76,92,109,117,
127,135,185,203; George
83,91,94(2),106,113;
George Davis 207; John
76,81,92(2),117,127,135,
155(2); Judith 106;

Saunders continued
  Mary 76(2),82,155,167,
  186; Rebecker 285; Sally
  206; Sarah 127; Susanna
  127,133,168; Tho. 130(2),
  135,166,187,273,280;
  Thos. 249; William 113,
  117,127,133(2),166; Wm.
  232
Savage, William 184
Sayre, Jane 198; Mary
  Grymes 161; Samuel
  William 281(2)
Scanderet, Margrett 184
Scanland, John 119(2),165;
  Keziah 119
Scarbrough, ffrances 43,47;
  Augustine 21,26,28;
  Dorothy 26,28; Maccrora
  43; Mary 26,28; William
  38,43,47(2)
Scinco, Anne 83
Scot, Bartholomew 167
Scott, Delphos 202
Scrosby, Anne 200; Dorothy
  204; Elizabeth 149,202;
  James 149(2),243,290,
  291,294; Jams. 249
Scrossby, James 240
Seagar, Anne 95; Jane 137;
  Margret 137; Oliver 75,
  137; Randolph 95; Wm. 95
Seager, ---- Mr. 50; Jane
  236,239; Jean 238,274;
  Jno. 239; John 28;
  Katherine 17; Mary 15,
  17,28,39,41,53(2); Mrs.
  41; Olliver 25; Randolph
  15,17,28; Mr. 38,39,41,
  50,53; Winifrid 15
Seagur, Anne 102; Catherine
  102; Jane 190; Mary 25,
  40; Randolph 25; Mr. 40;
  William 40,83,102,190
Seares, Catherine 167;
  Eliza. 79; Frances 116;
  Harry 97; Joseph 79,88
  (2),93,97,103,107(2),
  116,129,178; Mary 79,88,
  93,97,103,107,112,116,
  129; Thomas 103,129;
  Violetta 86,93
Sears, Constant 169;
  Elizabeth 148; Frances
  194; Harry 148,157,161;
  Henry 150,170,286; Jane
  148,150,157(2),161,286;
  John 150,186,208; Joseph
  112,193; Mary 112,200,
  286; Nancy 303; Philemon
  161; Philip 304; Sarah
  304; Thomas 186,205,303
Sebre, Nicholas 170
Seers, Betty 121; Joseph
  121; Mary 18,121
Segar, Ann 147; Anna 107;
  Anne 107,115,121,127,
  133; Henry 117,182;
  Jane 109,112(2),117,121,
  126,130,170; Mrs. 240;
  Jno. 230; John 121,130,
  172,193,197,215,229,233,
  241,242,245,247,260,262,
  263,264,266,268,273,277,
  308,311; Josiah 109;
  Judith 126,254; Margrett
  189; Mary 121,171,196(2),
  197,282; Oliver 109,112,
  117,121,126,127,130,163,
  189,209,210,213,216(2),
  220,224,229,233,235,245,
  247,266,269(2),271,277
  (3),310; Penelope 310;
  Polly Meacham 161;

Segar continued
  Priscilla 201; Randh.
  255; Randolph 171,196;
  Richard 133; Richard
  Miller 282; Richd. M.
  304; Thomas 147,171,196,
  197,282; William 107,
  115(2),121,127,130,133,
  161,193,196(2),208,210,
  213,216,224,260(2),262,
  265,269,270,305; Wm. 147
Selaman, Charles 69;
  Esther 69; Owen 69
Semour, Joannah 78; Thomas
  78; William 78
Serd, Elizabeth 153; John
  149(2),153; Susana 149;
  Susanna 153
Serdsborow, Frances 54;
  William 54
Seward, Ann 199; Anne 202;
  Benjamin 199(2),299,304;
  Bernard 159; Catharine
  207; Catherine 197;
  Elizabeth 197; John 159,
  197,200,294,295,299,302;
  John, Ser. 161; Lucy
  Blake 199; Nancy 199;
  Susana 159; Susanna 299
Shackelford, Francis 280;
  John 203; Robinson 202;
  Rose Berryman 207;
  William 201
Shackleford, James 35
Shakpurr, Samuel 176
Shanks, John 191
Sharlott, Elizabeth 84
Sharpe, Mary 26; Saml1.
  26; Samuell 22, Thomas
  26
Shaw, Ann 146; Mary 138,
  146,150(2); Thomas 138;
  Thos. 146,150; William
  138,208
Shay, Mary 164
Shecard, ----rles 288;
  John 288; Martha 288
Sheepherd, Henry 194;
  Samuel 194
Sheeres, John 20
Sheet, Richd. 292
Sheffield, William 22
Shelling, Eliza 79
Shelton, Benjamine 115;
  Catherine 104; Crisp 87;
  Crispin 140,236; Daniel
  126; Elizabeth 166; John
  110; Lettitia 140; Mary
  78,79,87,90,96(2),104,
  110,115,126,136,146(2),
  150,154,175,194(2);
  Micajah 154; Peter 34
  (2); Ralph 78,79(2),87,
  90,96,104,110,115,126,
  189,223,225,231,270;
  Reuben 90,136; Susanna
  34; Thomas 78,136,146,
  150(2),194; Thos. 154,
  194,277; William 140;
  Winney 202
Shepard, ---- Mr. 15,24;
  ---- Mr. 16; Catharine
  201; Mary 81
Shepherd, ----ley 285;
  Ann 57; Caty Price 284;
  George 302; Henry 160,
  285,299,300; Henry D.
  284; Henry Daniel 207;
  Josie 207; Mary 57,284,
  302; Nancy 206; Nanny
  160; Tabatha 299;
  Tabbitha 285; Tabitha
  160,300; William 300

Sheppard, ---- 53; Frances
  53; Jno. Mr. 53; John 8;
  William 29
Shereefes, ---- Mr. 10
Sheseld, William 120
Shetton, James 121; Mary
  121; Ralph 121
Shibley, Herodias 81
Shippey, Lettice 24,63;
  Mary 24,33; Richd. 24
Shiprel, Milicent 155;
  Tabitha 155
Shoare, Grace 9; Jone 9;
  Thomas 9
Shore, Ann 12; Grace 12;
  Tho. 12
Short, Jno. 274
Shorter, Elizabeth 115,166;
  Henry 115; Jno. 275;
  John 115,164,186,209,212,
  215,219,248
Shurle, Margrett 62
Shurley, Ann 61(2); Anne
  81,163; Judith 177;
  Richard 61(2); Richd. 61;
  Thomas 61,185
Shurlle, Ann 62; Richd. 62
Shurly, Ann 77; Judith 77;
  Richard 77
Siblee, Benson 159; Daniel
  Ball 170; Elizabeth 159;
  John 303; Lucy 303;
  Thomas 208; Thos. 159
Sibley, Ann 68; Benson 197;
  Daniel Ball 197; Eleaner
  68; Eliza. 81; Grace 46;
  John 46,54,184; Mary 162;
  Mildred 198; Susanna 197;
  Thomas 68
Siblie, ---- 197; Benson
  197; Susannah 197
Siddean, Edward 176
Siddon, Ann 60; Edward 60;
  Sarah 60
Sidorn, Ann 66; Edward 66
  (2)
Silvester, Alice 84
Simmons, Margaret 68(2);
  Margery 18; William 68
Simms, Ann 48(2); Elizabeth
  48; Tho. 48
Simonds, Margett. 79;
  William 79; Wm. 79
Simpson, John 39; Mary 22,
  23; Samuell 31
Sims, George 209
Sinah, John 287; Joseph
  287; Mary 287
Sinath, Joseph 291
Sittern, Anne 162
Sitterne, Edward 36; Jane
  36,37
Skelton, Ralph 167; Reuben
  85; Thomas 167
Skipwith, ---- Lady 20;
  Ann 29,32; Anne 56;
  Elizabeth 115,182; Fuller
  105; Gray 66; Henry 89;
  Robert 77; Sarah 96;
  Lady 56,66,77(2),89,96,
  105,115,185; William 77;
  Sr. 66,96; Wm. 56,77(2),
  89,105,115,209,214,220,
  214,220,227,229,265,272,
  306
Slanter, Anthony 15;
  Dorothy 15; Eliza. 35;
  John 8,15; Mary 15(2);
  Sarah 15
Slawter, Eliz. 27; Jno. 27;
  Margarett 27
Small, Joseph 255
Smether, Robert 167

Smith, ---- 13; Capt. 48;
Colonel 198; Revd. Mr.
198; ReverendMr 281;
Abigall 60; Agatha 183;
Alexander 108,183;
Alexdr. Mr. 36; Amey 9;
Ann 14(2),20,21(2),56(2),
57(2),58,69,103,143,151,
190(2),193,239,247,251,
252,253,256,279(3),292;
Anne 83,92(2),94,97,98,
103,104(2),108(2),110,
112,113,116,118(2),123,
131,182,222,230,234,272
Anne, junr. 271; Anthony
14,21,108,196,279; Arthur
46,60; Augustine 233,
234,264,272,309; Benja-
mine 147; Betty 118;
Caroline 131; Cary 94,
151,249,278; Catharine
159,298; Catherine 122,
156; Catherine George
283; Clara 113; Diana
116; Edward 193; Eliz.
15,237; Eliza. 17,26,50,
55,77,212,216,219,222,
224,229; Eliza., Senr.
227; Eliza., senr. 230;
Elizabeth 45(2),56,83,
112,113,118,119,122(2),
126(2),132(2),137,147,
151,167,190,216,218,224,
233(2),266; Elizth. 143;
Ellianor 46; Esther 201;
Frances 97,98,126,156,
191,200,222,226,267,271,
286,298; Franky 201;
George Meacham 284;
Henery 77; Henry 55,176;
James 56(2),58(3),69,94,
103,110,116,186,224,229,
230,260,266,272(2),283,
284,286,298; James, junr.
184; Jane 40,79,92,169,
298; Jno. 40,224,226,
229,235,239,271(2); Capt.
222; Jno., junr. 232;
Jno., senr. 271; Jno.,
junr. 236; Jno., Senr.
235; John 8,26,40,56,83,
84,92,97,98(2),103,108,
113,118,119,122,123,126,
131,132(2),151,156,159,
164,185,190,218,220,221,
242,244(2),246(3),249,
250(2),251,253,254,259(2),
262,263,264,267,269,272,
279,290,293,298,311;
Capt. 58(2),84,107,209,
308(2); Mr. 240; John
Richerson 283; John,
junior 260; John, junr.
226,251,253,263,279,280,
292(2),294(2),309,310,
312; John, sen. 271;
John, senr. 227,230,266,
312; John, Jr. 255;
John, Junr. 174,211,256,
259,261,305; John, Senr.
84,180,209,212,214,216,
306; John, junr. 243;
Joseph 35,50,113,118,
122,126(2),132,137,143,
147,151,163,195; Judith
151; Katherine 20,77;
Keziah 137; Margaret 22,
198; Margt. 9; Martha
98,151; Mary 23,46,60,
151(2),184,208,283,284,
286,298; Maurice 123,
210,214,265; Michael 94;
Moris 252; Morrice 115
(2); Morrice 110;

Smith continued
Oswald 110; Rachel 157,
170; Rachell 103; Ralph
9; Randolph 50; Rebecca
35; Robert 15,45,159;
Mr. 32,36(2),37; Ruth
56,122; Samuell 36,37;
Sarah 69,94(2),113,157,
202,208; South 157; Tho.
15,17,26,219,226,269,271,
272; Thomas 17,18,54,55,
56,57,85,92(2),98,104,
108,112,119,180,181,189,
209,223,265,268,269,271,
308; Thos. 230(2),234
(2),271,274(2); William
21,103,132,195,199
Smither, Mary 127; Moses
127; Richard 127
Smithey, Constant 170
Smother, Richard 162
Smyth, Ann 76,87,88;
Gregory 87; Henery 88;
James 76,88; John 10;
Capt. 74; Margaret 76;
Margt. 10; Mary 88;
Michaell 81; Rebecca 88;
Thomas 80; Thos. 87;
Unity 88
Snelling, Acquilla 106;
Alexander 95,147,169;
Ann 145; Anna 147;
Aquila 192,242; Aquilla
83,95,106,113(2),119,
125,130,134,137,145,167,
178,187(2),233,243;
Benjamine 137; Elizabeth
130,187; Henry 125; Lucy
134; Margaret 145; Marget
192; Margret 130,134;
Margrett 137; Mary 95,
106,113,119,125,147,187;
Priscella 81; Priscilla
119; Sarah 81
Snodgrass, ---- 286; David
147,170,286; Elizabeth
147; Hannah 286; Nathan
147
Snow, Cuthbert 284; Eliza-
beth 284; Henry 141(2),
147; Jane 147; Jone 141,
147; William Foster 284
Soanes, John 165
Sommers, Sarah 207
Sords, John 299; Susanna
299
Sorrow, Mary 141,169;
Samuel 141(2)
Sorry, Anne 134; Mary 134;
Samuel 134
Sourd, William 282
South, ---- 297; Andrew
91,160,287(2); Eliza.
287; Elizabeth 91,98,
165; George 297; John
83,91,98,160,181,304;
Rachel 160,297; Smith
98,297
Southall, Jane 281
Southern, Agatha 132;
Agnes 138,193; Averilla
148; Benjamine 130;
Catherine 66,173; Edward
132,138,158,286,298;
Elizabeth 304; Garret
132; James 135; Jane
158; Jno. 141; John 66
(2),111,118,123,130,135
(2),138,148,163,280;
John, Senr. 186; Joseph
123,189; Judith 286;
Lettice 83; Margaret
141,148; Margarett 141;
Margret 111,130;

Southern continued
Margrett 118,123,135(2);
Mary 134,140,151,158,
286,298; Samuel 135;
Sarah 151; Susanna 118;
Thomas 134; William 111,
140,151,167,194,298;
Wm. 134,140
Southren, Edward 286; Edwd.
288; Eliza. 286; Mary
286,288
Southward, John 40; Margt.
40; William 37,40
Southwort, Catherine 70;
Margaret 70; William 70
Southworth, Anne 110,111,
114,115,118,121; Cathe-
rine 125; Elizabeth 111,
125,172,180; Grace 180;
James 115; John 111,114,
118(2),121,163; Margret
177; Margrett 110; Mary
121; Thomas 114; William
85,110,115,125,163,165;
Wm. 221,226
Sovlt, Anne 195; Thomas
195
Spann, Mary 203; Thomas
280
Sparkes, Benjamine 86;
John 96,173; Mary 96;
William 96
Spencer, Ann 207; Anne
105(2); Frances 280;
Jeremiah 304; John 303;
Judith 29,33,107; Mary
107; Robert 105; Samuel
107; Thomas 53,206
Spotswood, Hugh 250,252,
254,279
Spratt, Charlotte 204;
Robert 200
Spyers, Anne 167
St. John, William 303
Stacey, Eliza. 15; Tho.
15; Thomas 15
Stacy, Charles 27; Eliz.
32; Eliza. 27; Tho. 32;
Thomas 27; Thoms. 36
Stake, Rose 18
Stalker, Henry 7; Richard
204
Stampar, Cary 86; John 89;
Mary 86,89; Powell 81,
86,89
Stamper, Cary 176; Dorcas
10; Elizabeth 8,12,208;
George 200; James 170;
Jno. 8,12(2); John 10,
23,140,144(2),148,153
(2),156,159,168,192(2);
Jonathan 102; Kerah 120;
Leonard 196; Letitia
113; Mary 96,102,113,
120,159,169; Mary, junr.
165; Mildred 196,199,
200; Nelson 303; Powel
113,185; Powell 96,102,
120,148; Robert 140,196,
199,200; Sally 280;
Samuel 199,303; Sarah
140,144,148,153,156(2),
159,192; Susannah 96
Stanard, ---- Mr. 248(2);
Mrs. 241; Anne 166; B.
279; Bev. 279; Beverley
109,252,253,290,294,301;
Eliz. 245,277; Elizabeth
102,106(2),109,113;
Elizah. 235; Elizth.
238; Eltonhead 14(2);
Mrs. 39; Sarah 14,113;
William 14(2),102(2),
106,109,113,162,176,188,

Stanard continued
William cont.: 212,215,
218,229(2),223,224,227,
264,268,270,306,309,312;
Wm. 212,219,232,239,258,
266,268,273,308(2),310
Standly, Mary 30; Rebecca
30,36; Tho. 30; Thomas
32
Stanly, Jonathan 18
Stannard, Ann 86(2); Mrs.
84; Eliz. 239; William
81; Wm. 86,275; Mr. 84
Stanton, Jane 165; Mary
54,65; Theodoret 65;
Theophilus 54,65,80
Stapleton, ---- Dor. 48;
ffrances 25,82,52;
ffrancis 40; Ann 52;
Elizabeth 116,140;
Frances 103; George 28,
178; Jane 64,164; John
25; Joyce 116; Lucy 140,
194; Mary 64,80,103;
Tho. 28; Tho, 25; Thomas
40,64,103,162; Mr. 40,
52; William 168; Wm. 140
Stark, Margaret 63
Staunton, Jane 70(2); John
70; Theophilus 63,70
Stedman, Frances 206
Steel, Thomas 172
Steeres, Mary 28
Steevans, Mabell 136
Steevens, Absalom 157; Ann
170; Anne 100; Benjamine
136; Elizabeth 152,200;
Elizth. 157; Frances 146;
John 91,146; Judith 200;
Lewis 142,200; Mabel 131;
Mabell 142,146; Mary 146;
Morris 107; Nathaniel
152; Priscilla 113;
Richard 83,91,96(2),100,
107,131(2),136,142,146,
165; Richd. 113,146,152,
157; Sarah 91,96,100,
107,113,182
Stephens, Isaac 304; Jphn
203; Judith 282; Lewis
282; Robert 7; Susanna
282
Steptoe, James 161; Sarah
R. 303; William 208
Stevens, Anne 82; Benjamin
201; Edmond Abbott 200;
Elizabeth 191,204(2);
John 169,200; Judith
282; Lewis 282; Mary 63,
200,202; Priscilla 194;
Richard 54(2); Sarah 54;
Susanna 282
Steward, Hugh 272; John
187,299; Martha 299(2);
William 208
Stewart, Hugh 132,188,229,
230,272; Jane 132,188;
Judith 132,168
Stiff, Anne 91,167;
Avarilla 134; Betty 200
(2),281(2),283; Constan-
tine 81; Edy 125; Eliza.
42,87,134; Elizabeth 91,
97,101,107,111,117,122,
125,128,175; Elizabeth
Baker 281; Jack Fearn
171; Jacob 30,81,87,97,
101,107,111(2),117,122,
128,134,188,194,195,217,
225,234,239,259(2),262,
267,271,278,279,300,
306,313; James 125,165,
200(3),201,281(2),283,
285; John 97,174;

Stiff continued
John Blake 200,281; Mary
195,208,280; Nicholas
42; Ruth 122,188; Sarah
30,81,101,170,171,285,
288,305; Tho. 30,42;
Thomas 23,87,107,117,
174,179; Thomas Meacham
283; William 128,171,
283,285,305; William
Nelson 305; Wm. 288
Stiffe, Elizabeth 59;
Elizabeth B. 302; James
59,170; John B. 303;
Nancy 302; Thomas 59;
Tom 302; William Nelson
302
Still, Eliz: 48; Elizabeth
48; Eloner 179; Tho. 48;
Thomas 179; William 113
Stodix, Elizabeth 201
Stone, Job 204; John 35
Storey, Mary 164
Stradford, Elizabeth 13;
Mary 13
Straughan, Catherine 66,
70; Edward 88; Katherine
64,88; Mary 70; Richard
63,64,66(2),70,88;
Thomas 64
Strauhan, Catherine 94;
Crispin 94; Richard 94
Street, Anne 205; Catharine
146,151; Catherine 157;
Mary 157; Richard 146,
151(2),157; Ruth 146;
Thomas 304
Stringer, ---- 285; Clara
199; Daniel 151(2),154,
158,161,170,246,285,291,
300; Elizabeth 154;
Hannah 151,154,158,161
(2),285,300; Lucy 158;
Sarah 154; William 300
Stuard, John 158(2); Mar-
tha 158
Stuart, Amey 92; Catherine
107; Charles 114; Dianah
136; Hugh 167,271; James
136,167; Jane 92,99,107,
114,136; John 90,92,99
(2),107,114; John, junr.
185
Stubbs, Martha Haines 281
Stureman, Robert 170
Suckling, Ann 18
Summers, ffrances 55; Ann
299; Eliz. 32,40; Eliza.
16,24,30,55; Elizabeth
16,40,180; Jno. 16,30,
32,40,55; John 24(2),
30,32; Wm. 299
Suthern, Catherin 61;
Edward 61; John 61
Sutton, Beamont 96;
Benjamine 120,187;
Chirstopher 14,62,65,
69,90(2),96,104,111,
116,120,125,135; Chris-
topher, Senr. 192;
Christopher 217,226,
228,232,259; Cussandra
9; Dorothy 24; Eliza.
14,26; Elizabeth 43,65,
167,206; Hope 65,69(2),
77,86,90,96,104,111,116,
120,125,135,243,250,255;
Jno. 9,14; John 26,77;
John Gayle 208; Lucy
303; Maria 304; Mary
199,204; Michal 125;
Nanny 201; Nathan 116,
182; Nathaniel 135;
Rowland 111;

Sutton continued
William Barbee 104;
Xtopher 77
Swepson, Mary 169
Swepstone, Jane 82
Swift, Eliz. 50; Elizabeth
53; Jno. 50; John 37;
Paul 50
Swords, Catherine 205;
Elizabeth 202
Syddern, Edward 175; Phebe
163
Sydnor, Johannah 22
Sykes, Frances 202; George
204
Sylvester, Joseph 202
Symes, Ann 67,72; Anna
165; Elizabeth 163; Hanna
67; John 72; Mary 164;
Thomas 67,72
Symons, Margett 83
Syms, Anne 163
Syphax, Jane 161

Taff, Anne 205; Elizabeth
199; Mary 171
Taliaferao, Mary Holden
257
Taliaferro, John 170
Tarpley, Lucy 201
Tatum, Isham 202
Tayloe, Christopher 109;
Honor 109; Richard 109
Taylor, ffrancis 52;
Ann 18,23; Ann Chowning
199; Benjamin 181;
Catherine 197; Eli 303;
Eliza. 52; Elizabeth
298; Frances 197,286,
298; Honor 105; Jane 52,
121; John 286,298; Kitty
283; Mary 121,283,286;
Rachel 197(2),199;
Richard 105(2),163,210
(2),215; Richd. 215,
216,269,301; Robert 11;
William 197(2),199,201
Teel, Elizabeth 23
Tegnall, Thomas 84
Tenoe, Ann 284,286; Stephen
284,286(2); Thomas 201,
284
Tenor, Anne 159; Elizabeth
159; Stephen 159
Terrey, William 37
Terrill, Eliza. 79; Mary
82
Terry, Andrew 83; Eliza-
beth 192
Thacher, Chicheley 252
Thacker, ---- Coll. 243;
---- 37; Coll. 243(2),
248; Mr. 10; ffrances
45; Alice 11,32,37; Ann
61; Anne 73,85,124,212,
214,215,218,220,224,259,
265,312; C. 168(2); C.C.
261; Chackeley 278;
Chicheley Corbin 131,188;
Chicheley 225,279;
Chichely 73; Chichley
Corbin 12; Chickely 276;
Coll. 245; Edward 11,
241; Edwin 61(2),101,
104(2),108,111,115(2),
119,124,128,131,138,139,
176,191,210,213,215,217
(2),218(2),221,223(3),
225(3),226,228(3),229
(2),230(3),231(2),232
(2),233,234,235,237(3),
239(3),245,246,252,258
(2),260(2),261(2),262,
265,269,271(2),272(2),

Webb, ffrances 26,35;
ffrancis 17; Anne 82;
Catharine 208; Elizabeth
17; Isaack 82; James 17,
20,26(2),32; Mary 104;
Milly 203; Tilley 204;
William 104(2),177;
William Crittenden 207
Weekes, ffran., Junr. 75;
ffrances 33; ffrancis
25; Abra. Mr. 22; Abra-
ham 10,97; Eliz. 36;
Eliza. 25,33; Elizabeth
78,218,222; Fran. 309;
Francis Jun. 75; Hobbs
33,78,80,87; Hobs 97,270;
Katherine 10; Lettice
Mrs. 53; Margt. 22;
Mary 78,81,87,97;
Millicent 10,87; Thomas
25
Weekes (alias), James 188
Weeks, Elizabeth 270(2);
Frances Mr. 58; Francis,
Junr. 49; Hobbs 305;
Hobby 211; Hobs 91,219,
225,263,311,313; Mary
91; Milicent Mrs. 49;
Thomas Hobs 91
Weight, Catherine 118(2);
Henry 118
Welch, Elizabeth 11; Jno.
11; Margt. 11; Mary 18;
Patrick 167
Wells, Ancoretta 18
Wennan, Thomas 164
West, Ann 18; George 202,
206; Hannah 19; John 19;
Nicho. 19
Weston, Anne 120,185,186;
Elizabeth 120,123,126(2),
129; John 120,123(2),
126,129,165,186; Mary
129
Weybole, Barbary 18
Whan, Jane 301
Wharry, Robert 182
Wharton, Abraham 119,125,
131,139,165,191; Eliza-
beth 83,125; John 139;
Mary 119,125,131,139,170;
Rebecca 119; William 131
Whately, John 80
Whealer, Ellianor 27;
Presilla 27; Tho. 27
Wheatherstone, Margaret 63
Wheeler, Elizabeth 83;
Mark 105; Sarah 105; Tho.
34; Thomas 34; William
82,105
Wheler, Ellianor 34
Whelling, Caleb 53; Eliza.
53
Whistler, Ann 144; Anne
92; Mary 92,177; Molly
144
Whitaker, Charles 184,204;
Edward 151,165; Eliza-
beth 151; Thomas 151,164
White, ---- 155; Eliza.
27,29; Elizth. 143;
Francis 155; James 27;
Jno. 169; Jno, 143;
John 155,246,249; Joseph
143; Thomas 27,85;
William 184
Whiteacre, Elizabeth 173
Whitehead, Jonathan 31
Whitely, John 206
Whiting, Mary Robinson 205
Whitlock, James 56; Jonas
56; Margaret 56
Whittacer, Edward 133;
Elizabeth 133(2)

Whittacre, Charles 122;
Edward 122; Elizabeth 122
Whittaker, Anne 126;
Charles 42; Edward 42,
126; Elizabeth 126;
Margt. 42; Walter Capt.
39
Whittakers, Edward 156;
Elizabeth 156(2)
Whittecar, Edward 300;
Eliza. 300; Persilah 300
Whittekar, Edward 161;
Eliza. 161; Mary 161
Whitteker, Robert 79
Whitters, Precilla 200
Whitticor, Charles 201
Wiat, John 201; Richard 83
Wiatt, ---- 303; James
302; Pitman 208; Thomas
204
Wignall, John 176
Wilberton, Ann 11
Wilburn, Margret 170
Wilch, John 9
Wilcox, ---- Capt. 290;
Ann 171; Isaac 171;
John 291,294(2); Martha
204; Nancy 171
Wilkeson, Ralph 37,53
Wilkines, Elizabeth 284;
James 284; Robert 284
Wilkings, Bridgett 120,
187; Elizabeth 132;
Robert 120(2),132(2)
Wilkins, Bridgett 127(2);
Eliz. 140; Elizabeth 171;
Elizth. 169; Jeremiah
140; John 284(2); Lucy
284,302; Robert 127,167,
284; Robt. 140,190
Willbourn, Frances 166
Willcock, Ann 146; Frances
146; John 146
Willcocks, Eliz 81; Mary
305; Sally 305
Willcox, John 250
Willes, Eliza. 79; Martha
79; Richard 79
William, Gardner 47
Williams, Aaron 181; Ann
12,64,89,146; Anne 80,
81,95,173,200,287; Aron
27; Benjamin 139,199,
201; Benjamine 127;
Billington 95; Bridgt
8; Bridgt. 23; Catherine
64,69,71,127,190; Charls
54,64; David 164; Edward
9,48,64(2),69,71; Elias
150,193(2); Eliza. 23,
26,27; Elizabeth 10,65,
71,77,95,103,118,178;
Eloner 179; Fanny 208;
Frances 89,177,181,199,
297; George 31,191;
Howard 64,198; Hugh 10;
James 15; Jane 111; Jno.
139,169,190(2); John 15,
17,26,27,29,33,81,89,95
(2),104,111,118,123(2),
127,132,151(2),154,156,
162,166,168,173,189,194,
273,287,297; John Thurs-
ton 199; Joseph 95,103;
Judith 69,71,103; Mar-
garet 12; Margarett 79;
Margt 8; Margt. 10;
Mary 15,17,31,80,104,
146,150,154,194; Michal
104,118,123,132,139,190;
Micholl 111; Rachel 200;
Reuben 132; Richard 8,9;
Richd. 12; Robert 146,
169; Robt. 77,150;

Williams continued
Sarah 8,9,144(2),193,
202; Steward 198;
Susanna 124,151,154,156
(2),168,194,297; Susannah
287; Tho. 10,17,26;
Thomas 8(2),9,23,31(3),
48,65(2),77,180; William
124,144
Williamson, ---- 25;
ffrances 19,79; Andrew
10,15,42; Aron 22;
Augustine 42; Benjamin
57,199; Benjamine 123,
182; Catherine 57,182;
Charles 44; Clara 284,
304; Eliz. 42; Elizabeth
101,106,111,115(2),123,
287; Ellianor 83; Frances
101; Henry 25; Jacob 55,
180; John 41; Kath. 28,
41; Katherine 19,28,38,
44,52,55,82; Margaret
15,52; Martha 38,217,
266; Mary 10,44,162,284,
287,298; Minor 106,179;
Robert 19,20,28,38,41,
44(2),52,55,57,101,106,
111(2),115,123,162,165,
182,215,218,264,310;
Robert, jr. 209; Robert,
junr. 214; Robert, jun.
310; Robert, Junr. 264;
Robt. 210,306; Robt.,
Senr. 262; Sarah 10,15;
Tho. 44; William 29,
284,287; Winifrid 25;
Wm. 298
Willis, Bridget 52; Bridgt.
30; Eliz. 141; Elizabeth
53; Ellianor 10; Isabella
30; John 10,39,78;
Martha 78; Mary 10(6);
Oliver 141; Richard 10,
78; Tho. 10(5); Thomas
10,201; William 23,30,
52(2); Willm. 141
Willkings, Bridgett 123;
James 123; Robert 123
Wills, Thomas 200
Wilson, Abraham 144;
Andrew 51; Elizabeth 90,
144; Isabella 51; John
51; Martha 144; Mary
16,24(2),171,174; Robert
90,205; Sarah 16;
Thomas 16,18,24,90
Wiltshire, Benjamin 281
Wily, John 167
Win, John 67; Richard 54,
67; Richd. 54; Sarah 54,
67
Winger, Thomas 37
Wingo, Anne 183
Winn, Anne 93; Elizabeth
61; Jane 78; Mary 46;
Owin 180; Richard 46,
61,78,82,93; Sarah 46
(2),61,78; Thomas 93,
172
Winning, Niels 206
Wisdale, Mary 180
Withers, ffrances 9(2);
Erasmus 9
Withnell, Christor Mr. 10
Wollace, Betty 156; Lucy
156; William 156
Wolley, George 16; Sarah
16
Wood, Ann 17,154(2),157,
160,168,284,299,300;
Anne 176,234; Catharin
Bushrod 144; Catharine
193; Catherine 105,134,168;

SLAVE INDEX OF CHRIST CHURCH

Listed in order of last name, first name in ( ), slave name & page no.

Bristow continued
 (Nicholas) Bess 307; Dina
 307; Dinah 258; Jack 266;
 (William) Ben 242; Rose
 235,248; Sarah 248; Will
 235,278; (Wm,) Hannah
 229; Rose 229
Brooks, (Jonathan) Brinah
 222; Hannah 227; Jenny
 236; Robin 222; Sarah
 245; Verena 227,245;
 Virena 236
Brown, (James) Milly 297;
 (Jams.) Brimer 294
Bryan, (John) Jone 209;
 Lettey 301; Letty 209;
 Phebe 301
Bryant, (Frances) James
 301; Nal 274; Oder 291,
 293; Prudence 294,301;
 (Francis, Frances) Simon
 256; (John) Odo 224; Peru
 224; Phebe 296
Buford, (Thomas) Ben 252;
 Deinah 230; Jenny 225,
 252,296; Joe 234; Lucy
 225,230,234,296; (Thomas,
 Senr.) Jonay 293; (Thos.)
 Frank 238; Jenny 290;
 Lucy 238; Poll 290;
 (Thos., Senr.) Frank 244;
 Lucy 244; (Thos., Senr.)
 Jone 255; Tom 255; (Wm.)
 Bess 274; George 274;
 Janna 292; Simon 292
Burford, (Thomas) Joe 275
Burk, (Eliz) Kate 279;
 (Eliz.) Kate 243; Sarah
 243; Sarah 243; (Eliza.)
 Annica 277; Harry 252;
 Judy 290; Kate 252,277,
 290; (Jno.) Judee 236;
 Kate 236; (John) Annica
 240; Ben 231; Cate 224,
 240; Jemmey 249; Kate
 227,231,249; Moll 227,
 271; Will 224
Burton, (Isaack) Catherine
 Lee 260

Campbell, (Jas.) Amy 249
Carter, (John) Cate 245;
 Hare 245; (Mary) Aga
 253; Cate 253
Causer, (Alice) Toney 221
Chainy, (Pennellope, Mrs.)
 Richard 49
Channing, Chowning,
 (William) Harry 220; Kate
 220
Cheadle, (Francis) Jenny
 230; Middlesex 230;
 (John) Ned 264,312; Sarah
 211,312; Toney 264; Tony
 211
Cheedle, (Frances) Europe
 236; Jack 226; Jenny
 226,236; (Francis,
 Frances) Jenny 223;
 Margery 223; (Jno.) Frank
 213; Sarah 213
Chelton, Chilton, (Thomas)
 Scipio 279
Cheney, (Thomas) Deila
 224; Della 270; George
 308; Harry 260; Mary
 271; Moll 220,266; Nan
 231; Peg 224,231,308;
 Pegg 220,307; Peter 265;
 Winney 307; Winny 268
Cheops, (Pat) Mary 253;
 Rose 253
Chilton, (Thomas) Rose
 293; (Thos.) Jane 254;

Chilton continued
 Judy 245; Phillis 278;
 Rose 245,248,254; Scipio
 248
Chouder, (Jeremiah) London
 274
Chowning, (George) -ewman
 293; Frank 293; (Robert)
 Cate 279; (William) Bob
 271; Cate 224,231; Dick
 270; Hampton 231; Harry
 269; Jenny 212; Robin
 224; Tom 212; (Wm.)
 Alice 297; Dick 220;
 James 297; Jenny 220;
 Kate 226; Mansor 297;
 Phillis 226
Churchhill, (----, Coll.)
 Antony 276; Beck 276;
 Ben 274; Betty 276(2);
 Billy 241,276; Bluff
 276; Brutus 275; Caesar
 276; (----, Collo.)
 Cress 263; (----, Coll.)
 Dick 275; Frank 241;
 (----, Collo.) Frank 263;
 (----, Coll.) Frank 275;
 Grace 276; Hannah 275;
 Harry 275; Jack 275;
 Jenny 276(2); Juno 276;
 Kate 275; Mingo 240,275
 (2); Nell 276; Punch
 275; Robin 276; Rosegill
 275; Sango 276; Scipio
 276; Tony 276(2); Venus
 276; Will 275; York 276;
 (----, Mr.) Flownder
 306; Jack 306; (Armistead)
 Abbie 256; Alice 229;
 Amy 221; Anthony 256;
 Antony 211; Betty 215,
 222; Billy 215; Bridgett
 220,268; Caesar 232,237,
 273; Cashus 270; Collo-
 nell 264; Cromwell 268;
 Cross 311; Daniel 225,
 267,271; Diana 309; Dick
 212,232,239,265,273;
 Flounder 216; Frank 226,
 261,276,309; Hagar 267;
 Hannah 216,237,266;
 Harry 311; Isaac 226;
 Isaack 225; Jack 222,
 235; Jemny 217; Jenny
 219,222,223,232,235,
 239,312; Judey 312;
 Judy 237; Kate 217;
 Laurence 276; Mary 223,
 225,226,309,312; Mat 276;
 Matt 238; Moll 229,238,
 309; Nanny 293; Nell
 212,219,238,265,268;
 Peg 211; Peter 267;
 Phill 237; Pompey 268;
 Pugg 312; Rachel 280;
 Richmond 272; Robin 270;
 Rosegill 217; Sam 267;
 Sarah 311; Sawney 312;
 Sue 312; Syfax 270; Toby
 264; Wouna,Wonna 217;
 (Armistead, Coll.) Ben
 274; Cenes,Caesar 277;
 Dick 277; Lucy 244; Moll
 244; Rachel 244; Titus
 277; (Armistead) Sarah
 218; (Armistead, Coll.)
 Ails 277; Moll 277;
 Rachel 277; (Eliza.) Tom
 259; (Thomas, mss-
 Armistead) Alice 213;
 Phillis 213; (William)
 Cott,Colt 62; Joan 62;
 Major 62; Mary 62; May
 62; Saturday 62;

Churchhill continued
 Sunday 62; Thursday 62;
 Tomboy 62; (William,
 Colloul.) Betty 49;
 Sarah 49; Sue 49; (Wm.)
 Jacob 258; Moll 258;
 Rose 258; Tony 259
Churchill, (beth) Mary
 309; Toney 309; (----,
 Coll.) Ben 236; Mary
 235; Phill 235; (Armi-
 stead) Annaca 239;
 Esther 256; Grace 239;
 Rachel 256; (Armstead)
 Annaca 275; Guy 246
Clark, (Edward) Billey
 Williamson 249; Cate
 267; Kate 218; Phillis
 218; Tom 267; (Edwd.)
 Dolly 292; (Mary) -emmy
 291; Cloe 296; (Thos.)
 Mary 292; Susanna 292
Clarke, (Ann) Nanny 238;
 Tom 238
Cooper, (Charles) Kate
 260,265
Corbin, (Gawen) Aaron 274;
 Aberry 267; Devonshire
 267; Frank 218; George
 267; Hampshire 267;
 Isaak 267; Joan 267;
 London 218; Ned 218,267;
 Robin 267; Rose 218;
 (Gawen, Coll.) Kate 241;
 Primus 241; (Gawin)
 Aaron 237; Alice 231,
 308; Arabella 221; Beck
 211; Betty 223,224,231,
 307; Bookry 275; Brad-
 ford 231,233,237;
 Bridgitt 309; Bristow
 211,264; Cate 222,231;
 Charles 306; Diamond
 271; Diana 210; Driner
 215; Easter 306; Essex
 306; Frank 210,222,224,
 264,306,307; Goy 221;
 Grasheir 222; Hannah
 210,307; Jack 307; Jef-
 frey 233; Jenny 227;
 Kate 227,235,238,308;
 Lucy 210,237; Mille 237;
 Moll 222,235,259,307,
 308; Newman 210; Per-
 cilla 210; Peter 227;
 Phillis 237,306,307;
 Pompey 307; Queen 223,
 231; Randall 306; Robin
 210,253; Rose 235(2),
 306,307; Rosse 215; Sam
 308; Sanco 308; Sandy
 238; Sarah 221,238,306
 (2),307,309; Sindab 258;
 Sue 210,237(2),307,308;
 Suke,Leeke 307; Syndab
 307; Tom 227,271(2);
 Will 238; Winney 227;
 (Gawin, Coll.) Alce 249
 (2); Alice 242; (Gawin,
 Col.) Bradford 243;
 (Gawin, Coll.) Jane 242;
 (Gawin, Colo.) Joe 252;
 Kate 252; (Gawin, Coll.)
 Sacco 279; (Gawin, Col.)
 Tom 243; (Gowen) Azor
 275; (Gowin) Ben 275;
 Phebe 275; (Henry, Coll.)
 Billy 241; (Rich.) Aaron
 292; Beller 292; Dick
 292; Grace 292; Isbell
 292; Jilson 292; Nona
 292; Sampson 292;
 (Richard) Billey 244;
 Dorender 243; Frank 248;

Corbin continued
  Harrow 243; Isaac 255,
  280; Jack 248; Jenny
  244; Letty 245,278; New-
  man 246; Phebe 244; Robin
  280; Robing 254; Sarah
  245; Sary 244; Stafford
  278; Tamar 244; (Tho.,
  Collo.) Philip 240;
  (Thomas) Ben 236; Davy
  238; Dick 233; Doll 236,
  274; Mack 234; Roger
  241; Susan 234; Tom 236;
  (Thos.) Beck 272; Frank
  273; (----, Capt.) Eliza.
  Phillips 25; Jane Phillips
  25; Phillip Phillips 25;
  Thomas Phillips 25
Crockford, (John) Beck 227;
  Bob 227,271; Jack 265;
  Judy 223,269; Molly 223;
  Nan 272; Toney 273
Crosbie, (James) Moll 235;
  Nany 235
Crosby, (James) Bess 242;
  Harry 242
Crutchfeild, (Wm.) Carter
  228; Rose 228
Curtis, (James) Aleck 261;
  Nanny 261; Will 261;
  (James, junr.) Clarinda
  310; Mingo 262; (James,
  Sen.) 58; (James, Senr.)
  Frank 58; Harry 58;
  (James, Sen.) Nanney 58;
  Phillis 58; (James, Senr.)
  Tony 58; (James, Junr.)
  Jenny 213; Judy 213;
  (Jno.) Dinah 274; Jenny
  275; Peter 274; Robin
  273; (John) Beck 271;
  (Rice) Dick 266; Dinah
  267; Enos 214; Frank 211;
  Jack 216; Janey 308;
  Jeney 306,307; Jenney
  209; Jenny 216,311; Jone
  214; Mintar 266; Minter
  214; Nanny 306; Natt 307;
  Ned 209; Phillis 214,218;
  Sam 308; Tom 266; Will
  218; Winne 216; Winney
  263,311; (Rice, Mr.)
  Mingo 60; Nan 60; (Rice,
  Mr.) ffrank 74; Judith
  74; Sarah 74
Daniel, (----) Beck 292;
  Jane 292; (Ann) Clara
  290; (Charles) Anthony
  249; Bob 279; Bowker
  242; Jack 246; Jeney 255;
  Judy 256; Kate 242,249,
  250,255,293; Lucy 254;
  Nan 250; Nana 254; Nann
  293; Robin 250; Sarah
  254; Will 250; (Clary)
  Alce 279; (Constant)
  Cate 245; Harry 245;
  (Frances Meacham) Hannah
  295; Judy 295; (Garret)
  Hannah 240; Jemmy 240;
  (Garrett) Cate 230;
  Hannah 230,236; Jack
  236; (Henry) Bristow 238;
  Cate 229; Dillah 221,
  229,234,238; Dinah 237;
  Frank 247,296; Jone 247,
  250; Jude 278; Nan 221,
  268; Peter 250; Sarah
  296; Toby 234; Wingo,
  Mingo 237; (James) Cate
  296; Hannah 238,296; Jack
  264; Juday 296; Judy 238;
  Phillis 232; Sally 296;

Daniel continued
  Tom 263; (James, Junr.)
  Gawin 235; Phillis 235;
  (John) Frank 211; Kate
  211; (Margret) Alice
  226; Amy 271; Margery
  226; Will 272; (Margrett)
  Alice 230; Ben 229; Billy
  230; Cate 272; Crozier
  221; Daphny 221; Dinah
  229; George 212; Kate
  210,212,221; Toby 210,
  264; (Obediah) Rachel
  253; (Robert) Amey 226;
  Captain 259; Frank 226;
  Gloster 277; Harry 265;
  Juda 249; Judy 246,277;
  Peter 246; Phill 290;
  Sampson 249,278; (Robert,
  Mr.) Cate 49; (Robt.)
  Frank 232,274; Gloster
  242; Jack 277; Judy 242;
  Sam 274; Winney 232,272;
  (Robt., Senr.) Alice
  305; Dinah 305; (William,
  jr.) Sarah 267; (William,
  Senr.) Jenny 262; (Wm.)
  Alice 233; Annaka 253;
  Daffery 256; Dinah 236;
  Judy 233,253; Letty 236;
  (Wm. junr.) Judy 229;
  Lucy 229; Margery 229;
  (Wm., junr.) Charles 271;
  Jack 269; Judy 213,271,
  309; Margery 272; Nan
  309; Sary 213; Winny 271;
  (Wm., Junr.) Jack 259
Daniell, (Henry) Dillah
  223; Judy 223; (James)
  Jack 306; Wan,Nan 306;
  (Margrett) Alice 221;
  Amy 221; Kate 216; Winne
  216; (Robert) Alice 310;
  Ben 270; Judy 308,310;
  Phillis 308; (Robert Cap.)
  Winnie 75; (Robert Cap.)
  Mingo 75; (Robert, Capt.)
  Alice 59; Ben 59; Cap-
  tain 59; (William) Betty
  32; (William, junr.)
  Judy 312; Kate 312;
Daniell, (Wm. jr.) Judy
  219; Winney 219
Darrill, (Sampson) Jemmy
  228; (William) Harry
  261
Davis, (Andrew) Moll 228;
  Nat 228; (John) Letty
  231; Phillis 231;
  (William) Beck 309; Bob
  309; (Wm.) Dinah 246;
  Sue 246
Degge, (John) Flora 311;
  Hannah 309; Jeney 308;
  Jeny 307; Judy 213,309,
  311; Nell 213; Sarah
  264; Toney 308; Wonna
  307
Digge (mss says Degge),
  (John) Judy 210; Sarah
  210
Dillard, (Edward) Ben 250;
  Jane 254; Margree 241;
  Mingo 239; Unity 239,
  250; (Edwd.) Ann 292;
  Unity 292; (Nicholas)
  Beck 294; Cate 250;
  Hannah 297,300; Jane
  255; Kitt 295; Margery
  293(2),301; Margre 255;
  Moses 297; Sam 246;
  Sarah 295; Will 253
Dillion, (Edmund) Dinah
  280

Dodson, (John) Sarah 265
Dudley, (Elizabeth, Mrs.)
  Rose 58; (James) Judy
  224; Miny 229; Peter
  224; Samson 270; (Jane)
  Daniel 256; Sabrina 256;
  (Robert) Billy 251;
  Margery 260; Robbin
  Mingoll 58; (Robt.) Judy
  307; Margery 307;
  (Thomas) Charles 308;
  Guinea 307; Harry 307;
  Jenny 270; Nanny 209
Dunlevy, (James) George
  Caine 242; Judy 242

Elliot, (Robert) Milley
  254; Peter 254
Ellis, (Hezekiah) Eve 209,
  214,306,311; Jenny 214;
  Phillis 311; Rose 209;
  Venus 306
Faulkner, (Tho.) Robert
  223; (Tho., Senr.) Robert
  269
Fearn, (Geo.) Jane 296;
  (George) Frank 289;
  Jane 289,294,295; Kate
  294; Lewis 295; (John)
  Toby 268; (John, Senr.)
  Bess 245; Phillis 245;
Frazar, (Alexander)
  Middlesex 276
Frazeir,Frazier, (Alexan-
  der) Jemmy 237; Kate
  237
Frazier, (Alex) Bess 239;
  Doctor 239; (Alex.)
  George 247; Jane 239;
  Kate 247; Lucy 247; Moll
  239,247,293; (Alexander)
  Beck 240; Bess 246(2);
  Buchan 237,274; Caesar
  240; Frank 244; Haring-
  ton 280; Jack 237; Judy
  240,254,275; Kate 237,
  240,244; Maulkam 270;
  Micclesex 276; Mole 254;
  Molly 237; Nanny 277;
  Robin 244; (Alexdr.)
  Abram 290; Bess 242,249,
  290; Easter 249; Jeny
  242; (Alexer.) Bess 255;
  Clara 255; Kate 255;
  Tom 255; (Alexr.) Davie
  292; Jeany 300; Moll
  292; Sue 294,297
Fretwell, (Wm.) Dina 247;
  Jenny 247
Fureman,Tureman, (Robert)
  Jenny 278

Gail, (----) Dinah 251;
  Nan 251
Gaile, (----, Mr.) Dick
  248; Hannah 248;
  (Mathias) George 278
Gaille, (Mathias) Hannah
  244; Harry 244
Ga;e, (----) Betty 297;
  George 296; Hannah 252;
  Hope 297; James 290;
  Kate 297; Tom 252; Will
  289; (Mathew) Bess 237;
  Sue 237; (Matthew) Glas-
  gow 279; (Matthias)
  Bess 256; Cate 256,293;
  Chance 256; Doll 240,
  275; Hanah 274; Hannah
  240; Jack 273; Jeny 250;
  Joe 293; Kate 275; Nan
  247; Sampson 247,278
Gardiner, (William, Senr.)
  Tom 248; (Wm.,Senr.)Judy
  244

Gardiner continued
Lucy 244
Gardner, (John) Moll 296;
(Wm.) Jemmy 255; Jude
255
George, (David) Ben 309;
Frank 214,309,313; Mingo
214; Poll 268; (John)
Tom 268; (Robert) Alice
231; Jack 218; Kate 218,
220; Maria 220; Winney
231; (Robert Senr.)
George 229; Kate 229;
(Robert, junr.) Beck 214,
220; Jane 214; Phillis
220; (Robert, senr.)
Della 262; Jemmy 262;
Sarah 263; (Robert, Senr.)
Kate 214; Phillis 209;
Will 214; (Robt.) Jack
266; (Robt., junr.) Beck
311; Hannah 311; Sarah
260; (Robt., Senr.)
Venus 263
Gibbs, (John) Anne 264;
Bess 268; Billy 216;
Kate 209,212,216; Nanny
209; Violett 212; (Mary)
Bess 220; Kate 220;
(Zacarias) Gabriel 226
Gilpen,Gilpin, (Henry)
Juno 222
Gilpin, (Henry) Kendall
214; Sprigg 311; (Joseph)
Beck 212; Charles 264;
Jenny 266; Sampson 212;
(William) Beck 231;
Sawney 231
Goodloe, (Henry) Guy 262
Goodwin, (Jno.) Sarah 238;
Will 238
Gordon, (Wm.) Bess 228,232;
Chance 228; Hannah 211,
214; Jenny 212; Kate
212,264; Lander 270;
Mingo 232,273; Nan 214;
Robin 267; Sampson 267
Gour (mss says Goar),
(Joseph) Beck 209;
Charles 209
Graves, (Alexander) Ben
224; Bristol 235; Bris-
tow 274; Dublin 262;
Frank 306; Hannah 237;
Jemmy 212; Jenny 217;
Judy 228; Mingo 244;
Robin 268,312; Sarah 212,
217,234,235,237,306,312;
Tom 264; (Alexr.) Dick
244; (Mary) John 279;
Sarah 278
Gray, (William) Antony
212; Caesar 268; Hannah
212,222,311; Pompy 222;
Ross 311
Green, (James) Elizabeth
301; (Jn.) Chloe 143;
Henry 143; Sarah 143;
Willm. 143
Grymes, (----,Coll.) Adam
253; Ann 242; Charles
277; Cloye 242(2);
Hannah 242(2); James 242;
Margery 253; Minter
277; Moll 253; Peter
253; Rachel 277; Silvia
242; (Charles) Alice
235; Sarah 235; (Jno.)
Alice 307(2); Beck 232;
Cress 234,237; Daffany
237; Eve 239; Flora 236;
Hannah 232; Harry 234;
Jack 236; Jemmy 237;
Joan 220(2); Mingo 220;

Grymes continued
Moll 220; Oliver 237;
Winney 239; (Jno., Hon-
ble.) Harry 274; Rose
274; (John) Abigall 211,
220; Abigal 216; Abigall
270; Absolom 262; Alice
259; Ambrose 273; Arminto
214; Bacchus 274; Beck
225,226,227,229,267,269;
Ben 225; Betty 267,312;
Bluff 274; Bungy 266;
Cate 269; Charles 218;
Chris 230; Ciss 214;
Cris 225; Cromwell 229,
274; Daffine 226; Daniel
313; Daphney 229; Del
211; Dick 260; Dinah
220,247; Edward 222;
Esther 216,233,274; Eve
231; Flora 229,232,273,
308,313; Grace 231,234;
Harry 262; Hector 267;
Jack 260; James 308;
Jane 308; Jenney 222;
Jenny 312; Jeptha 214;
Joe 231,272; John 308;
Jude 247; Judy 308;
Kate 211; Lucy 308; Mar
231; Margery 211,312,
313; Mars 267; Mary 309;
Mentas 308; Mingo 222,
227,269,270; Minter 221;
Ned 225,230,272; Nocco
274; Pancha 270; Peg
216; Peter 308; Phebe
214; Phillis 211; Rachel
216; Rachell 218; Ralph
267; Robin 308; Roger
233; Rose 267,308,309
(2),313; Ruth 267; Sancho
234; Sarah 308,312;
Sawney 211; Sawny 262;
Scipio 214,309; Simon
214,265; Sue 308,309;
Tom 269; Winny 233;
(John, Coll.) Abraham
276; Benjamin 243;
Charles 241; Cresce 248;
Cress 242; Daphney 244;
Grace 243,248; Jack
Wilshire 279; Pat 244;
Will 242; (John, Colo.)
Mirah 250; Sue 250;
(John, Esq.) Cress 240;
Dinah 240; Isaac 240;
Pegg 240; (John, Esqr.)
Daphne 280; (John,
Honble., Esqr.) Daffiny
247; Robin 247; (Phillip)
Ann 255; Thos. Goselen
255; (R.) Ben 307; Soll
307;
Gunter, (Charles) Dinah
300; Peg 300; (Judith)
Sarah 290

Hackett, (Thomas) Jeffrey
215; Winny 215
Hacknay, (Willm.) Dinah
236; Nan 236
Hackney, (William) Avith
240; Cate 249; Harry
264; Jemmy 307; Judah
249; Judy 312; Juno 232;
Kate 312; Nan 232,240,
292; (William, Junr.)
Fillis 254; Peter 254;
(William, Senr.) Jenny
251; Nan 251,254; Sara
254; (Wm.) Hannah 229;
Lucy 244; Nan 229,244,
247; Randol 247; (Wm.,
junr.) Mill 290; Phillis
293

Hadley, (Sarah) Betty 258
Hadly, (John) Lily 49
Hardee, (Curtis) Jemima
243; Kezia 250; Verena
243; (John) Hampton 248;
Verena 248; (Joseph)
Charles 213,266; Dinah
209,213,218; Moll 218;
Sam 209
Harden, (George) Hannah
310; Juno 310
Hardin, (Eliza.) Beck 255;
(Elizabeth) Ralph 254;
(Geo.) Busbee 278; Buzbe
246; Hannah 242; Jenny
237; Judy 246,278; Rose
237; Simon 242; (George)
Blade 233; Chance 242;
Charles 242; Cupid 226;
Dick 278; Hanah 223;
Hannah 231; Harry 278;
Judy 242,269,278; Juno
241; Lewis 250; Neeton,
Neeten 223; Nell 231;
Rose 224,226,233; Sprig
241; Tamar 278; Wonder
224,270; Wonna 250
Hardine, (George) Hannah
216; Wonah 216
Harding, (George) Bess
262; Dick 307; Dinah
306; Hannah 210; Jacob
271; Phil 219; Rose 219;
Sarah 271,306,307,311;
Sprigg 210; Tamar 311
Haselwood, (Thomas) Adam
262; Della 308; Dellow
211; Harry 308; Walley
211
Haslewood, (Thomas) Dellah
217; Dick 217
Hazelwood, (Tho.) Dellow
310; Will 310
Hazlewood, (Thomas) Jack
75
Hill, (Richard) Betty 306;
Hannah 279; Mary 223;
Nanny 210,278; Peter
223; Sarah 306; Tom 210,
264; (Richd.) Mary 269;
(William) Jeane 279;
Jenny 228; Lucy 234;
Nan 234; Robin 228;
(William, Senr.) Nan
241; Tamar 241; (Wm.)
Dey 256; Harry 237;
Jenny 237; (Wm., junr.)
Dick 251; Dy 251; Moll
312
Hipkings, (James) Moll 312;
(John) Harry 271; Judy
212,217; Lettey 272;
Letty 212; Robbin 49;
Sampson 217
Hipkins, (Jno.) Dye 239;
Judy 239; Simon 275;
(Jno. Mr.) Dick 74;
(John) Caesar 222; Jude
233; Judy 222,227;
Sangro 233; Simon 227;
(Thomas) Mary 58
Hoar, (John) Kate 85
Holderness, (Robert) Kate
214; Manuel 216; Pegg
222; Peter 222; Phillis
216
Hord, (John) Ben 307; Cate
307
Hoyll, (Samuel) Nell 49
Hudson, (Peter) Averilla
247
Humphris, (John) James
295
Hunt, (Mary) Ben 241;

Hunt continued
Jack 268; Janne 241;
Jenney 232(2); Yassum
276; (Mathew) Frank 210;
Harry 263; Jenny 210;
(Mathew, Matthew) Billy
225; Jenny 225; (Matt.)
Beck 310; Jenney 310;
(Matthew) Ben 259; Betty
221; Charles 218,261,268;
Jenny 215,218,221; Judy
215; Kate 261; Robina
50
Jackson, (Mary) Ann 294;
Daniel 296; James 251;
Lucana 255; Mille 243;
Nan 243,247,255; Will
247; (William) Ambrose
161; Jenny,Jemmy 161
Johnson, (Henry) Sarah 290;
(Jonathan) Jack 264;
(Margaret) Newman 254;
Ruth 254,293; (Robt.,
Senr.) Benjamine 223;
Hagar 223
Jones, (Anne) Charles
Nelson 161; John Saun-
ders 161; Toney 295;
(Charles) Dinah 310;
Kate 310; (Churchhill)
Ambrus 292; Antho. 254;
Ben 294; Charles 292;
Dinah 296; George 250,
295; James 252; Jemmy
296; Judy 295; Moll 289;
Phillis 300; Rachel 289;
Serinah 289; Tamer 255;
(Churchill) Kate 251;
Peter 278; (Humphery)
Della 262; Gawin 310;
Jefferey 305; Jenney
305; Nell 306,310; Roger
262,306; (Humphrey)
Abygall 243; Avey 214;
Bess 220; Charles 209;
Delah 209; Hannah 227;
James 235; Jenny 217;
Judy 244,277; Lucy 235,
244,294; Megg 75,213,
217,227; Mill 235; Nan
238; Nell 209,220,235,
243; Phill 238; Sam 214;
Seberina 209; Tom 213;
Winny 241; Wooser 270;
(Humphry) Cate 231;
Dellah 216; Edy 231;
Frank 225; Joan 216;
Kate 225; Lucy 231; Matt
215; Murreah 225; Nan
275; Nell 215,225; Ralph
231; Sambo 266; (Humphry.)
Jacob 290; (Humpry.)
Thomas 290; (John) Dap-
hne 292; Lette 256;
Meriah 250; Nanna 292;
Sam 252; Sary 255; Win-
ney 290; (Mary) Chaney
292; James 292; (Rice)
Bess 263; Peter 229;
(Roger) Bess 265; Dinah
312; Dum 233; Frank 233,
236; Hagar 244; Hannah
240; Jack 311; Joe 215;
Judith 277; Kate 215,312;
Moll 305; Pat 271; Patt
226; Peter 305; Phil
223; Phillis 308,311;
Ralph 261; Ruth 228;
Sampson 308; Sawney 220;
Siller 236; Tom 263;
Will 58; (Roger, Mr.)
ffrank 74; Sarah 74;
Toney 74; (Roger, Mr.)

Jones continued
Cesar 58; Thamer,Thamar
49; (Rogr.) Frank 245;
Peter 245; (Sarah) Criss
301; Davy 223; Nann 301;
Nanne 294; (William)
Dinah 249; Morear 245;
Rose 300; (Wm.) Bess
301; Sam 301
Kelley, (Patrick) Peter
262
Kemp, (----, Capt.) Mary
46; (----, Maj.) Dido
277; Tony 277; (----,
Majr.) Dido 241; Tony
241; (----, Mrs.) Daniel
248; Jenny 248; Judy
248; Pressilla 248;
(Mary) Charles 255;
Nanny 253; (Mathew) Bess
212,233,278; Betty 278;
Caesar 260; Cate 233;
Frank 213,265; Hannaball
272; Harry 213,261,306;
Jamey 216; Jenny 220;
Joice 262; Judy 233,239;
Juno 312; Nanny 233;
Peter 239; Phillis 220;
Robin 214,266; Roger 263,
312; Rose 216; Sampson
212; Toby 263; Tom 265,
311; Wonna 306; Wonne
311; (Mathew, Matthew)
Dido 226; Kate 226;
(Mathw.) Bess 239; Sam
239; (Matt, Major) Jenny
240; (Matth.) Jemmy 236;
Johnny 236; Sam 236;
(Matthew) Abraham 218;
Bess 242(2); Charlotte
218; Dan 216; Dick 309;
Dido 244,309,311,312;
George 264; Grace 244,
278; Jack 277; Jenny
244,278; Joe 277; Joice
311; Judy 243; Juner
244; Juno 219,230,307;
Kate 277; Lucy 230,272,
305; Ned 244,278; Pat
219; Paul 264; Peter
277; Phill 260,307; Rose
243; Sampson 260,309;
Scipio 269; Simon 244,
278,313; Toney 269; Will
277; York 270; (Richard,
Mr.) Cress 59; Dinah 59;
Juda 59; Moll 59; Nedd
59; Nora 59; (Thomas, Mr.)
Joanna 67
Kemp (Stiff), (Mathew,
Jacob) Frank 238
Kidd, (John) Bristow 254;
Jeney 254; (William)
Peter 265
Klug, (S.) Fanny 257;
Frank 257; Levie 257;
Mary 257; Nancy 257;
Peggy 257; Peter 257;
(Samuel) Abram 257;
Billy 257(2); Dolly 257;
George 257; Jack 257;
James 257; Jesse 257;
Kate 257; Mary 257;
Matt 257; Nancy 257;
Nanny 257; Ned 257;
Peggy 257; Randolph 257;
Tom 257
Laughlin, (Tho.) Hannah
279; Joe 279; Moll 279;
(Thomas) Judith 250;
Phil 243; (Thos.) Dido
250; Fortin 250,254;

Laughlin continued
Fortune 247,278; Frank
247,278; Hannah 247,279;
Harry 255; Jenney 255;
Lewey 255; Mole 247;
Moll 255; Rachel 254;
Will 238
Lawson, (William) Betty
240; Frank 240; Jack
240; Toney 277
Lee, (Charles) Frank 251;
Jack 258; Kate 301;
Mary 251; Robert 301;
(George) Hannah 255,292,
293; Judy 292; Sampson
255,280
Lewis, (Eusebius) Ben 254;
Davy 292; Frank 254,292
(2); (Jno.) Beck 239;
Cupid 239; (John) Alice
246; Beck 227,232,241,
246,250,292; Doll 261;
Hampshire 227; Jeny 279;
Newman 250; Orson 241;
Pheebe 232; Sarah 292;
(Mary) Beck 247; Frank
247,251; Jemmy 251
Listney, (Daniel) Venus
268
Loe, (Sam) Jack 260
Machan, (James) Jack 292;
Jone 253; Tom 253
Machen, (Mary) Gabriel
234,273; Phill 237;
Phillis 228,234,237,272,
275; (Tho.) Betty 258;
Grasheir 258; Isaac 211;
Judith 221; Phillis 211,
221; Rebecca 211;
(Thomas) Charles 270;
Davy 217; Lettice 267;
Nero 311; Phillis 217,
311; Sampson 271; (Thos.)
Charles 224; Old Phillis
224; Sampson 224; Young
Phillis 224
Mackneele, (John) George
253
Majorn, (Gawin) 215; Winey
215
Marshall, (Jno.) James
229; Kate 229; (John)
Caesar 231; Hannah 232;
Kate 231,272; Peter 232;
(Mary) Joyce 247
Marston, (John) Dinah 312;
Toney 312; (John, Senr.)
Dye 215; Rose 215;
(Thomas) Judy 251; Tom
251
Mayo, (Anne) Ben 313;
Felicia 310; Nan 261,
310; Phillis 306,313;
Robin 306; (James) Beck
242,245; Dick 245; Nan
242; (John) Lucy 213;
Phillis 213
Meacham, (James) Jack 262;
Lucy (free negro) 221;
Peter 261; Sarah (free
negro) 221; (John) Betty
300; Jane 296; Sue 296,
300; (John, Mr.) Moll
49; Peter 49; (Mary)
Will 274; (Tho.) Phillis
306; Rose 306; (W.) Moll
Carter 295; Unity Carter
295; (Wm.) Cate 300;
Phill 296
Michelborough, (Edmund)
Ben 228; Sarah 228
Michelborough, Mickle-
burrough, (Edmund)

Mickelborough continued
Alice 225; Frank 225;
Numan 225; Sary 225
Mickelborough, (Edmond)
Frank 211; Will 211;
(Edmund) Frank 230;
Lucy 230; (Henry) Hannah
228; Jack 228; Penny 301
Mickelburrough, (Edmd.)
Dick 238; Sarah 238;
(Hen.) Hannah 238; Sary
238; (Henry) Annaca 245;
Glasco 247; Jane 248;
Lucia 294; Nan 248; Nell
294
Mickleburrough, (Edmd.)
Sarah 234; (Edmund)
Alice 270; Frank 217,220,
311; Judy 217; Kate 307;
Moll 311; Nan 220; Toney
270; Will 265; (Henry)
Gawen 269; Gawin 223;
Hannah 223; Jack 252,271;
Jenny 252; Jeny 256;
Lewis 256; (Robert) Sarah
247(2)
Miller, (Christian) Amee
253
Minor, (Doodis) Betty 11;
Deco 11; James 11; Mary
11; Nann 11; Pallas 11;
Phelis 11; (Garrett)
Peter 75; Tenny 75;
(Garret, Mr.) Hannah 49;
Nan 49; Palles 49;
(Garrit) Dego 311; Lucy
313; Poll 311; (Garritt)
Betty 305; Degar 263;
Dinah 214; George 263;
George Hooper 307; Han,
Hannah 307; Hannah 214,
268,311; Jemmy 263,311;
Nan 211; Nanny 264; Poll
211,305,306; Sarah 263,
306; (John) Hannah 217;
Jemmy 217; Poll 218; Sam
218; (Minor) Degal 58
Montague, (Thomas, Mr.)
Ben 49; Moll 49; Sam 49;
Sara 49
Moseley, (Jno.) Bristow
236; Hannah 236; Kate 236;
Sue 236; (John) Ben 220;
Bett 227; Cate 230; Cato,
Cate 220; Dy 219,232;
Dye 224; Harry 219;
Jeney 271; Jenny 227;
Letty 264,311; Mingo 224;
Rose 232; Will 230;
(Marvell) George 269;
(Marvil) George 219; Jack
261; Nathan 219
Mosely, (John) Dy 216;
Jack 216
Mosely, Moseley, (John)
Dye 305; Hannah 305
Mountague, (Lewis) Great
Nan 296; Harry 294; James
296; Moll 294,296,300;
Rachel 294; Sam 300;
Sarah 294; (Penelope)
Jane 295,296; Will 295;
(Peter) Jack 307; Moll
307; (Philip) Bristow
296; Easter 296; George
295; Hannah 295,296;
Nanny 296; (Tho.) Caesar
310; Eugene 310; Frank
310(2); Hampton 215;
Hannaball 262; Jack 310;
Judy 215,312; Letty 309;
Moll 309,310; Pen 312;
Penn 263; Phebe 309;
Phillis 309; Sampson 310;

Mountague continued
(Thomas) Cate 75; Daphne
291,301; Edee 251; George
210; Hannah 296; Hary,
Harry 296; Jack 296;
Jamey 247; Jane 247,296;
Jenny 313; Jude 246;
Judith 230,251; Judy
210; Nancey 230; Phebe
308; Phillis 263; Venus
246; Wall 301; Will 308;
(Thos.) Agga 290; Daphne
232,289; Essex 224;
Hannah 225; Harry 244;
Jack 242; Jane 256,290,
301; Janey 252; Judeth
248; Judith 239,242,278;
Judy 224,225,232,238,
244; Lucy 238; Mill 256;
Nat 248; Natt 278; Peter
301; Sam 239; Tom 252;
Winney 289; (William)
Cate 250; Hannah 220;
Letty 250,276,278; Moll
220; Poll 217; Winny
217,267; (Wm.) Abram
256; Cate 253,256;
Clarinda 247; Corender
253; Corinder 244;
Creasey 253; Frank 213,
256; Hannah 256; Isaac
256; Jacob 256; Jemmy
274; Joe 247; Kate 313;
Letty 244; Lucretia 251;
Marlburrough 272; Marle-
brough 233; Moll 213,
231,233; Patty 253;
Phillis 251,253; Sampson
231; Venus 253; (Wm.
junr.) Moll 226; Winney
226; (Wm., junr.) Sam
264
Mt'gue, (Lewis) -ccas 291;
Sarah 291; (Thos.)
Nancey 291; Rey 291
Murrah, (John) Hannah 228;
Jemmy 219; Jenny 219,
234; Petro 268; Sue 234;
(Mary) Hannah 278; (Sarah)
Tom 268
Murray, (John) Peter 216
Murrey, (Mary) Ben 279
Murry, (John) Billy 212;
Corey 259; Jack 255,259;
Jenny 212; (Mary) Ben
248; Betty 244; Jany
244; (Mary, Seignr.)
Chales 239; Jenny 239

Norman, (Tho.) Carter,
Cartee 217; Phillis 217;
(Thomas) Carter 212;
Frank 264,311; Lucy 212,
265

Ogilvie, (William) Betty
259
Orrel, (Laurance) Ann 279
Orrell, (Laurance) Moll
270; (Lawrence) Hannah
274
Orrell, Orrill, (Laurence)
Crispin 221; Hannah 221;
Hannah 221; Sam 221
Oril, (Frances) John 301;
(Lawrance) Ann 248;
Judy 248; (Martha) Ben
296; Lucy 296
Orrill, (Laurance) Crispin
269; Hampton 268; Hannah
234; Johny 234; Sam 269;
Willmott 233; York 233;
(Laurence) Hannah 227;
Lucy 227; York 275;

Orrill continued
(Law.) Judy 251; Phillis
251; Tony 279; Willmott
279; (Lawrance, Laurance)
Gloster 225; Hanah 225;
Moll 225; Wilmuth 225;
(Lawrence) Caesar 246;
Judy 246; Sarah 228;
Willmut 228
Owen, (Augustine) Betty
212; Margery 212; Sharp
266; (Clement) Harry
219; (John) Peg 213;
Will 213,266; (William)
Alce 240; Ben 235; Dido
232; Filles 243; Jack
276; James 228; Joe 243;
Peg 228; Pegg 235,240;
Yangar 232; Yango 273;
(Wm.) Lucy 266; Primas
270

Page, (----, Mrs.) Betty
240; Molly 240
Parrott, (Penelope, Mrs.)
Frank 58
Perrott, (Curtis) Maggy
270; (Richard) Harry
219; (Richard, Mr.)
ffrank 11; Hannah 11;
Kate 11(2); Richard 11;
Sampson 11; Sarah 11;
Thomas Mack 11; Toney
11(2); Tugg 11; Wm. 11
Philpots, (Paul) Bess 231;
Joe 231
Philpott, (Paul) Boston
270
Philpotts, (Paul) Boston
226
Porter, (Francis) Betty
221,270; Frank 215,270;
Jack 215; Nanny 215; Sue
215,221
Price, (John) Alice 310;
Ben 266; Betty 310;
Bristow 312; Caesar 266,
312; Cromwell 266; Han-
nah 212; Judy 212,215,
217,268,310,312; Letty
215; Mary Whistler 310
(2); Mingo 217,267; Moll
212; Sue 212,310,312;
Tom 264; Toney 310; Tony
266; Will 310; (Tho.)
Lucy 222; Phillis 222;
(Thomas) Lucy 272; (Thos.)
Daphne 243; Lucy 243;
Mille 237; Newman 243;
Phillis 243,256; Sue
237,243,256; Winney 243
Pryor, (William) Winney
161

Ransom, (Frances) Frank 305;
Jane,Jone 305
Ransome, (Frances) Dina
262
Reade, (Alexr.) Phillis
290; William Jackson
290
Reed, (James) Fergus 274
Reeves, (----, Mr.) 11;
James 11; Tom 11
Reid, (James) Back 250;
Beck 230,235,238,241,
247,290,291; Bett,Beck
226; Betty 300; Frank
230,290,294; Harry 297;
Kate 226; Lucy 241,294,
297; Molly 250; Nanna
291; Nanny 238,294,297,
300; Robin 235; William
247,294

Smith continued
Antony 271; Betty 229,235;
Dido 224; Hannah 239;
Harry 239; Judee 235;
Judy 232; Maud 232; Nanne
229; Nanny 226; Randolph
224; Sue 229; Tom 226;
(Jno., Capt.) Antony 222;
Betty 222; (Jno., Junr.)
Judee 236; Sam 236; (Jno.,
Senr.) Liddey 271; Nan
235; Sary 235; (John)
Abraham 272; Adam 254;
Anne 253; Beck 221; Ben
311; Cate 246; Dinah 220;
Eliza 246; Frank 84,269;
Hannah 246; Ibbo 259;
Jack 249,250,263; Jeney
311; Jenny 221,250; Joe
264; Judy 220,244(2),249,
250,251; Kate 218; Maud
220,293; Moll 218; Muria
246; Nan 220,246,271;
Oliver 242; Parker 244;
Peg 246; Phillis 246;
Pompey 290; Rose 254,290;
Sam 279; Sarah 267; Tom
271; Wouna 246; (John
Cap.) Jane 107; (John
Senr.) Kate 230; Mingo
230; (John, junior) Jenny
260; (John, junr.) Adam
280; Anthoney 253; Betty
253,294; Billy 305; Book-
er 251; Charles 309;
Frank 226; George 280;
Hannah 280; Judy 226;
Kate 211; Lura 263,312;
Lyddee 211; Peter 294;
Robin 279; Rose 280;
Sarah 305,309,312; (John,
senr.) Betty 216; Dido
216; Kate 227; Sambo
227; (John, Capt.)
Anthony 58; Ben 84; Betty
308; Charls 58; Dido
209,308; Frank 58,308;
Jenney 308; Judith,Judeth
58; Ned 308; Nimine 308;
Tom 58; Will 209; (John,
Jr.) George 255; Hannah
255; (John, Junr.) Char-
les 262; Esther 256;
Hannah 243; Margery 256;
Mille 243; Ned 310; Rose
292; Toby 261; Will 292;
(John, Sen.) Frank 271;
George 259; Jenny 271;
Judy 259; (John, Senr.)
Anthony 266; Betty 209,
214; Frank 212; Harry
214; Ishmael 312; Jack
84; Jenny 209; Judy 212;
Moll 306,312; Robin 306;
(Maurice) Amey 265; Amy
214; Hannah 210,214;
Letty 210; (Moris) Cate
252; Hannah 252; (Morrice)
Anna 115(2); Judith
Johnson 115; Lettice 115;
Peter Johnson 115(2);
(Robert, Mr.) Betty 32;
(Tho.) Betty 226; Charles
226,271; Dinah 219,226;
Gilbert 272; Harry 269;
Jenny 219; (Thomas) Betty
308; Bucker 209; Cummah
308; Jenny 271; Moll 209,
268; Thom 223,269; Will
265; (Thos.) Adam 234;
Bellah 230; Betty 271;
Billah 234; Dinah 230,
234; Gilbert 230; Gunner
274; Ishmael 274; Jemmy 234;

Smith continued
Sango 230
Smith (Aldin), (John)
Judy 240; Tamar 240
Smith, Smyth, (John, Mr.
Senior) Dinah 74;
Ffranke 74; Hally,Harry
74; Hannah 74; Judy 74;
Moll 74; Sanco 74
Smyth, (John, Capt.) Ben
74; Janey 74
Snelling, (Aquila) Simon
242; Venis 242; (Aquilla)
Jenny 233; Simon 243;
Venus 233,243
Southworth, (Wm.) Harry
226; Sarah 221; Venus
221,226
Spotswood, (Hugh) Dinah
252; Hannah 254; Robin
254; Simon 250,279
Stanard, (----, Mr.) Diana
248; Letty 248; Phillis
248; Sukey 248; (----,
Mrs.) Ealce 241; Letty
241; (B.) Letty 279;
Margret 279; (Bev.)
Sampson 279; (Beverley)
Betty 253,290,301;
Billey 290; Dilce 301;
Francis 253; Irenah 252;
Kate 294; Lucy 294;
Margaret 290; Moses 294;
Penelope 294; Penelopy
294; Phillis 252,290,294;
(Eliz.) Alice 245; Billy
245; Joe 245; Judith
245(4); Lemuel 245; Letty
245(2),277; Margret 245,
277; Sarah 245; (Elizth.)
Duncan 238; Sary 238;
(William) Abigal 224;
Agie 227; Alice 270;
Clarinda 309; Cyrus 306;
Dianah 223; Frank 312;
Irene 215; Jane 268;
Jerrell 215; Judy 215,
220,224,227,306; Juno
220; Kate 309; London
218; Merenry-Mercury
264; Moll 215; Sarah
212,218,220,223,312;
Titan 212; Winny 220;
(Wm.) Alice 219,308(2);
Apollo 258; Bacchus 268;
Hannah 308; Hester 258;
Irene 266; Judy 212,232,
310; Letty 308(2); Mer-
cury 310; Molly 308;
Nimrod 219; Phillis 212;
Scipio 232,273
Stannard, (Eliz.) Judith
239; Lemuel 239; (Wm.)
Harry 239,275; Letty 239
Stapleton, (----, Dor.)
Robert 48
Steward, (Hugh) Dinah 272
Stewart, (Hugh) Jane 230;
Marjory 229; Phillis
230; Rosa 229,272
Stiff, (Jacob) Cate 262;
Dina 306,313; Dinah
217,267; George 259;
Gumbe 279; Gumbee 225;
Hagar 234,300; Jack
259,271; Johnson 300;
Judy 313; Kate 306;
Margere 279; Margery 217;
Nassau 278; Phillis
225,234,239; Simon 239
Stringer, (Daniel) Daphne
291; Jenny 246; Peter
246
Stuart, (Hugh) Jupiter 271

Sutton, (Christopher)
Dick 259; Hannah 217;
Judy 217; Lucy 226,232;
Peter 226; Phil 228;
Sue 232; (Hope) Judy
243,255; Sarah 243;
Simon 255; Sue 250;

Taylor, (Richard) Billy
215; Letty 210(2);
Peter 210; Sarah 210;
Sue 215; (Richd.) Betty
216; Daphney 301; Dick
269; Frank 301; Letty
215; Nan 215; Sarah 216
Thacher, (Chicheley) Lucy
252; Phalmoth 252
Thacker, (----, Coll.)
Alice 243,245,248;
Annaka 243; Betty 245;
Frank 243; Hezekiah 243;
Kate 243(2); Rachel 245;
Richard 248; Rose 243;
Sarah 245; Susannah 243;
(Alice) Peter 32; (Anne)
Betty 212,265; Frank
214,218,224,312; Jemmy
224; Jenny 220; Kate
312; Letty 214; Moll
212,215,220; Nanny 215;
Ned 218,259; (C.C.)
Jemmy 261; (C. Henry)
(H)arry 291; Jenny 291;
Juda 291; (Chackeley,
Chechiley) Sambo 278;
(Chicheley) Dick 279;
Mertilda 225; (Chickely-
Chichely) Jenny 276;
(Edward) Kate 241;
(Edwin) Abraham 217;
Affrica 239; Agy 217;
Alice 213,221,225,229,
232,237; Amey 271; Amy
223; Anaca 252; Anakey
225; Annakey 231; Ave
239; Beck 228; Betty
230,260,272; Billey 260;
Billy 306; Bob 230;
Bristow 245; Charles
218; Criss 225,271;
Cyphax 273; Cyrus 273;
Davy 261; Dick 232,237;
Dinah 228; Doll 223;
Dorinda 273; Dye 234;
Edy 229; Eliza. 252;
Eve 223,230,232,237;
Gawen 235; Gowin 239;
Great Alice 252; Guy
225; Hannah 233,237,258;
Harry 272,277; Jack 233;
Jemima 218; Jemmy 261;
Jenny 231; Joan 217;
Joe 225,273; Jone 252;
Jubia 246; Judee 237,
274; Judy 262,311;
Jupiter 261; Kate 217,
223,228,233; Kitt 258;
Lettey 306; Letty 228,
237; Little Alice 252,
279; Lucy 217,221,225,
230,234,239; Mary 252;
Nan 221,269; Numan 229;
Pattey 231; Pen 210,
265; Peter 232,252,274;
Phillis 226; Priscilla
221; Ralph 252; Richard
Cooper 138; Robin 230,
272; Rose 218,226,231,
237,246; Ruben 252; Ruth
228; Sabina 223,229;
Sabina-Sabrina 217;
Sabrina 139,213,235;
Sarah 233,239,245,261;
Tony 223; Will 223,252;